Subterranean Fire

Subterranean Fire

A History of Working-Class Radicalism in the United States

Updated Edition

Sharon Smith

Chicago, Illinois

Subterranean Fire
© 2006 Sharon Smith

First published in 2006 by Haymarket Books
This edition published in 2018
PO Box 180165
Chicago, IL 60618
773-583-7884
www.haymarketbooks.org

Cover design by Eric Kerl.

This book was published with the generous
support of the Wallace Global Fund.

Library of Congress Cataloging in Publication Data is available

Printed in Canada by union labor.

Contents

For Kamal and Ahmed

But if you think that by hanging us you can stamp out the labor movement—the movement from which the downtrodden millions, the millions who toil and live in want and misery, the wage slaves, expect salvation—if this is your opinion, then hang us! Here you will tread upon a spark, but here, and there and behind you, and in front of you, and everywhere the flames will blaze up. It is a subterranean fire. You cannot put it out. The ground is on fire upon which you stand.

—August Spies, Haymarket martyr,
speech at trial, October 7, 1886

Men make their own history, but they do not make it just as they please; they do not make it under circumstances chosen by themselves, but under circumstances directly encountered, given and transmitted from the past.

—Karl Marx, *The Eighteenth Brumaire of Louis Bonaparte*

Acknowledgments

Thanks to all the folks at Haymarket Books. Anthony Arnove has always offered encouragement and is available for advice around the clock. Julie Fain oversaw the entire project with diligence, good humor, and heroic patience. Dao Tran's careful reading and insightful comments brought political clarity when it was lacking in the original manuscript. Tristin Adie's meticulous reading of the final manuscript has spared me much embarrassment. And Ahmed Shawki's editorial work was invaluable in giving this book its final form. To each of them, I express my heartfelt gratitude. Any remaining errors are, of course, my own.

In addition, I am very fortunate to be surrounded by an incredible team of coworkers and collaborators in Chicago: Alan Maass, Marlene Martin, Paul D'Amato, Lance Selfa, Lee Sustar, Elizabeth Schulte, Nicole Colson, Joel Geier, David Whitehouse, Sherry Wolf, Bill Roberts, Eric Ruder, Adam Turl, and Sarah Macaraeg.

This book owes an enormous debt to the many radicals and union militants who have dedicated their lives to building the class struggle in all its elements. Their experiences and politics point the way forward for those of us today urgently seeking a new path for the working-class movement. We truly stand on the shoulders of giants.

Preface to the Second Edition

Ifinished writing the first edition of *Subterranean Fire* in early 2006. Back then, George W. Bush was still president and Barack Obama was still a U.S. senator with presidential ambitions. Much has changed! This edition includes an additional section, part V, "From George W. Bush to Donald J. Trump," covering the key events of the last decade along with the flashpoints of class and social struggle that have begun to shape a new resistance.

The Great Recession looms large in part V—as it still hangs over U.S. society a decade after it began. This is partly because the recession exposed the extreme excesses of modern capitalism, but also because since then a new generation of young people has become radicalized by the rising class and social inequality—including racist police violence—which has accelerated during and after the recession. The popularity of self-described socialist Bernie Sanders's campaign for president in 2016 was a product of the already-growing support for socialism, especially among the younger population, while Sanders's campaign also boosted the youth radicalization yet more broadly.

But those who campaigned for Sanders instead got Trump as their president in 2016. The election of this deeply misogynist, xenophobic, racist, billionaire demagogue further polarized an already divided population. On the one hand, Trump has reinvigorated the entire right wing of U.S. politics, from the Republican Party establishment, to "alt-right" white nationalists, to openly fascist organizations. At the same time, the Trump administration has injected a sense of urgency for resurrecting the politics of solidarity in order to build the largest possible resistance—even reviving the slogan "an injury to one is an injury to all"—that represents the best elements of the labor movement historically.

Thus, Trump's presidency has lit a fire under a new generation of activists who have known nothing but declining living standards and rising bigotry during their lifetimes. As I write this preface, I am frightened by the far-right resurgence but also filled with a tremendous sense of hope because, after forty years of one-sided class war, there is no doubt in my mind that this generation is destined to lead the struggles that can revive the tradition of working-class radicalism.

Resistance to the status quo has continued to unfold since I submitted the updated manuscript in early October 2017. The #MeToo movement rose like a rocket just weeks afterward, bringing down—in a matter of days—the seemingly untouchable Harvey Weinstein, one of the most powerful producers in Hollywood, and exposing him as a decades-long rapist and abuser. Hollywood actors first brought the issues of sexual assault and harassment into the national spotlight, and they inspired millions of working-class women to gain the courage to speak out about their own sexual abuse, exposing it as a *workplace* epidemic—in which men in positions of authority routinely harass and assault those under their control. Indeed, the Alianza Nacional de Campesinas, an organization of current and former women farmworkers, issued an open letter in solidarity with Hollywood actors who have faced sexual abuse on November 10, 2017. They wrote, "Even though we work in very different environments, we share a common experience of being preyed upon by individuals who have the power to hire, fire, blacklist and otherwise threaten our economic, physical and emotional security."

In addition, in early 2018, between February 22 and March 6, we witnessed the most successful working-class strike in four decades: West Virginia teachers, bus drivers, cafeteria workers, and other school employees went on a statewide strike, shutting down all fifty-five counties in the state for nearly two weeks—and *won*. This strike was significant both because it was illegal from its beginning, according to West Virginia law, and because the strikers stayed out even after their union leaders announced they had settled the strike based on nothing but promises from West Virginia Governor James Justice.

The West Virginia strikers showed us once again that periods of "labor peace" do not necessarily indicate working-class satisfaction with the status quo. Usually, it is very much the opposite. There is never a stalemate in the class struggle—one side is always either winning or losing ground at the expense of the other side. The last four decades in West Virginia, as in so many other working-class communities in the industrial heartland, have witnessed an epidemic of job loss and poverty—and all the aspects of social crisis that go with that epidemic. Even though the labor movement seems calm from the outside, working-class lives have been upended to the point that the class struggle provides the only possible way to move forward.

It's also fitting that the coal counties in the southern part of the state played such a key role in starting and sustaining the struggle. Many commentators have taken to ridiculing these communities as "Trump country" without regard to their strong union traditions and history of class consciousness. But there is a reason why Bernie Sanders won in the West Virginia primary—even if the state went to Trump in the general election.

However dire the state of the labor movement is today, the main takeaway from the West Virginia teachers' strike is that the future is far from hopeless. The teachers' struggle answered a question that has been haunting many of us—namely, after so many decades, how can long-standing working-class traditions be transmitted to those who came of age in the last four decades, never having had the opportunity to experience the highs and the lows of the class struggle that were once commonplace among workers? Solving this dilemma turns out to be less difficult than we might have imagined, at least in coal country, where union traditions survived long enough to play a role in this new phase of struggle. These traditions helped guide West Virginia teachers through to victory in their strike, even as they injected new elements such as using social media to organize teachers across the state. In so doing, they provided fresh lessons that can play a role in rebuilding the labor movement from the bottom up.

Marxism is neither a religion nor a product of wishful thinking. It is a science, based on the understanding that the two main antagonistic classes in society—capitalists and workers—are ultimately on a collision course. I hope that this book can offer some lessons from the past that will help to arm a new generation who will undoubtedly lead the way forward in the class struggle.

In solidarity,
Sharon Smith
March 28, 2018

Introduction

The United States ranks not only as the richest society in the world today but also as the most unequal among advanced industrialized nations.[1] The scale of poverty among the poorest Americans, according to the United Nation's 2005 *Human Development Report,* is comparable to that in parts of the Third World.[2] The U.S. infant mortality rate matches that of Malaysia. African Americans living in Washington, D.C., have a higher infant mortality rate than residents of the Indian state of Kerala.[3] Across the United States, Black mothers are twice as likely as whites to bear low-birth-weight babies, and Black children are twice as likely to die before their first birthday.[4]

Child poverty rates in the United States have been rising steadily since 2000, following twenty years of decline, and, mirroring Mexico, surged past 20 percent in 2005. On average, a male child born into the wealthiest 5 percent of the U.S. population will live 25 percent longer than a male child born into the poorest 5 percent.[5]

From its earliest years, U.S. capitalism has relied upon massive social and class inequality, despite all rhetoric to the contrary. Even during periods of economic boom and rising median incomes, a significant portion of the working class has consistently lived in extreme poverty. This cold fact was easier to hide during the economic boom that followed the Second World War, when the wages of unionized manufacturing workers in the United States were the highest in the world.

When the postwar boom came to a halt in the mid-1970s, however, U.S. employers united to launch a sustained attack intended to shift the balance of class forces decisively in favor of capital, by forc-

ing down working-class living standards and destroying union organization. Class inequality has increased almost without interruption
ever since, through boom and slump alike, and has now returned to
the record levels of the 1920s, the decade before the Great Depression.[6] In 1970, the average real compensation for the CEOs of the
top one hundred U.S. corporations was thirty-nine times the pay of
the average worker. By 2002, they earned more than a thousand
times the average worker's wage.[7]

As Warren Buffett, the world's fourth-richest man, commented
in his 2004 annual letter to the shareholders of Berkshire Hathaway,
"If class warfare is being waged in America, my class is clearly winning."[8] Shifting the balance of class forces is the urgent challenge facing the working-class movement today. The working class is facing a
profound social crisis in the twenty-first century. Yet this crisis rarely
merits a mention in the nightly news or on the floor of Congress.
Tracing the roots of this crisis requires a historical perspective—but
one aimed at pointing the way forward.

Union organization is, of course, crucial to the success of the
labor movement. Yet labor unions have never represented a majority of U.S. workers. Union membership peaked at 35.5 percent of
the workforce at the end of World War II.[9] Since the 1980s, union
membership and strength has been in a downward spiral. In 2004,
just 12.5 percent of wage and salary workers belonged to a union,
according to the U.S. Bureau of Labor Statistics. The rate for workers in the private sector dropped to 7.9 percent in 2004—roughly
half of what it was in 1983.[10] In the interests of building a stronger
union movement in the future, this book examines why union membership has remained comparatively low and why it has declined so
much in recent decades.

The strikes and struggles that led to permanent organization represent labor's biggest victories. But some important battles that were
lost nevertheless impacted the balance of class forces. To understand
the dynamics of class struggle in the United States, it is important to
look at both the victories and defeats of the U.S. labor movement.
Likewise, some relatively short-lived labor organizations have been
as important to shaping the character of the working-class movement as those that survived and prospered.

The Knights of Labor, the most powerful union organization in
the 1880s, vanished as a significant force by the late 1890s. The In-

dustrial Workers of the World (IWW) peaked in influence in the first two decades of the twentieth century, but faded as a major force well before the rise of the Congress of Industrial Organizations (CIO) in the 1930s. Yet both the Knights of Labor and the IWW played a crucial role during key periods of class struggle, advancing the cause of industrial unionism and training activists who played a role in organizing the next generation of workers.

The Dodge Revolutionary Union Movement (DRUM), an organization of Black autoworkers that grew out of a wildcat strike at General Motors' Dodge Main plant in 1968, lasted just a few short years. But during its brief existence, DRUM showed the potential for African-American workers to wage a powerful fight against racism, while winning solidarity from a sizeable layer of white unionists.

In addition, because race and class are so closely intertwined in this historically segregated society, movements against racism have often profoundly impacted the direction of the class struggle, even when they have taken place outside the arena of organized labor.

The battle for Reconstruction after the Civil War shaped the character of the labor movement for generations to follow. The urban rebellions that rocked U.S. cities in the 1960s were struggles against racism and poverty, and helped to transform the political landscape alongside the powerful civil rights and Black Power movements.

The 1992 Los Angeles rebellion erupted in response to the acquittal of four white police officers captured on videotape beating Black motorist Rodney King. That outpouring of rage lasted four days—put down only by thousands of National Guard and federal troops occupying the city—forced the issues of racism and police brutality into mainstream discourse.

The Working-Class Majority

The working class is often caricatured as white, male, and blue collar. In reality, the working class includes skilled and unskilled workers in factories, laundries, restaurants, schools, offices, and sweatshops; sharecroppers, tenant farmers, and migrant workers laboring in fields; women workers and the non-working wives of male workers; and those who have jobs and the currently unemployed.

White males, in fact, hold a minority—just 46 percent—

of working-class jobs, according to economist Michael Zweig. He estimates that women make up 47.4 percent of those in working-class occupations. Zweig also finds that "[B]lacks and Hispanics are over-represented in the working class." African Americans make up 10.7 percent of the labor force, but 12.6 percent of those in working-class jobs. Latinos made up 9.2 percent of those employed, but 11.3 percent of those in working-class occupations.[11]

Zweig estimates that the working class makes up roughly 62 percent of the U.S. population, a clear majority. But Zweig probably *underestimates* the proportion of workers in the population. Zweig correctly regards those who have a degree of "independence and authority" at work to be middle-class professionals. This category includes most lawyers, doctors, and computer scientists.

But Zweig also includes public schoolteachers and university professors in the "middle class" category, although teachers have been well represented in the union movement for decades. Like registered nurses and many social workers, teachers have experienced the progressive deskilling of their once-professional occupations in recent decades, with their work process increasingly dictated by authority from above. The growing number of doctors employed by profit-making managed care corporations likewise have little "independence and authority" over their professional medical decisions.[12]

Zweig acknowledges, "By the way, the Department of Labor comes up with an even larger number for what might be considered the working class than I do. The Department notes that 82 percent of the one hundred million non-farm, private-sector employees in the United States in 1996 were "non-supervisory" employees."[13] Since the Department of Labor statistics include accountants, doctors, lawyers, and other professionals in private practice, the actual proportion of Americans in working-class jobs probably measures somewhat less. The real figure is likely to fall somewhere between Zweig's estimate and the Department of Labor's—numbering more than 70 percent of the U.S. population, a large majority.

Working-class struggle has advanced only through building solidarity, uniting workers in a class-wide movement. The examples of such solidarity are hidden from mainstream historical texts, and their importance is often downplayed or ignored even in recent labor history. This study devotes considerable space to the high points of class unity because understanding how workers have overcome divisions in the past is crucial to charting a course for future solidarity. Viewing working-class history in all its complexity also challenges the existing myths about the gender and racial composition of the labor movement and the American working class as a whole.

White, male, skilled workers were well represented within the ranks of the skilled crafts that dominated the American Federation of Labor (AFL). But the Knights of Labor, the IWW, and other labor and political organizations drew unskilled Black, immigrant, and women workers into some of the most important class battles in history well before the CIO in the 1930s broke through the exclusivity of craft unionism.

Too often, labor historians have downplayed or ignored the role of working-class women in the class struggle. To be sure, many unions made no effort to organize in female-dominated occupations until the 1960s. But those who assume that women have been passive bystanders to the labor movement will be surprised to learn the heroic role women have often played in important strikes. During the highest points of class struggle, strikes have traditionally drawn entire families into battle, on and off picket lines.

In the case of mining, for example, women were rarely employed as coal miners, but fought in solidarity with husbands, brothers, and sons, in some of history's most bitter and violent confrontations between labor and capital. It is no accident that Mother Jones, the charismatic woman who traveled the country in support of striking miners a century ago, is one of the most legendary figures in working-class history.

Typically, mining companies evicted miners and their families from company housing as soon as a strike began, forcing entire communities into homelessness for the weeks or months of the strike. Striking families would set up tent colonies, often near the mine entrance, and entire families would band together to block the roads from strikebreakers. In the infamous Ludlow, Colorado, strike in 1913, women did not merely organize the tent communities to feed and give shelter to the ten thousand miners and their families—they also joined the men on pickets and organized international solidarity.[14]

Women workers, when given the opportunity, have often been willing to fight inside the union movement for their rights as women.

Although such examples are often anecdotal, they offer a powerful challenge to gender stereotypes. In just one example, women were "especially prominent" among the delegates to the Washington state convention of union boilermakers in June 1919, "and when they heard a proposal to denounce the employment of married women, in the words of one reporter, they 'beat it to a frazzle.'"[15]

Politics and Struggle

Those who focus only on the machinations of the official union apparatus can easily underestimate the potential of the rank and file below. The growth of union membership has never proceeded as a seamless advance, but has been concentrated within relatively short periods of social turmoil. As socialist historian Bert Cochran noted in 1959,

> Large-scale union growth never takes place in isolation from large social events but is one of the components of a generalized labor surge. . . . If we set the 1880s as the beginning of the modern labor movement, and go over the figures from that date to the present, we are immediately struck with a startling result: *The growth of American trade unions occurred in five brief explosions concentrated in relatively short periods of time against a background of major social upheavals brought on by depression or war.*[16]

These explosions in struggle, and the competing strategies for the direction of the class struggle in each of these eras, are a central concern of this book. Below is a table of the five periods:

TABLE OF PERIODS OF RAPID UNION GROWTH[17]

Period	Years	Number of Years	Approximate Membership Growth
I	1884–86	3	110,000 to 950,000
II	1897–1903	7	447,000 to 1,914,000
III	1917–20	4	3,061,000 to 5,048,000
IV	1934–38	5	3,609,000 to 8,000,000
V	1940–43	4	8,500,000 to 13,500,000

Cochran was writing after union membership as a share of the U.S. workforce had already entered the steady decline from which it has yet to recover. One key argument of this book is that this decline in union membership coincided with a dramatic fall in working-class radicalism—the direct consequence of the anticommunist witch-hunt in the 1940s and 1950s known as "McCarthyism" (named after its most ardent proponent, Senator Joseph McCarthy). The witch-hunt, initiated at the highest levels of government, purged radicals from the labor movement, permanently uprooting radical traditions from their historic base inside the working class.

No longer faced with the pressure that working-class radicals so often provided in the past, union leaders have pursued a strategy that seeks collaboration and avoids class conflict over the last fifty years. This strategy has proven disastrous for the union movement and the working class as a whole.

Working-Class Radicalism

Radicalism is by no means alien to America, as has been so often assumed in recent decades. Indeed, the struggle for the abolition of slavery and the battle for Reconstruction that followed were *radical* movements that proved decisive to the future of the working-class movement, North and South. The victory of abolition created the possibility for a multiracial labor movement. Subsequently, the defeat of Reconstruction represented the triumph of modern racism—the key obstacle to working-class unity ever since. The ongoing competition of a low-wage, non-union labor force in the South has shaped the character of the entire working-class movement, giving Northern employers an inbuilt advantage when their workers seek higher wages.

Key points of class struggle have typically involved a strong radical component. Strategies are informed by politics, and radical politics have tended to rise in influence among workers whenever the labor movement has advanced and confidence has risen.

Until the McCarthy era, political debates were aired *inside* the labor movement at virtually any given moment, and at various junctures, anarchists and socialists played a key role in leading the movement forward. Studies of labor's formative years provide tremendous insight into the turbulent dynamics inside and well outside the AFL many decades before the dominance of craft unionism gave way to the rise of mass industrial organizing in the 1930s.

Labor's first "Great Upheaval" during the 1880s—when the Knights of Labor swelled from 60,000 to 700,000 between 1884 and 1886—was, as historian John R. Commons described, a movement that "bore in every way the aspect of a social war. A frenzied hatred of labor for capital was shown in every important strike."[18]

Labor party efforts surged around the country during this period, including the union-backed 1886 New York mayoral campaign of Henry George, running on an independent ticket. Election Day in New York City was marked by massive voting fraud. According to historian Eric Chester, "At certain polling places, gangs of toughs, with the complicity of police, made sure that only Democratic voters could cast their ballots. . . . Ballot boxes were stuffed with spurious ballots, while other containers holding votes for Henry George were cast into the East River." Even so, George received 68,000 votes, one-third of the total.[19]

Chicago anarchists August Spies and Albert Parsons, two founders of the International Working People's Association, helped lead the 1886 strike for the eight-hour day and ultimately paid with their lives for their leading role. The organization's founding manifesto, issued in 1883, set as its key objectives, according to historian Paul Avrich:

> FIRST—Destruction of the existing class rule, by all means, i.e., by energetic, relentless, revolutionary, and international action.
>
> SECOND—Establishment of a free society based upon co-operative organization of production.
>
> THIRD—Free exchange of equivalent products by and between the productive organizations without commerce and profit-mongery.
>
> FOURTH—Organization of education on a secular, scientific and equal basis for both sexes.
>
> FIFTH—Equal rights for all without distinction of sex or race.
>
> SIXTH—Regulation of all public affairs by free contracts between the autonomous (independent) communes and associations, resting on a federalistic basis.[20]

The anarchist manifesto described above concluded with Marx's famous phrase, "Workmen of all countries unite! You have nothing to lose but your chains, you have a world to win!"[21] Elements of Marxism, reform socialism, and the "revolutionary socialism" of anarchist trade unionists often overlapped during this formative period, reflecting the political fluidity and debates among labor radicals in the late nineteenth century.

The twentieth century brought the consolidation of the AFL—but also witnessed yet another upsurge in class struggle, accompanied by the rise of the anarcho-syndicalist IWW and the founding of the Socialist Party. By the early twentieth century, as labor historian David Montgomery argues in *The Fall of the House of Labor*, "[s]ocialists, Democrats, and independents were all competing effectively for the votes of workers in search of a new political regime." A 1910 voting survey of three Pennsylvania mining towns, for example, found that socialist votes were nearly double those for Democrats and almost equal to those for Republicans.[22]

The working-class upsurge of 1917–20 involved a broad reaction against an unpopular war coupled with the global inspiration provided by the victory of a working-class government in the 1917 Russian Revolution. Montgomery noted, "The appearance of workers' councils in Russia and Germany, and even in the creameries of Limerick in Ireland" deeply impacted U.S. workers' consciousness: "By 1919, 'council' and 'delegate' were words with revolutionary resonance similar to what 'convention' and 'citizen' had carried in 1789."[23]

The radicalization that followed the Russian Revolution involved a generation of workers, many of them veterans of the Socialist Party and the IWW. Many of these radicals went on, as communists, socialists, or Trotskyists, to play a leading role in the most important era of class struggle in U.S. history—the Great Depression.

The labor insurgency of the 1930s was a revolt against mass unemployment and poverty caused by economic depression. The Depression decade is unparalleled in the size and scope of working-class radicalization that grew out of a wave of unprecedented victories for organized labor. Membership in the Communist Party swelled to tens of thousands, while socialists, communists, and other radicals emerged as rank-and-file leaders in key strikes. This high point of class struggle offers invaluable lessons about the dynamic between struggle and radicalization, and directly challenges the notion that U.S. workers are inherently too conservative to embrace radical ideas.

The final period of union growth noted by Cochran, between 1940 and 1943, took place during and immediately following the Second World War. While the war was followed by a massive strike wave, this period was significantly different in political character from previous advances for unions. Left-wing opposition to the war was dwarfed by the Communist Party's enthusiastic support for the U.S. war effort and the strike ban. This period cemented union leaders' alliance with the global aims of U.S. imperialism for more than six decades, and set the stage for the success of McCarthyism in persecuting left-wing unionists in the postwar era.

Since Cochran's analysis in 1959, the class struggle saw another major spike—in the years between 1967 and 1974, in the context of a social upheaval against war, racism, and other injustice, which reverberated inside the working class. This upsurge witnessed a wave of wildcat strikes, major advances for public sector unionization, and the rise of significant rank-and-file union movements in major industries. But unions were nevertheless unable to prevent the onset of an employers' offensive that has continued without interruption since the mid-1970s.

For those interested in the potential for revitalizing the labor movement today, past political debates and struggles are as important as the outcome at any given point in labor history. In essence, the outcome is rarely a foregone conclusion and involves a battle over strategies, often shaped by competing sets of politics. The interests of the working-class movement are best served not when these debates are avoided, as they have been since McCarthyism, but when radical viewpoints are welcomed and discussed inside the labor movement.

The arguments that follow—admittedly and unapologetically informed by Marxism—are offered in this spirit.

Sharon Smith
January 2006

PART I

Class Struggle in the "Land of Opportunity," 1865–1930

CHAPTER ONE

Are American Workers Different?

I n 1886, the first May Day of the world working-class movement
was marked in the United States by a massive political strike wave
of more than three hundred thousand workers—forty thousand
in Chicago alone—demanding the eight-hour day. The anarchist-led
Chicago Labor Union, called "upon all wage workers the necessity
of procuring arms before the inauguration of the proposed eight-
hour strike, in order to be in a position of meeting our foe with his
own argument, force." [1] During this tumultuous period, newspaper
headlines nationwide expressed the alarm of business leaders, asking,
"The Revolution?" [2] The struggle culminated in a police massacre in
Chicago's Haymarket Square, and the trial and execution of four of
the movement's leaders, including August Spies and Albert Parsons.

The scope and violence of the 1886 strike wave convinced Karl
Marx's collaborator Frederick Engels that class consciousness was
rising on a mass scale amid rapid industrialization. As he wrote to
Florence Kelley Wischnewetsky, "the American working class is
moving, and no mistake. And after a few false starts, they will get
into the right track soon enough. This appearance of the Americans
upon the scene I consider one of the greatest events of the year." [3] To
be sure, Engels recognized that the road to an independent workers' party would not be a smooth one. In 1893, Engels wrote, in a
letter to German socialist Adolph Sorge, "[I]t cannot be denied that
American conditions involve very great and peculiar difficulties for
a steady development of a workers' party." [4] But Engels remained
optimistic until the end of his life that workers in the United States
would, as elsewhere, eventually form an independent political party.

3

More than a century later, however, workers in the U.S. still have no political party independent of the corporate-backed Democrats and Republicans. In this important way, the U.S. working class hasn't followed the same path as workers' movements in most other industrialized countries, which have developed and sustained labor or social democratic parties. At the same time, U.S. workers have historically shown an enormous capacity to battle their employers. The labor movement's formative period, in the fifty years after the Civil War, took place amid sharp economic booms and slumps matched by dramatic ups and downs in class struggle.

Between 1881 (the first year for which reliable figures are available) and 1905, 7.5 million workers took part in a total of 38,303 strikes across the United States. In that same time period, 198 strikers or sympathizers were killed, 1,966 were wounded, and 6,114 arrested.[5] For more than a century, the class struggle in the United States fit a pattern of (sometimes long) periods of calm, punctuated by huge explosions of struggle. Most often those periods of calm, far from representing class harmony, witnessed dramatic setbacks for the labor movement. Then years of pent-up bitterness and class anger gave way to massive eruptions of struggle, in an American parallel to British historian E. J. Hobsbawm's apt description of "collective bargaining by riot."[6]

Historian Jeremy Brecher described the Southwestern Railroad strike in 1886: "The characteristic response of the workers to [management's] attempts to break the strike was the 'killing' of the engines. This was done by putting out the engine's fire, letting out the water, displacing engine connections, and destroying part of the machinery."[7] The Russian revolutionary Leon Trotsky noted the extraordinary militancy of U.S. workers in his 1934 article, "If America Should Go Communist":

> The American temperament is energetic and violent, and it will insist on breaking a good many dishes and upsetting a good many apple carts before Communism is firmly established. Americans are enthusiasts and sportsmen before they are specialists and statesmen, and it would be contrary to the American tradition to make a major change without choosing sides and cracking heads.[8]

But American workers' breathtaking combativeness has coexisted alongside a weak political tradition. Although the Chicago Haymarket massacre helped to establish May Day as a holiday for workers worldwide, this holiday is still not celebrated in the United States. Indeed, many active unionists have never heard of May Day nor are they aware of its origins in American workers' struggle for the eight-hour day. Likewise, the 1909 New York City garment workers' strike inspired another socialist holiday, International Women's Day—celebrated on March 8 each year around the world.[9] But like May Day, International Women's Day remains part of the hidden history of the labor movement, unknown to the vast majority of American workers.

The Myth of "American Exceptionalism"

U.S. employers have always been keenly aware that the promise of prosperity could be a useful weapon in the class struggle—a corresponding carrot to the stick of repression they so often wielded. As Julius Rosenwald, founder of the Shefferman union-busting firm, remarked in 1926, "Don't imagine, however, that anything we do for our people in the way of profit sharing, or enabling them to acquire stock, or providing meals at low rates, medical attention, recreation grounds, vacations, and so forth is done from philanthropic motives—not in the least. Whatever we do for our employees we do because we think it pays, because it is good business." [10]

Yet a range of theories have long asserted that the promise of upward mobility has rendered the American working class uniquely incapable of sustaining class consciousness, much less a class-wide movement for socialism. Broadly grouped, these theories fall into the category of what has become known as "American exceptionalism."

Theories of American exceptionalism have been around since the days when immigrants were first lured to America with tales that the streets were paved with gold and claims that anyone could strike it rich in the "land of opportunity." In 1831, French historian and sociologist Alexis de Tocqueville marveled at the "democracy" he found in the U.S., especially as compared to the continued existence of a landed nobility throughout Europe. "The position of the Americans is quite exceptional," he commented, "and it may be believed that no democratic people will ever be placed in a similar one." [11] De Tocqueville's enthusiastic comments are often cited by proponents of American exceptionalism.

De Tocqueville's enthusiasm, however, was tempered by the

gaping class inequality he also observed in the United States, where there are "some men who are very opulent and a multitude who are wretchedly poor." De Tocqueville expressed reservations that America's "manufacturing aristocracy which is growing up under our eyes is one of the harshest that ever existed in the world." [12]

Those seeking to prove that American society has successfully contained working-class consciousness rarely acknowledge de Tocqueville's lack of enthusiasm for the rising manufacturing class.[13] Yet this offers insight into the limits of "democracy" and class mobility in U.S. society, even in the early nineteenth century.

As editors Rick Halpern and Jonathan Morris argued in *American Exceptionalism? U.S. Working-Class Formation in an International Context,* the approach guiding most theories of American exceptionalism is problematic because "absence rather than presence is seen to hold the key to American distinctiveness." As they explain,

> The lack of a sufficient degree of "class consciousness," characterized by the failure to establish a labour party, renders intelligible both the relative weakness of early twentieth-century trade unionism in the U.S. as well as the uncontested dominance of the two major parties. Of course, this framework precludes all sorts of interesting and important investigations into actual working-class politics, radicalism, organization, and activity. . . . If the proponents of exceptionalism found no evidence of class conflict, then the labour historians would uncover a history of struggle that rivaled that of any European proletariat.[14]

Indeed, the massive struggles that shook U.S. society in the latter half of the nineteenth century exposed the brutal underbelly of America's "unique" democracy and the explosive nature of class conflict. As historian Neville Kirk argues, "The immediate post-bellum years [following the Civil War] in the North saw a revived labour movement commit itself to the principle of independent labour politics. In the South, the desires of free Black people . . . for control over their labour and ownership of land flatly contradicted bourgeois expectations that freedom for Black people would equal the freedom to earn a wage and sell their labour power to capitalist employers." [15] The violent battles of this period, Kirk writes, showed "the far less consensual, neutral and pluralistic sides of the American liberal state and ruling bloc: capital accumulation and the employer's 'right' to absolute mastery in the workplace were to be guaranteed at all costs." [16]

Some exceptionalism themes nevertheless deserve consideration and can aid in understanding the character of class consciousness during the labor movement's formative years.[17]

First, as de Tocqueville argued, the character of American society was different than that found in Europe because the United States had no feudal past, and therefore no landed aristocracy. In contrast to the development of European bourgeois democracy, the American Revolution granted universal suffrage (for white males) from the outset. All women were denied the vote, and America's Black population lacked any rights of citizenship, but U.S. workers had no immediate class-wide impetus to form independent workers' movements to struggle for democratic rights.

Second, upward class mobility was a possibility for a significant minority of workers. U.S. industry expanded rapidly in the decades following the Civil War. In 1860, American iron and steel production amounted to one-fifth of British output. By the turn of the century, the United States was the largest steel manufacturer in the world.[18] Despite brutal working conditions, workers could aspire toward management and even entrepreneurial pursuits. In addition, the U.S. government opened the door to massive Western migration after the Civil War by granting ownership to anyone who settled on land owned by the government. Migration to the Western frontier contributed to a turnover among workers who might otherwise have stayed and fought for better conditions.

Third, immigrants made up a sizeable proportion of the U.S. working class, and they were separated by language and cultural differences in an already racially and ethnically divided society. Moreover, many immigrants were only a "temporary proletariat," who could move to the West, aspire to rise up the social ladder, or return home. Thus immigrants alone could not constitute the basis for the development of a permanent working-class movement.

Taken as a whole, the themes described above can help to explain why a substantial layer of workers would seek individual, rather than collective, solutions during the second half of the nineteenth century. But the importance of these factors should not be exaggerated. These theories describe temporary, not permanent, features of American society. These factors made it more difficult for U.S. workers to develop class-wide organizations, but only until the first decades of the twentieth century. By 1886, Engels already foresaw these factors fading as obstacles to class-wide consciousness:

There were two circumstances which for a long time prevented the un-avoidable consequences of the Capitalist system from showing them-selves in the full glare of day in America. These were the easy access to the ownership of cheap land and the influx of immigration. They allowed, for many years, the great mass of the native American popu-lation to "retire" in early manhood from wage-labour and to become farmers, dealers, or employers of labour, while the hard work for wages, the position of a proletarian for life, mostly fell to the lot of immigrants. But America has outgrown this early stage. The boundless backwoods have disappeared, and the still more boundless prairies are faster and faster passing from the hands of the Nation and the States into those of private owners. The great safety-valve against the forma-tion of a permanent proletarian class has practically ceased to act. A class of life-long and even hereditary proletarians exists at this hour in America.[19]

By the dawn of the twentieth century, no Western frontier re-mained to be conquered. And though U.S. capitalism continued to expand in the twentieth century, employers turned toward raising the productivity of labor rather than relying on an ever-growing labor force. By the 1920s, immigration was severely curbed for sev-eral decades, and upward mobility ceased to be a possibility for the vast majority of workers.

If the potential to develop mass working-class organization hadn't existed in the nineteenth century, it certainly did by the twen-tieth. As British socialist Duncan Hallas argued, "All the special fac-tors which can be shown to have operated in the United States until 1900 or 1920 were now of steadily diminishing importance. So the presence or absence of a political labour movement has to be judged in terms of certain specific events and struggles." [20]

Prosperity and Class Consciousness

The most persistent claim of exceptionalism theorists, however, is that prosperity alone has permanently thwarted class consciousness in the United States. The most influential proponents of this claim have not been the gleeful defenders of the class status quo, but most often academic "experts" in the field of sociology.

As early as 1906, sociologist Warner Sombart had already de-clared that the U.S. working class was too enamored by capitalism to build a socialist movement. In his book, *Why Is There No Social-ism in the United States?* Sombart asserted that the United States was "the promised land of capitalism" where "on the reefs of roast beef and apple pie socialistic Utopias . . . are sent to their doom."[21] Sombart drew this conclusion at a time when millions of workers crowding city slums and shantytowns across the United States rarely got a decent meal, and class war had long been raging in the "land of opportunity." Indeed, in 1903, David M. Parry, president of the National Association of Manufacturers (NAM), railed against "the present program of violence, boycotting, and tyranny now being carried out by the majority of labor unions," as he called for combating "legislation of a socialistic nature."[22] Moreover, while average wages were higher in the United States than in Europe, the gap between the wages of skilled and unskilled workers was greater.[23]

Theories of American exceptionalism became popular once again during the long economic boom following World War II, when more than two decades of unprecedented prosperity temporarily blunted working-class consciousness in the shadow of the "American Dream." Sociologist Daniel Bell famously proclaimed "the end of ideology" in 1960, adding later, "Abundance . . . was the American surrogate for socialism."[24] In 1973, sociologist Benjamin S. Kleinberg argued that American workers' interests coincided with those of American capitalism: [R]esolving the tensions between different social classes requires no fundamental redistribution of the social product, only its continued growth. Growth of the national product is viewed as a good in itself. . . . To the extent that individuals can satisfy their desires for a material improvement of living standards, they lose interest in ideology and even in politics itself.[25]

Decades of falling wages and living standards since Kleinberg made this statement have exposed the shortsightedness of this view. "Four out of five households take home a thinner slice of the economic pie than they did a quarter century before," labor historian Lichtenstein noted in 2002. Today, CEOs earn more than a thousand times the average worker's wage.[26] Young male workers have experienced the steepest decline in real wages—25 percent between the early 1970s and the early 1990s.[27]

American exceptionalism nevertheless experienced a reincarnation during the 1990s, albeit on shakier grounds. As Halpern and Morris commented, "Books and articles dealing with exceptionalism form a small growth industry in academic publishing on both sides of the Atlantic."[28]

Political analyst Seymour Martin Lipset's particular variation on American exceptionalism rests not on promises of prosperity, but on ideology alone. In his 1997 book, *American Exceptionalism: A Double-Edged Sword,* Lipset acknowledges,

> The United States continues to be exceptional among developed nations in the low level of support it provides for the poor through welfare, housing, and medical care policies. As a result, though the wealthiest country, it has the highest proportion of people living in poverty among developed nations, according to the detailed statistical analyses of the Luxembourg Income Study data, the most comprehensive available. The United States also ranks last among ten countries (six in Europe, plus Australia, Canada, and Israel) as the most unequal in comparisons of income distribution.[29]

Lipset further admits that Americans have grown increasingly distrustful of political leaders and institutions for the last three decades. "This erosion of trust in American government is troubling," he writes. But U.S. society is permanently cushioned from the threat of a left-wing revolt, Lipset argues, due to popular acceptance of a unique set of "American values," including a strong sense of morality and an American work ethic that ensures "the survival of the American Dream." [30]

Traditional theories of American exceptionalism would be easy to dismiss as either obsolete or unproven. But left academics often echo the same arguments as their more mainstream counterparts, particularly during longer periods of labor calm. More than one left-wing writer has dismissed the potential for mass working-class struggle—only to be proven wrong by the next labor upsurge.

Are American Workers "Bought Off"?

During the 1960s in particular, many leftists regarded the working class living in the heart of U.S. imperialism as part of the problem, rather than as a potentially powerful part of the struggle against capitalism and the war in Vietnam. A host of left-wing theorists argued that the promise of owning a house in the suburbs and a color TV had permanently diverted the class interests of U.S. workers. In 1967, the German-American philosopher Herbert Marcuse, a guru of the 1960s counterculture, argued that the system provided a "comfortable, smooth, reasonable, democratic unfreedom. . . . Under the conditions of a rising standard of living, non-conformity with the system itself appears to be socially useless."[31] Marcuse's observation was proven wrong by the end of the 1960s by a series of working-class revolts and the rise of a working-class majority opposed to the war in Vietnam. The number of unauthorized strikes across all industries doubled between 1960 and 1969, from 1,000 to 2,000. The year 1970 witnessed a veritable strike wave—including a 67-day strike against General Motors—which was part of a rise in class struggle that subsided only in 1974.[32]

Some of these struggles were political as well as economic. In 1969, 95 percent of West Virginia's coal miners went out on a wild-cat strike demanding government legislation covering Black Lung, a disease that kills so many miners. Other struggles were led by groups of workers influenced by the antiwar and Black Power movements. The most significant of these struggles led to the formation of the Dodge Revolutionary Union Movement (DRUM) in 1968. After shutting down production at the Dodge Main assembly plant in a wildcat strike, Black workers formed DRUM to combat both company and union racism.[33]

Many of the strikes during this period involved some of the most highly paid workers in the U.S.—including autoworkers and Teamsters. Theorists like Marcuse, who had dismissed these workers as overpaid and part of the bulwark of the system, were proved wrong. The labor upsurge between 1967 and 1974 validated once more the historic role of the working class in Marxist theory.

Exploitation and Class Struggle

Karl Marx understood the revolutionary potential of the working class as an objective consequence of exploitation. The Marxist definition of the working class, therefore, has little in common with those of sociologists. Although income levels obviously bear some relationship to class, neither income level nor degree of class consciousness determines social class. Some workers earn the same as or more than some people who fall into the category of middle class. And many people who consider themselves "middle class" are in fact workers. Nor is class defined by categories such as "blue collar" versus "white collar." For Marxists, the working class is defined by its relationship to production. Broadly speaking, workers are those who do not control production but rather are controlled from above, and are forced to sell their labor power to employers. This definition includes the vast majority of employees in the United States.

Exploitation reduces individual workers to mere cogs in the wheels of mass production, thus depriving, or alienating, workers from the fruits of their labor. As Marx wrote in *Capital,* "All means for the development of production transform themselves into means of domination over, and exploitation of, the producers; they mutilate the laborer into a fragment of a man, degrade him to the level of an appendage of a machine, destroy every remnant of charm in his work and turn it into a hated toil." [34] Elsewhere in *Capital,* Marx added, "It follows therefore, that in proportion as capital accumulates, the lot of the laborer, be his payment high or low, must grow worse." [35]

"Scientific management" techniques were first championed by corporate consultant Frederick Winslow Taylor in the early twentieth century and have been steadily refined ever since. But Taylor's operating principles—tightly timed production quotas and a strict division of labor—have been universally adopted by mass production industries, robbing workers of any control over the production process. Today, for example, workers at the Toyota NUMMI plant in California are in "motion" on the assembly line for 57 seconds out of every minute. [36]

In the 1960s, American workers were the highest paid in the world, but they paid a steep price through a drastic rise in their rate of exploitation. Output per worker more than doubled between 1947 and 1972. While the number of manufacturing workers grew by 28.8 percent between 1950 and 1968, manufacturing output grew by 91 percent. In 1950, U.S. steel mills produced half the world's steel; U.S. auto companies were responsible for 76 percent of world vehicle production. [37] The real beneficiaries sat on the boards of directors of the biggest U.S. corporations.

The Labor Upsurge of 1967–74

In 1972, eight thousand workers voted by a margin of 97 percent to strike General Motors' Lordstown, Ohio, plant. Led by young workers and Vietnam veterans, the Lordstown strike was a collective response to rising exploitation. Through a combination of automation and assembly line speedup, the Lordstown plant raised its output from 66 cars per hour in 1966 to over 100 per hour in 1971.[38] The 29-year-old president of the United Auto Workers (UAW) local told author Studs Terkel, "If the guys didn't stand up and fight, they'd become robots too. They're interested in being able to smoke a cigarette, bullshit a little bit with the guy next to 'em, open a book, look at something, just daydream if nothing else. You can't do that if you become a machine." [39]

It was this understanding of class struggle being shaped by material conditions that led socialist historian Hal Draper to argue:

> To engage in class struggle it is not necessary to "believe in" the class struggle any more than it is necessary to believe in Newton in order to fall from an airplane. . . . The working class moves toward class struggle insofar as capitalism fails to satisfy its economic and social needs and aspirations, not insofar as it is told about struggle by Marxists. There is no evidence that workers like to struggle any more than anyone else; the evidence is that capitalism compels and accustoms them to do so.[40]

Though Marcuse's pessimistic conclusion was wrong, his and similar theories continued to influence the generation of 1960s student radicals, perpetuating the belief that American workers were "bought off" by the system. Indeed, even in the twenty-first century, many who oppose global injustice frequently mistake the prosperity of U.S. capitalism for the prosperity of its population, despite the gaping inequality within the U.S. population.

Like Sombart's, most left-wing theories of American exceptionalism hold partial truths, but none of the factors they describe has been decisive. There is nothing fundamentally different about the American working class that makes it incapable of acting as a class, or which can explain why workers in the United States have not yet developed an independent political tradition. This was certainly the conclusion drawn by leading Marxists who studied the conditions of the U.S. working class before and after the dawn of the twentieth century. As Mike Davis wrote, "At one time or another, Marx, Engels, Kautsky, Lenin, and Trotsky all became fascinated with the prospects for the development of a revolutionary movement in the United States. Although each emphasized different aspects of contemporary social dynamics, they shared the optimistic belief that 'in the long run' the differences between European and American levels of class-consciousness and political organization would be evened out by objective laws of historical development." [41]

Most Marxists held a balanced view of the strengths and weaknesses of the U.S. working class. Leon Trotsky, who gained a great deal of familiarity with the Depression-era class struggle in the United States during his final exile in Mexico, reiterated this theme. When asked about the "backwardness" of U.S. workers, he responded, "The backwardness of the United States working class is a relative term. . . . The American worker is very combative—as we have seen during the strikes. They have had the most rebellious strikes in the world. What the American worker misses is a spirit of generalization, or analysis, of his class position in society as a whole." [42]

As Kirk argued, "As seen in the pre-1914 fortunes of the Socialist Party, there did exist considerable popular support for socialism in America, both inside and (especially) outside the AFL. . . . [I]t is not the absence of moves to independent labor and/or socialism which demand explanation, as suggested by proponents of 'exceptionalism,' but rather both the frequency and short-lived character of such moves." [43]

CHAPTER TWO

The Peculiarities of American Capitalism

Most theories of American exceptionalism emphasize the income advancement opportunities in the United States as it developed into the world's richest economy, and the real and perceived effects on working-class consciousness. But that focus misses the point, because the enormous wealth produced by American capitalism has never been distributed remotely equally.

Engels remarked in an 1892 letter to German-American socialist Hermann Schlüter, "[Y]our bourgeoisie knows much better even than the Austrian Government how to play off one nationality against the other: Jews, Italians, Bohemians, etc., against Germans and Irish, and each one against the other, so that differences in the standard of life of different workers exist, I believe, in New York to an extent unheard of elsewhere." [1]

Already in 1881, Marx observed that capitalism in the United States was developing *"more rapidly* and *more shamelessly* than in any other country." [2] American rulers have traditionally used every means at their disposal to divide and weaken the working class movement—and made every attempt to crush it when it rises up. Nineteenth-century railroad baron Jay Gould once boasted that he could "hire one half of the working class to kill the other." [3]

The U.S. ruling class is not fundamentally different in nature when compared with its European counterparts—all seek to advance their class interests, politically and economically. The United States is distinctive, however, in the aggressiveness of its rulers toward threats from below. Socialist historian Leo Huberman observed, "It took American workers a century and a half of militant battling before they succeeded in having written into law their right to organize into unions and bargain collectively without interference from the employers."[4]

As labor historian Stephen H. Norwood notes:

> The United States during the early twentieth century was the only advanced industrial country where corporations wielded coercive military power. In Europe, employers did not hire armed mercenaries. . . . Paradoxically, the nation that never experienced feudalism and that pioneered in introducing civil liberties allowed corporations to develop powerful private armies that often operated outside the law, denying workers basic constitutional rights. . . . During the 1930s, Ford Motor Company's Service Department, directed by ex-pugilist Harry Bennett, formed to suppress union organizing and strikes, constituted the world's largest private army, numbering between 3,500 and 6,000 men.[5]

Kirk makes the same comparison, describing the post-Civil War era: "Labour relations in the United States were increasingly characterized by degrees of violence and official repression and coercion generally unmatched in the 'Peaceable Kingdom' of Britain."[6]

Furthermore, Kirk argues,

> The more inflammatory nature of class and social relations in the United States, as compared with Britain, was intimately related to the stages of development and characteristics of capitalism in the two countries. The more acute nature of the crisis of competitive capitalism in the late nineteenth century U.S. . . . and that country's more rapid, uncontrolled and disruptive transition from competitive to monopoly capitalism; the relative weakness of the cushion of formal empire and "gentlemanly" practices for American capital; the far more aggressively individualistic and transforming strategies (centrally embracing the "open shop" and Taylorism) of hegemonic U.S. employers and their powerful, "unrepublican" allies in the judiciary and other parts of the state machinery . . . [all] combined to generate higher levels of conflict and turbulence in the United States.[7]

The lawlessness of nineteenth century magnates such as Cornelius Vanderbilt and Andrew Carnegie was not limited to labor relations. Cutthroat competition meant that capitalists facing frequent booms and savage slumps were equally at odds with one another, using bribery, raiding tactics, and blackmail to gain dominance. Shipping owner Vanderbilt famously declared on one occasion, "Law? What do I care about law? Hain't I got the power?"[8] After an attempt by associates to seize control of one of his properties, Vanderbilt responded with this crisp piece of correspondence:

Gentlemen:

You have undertaken to cheat me. I will not sue you, for law takes too long. I will ruin you.

Sincerely yours,

Cornelius Vanderbilt[9]

Historian Sidney Lens argued that nineteenth century economic growth "was accompanied by an orgy of corruption and thievery such as the nation had never seen before." During the Civil War, financier J. P. Morgan "bought defective rifles, already condemned, *from* the government, for $17,500 one day, and resold them to the government the next day for $110,000." In May 1901, a fierce stock market war between Morgan and E. H. Harriman led to a financial crash, throwing thousands of investors into financial ruin. Yet when a reporter asked Morgan whether he should offer an explanation to the public, Morgan responded, "I owe the public nothing."[10]

U.S. manufacturers abandoned their individual rivalries, however, to unite as a class against labor early on, adopting a number of ruthless methods to enforce corporate rule that set them apart from their European counterparts. These methods *combined* contributed both to the explosiveness of the class struggle and the failure of repeated attempts by workers to form a political alternative to the rule of the dominant capitalist parties.

The following factors will be explored:

- A degree of racism and racial segregation exceeding that of every other industrial society, with the exception of South African apartheid
- a political system based upon the shared rule of two corporate parties, the Democrats and the Republicans, in which one of those parties—more recently the Democrats—successfully masquerades as an ally of the downtrodden
- reliance on extraordinary levels of political repression, including a combination of armed violence, high levels of incarceration, execution, and legal and ideological warfare to suppress oppositional movements

"Divide and Conquer"—the Role of Racism

In the late 1960s, President Lyndon Johnson appointed a government-sponsored study on the causes of Black ghetto rebellions then sweeping U.S. cities. The Kerner Commission report, issued in 1968, concluded that the United States was "moving toward two separate societies, one Black, one white—separate and unequal." The report continued, "What white Americans have never fully understood—but what the Negro can never forget—is that white society is deeply implicated in the ghetto. White institutions created it, white institutions maintain it, and white society condones it."[11]

To coincide with the thirtieth anniversary of the Kerner Commission report in 1998, the privately funded Milton S. Eisenhower Foundation released its own study, "The Millennium Breach," which echoed the conclusions of the Kerner Commission. The Eisenhower Foundation found that, even with the nation's unemployment rate below 5 percent, unemployment rates for young African-American men in urban areas such as South-Central Los Angeles were more than 30 percent. The U.S. incarceration rate of Black men was four times higher than that in South Africa under apartheid. The U.S. child poverty rate was four times the average of Western European countries. More than half of the 43 percent of the children of African Americans and other racially oppressed groups attending public schools were living in poverty.[12]

Indeed, by 2003—nearly sixty years after the U.S. Supreme Court issued its 1954 *Brown v. Board of Education of Topeka* decision striking down school segregation and more than thirty years after Court-ordered school desegregation—U.S. schools have resegregated to the same level as before busing began.[13]

White students today attend schools that are, on average, 80 percent white. The most racially segregated schools are in the North—in New York, Illinois, Michigan, and California. Many rich suburban schools tend to be all white and many of the poorest inner city schools are exclusively Black or Latino.[14] In 2000, according to the Education Trust, New York school districts with the highest concentration of white students received $2,034 more per student in state and local funding than those with the highest concentration of racial minorities.[15]

School segregation is not isolated from other aspects of racism, like housing, because government policies have historically restricted Blacks from settling in more prosperous white areas. Federal housing programs that helped millions of white families buy homes from the 1940s through the 1960s excluded most African Americans by catering to local racist ordinances. Even when Blacks managed to get mortgages, racist mobs often terrorized their families to drive them out, firmly establishing all-white enclaves across the country.

As social scientists Douglas S. Massey and Nancy A. Denton wrote in 1993, "No group in the history of the United States has ever experienced the sustained high level of residential segregation that has been imposed on Blacks in large American cities for the past fifty years." [16]

The Chicago Urban League's Paul Street asked rhetorically in 2002,

> Why are African Americans twice as likely to be unemployed as whites? Why is the poverty rate for Blacks more than twice the rate for whites? . . . Why do African Americans make up roughly half of the United States' massive population of prisoners (two million) and why are one in three young Black male adults in prison or on parole or otherwise under the supervision of the American criminal justice system? Why do African Americans continue in severe geographic separation from mainstream society, still largely cordoned off into the nation's most disadvantaged communities thirty years after the passage of civil rights fair housing legislation? Why do Blacks suffer disproportionately from irregularities in the American electoral process, from problems with voter registration to the functioning of voting machinery? Why does Black America effectively constitute a Third World enclave of sub-citizens within the world's richest and most powerful state? [17]

Capitalism and Slavery

The system of slavery engraved racism at the very core of the global capitalist system. As Marx argued, "Without slavery there would be no cotton, without cotton there would be no modern industry. It is slavery which has given value to the colonies, it is the colonies which have created world trade, and world trade is the necessary condition for large-scale machine industry." [18] Nowhere was this truer than in the United States, where slave labor on Southern plantations laid the basis for the development of the Northern industrial economy.

But Marx also argued that the existence of slave labor allowed industrial capital to expand rapidly by increasing the rate of exploitation of wage workers: "In fact the veiled slavery of the wage laborers in Europe needed the unqualified slavery of the New World as its pedestal. . . . Capital comes dripping from head to toe, from every pore, with blood and dirt." [19]

As historian Theodore Allen argued,

Why was it that . . . in the United States the industrial bourgeoisie was barred by law from meeting its growing labor needs by employing African Americans fleeing from racial oppression in the South? The answer is that in the United States the government was constituted on the strict condition of giving full faith and credit recognition to slavery, and the sixty percent [sic] electoral bonus to slaveholding states. It was as a consequence of this fact that the country was dominated by the Southern slaveholders from the American Revolution until the Civil War, and white supremacism was established as a sort of American super-religion, with appropriate penalties for "backsliders." Under the circumstances, "white" identity was made to appear to be an unrefusable offer. But it would prove to be as unhelpful to the class interests of European-American workers as "salvation," or reliance on an imminent Judgment Day was to the class interests of the workers in England.[20]

Slavery was abolished, but white supremacy flourished in its aftermath, used first to defeat Reconstruction in the South and thereafter to systematically combat the potential for multiracial class unity that threatened the onward march of industrialization. Racism has been the centerpiece of ruling-class strategy ever since, intended to keep different sections of the working class permanently divided.

At the end of the Civil War, however, which system would replace the rule of slave-owners was an open question—resolved only after a lengthy struggle for Reconstruction, aiming to rebuild Southern society on a different basis.

The Battle for Reconstruction

With federal troops occupying the South to enforce national law, freed African Americans and Northern radicals seized the moment to transform the postwar South. Congress ratified the Thirteenth Amendment in 1865, banning slavery anywhere in the United States. The Fourteenth Amendment followed in 1868, guaranteeing citizenship to African Americans and prohibiting former Confederate secessionists from holding federal or state office. The Fifteenth Amendment, passed in 1870, declared that no citizen could be deprived of the right to vote because of race, color, or previous condition of servitude. When Congress granted Blacks the right to vote, it also disfranchised 100,000 white Confederates.[21]

Between 1867 and 1868, Congress passed a series of Reconstruction Acts, dividing the former Confederacy (except Tennessee) into five districts under military commanders authorized to force Southern states to write new constitutions and to ratify the Fourteenth Amendment. Congress passed the Reconstruction Acts over the veto of President Andrew Johnson—Abraham Lincoln's Democratic, racist vice president—who assumed the presidency after Lincoln's assassination.

During the first years after the Reconstruction Acts, poor whites began, for the first time, signing up with the Republican Party alongside Blacks in Southern states, on the basis of common class interests. Radical Republicans advanced policies of debtor relief, the eight-hour day and other workers' rights, and many states adopted free public education for all citizens for the first time. In addition, small farmers were given tax relief while large plantation owners found their taxes raised.[22]

As W. E. B. Du Bois argued, "The lawlessness in the South since the Civil War . . . became a labor war, an attempt by impoverished capitalists and landholders to force laborers to work on the capitalist's terms."[23] The outcome of the struggle for Reconstruction was impossible to predict beforehand. Before "racist oppression was made into the glue that held the whole system together," argued historian Jack Bloom,

> Virtually all possible combinations came into being at one or another point. Upper-class whites developed a paternalistic relationship with Blacks, which they used to hold back the class aspirations of lower-class whites. Upper- and lower-class whites allied to suppress Blacks whenever Blacks sought to challenge the economic and social arrangements that were the basis of the oppressive conditions of their lives. Lower-class whites and Blacks united against the class prerogatives of the upper class. But the main dynamic in this process was provided by upper-class whites' successful effort to retain their economic and political domination of the region.[24]

Newly freed African Americans made clear their intention to transform Southern plantation society into a participatory democracy. Fourteen Blacks were elected to Congress from six southern states, and two African Americans from Mississippi were elected to the U.S. Senate.[25] In contrast, the first Northern Black congressman was not elected until the 1920s, and the first

Northern Black U.S. senator was elected only in the 1960s.[26] South Carolina voters elected an African-American governor, and Blacks held a majority in several Southern state legislatures, tipping the balance in favor of Reconstruction.[27]

Florida's agent from the Bureau of Refugees, Freedmen, and Abandoned Lands, Jacob A. Remley, was astonished to find that "the freed people exhibit a knowledge of their political situation and their relations to it, which could scarcely be expected from a people heretofore prohibited from acquiring a knowledge of such matters."[28] As a group, African Americans articulated the desire for the right to vote and for "fair labor contracts with growers and to purchase land," historian Paul Ortiz described.[29]

African Americans embraced political activism and posed an articulate challenge to corporate rule. Florida's Black legislators, for example, collectively stated their opposition to a pro-corporate bill in 1872:

> Capital needs no legislation in order to provide for its use. Capital is strong enough to take care and provide for itself, but corporations are a dangerous power, especially large or consolidated corporations, and the American people fear them with distrust. We want no Tom Scotts, Jim Fisks, or Vanderbilts in this State to govern us, by means of which they would influence legislation tending to advance personal interests. The great curse of Florida has been dishonest corporations, with an eye single to their central interest.[30]

At the same time, however, former slaveholders were determined to approximate as closely as possible the conditions of slavery in its aftermath. White supremacists' slogan for the defeat of Reconstruction was "Redemption." The Redeemers did not attempt to overturn Reconstruction at the federal level, but by defeating Republicans at state polls using violence and voting fraud.

As historian C. Vann Woodward argued, the Redeemers "frankly constituted themselves champions of the property owner against the propertyless and allegedly untaxed masses."[31] In the Black-majority Nachitoches Parish in Louisiana, "not a single Republican vote was counted in 1878, more than fifty Negroes were killed and others driven from their homes during the campaign, according to a report by the United States District Attorney."[32] Jack Bloom described the situation in Alabama: "In one county, the polling place was stormed as the ballots were being counted; the judge who was counting was fired upon, his son was killed, and the ballot box was stolen."[33]

The Ku Klux Klan (KKK) was the Redeemers' primary vehicle for lynching, home burnings, and other forms of racial violence used to defeat Reconstruction. Leading members of the Democratic Party used the KKK to drive out radical Republicans, both Black and white, after the Civil War:

> The one really new ingredient of regular [Klan] activity after 1867 was opposition to the radicals. And so far as the Klan loomed larger than the earlier vigilante groups, this was undoubtedly the reason. Only now did upper class elements and Conservative political leaders take much interest in the idea. In many places some took over Klan leadership, at least temporarily. The Klan became in effect a terrorist arm of the Democratic Party, whether the Party leaders as a whole liked it or not.[34]

The Republican Party, committed to securing the dominance of free (or wage) labor over the system of chattel slavery, opposed the Confederacy in the Civil War. But the Republicans shared common class interests with Democrats, including a strong allegiance to manufacturers' right to make their profits with workers "free" from labor unions. The Republican Party establishment ultimately defeated its own radical wing, uniting with Democrats to enact the Compromise of 1877, withdrawing federal troops from the South—dealing Reconstruction its final blow.

In so doing, the Republican Party, once the party of abolition, turned its back on the democratic demands of African Americans and enabled the victory of white supremacy. Radical Republicans were removed from office in every Southern state by the late 1870s, and the programs and rights ensured by Reconstruction legislators were immediately dismantled. Southern legislators reinstated Black Codes first imposed by slaveholders during the first two years after the Civil War—criminalizing African Americans under "vagrancy" and other laws.[35]

The Black Codes thus ensured a large supply of Black prisoners, who were leased out as convict labor in conditions closely approximating those of slavery. As Mississippi plantation records in the 1880s documented, "the prisoners ate and slept on bare ground, without blankets or mattresses, and often without clothes. They were punished for 'slow hoeing' (ten lashes), 'sorry planting' (five lashes) and 'being light with cotton' (five lashes). Some who attempted to escape were whipped 'til the blood ran down their legs.'" [36]

White racists went on the rampage after the defeat of Reconstruction, using lynching, castration, and other mob violence to impose a reign of terror on the African-American population. "Between 1882 and 1903, 285 people were lynched in Louisiana, 232 of them Black, and many of the rest immigrant workers." [37] The perpetrators were rarely "found" by local police, who generally made no pretense of hunting for them. In fact, police often joined groups of whites in cheering on the vigilantes. Lynching continued as a means of terrorizing the Black population well into the twentieth century. [38]

Segregation Imposed from Above

Southern lawmakers passed segregation laws (nicknamed "Jim Crow" laws) and voting restrictions disfranchising African Americans across the South as the century drew to a close. Jim Crow banned all forms of racial integration, forbidding poor whites and poor Blacks from having any social contact. It is well known that Jim Crow made it illegal for Blacks and whites to eat at the same restaurants, use the same toilets, or drink from the same water fountains. Each locality, however, could—and did—add its own refinement of segregation laws. By the early twentieth century, the city of Atlanta required that Black and white court witnesses swear on different bibles, and the city of New Orleans set up segregated prostitution districts. In Birmingham, Alabama, in the 1930s, arrest was the punishment for the "crime" of "advocating social equality between whites and Negroes." [39]

Moreover, a series of decisions by the U.S. Supreme Court between 1873 and 1898 upheld the "constitutionality" of racial segregation. In its infamous 1896 *Plessy v. Ferguson* decision, the Court upheld a Louisiana law mandating separate railway cars for whites and Blacks, ruling that sweeping segregation ordinances violated neither the Thirteenth nor Fourteenth Amendments to the U.S. Constitution. The Court's sanction paved the way for the absurd segregationist slogan "separate but equal" that would remain in place for almost sixty years, until 1954.

Northern states did not pass sweeping segregation laws, but practiced racial segregation nonetheless. In the early twentieth century, the city of Topeka, Kansas, formally segregated its high school system. Many of Boston's hotels and restaurants refused to serve Blacks. Most Northern employers refused to hire African Americans until the massive labor shortages produced by World War I—but deliberately recruited Blacks as strikebreakers during major strikes, to stir up racial hatred that undercut unions. Black and white soldiers were segregated throughout the U.S. Army through World War II.[40]

Nor was racist violence limited to the Southern strongholds of white supremacy. As Norwood described,

> Blacks' increasing insecurity and vulnerability in the North was dramatically illustrated in violent white attacks on African-American communities in towns previously considered hospitable to Blacks, and where they had long resided. Bloody, anti-Black riots occurred in Springfield, Ohio, in 1906, which had been on the line of the Underground Railroad, and in Springfield, Illinois, "within the pale of influence of the tomb and home of Lincoln the Emancipator."[41]

But white Southern workers and poor sharecroppers did not benefit even slightly from the extreme level of racism. In fact, the higher the level of racism, the more they lost. When the racist poll tax was passed in the South, imposing property and other requirements designed to shut out Black voters, many poor whites also lost the right to vote. After Mississippi passed its poll tax law, the number of qualified white voters fell from 130,000 to 68,000.[42]

Civil rights leader W. E. B. Du Bois argued that Black disfranchisement strengthened the Southern vote in relation to the North because "the White Southerner marches to the polls with many times as much voting power in his hand as a voter in the North."[43]

Due to the system of white supremacy, he added, "The South does and must vote for reaction. There can be, therefore, neither in the South nor in the nation a successful third party movement. . . . A solid bloc of reaction in the South can always be depended upon to unite with Northern conservatism to elect a president."[44]

The effects of segregation extended well beyond the electoral arena. Jim Crow empowered only the rule of capital. Whenever employers have been able to use racism to divide Black from white workers, preventing unionization, both Black and white workers earn lower wages. This is just as true in recent decades as it was 100 years ago. Indeed, as socialist Ahmed Shawki argued of the 1970s, "In a study of major metropolitan areas Michael Reich found a correlation between the degree of income inequality between whites and Blacks and the degree of income inequality *between whites.*"[45] One 1970s study concluded:

> But what is most dramatic—in each of these blue-collar groups, the Southern white workers earned less than Northern Black workers. Despite the continued gross discrimination against Black skilled craftsmen in the North, the "privileged" Southern whites earned 4 percent less than they did. Southern male white operatives averaged . . . 18 percent less than Northern Black male operatives. And Southern white service workers earned . . . 14 percent less than Northern Black male service workers."[46]

After the Redeemers' victory, the history of Reconstruction was quickly rewritten in major texts, assigning key roles to greedy Northern "carpetbaggers" while falsely charging Reconstruction regimes as rampant in their corruption. No attempt was made to hide the racist aspect of this assessment. Du Bois described submitting a (solicited) manuscript to the *Encyclopedia Britannica*'s fourteenth edition—only to discover that the editor removed all references to Reconstruction from the manuscript. Instead of Du Bois' description of Reconstruction, the following replacement appeared: "Reconstruction was a disgraceful attempt to subject white people to ignorant Negro rule; and that, according to a Harvard professor of history (the italics are ours), 'Legislative expenses were grotesquely extravagant; the *colored members in some states engaging in a saturnalia of corrupt expenditure.*' "[47]

U.S. rulers claimed "science" was on their side as they promoted racist ideology against African Americans. The definition of the word "Negro" in the 1903 edition of *Encyclopedia Britannica*, included the following pseudo-scientific phrases:

> Weight of brain, as indicating cranial capacity, 35 ounces (highest gorilla 20, average European 45; . . . thick epidermis . . . emitting a peculiar rancid odour, compared . . . to that of a buck goat; . . . the inherent mental inferiority of the blacks, an inferiority which is even more marked than their physical differences. . . . No full-blood Negro has ever been distinguished as a man of science, a poet or an artist.[48]

Social Darwinism: " Survival of the Richest"

The poisonous and sustained racism directed against African Americans has been unparalleled in U.S. society. But since the first wave of Irish immigration in the late 1820s, America's wealthy elite has also aggressively cultivated racist ideas against nearly every group of foreigners arriving on U.S. shores. Hostility greeted each successive wave of European immigrants, especially from Eastern and Southern Europe, who were viewed as lesser breeds by nineteenth and early twentieth century employers.[49]

Even during the many periods when employers have encouraged massive immigration to fulfill their need for labor, they stoked anti-immigrant hysteria from above. Racist ideology serves the convenient purpose of justifying harsh and degrading treatment of immigrant labor, while driving a wedge between white and foreign workers.

The Chinese Exclusion Act of 1882 placed a ban on Chinese immigration, even though railroad companies had brutally exploited Chinese workers to build the nation's railroads in the 1860s and 1870s. In 1867, ten thousand Chinese railroad workers staged one of the most important strikes of the century. They demanded higher pay, shorter working hours (including an eight-hour day for tunneling workers) a ban on whipping and the right of workers to quit their jobs. But no one else in the labor movement came to their support, and within a week the strike was crushed.[50]

· Mexican workers have traditionally filled a unique role for U.S. agriculture. In the 1920s, while curtailing immigration overall, U.S. law allowed unlimited immigration from Mexico. This, Montgomery argued, "institutionalized a revolving door for migrant field workers from Mexico, who numbered at harvest time as many as all immigrants from the rest of the world combined but could be, and were, returned to Mexico en masse when large growers did not need their labor."[51]

Immigration laws have undergone a variety of changes since then, but this employment pattern for Mexican workers has remained. Even when federal law bans Mexican migration, immigration officials typically look the other way while employers openly flout the law—reserving occasional punishment for undocumented workers, arrested and deported in showcase immigration "raids."

Agricultural firms have thus permanently enjoyed a virtually unlimited supply of temporary Mexican labor—a low-wage workforce made up of entire families without legal rights who toil long hours at backbreaking work.

But if the rapid expansion of capitalism brought misery to the vast majority of workers, America's rulers developed a "scientific" explanation as the twentieth century dawned. The massive inequality between the wealthy corporate elite and the nation's laborers was explained away by a school of academia known as "eugenics," a bizarre twist on Darwin's theory of evolution. In a reactionary interpretation of "the survival of the fittest" (something Darwin surely never intended), the dominant wing of the eugenics movement regarded the wealthy portion of society as genetically superior to the poor, and whites overall as superior to other races and ethnic groups.

Eugenics, the "science" of "improving heredity," (in the image of wealthy white Anglo-Saxons) counterposed the "aristogenic" population (those with good genes) with the "cacogenic" majority (those with bad genes). The eugenics movement was initiated and funded by corporate powerbrokers, backed by willing teams of biologists, psychologists, and anthropologists, who provided a plethora of "evidence" that social inequality was merely the result of some people possessing much better genes than others. Those at the top of the social ladder had proven their racial superiority, while those at the bottom were biologically incapable of success, according to these scientists.[52]

This theory rose to national prominence in the immediate aftermath of Jim Crow segregation and Black disfranchisement in the South. The eugenics movement doubtless provided considerable comfort to segregationists who enacted color bars on African-American labor and to the majority of Northern employers who refused to hire Blacks except as strikebreakers. In addition, many employers justified mistreating foreign-born workers on the basis that immigrants were genetically inferior. During the 1902 coal strike, Reading Railroad president George Bayer responded to reports that 145,000 strikers and their families were starving with the following retort: "They don't suffer. Why, they can't even speak English."[53]

Corporate leaders such as Alexander Graham Bell and Mrs. E. H. Harriman (married to the president of Union Pacific Railroad) helped to spearhead the eugenics movement through the Eugenics Section of the American Breeder's Association, founded in 1906. John D. Rockefeller donated $21,432 to this organization between 1910 and 1917. A different organization, the Race Betterment Foundation, founded by the Kellogg (cereal) family, enjoyed the support of the Rockefellers and the Carnegies, in addition to the Ford Motor Company, the U.S. Steel Company, and other leading corporate interests.[54]

As historian David Gersh argued, the eugenics movement was funded by corporate money, supported by charitable and political groups, and legitimized by academics. Harvard psychologist Robert Yerkes of the Organization on Prisons and Prison Labor, for example, advocated "[b]oth positive eugenics (superior people should marry one another and have lots of children) and negative eugenics (sterilization, segregation, marriage restriction, and immigrant restriction for those declared inferior)."[55]

The rise of U.S. imperialism gave further impetus to the eugenics movement in the early twentieth century. It was much easier to justify the colonization of other nations by the U.S. military if the conquered were regarded as inferior beings. Rudyard Kipling's poem, "The White Man's Burden," was used to justify the U.S. takeover of the Philippines after the Spanish-American War, and was greeted by popular acclaim, enjoying broad publication in 1899.[56]

Hiring policies based on eugenics were quickly incorporated into the scientific management techniques that guided corporate policies by the early 1920s. As Montgomery described, managers sought

> to select workers of the right nationality, race, and sex for each position. All managers seem to have agreed with International Harvester's H. A. Worman that "each race has aptitude for certain kinds of work," even though they often disagreed as to just which "race" was best for what. . . . At Pittsburgh's Central Tube Company, the personnel manager analyzed the "racial adaptability" of thirty-six different ethnic groups to twenty-four different kinds of work under twelve sets of conditions and plotted them all on a chart to guide his hiring practice.[57]

Those "Fit" and "Unfit" to Bear Children

Socialist Margaret Sanger was an early pioneer in the fight for birth control during the early years of the twentieth century. Sanger's early projects enjoyed the support of radicals from the IWW and the

Socialist Party, driven by a desire to help working-class women gain access to contraception as a means of bettering their lives. In March 1914, Sanger began producing a newspaper, the *Woman Rebel,* espousing birth control and women's rights more generally. The U.S. Postal Service immediately pronounced the newspaper "obscene" and banned it from the nation's mail system.[58]

Over the next few years, however, Sanger's radicalism faded. She became swayed by eugenics arguments as she sought allies in the propertied class to fund more ambitious projects—including the eventual founding of Planned Parenthood. By 1919, Sanger's publication, *Birth Control Review,* demanded, "More children from the fit and less from the unfit—that is the chief issue of birth control."[59]

Those "unfit" to bear children, according to the Eugenicists, included the mentally and physically disabled, prisoners, and the non-white poor. They acted on this conclusion, spearheading laws enacted in 27 states by 1932 calling for compulsory sterilization for the "feeble-minded, insane, criminal, and physically defective."[60]

In 1939, the Birth Control Federation of America, as historian Dorothy E. Roberts describes, "planned a 'Negro Project' designed to limit reproduction by Blacks who 'still breed carelessly and disastrously, with the result that the increase among Negroes, even more than among whites, is from that portion of the population least intelligent and fit, and least able to rear children properly.' "[61]

Population control programs left large numbers of Black women, Latinas, and Native American women sterilized against their will or without their knowledge through much of the twentieth century. In 1974, an Alabama court found that between 100,000 and 150,000 poor Black teenagers had been sterilized each year in Alabama during this time period. A 1970s study showed 25 percent of Native American women had been sterilized under federally funded programs, and that Black and Latina married women had been sterilized in much greater proportions than married women in the population at large.[62] By 1968, one-third of women of childbearing age in Puerto Rico—still a U.S. colony—had been permanently sterilized. Many of these women were sterilized without their clear consent, or without telling them the operation was permanent.[63]

Racism and the Labor Movement

This extreme level of racism left a permanent stamp on the labor movement. The South remains a nonunion stronghold today, largely because the legacy of white supremacy has not yet been destroyed. The existence of a nonunion, low-wage Southern workforce has hung like a noose around the neck of the U.S. labor movement historically. But until the 1930s, instead of championing working-class interests by challenging racist segregation and bigotry, all too often the labor movement tolerated it—and sometimes actively supported it.

In the debate over slavery itself, the early American labor movement failed to ally with the cause of abolition. While a minority of Northern workers became actively committed to ending slavery, the main labor organizations linked themselves to the pro-slavery Democratic Party. As Davis argues, the consequences were far-reaching: "In the absence of a working-class anti-slavery current, labor lost the chance to forge its own links of unity with the Black masses of the South or to create its own revolutionary-democratic tradition.[64]

To be sure, this alliance was based *partly* on the Democrats' ability to convince white workers that the Republicans were a party of big business. The Democrats argued that Republican policies would give "bounties to particular interests to the detriment of the great industrial classes of the Country . . . and sought to aggrandize the few at the expense of the many." In addition, Democrats warned white workers that the abolition of slavery would "bring the Negroes into the Northern states to take the place of white laborers."[65]

The New York City antidraft race riot in 1863 was an explosion of racist violence by Irish immigrants—who were *also* targets of vicious bigotry at that time. The rioting was directed both against the class-based conscription system, which exempted the rich from fighting, and against Blacks. Davis argued that it "exhibited the schizophrenic consciousness of the immigrant poor: their hatred of the silk-stocking rich and their equal resentment against Blacks.[66]

After the Civil War, some sections of the labor movement opened their doors to Black workers. The National Labor Union, formed in 1866, invited Blacks to join. But when some member craft unions protested the idea of racial integration, they were not challenged. More significant was the rise of the Knights of Labor in the 1880s, organizing Blacks, women, and most immigrants into the first mass industrial union in U.S. history. The Knights also introduced the slogan "an injury to one is the concern of all," a guiding principle of class struggle ever since.[67] At the height of the Knights' strength in 1886, it claimed roughly 60,000 Black workers as members. By 1887, an estimated 65,000 women were enrolled in the order. [68]

Montgomery described the Knights' role in the bitter 1886 strike against Jay Gould's Southwestern Railroad line:

> They supported rallies, press campaigns, and boycotts that brought men and women, Black and white workers of many occupations into the railroad towns' various local assemblies, to the increasing anxiety of the local elites. The Knights' gospel of "universal brotherhood" assumed an especially militant aspect when District Assembly 101 was formed, demanded recognition from the southwest lines as agent for all railwaymen, and presented wage demands for yard and section hands.[69]

The Knights of Labor was politically backward, however, on the issue of Chinese immigration. While the Knights welcomed many immigrants into the order, it also joined other unions to campaign for an end to Chinese immigration.[70] This contradiction weakened the Knights' otherwise path-breaking steps toward uniting the labor movement across racial lines.

The Knights of Labor was also confused on other key issues. The order's eccentric leader, Terence Powderly, opposed the strike weapon as a "relic of barbarism" that provided only "temporary relief" to workers. In addition, while emphasizing class solidarity, the Knights explicitly rejected radical politics, refusing to march behind red banners or contingents of armed workers in mass demonstrations for the eight-hour day in 1886. Nevertheless, over Powderly's opposition, general assemblies of the Knights responded to the call for a national strike on May 1, 1886, and "embraced it jubilantly." [71]

Despite its weaknesses, the Knights' defining feature was its commitment to industrial unionism, thus for the first time laying the basis for united working-class action. As Engels argued at the time, the Knights provided a model for future generations of American workers:

> The Knights of Labor are the first national organization created by the American working class as a whole; whatever be their origin and history, whatever their shortcomings and little absurdities, whatever their platform and their constitution, here they are, the work of

practically the whole class of American wage-workers . . . here is the raw material out of which the future of the American working-class movement, and along with it, the future of American society at large, has to be shaped.[72]

But by the 1890s, the Knights began fading in influence alongside the rising dominance of the AFL as a craft federation, and the course of the American labor movement made a sharp shift rightward. The AFL not only refused to organize the unskilled, but also refused to force its member unions to organize Blacks into the same unions with whites.

The AFL technically opposed a color bar on Black workers. But in the 1890s, the Federation admitted the International Association of Machinists (IAM), which in practice refused to allow Blacks as members. In 1899, two unions with formal color bars—the Order of Railroad Telegraphers and the Brotherhood of Railway Trackmen—joined the Federation.[73] The following year, the AFL amended its constitution to permit the chartering of segregated unions for Blacks who were excluded from whites-only unions. By the turn of the century the precedent had been set: the AFL was a segregated union federation, in deed if not in word. Its membership was only 3 percent Black, with the vast majority of its Black members organized into segregated union locals, even when they worked side by side with whites for the same employer.[74]

The AFL's exclusionary policies were not limited to African Americans, but extended to immigrants and women who filled the ranks of unskilled labor and were categorically shut out of most craft unions. In contrast to industrial unions, which united skilled and unskilled workers into common organizations, craft unionism first arose as a means of protecting tradesmen from the deskilling of their crafts that accompanied the rise of factory production. This strategy was largely unsuccessful in this aim and failed to prevent the decline or even disappearance of most dominant nineteenth-century trades, such as iron rollers, puddlers, and finishers.[75] Moreover, this sectional craft strategy undermined class-wide solidarity, often pitting craft unions against the unskilled seeking to join unions.

AFL president Samuel Gompers was an unapologetic racist who shared the ideology of the eugenics movement. Although Gompers was a socialist as a young cigar maker in New York, he embraced conservatism as he advanced within the leadership of the AFL. In

his autobiography, Gompers defended "the principle that the maintenance of the nation depended on the maintenance of racial purity
and strength." When he advocated literacy tests as a means to exclude immigrants, he said these "would exclude hardly any natives
of Great Britain, Ireland, Germany, France or Scandinavia. It will
shut out a considerable number of South Italians and of Slavs and
other[s] each or more undesirable and injurious." [76]

Gompers routinely referred to Blacks as "darkies," who he described as lazy, ignorant, and immoral.[77] Although most AFL unions
excluded African Americans, Gompers refused to admit that the
labor movement bore any responsibility for Black workers who
then became strikebreakers. He vowed to unleash upon Black strikebreakers, "a race hatred far worse than any ever known." [78]

His threat was realized in East St. Louis in 1917, when local
AFL leaders, having refused to organize Blacks into unions, turned
around and declared war on them. When large numbers of Blacks
began to migrate North during World War I, AFL leaders in East
St. Louis claimed that the "growing menace" they posed to organized labor was so great that "drastic action must be taken . . . to get
rid of a certain portion of those who are already here." [79]

Within a week, the East St. Louis riot began. As Philip Foner
described,

> [E]nraged mobs of white residents took to the streets and began shoot-
> ing, lynching, and burning Blacks whenever they found them, killing
> men, women, and children. For almost two days the rioting raged until
> order was finally restored. At least thirty-nine Blacks and eight whites
> lost their lives in the riot, with a hundred or more injured . . . making it
> one of the worst anti-Negro riots, in terms of lives lost, of the twentieth
> century.[80]

Although AFL leaders had incited the East St. Louis riot, the
Federation refused to denounce racial segregation and violence a
few months later, at its 1917 convention. The AFL majority rejected
a resolution proposed by its left wing, denouncing discrimination
against Blacks. The resolution, against disfranchisement, segregation, lynching, and other aspects of racial discrimination, called on
the AFL to use its influence "to the end that all the political, civic,
and economic disabilities so offensive and destructive to the rights of
Negroes as human beings and American citizens be removed." The
resolution was roundly denounced before it was voted down.[81]

The Multiracial UMWA

The United Mine Workers of America (UMWA) was an important exception to the AFL's racist record. Because mining is so hazardous, miners' safety has traditionally depended on trust between skilled and unskilled workers, whose lives literally depend on each other. In addition, a large number of miners were African American while immigrant workers also entered the mining industry in substantial numbers.

Furthermore, most mining companies forced their workers' families to live on company property in company housing and to shop at expensive company stores. The company was therefore not only an employer, but also a landlord and retailer to whom the miners were constantly in debt. This instilled an intense hatred of the company within mining communities, boosting loyalty to the union among entire mining families. Miners' children went on strike at fourteen Pennsylvania schools to protest scabbing by their teachers' fathers and brothers during the 1902 coal strike.[82]

As Montgomery noted, miners' "bulwark—almost their secular church—was the union. No other AFL union of the 1910s evoked such loyalty from members, such fervent responses to strike calls from miners who were not members, such rank-and-file fury at leaders' misdeeds . . . as did the UMWA."[83]

The miners' union was part of the AFL but was industrial in structure. By 1900, earlier segregation policies had been overturned, and the vast majority of UMWA locals were "mixed," bringing immigrants, Blacks, and whites into the same locals. This was true even in the segregated South. In Alabama, where by 1904 half of the union's 12,000 miners were Black, one observer wrote, "Some camps whose living conditions were almost completely segregated met at union halls, heard reports from Black officers, and elected Black men as local committeemen and as convention delegates."[84]

All told, by 1902, the UMWA could claim 20,000 Black miners as union members, between 10 percent and 15 percent of the total membership. Fines and other disciplinary actions were taken against miners' locals that discriminated on the basis of race. In 1912, the UMWA insisted that a regional contract covering Illinois, Indiana, Ohio, and Pennsylvania include a clause "that no worker shall be discriminated against in any way on account of race, creed, nationality, or color." [85] In 1919, the UMWA staff included organizers of many races and nationalities, including a sprinkling of Chinese and Japanese staffers. [86]

The UMWA provides the earliest and most important example of a multiracial industrial union that thrived even in the segregated South. This union was the exception, rather than the rule, however, until the rise of the CIO in the 1930s finally challenged the dominance of craft unionism—and the labor movement finally began to break down racial barriers on a national scale.

The miners' principled tradition therefore only highlights the terrible deficiencies of the AFL.

While the UMWA leadership was not radical, many of its members were drawn to socialism, as Lens describes:

> The UMWA under [President John] Mitchell—and subsequently under John L. Lewis—was a strange combination of militancy and radicalism at its base and moderation at its apex. During [the 1902 coal strike], for instance, the Socialist Party was able to form as many as three or four locals per day in the colliery regions. "The Coal strike," reported one of the party's organizers, "has done more for the cause of Socialism than all of the events that ever happened in the United States before." [87]

Multiracial Unity in the Segregated South

Southern employers relied upon—and viciously fought to maintain—the system of white supremacy. Their motivations included a strong desire to keep the working class divided by race. But Black and white timber workers in Louisiana, separated into "biracial" unions (Black and white locals within the same union), fought hard to overcome the many obstacles to class unity workers faced in the early twentieth century. Their attempts to organize were defeated—but by company violence, not by racial animosity.

Louisiana lumber companies used private armies to crush the biracial Brotherhood of Timber Workers (BTW) after it formed in 1911. The company's army broke up union meetings, beating and flogging the workers, and drove entire union families out of their homes. BTW members carried their own guns for protection when they went on strike. Ultimately, the company prevailed. Norwood noted, "Although the companies proved unable to exploit racial divisions among the strikers, they prevailed because of superior fire-power." [88]

A few years later, the Great Southern Lumber Company added "cold-blooded murder" to the methods it used to defeat a biracial AFL organizing drive in Bogalusa, Louisiana. The company ordered its troops to hunt down and capture the leader of the Black saw-mill and loggers' union. He hid at union headquarters, protected by white unionists. The company's private army surrounded the building, massacring four of the white workers, while the African-American unionist escaped. It is again worth noting that the com-pany violence did not weaken the racial solidarity of the workers, even in defeat. [89]

The government's role in backing employers' efforts to com-bat racial solidarity should not be underestimated. As Montgom-ery argued,

> Working-class efforts did circumvent the barriers of racial separation during the 1880s in many parts of the South—and even after disen-franchisement and legal segregation of Afro-Americans had been fully accomplished—in the coal mines of Alabama and West Virginia, on the New Orleans docks, and in the timber camps of Louisiana. All such ef-forts, however, had to confront not only the economic power of the em-ployers and the mutual suspicion of white and Black workers but also the ultimate bulwark of white supremacy and segregation: *the state*. [90]

Nevertheless, at certain key points, workers and sharecroppers managed to successfully forge solidarity in the segregated South. The 1890s witnessed two noteworthy examples: the Populist move-ment, of which some Southern populists were the most radical, and the New Orleans general strike of 1892. Neither of these attempts to forge multiracial unity survived over the long term. But both provide insight into the volatile dynamics of race and class.

The Populist Movement

The People's Party, launched in 1892 as a third-party alternative, gave expression to the widespread hostility toward the industrial barons who dominated both the Democratic and the Republican Parties. The Populists aimed to represent "the common people" and denied merchants and landowners the right to membership. Among its other planks, the Populist movement called for "collective ownership by the people of the means of production and distribution." [91] Its platform also declared, "the interests of rural and civil labor are the same," and demanded shorter working hours and a ban on the Pinkerton strikebreaking agency.[92]

The Populists' other demands included, as noted by Lens, " 'free and unlimited coinage of silver and gold at the present legal ratio of sixteen to one,' government ownership and operation of the railroads, telephones, and telegraphs, a progressive income tax, and reclaiming land owned by railroads and other corporations 'in excess of their actual needs.' " [93]

Some Populist leaders aimed to win poor whites to a common class program with poor African Americans. But Populism rose at the historic moment when the system of white supremacy was poised to triumph throughout the South. The Party platform did not offer a broad challenge to segregation laws or Black Codes, and its constituencies varied from one locality to the next.

The People's Party did, however, articulate a program of racial solidarity based upon class interests. Populist leader Tom Watson, for example, argued for racial unity in terms echoing those of abolitionist Frederick Douglass: "You are made to hate each other because upon that hatred is rested the keystone of the arch of financial despotism which enslaves you both. You are deceived and blinded that you may not see how this race antagonism perpetuates a monetary system which beggars you both." [94]

Although the movement's leaders were overwhelmingly white, many Populists directly challenged the system of white supremacy. In Georgia, which led all states in the number of lynchings, Populists organized to defend African Americans against racial violence. In one instance, two thousand white sharecroppers came together to defend a Black Populist from a threatened lynching. In Mississippi, Texas, and North Carolina, Populists pledged to set up free public schools for African-American and white children. In North Carolina, Populist legislators changed voting district boundaries in order to elect a Black congressman.[95]

The party held mass meetings frequently numbering in the thousands. At its height, the People's Party succeeded in winning the votes of millions of poor Blacks and whites, in a grand coalition against the wealthy and powerful in the face of worsening conditions for small and tenant farmers.

As Bloom noted,

> In 1894, the People's Party polled 44.5 percent of the vote despite massive fraud and vote manipulation. They took two Congressional and many legislative seats in Alabama, and in Mississippi they won one third of the vote. In 1896 they won control of the senate in North Carolina and shared control of the House with the Republican Party. In that year, the Populist candidate for governor of Louisiana won 44 percent of the vote.[96]

In response to the widespread success of the Populist movement, Southern states passed laws intensifying the system of white supremacy—voting restrictions, including the poll tax disfranchising Blacks, and Jim Crow segregation laws. In addition, as Bloom argued, "The Populist movement, to which the Southern elite had responded by driving Blacks out of politics, may have caused a similar reaction in the North. The movement was, after all, directed against Northern business interests, and it sought to unite the South and the West against them."[97]

The New Orleans General Strike of 1892

Black and white workers labored side by side on New Orleans docks, and Black workers formed a large segment of the city's labor force—described as the most integrated in the United States in 1911. New Orleans workers had established a strong biracial union tradition well before the 1892 strike.[98] But New Orleans was also a bastion of white supremacy. Each step forward for the labor movement was a setback for white supremacy, and vice versa, in a shifting balance of forces from the end of the Civil War through the early twentieth century.

The New Orleans general strike of 1892 took place in the midst of the Populist upsurge. In the 1892 election, Louisiana's Democratic and Republican Parties were both split by the Populist vote. The platform of the Louisiana People's Party read in part, "You Colored Men . . . you must now realize that there is no hope of any further material benefit to you in the Republican Party, and that if you remain in it you will continue to be hewers of wood and drawers of water in the future as you have been in the past . . . Democrats. . . . The specter of Negro supremacy has been used to keep you in the toils of the scheming machine politicians."[99]

In a stunning show of solidarity, 25,000 workers—nearly the entire New Orleans workforce, Black and white—went on strike. The vast majority of the strikers belonged to biracial unions. But one of the five strike leaders was an African American, and the striking unions held together in solidarity throughout the strike. One sympathetic unionist described, "There are fully 25,000 men idle. There is no newspaper to be printed, no gas or electric light in this city, no wagons, no carpenters, painters or in fact any business doing. . . . It is a strike that will go down in history." [100]

Faced with Populist strength at the polls and racial unity within its local working class, New Orleans employers fought back with a vengeance. The strike ended in defeat after eleven days, following the threat of military force, in a monumental blow to working-class unity.

In the years that followed, Louisiana's state legislature instituted stringent Jim Crow laws, adding a property requirement for voting in 1900. Within several years, the Black vote in Louisiana dropped by 90 percent, and the *white vote* dropped by 60 percent, leading to the collapse of the Populists.[101] The defeat of the strike and the collapse of the People's Party left white supremacy unchallenged in New Orleans—in a period of accelerating racist violence across the South. Racial tension was such that, during an incident of police brutality in 1900, a Black man shot 27 whites, including seven police. The incident touched off a massive race riot against African Americans in New Orleans, in which the Black shooter was lynched and five other Blacks were killed.[102]

But the riot was followed by another, equally rapid, reverse shift in consciousness, as biracial solidarity revived in concert with the labor movement. In 1907, Black and white workers again united to completely shut down the city's port for three weeks—this time, winning their demands. Afterward, a Port Inquiry Commission made up of local politicians identified the port's greatest problem as its *lack* of racial segregation. "One of the greatest drawbacks to New Orleans is the working of the white and negro races on terms of equality," it concluded, recommending that in the future Blacks and whites be separated "for sociological reasons." [103]

Race, Class, and "Whiteness Theory"

Given the depths of racism in U.S. society, it is not surprising that Black separatism is an important political current historically. Black nationalism is a legitimate response to the colossal and sustained level of racism directed against African Americans since slavery. Black nationalism has risen in influence among African Americans particularly when the level of class struggle is low and the possibility for multiracial class unity appears hopeless. As Ahmed Shawki argues in *Black Liberation and Socialism,* "Above all, the main factor that gives rise to Black nationalism is white racism." [104]

The notion of "white skin privilege," that all whites share a common interest in upholding a system of white supremacy, has provided the unifying core for Black nationalism—from the conservative nationalism of Marcus Garvey's "Back to Africa" movement in the 1920s to the revolutionary nationalism of the League of Revolutionary Black Workers that launched DRUM in the 1960s.

But who is responsible for the perpetuation of racism—both ideologically and structurally—in U.S. society? And who stands to benefit? In recent years, the notion that all whites gain from racism and are equally responsible for Black oppression has gained acceptance, especially in academic circles. "Whiteness theory," now in vogue among many current labor historians, also strikes the theme of white skin privilege. But the theoretical framework of whiteness theory has more in common with postmodernism than with the ideas or politics of Black nationalism. Historian David Roediger helped launch this academic trend with the publication of his 1991 book, *The Wages of Whiteness.* Despite the legally sanctioned and violently enforced system of white supremacy, backed by both political parties after Reconstruction, Roediger asserts, "working class 'whiteness' and white supremacy [are] creations, in part, of the white working class itself." [105]

Roediger accuses Marxists of reducing racism to something that merely "trickles down" from on high, and criticizes Marxists' tendency "to concentrate on the ruling class's role in perpetuating racial oppression and cast white workers as dupes, even if virtuous ones." [106]

To be sure, Roediger pays homage to revered civil rights leader W. E. B. Du Bois. Indeed, the phrase "wages of whiteness" harks back to Du Bois' classic work, *Black Reconstruction in America,* noting the effects of racism on Southern white workers: "[T]he white group of laborers, while they receive a low wage, were compensated in part by a sort of public and psychological wage. They were given public deference and titles of courtesy because they were white. They were admitted freely with all classes of white people to public functions, public parks, and the best schools." [107]

But Du Bois' quote, taken out of context, is misleading. Du Bois positions the above comment between two others that clearly show his intention to explain how the ideology of white supremacy prevented Black and white workers from uniting as a class, to the detriment of *both*. First, Du Bois argues, racism "drove such a wedge between the white and Black workers that there probably are not today in the world two groups of workers with practically identical interests who hate and fear each other so deeply and persistently and who are kept so far apart that neither sees anything of common interest." [108]

A few paragraphs later Du Bois adds, "The result of this was that the wages of both classes could be kept low, the whites fearing to be supplanted by Negro labor, the Negroes always being threatened by the substitution of white labor." [109]

For Roediger, in contrast, the "psychological wage"—and psychology generally—is paramount. Roediger argues, "working class whiteness reflects, even in the form of the minstrel show, hatreds that were profoundly mixed with a longing for values attributed to Blacks." [110] Labor historian Brian Kelly remarked that this emphasis by the whiteness wing of labor historians "leaves one wondering whether white supremacy served any function *other* than defending the material and psychological interests of working-class whites." [111]

But the important instances of racial unity even during the era of segregation merit explanation. Roediger himself admits, "The popular working class consciousness that emerged during the later stages of the Civil War, especially in the North, saw the liberation of Black slaves as a *model,* and not just as a threat. Like freedpeople, white workers came to see the Civil War as a 'Jubilee' and, in the words of Detroit labor leader Richard Trevellick, to hope that 'we are about to be emancipated.'" [112]

Nevertheless, Roediger concludes, "The meager record of biracial organization does not allow us to fall back on the generalization that Black-white unity automatically places labor in a better tactical position from which to attack capital." [113]

Although Roediger claims otherwise, [114] the political framework for whiteness theory appears deeply indebted to an offshoot of post-modernism known as "identity politics," popular among much of the post-1970s academic left. [115]

Whiteness Theory and the Politics of "Difference"

Ernesto Laclau and Chantal Mouffe—self-described post-Marxists—first articulated the theoretical framework for identity politics in their 1985 book *Hegemony and Socialist Strategy: Towards a Radical Democratic Politics.* [116] Laclau and Mouffe's (extremely) abstract theory divorces every form of oppression not only from society generally, but also from each other. As they put it, society is a field "criss-crossed with antagonisms" in which each form of oppression exists as an entirely autonomous system.

According to this schema, social class is just another form of oppression, separate from all others, leaving the system of *exploitation* equally adrift. Furthermore, each separate system of oppression has its own unique set of beneficiaries: all whites benefit from racism, all men benefit from sexism and all heterosexuals benefit from homophobia—each in a free-floating system of "subordination."

Not surprisingly, Laclau and Mouffe argue," '[T]he possibility of a *unified discourse* of the left is also erased. If the various subject positions and the diverse antagonisms and points of rupture constitute a *diversity* and not a *diversification*, it is clear they cannot be led back to a point from which they could all be embraced and explained by a single discourse." [117] So identity politics, the politics of "difference," seeks to refute the unifying potential of working-class interests.

Significantly, Laclau and Mouffe insist that the state itself is autonomous, and take great pains to refute the Marxist assumption that the state consistently acts on behalf of society's ruling class. [118] This theory, if it were grounded in reality, would have enormous implications for the origin of white supremacy. White supremacy then *could* be a creation "in part, of the white working class itself," as Roediger asserts.

But, as historian Gregory Meyerson responded to this analysis,

[W]hile it is true that the various identity categories intersect—class is lived through race and gender etc.—and while I am also willing to accept that no experience of oppression should be privileged over another, it does not follow that multiple oppressions require multiple structural causes . . . [Roediger's] working class appears too autonomous, at times nearly sealed off from ongoing processes of class rule. This autonomy, inconsistently maintained . . . requires Roediger to supplant class analysis with psychocultural analysis.[119]

Who Benefits from Racism?

Central to Roediger's critique is the notion that Marxism minimizes the importance of race:

The point that race is created wholly ideologically and historically, while class is not wholly so created, has often been boiled down to the notion that class (or "the economic") is more real, more fundamental, more basic or more *important* than race, both in political terms and in terms of historical analysis. . . . In a quite meaningless way, the "race problem" is consistently reduced to one of class.[120]

But Roediger's analysis is flawed, on several counts. First, he appears to assume that working-class interests have been defined historically *only* by the actions of white males, as if women and African Americans—not to mention other oppressed populations—have not played an active role in defining working-class identity. Second, Roediger falsely assumes that by designating class as the primary antagonism in capitalist society, Marxism discounts the importance of race. Most significantly, Roediger's entire thesis rests on the assumption that white workers benefit from the existence of racism.

Meyerson counters this set of assumptions, proposing that Marx's emphasis on the centrality of class relations brings oppression to the forefront, as a precondition for working-class unity:

Marxism properly interpreted emphasizes the primacy of class in a number of senses. One, of course, is the primacy of the working class as a revolutionary agent—a primacy which does not, as often thought, render women and people of color "secondary." Such an equation of white male and working class, as well as a corresponding division between a "white" male working class identity and all the others, whose identity is thereby viewed as either primarily one of gender and race or hybrid, is a view this essay contests all along the way. The primacy of class means that building a multiracial, multi-gendered international working-class organization or organizations should be the goal of any revolutionary movement: the primacy of class puts the fight against racism and sexism at the center. The intelligibility of this position is rooted in the *explanatory* primacy of class analysis for understanding the structural determinants of race, gender, and class oppression. Oppression is multiple and intersecting but its causes are not.[121]

Designating class as the primary antagonism in capitalist society bears no inference on the "importance" of racism, as Roediger claims. Marxism merely assumes a *causal* relationship—that white supremacy as a system was instituted by capital, to the detriment of labor as a whole. Marxist theory rests on the assumption that white workers do *not* benefit from a system of white supremacy. Indeed, Marx argued of slavery, the most oppressive of all systems of exploitation, "In the United States of America, every independent workers' movement was paralyzed as long as slavery disfigured part of the republic. Labor cannot emancipate itself in the white skin where in the black it is branded." [122] Marx was not alone in assuming that racism, by dividing the working class along ideological lines, harmed the class interests of both white and Black workers. Frederick Douglass stated unambiguously of slaveholders, "They divided both to conquer each." [123]

Douglass elaborated, "Both are plundered and by the same plunderers. The slave is robbed by his master, of all his earnings above what is required for his physical necessities; and the white man is robbed by the slave system, because he is flung into competition with a class of laborers who work without wages." [124]

Capitalism forces workers to compete with each other. The unremitting pressure from a layer of workers—be they low-wage or unemployed—is a constant reminder that workers compete for limited jobs that afford a decent standard of living. The working class has no interest in maintaining a system that thrives upon inequality and oppression. All empirical evidence shows quite the opposite. Racism against Blacks and other racially oppressed groups serves both to lower the living standards of the entire working class and to weaken workers' ability to fight back. Whenever capitalists can threaten to replace one group of workers with another—poorly paid—group of workers, neither group benefits.

The historically nonunion South has not only depressed the wages of Black workers, but also lowered the wages of Southern white workers overall, as noted previously—and prevented the labor movement from achieving victory at important junctures. So even in the short term the working class as a whole has nothing to gain from oppression.

A Question of Consciousness

But Marxist theory is careful to distinguish between material benefits and the psychology, or consciousness, regarding race. Whereas material (i.e., class) interests are fixed and objective, consciousness is fluid and subjective.

When Marx identified the working class as the agent for revolutionary change, he was describing its historical potential, rather than its actuality or as a foregone conclusion. Without the counterweight of the class struggle, competition between groups of workers can act as an obstacle to the development of class consciousness, and encourage the growth of what Marx called "false consciousness." Marx did not regard white workers as "dupes" as Roediger claims in his caricature of Marxism.[125] Rather, Marx merely understood, as he argued in the *Communist Manifesto,* "The ruling ideas of each age have ever been the ideas of its ruling class."[126]

Ruling-class ideology in its various forms serves to justify the class status quo, pitting workers against each other, and impeding workers' ability to unite in struggle against their employers. Racist ideology, so strongly asserted by Southern segregationists and the eugenics movement, did exercise a strong deterrent to class unity at its height. And racism remains the key division within the working class.

But consciousness is a changing, not static, phenomenon. The dynamic is such that workers' objective circumstances are always in conflict with bourgeois ideology, as evidenced by the exceptional instances of multiracial unity even in the South during Jim Crow.

Roediger's analysis misses this *active* dynamic of class struggle central to Marxist theory—in which workers' objective class interests collide with "the ideas of its ruling class." New Orleans workers demonstrated the volatility of this dynamic, in a racially united general strike in 1892, followed by murderous race riots in 1900, and then a successful union struggle of white and Black workers in 1907. Marx described in the *Communist Manifesto:* "This organization of proletarians into a class . . . is continually being upset again by the competition between the workers themselves. But it ever rises up again, stronger, firmer, mightier." [127]

Much as the Knights of Labor contradicted itself by campaigning against Chinese immigration while admitting women, Blacks, and most immigrant workers, individual workers also hold contradictory ideas inside their own heads. Workers are neither dupes nor romantic heroes, but active agents in a process of determining their genuine class interests.

Because consciousness is subjective, no segment of the working class can be expected to behave in a predetermined way. Marx distinguished between a class "in itself" and a class "for itself," which has reached broad class consciousness. The political intervention of radicals within the working-class movement has frequently played a crucial role in advancing class consciousness.

As Marx wrote, "The revolution is necessary, therefore, not only because the *ruling* class cannot be overthrown any other way, but because the class *overthrowing* it can only in a revolution succeed in ridding itself of all the old crap and become fitted to found society anew." [128] Racism and segregation have historically been the key obstacles to working-class unity in the United States—the worst of the "old crap" that must be conquered if the labor movement is to succeed.

The Corporate Duopoly

The Democratic Party was a pro-slavery party in the Civil War, while the Republicans represented both radical reformers and the Northern industrial capitalist class. After the Northern victory in the Civil War established the dominance of industrial capital, the old Southern plantation owners provided the segregationist backbone for the Democratic Party until the Reagan era of the 1980s, when many Southern "Dixiecrats" began shifting toward the more conservative Republican Party.

The Democrats and Republicans, as two wings of the capitalist class, have shared political power between them for 150 years. Historian Matthew Josephson described the relationship between the "captains of industry" from railroads, mining, and banking and the two main parties during the late nineteenth century:

> The masters of business who sat in the upper chambers of Congress (or "Millionaires' Club," as it was humorously called), or their close associates who became Representatives or governors of states, make up a long and distinguished roll call [of Republicans]. . . . Furthermore, the opposing party [the Democrats], the "outs," were like the Republicans, who were usually the "ins," also led by masters of business or corporation lawyers.[129]

Even in the era of slavery, the Democrats' appeal was double-edged: Democratic Party politicians appealed to workers on the basis of class, by promising pro-working class reforms,[130] *and also* stirred up race resentments. On this basis, the Democratic Party managed to gain a considerable following among white workers, mainly among Irish and other immigrants, even before the Civil War.

At least part of the Democratic Party's appeal for immigrant workers, as David Brody argued, was that "immigrant workers, always at the receiving end of nativist hostility, now had in the Black man a suitable target on whom to discharge their own rage."[131]

The Democratic Party has always been every bit as much a ruling-class party as the Republicans. Yet, for well over a hundred years it has consistently portrayed itself, with considerable success, as more responsive to the needs of workers and the poor. At each point when workers have put their faith in the Democrats, however, their hopes have been betrayed.

The consistently bourgeois base of the Democratic Party should be a central concern for the labor movement, yet the Democrats' professed class loyalties (most notable during election campaigns) have traditionally confused labor activists and even much of the political left.

The Graveyard of Social Movements

Setting a lasting pattern, the Democrats managed to absorb—and thereby destroy—the Populist movement of the 1890s. The Populists' success at the polls posed a direct threat to the Southern dominance of the Democratic Party. For this reason, William Jennings Bryan, the Democrats' 1896 presidential candidate, set his sights on winning votes away from the People's Party.

Although Bryan lost the 1896 election to the Republican candidate, William McKinley, he won most of the Populist vote. The

People's Party collapsed in the wake of this spectacular defeat. Populist leader Tom Watson defected to the Democratic Party, abandoning the struggle for racial unity and embracing the Democrats' message of white supremacy. The Populist debacle thus marked the Democratic Party's first foray as the "graveyard of social movements."

Bryan, for his part, went on to become Secretary of State in 1913 under Democrat Woodrow Wilson. In his new role as imperialist enforcer, Bryan led the U.S. invasions of Haiti, Nicaragua, Mexico, and the Dominican Republic. Baring his racist Democratic Party roots, he exclaimed upon learning that rich Haitians educated their children in France, "Dear me. Think of it! Niggers speaking French!" [132]

While the Populist movement debated whether to break with the two-party system, a parallel struggle was taking place within the AFL. Like the Populists, socialist delegates to the 1893 AFL convention won a majority to endorse the principle of "collective ownership of the means of production." Gompers and other conservatives banded together to overturn the collective ownership demand a year later. The socialists in the AFL retaliated by removing Gompers by majority vote as AFL president. [133]

But by 1895 Gompers regained office, this time permanently. Under his leadership, the AFL became more integrated into the two-party system. This move was encouraged by many local union leaders who found it personally useful to ingratiate themselves to local politicians in cities such as New York and Boston, where Democratic mayors ran developed patronage machines. Although socialists remained a thorn in Gompers' side (up to 40 percent of AFL delegates continued to support socialist resolutions until World War I), the conservatives carried the day.

The AFL finally cemented its alliance with the Democrats by supporting Woodrow Wilson for president in 1912. Gompers rejected the idea of a labor party on the grounds that labor would lose its bargaining power with both Democrats and Republicans unless the AFL supported one or the other. [134] On this basis, trade union leaders have been tied to the coattails of the Democratic Party ever since.

The Great Pretender

President Franklin Delano Roosevelt secured the loyalty of working-class Americans to the Democrats during the Great Depression of the 1930s. For many generations since, Roosevelt has held legendary stature as a friend and ally to unions and the poor.

Roosevelt frequently voiced compassion for the poor, and his administration instituted major policy changes from those of his haughty predecessor, Republican Herbert Hoover. Roosevelt declared in 1933, "No business which depends for its existence on paying less than living wages to its workers has any right to continue in this country." [135] Roosevelt granted some important reforms to workers—including the National Labor Relations Act (Wagner Act) in 1935, finally granting the legal right to join unions.

But Roosevelt granted these reforms because he recognized that working-class discontent was reaching a boiling point in the early 1930s, and hoped to prevent working-class rebellion. Although he is widely remembered as a social reformer, he summed up his own philosophy this way: "A true conservative corrects injustices to preserve social peace." [136]

Roosevelt's policies were aimed at restoring stability to U.S. capitalism after the 1929 stock market crash and the onset of the Great Depression. As Lens argued,

> If America was not close to revolution in 1932 it was only because it still had considerable resources to ease the plight of the hungry and destitute. But the situation was not one to be regarded lightly, and the New Deal, when President Roosevelt took office in March 1933 could not risk the kind of frontal assault against labor, which included the poor, that other administrations had conducted in the past. . . . Some historians have claimed that it was Roosevelt who gave unions their impetus in the 1930s, but the actual facts do not reflect this conclusion. Though there was an interplay of cause and effect, it was the irresistible pressures of millions of people, flailing out of frustration, that drove the New Deal to the appeasement of unionism. [137]

But even at the height of working-class discontent in 1937, Roosevelt asserted, "I am the best friend the profit system ever had." [138] Indeed, Roosevelt aimed for nothing less than "the salvation of American capitalism." [139]

Roosevelt won a section of capital to back the Democratic Party program—state intervention at home and internationalism abroad—to pull the U.S. economy out of crisis. Although these capitalists made up only a minority of business leaders, they were among the most powerful. Roosevelt's backers included top executives from some of the biggest corporate interests, including General Electric, IBM, R. J. Reynolds, and Standard Oil of New Jersey and California.

These corporate giants joined forces with leading international financiers to back the Democratic program. All told, Roosevelt received roughly 25 percent of all his campaign contributions of over $1,000 from rich bankers and stockbrokers in the 1932 election.[140]

As historians Joel Rogers and Thomas Ferguson described,

> At the center of [the New Deal coalition] were not millions of farmers, Blacks and poor that have preoccupied liberal commentators, nor even the masses of employed or striking workers who pressured the government from below (and later helped implement some of the New Deal's achievements) but something else—a new power bloc of capital-intensive industries, investment banks, and internationally oriented commercial banks.[141]

Many militant workers sought to break with the Democrats during the Depression decade, but union leaders prevailed on this decisive issue. The labor movement's loyalty to the Democratic Party has been unswerving ever since, on the grounds that the Democrats represent the "lesser evil" compared with the Republicans. But the union movement's long-standing commitment to the corporate-based Democrats has severely weakened labor's bargaining power with capital. The Democrats have been able to take the working-class vote for granted while pursuing pro-corporate policies, generation after generation, since Roosevelt—without fear that unions will pursue an independent political course.

Violence and Class Conflict

Frederick Engels once wrote of the American ruling class, "nowhere else in the whole world do they operate in such an impudent and tyrannical way as over there."[142]

In *Hammer and Hoe,* describing communists' experiences organizing among Black Alabama sharecroppers in the 1930s, Robin Kelley wrote, "When we ponder Warner Sombart's question, 'Why is there no socialism in the United States?' in light of the South, violence and lawlessness loom large." Communists and unionists in Alabama at that time faced "the possibility of imprisonment, beatings, kidnapping, even death." [143] Ruling-class violence alone could not prevent workers from organizing—the Alabama Share Croppers' Union (SCU) swelled to 10,000 members by 1935. But violence and repression *were* the reasons why the SCU was an armed, underground organization.

Ruling-class violence and repression were ongoing features of the segregated South. But U.S. rulers, North and South, have routinely responded violently during high points of struggle. When George H. W. Bush sent in federal troops to crush the Los Angeles rebellion in April 1992, he was upholding a long-standing tradition.

This tradition was established early on, in the strike waves during the last decades of the nineteenth century. The largest corporations, especially in railroads and steel, wielded enormous financial resources. They could afford to hire private armies of strikebreakers, such as the well-known Pinkertons, while their close allies in government provided them with favorable court rulings and contributed government troops to attack strikers.

Davis describes "the exceptional violence of the battle for union recognition in the United States":

> To make a comparison with the British case: if American workmen possessed an unrestricted vote over half a century earlier than their English counterparts, they also had to struggle a generation longer in the face of hostile courts and intransigent employers to consolidate their first craft unions. American labor may never have had to face the carnage of a Paris Commune or defeated revolution, but it has been bled in countless "Pinkerloos" at the hands of Pinkertons or the militia.[144]

The Homestead Strike

The violence of employers has doubtless contributed to the explosive character of the class struggle in the United States historically. The Homestead Steel strike of 1892 is one example of the scale of class war in the late nineteenth century. Henry Clay Frick, a notorious union-buster, deliberately provoked a strike by slashing wages at his steel mills in Pittsburgh. Frick then hired three hundred Pinkerton detectives and brought them by boat to the Homestead factories, located next to a river. A mob of armed workers initially kept the Pinkertons from reaching the riverbank. As Brecher described,

> The strikers, joined by large numbers of armed supporters from other towns, now tried to find a way to drive the Pinkertons out of the barges. First they built barricades of steel and pig iron from which they could fire with safety on the barges, firing at point-blank range. Half-pound sticks of dynamite were hurled onto the barges, blowing holes in the sides but failing to sink them. . . . Workers flooded the river around them with oil, but were unable to set them afire. A flaming raft was floated toward them, but the current carried it past. A natural gas main was directed toward the barges and the gas ignited with Fourth of July firecrackers, but only a small explosion was triggered. . . . By the end of the day the Pinkertons were faced with a mutiny of their own men.[145]

By the end of this battle, forty workers had been shot and nine killed. But twenty Pinkertons were shot, seven died—and scores more were injured. Although other workers struck in solidarity, the Homestead strikers were defeated in the end. Pennsylvania militia occupied the town, and after several months the strikers returned to work, their union crushed.[146]

The Ludlow Massacre

"No strikes in American history . . . were so naked an expression of the class war, so akin to actual war, as those in the hard-rock mining communities of the West," Lens argued. As he described,

> Though fought by small numbers—a few hundred, a few thousand, and though their effect on the nation's economy was marginal, they embodied the extreme in labor-capital confrontation. . . . Employers called on county sheriffs, hired guards, state and federal troops repeatedly; while miners grabbed instinctively for their Winchesters or sticks of dynamite. Shoot-outs, dynamitings, outdoor bullpens, injunctions, deportations were widespread and commonplace.[147]

The infamous Ludlow massacre illustrates the level of wanton violence corporations inflicted upon striking workers in this era. On the morning of April 20, 1914, the private army of John D. Rockefeller's Colorado Fuel & Iron Company, along with state troops, opened fire upon striking mining families sleeping inside their tent colony. The miners fired back for hours, but eventually ran out of ammunition. The guards then went on the rampage, drenching the tents with oil and setting them on fire, beating and shooting the now-unarmed miners while smashing up their personal belongings. Thirteen women and children burned to death, and three strikers were executed on the spot.

The strike did not end there—rather, it turned into an all-out war. The UMWA, the Colorado Federation of Labor, and the Western Federation of Miners issued a joint call for their members to take up arms, distributing weapons and ammunition. On April 29, the miners defeated both state and private troops. President Wilson responded by sending the U.S. Army to occupy the region, which they did until delegates to a UMWA conference finally surrendered in December, after more than a year on strike.[148]

The Court Injunction and the 1894 Pullman Strike

As the examples above show clearly, corporate repression has traditionally enjoyed the active support of government. Court injunctions criminalizing large pickets and even entire strikes have provided employers with the legal sanction to attack strikers for well over one hundred years. The experience of the American Railway Union's (ARA) 1894 Pullman strike demonstrates how the courts established legal precedent early on—imposing injunctions not because of a breakdown of law and order but in defense of corporations' unbridled rights to make profits.

The Pullman strike was initially notable for its *lack* of picket line violence relative to the times. The union's president, Eugene Debs, called on strikers to "respect law and order," and most did in the early weeks of the strike.[149] But the strike generated an immense show of solidarity because of universal working-class hostility toward the railroad magnates—known as the "robber barons" in popular culture. Hundreds of thousands of strike supporters across the country wore the ARA's white ribbon to express their solidarity. California militias called in to attack the strikers refused their orders. A reporter from Battle Creek, Michigan, commented, "The Company has no men here that it can use to pull the trains if there were 1,000,000 soldiers here, and it is esteemed unwarranted." [150]

Working hand in glove with Pullman management, U.S. Attorney General Richard Olney applied within weeks for an injunction against the strike, arguing that the striking union was involved in a conspiracy "in restraint of trade." The government ruled that the Pullman strike violated both the Sherman Anti-Trust Act and the Interstate Commerce Act, although both pieces of legislation were intended to curb corporate monopolies, not to aid them. Federal judges quickly granted an injunction against the strike, immediately putting the 150,000 striking workers in violation of the "law." [151]

Within a matter of days after the injunction, 6,000 federal and state troops were occupying the city of Chicago, alongside 3,100 police and 5,000 deputy marshals. The troops moved in even as the company rejected Debs' repeated offer to end the strike if management would agree to arbitration. The troops attacked first with bayonets, then with guns.

Mob violence was the only effective counterweight to troop strength, meeting with some initial success. Thousands of men, women, and children surrounded—and often successfully stopped—trains manned by strikebreaking soldiers on the railroad tracks. The strikers and their supporters learned that just thirty to forty people could push over a railroad car by rocking it back and forth, as they demonstrated repeatedly.

A week later, President Grover Cleveland banned any assembly of people throughout Illinois, extending the ban to other strike hot spots such as Wyoming, North Dakota, Idaho, Colorado, Washington, and California.

But solidarity was so strong that even a group of Army officers, meeting in Chicago, declared their support for the strike and objected to using the Army as a strikebreaking force. (They were court-martialed for their protest.) Authorities went on the offensive, arresting Debs and three other strike leaders, ransacking their union offices, and charging them with criminal conspiracy. Two sympathetic saloonkeepers bailed them out, since the union had no money. [152]

The Chicago Trades and Labor Council called a citywide sympathy strike, but only 25,000 workers turned out because of the military occupation of the city. Debs wisely asked the AFL to call a national sympathy strike. As Lens argues, such a national call "would undoubtedly have brought to the streets several million working men, and might have forced President Cleveland to a more neutral position." [153]

Once again, however, Gompers squandered the opportunity for a class-wide fight-back. The AFL declared, "a general strike at this time is inexpedient, unwise, and contrary to the best interests of working people." [154] More likely, Gompers was watching out for his own "best interests," sensing in Debs and the American Railway

Union (ARU)—an industrial union—a threat to the AFL's dominance within the labor movement.[155]

Within weeks, the strike ended in spectacular defeat, the ARU destroyed. Southern Pacific Railroad introduced a "yellow dog contract" forcing its workers to sign a pledge that they would never join a union. The U.S. Supreme Court upheld the Pullman strike injunction in its entirety a few months later. Indeed, the Court added that such a preemptive action was deemed necessary because the strike amounted to a "malicious conspiracy" to damage the "probable expectancies" of management for its profits.[156]

Red Scares and the Penal System

The U.S. employers' arsenal, aided by a complicit government and a compliant media, has always included a strong ideological component. During the 1894 Pullman strike, a *Chicago Tribune* headline screamed, "Mob Is in Control," despite picket lines being at that point orderly and law-abiding. Based on information "leaked" to the press by the publicity bureau of the employers' General Managers Association, newspaper headlines across the country raised the following charges against the Pullman strikers: "Anarchists on Way to America from Europe"; "From a Strike to a Revolution"; "Anarchists and Socialists Said to Be Planning the Destruction and the Looting of the Treasury." [157]

Two decades before the Pullman strike, hysteria against communists and anarchists was already in full bloom. By the late 1870s, in the wake of the 1877 railroad strike, Chicago entrepreneur Marshall Field initiated a "Citizens' Association"—its stated purpose, "to fight communists." [158]

The Haymarket Martyrs

U.S. rulers have generated full-throttled anti-red hysteria whenever radical movements have gained a foothold among large numbers of workers. The first national "red scare" greeted the 1886 eight-hour movement, led by anarchists, culminating in the Haymarket incident in Chicago on May 3.

The Haymarket incident has been described as a "riot," a "massacre," or a "bombing," depending on the writer's class viewpoint. The chronology of events is straightforward, taking place during an enormously successful national movement demanding the eight-hour workday—involving 300,000 workers, with 190,000 on strike by the second week of May 1886. The strike's momentum grew despite opposition to participation by the leadership of the then-powerful Knights of Labor.[159]

So great was the influence of Chicago anarchists Albert Parsons and August Spies within Chicago's labor movement that the *Chicago Mail* named them in an ominous editorial on May 1: "There are two dangerous ruffians at large in this city; two skulking cowards who are trying to create trouble. One of them is named Parsons; the other is named Spies. . . . Mark them for today. . . . Make an example of them if trouble does occur." [160]

Forty thousand workers struck for the eight-hour day in Chicago, culminating in an altercation with strikebreakers on May 3 outside the McCormick Harvester Works, where police killed four workers, injuring many more. A rally called for the next day at Haymarket Square to protest the police brutality attracted a relatively small crowd of twelve hundred, dwindling to three hundred when rain began to fall. Just as the speeches were concluding, a line of police entered the square and ordered the rally to disperse. As the speakers were leaving, a bomb was thrown into the crowd of police, killing eight and injuring 67 police. In response to the bomb, the police opened fire on the crowd, killing and wounding civilians and police alike.[161]

Without evidence, eight Chicago anarchists were tried and convicted—not of actual murder, but of "conspiracy to commit murder"—for "inciting," rather than committing, violence in Haymarket Square. On November 11, 1887, after the U.S. Supreme Court rejected their appeals, four were executed by hanging (a fifth had been sentenced to death but committed suicide in his cell). The other three received lengthy prison terms.

In 1893, Illinois governor John Peter Altgeld finally issued a pardon, acknowledging that no evidence incriminated any of those convicted in the bombing.[162] The actual bomb-thrower was never caught. Parsons blamed the bombing on a police agent intent on inciting violence. Labor historian Samuel Yellen commented, "The possibility of an agent *provocateur* must not be dismissed out of hand. The police officials in Chicago were at this time equal to such a scheme." [163]

Nonetheless, the Haymarket incident unleashed a wave of antiradical hysteria by all the "leading molders of public opinion," as Avrich described. Newspaper headlines blamed "Dynamarchists" and "Red Ruffians" for the bombing, screaming for revenge. "There are no good anarchists except dead anarchists," bellowed the *St. Louis Globe-Democrat*. [164]

Because German immigrants provided the largest base for anarchism at the time, the press vilified European-born workers. The *Chicago Times* described America's "enemy forces" as "rag-tag and bob-tail cutthroats from the Rhine, the Danube, the Vuistukla and the Elbe." [165]

Chicago's wealthiest citizenry, including Marshall Field, donated more than $100,000 to aid the police in stamping out radical "subversion," in a pattern that continued through 1891. Chicago police seized the opportunity to raid radical newspaper offices, wrecking equipment and seizing mailing lists, invading meeting halls and entering the homes of radicals in order to beat and arrest them. "Make the raids first and look up the law afterward," instructed State's Attorney Julius S. Grinnel. [166]

Sacco and Vanzetti

The same fate of the Haymarket martyrs would await two Italian anarchists, Nicola Sacco and Bartholomeo Vanzetti, in 1927. After their friend and fellow anarchist, Andrea Salsedo, mysteriously "jumped" to his death from the fourteenth floor in 1920 while being detained by the FBI, Sacco and Vanzetti armed themselves, and were soon arrested for robbery and murder. An international campaign failed to save their lives during the red scare of the 1920s that followed the 1917 Russian Revolution. [167]

The red scare provided a useful ideological rationale for cracking down on the working-class movement that surged in the aftermath of the revolution. Immediately after the Bolshevik Revolution began, the U.S. government went on the rampage against socialist, anarchist, and immigrant union militants. The Espionage Act of 1917, passed under Democrat Woodrow Wilson, made it illegal to make any public statement against U.S. participation in World War

I or to take any action that might interfere with the war effort. By the end of 1917, nearly all mail was subject to government approval—all "unacceptable" mail was banned from the U.S. postal system.

Socialist Party offices were raided, and government agents occupied the party's Chicago offices for three days. In South Dakota, troops broke up a Socialist Party convention. In the West, activists from the Industrial Workers of the World suffered mass arrest under the Espionage Act, and were "tarred and feathered, beaten, jailed, [and] dumped without food or water in the desert." [168]

Presaging the anticommunist witch-hunt that would begin in the 1940s, the government formed the American Protection League, with 250,000 volunteers whose job it was to uncover any disloyal activities in their factories and neighborhoods. Meanwhile, all those who were foreign-born were forced to register with the government, which then decided to "detain" 6,000 immigrants in jails. All told, 1,532 people were arrested for disloyalty under the Espionage Act. [169]

Ethel and Julius Rosenberg

History would repeat itself yet again when Ethel and Julius Rosenberg were executed in 1953, at the height of the anticommunist hysteria known as McCarthyism. Both Ethel and Julius Rosenberg had been long-standing Communist Party members. She had led a strike of shipping workers in 1935 at the age of nineteen, and the two of them had been active in the fight against fascism. [170]

The Rosenbergs were convicted on hearsay evidence of having passed atomic secrets to Russia during World War II. FBI communiqués admitted that the government had no evidence that Ethel Rosenberg was involved in espionage, but would keep her on death row as a bargaining chip to pressure her husband to confess. Even if government accusations against Julius Rosenberg were true—that he tried to share atomic information with Russia so that no nation could ever again use the atomic bomb against another—his motives were admirable. [171] This was especially the case so soon after the massive death and destruction caused there when the United States dropped atomic bombs on Hiroshima and Nagasaki at the end of World War II.

An enormous outpouring of protest emerged internationally on behalf of the Rosenbergs. Even the Pope, himself an anticommunist, called for clemency. But the U.S. Supreme Court refused to stop the execution at the last minute, and President Eisenhower refused to grant clemency.[172] On June 19, 1953, Ethel and Julius Rosenberg were executed, leaving behind two young sons.

Throughout their three years in prison awaiting execution, the Rosenbergs insisted they were innocent, and they refused to plea bargain. A letter from Julius to Ethel while they were imprisoned at Sing Sing showed that he understood how the government was using their pending execution to terrify others on the left. "Our case is being used as a camouflage to paralyze outspoken progressives and stifle criticism of the drive to atomic war." Jean Paul Sartre described the execution of the Rosenbergs as "a legal lynching that has covered a whole nation in blood." [173]

The United States remains one of the few nations in the developed world that still routinely uses the death penalty. But its massive prison system has also played a central role historically in enforcing class rule in the United States, including the system of white supremacy in the South. The Thirteenth Amendment banning chattel slavery allowed an exception for those convicted of a crime to be held in involuntary servitude or slavery while serving their sentences. African-American scholar Joy James described the role of Black prison labor in the post-Civil War Deep South:

> A hundred years ago, more African Americans died in the convict leasing system than they did during slavery, worked to death by a business venture coordinated by both state and private industry that replaced plantation labor with prison labor, a commodity that could always be replenished by sweeps arresting Blacks because they were Black.[174]

"The U.S. has the highest incarceration rate in the industrialized world," James added. Of the over two million people currently serving time in U.S. jails, the vast majority is poor. Seventy percent are Black or from another racially oppressed population. In June 1997, the number of women serving time in U.S. prisons was ten times that of Spain, England, Scotland, Germany, and Italy combined.[175]

PART II

The Battle for Industrial Unions—
The View from Below

CHAPTER THREE

The Rise of the Labor Left, 1900–1930

T he anticommunist witch-hunt that enveloped U.S. society in the 1940s and 1950s is typically remembered as an attack on Hollywood movie actors, directors, and screenwriters, mercilessly interrogated by Senator Joseph McCarthy during the showcase hearings of the House Un-American Activities Committee (HUAC). But McCarthyism vilified the entire left, from communists to pacifists, in every arena of activism. Thousands of socialists and union militants were driven out of their jobs and their unions or thrown in prison for expressing their political beliefs at the height of the anticommunist hysteria in the early 1950s.

McCarthyism *physically* removed radicals from the American labor movement—and with them, any memory of the role groups of socialists and other radicals so often played in advancing the class struggle during the first three decades of the twentieth century. The long-term effect of McCarthyism has been to erase this history—of the mass struggles that built the union movement—replaced by the myth that radicalism has always been alien to the American working class.

The reality is quite different. Anarchists played a leading role in the eight-hour-day movement in the 1880s. The Populist movement grew into an electoral threat to the Democratic Party in the 1890s South. Anarcho-syndicalists from the Industrial Workers of the World (IWW) led some of labor's most important strikes during the first two decades of the twentieth century.

In addition, two political organizations, the Socialist Party and later the Communist Party, showed the potential to grow into mass working-class organizations at crucial junctures of the class struggle. In the end, neither party was successful. Understanding why this was the case is key to explaining the subsequent conservative course of the U.S. labor movement.

The Dawn of U.S. Empire

The United States emerged as a world power as the twentieth century dawned, having defeated Spain in the 1898 Spanish-American War. The U.S. military, after invading the Spanish colonies of Guam, Cuba, Puerto Rico, and the Philippines in 1898, acquired three of those colonies—Puerto Rico, Guam, and the Philippines—and established a permanent U.S. military base, Guantánamo Bay, on the fourth, Cuba. As it turned out, the population of the Philippines wanted independence—having already endured Spanish colonial rule since the sixteenth century. When the United States began the occupation of their country, Philippine leaders launched a war for independence that lasted until 1913. Between 1900 and 1903, the U.S. forces killed more than one million people in the Philippines—all for the cause of "civilizing" its native population. U.S. Army General Shefter explained, "It may be necessary to kill half of the Filipinos in order that the remaining half of the population may be advanced to a higher plane of life than their present semi-barbarous state affords."[1]

The United States—itself a former British colony—thus acquired colonies of its own. From this point forward, the themes of American patriotism combined the expansionist aims of U.S. imperialism with traditional pride in its *anti*-colonialist victory against Britain in 1776. The Spanish-American War's impact on U.S. domestic politics is evidenced by the popularity of Theodore Roosevelt, president between 1901 and 1909—a Spanish-American War hero who led the 1898 "battle of San Juan Hill" in Cuba. Roosevelt, in turn, was succeeded by William Taft, who served as the U.S. occupation's first civilian Governor-General of the Philippines between 1901 and 1903.

The rise of U.S. imperialism brought with it a surge of patriotism from America's rulers, who trumpeted the spread of America's uniquely "democratic" values as a justification for war abroad. The Democratic and Republican Parties henceforth stood united in merging the aims of the U.S. empire with domestic policy. The promotion of "American" values, reaching a fever pitch during major wars, provided an added ideological advantage when cracking down on "un-American" radicals at home.

Meanwhile, white supremacy reigned unchallenged in the "land of the free and home of the brave" throughout this period. The mass disfranchisement of African Americans rendered their interests irrelevant as far as the politicians of either party were concerned. The Republican Party, chasing after the votes of the Democrats' Southern segregationist base, severed any remaining connection to its anti-Confederate past. President William Howard Taft remarked in 1908 that African Americans were "political children, not having the mental status of manhood."[2] He easily paved the way for his successor, Democrat Woodrow Wilson, whose election, according to historian Harvard Sitkoff, "led to the most Southern-dominated, anti-Negro, national administration since 1850."[3]

White supremacy reached increasingly sordid extremes in the twentieth century—regardless of which Party occupied the White House. In 1911, the city of New Orleans barred African Americans from attending the city's annual Mardi Gras festival.[4] That same year a Livermore, Kentucky, theater sold tickets for a lynching of an African American. Those in orchestra seats paid top dollar to fire as many shots at the hanging body as they wished; those in cheaper seats were limited to a single shot. In 1916, a mob of ten thousand gathered in the Waco, Texas, town square to cheer on "the stabbing, mutilation, and burning alive" of a mentally handicapped Black youth.[5]

Most employers, who continued fighting tooth and nail to prevent their own workers from unionizing, joined in the fit of patriotism—claiming they were fulfilling their patriotic duty to confront unions' "un-American" threat to freedom and individual liberty. The National Association of Manufacturers (NAM), founded in 1895, lobbied vigorously against any and all pro-labor legislation. In 1903, the Association launched its fight for the "open shop" under the guise of "protecting" workers' rights to refuse to join unions.[6]

But even the most recalcitrant companies felt under considerable pressure to find some solution to the frequent disruption of production caused by strikes. And this required some degree of rational negotiation, or at least the appearance thereof. To this end, a group of manufacturers formed the National Civic Federation (NCF) in 1900. Many of the NCF's prominent leaders were also active in the NAM, but represented a wing of capital hoping to establish a more stable relationship with those union leaders considered "responsible," while undermining union radicals and militants.[7]

The NCF attempted to project itself as an objective third-party mediator in industrial disputes, promoting an image of labor-management collaboration. But the Federation's invitation-only membership ensured industrialists a favorable outcome on all strike settlements. Two-thirds of its membership was reserved for business leaders and their allies in government; labor representatives were never allowed to exceed one-third. Former President Grover Cleveland, who had sent in federal troops to crush the 1894 Pullman strike, accepted the NCF's invitation to join as a representative of "government."

Invitations to join the NCF were extended only to AFL leaders who shared the manufacturers' hostility to radicals. Gompers was "delighted" to join the NCF and served as its first vice-president. Historian Philip Yale Nicholson noted, "Gompers always loved the praise and flattery he received from businessmen." UMWA president John Mitchell and an assortment of officials from the AFL's railroad brotherhoods added to labor's willing presence on the NCF.[8]

The NCF mediated strikes in twenty-two states in 1901. But it proved largely unsuccessful at achieving any genuine collaboration between labor and capital. Mitchell's membership in the NCF did not prevent class war from continuing to rage in the nation's mines. This was evidenced during the 1902 coal strike, when 14 miners were killed, 42 were injured, and 67 were charged with aggravated assault. In addition, 22 buildings were set on fire, and 69 separate "riots" took place.[9] Nevertheless, business leaders awarded Mitchell with a $1,000 diamond ring to express their gratitude for the settlement of the 1902 strike.

Few in the labor movement were favorably impressed by the NCF, or Gompers' participation. As socialist Morris Hillquit ridiculed, "The game played by the Civic Federation is the shrewdest yet devised by the employers of any country. It takes nothing from capital, it gives nothing to labor and does it all with such an appearance of generosity, that some of the guileless diplomats of the labor movement are actually overwhelmed by it."[10]

Although the NCF faded from influence by 1905, it had set a precedent that would guide labor's future collaboration with government and business during the First and Second World Wars. In 1903, Mitchell declared confidently, "The trade union movement in this country can make progress only by identifying itself with the state."[11]

The labor movement began to strengthen as an effective force during a sharp rise in struggle that began in the late 1890s and continued through 1904. The number of strikes in the mid-1890s averaged 1,000 to 1,300 per year. By 1904, the number rose to nearly 4,000. The AFL's membership grew from 350,000 to 1,650,000, while union membership overall quadrupled between 1899 and 1904—from 447,000 to 2,072,000. Although the American Railway Union (ARU) had been destroyed by the 1894 Pullman defeat, railroad craft brotherhoods represented 200,000 workers by 1904. The bitter struggles of the nineteenth century had not been fought in vain.[12]

As radical historian Sidney Lens argued, "No union gained its objectives without some duty on the picket line, some violence, arrests, killings. But in certain fields, mainly the decentralized industries, management recognized that it could not destroy its nemesis, and concluded that some sort of collaboration was preferable to war. Indeed, under some circumstances, collaboration could be profitable." Unions in the building trades, Lens continued, achieved an "arms length accommodation with management," while the UMWA was able to "establish an armed truce" with the mine-owners.[13]

But the character of the U.S. labor force was also changing. The advance of factory production relied upon progressively deskilling the manufacturing workforce, relying increasingly on semi-skilled and unskilled workers—the very workers disparaged by the AFL. Although the AFL grew, many important nineteenth-century craft unions faded into insignificance by the early twentieth century, including the once-powerful Amalgamated Association of Iron, Steel, and Tin Workers. And the vast majority of unskilled workers remained unorganized.

The Uprising of the 20,000

The 1909 uprising of New York City garment workers marked the earliest and most important struggle of women working in a female-dominated industry. It began with a strike at the Triangle Shirtwaist factory. The company locked out all its workers and began advertising for strikebreakers on September 28, 1909, after its workers started joining Local 25 of the International Ladies Garment Workers Union (ILGWU). Although the ILGWU was an AFL craft union, Local 25 was set up to organize the garment industry on an industrial basis, uniting skilled and unskilled workers in one union.

Thugs broke up picket lines on the first day of the Triangle strike, touching off a thirteen-week general strike throughout the garment district, with workers walking off their jobs in droves and literally swarming union offices. Within a few weeks, an estimated twenty thousand to thirty thousand garment workers—75 percent of the city's garment workforce—had joined the strike. Three-quarters of these striking workers were women, many of them Jewish teenagers. Their main demand was union recognition—a closed shop, requiring all workers to join the union.

Despite this militant demand, the plight of these young workers attracted the support not only of Socialists and committed suffragists, but also some wealthy socialites, who helped raise money and publicize the strike.

The Women's Trade Union League (WTUL), an organization led by middle-class women, devoted itself to organizing on behalf of the garment workers. Picketers endured regular beatings and arrests at the hands of the police, and on December 3, the WTUL led ten thousand strikers to the Mayor's office with a petition against police brutality. As feminist historian Meredith Tax described,

> The solidarity the strikers built was their greatest achievement, and it is this that makes their strike memorable. They showed the world that the slow entry of millions of women into the U.S. industrial workforce had set new conditions for women's struggle and had liberated women from the privacy of household drudgery in sufficient numbers for them to be able to act together. A number of observers saw them as a working-class analogue to the suffragists, showing what the women's movement could be like when the issues included survival.[14]

At a meeting on December 27, union leaders announced they had reached a compromise with the garment manufacturers that failed to grant union recognition. The two thousand workers at the meeting shouted them down, yelling, "Send it back, we will not consider it!" and "We want recognition of the union!" This was the beginning of the end, however. After the strikers rejected the union's compromise, Tax noted, many suffragists and even the AFL "deserted the strike because it was becoming too radical."

The strike dragged on until February 15, 1910, when the union officially declared it over—although thirteen shops were still on strike. Just over a year later, on March 25, 1911, the Triangle shirtwaist factory went up in flames. The strikers had failed to win their demand for an end to the company's policy of locking its workers inside the building. Trapped inside as the fire raged, 146 of the five hundred Triangle workers were killed and many more were seriously injured.

The Socialist Party of America

The Socialist Party (SP) was founded in 1901, in the midst of a sharp rise in class struggle. Its membership peaked at more than one hundred thousand members in 1912—the same year the party's presidential candidate, Eugene Debs, received nine hundred thousand votes, nearly 6 percent of all votes cast. In 1912, twelve thousand socialists were elected across the country, mainly to local office—including as mayors of seventy-nine cities. The Party's newspaper, *Appeal to Reason,* reached a circulation of 250,000 in 1908, rising to more than five hundred thousand by 1912. *The Jungle,* Upton Sinclair's vivid exposé of conditions in the meatpacking industry, made its first appearance as a serialized story in the pages of *Appeal to Reason.*[15]

Socialists also made up a significant minority of the AFL, regularly challenging Gompers' conservatism at annual conventions. In 1912, the Socialist Party's candidate for AFL president won a third of the vote against Gompers.[16] In response to this burgeoning threat, Gompers began helping to build the Militia of Christ, formed in 1912 as a conscious attempt to counter socialist influence among Catholic workers.[17] The Militia seems to have succeeded in at least irritating socialist unionists, as the party's Latvian federation reported to the 1912 Socialist Party convention:

The church tries to organize strikers according to their creeds, as was seen in the recent Illinois Central Railroad strike. Thus the class solidarity of the workers is impaired and their enemies triumph. The dragging in of the Carpenter of Nazareth into discussions at trade union conventions is a silly attempt to distract the worker's attention from the main issues. The "Militia of Christ" has become an active enemy of the workers and is helping the state militia to crush the strikers. The role of the church as a strike-breaking agency should be made plain to the workers.[18]

Socialists, Democrats, and Imperialist War

The Socialist Party managed to bring together representatives from nearly every left-wing current, from died-in-the-wool reformists to militant union leaders and fiery revolutionaries. Thousands of left-wing Populists who had abandoned the People's Party after it folded into the Democrats quickly signed up with the Socialist Party. Some of labor's most militant leaders were also founding members of the SP—including the charismatic Debs, who soon became the party's most popular spokesperson, "Big Bill" Haywood from the Western Federation of Miners, and mining legend Mother Jones.

But the far more conservative labor lawyer Morris Hillquit and Milwaukee newspaper editor Victor Berger permanently seized the party's leadership apparatus. Hillquit had led a "constitutionalist" split from the radical Socialist Labor Party (SLP) in 1899. Berger was a former populist. Both were committed to building the Socialist Party as an electoral force, and both ran for office numerous times. Milwaukee voters elected Berger five times to serve in the House of Representatives between 1910 and 1929.[19]

The Socialist Party quickly affiliated with the Second International, a global federation of socialist and labor parties.[20] The party's diverse membership united around an uncompromising rejection of the Democratic Party, its constitution pledging complete independence from either capitalist party. The Socialists never bent on this issue. The party stood firm even when Democratic President Woodrow Wilson gained broad liberal support for reelection in 1916. His campaign slogan, "He kept us out of war," led most voters to believe Wilson would continue to keep the United States out of World War I. Once reelected, however, Wilson adopted a new slogan: war would "make the world safe for democracy." He declared war against Germany in April 1917.[21]

The socialists opposed the United States's entry into World War I and maintained a principled opposition throughout, despite enormous pressure. "Gompers dropped the AFL's earlier objection to the war in the fall of 1916, just in time to be named by President Wilson as a civilian advisor to the newly formed Council of National Defense," commented Philip Nicholson. Gompers "was eager to assist the government in the suppression of the Socialist Party and the outright destruction of the IWW, his two main rivals for the leadership of labor." Indeed, Nicholson added, "When the question of whatever happened to labor militancy and socialism in the United States is asked, the beginning of the answer can be found in the entry of the nation into the Great War. With the declaration of war, President Wilson made Gompers the official spokesman for all labor, and the two set out to break or destroy opposition to the goals of capital at home and abroad." [22]

But the war remained unpopular among large segments of industrial workers, including the large number of immigrant workers who felt no deep loyalty to the U.S. government. The IWW proposed turning the imperialist war into a "class war," and thousands of socialists dedicated themselves to building grassroots opposition to the war. [23]

In December 1914, for example, the Oklahoma Socialist Party adopted a resolution, "If War is declared, the Socialists of Oklahoma shall refuse to enlist; but if forced to enter military service to murder fellow workers, we shall choose to die fighting the enemies of humanity in our ranks rather than to perish fighting our fellow workers." [24]

After the United States entered the war, several thousand poor Oklahoma farmers formed secret antiwar societies—with names such as the "Working Class Union," linking their opposition to war with their opposition to capitalism. In August 1917, one Oklahoma antiwar society armed its one thousand members and rose up, declaring, "We decided we wasn't gonna fight somebody else's war for 'em and we refused to go." Oklahoma troops were quickly called in to put down the uprising. In the battle that followed, known as the Green Corn Rebellion, several socialists were killed, and many more were wounded.[25]

Socialist Party leaders were easy targets of the government repression that accompanied the onset of war. By the end of World

War I, nearly every leading member of the Socialist Party, including Debs and Berger, was in prison for "disloyalty" under the Federal Wartime Espionage and Sedition Acts of 1917–18. Marxist sociologist Rhonda Levine commented of this period,

> Whereas the use of private repression was used during the nineteenth century to quell labor militancy, state and local repression came to the forefront during the early years of the twentieth century and was followed by federal repression on a massive scale during World War I and the immediate postwar years. The tremendous amount of political repression severely weakened the leftist opposition in the United States during the 1920s.[26]

Debs went to prison for delivering a fiery antiwar speech to an audience of twelve hundred at the Socialist Party's Ohio state convention in Canton, Ohio, on June 16, 1918. He was convicted for "uttering words intended to cause insubordination and disloyalty within the armed forces of the United States, to incite resistance to the war, and to promote the cause of Germany." [27] Debs ran for president in 1920 from his prison cell and won nearly a million votes. Debs' speech, recorded by a government stenographer, read in part:

> Every solitary one of these aristocratic conspirators and would-be murderers claims to be an arch-patriot; every one of them insists that the war is being waged to make the world safe for democracy. What humbug! What rot! What false pretense! These autocrats, these tyrants, these red-handed robbers and murderers, the "patriots," while the men who have the courage to stand face to face with them, speak the truth, and fight for their exploited victims—they are the disloyalists and traitors. If this be true, I want to take my place side by side with the traitors in this fight. [Great applause.] . . .
>
> And here let me emphasize the fact—and it cannot be repeated too often—that the working class who fight all the battles, the working class who make the supreme sacrifices, the working class who freely shed their blood and furnish the corpses, have never yet had a voice in either declaring war or making peace. It is the ruling class that invariably does both. They alone declare war and they alone make peace. . . .
>
> In passing I suggest that we stop a moment to think about the term "landlord." "LANDLORD!" Lord of the Land! The lord of the land is indeed a super-patriot. This lord who practically owns the earth tells you that we are fighting this war to make the world safe for democracy—he who shuts out all humanity from his private domain; he who profiteers at the expense of the people who have been slain and mutilated by multiplied thousands, under pretense of being the great American patriot. It is he, this identical patriot who is in fact the archenemy

of the people; it is he that you need to wipe from power. It is he who is a far greater menace to your liberty and your well being than the Prussian Junkers on the other side of the Atlantic Ocean. [Applause.][28]

In 1918, while still under indictment under the Espionage Act, Berger was elected to the House of Representatives by Milwaukee voters. But Congress refused to seat him on the grounds that he was a convicted felon and against the war. Berger was again elected in 1919 in a special election, and again Congress refused to seat him. Berger was elected a third time in 1921, and this time he was seated without Congressional opposition.[29]

Reform versus Revolution

Thus, the socialists stood firmly united on the class nature of the Democratic Party, opposing its entry into imperialist war. The SP maintained its staunch opposition to the war even after almost every other affiliate of the Second International collapsed into patriotism, with each national party supporting victory for its own country's rulers. Despite the enormity of this crisis, however, the socialists did not break with the politics of the Second International.

In contrast, a group of prominent European revolutionaries—including V. I. Lenin in Russia and Rosa Luxemburg in Germany—abandoned the Second International at the start of the First World War. This revolutionary wing of the socialist movement went on to found the Third International (also known as the Communist International, or Comintern) after the Russian Revolution of 1917. The disagreement over the war had been symptomatic of a much larger difference—whether socialism could be won simply through electoral reform or required a revolution. Lenin, in particular, argued for the creation of explicitly revolutionary organizations inside each country, to build a mass working-class movement for socialism.[30]

The Socialist Party of America refused to join the Third International, remaining firmly committed to a strategy of gradual reform. Indeed, socialist leaders were thoroughly hostile to the revolutionary wing of their own party. The party's right and left factions were in constant conflict over a range of crucial political questions, accelerating with the passage of time. The right wing oriented only to the AFL, while the left wing helped found the anarcho-syndicalist IWW. The right wing spouted racist dogma while the left wing opposed racial segregation. The right wing denounced the Russian Revolution of 1917, while the left wing embraced it.

But time and again, the right wing carried the day. The reason was simple: the right wing controlled the leadership apparatus, while the left wing generally remained aloof from party organization in its formative years. Some of the party's most important working-class leaders thus played no direct role in shaping its policies. In Debs' twenty-five years as a member of the Socialist Party, he attended only one convention after it was founded. This arrangement allowed for a relatively peaceful, if mutually disdainful, coexistence.

In another example of the left wing's abstention from party organizing, Big Bill Haywood refused to run for a party leadership position for many years. When he finally changed his mind, he was elected to the party's national executive committee on his first try, in January 1912. By then, however, the right wing had long been in firm control of the party machinery. Faced with the rising influence of Haywood and other revolutionaries inside their own party, the right wing forced a showdown with Haywood. This they did, however, from a position of organizational strength.

Until that point, the party's right wing was allowed to lead the organization virtually unchallenged. The strategy embraced by Hillquit and Berger presumed the United States could simply "evolve" toward socialism by electing ever-greater numbers of party members into government office. Hillquit stated bluntly, "so far as we Socialists are concerned, the age of physical revolution . . . has passed." [31] As the years passed, the right wing increasingly viewed success strictly in terms of how many SP votes came in on election day.

Moreover, the party's electoral strategy tended to limit socialist leaders to *advocating* social change during political campaign speeches, rather than *building* class-based struggles to fight for reforms on the ground. The party's influence was broad but its base of support did not come mainly from the labor movement. As Duncan Hallas noted, the Socialist Party's voting base was not "at all closely associated with trade union organization. This is confirmed by the pattern of its electoral success. By 1912 the American Socialist Party had one hundred thousand members. Its strongest vote, however, was not in the Eastern seaboard, which was still the major industrial area, but in the West—an area only recently settled." [32]

In the eyes of the party leadership, the class struggle could and did get in the way of electoral success. The SP's right wing stood adamantly opposed to class confrontation, including most strikes—on the grounds that these often involved "illegal" activity. While campaigning for Congress in Milwaukee in 1906, Berger assured local industrialists not to fear a Socialist Party victory because, "I can say from actual experience that the Social-Democrats in this city have opposed almost every strike that has ever been declared here." [33]

Later, Trotsky reminisced about this stodgy band of Socialist Party leaders in his autobiography:

> To this day I smile as I recall the leaders of American Socialism. . . . In the United States there is a large class of successful and semi-successful doctors, lawyers, dentists, engineers, and the like, who divide their precious hours of rest between concerts by European celebrities and the American Socialist Party. . . . [T]hey are simply variants of "Babbitt," who supplements his commercial activities with dull Sunday meditations on the future of humanity. [34]

In contrast, Eugene Debs personified the Socialist Party's left wing. Debs was radicalized when Democratic President Grover Cleveland broke the Pullman strike in 1894. Debs never voted Democrat again and was already a committed revolutionary socialist by the time he joined the Socialist Party. For the rest of his life, Debs remained dedicated to building a revolutionary working-class movement. After the 1917 Russian Revolution, he declared, "From the crown of my head to the soles of my feet I am Bolshevik, and proud of it. The Day of the People has arrived!" [35]

Although Debs ran for president on the Socialist Party ticket five times, he held no illusions that voting alone could win a socialist society. For Debs, a presidential campaign was simply another excuse to embark on a national speaking tour. He spent most of his time on the road, drawing large crowds and mesmerizing his audiences with a sense of optimism, using plain language and humor to explain the ideas of socialism. "Voting for socialism is not socialism any more than a menu is a meal," Debs argued in a 1911 speech. "The working class must get rid of the whole brood of masters and exploiters, and put themselves in possession and control of the means of production. . . . It is therefore not a question of 'reform,' the mask of fraud, but of revolution. The capitalist system must be overthrown, class rule abolished and wage slavery supplanted by cooperative industry." [36]

Segregated Socialism?

Because the Socialist Party's left wing did not effectively fight for its positions within the party, even the most reactionary policies could carry the day. The party's right wing contained within it open racists and segregationists, who saw no contradiction between socialist principles and the ideology of white supremacy. In fact, influential leaders of this grouping believed that the victory of socialism would solve the "race question" once and for all—with *complete segregation* of the races. Berger was among them. Berger summarized his views in 1902:

> There can be no doubt that the Negroes and Mulattoes constitute a lower race—that the Caucasian and indeed the Mongolian have the start of them in civilization by many thousand years—so that Negroes will find it difficult ever to overtake them. The many cases of rape which occur whenever Negroes are settled in large numbers, prove moreover, that the free contact with the whites has led to the further degeneration of the Negroes, as of all other inferior races.[37]

Berger predicted that *segregation* would end racial "degeneration" in a socialist society, echoing the philosophy of the eugenics movement. Most Southern branches of the Socialist Party refused to allow African Americans to join. A 1904 article in the *Social Democratic Herald* declared that Blacks were inferior and depraved scoundrels who went "around raping women and children."[38] Its substantial number of segregationists prevented the Socialist Party from ever taking a formal position against the lynching and disenfranchisement of African Americans, or even Jim Crow segregation laws.

Fortunately, the Party's left wing contained an equally large number of antiracists. Black socialist Hubert Henry Harrison argued in a 1912 speech,

> It pays the capitalist to keep the workers divided. So he creates and keeps alive these prejudices. He gets them to believe their interests are different. Then he uses one half of them to club the other half with. In Russia when the working men demanded reform, the capitalists sick them on the Jews. In America they sick them on the Negroes. That makes them forget their own condition; as long as they can be made to look down upon another class.[39]

Debs was also a committed opponent of racism. He argued, "The whole world is under obligation to the Negro, and that the white heel is still upon the Black neck is simply proof that the world is not yet civilized. The history of the Negro in the United States is a history of crime without a parallel." [40]

Debs fought racism wherever he encountered it. He consistently refused to speak before segregated audiences when touring the South, and he denounced Jim Crow laws. When the film *Birth of a Nation* was released in 1915, glorifying the Ku Klux Klan and degrading African Americans, Debs called on socialists to picket the film—joining a picket against the film in his hometown of Terre Haute, Indiana.

Eugene Debs was far in advance of most socialists of his time. But Debs did not understand that the extreme racism of the U.S. ruling class *required* the socialist movement to forge a principled opposition to racism in all its forms. Debs rejected the idea that the Socialist Party should fight explicitly against racial oppression. He stated, "We have nothing special to offer the Negro, and we cannot make separate appeals to all races. The Socialist Party is the Party of the working class, regardless of color—the whole working class of the whole world." [41] Thus, Debs' opposition to racism was politically inadequate in a society dominated by racial segregation.

Still, on the issue of segregation, the right and left wings of the SP were miles apart. The two wings were also divided on the desirability of women's suffrage. In 1910, Berger declared, "Now it is clear, and no one will deny that the great majority of women of the present day—and that is the only point we can view now—are illiberal, unprogressive, and reactionary to a greater extent than the men of the same strata of society. . . . Now if all this is correct, female suffrage, for generations to come, will simply mean the deliberate doubling of a certain church—will mean an addition to the forces of ignorance and reaction." [42]

In addition, the party was sharply polarized over the issue of immigration. Berger argued that socialism would only come to the United States and Canada if they remained "white countries." He warned that unless immigration was severely restricted, especially against the "Jap" and the "Chinaman," "this country is sure to become a black-and-yellow country within a few generations." He chastised his critics in one debate, reminding them that socialists' first duty is to their class and families, as if this perverse logic was self-evident. [43]

The immigration issue was debated bitterly at the 1908 and 1910 Socialist Party conventions, without deciding on a position. The left wing did not put forward its own proposal, so the debate involved varying degrees of support for restricting immigration to the United States. Although Debs was not a delegate to either convention, he angrily condemned the SP for its reactionary stand against foreign-born workers: "[I]f socialism, international, revolutionary socialism, does not stand staunchly, unflinchingly, and uncompromisingly for the working class and for the exploited and oppressed masses of all lands, then it stands for none and its claim is a false pretense and its profession a delusion and a snare."[44]

The SP finally decided its position on immigration at its 1912 convention. The right wing presented a resolution on immigration which, according to historian Ira Kipnis,

> made the 1910 majority report seem pro-Asiatic in comparison. It called for strengthening and strict enforcement of existing exclusion laws. It said race feeling was a product of biology and therefore could not be eradicated. Racial antagonism would persist under socialism and play an important part in economic life. "If it should not assert itself in open warfare in a socialist form of society, it will nevertheless lead to a rivalry of races for expansion over the globe as a result of the play of natural and sexual selection."[45]

Although this resolution did not pass, its replacement was not much better. Proposed by Hillquit, it read, "The Socialist Party of the United States favors all legislative measures tending to prevent the immigration of strike-breakers and contract laborers, and the mass immigration of workers from foreign countries brought about by the employing classes for the purpose of weakening American labor, and of lowering the standard of life of American workers."[46]

The IWW's Revolutionary Unionism

In June 1905, Debs and Bill Haywood joined others from the Socialist Party's left wing to help found the IWW—its members popularly known as the "Wobblies." Besides Debs, the 203 delegates to the founding meeting in Chicago included some of labor's most legendary figures: Haywood, secretary-treasurer of the Western Federation of Miners; Lucy Parsons (widow of Haymarket martyr Albert Parsons); Mother Jones; labor firebrand Elizabeth Gurley Flynn;

Charles O. Sherman, leader of the United Metal Workers (an industrial union that split off from the AFL's International Association of Machinists).

The Socialist Party's right wing chose to boycott the IWW's founding convention, however. Party leaders rationalized this decision on the grounds that Socialist Party delegates had just won an AFL convention resolution calling for "the overthrow of the wage system," which they presumably believed made the need for revolutionary organization unnecessary.[47]

Haywood declared from the podium:

> Fellow workers, this is the Continental Congress of the working class. We are here to confederate the workers of this country into a working class movement that shall have for its purpose the emancipation of the working class from the slave bondage of capitalism. . . . The aims and objects of this organization should be to put the working class in possession of the economic power, the means of life, in control of production and distribution, without regard to capitalist masters.[48]

Convention delegates paid tribute to the Haymarket martyrs and passed a resolution in support of the 1905 Revolution then underway in Russia. The IWW constitution stated that class "struggle must go on until all the toilers come together . . . and take and hold that which they produce by their labor." The delegates explicitly rejected the organizing model of craft unionism, instead forming thirteen industrial unions based in agriculture, mining, transportation, construction, railroad, and other major industries.

The IWW's founders sought a firm break with the conservative craft unionism of the AFL. Haywood established the Wobblies' negative view of AFL leaders, calling UMWA's Mitchell a "jackass" and labeling the entire AFL leadership "labor fakers." IWW spokespeople frequently referred to the American Federation of Labor as the "American Separation of Labor."[49]

The IWW aimed to organize a mass industrial union, enthusiastically welcoming all unskilled workers, and committed itself to organizing among occupations dominated by African Americans, women, and immigrants. The Wobblies consciously built strikes from the bottom up, through mass pickets and solidarity actions. This strategy foretold the class solidarity that built the Congress of Industrial Organizations (CIO) decades later during the Great Depression of the 1930s. Hundreds of thousands of workers were schooled in class struggle during the heyday of the IWW in the first two decades of the twentieth century. Indeed, many labor radicals who helped lead the rank-and-file battles of the 1930s had gotten their initial training as Wobblies.

From its beginning, the IWW also pledged it would not settle for advancing workers' rights under capitalism, but rather build "one great industrial union" that would form "the structure of the new society . . . within the shell of the old." [50] The politics of anarcho-syndicalism, or revolutionary unionism, dominated among the IWW's founders. Anarcho-syndicalists conceived of their organization not just as an industrial union, but also as a revolutionary organization. Anarcho-syndicalists shunned the idea of political organization in principle, insisting that workers' strike action alone could lead to the revolutionary transformation of society, in one mass strike that could paralyze capitalism and give birth to a new society. So even within the revolutionary IWW, there was little agreement between Socialists and anarcho-syndicalists on what a revolution might mean, or how it might come about.

Haywood on Trial

The Wobblies had little time to savor the success of their founding meeting, since IWW leaders were immediately targeted for government repression. Just seven months after the IWW was formed, Haywood was arrested on trumped-up murder charges. Authorities accused Haywood, along with Western Federation of Miners' president Charles Moyer and Federation sympathizer George A. Pettibone, of assassinating the notoriously antiunion former governor of Idaho, Frank Steunenberg. In addition, Haywood was charged with ordering the murders of another twenty-five mining bosses over the years. Pinkertons hired by the governor of Colorado kidnapped all three men and immediately transported them to Idaho. "They will never leave Idaho alive," Denver Pinkerton James McPharlan told the *Chicago Tribune* in February 1906. [51]

An outraged Debs, drawing the obvious parallel with the persecution of the Haymarket martyrs, wrote in *Appeal to Reason*, "Nearly 20 years ago the capitalist tyrants put some innocent men to death for standing up for labor. They are not going to try it again. Let them dare! There have been 20 years of revolutionary education, agitation, and organization since the Haymarket tragedy, and if an attempt is made to repeat it, there will be a revolution." [52]

Haywood's cause resonated far beyond Wobblies and left-wing socialists. Hillquit himself spoke to a rally of twenty thousand Haywood supporters at New York City's Grand Central Palace. The Socialist Party produced a special edition of *Appeal to Reason,* printing a million copies as part of Haywood's defense campaign. Even Gompers denounced the kidnapping at the 1906 AFL convention, and the AFL joined unions from all over the United States to raise money for Haywood's defense. [53]

In Boston, fifty thousand unionists demonstrated on Moyer and Haywood's behalf, chanting: "If Moyer and Haywood die; If Moyer and Haywood die; twenty million unionists will know the reason why." [54] When President Theodore Roosevelt publicly labeled the three accused men "undesirable citizens," thousands of defiant college students expressed their solidarity with Haywood, donning buttons declaring, "I am an undesirable citizen." [55]

Radical attorney Clarence Darrow—who had defended Debs during the Pullman strike—represented Haywood at his murder trial in 1907. Before the trial even started, however, the government's case began to fall apart when one of the prosecution's two main witnesses recanted. Haywood's defense showed the remaining witness had a history of perjury and confessing to crimes he had not committed. The jury voted to acquit Haywood on July 29, 1907. Pettibone was acquitted soon after, and the charges against Moyer were dropped. [56]

But Haywood had languished in prison for fifteen months, battling for his life. During his prolonged absence, a bitter struggle was dragging on *inside* the IWW. On one side were those who believed the IWW should focus its efforts on the day-to-day union struggle; on the other was a group insisting the emphasis should be on revolutionary activity. Daniel DeLeon, the doctrinaire leader of the Socialist Labor Party, threw his weight behind the "revolutionary" side, undoubtedly adding to the level of animosity during the debate. In 1906, IWW president Charles O. Sherman quit the organization. In 1907, the 27,000 members of the Western Federation of Miners voted to disaffiliate in a two-to-one vote. [57]

Internal strife continued to plague the young organization after Haywood's return. By its 1908 convention, the IWW was again divided, this time between Socialists and anarcho-syndicalists. As Lens described,

> In part this was a matter of temperament, in part, philosophy. The west-
> ern migratory workers who poured into Chicago in blue denim over-
> alls, black shirts, and red ties, singing, "Hallelujah, I'm a bum" were
> not particularly enamored of the ballot box. They accepted Marx's
> doctrine of the class struggle, and many carried joint membership in
> the IWW and the Socialist Party. But they considered electoral action
> an effete trap, and wanted to confine the IWW's work to the economic
> front. Vincent St. John, the metal miner from Telluride, expressed their
> misgivings, as did Haywood, who had been converted to syndicalism
> on a trip to France. Daniel DeLeon, on the other hand, insisted on both
> efforts on the part of the union, economic and electoral. . . . Eugene
> Debs, caught between the two factions, alienated by the apolitical trend
> of his brain child, but nonetheless warmly sympathetic to its industrial
> and revolutionary approach, refused to attack the IWW publicly, but
> he did permit his membership to lapse.[58]

Debs' vision of industrial unionism proved more akin to what eventually became the CIO in the 1930s. Debs remained a loyal, though often critical, member of the Socialist Party until his death in 1926.

DeLeon, who disparaged his opponents in the 1908 debate as "slum proletarians" and a "bummery," quit the IWW at its 1908 convention.[59] Though DeLeon's departure was no loss, it would be wrong to dismiss the content of these debates as merely sectarian squabbles. These disagreements inside the IWW involved crucial is-sues of strategy that determined the course of the radical wing of the union movement for more than a generation.

By the end of 1908—just three years after its founding—the IWW was much weaker, having lost Debs and a number of other union leaders, and without a strong base in existing unions. The Wobblies' strength, however, continued to lie in its members' dedica-tion to rank-and-file solidarity. In December 1906, a group of three thousand Wobblies at General Electric's Schenectady, New York, plant led the first sit-down strike in U.S. history. When management fired three IWW members, their comrades shut down production and sat down for sixty-five hours—completely idling the plant's seventeen thousand workers.[60] In the years after 1908 the Wobblies experienced rapid growth and influence. The IWW enthusiastically organized support for farm laborers, mill workers, lumber workers, and any other group of workers on strike in every region of the country.

Many of the Wobblies' greatest successes took place under the sole leadership of anarcho-syndicalists. And some key IWW leaders, including Haywood and Gurley Flynn, continued to maintain their membership in the Socialist Party. Gurley Flynn, known as the "Rebel Girl," helped to lead some of the IWW's most important strikes—most notably the 1912 strike of Lawrence, Massachusetts, textile workers. The Lawrence strike illustrates the IWW's most important strength—its unparalleled commitment to workers' self-. organization.

The 1912 Lawrence Strike

The textile operators in Lawrence, Massachusetts, deliberately recruited immigrant workers from "as many different language groups as possible in order to prevent them uniting to make trouble; if they competed rather than combined, wages could be kept down," wrote Meredith Tax. She added:

> By 1912 there were twenty-five different ethnic groups in Lawrence mills. . . . Immigrants were drawn to Lawrence by posters placed in towns throughout the Balkans and the Mediterranean showing happy workers carrying bags full of money from the factory gate to the bank. In many workers' tenement rooms, these posters were the only decoration. Their dead hopes stared down from the wall.[61]

Half the workforce was made up of women and children who were *literally* starving to death. As Tax noted, "The average spinner died at the age of thirty-six—twenty-nine years less than the average lawyer or clergyman," while "the infant mortality rate in Lawrence was 172 out of 1,000." [62]

In January 1912, neither the AFL nor the IWW had more than a few hundred members in this New England textile center. Yet, after management cut workers' pay by more than thirty cents per week, thousands of Lawrence workers went on strike. IWW organizers had begun agitating in Lawrence months earlier, when weavers at the Atlantic Cotton Mill went on strike for four months after management announced piece rates would drop from seven looms at 79 cents to twelve looms at 49 cents. The Wobblies sent in organizers Gurley Flynn and J. P. Thompson, printed up thousands of leaflets and stickers calling the speedup "murder on the installment plan," and began holding meetings at the factory gates. As Gurley Flynn described their speeches, "We talked Marxism as we understood it—the class struggle, the exploitation of labor, the use of the state and armed forces of government against the workers. It was all there in Lawrence before our eyes. We did not need to go far for the lessons." [63]

The strike itself began spontaneously when management handed out the smaller pay packets on January 11, 1912, and outraged workers began shutting down their machines from one mill to the next by the following day. Squads of flying pickets marched through the town with the rallying cry, "Better to starve fighting than to starve working." By the end of the first day, ten thousand workers were out on strike. As Lens noted, "In a single day four times as many people had been unionized as in the previous six years." [64]

When informed that the sidewalks outside the mills were legally considered private property, the Lawrence strikers created a moving mass picket, in which thousands of workers simply "walked" around the plant, booing "boisterously" when someone crossed the picket line. The workers, carrying signs that read, "Don't be a scab," picketed the plants en masse twenty-four hours a day and held frequent demonstrations of up to ten thousand, marching through town singing "Solidarity Forever" and other IWW tunes. [65]

The AFL, for its part, wanted nothing to do with these unruly strikers. Gompers later dismissed the Lawrence strike as "a passing event," while local AFL leaders ordered their skilled craftsmen to *cross* picket lines in the hopes that the mill-owners would return the favor to the AFL with union recognition. [66]

When labor hero Big Bill Haywood arrived in Lawrence on January 24, fifteen thousand strikers turned out to greet him in a festival with three marching bands. Haywood explicitly enjoined the strikers to avoid violence, despite the Wobblies' media reputation for instigating bloodshed and industrial "sabotage." A group of Lawrence's leading citizens, however, *were* arrested for planting three caches of dynamite around town, in the hopes of blaming it on the IWW. [67] Apart from a few minor skirmishes, the strikers were largely peaceful—yet the local Commission of Public Safety soon declared there would be "no more toying with these lawless strikers," ordering police and militia henceforth to "shoot to kill." [68]

When mill owners announced they would open the factories on

January 29, thousands of strikers filled Lawrence's streets. Police used the mass demonstration as an excuse to fire into the peaceful crowd, killing a young striker. Although police bullets killed the striker, they nevertheless blamed it on a mysterious "man in a brown overcoat" and arrested striker Joseph Caruso as an accessory to murder. They also arrested IWW leaders Joe Ettor and Arturo Giovannitti (who were two miles away during the incident) for having implicitly caused the murder by "inciting a mob to riot." [69]

The three—all Italian nationals—spent the rest of the strike in jail. One Boston newspaper praised the arrests, declaring, "The passing of Ettor means the ascendancy of the white-skinned races at Lawrence." [70]

Losing two of their union leaders did not, however, paralyze the strikers' organization. A befuddled police captain reported, "I will tell you—there were no leaders in the streets. . . . The crowds on the street were usually led by women and children." [71] The IWW made a special effort to encourage the women strikers to take leadership, as they did in all strikes, and women made up a significant part of the Lawrence strike committee. As Gurley Flynn explained, "The IWW has been accused of putting the women in the front. The truth is, the IWW does not keep them in the back, and they go to the front." [72]

The strike's turning point came when the Italian Socialist Federation of New York offered to place the children of strikers in the homes of supporters for the rest of the strike. Margaret Sanger traveled to Lawrence to escort the first 119 children to Grand Central Station in New York City—where they were greeted by a ceremonious gathering of five thousand socialists and Wobblies singing the *Internationale*. [73]

A week later, another 126 children were sent out of Lawrence. But Lawrence police began arresting the children and on February 24 attacked a group of parents and children arriving at the railroad station—beating them with clubs and arresting thirty parents and children on charges of "congregation." The incident was so shocking that many prominent citizens, including First Lady Helen Herron Taft, traveled to Lawrence to view the strike situation. They were followed by a bevy of reporters who finally began telling the strikers' side of the story. [74]

Backed by unions across the country, socialist Congressman

Victor Berger demanded a congressional investigation into the children's undernourished condition. Although Gompers reserved his testimony at the preliminary hearings to make "his usual charges against the IWW and its anarchy and revolution," according to Lens, the testimony of the children themselves focused national attention on the starvation wages paid to Lawrence textile workers. One fourteen-year-old girl, who had been severely injured when her hair got caught in a machine, said simply that she went on strike "because I didn't get enough to eat at home."[75]

Within a week, the textile operators capitulated, and the twenty thousand strikers voted unanimously to accept their offer at a mass meeting on March 14. The IWW's ability to forge solidarity between immigrant workers was vividly illustrated at the strikers' victory celebration, when the Lawrence workers sang the *Internationale* in more than a dozen different languages.

The Limits of Anarcho-Syndicalism

The IWW's opposition to capitalism as a system and its dedication to bring all workers together in "one big union," marked some of labor's highest points of struggle. At the same time, however, the Wobblies' commitment to anarcho-syndicalism hampered their ability to create an organizational alternative to either the Socialist Party's conservative leadership or to the dominance of AFL craft unionism. IWW leaders' aversion to "politics" prevented them from providing an effective revolutionary challenge to Socialist Party policy—even though the left wing often claimed more numbers than the right.

Furthermore, the IWW refused to sign union contracts with employers, limiting its impact even as a labor union over the long term. The Wobblies strongly preferred to rely on the strike weapon rather than sign contracts to enforce agreements with employers. This proved especially problematic at the time, when most strikes were waged primarily for union recognition, and employers often reneged on verbal agreements. For this reason, the IWW's impact in most localities was short-lived, despite its frequently spectacular role in advancing the class struggle. The Lawrence strike illustrates this shortcoming. Immediately after the strike, the IWW had fourteen thousand members in Lawrence. A year later, membership there had fallen to just a few hundred. Although the Wobblies organized an estimated million workers, its membership never numbered more than 100,000 to 120,000 members.[76]

The IWW's goal of revolutionary unionism proved unattainable. By definition, unions are reform organizations, necessary to strengthen the bargaining power of workers in relation to capital in the ongoing class struggle. Revolutionary organizations are formed to challenge and ultimately overthrow the rule of capital. Anarcho-syndicalism attempts to combine these two goals—one based on reforming the system, the other on overthrowing it—in a single class-wide organization.

Yet reform is a necessary precondition to revolution. Stable union organization makes possible the growth and strengthening of working-class confidence, crucial to taking the offensive in the class struggle. Moreover, while a mass strike can paralyze the capitalist system, it leaves the state untouched. An elaborate government apparatus enforces corporate rule, so an effective revolutionary challenge must recognize the importance of explicitly political organization.

Still, most socialists, including those with dual membership in the IWW, regarded "political" action as campaigning for Socialist Party candidates, rather than building a political party dedicated to winning workers to the project of revolution. For many revolutionaries, rigidly separating "politics" from class struggle proved inadequate as a strategy. By the early 1920s, as Lens noted, "The IWW had been decimated by the conversion of innumerable adherents to communism." [77]

The Socialist Party Shifts Right, and the Workers' Movement Shifts Left

By 1912, the Socialist Party leadership had paved the way for the elimination of most IWW revolutionaries from its ranks. Haywood, newly elected to the party's national executive committee and fresh from the Lawrence strike victory, was finally ready to challenge the right wing's dominance. Part of this challenge, which gained considerable support, was his effort to democratize the party. As Kipnis described, "The executive committee, wrote Haywood, must abandon its practice of acting as a supreme court on all local matters. It must also cease appropriating to legislate in all party affairs." [78]

Party leaders had begun to prepare months earlier to keep Haywood off the executive committee, orchestrating a smear campaign based on his IWW affiliation. But at the heart of the debate was a principled difference between a strategy of reform and revolution: whether elections or the class struggle would ultimately win a socialist society. Hillquit launched the attack, falsely accusing Haywood of having renounced voting in favor of labor "lawlessness." [79]

In reality, Haywood—who ran for Colorado governor while jailed there in 1906—was a loyal party member who had continued to advocate voting socialist. He did, however, argue that capitalist law functioned on behalf of U.S. rulers, allowing them to kill strikers and their children. "Do you blame me when I say that I despise the law?" he asked a cheering audience at New York City's Cooper Union in January 1912. "And I am not a law-abiding citizen," he continued. "We should say that it is our purpose to overthrow the capitalist system by forcible means if necessary." [80] Hillquit countered that the party worked for change only "by the regular and lawful methods established for that purpose." In his reply, Haywood asked whether Hillquit planned "to stand behind a barricade of law books firing a series of well-written briefs at the advancing army of capitalistic minions?" [81]

At the convention, having manipulated local votes to elect a "great majority" of "professionals, businessmen, and leaders in the craft unions" as delegates, according to Kipnis, the right wing passed the following amendment: "Any member of the party who opposes political action or advocates crime, sabotage, or other methods of violence as a weapon of the working class to aid in its emancipation, shall be expelled from membership in the party." [82] Debs, while refusing to attend the convention, made his opinions known. He took a middle-road position, opposing "anarchistic tactics" while arguing that expulsion was too severe a penalty.[83]

The Party leadership used this amendment to push Haywood off the national executive committee in February 1913. Haywood declined to renew his party membership that year, and thousands of revolutionary socialists followed suit.

The campaign against Haywood coincided with a related development in the Socialist Party—a decisive turn away from union struggle. In 1912, the party contributed more than $21,000 in strike support and labor defense cases. That figure dropped to $400 in 1913, and to zero in 1914.[84]

A few years after the party expelled the bulk of its IWW revolutionaries, the labor movement experienced massive growth, accompanied by a growing radicalization among workers. But the Socialist Party's right wing, united in opposition to labor militancy, was unable to identify with this radicalization. After the victory of the 1917 Russian Revolution, tens of thousands of immigrant workers joined the Socialist Party's foreign language federations, only to discover that the party's leadership opposed the Bolsheviks. And the party's own conservatism prevented it from fighting effectively against the crackdown on its own members in the years that followed.

During the First World War, Gompers agreed to ban all AFL strikes and to allow the government to set wages for the duration of the war. In exchange, the AFL was assured the right to unionize workers under government jurisdiction. But as soon as the war ended on November 11, 1918, the class struggle exploded once again. Between 1914 and 1920 the organized labor movement doubled in size. Four million workers took part in strikes in 1919. Mine workers demanded that mines be nationalized and called for a six-hour workday. In 1918–19, labor parties grew up in more than forty U.S. cities.[85] In 1920, as labor historian David Montgomery notes, 253 strikes were unauthorized by unions—involving "850,837 workers, or 58 percent of all the year's strikers."[86]

The victory of a workers' revolution in Russia in 1917 boosted the confidence of workers around the world. U.S. workers were no exception. A 1920 study by the Interchurch World Movement reported, "the Russian government is a laboring man's government and it has not fallen down yet. Two years of newspaper reports that the Russian republic is about to fall seem to have given workingmen, even here, a sort of class pride that it hasn't fallen."[87] The radical upsurge infected the AFL itself—when convention delegates, over Gompers' objection, passed a resolution for "public ownership and democratic management" of the nation's railroads.[88]

The 1919 Seattle General Strike

The high point of this rise in struggle was undoubtedly the Seattle General Strike, when 65,000 striking workers took over the city between February 6 and February 11, 1919. The strike was remarkable not only for its immense showing of class solidarity, but also for its conscious identification with the Russian Revolution.[89]

From its beginning, the struggle incorporated both political and labor demands. As historian Jeremy Brecher described, "When a socialist and former president of the Seattle AFL, Hulet Wells, was convicted for opposing the draft during the war and then tortured in prison, the Seattle labor movement erupted with giant street rallies." He added, "Even the more conservative members of the Seattle labor movement supported the Bolshevik revolution and opposed U.S. intervention against it."[90]

On January 21, 35,000 Seattle shipyard workers went on strike for higher pay. But the strike quickly took on a political dimension when a representative of the government's United States Shipping Board Emergency Fleet Corporation telegrammed the shipyard owners to demand they grant no wage increases. The telegram, addressed to the employers' Metal Trades *Association,* was accidentally delivered to the workers' Metal Trades *Council.* The outraged strikers asked the city's Central Labor Council to poll their unions' members on authorization for a general strike. Within two weeks, 110 local unions had granted authorization and formed a three hundred-member general strike committee, with a fifteen-member executive committee, charged with running the strike. As Brecher described, the strike committee formed "virtually a counter-government for the city." He continued,

> Workers in various trades organized themselves to provide essential services with the approval of subcommittees of the executive committee, which granted them exemptions from the strike. Garbage wagon drivers agreed to collect wet garbage that would create a health hazard, but not paper and ashes. Firemen agreed to stay on the job. The laundry drivers and laundry workers developed a plan to keep one shop open to handle hospital laundry; before the strike they instructed employers to accept no more laundry, then worked a few hours after the strike deadline to finish clothes in process so they would not mildew. Vehicles authorized to operate bore signs reading, "Exempted by the General Strike Committee. . . . Employers and government officials as well as strikers came before the Strike Committee to request exemptions.[91]

Uniformed war veterans provided security for the city throughout the strike.[92] The workers organized twenty-one dining halls around Seattle that served workers and their families more than 30,000 meals per day.[93] There was no violence during the Seattle

General Strike, and arrests declined by nearly half for its duration. The lack of violence did not prevent Seattle Mayor Ole Hanson from calling for federal troops, who, along with National Guard, local police, and 2,400 hurriedly sworn-in special deputies, occupied the city on February 7. Hanson later credited himself with having prevented an insurrection: "The intent, openly and covertly announced, was for the overthrow of the industrial system; here first, then everywhere. . . . True, there were no flashing guns, no bombs, no killings. Revolution, I repeat, doesn't need violence."[94]

The troop presence alone, however, did not force Seattle's workers into submission. The strike committee finally ended the strike on February 11, citing "[p]ressure from international officers of unions, from executive committees of unions, from the 'leaders' in the labor movement, even from those very leaders who are called 'Bolsheviki' by the undiscriminating press."[95]

Seattle workers' support for the Russian Revolution continued, however—evidenced in the fall of 1919, when longshoremen refused to load arms destined for an anti-Bolshevik general (fighting to overthrow the workers' government) and "beat up strikebreakers who tried to load them."[96]

The Socialist Party grew throughout this period, though not exceeding its 1912 record. In 1917 local elections, SP candidates in New York received 22 percent of the vote; in Chicago and Toledo, each 34 percent, and in Dayton, 44 percent.[97] By 1919, the Socialist Party's membership approached one hundred thousand for the second time.[98]

The Birth of American Communism

It was inevitable, however, that the Socialist Party's long-standing internal divisions would lead to a final split between reformists and revolutionaries. That split took place at the 1919 Socialist Party convention, when its leaders faced a majority in support of the Russian Revolution, intent on affiliating with the Comintern. To regain its own majority, the SP leadership simply expelled two-thirds of its membership, including six foreign language federations.

The Socialist Party never recovered. By 1929, its membership had plummeted to a mere six thousand on paper—and far fewer in reality. As Howe described,

Hillquit was frank about the Party's condition, admitting that, at best, it came to fitful life in a few cities during electoral campaigns and then lapsed back into slumber. Somewhat later he said to [another Party leader]: "You'll have to remember that the comrades in New York have elevated inaction into a theory." Competing leftists often called the Socialist Party "a retirement home." [99]

Although the Socialist Party would revive in the 1930s, most of that generation's militant workers looked elsewhere for political leadership.

The immediate prospects for a new revolutionary party, however, did not look promising in 1919. The expelled socialists, numbering perhaps fifty thousand, were unable to agree on a common strategy and quickly split into two competing camps: the English-speaking group planned to crash an emergency convention called by party leaders, to demand their reinstatement. The other, somewhat larger, group, representing the foreign language federations, wanted to split to form its own organization. The first group's plans proved entirely unsuccessful: upon entering the convention hall, police immediately tossed them out.

In the end, the two competing factions founded two separate parties with indistinguishable political principles. The Communist Labor Party was formed on September 1, 1919, in Chicago, while the Communist Party of America was formed one day later, on September 2, 1919, also in Chicago. Both parties immediately affiliated with the Comintern. At the insistence of the Comintern, the two groups came together to form the United Communist Party in 1921, but they continued to squabble incessantly. [100]

American communism was thus born in the context of two competing factions. Not surprisingly, factionalism continued to characterize its existence for the next eight years. As Hallas described the Communist Party of the early 1920s:

> The Communist Party, on the other hand—the product of a fusion in 1919–20—was essentially a federation of factions. It must have been one of the very worst parties in the Comintern—and that's really saying something. It was internalized, fraught with problems, and ineffective until two events coincided. One was the onset of the world slump. The impact of the slump in the U.S. was enormous. In the years 1929–32 there was a catastrophic drop in industrial output of 40 percent. Secondly, by 1929 the American Communist Party had been effectively Stalinized—all the warring factions were done away with. [101]

Maintaining a strong allegiance to the IWW—and incorporating the Wobblies' hostility to the AFL—the American communists initially refused to work within the AFL. On this issue, they quickly found themselves in conflict with the Comintern's emphasis on working within *all* existing trade unions. In July 1921, the Comintern, comparing the U.S. situation with the rise of revolutionary workers' movements in Europe, issued an explicit rebuttal to the American communists' refusal to work within the AFL:

> The same revolutionary process is occurring in *America*, though more slowly. Communists must on no account leave the ranks of the reactionary Federation of Labor. On the contrary, they should seek to gain a foothold in the old trade unions with the aim of revolutionizing them. It is vital that they work with the IWW members most sympathetic to the Party; this does not, however, preclude arguing against the IWW's political positions.[102]

Won over, the competing factions permanently united to form the Workers' Party (the Communist Party), its purpose "to coordinate the entire left wing of the American labor movement within the existing unions." William Z. Foster, who joined the communist movement in 1921, greatly contributed to this aim. Foster was already an established union activist who had formed the Trade Union Education League (TUEL) in 1920 as a broad labor formation that quickly established a base in a number of AFL unions. As Montgomery described, "The TUEL was most influential in unions that had shown a progressive orientation by 1921, especially the miners, ladies' garment workers, amalgamated clothing workers, carpenters, and machinists." [103]

But by 1923 in the atmosphere of anticommunist hysteria that pervaded U.S. society, the TUEL found itself increasingly isolated, even by Foster's AFL allies. By that time, the AFL itself was devoting its efforts to a campaign to curb immigration. Once Foster's communist affiliation became publicly known, he was shunned even in his home base of Chicago, where he had enjoyed a collaborative relationship with AFL leaders for years.

In 1924, the TUEL joined forces with the Chicago Federation of Labor in an ill-fated attempt to support the independent presidential campaign of maverick Republican Senator Robert M. La-Follette. As Montgomery noted, "So intense was the pressure from the AFL . . . against that move, however, that few prominent progressives attended. As a result, the convention was easily dominated by the communists, who captured the determination of those people who had come for immediate action and brushed aside the hesitant leaders of the Chicago Federation of Labor. The latter abruptly abandoned the movement."[104]

By the mid-1920s, it would have been difficult to predict that the Communist Party would achieve mass influence in the labor movement just a decade later.

The 1920s Red Scare

American communism was born in the midst of the wave of political repression that accompanied the U.S. entry into war. The repression accelerated in response to the radicalization that followed the Russian Revolution. The red scare of this period, like the McCarthy era that followed in the 1940s and 1950s, had the dual purpose of bolstering U.S. rulers' foreign policy aims while stamping out working-class opposition at home.

Socialists and Wobblies alike were sent to prison or deported for "betraying" America under the Espionage Act. The U.S. Postal Service suspended or banned all antiwar publications from delivery by U.S. mail. The employers who crushed strikes during this era justified their actions in the language of patriotism. The IWW was singled out with a vengeance. In Jerome, Arizona, copper mine owners formed the "Jerome Loyalty League" to destroy an IWW-led miners' strike in 1917. In Bisbee, Arizona, an army of two thousand "deputies" attacked another miners' strike, and as Nicholson described, "The workers, and every local labor advocate, IWW member and sympathizer (including several local businessmen), were packed into railroad cattle cars with minimal provisions and stranded in the midst of the New Mexico desert."[105] In Butte, Montana, mine owners arranged the murder of IWW organizer Frank Little, whose "tortured and mutilated body was found hanging from a railroad trestle bridge" in August 1917.[106]

The wartime repression long outlasted the war itself. In September 1919, Congress created the American Legion as an arm of the National Association of Manufacturers (NAM), as Nicholson wrote, "for the stated purpose of combating radicalism, especially as it manifested itself in the labor goal of the closed or union shop":

Before 1919 was over, Legionnaires had helped break a streetcar work-ers' strike in Denver, Colorado (August), and attacked the IWW meet-ing hall in Centralia, Washington (November). When they were met with armed Wobbly resistance in Centralia, Legionnaires captured, castrated, and lynched the IWW leader, Wesley Everest, a decorated World War I veteran. The patriotic vigilantes of the American Legion made no secret of their political ideals. The featured guest speaker at the American Legion Convention in San Francisco in 1923 was one of their heroes, the Italian Fascist dictator, Benito Mussolini.[107]

In 1920, thirty-two states banned the flying of a red flag, and New York State declared the Socialist Party an illegal organiza-tion.[108] By 1921, Montgomery noted, only eleven of eighty-eight major cities had removed their wartime bans on street meetings." The U.S. Justice Department worked hand in glove with the Labor Department, including its Immigration Bureau, to persecute "dan-gerous radicals," while immigration laws were used to arrest and deport foreign-born radicals and union activists.[109]

Between 1917 and 1920, many states passed laws effectively outlawing the IWW for the crime of "criminal syndicalism." On November 19, 1919, Attorney General A. Mitchell Palmer (then seeking the Democratic Party presidential nomination), with the aid of a young J. Edgar Hoover, directed Justice Department agents to raid radical offices in more than twelve cities, arresting two thou-sand alleged radicals in New York alone. On January 2, 1920, the Palmer raids resumed, as agents staged simultaneous attacks on communists and IWW members in thirty-three cities—deporting between five thousand and ten thousand immigrants for allegedly belonging to a radical organization. As Lens described, "Seldom had America witnessed such police state tactics. Five hundred men and women were arrested in Boston, shackled, and driven through the streets."[110] Levine noted, "The raids virtually destroyed local Com-munist organizations."[111]

Meanwhile, Congress set its sights on excluding immigrants "... 'of undesirable' nationalities, without closing the doors to Northern Europeans or depriving western farm operators of mi-grant hands," according to Montgomery.[112] Merging eugenics with anticommunism, Washington's activist senator Albert Johnson op-posed allowing the entry of those who were "filthy, un-American, and often dangerous in their habits."[113]

The red scare was closely tied to government efforts to curb the class struggle, evidenced by Congress' attempt to make it a crime to "advocate a railway strike" in 1919. [114] But its efforts did not always succeed. Although the Senate incorporated a strike ban in a railroad postwar reprivatization bill, the ban was removed in committee— after the International Association of Machinists (IAM) threatened a nationwide strike if it passed.

AFL unions joined in the anticommunist hysteria. In 1923, the UMWA ordered the expulsion of all communists from membership. In 1924 and 1925, the carpenters' and machinists' unions followed suit. The AFL's October 1923 convention expelled its only known communist delegate, union member William Dunne. [115]

The repression culminated in the 1927 execution of Sacco and Vanzetti. The two Italian anarchists became symbols of persecution against foreign-born workers, and as their execution date drew near, protests and strikes spread from New York City's garment workers to Midwestern coal miners. When the IWW called for strikes on the anarchists' behalf, miners as far away as Colorado walked out. [116] By the late 1920s, the number of *annual* deportations rose to more than 38,000. [117]

The "Roaring Twenties": A Bosses' Paradise

By 1920, a majority of the U.S. population was concentrated in industrial cities for the first time. [118] The decade saw the growing concentration of capital and wealth, with more than twelve hundred mergers in manufacturing between 1918 and 1928. [119] Income tax rates for the wealthiest Americans fell from 77 percent during World War I to just 25 percent in its aftermath. As Levine notes, "By the end of 1929 the two hundred largest business corporations possessed nearly half the corporate wealth of the United States, 38 percent of the business wealth, and 20 percent of the total national wealth." [120] With good reason, the 1920s became known as the "Roaring Twenties" for its soaring profits and unbridled ruling-class opulence.

The rise of mass-production industries that followed World War I greatly accelerated labor productivity: between 1914 and 1927, productivity increased by 55 percent in iron and steel, 178 percent in auto, and 292 percent in rubber. [121] During the long boom of the 1920s, leading economists proclaimed capitalism's booms and slumps to be a thing of the past, declaring that the U.S. economy could look forward to "permanent prosperity." The banking magnate Melvin A. Traylor declared confidently, "We need not fear a recurrence of the conditions that will plunge the nation into the depths of the more violent financial panics such as have occurred in the past." [122]

Corporate leaders spent the decade slashing wages and breaking unions, with widespread success, while promoting their own toothless company unions. The Supreme Court's 1923 *Adkins v. Children's Hospital* ruling pronounced minimum wage laws as violations of the Constitution's "protection of liberty of contract." During the 1920s, corporations used twice as many court injunctions against strikes than "in any comparable period," according to Nicholson.[123]

Employers were further aided in their efforts by the government's red scare that lasted well into the 1920s. The National Association of Manufacturers went on an antiunion offensive. Dovetailing with the red scare, the Association organized a mass literature campaign to discredit unionism as linked to "Communist activities." [124] Corporations across the country enrolled in a campaign calling itself "the American Plan," in a patriotic challenge to the tyranny of "un-American" unionism. As Lens described, "From a thousand different but coordinated forums, the disciples of 'Americanism' shouted that unions desecrated the worker's right to 'free choice.' " [125]

Many employers took the opportunity to force workers to sign pledges that they would never join a labor union—widely derided as "yellow dog contracts" in the union movement. Bethlehem Steel refused to sell its steel to contractors "who were so unpatriotic as to hire union labor." [126]

Although 688,538 workers took part in more than eleven hundred strikes between 1922 and 1926, most went down in defeat. "Victory" was relative, and usually involved a wage cut—but one lower than employers initially demanded. By 1929, the AFL had lost a million members, dropping from four million in 1920, to three million at the end of 1929.[127] The UMW represented just 80,000 miners by 1928, its membership falling to 40,000 by 1932.[128]

Heading South to Escape Unions

One of the worst labor defeats of this era was reserved for Southern textile workers, by an employing class intent on preserving the South's status as a nonunion haven for employers.

In the late 1920s, many textile manufacturers had already begun escaping unionization in the North by relocating to the Deep South. By 1927, cotton textile production was concentrated in the South, 67 percent as measured by yards produced and 56 percent by value.[129] The North-South wage differential was enormous. In 1928, the Bureau of Labor estimated that hourly wages were 43.6 percent lower in the South in a survey of seventeen occupations. That same year, wages in Southern textile mills stood at 29.1 cents per hour, compared with 41.4 cents in New England.[130] *Business Week* described this significant wage differential as "the lure dangled before the noses of harassed New England mill owners." [131]

Plagued with problems of chronic overproduction due to seasonal fashion fluctuations, textile companies fought ruthlessly to guard their interests against labor reform of any kind.[132] As one South Carolina mill owner declared candidly: "We govern like the Czar of Russia." [133] Historian Irving Bernstein noted of this period,

> On issues that affected their interests the mill owners exercised firm control over the machinery of state and local government. Nearly all representatives and senators from the Southern textile states in Washington felt it was their sacred duty to protect the industry against outside encroachment in such matters as foreign competition, the child labor amendment, and federal investigation of working conditions. When an occasional critical voice was raised in protest . . . the mill owners' hostility guaranteed that it would not be heard.[134]

Southern mill owners controlled all institutions in company towns—including the clergy. As one manager put it: "We had a young fellow from an Eastern seminary down here as pastor . . . and the young fool went around saying that we helped pay the preachers' salaries in order to control them. That was a damn lie—and we got rid of him." [135]

Hiring policies virtually barred Black workers from jobs in the Southern textile industry: of a hundred thousand North Carolina textile workers in 1930, fewer than three thousand were African American, all employed in the worst and most dangerous jobs.[136] But Southern textile manufacturers paid poverty wages to their largely white workforces. In 1919, a Senate investigation showed textile wages were the lowest in manufacturing, with the possible exception of tobacco.

Southern 1920s-era laws upheld the sixty-hour week and ten- to twelve-hour days that were typical in the textile industry. Alabama law placed no limit on work hours. North Carolina and Georgia allowed up to a sixty-hour workweek. Children under the age of fourteen were common in the textile workforce. South Carolina provided no workmen's compensation for those injured on the job.

Those labor laws that did exist went largely unenforced. A 1929 investigation by the South Carolina House of Representatives found the office of the state's Commissioner of Agriculture, Commerce, and Industry "in a state of inertia and lethargy." The investigation concluded, however, that the commissioner himself was "quite wakeful" in making sure "to suppress and excuse practically every violation of labor laws."[137]

The United Textile Workers (UTW), an AFL union, was singularly unsuccessful in organizing in the 1920s, although it was unclear how hard it had tried. The UTW's membership shrank during the course of the decade, by 1929 representing less than 3 percent of the nation's 1.1 million textile workers—all in the North. Labor scholar Robert R. R. Brooks observed, "The union appeared to consist almost entirely of a suite of offices, a complement of officers, and a splendid array of filing cabinets."[138]

The UTW was ill-prepared to face the wrath of Southern textile manufacturers when members of its Local 1630 in Elizabethtown, Tennessee—facing widespread speedups (called "stretch-outs" in textiles) and wage cuts—went out on strike in April 1929. The towns' leading citizens responded by organizing vigilante mobs who were "determined that the strike menace be nipped in the bud."[139] Armed gangs, led by Elizabethtown businessmen and police, drove two union organizers over the state border and warned them never to return. One organizer reported that the local president of the First National Bank led the armed gang that seized him, telling him at gunpoint that he would "fill me full of holes if I returned." Another union member was beaten by a mob—headed by a local leader of the Presbyterian Church—after they entered his home in the middle of the night. His sister arrived with a rifle, and after exchanging gunfire, the thugs left.[140]

AFL President William Green (who succeeded Gompers) traveled to Elizabethtown to pledge the federation's support to a gathering of four thousand strikers. The company subsequently fired all members of Local 1630. The union called a second strike in response, shutting down two Elizabethtown mills. This time, the strikers were met by eight hundred state police and sheriff's deputies—paid for by management: $1,000 per day to the state of Tennessee for the service of its police force and $50,000 to the county in a "goodwill" gesture for the use of its deputies. The troops reported directly to plant managers—arresting 1,250 striking workers from the picket line. The violence that ensued culminated in the firebombing of the town's main water line.[141]

On May 25, union officials and management finally reached an agreement, one that did not recognize the union but mandated management to meet with an employee committee to discuss grievances. But on September 19, the company posted a notice stating, "The management does not intend at any time to discuss any matters . . . with outside individuals or organizations." Those workers who objected were told they should not "remain in our employ."[142]

The defeat of the UTW highlighted the enormous odds that would confront labor in the South—and especially in the textile industry. There were more defeats to follow, but also the potential for some very significant advances in the years to come.

The Triumph of Stalinism and "Third Period" Communism

The Russian Revolution of 1917 was an inspiration to most radicals and revolutionaries, even if they were not 100 percent behind the policies of the new Bolshevik regime. The situation changed dramatically over the next decade. By 1928, the year Stalin exiled Trotsky, the Russian regime oversaw the complete reversal of every gain won by the working class in the 1917 revolution.[143] From then on, Communist Parties internationally were required to uncritically adopt each twist and turn in Stalin's foreign and domestic policy as their own. While this rid the American Communist Party of its perpetual factionalism, the organization became a caricature of the machine that Stalin built to rule Russia. As American Communist Party leader Earl Browder argued in the mid-1930s, "If one is not interested in directives from Moscow, that only means he is not interested in building socialism at all."[144]

In 1928, when Stalin first secured control over the Russian Communist Party, he announced that capitalism was entering a new period of economic crisis and revolution would soon be on the global agenda. Soon the only alternatives would be communism or fascism, he pronounced. The duty of communists the world over was therefore to prepare for the upcoming revolutionary crisis—by declaring war on all liberal and social democratic leaders, whom Stalin labeled "social fascists," or secret supporters of fascism masquerading as social reformers.

Thus, at Stalin's behest, Communist Parties around the world entered their wildly sectarian Third Period era in 1928, seeking to enhance their own revolutionary image by denouncing all other forces on the left as traitors to the "Bolshevik tradition." The Third Period had nothing to do with world politics, however, but was the product of Stalin's "revolutionary" justification for the forced collectivization of agriculture underway inside the USSR.[145]

During the Third Period, lasting from 1928 until 1934, American communists dutifully denounced members of the Socialist Party and other reformers as "social fascists." In the midst of the 1929 stock market crash that ushered in the Great Depression, the October 28 issue of the communist newspaper, the *Daily Worker,* reserved its main editorial for an attack on Socialist Party leader "Norman Thomas, Candidate of the Third Capitalist Party."[146]

But the Stalinists reserved their fiercest hostility for the tiny Trotskyist movement, then attempting in very difficult circumstances to build an alternative to Stalinism. Following Stalin's lead, the American CP expelled its own Trotskyist faction in 1928. From that point on, communists engaged in a relentless campaign against Trotsky and his political allies, (falsely) accusing them of being in league with Hitler himself. The persecution against Trotsky culminated in his murder at the hands of Stalin's assassin in Mexico in 1940.[147] The American Communist Party's campaign against Trotskyists also periodically included physical assaults, from the late 1920s and continuing into the 1940s.[148]

In its Third Period, communists managed to also alienate organized labor when it formed rival "red" unions to compete with the AFL. In 1929, the CP replaced its broadly oriented Trade Union Education League (TUEL) with the "revolutionary" Trade Union Unity League (TUUL), completing its shift to red unionism. The TUUL was, by all accounts, unsuccessful in all its aims.[149]

CHAPTER FOUR

Depression Decade:
The Turning Point

The 1920s-era economists who declared a "permanent end" to booms and slumps had spoken much too soon. Before the decade was over, the U.S. economy plunged into its worst depression in history. The October 1929 stock market crash that marked the beginning of the Great Depression ushered in an extended period of misery for the entire working class. By 1932, fully 23.6 percent of the population was unemployed. But certain sectors of industrial workers were hit even harder, particularly in textiles and auto. Employment at the Ford Motor Company, for example, dropped from 128,142 in 1929 to just 37,000 in 1931.[1]

As Nicholson noted,

> For every publicized suicide of a failed businessman or stock specula-
> tor, thousands of innocent workers, women, and children died of star-
> vation, malnutrition, or exposure. No one will ever know how many
> working-class women died of botched abortions, or how many infants
> were killed or died because of the effects of the Depression. No labor-
> ing family was untouched. . . . By the terribly cold winter of 1932–33
> a full third of the labor force was unemployed and without regular
> income. In large cities and industrial centers the unemployment rate
> was 40 to 50 percent.[2]

But there was little sympathy for the starving masses among U.S. rulers. Indeed, employers used the threat of unemployment to force down the wages of those who still had jobs. By 1930, real weekly earnings had fallen by 20 percent across all industries, and by 15 to 30 percent in manufacturing and mining.[3]

Republican President Herbert Hoover opposed every measure

to grant federal assistance to feed the hungry or help the homeless. Hoover refused even to acknowledge the existence of mass unemployment and did nothing to provide relief, besides appointing a government commission to "investigate" the problem. With good reason, shantytowns of impoverished workers were widely known as "Hoovervilles." Even "Mickey Mouse" could have defeated Hoover in 1932, as was frequently noted at the time.[4]

Hoover did, however, grant some important labor reforms. Perhaps sensing the threat of a coming upturn in class struggle, he signed legislation outlawing yellow dog contracts and restricting the use of court injunctions against strikes. Nicholson commented, "The concept of the federal protection for the right of workers to form collective organizations for representation, however, would soon become one of the foundations of the rapid expansion of unions during the New Deal. That right is usually credited to the new president, Franklin Delano Roosevelt, but actually began in its advance in the administration of Herbert Hoover."[5]

Most employers nevertheless flatly refused to bargain with any union in the early 1930s.

The Limits of the New Deal

When Roosevelt campaigned for president in 1932, his platform differed little from the Republicans, other than a vaguely worded promise for a "new deal for Americans" and a promise of limited unemployment benefits. But neither Roosevelt and the Democrats, nor the Republicans, objected when the U.S. Army attacked a protest of 15,000 unemployed workers "using tanks and tear gas" in Washington, D.C., in the summer of 1932.[6]

As Nicholson argued, "Until the banking crisis of 1933, and the first hundred days of the New Deal, the government did not intervene on behalf of the people in the same way as it responded to demands for help on behalf of business. Helping to relieve the distress of business was accepted as a legitimate course of government action, whereas helping impoverished people was not."[7]

Police repeatedly fired upon hunger marchers in the early 1930s. In 1932, the Detroit police used machine guns to mow down a hunger demonstration of several thousand. Four demonstrators were killed and more than sixty were injured. Yet afterward a city prosecutor commented, "I say I wish they'd killed a few more of those damn rioters." [8] When faced with opposition from its impoverished population, U.S. rulers systematically responded with violence. But in so doing, they unleashed an unparalleled era of working-class upheaval.

Even before Roosevelt's inauguration in March 1933, the union movement was already rising, particularly among young workers. Auto manufacturers, for example, generally refused to hire anyone over the age of forty, preferring young workers who could keep up with the rapidly moving assembly line. [9] But these young workers also proved to be energetic fighters on picket lines. In January 1933, fifteen thousand autoworkers went out on strike, demanding the right to organize. That same year, Hormel meat-packers in Austin, Minnesota, went on the first sit-down strike of the decade, and won. [10]

In May 1933, Roosevelt granted workers the right to organize into unions in Section 7(a) of the National Industrial Recovery Act (NIRA), and workers rushed to organize unions. Section 7(a) provided a minimum wage and maximum hours. But its most important passage read, "employees shall have the right to organize and bargain collectively through representatives of their own choosing, and shall be free from the interference, restraint, or coercion of employers." [11] In 1933, there were 1,695 work stoppages, double the figure for 1932, and they involved 1,117,000 workers—nearly four times the number for the previous year. In 1934, the figures rose a bit higher: 1,856 strikes, involving 1,470,000 workers. [12] But everywhere employers put up violent resistance.

The Bloody Textile Strike of 1934

Like workers across the country, textile workers interpreted the NIRA as an invitation to organize. The AFL's United Textile Workers of America (UTW), with just fifty thousand members in 1933, ballooned to four hundred thousand by mid-1934. But as a group, textile manufacturers had no intention of surrendering to collective bargaining, and summarily fired these new union members whenever they protested the flagrant violations of wage and hour laws that characterized the industry.

A meeting of UTW delegates on August 31, 1934, called a national strike—demanding union recognition, reinstatement of all workers fired for union activity, and a thirty-hour workweek at the forty-eight-hour week pay scale established by the NIRA. Nearly four hundred thousand East Coast textile workers responded to the call, from New England to the Deep South. The workers formed flying pickets, traveling from one mill town to the next, calling other workers out on strike.

The *New York Times* sounded the alarm at the flying pickets, warning that women were "taking an increasingly active part in the picketing, egging on the men" and were "apparently prepared to stop at nothing to obtain their objectives." The *Times* added, "The growing mass character of the picketing operations is rapidly assuming the appearance of military efficiency and precision and is something entirely new in the history of American labor struggles." [13]

The manufacturers retaliated with a reign of terror in one of the bloodiest labor defeats in U.S. history. Brooks observed, "The thousands of militiamen, sheriffs, and armed strikebreakers which were thrown into strike territories and the numerous deaths at the hands of drunken deputies and nervous guardsmen linked the forces of law and order so clearly with the interests of the textile employers that northern newspaper reporters repeatedly referred to the situation as 'the employers' offensive.'" [14]

In the South, the employers justified the armed mobs attacking strikers with a torrent of racism, combined with anticommunism. The *Gastonia Daily Gazette* ran "Communism in the South. Kill it!" as a front-page headline. Employers distributed antiunion leaflets to white workers asking, "Would you belong to a union which opposes white supremacy?" [15]

In Gastonia, North Carolina, National Guardsmen, joined by armed strikebreakers, were ordered to "shoot to kill" unarmed strikers: "Without warning came the first shots, followed by many others, and for a few minutes there was bedlam. Striker after striker fell to the ground, with the cries of wounded men sounding over the field and men and women running shrieking from the scene." [16] In Burlington, North Carolina, troops bayoneted five picketers in a group of four hundred, all wearing "peaceful picket" badges. Georgia Governor Eugene Talmadge declared martial law and threw strikers into prison camps. [17]

National Guard troops occupied mill towns throughout New

England. Rhode Island's Democratic governor declared the strikers were leading "a communist uprising and not a textile strike in Rhode Island," and declared a state of insurrection. In Sayles, Rhode Island, state troopers fired at pickets with machine guns. In Woonsocket, troops used teargas on a crowd of two thousand strikers and fired into the crowd, killing one and injuring four.[18]

Once again, the AFL failed to provide the leadership needed to win the strike. Rhode Island UTW leader Frank Gorman refused to sanction the flying pickets and blamed the violence on communists.[19] Lens wrote, "Leftists who offered the union help were rebuffed or even castigated. No effort was made by the UTW to call city or state strikes, or to involve the garment industry unions, beyond securing financial help from them."[20] The union declared the strike a "victory" and called it off after three weeks, with nothing gained. Thousands of strikers lost their jobs; others were forced to sign yellow dog pledges to leave the union.

But in the strike's aftermath, textile workers began to clamor for a labor party. As Eric Leif Davin argued,

> In both the South and New England, the United Textile Workers' strike taught mill workers to distrust the Democratic Party, whose representatives had fought the strike. The Massachusetts Committee for a Labor Party declared in March 1936, "The New Deal was supposed to give us the right to organize. Yet when the textile workers went on strike in 1934 for recognition of their union and to stop speed-up, Democratic governors in 12 states called out the militia to drive the workers back to work and break the strike. In fact, 14 workers were killed by militia called out by Democratic governors."[21]

Even Gorman, who had helped to lead the textile strike to defeat, was convinced of the need for a labor party by his experience. "Many of us did not understand what we do now," Gorman acknowledged. "We know now that we are naive to depend on the forces of government to protect us."[22] Gorman brought the fight to the 1935 AFL convention, where he proposed one of a total of thirteen labor party resolutions. Despite considerable bureaucratic stonewalling by AFL leaders, his resolution lost by just four votes, with a total of 108 to 104.[23]

The Tide Begins to Turn

As the NIRA strengthened more workers' resolve to unionize, the center of struggle shifted away from hunger and unemployed marches toward strikes for union recognition in key industries. The left also began to grow again in this period. The Communist Party grew from eight thousand to twenty-four thousand members, and even the Socialist Party experienced an increase in membership.

These two developments were related since, as Lens argued, "One or two leftists among a thousand workers was enough to give the group direction and stimulus, and there were plenty of young leftists around. A new generation, active at first in the battles of the unemployed, and then in the plants, talked openly of revolution as if it were the first order of business on the historical agenda." [24]

In 1934, the tide began to turn. Although the textile workers were defeated that year, three other strikes, in San Francisco, Toledo, and Minneapolis—fought almost simultaneously in the spring and summer of 1934—began to shift the momentum in favor of workers. Each strike proved in practice that working-class solidarity could win, however well-armed and -funded the employers' side. Labor radicals played a key role in leading all three strikes to victory, relying on the strength of class solidarity alone and rejecting any collaboration with the employers.

The Toledo Auto-Lite Strike

Local 18384 of the AFL first called a strike at Toledo's Auto-Lite parts plants and two affiliated companies on February 23, 1934. But the union was designated a "federal" affiliate of the AFL, allowing it no autonomy from national control, and AFL president William Green quickly ordered the strikers back to work. A month and a half later, under continuing duress, four thousand Auto-Lite workers again went out on strike. But the strikers represented fewer than half the workers employed at Auto-Lite, making it relatively easy for the company to keep the plant running. To further demoralize the workers, a court soon issued an injunction limiting the number of pickets to twenty-five. The AFL decided to accommodate the court ruling, allowing strikebreakers to enter the plant freely. [25]

In April 1934, no one could have expected that this strike would end in victory. But the American Workers Party, a small organization led by A. J. Muste, built a solidarity movement that united employed and unemployed in a common struggle. Muste was a unique type of 1930s radical, a religious pacifist wary of Stalinism but sympathetic to socialism—and dedicated to building the union movement.[26]

With one-third of Toledo's residents out of work, the company could have quickly assembled a large army of strikebreakers. Thus, the most immediate threat to the strike came from the city's large number of unemployed. But the unemployed proved key to winning the strike. Through Muste's Lucas County Unemployed League, the strikers managed to convince thousands of unemployed workers that their own interests lay not in stealing the strikers' jobs but in helping the union to win its strike.

Lens described,

> The league, like the federal [AFL] local, had been enjoined from picketing, but its officers had less respect for the sanctity of the courts. Unity of the jobless with strikers was a cardinal principle, almost a religious dogma, with the revolutionaries of the American Workers Party. . . . True to their word, they mobilized 1,000 unemployed before the Auto-Lite gates on the first day, 4,000 on the next, and 6,000 on the third.

Pickets were generally peaceful until May 23, when a strike-breaker threw a bolt at a woman striker, and some strikers responded in kind. The Associated Press reported, "Suddenly, a barrage of tear gas bombs was hurled from upper factory windows. At the same time, company employees armed with iron bars and clubs dragged a fire hose into the street and played water on the crowd. The strike sympathizers replied with bricks, as they choked from gas fumes and fell back."[27] Although police went in swinging, they had to give up, also choking from tear gas. A fifteen-hour battle ensued, after which nine hundred National Guard troops finally rescued the strikebreakers trapped inside.

The troops opened fire on the strikers, killing two and injuring dozens, but the workers did not back down. They fought the National Guard for a total of six days, with numerous injuries on both sides. Finally, on May 31, the company agreed to close the plant to strikebreakers and the troops were removed. The next day, forty thousand workers protested outside the Lucas County Courthouse against the arrests of two hundred strikers—and ninety-eight of the city's ninety-nine local unions pledged to call a general strike in sympathy. The company finally backed down on June 4, granting union recognition to Local 18384 and agreeing to rehire all strikers.[28]

The San Francisco General Strike

Like the Toledo strike, San Francisco longshoremen defied their own union leaders when they called a West Coast strike in May 1934. The International Longshoremen's Association (ILA) had already negotiated a secret agreement with the employers that would have weeded out young union militants from the docks when the San Francisco longshoremen voted unanimously to call a strike for May 9. Despite frantic telegrams urging a postponement from both the U.S. Department of Labor and ILA officials, the strike went on as scheduled.

By May 11, fourteen thousand longshoremen were on strike from San Diego to Seattle. The strikers demanded a closed union shop and a thirty-hour workweek to replace the forty-eight-hour week then in place. One of their most important demands was for a union-controlled hiring hall to replace the system by which foremen could pick out those they wanted to work each day—in a long tradition of favoritism, by which payoffs and bribes to supervisors were necessary to get hired.

Rank-and-file union members elected communist Harry Bridges as chairman of the San Francisco strike committee.[29] From the beginning, the strike was remarkable for its immense solidarity, with daily mass meetings and round-the-clock pickets. The thousand burly San Francisco pickets were extremely successful at keeping scabs away: only five union members successfully crossed the picket line. As Lens commented, "No sensible person would have tried to cross that picket line without a few squads of police to shepherd him through, and even then he might not have made it. The pickets did not have to resort to violence often, for their mere presence was a discouragement to those who had designs on their jobs."[30]

"It is a different strike from any the Coast has ever known," remarked the liberal *Nation*.[31] Squads of longshoremen at the docks personally appealed to rank-and-file truck drivers and merchant marines to support their strike—and those rank-and-filers, in turn, pressured their own union leaders to call a sympathy strike. Within a week, the Teamsters' union refused to haul cargo to or from the docks and twenty-five thousand maritime workers were on strike in solidarity up and down the West Coast.[32]

AFL president William Green, meanwhile, denounced the strikers as "communists." But ILA leaders who tried to push through an agreement without the union hiring hall demand in mid-June were booed down by a mass meeting of strikers. Two months into the strike, the city's business community pulled together to open the port. On the morning of July 5, the city sent in its entire police force, which opened fire on the crowd, launching a daylong pitched battle, known as "Bloody Thursday." The pickets dispersed, only to reassemble hours later—this time joined by substantial numbers of workers from other unions. In the melee that followed, four workers were killed and hundreds more wounded. Later the workers placed flowers at the site where two workers were killed, with the words, "Two men killed here, murdered by police." [33]

If the longshoremen had surrendered, the defeat would have reverberated through all unions, reaching up and down the West Coast. Instead, the San Francisco strike committee decided to expand the strike to other unions. By July 14, representatives of 115 local unions voted to go out on a general strike in their support.[34]

Although a citywide general strike was the last thing AFL leaders wanted, there was nothing they could do to head it off. So they immediately assumed leadership of the strike in order to quickly bring it to a close. The Central Labor Council called a general strike, bringing 130,000 workers out, paralyzing the entire city for four days—but effectively seizing leadership from the strike committee.

Police and National Guard Troops (now numbering forty-five hundred) unleashed a wave of repression on strikers all over San Francisco, while vigilante squads raided union offices and attacked workers wherever they gathered. As Art Preis noted, "Thirty-five gangs of vigilantes, heavily armed, raided headquarters of the Communist, IWW and Socialist groups. . . . In some instances, the police who arrived after the vigilantes left completed the work of destruction. They jailed more than 300 persons." [35]

Instead of leading the strike forward, the AFL leadership deliberately wound it down. By the third day of the strike, they began to demand the strikers should end it. By the fourth day, the strike was over:

[Immediately] President Green of the AFL disowned the strike. The second day of the strike the General Strike Committee called for arbitration of all issues, thus giving up the basic demand which the strike was all about, the union hiring hall. The third day it reopened all union restaurants and butcher shops and ended embargoes on gasoline and fuel oil. . . . By the fourth day the General Strike Committee voted 191 to 174 to end the general strike.[36]

The longshoremen won union recognition but were forced to compromise on the demand for a union hiring hall—a partial victory, but far short of what would have been possible had the general strike continued. In the strike's aftermath, Nicholson noted, "the entire area seethed with class hatred."[37]

Minneapolis Teamsters Strike

The 1934 Minneapolis Teamsters strike occurred in three waves of struggle: as a truck drivers' strike in February that expanded to include warehouse workers in May and ended in victory in July. Rank-and-file leaders of Minneapolis Teamsters Local 574 were able to maintain control from start to finish. The national Teamsters' union, then numbering just ninety-five thousand, was much too weak to impose its will on the upstart local, although the union's president, Daniel Tobin, remained hostile through every phase of the strike.

Local 574 wrote to Tobin in February, requesting permission to go on strike. The local finally received a reply from Tobin, refusing to give the unions permission to strike—but not until two days *after* the first phase of the strike ended in February. "By that time we'd won and had signed a contract with increased pay," explained Local 574 president Bill Brown.[38]

For emphasis, Tobin denounced the Minneapolis strike leaders as "radicals and Communists" in the Teamsters magazine.[39] AFL officials thus played no role in winning the victory in Minneapolis. The strike's leaders were rank-and-file truck drivers. In particular, a group of Minneapolis Trotskyists—Karl Skoglund and brothers Vincent, Miles, and Grant Dunne—played a decisive role in shaping the character of the strike. Another strike leader, coal driver Farrell Dobbs, joined the Trotskyists as a result of his experience in 1934. Dobbs, a young worker who had voted for Hoover in 1926, hardly fit the stereotype of an "outside agitator" so commonly associated with radicals.

As in Toledo and San Francisco, the Minneapolis strike "displayed radical leadership's reliance on the rank and file, advance planning as meticulous as that of an army and a defiance of what is commonly called 'law and order' when law and order was specifically directed at crushing their union," Lens observed.

By May, five thousand Teamsters were on strike, but the union's various operations involved thousands of Minneapolis workers beyond Local 574. The strike itself expanded dramatically when thirty-five thousand building workers walked off the job in solidarity, and the city's taxi workers followed suit. Even the city's Central Labor Council endorsed the strike.[40]

Each step of the way, the union's seventy-five-member strike committee—made up of rank-and-file truck drivers—ran the struggle democratically, through nightly mass meetings with all striking workers and publishing a daily strike newspaper with a circulation that reached ten thousand. The strikers organized their own hospital and kitchen out of the garage that served as strike headquarters, treating the injured and feeding up to ten thousand workers per day.

Teams of strikers constantly patrolled the streets of Minneapolis in "cruising picket squads"—trucks filled with picketers who could be immediately dispatched to confront scab trucks moving anywhere in the city. The trucks phoned into union headquarters every ten minutes with progress reports, such as "Truck attempting to move load of produce from Berman Fruit, under police convoy. Have only ten pickets, send help."[41]

Two thousand Minneapolis businessmen, organized under the neutral title of the "Citizens' Alliance," organized an antiunion movement to counter the strikers. The Alliance organized its own "mass movement of citizens" including a "citizens' army"—which city authorities immediately deputized as a "special police force." Like Local 574, the Alliance organized its own "strike headquarters" to feed its thousands of supporters and provide medical care to injured strikebreakers.[42]

The police and their "deputies" attacked the Minneapolis strikers time and again, with high casualties on both sides. But as Dobbs argued in his eyewitness account of the strike, *Teamster Rebellion,* "Contrary to bosses' hopes and expectations, the strikers were not exactly paralyzed with fear at the prospect of facing an army of cops and deputies."[43] In one such confrontation on May 22, fifteen hundred police and armed strikebreakers, who had been quickly sworn in as deputies, attacked a gathering of twenty thousand strikers. But as Preis described, the police were the losers in what was later called "the Battle of Deputies' Run":

> The pickets charged the deputies first and noticed that many uniformed cops were tending to hang back. . . . Sensing this mood among some of the cops, the pickets continued to concentrate mainly on the deputies. Soon even the bystanders were getting their licks in support of the strikers. Finding themselves mousetrapped, many deputies dropped their clubs and ripped off their badges, trying with little success to seek anonymity in the hostile crowd. By this time the pickets were also zeroing in on uniformed cops who had gotten into the thick of the fight. The scene of the battle spread as cops and deputies alike were driven from the market. The deputies were chased clear back to headquarters, the strikers mopping up on stragglers along the way. In less than an hour after the battle started, there wasn't a cop to be seen in the market, and pickets were directing traffic.[44]

Minnesota Governor Floyd B. Olson, representing Minnesota's Farmer-Labor Party, initially supported the strike. Declaring, "I am not a liberal . . . I am a radical," he even donated $500 to the strike fund.[45] But as the strike wore on in May, involving increasingly bloody confrontations between police and strikers, Olson apparently changed his mind and put thirty-seven hundred National Guard troops on alert. Olson retreated only when the employers agreed to settle the strike on May 25.

But the strike resumed again on July 16 after the employers reneged on the settlement. Local newspapers warned of "Reds" and "Bloody Revolution," as the strike entered its bloodiest phase. Meanwhile, city police carried out a murderous attack on unarmed pickets, killing two strikers and injuring fifty-five on July 20, in an incident known as "Bloody Friday."[46] A government investigation of the incident reported later, "Police took direct aim at the pickets and fired to kill. Physical safety of the police was at no time endangered. . . . At no time did pickets attack the police."[47]

Nevertheless, the "radical" Governor Olsen responded to "Bloody Friday" by declaring martial law and finally calling in the National Guard, making no pretense that the troops would defend the strikers.[48] The Guard immediately raided the union's headquarters, arresting the Dunne brothers in a roundup of one hundred strike leaders. But all union taxis, ice, beer, and gasoline trucks responded by going out on strike. Forty thousand people marched in the funeral procession for striker Harry Ness, killed on "Bloody Friday." Authorities released the strike leaders after a demonstration of forty thousand angry workers demanded it.

Eventually the number of troops nearly matched the number of strikers. In a face-off that lasted five weeks, the strikers continued using cruising picket squads to stop scab trucks while Roosevelt's labor board mediators worked to negotiate a settlement. The employers finally caved in on August 22, granting the union's main demands. The "radicals and communists" so despised by Tobin had won the International Brotherhood of Teamsters its first major victory of the 1930s.[49]

The CIO Opens Its Doors

Conditions were overripe for mass industrial unionism in the United States by the 1930s. Industrial productivity had risen by less than 10 percent between 1899 and 1914, but between 1920 and 1930 it had increased by 7 percent each year. Unskilled and semi-skilled workers moved to the forefront of manufacturing. In 1926, the Ford Motor Company announced that 43 percent of its jobs required only one day's training.[50]

Most importantly, the working class was no longer completely segregated along racial lines. The slowdown in immigration after 1914 brought with it a corresponding increase in internal migration. A half-million Southern Blacks moved North during World War I to fill widespread labor shortages. By 1930, more than 25 percent of African-American men were employed in industrial jobs, compared with just 7 percent in 1890. By the mid-1930s, Black workers made up 20 percent of laborers and 6 percent of operatives in the steel industry nationally. One-fifth of the workforce in Chicago's slaughterhouses was African American. White workers could not hope to win unless they united with Black workers, and that could not happen unless unions organized on the basis of at least formal equality.[51]

Yet despite the sharp rise in industrial struggle by the mid-1930s, most AFL leaders continued to cling to the exclusivity of craft unionism. In 1932, the AFL still opposed federal unemployment compensation.[52] At the 1934 AFL convention, during a debate about organizing the unskilled, Tobin repeated Gompers earlier insults, calling unskilled workers "garbage."

In the early 1930s, unskilled workers who wanted to unionize had no choice but to apply for membership in the AFL, but soon became disillusioned by the indifference—and hostility—directed toward them by union leaders. Unskilled and semiskilled workers who joined the AFL were quickly shuffled off into "federal locals"—subsidiaries with fewer rights than the brotherhoods of skilled workers. Thousands of rubber- and autoworkers rushed into the AFL after the NIRA granted the right to unionize—but many rushed out again just as quickly in frustration.

Furthermore, while the AFL began to admit larger numbers of Black workers into its unions, it made no attempt to break with its own racist tradition. In 1924, the National Association for the Advancement of Colored People (NAACP) issued an open letter to the AFL, which read:

> For years and years, the American Negro has been requesting his admission into the ranks of the organized labor movement. The Negro movement as a whole is outside the ranks of the organized labor movement. The white labor movement will not have the Negro movement within it. If we come to allow the formation in America of a powerful bloc of non-unionized Black workers, workers who would be entitled to hate the trade union idea, all workers, Black and white, will suffer the consequences.[53]

The NAACP proposed to the AFL "the formation of an interracial workers' commission to promote systematic propaganda against racial discrimination in the unions." In 1929, the NAACP again appealed to the AFL to fight racial discrimination. In both instances, the AFL did not even bother to respond.[54]

But a section of the AFL's top leadership, led by UMWA president John L. Lewis, broke with craft unionism, forming the CIO (the Committee for Industrial Organization, later changing its name to the Congress of Industrial Organizations) as a wing of the AFL in 1935. The CIO leaders at the 1935 AFL convention included Lewis; Charles Howard, president of the International Typographical Union; Sidney Hillman, president of the Amalgamated Clothing Workers; and David Dubinsky, president of the International Ladies Garment Workers Union.[55]

Lewis was no left-winger. In fact, Lewis supported Republican Herbert Hoover in the 1932 presidential election.[56] In 1922, Lewis expelled hundreds of rank-and-file oppositionists from the UMWA after they criticized his leadership in a strike. During the 1920s, he systematically drove communists and socialists out of the miners' union. At one miners' convention, Lewis halted the proceedings and pointed to a group of known communists sitting in the balcony, ordering them to leave. Then, at Lewis' behest, a group of loyalists beat the communists senseless in public.[57]

Lewis ran the UMWA as an exceedingly bureaucratic, top-down machine. He was woven of the same cloth as the rest of the AFL leadership. But unlike the others, Lewis recognized that if the AFL did not open its doors to the unskilled, another rival union organization would grow out of the mass organizing drives already taking place. As Saul Alinsky, Lewis' biographer, concluded, Lewis merely "read the revolutionary handwriting on the walls of American industry," when he pushed to organize an industrial union federation.[58]

Lewis and other AFL leaders, including Hillman, tried to convince their more conservative colleagues that the future lay with industrial unionism. But they got nowhere. At the 1935 AFL convention, this division finally brought a formal split between the two sides. The break was dramatized by an actual scuffle on the convention floor, when "Big Bill" Hutcheson, the conservative president of the carpenters' union, called Lewis a "bastard"—and Lewis scrambled over a row of chairs to punch him in the jaw.[59] The split was official.

Lewis had been right. When the CIO formally opened its doors as a section of the AFL in 1935, industrial workers flooded in. Auto- and rubber workers, already at the forefront of the class struggle, quickly affiliated their unions with the CIO. In 1938, when the AFL finally expelled the CIO and its million members, the CIO emerged as a rival union federation to the AFL.

John L. Lewis and other union leaders who formed the CIO hoped to model it after the United Mine Workers: a highly bureaucratic union machine, but one willing to organize any and all workers, Black and white, skilled and unskilled, on an equal basis. The severity of racism and its divisive effect on the labor movement *required* the CIO to take a stand against lynching and segregation, and to condemn racial discrimination.

The CIO issued special outreach publications for African-American workers, making clear that the CIO represented a new breed of unionism that no longer barred the participation of Black workers. A CIO brochure, *The CIO and the Negro Worker—Together for Victory*, stated, "Negro Workers, join the CIO union in your industry. The CIO welcomes you. It gives you strength to win justice and fair play. The CIO unites you with fellow workers of all races and all creeds in a common struggle for freedom, for democracy, for a better life." [60]

The CIO's concrete commitment to ending racial discrimination often proved no more than symbolic, but even this represented a sharp break with past AFL practice—making it possible, for the first time, to build a multiracial labor movement in the United States. By the end of the 1930s, a half-million Black workers had joined a CIO union. [61]

Roosevelt's Balancing Act

When Roosevelt signed the National Industrial Recovery Act in 1933, he hoped that granting some reforms could placate workers enough so that he could get on with the business of stabilizing the U.S. economy. NIRA created a National Recovery Administration (NRA) that would promote compliance with the act's provisions. In a 1933 radio address, he specifically urged workers *not* to struggle to win the right to unionize: "The workers of this country have rights under this law which cannot be taken from them, and nobody will be permitted to whittle them away but, on the other hand, no aggression is necessary now to attain these rights. . . . The principle that applies to the employer applies to workers as well and I ask you workers to cooperate in the same spirit." [62]

These words undoubtedly began to ring hollow to workers whose governors called out the National Guard when they tried to exercise their legal right to unionize. It soon became clear that Roosevelt had only grudgingly consented to grant workers the right to unionize, and he deliberately wrote Section 7(a) of the NIRA so vaguely that it could easily be interpreted as ensuring the "rights" of employers to form company unions. Many employers found it convenient to interpret the NIRA in just this way in order to crush genuine union drives. Soon, many workers were referring to the NRA as the "National Run Around." [63]

Until 1935, Roosevelt was caught in a delicate balancing act. As Mike Davis notes, Roosevelt managed to successfully

> draw support both from the majority of the unions and from the so-called "progressive" wing of capital (advocates of greater corporatism, including the management of GE, U.S. Steel, the Rockefeller oil interests, and even the President of the U.S. Chamber of Commerce). He balanced this conflictual alliance by offering the AFL a more or less pro-union interpretation of NRA codes in lighter (and Northern) industries, as well as energetic relief measures; to big business, on the other hand, he ceded an interpretation of the NRA code in heavy industry which . . . buttressed the "company unions" that had been thrown up as roadblocks to genuine organization. [64]

African Americans had an additional reason to be angered by the NRA—it institutionalized racist wage scales. Conditions for many Black workers actually *worsened* after the NRA came into being. In order to appease the Southern segregationist wing of the Democrats' New Deal coalition, Roosevelt allowed the NRA to legalize racial discrimination practiced in the South, and to generalize it to all U.S. industry.

Blacks were effectively excluded from receiving minimum wages established in particular industries because the NRA allowed employers to exempt predominantly Black job categories from coverage. In the South, where the majority of Black workers remained concentrated, workers were routinely paid less than Northern workers for the same jobs in the same industries. And in industries in which Black and white workers' wages were made equal, it was common practice for racist employers to simply fire all their Black workers and replace them with whites, arguing that the NRA wage minimums were "too much money for Negroes." With good reason, within a matter of months, the NRA was known among Black workers as the "Negro Removal Act" and the "Negro Robbed Again." [65]

But as the level of working-class struggle grew and the economy began to stabilize in 1935, corporate interests started to abandon the Roosevelt administration. As Davis points out, "It was this mass desertion of business from the administration in 1935 that drove a *reluctant* Roosevelt temporarily into the arms of Lewis and the CIO insurgents." [66] Roosevelt needed the working-class vote in order to win reelection in 1936, and he shrewdly tailored his campaign to win the hearts and minds of workers. He put on quite a convincing show, declaring during the campaign that if big business hated him, "I welcome their hatred," and promising, if given the chance to serve a second term, they will have "met their master." [67]

It was toward this end that Roosevelt made several far-reaching concessions to workers in 1935. He pushed through the National Labor Relations Act (the Wagner Act), finally making it illegal for employers to refuse to bargain with unions. He also secured passage of the Social Security Act, by which the U.S. government agreed to provide a minimal standard of living for the poorest families and for the elderly. Finally, he established the Works Progress Administration (WPA), later renamed the Works Projects Administration, offering government jobs to unemployed workers, primarily in construction projects.

These concessions earned Roosevelt his legendary status as an ally of the working class. But these reforms, while important, were a calculated move to capture the loyalty of the ascending labor movement for the Democratic Party. Although Roosevelt promised workers during his 1936 reelection campaign, "we have only begun to fight," he granted no more significant reforms during the remainder of the Depression decade.[68]

Mass Radicalization

Labor leaders were all too happy to deliver the working-class vote to Roosevelt in 1936. Raising the slogan, "The President wants you to join the union," at picket lines across the country, the CIO leadership virtually guaranteed Roosevelt's continued popularity among the mass of workers. In 1936, the CIO created Labor's Nonpartisan League, portrayed by its founders as a bold step in the direction of forming a labor party. But it was nothing of the kind. On the contrary, it placed labor securely in the pocket of the Democratic Party. In fact, it was specifically organized to campaign for Roosevelt's reelection.

Historian Davin argued, "[A]t the grassroots level among labor's rank and file, Labor's NonPartisan League was crucial to securing and hammering home labor's loyalty to Roosevelt and the Democrats." [69] He added,

> [Historians] "have tended to ignore the additional reason Labor's NonPartisan League was formed: to wean organized labor, especially the new CIO unions in the mass-production industries, away from independent politics, away from a labor party for which so many were then clamoring.... It is this resulting civil war *within* "labor's civil war" that has remained unchronicled.... The loyalty of organized labor and the new urban, working-class voter to FDR and the Democrats was therefore *not* a foregone conclusion and had to be won after intense, continuing, and delicate internal struggle. In this struggle the labor party idea lost.[70]

Through the Nonpartisan League, the CIO raised $750,000 for Roosevelt, which helped make up for Roosevelt's loss of corporate campaign dollars. During the final weeks of the presidential campaign in 1936, the CIO also suspended its organizing drives in order to devote its full organizational resources to Roosevelt's reelection.[71]

Although Roosevelt remained popular, many workers also became frustrated with the Democratic Party. Once the union movement began to challenge the class status quo, compassionate New Deal rhetoric went out the window as most Democratic politicians proved in practice that they stood firmly on the side of the employers. In 1934, twelve Democratic governors called in the National Guard to break strikes in their states.[72]

A 1937 Gallup poll showed that at least 21 percent of the population supported the formation of a national farmer-labor party as an alternative to the Democrats and Republicans. Gallup polls between December 1936 and January 1938 showed between 14 and 18 percent of respondents saying they "would join" a labor party.[73] Inside the labor movement, this sentiment was even stronger than in the population at large, particularly among workers at the forefront of struggle. The "young workers in auto, rubber, textiles, and steel who poured into the CIO and supported the concept of industrial unionism were the same people who so vocally demanded labor's move toward independent political action," Davin commented. "[T]he two movements—industrial unionism and independent political action—appeared as inverse sides of the same coin."[74] At both the AFL and various CIO conventions in 1935 and 1936, resolutions in support of forming a labor party gained considerable support.

By 1936, "the UAW, the ILGWU, the Mine, Mill and Smelter Workers, the Southern Tenant Farmers' Union, [A. Philip] Randolph's Brotherhood of Sleeping Car Porters, the United Textile

Workers, and the American Newspaper Guild" had endorsed resolutions in support of a national farmer-labor party.[75]

The 1936 United Auto Workers convention voted unanimously
to actively support the formation of a national farmer-labor party.
Even more significantly, after a heated debate, UAW delegates *voted
down a resolution supporting Roosevelt for president.*[76]

CIO leaders faced a serious dilemma: having promised to deliver
union support to Roosevelt, they now faced the possibility of a mutiny within the ranks of one of the fastest-growing unions in a key
industry. That the UAW delegates had already voted, however, did
not stop CIO leaders from taking quick action to ensure the union's
support for Roosevelt.

Union officials were willing to use any means necessary, including blackmail, to convince the UAW delegates to reverse the vote.
Adolph Germer, John L. Lewis' personal representative to the convention, simply pulled the UAW leaders aside and explained that
either the convention would agree to support Roosevelt or the CIO
would revoke the UAW's funding to organize the auto industry.
Once UAW president Homer Martin explained to the delegates that
the vote would have to be reversed "because of the effect it may have
on the future of our Organization," the convention quickly passed a
new motion in support of Roosevelt.[77]

Other union leaders were equally devious in gaining working-
class votes for Roosevelt's reelection. Worried that socialist traditions among New York's garment workers would prevent them from
voting Democrat, Hillman spearheaded the formation of a pseudo-
labor party in 1936. Its name, the American Labor Party, implied it
was both national in scope and nonpartisan. In reality, it was neither.
The American Labor Party existed as an electoral force almost exclusively in New York; while running its own local candidates, the party
endorsed Roosevelt for president in 1936. As Preis explained,

> For Hillman the first and most important task was to "sell" the idea to
> his own union people. . . . Many of the union members, especially in
> New York and Chicago, had grown up in the tradition of supporting
> the Socialist Party, at least locally, and shunning our Tammany Halls.
> The new league . . . was to function mainly through one of the two
> major parties, and particularly the Democratic Party, in order to ensure
> Roosevelt's re-election. . . . The thought was to channel "regular" so-
> cialists into Roosevelt's camp.[78]

When Hillman "sold" the idea to the board of his union, the Amalgamated Clothing Workers (ACW), he introduced rhetoric that cast the Democratic Party as a lesser evil compared with the danger of a Republican administration—rhetoric that would be repeated by labor leaders in every election year since. Hillman told the ACW board in April 1936, "I say to you that the defeat of Roosevelt and the introduction of a real Fascist administration such as we will have is going to make the work of building a labor movement impossible." [79]

The pressure to support Roosevelt was enormous, even among many socialists. By the time the ACW convention took place in May, its board had been convinced by Hillman and "stifled the anticipated resolutions by militant rank-and-file advocates of a national farmer-labor party." [80] Even the Minnesota Farmer-Labor Party fell into step behind the New Deal coalition, its politics virtually indistinguishable from Roosevelt's by that time. Many long-standing members of the Socialist Party also succumbed to the pressure to campaign for Roosevelt in 1936. Long-time socialist David Dubinsky left the SP to help form the American Labor Party in 1936.

Roosevelt's reelection was one issue on which the AFL and CIO rivals saw eye to eye. Preis argued, "It should be noted that AFL leaders who could not stomach the CIO as organizer of the unorganized industrial workers could join with it in a 'non-partisan' body to harness the workers to capitalist politics for the reelection of the 'New Deal' President." [81]

The CIO's loyalty to the New Deal coalition effectively prevented the rise of a labor party in the pivotal election of 1936. As Preis explained,

> The history of the CIO was to constantly appear as an admixture of two elements. On the one hand, mass organization of the industrial workers was to lead to titanic strike battles, most often initiated by the militant ranks despite the leadership. On the other, the workers were to be cheated of many gains they might have won because of the intervention of the government, which had the backing of the CIO leaders themselves. Unwilling to "embarrass" the Democratic administrations . . . the CIO leaders kept one arm of the CIO—its political arm—tied behind its back. [82]

But Roosevelt's reelection did not reverse the working-class radicalization by then well underway. Roosevelt's concessions to workers continued to fuel both confidence and anger. For a very short period of time, between 1936 and the end of 1937, the level of radicalization was such that the workers at the forefront of CIO organizing drives—autoworkers in particular—took the offensive. They did so from a position of strength, demonstrated vividly by the Flint sit-down strike during the winter of 1936–37, touching off a sit-down strike wave that swept the nation in the months that followed.

Thus, the Depression decade marked the historic turning point for the U.S. labor movement. All the elements existed to finally confront U.S. employers' traditional attempts to divide and weaken the labor movement: breaking down racial barriers to build genuine unity; preparing to confront the violence of the bosses; challenging anti-communism; breaking with the Democrats and the Republicans to form an independent working-class party.

As Levine explained, "The shift in the balance of class forces engendered a chaotic situation in which capitalists—who themselves were increasingly being fragmented both economically and politically—were gradually losing the iron grip that during the 1920s boom period they had enjoyed over the working class in general and the increasingly restive industrial working class in particular. . . . By the middle 1930s, the growing round of strikes was the most visible sign that the industrial working class had actively intervened to determine the course of industrial production." [83]

For the first time, the potential existed to build an independent working-class party. Such a party could have developed into a political alternative to the Democrats, even after Roosevelt's reelection in 1936. But this would have required an effective political leadership inside the working-class movement. Instead, there was the Communist Party.

The Communist Party

The Communist Party was by no means the only socialist organization contending for leadership inside the working-class movement during the Depression era. The three 1934 strikes that helped tip the balance of class forces were led by three different groups of radicals. The Trotskyists, in particular, showed through their brilliant execution of the 1934 Minneapolis Teamsters strike that they were up to the task of providing organizational and political leadership for a democratic labor movement. But they were far too small to play this role nationally.

The Communist Party quickly moved ahead of all other left-wing organizations, winning the allegiance of hundreds of thousands of workers who became radicalized during the 1930s—some who joined, others who remained within its broader periphery.

The Communist Party was the only organization to play a crucial role in the labor movement nationally during this decisive era, for several reasons. First, the CP was comparatively larger. Even at the start of the Depression, the Communist Party claimed a membership of seventy-five hundred, compared with the Trotskyists' meager 131 members in 1931. At the end of 1938, the CP had grown to eighty-two thousand, while the number of Trotskyists, by then in the Socialist Workers Party (SWP), peaked at twenty-five hundred. Meanwhile, the Socialist Party continued its long process of decline, still consumed by internal turmoil as its right and left wings continued to battle. SP membership actually *fell* in 1935—a pivotal year of growth in class struggle.[84]

Moreover, the Communist Party built a genuine base among industrial workers, containing within its membership many of the same shop-floor leaders who led the strikes that built the CIO unions. In 1935, communist membership among autoworkers numbered 630, nearly doubling to eleven hundred in 1939—with a much larger periphery of sympathizers. In 1937, the CP had twenty-eight shop nuclei in the Detroit auto industry, while CP members were active in nearly every major autoworkers union local.[85]

Likewise, rank-and-file communists played a leading role in some of the most important rubber workers' strikes that swept through Akron, Ohio, in 1936. Communists were part of the Firestone strike committee, while the chief picket captain of the Goodyear strike was a party leader. That same year, the CP's Akron organizer was asked to address a meeting of all the strike's picket captains.[86]

Furthermore, communists still successfully claimed they were the inheritors of the 1917 Russian revolutionary tradition. The extent of Stalin's atrocities was not well known outside of Russia until the 1950s. In the 1930s, the memory of the 1917 Russian Revolution continued to provide inspiration to working-class people struggling the world over. In the face of victorious fascism in Germany, Italy, and Spain, Stalin could pose as a sincere defender against fascism in international politics for the better part of the 1930s. These factors undoubtedly contributed to the Communist Party's widespread influence among workers in this era.

No matter what its size or how deep its roots among militant workers, however, Stalinism led the Communist Party down a path that ultimately proved disastrous for the working-class movement in the 1930s.

Building a Multiracial Movement

For all the weaknesses of the American Communist Party, however, its commitment to fighting racism was exemplary. As Nicholson noted, the CP was "the only organization among the working class to combat racism actively. They forced the issue to the foreground of the labor movement and the nation when no other group outside of the Black community would take it up." [87] In fact, the CP in the 1930s provides a model for building a working-class movement that puts fighting racism at its center.

This was true despite the CP's bizarre "Black Belt" theory, a product of the party's ultra-sectarian Third Period between 1928 and 1932. Stalin instructed American communists to advocate "self-determination for the Black Belt" in the United States. He told them to call for a separate Black republic in the Southern states, where a majority of Blacks still lived—even though no demand for such a racially separate republic had ever been raised by African Americans themselves.

Perhaps for this reason, the Black Belt theory had virtually no influence on the Communist Party's practice and was rarely even mentioned in its literature. The communists did adopt the following perspective on combating racism on October 26, 1928, which proved to be of much greater consequence. The party pledged to regard "the struggle on behalf of the Negro masses . . . as one of its major tasks. . . . [T]he Negro problem must be part and parcel of each and every campaign conducted by the Party." [88]

The communists consistently made a priority of antiracist activity throughout the Depression decade. Moreover, they understood that the labor movement's success depended upon systematic confrontation with the system of white supremacy in the South and racism in the North. Although these efforts did not overcome the problems of Stalinism, the party's commitment to fighting racism marked an enormous step forward from the indifference of earlier socialist organizations, the Socialist Party in particular.

Communists in Alabama

Even in Alabama, where the communist movement made its earliest inroads in recruiting African Americans, the party did not organize around the demand for a Black republic. But communists *did* incorporate the fight against racism into the day-to-day class struggle. Indeed, they had no choice, given the high level of racism in Alabama society. Three white CP organizers traveled to Birmingham, Alabama, in 1929 to build a union among Black sharecroppers. As they began to gain a hearing among African Americans over the following years, the Ku Klux Klan (KKK) responded by directing most of its energy toward fighting communism.

In 1934, the KKK organized forty-four new klaverns in northern Alabama, while a group of affiliated fascists began publishing the Alabama *Black Shirt*. They distributed leaflets warning, "Negroes Beware. Do not attend Communist meetings. . . . The Ku Klux Klan is watching you." [89] In 1934, as Robin D. G. Kelley described, "[white Communist] Clyde Johnson survived at least three assassination attempts. Black Communist Steve Simmons suffered a near-fatal beating at the hands of Klansmen in North Birmingham, and a few months later his Black comrade in Bessemer, Saul Davis, was kidnapped by a gang of white TCI employees, stripped bare, and flogged for several hours. These examples represent just a fraction of the anti-radical terror that pervaded the Birmingham district in 1934." [90]

In the pursuit of local communists, the KKK enjoyed the full support of the Birmingham police department's "Red Squad," which beat up and arrested communists on a regular basis. With any number of local ordinances at its disposal for use against communists, the Birmingham city council nevertheless pushed through an ordinance aimed specifically at radicals. The "Downs Literature Ordinance," passed in 1934, made it illegal to possess one or more copies of "radical" literature—broadly defined to include antiwar or antifascist materials and pro-labor and liberal publications. [91]

Birmingham newspapers regularly ran headlines such as, "Communists Tell Negroes to Force Social Equality throughout the

South." The local Birmingham Trades and Labor Council echoed this theme. The *Labor Advocate* warned against communists who "openly preach social equality for the Black race . . . Any man who seeks to disturb the relations between the races is a dangerous character, and should be squelched NOW!" [92]

Both the Communist Party and the Share Croppers' Union (SCU) were forced to arm themselves in self-defense, and most meetings and activities were conducted underground. CP leader Harry Haywood described "a small arsenal" of weapons at a union meeting he attended: "Sharecroppers were coming to the meeting armed and left their guns with their coats when they came in." [93]

Whether communist or union, all literature was secretly distributed. As Kelley described,

> [M]any Black Alabama Communists expressed great pride in their ability to outsmart the bosses, as revealed by the ingenious ways activists distributed leaflets in direct violation of seditious literature ordinances and constant police surveillance. In Birmingham, Black women posing as laundresses picked up bundles of leaflets, stencils, and paper from the homes of white Communists and smuggled the materials out in baskets of laundry. [94]

In Montgomery, Black communist leaders "produced SCU leaflets with a mimeograph machine they kept hidden in their home and surreptitiously left packages at Al Jackson's barbershop (another Black Montgomery Communist) for organizers who regularly came by for a 'trim.'" [95]

Birmingham communists issued their own leaflet in response to the Ku Klux Klan, which read, "KKK! The workers are watching you!" [96] In the spring and summer of 1935, the SCU organized successive strikes of cotton choppers and cotton pickers in the area. In the second strike, most local WPA workers refused to act as strikebreakers, and the majority joined the strike. Although solidarity was enormous, both strikes met with a bloodbath against union activists; police and mobs of local vigilantes beat, arrested, murdered, and lynched strike leaders throughout the area in a rampage of terror. [97]

Given this scale of repression, both the communists' and the SCU's inroads in Alabama were stunning. After three members of the Share Croppers' Union were shot and killed by police in 1932, three thousand people marched in a funeral procession for six miles, following caskets that were draped in banners with the communist hammer and sickle, while a thousand stood along the route in trib-ute.[98] By 1934, the Communist Party claimed a thousand members in Birmingham, mostly Black. During the bloody strikes of 1935, SCU membership approached ten thousand.[99]

Fighting Racism in the North

In the North as well, communists made a priority of fighting rac-ism in every arena of struggle. Their job was made easier because the Depression had already raised the level of class consciousness among many workers. White as well as Black workers faced unem-ployment, evictions, and hunger—and many workers were receptive to the communists' calls for multiracial unity.

In the early 1930s, Harlem communists divided their time equally between organizing against unemployment, demonstrating against racist hiring policies, and protesting against lynching. In 1933, when communists and their allies traveled to Washington for a demonstra-tion to free the Scottsboro Boys, they stopped off on the way to hold sit-ins at restaurants that refused to serve blacks—a tactic popular-ized decades later by the civil rights movement. Black communist Cyril Briggs described the effects of the march on the self-confidence of the Harlem contingent as a breakthrough: "The march marks a new stage in the struggle of the Negro people, with the Negro work-ers emerging as the leaders of these struggles . . . and supplanting businessmen, preachers, and professional self-elected leaders who have consistently betrayed our struggle in the past." Within weeks after the march on Washington, the party-sponsored International Labor Defense claimed nineteen chapters, with seventeen hundred members in Harlem alone.[100]

In 1935, New York City communists organized a traveling squad of working-class women, starting in Jewish neighborhoods and spreading to Harlem. In Harlem, hundreds of women, mainly African American, marched to demand that local butchers lower their prices by 25 percent. As the *Daily Worker* reported June 3, 1935,

> More than a thousand consumers formed a flying squad and moved down Lenox Avenue holding meetings in front of all open stores. . . . So great was the sense of the power of the workers that when butchers agreed to cut prices, housewives jumped up on tables in front of stores

and tore down old price signs and put up new ones. . . . No store held
out for more than five minutes after they arrived.[101]

In 1936, across the United States, young communists circulated
petitions against segregation in baseball, in a campaign featuring white
and Black ball players calling for integration in professional sports.
As *Daily Worker* sports editor Lester Rodney later recalled, the idea
came from "some kids in the YCL (Young Communist League)" who
suggested, "'why don't we go to the ballparks—to Yankee stadium,
Ebbets Field, the Polo Grounds—with petitions?' . . . We wound up
with at least a million and a half signatures that we delivered straight
to the desk of [baseball commissioner] Judge Landis."[102]

The Scottsboro Boys

The Communist Party developed its first national campaign against
racism through its years-long effort to free the Scottsboro Boys.
The Scottsboro Boys case began in 1931 and dragged on for nearly
twenty years, making it one of the most important antiracist struggles in U.S. history. But it was also important because it marked the
first time in the United States that Black and white workers joined
together in large numbers in a campaign explicitly against racism.

The Scottsboro Boys were nine Black youths, aged thirteen
to twenty-one, indicted in Alabama on March 30, 1931, on a
trumped-up charge of gang-raping two white women on a freight
train. There was no evidence to support a charge of rape, but that
did not matter, since it was common practice throughout the South
to convict Black men on unsubstantiated charges of raping white
women. Within two weeks of the incident, the Scottsboro Boys had
been tried, convicted, and sentenced to death by an all-white jury—
all while a large lynch mob of white racists stood inside and outside
the courtroom.

Although the Scottsboro Boys case was a clear-cut issue of racism, it nevertheless divided the Black population along class lines.
The middle class–oriented NAACP refused to touch the case in the
first instance. As Mark Naison described, "[T]he last thing they
wanted was to identify the Association with a gang of mass rapists
unless they were reasonably certain the boys were innocent or their
constitutional rights had been abridged."[103] But the Communist
Party had no such reservations. It immediately sent a legal delega-

tion from the ILD to offer to defend the Scottsboro Boys in court.

When the NAACP finally got involved in the case, it aimed to limit the defense to ensuring that the youths were given a "fair" trial. But the Communists correctly responded in the Party's Black newspaper, the *Liberator,* "There can be no such thing as a 'fair trial' of a Negro boy accused of rape in an Alabama court." The ILD's strategy was to "give the boys the best available legal defense in the capitalist courts, but at the same time to emphasize . . . that the boys can be saved only by the pressure of millions, colored and white, behind the defense in the courts." [104]

The party developed a national campaign against the "Scottsboro legal lynching" through the ILD and the National Scottsboro Action Committee, with a strategy relying on mass mobilization and protest.[105] The campaign, in its first phase, organized hundreds of Black and white workers, marching side by side, in Scottsboro demonstrations that grew into thousands as the campaign built strength. Communists organized local street meetings and toured the parents of the Scottsboro Boys, who spoke to packed meeting halls in the early 1930s. Ruby Bates, one of the white plaintiffs, joined the speaking tour after she came forward to state that the police had made her lie—she hadn't been raped after all.

As the Scottsboro campaign dragged on, the Communist Party gained new respect among African Americans, while the NAACP's reputation took a nosedive among Harlem's Black residents. As one NAACP leader described the consequences of the Scottsboro campaign, "on every corner up here now, the NAACP is catching hell, and anyone who lifts his voice in the interest of the organization also catches hell." [106]

The Scottsboro Boys case was not fully resolved until 1950, when the last defendant was finally released from prison. But through its campaign in the 1930s, the Communist Party proved in practice that Black and white workers could unite to fight racism. This experience strengthened the working-class movement in the 1930s and also impacted the racial composition of the party. At the time of the stock market crash in 1929, the Party had only fifty black members. By the mid-1930s, the Communist Party's Black membership had grown to roughly 9 percent nationally.[107] This represented a small, but significant, step toward a achieving a multiracial socialist movement in the United States.

The Party's first real success at recruiting among Blacks took place in the context of the 1934–35 upsurge in strikes that led to the founding of the CIO. Communists' reputation as sincere antiracists no doubt helped them to convince larger numbers of African Americans to join the union movement. For the first time in the history of the U.S. labor movement, Black workers began joining unions in much larger numbers, often playing a leading role in the strikes for union recognition that built the CIO in 1936 and 1937.

Indeed, one of the most effective sit-down strikes of the Depression era took place in Birmingham, Alabama. On December 24, 1936, Black steel workers, led by two members of the Communist Party, went on strike against the American Casting Company. Within a few days, the strikers won a major victory when the company granted a 20 percent wage increase and overtime pay.[108]

From Third Period to Popular Front

In 1935, Joseph Stalin made a complete about-face in foreign policy, which lasted until 1939. After Hitler came to power in Germany, Stalin began to worry that Hitler represented a potential military threat to the Soviet Union. He therefore started seeking allies among other world powers, including President Roosevelt in the United States. To this end, the Soviet Union joined the League of Nations in September 1934, and Stalin unveiled a new policy called the "Popular Front," a sharp departure from Third Period communism. In the United States and other countries where Stalin sought to ingratiate himself to ruling parties, communists would have to do likewise.

Thus, after spending the previous seven years denouncing as social fascists not just Roosevelt and the Democrats, but also liberals and reform socialists, American communists were instructed to become virtually indistinguishable from them. As the 1936 presidential election approached, the Popular Front required the Communist Party to help ensure Roosevelt's victory. Communists were to become loyal, if uninvited, members of Roosevelt's New Deal coalition.

By this time, Communist Party leaders were quite used to reversing policies on a moment's notice when the word came from Moscow. The transformation from Third Period to Popular Front took place gradually between 1935 and 1936, without formal acknowledgment of a change in position.

As late as January 1935, the *Daily Worker* described Roosevelt as "the leading organizer and inspirer of fascism in this country." But by the end of 1936, the Communist Party had changed its tune. While the party did not formally support Roosevelt in the election (voicing fear that open communist support might hurt his campaign), the CP made it clear that it hoped he would win. By 1938, Party leader Eugene Dennis abandoned the idea of forming a third political party in the U.S., arguing that the Popular Front could "take the form of a political federation, operating insofar as electoral activity is concerned, chiefly through the Democratic Party." [109]

In 1937, Roosevelt delivered a speech arguing that the United States should join the "peace-loving" nations of the world to "quarantine" aggressor countries. Despite Roosevelt's talk of "peace," his speech actually brought the United States a step closer to going to war. But the Communist Party stood behind the president, issuing a statement using the same double-speak: "Everyone must line up on one side or the other. Whoever is opposed to collective action for peace is an enemy of peace, an agent of the international bandits." [110]

A similar transformation occurred in the CP's attitude toward liberals and labor leaders. During the Third Period, these were lumped together as social fascists, on the basis that fascism "must find indirect support. This it finds in the Socialist Party and the reformist trade union officialdom." But by the time the Popular Front was in full swing in 1937, CP leader Earl Browder issued this gushing praise of John L. Lewis and the CIO: "Democracy today is destroyed in much of the capitalist world. It is fighting for its life in the remainder. It can survive under capitalism only to the degree to which there are successfully carried out programs such as those of John L. Lewis and the Committee for Industrial Organization and the economic reforms and the peace program of President Roosevelt." [111]

The communists' stance toward liberal Black organizations also shifted markedly. Naison commented that the CP, organizing in Harlem in the early 1930s, "devoted as much attention to attacking other Harlem organizations as to publicizing its own activities." In 1930, for example, communists disrupted a Harlem conference on unemployment, chaired by A. Philip Randolph, civil rights activist and president of the Brotherhood of Sleeping Car Porters. The conference's demands included a call for a five-day workweek, an eight-hour day, and public works programs for the unemployed. But Black communists who attended (and were eventually thrown out for disrupting the meeting) called the participants "traitors," "scab herders," and "sky pilots." [112]

In the early 1930s, communists' hostility to the NAACP was so great that they would not allow NAACP lawyers to participate in the legal defense of the Scottsboro Boys, even though NAACP participation would have helped to broaden support for the campaign. When renowned lawyer Clarence Darrow offered to help defend the Scottsboro Boys in 1931, ILD attorneys said they would accept his help only if he renounced the NAACP. Darrow refused and withdrew from the case. [113]

But the Popular Front ushered in an entirely new posture. In 1936, the CP joined forces with a cross-section of Black professionals and reformists to launch the National Negro Congress—which elected former nemesis A. Philip Randolph as its first president. The NAACP withheld its formal support, but not for lack of effort on the part of the communists. In 1935, Browder submitted an article to the NAACP magazine, *Crisis,* pleading for reconciliation between the two groups. Browder asked, "Would it not be better if instead of attacking us, you would combine forces with us in fighting for Negro rights, for Angelo Herndon, for the Scottsboro Boys, and for the defense of Ethiopia. We would welcome cooperation with you for these things, in place of having to answer your attacks, which is indeed an unpleasant duty." [114]

Naison described how, at the founding conference of the National Negro Congress, "Communists filled their speeches with references to American history and proclaimed respect for the American political tradition. 'It was not Marx, Lenin, and Stalin whom Communists cited in their addresses,' the *Amsterdam News* reported. 'Rather it was Douglass, Lincoln, and the heroes of the American Revolution from whom they drew their inspiration.'" [115]

"Communism Is Twentieth Century Americanism"

The American Communist Party went far beyond the call of duty in carrying out the Popular Front policy. Communist leaders' stated aim to remold the party's image as a "responsible American organization" soon emerged as unadulterated patriotism. As Chester describes,

Patriotic appeals became the mainstay of Communist rhetoric. The Party insisted that it was "carrying on the work of Jefferson, Paine, Jackson and Lincoln." During the 1938 election, the Communist Party's chief slogan was "Communism is Twentieth Century Americanism." Browder even upheld the CP as "the most consistent fighter . . . for the defense of our flag and [the] revival of its glorious revolutionary tradition." [116]

Between 1937 and 1939, the party retreated yet further from the notion of an independent working-class party, as the Popular Front gave way to an even broader class alliance called the "Democratic Front." Defined as a coalition "of the forces opposed to the fascists," the Democratic Front included workers, farmers, the middle class, and "important sections of the upper middle class and certain liberal sections of the bourgeoisie." [117]

Browder's attempt to incorporate the Communist Party into the mainstream of U.S. politics led him to instruct party members to court the Catholic Church in order to "help influence the integration of the Catholic community into the Democratic Front." Toward this end, the party hailed St. Patrick as "a People's saint," and Browder asserted, "[Q]uestions of family and social morality furnish no practical division between Catholics and Communists. . . . Communists are staunch upholders of the family. We consider sexual immorality, looseness and aberrations as the harmful product of bad social organization. . . . We combat them as we combat all other harmful social manifestations." [118]

The Communist Party more than tripled in size during the Popular Front period, from twenty-six thousand members in 1934 to eighty-two thousand members in 1938. But it would be wrong to credit Popular Front policies for this growth as a step forward from the Communists' self-imposed isolation of its Third Period. The party's membership also tripled in size between 1930 and 1934, when it grew from seventy-five hundred to twenty-eight thousand—while still in its Third Period phase. [119]

From 1928 on, the CP never decided its strategy based upon what was needed to move the labor movement forward in the United States. As long as it received its directives from Moscow, based on the changing goals of Stalin's domestic or foreign policy, the American Communist Party could not aim to build an independent workers' movement inside the working class—during either the

Third Period or the Popular Front. In shifting from the Third Period to the Popular Front, the Party merely traded one disastrous policy for another, shifting from outlandish sectarianism to the adoption of equally outlandish patriotism.

Moreover, the Communist Party's growth and influence among workers during the 1930s only made the consequences of its misguided policies more tragic. The onset of the Popular Front period coincided with the height of the CIO strike wave in 1936–37. Thus, at the very same time that workers were becoming radicalized on a fairly large scale, creating the potential for the creation of a revolutionary workers' party, the Communist Party did everything it could to halt that process.

In the pivotal year of 1936, communist shop-floor leaders were instructed to help the CIO leadership in delivering the working-class vote to the Democrats. Despite the fact that many militant workers were already willing to break with the Democratic Party, Roosevelt was reelected in 1936 in one of the biggest landslides in U.S. history.

But the consequences of the Popular Front spread far beyond the electoral arena. Many African-American party members resigned in protest in 1935 when they discovered that, while the Communist Party was campaigning for Ethiopian independence after Mussolini's invasion, the Soviet Union continued to trade with Italy.[120]

1936–37: The Class Struggle Peaks

By 1936, working-class confidence was already surging, especially among workers in the tire and auto industries. An economic upturn that began in 1935 and lasted until the fall of 1937 boosted militancy still further. A wave of sit-down strikes spread through the center of rubber production, Akron, Ohio, beginning in early 1936. As Brecher described,

> A week seldom passed without one or more sit-downs. . . . The Goodyear management, for instance, assigned two non-union inspectors to a department with instructions to disqualify tires produced by known union men. After pelting them with milk bottles for a while, the men sat down and refused to work till the inspectors were removed. The company rushed in forty factory guards with clubs, but a 65-year-old union gum miner met the army at the entrance and told them to "beat it." They went—and the non-union inspectors were replaced. [121]

Although the leadership of the United Rubber Workers did not approve of these strikes, the Akron sit-down successfully won most of the workers' immediate demands, though not URW recognition. Most sit-downs were fought over wage and work issues, but Goodyear rubber workers also sat down for a full day in the fall of 1936 after company goons beat up a local union leader. The next night, the same group of workers sat down again—this time, to protest a KKK cross-burning in view of their Akron plant.[122]

Neither top CIO officials nor Roosevelt's emissaries could dampen the Akron rubber workers' defiant mood. In late February 1936, Roosevelt sent his own mediator to convince Goodyear workers to end a two-week, company-wide sit-down. Four thousand workers assembled at a mass meeting responded to the mediator's suggestion that they return to work with the chant, "No, no, a thousand times no, I'd rather be dead than a scab!" After a month on strike, the Goodyear workers went back to work with some gains, but no union contract. Rubber workers did not win union recognition from Firestone, Goodyear, Goodrich, or U.S. Rubber until a year later—after the UAW's victorious Flint sit-down strike.[123]

The Flint Sit-Down: Strike of the Century

In November 1936, the sit-downs spread to the auto industry, reaching Detroit in late November, when twelve hundred steelworkers occupied the Midland Steel auto-body plant, setting off an organizing frenzy. As Cochran describes:

> After the Midland victory, Detroit went into a fever of union agitation and organization. Workers would repeatedly call up union offices demanding that an organizer be sent to their shop to sign them up, or take care of their grievance, or call a strike. Delegations would descend on union headquarters for union books and equipment. There were sit-downs at Gordon Baking, Alcoa, National Automotive Fibers, Bohn Aluminum, and Kelsey Hayes.[124]

The legendary Flint sit-down strike turned the tide more dramatically than any other 1930s strike. During the course of the Flint struggle, which began on December 28, 1936, and lasted until February 11, 1937, 140,000 General Motors (GM) autoworkers—out of the company's workforce of 150,000—either sat down or went out on strike. But the strike's importance reached far beyond the auto industry. The attention of the entire nation was riveted on the Flint autoworkers as they took matters into their own hands—confronting the company and, at various points, the CIO leadership, the police, the company's hired thugs, and even Roosevelt—and *won*.[125]

By the time the Flint sit-down began, auto manufacturers had developed an elaborate apparatus to undermine unions. GM contracted with the Pinkerton Agency to develop an elaborate spy network against union organizers. "Those whom spies identified as unionists were often beaten up or had 'accidents' happen to them," according to Norwood.[126] He explained,

> Fiercely determined to prevent unionization, the auto manufacturers and their parts suppliers developed sophisticated and extensive espionage systems and assembled formidable arsenals of tear gas and firearms, which they shared with municipal police departments in the Detroit area and Flint, active agents in the anti-union campaign. Management's commitment to use violence to derail the union effort, its ability to employ the police as an anti-union instrument, and GM's mobilization of vigilante armies in Flint and Anderson, Indiana, precipitated a seemingly endless series of physical confrontations with those attempting to organize the industry.[127]

Flint was the center of the General Motors manufacturing empire. GM employed roughly 47,000 Flint workers in 1936. UAW membership in Flint grew from 150 at the end of October to 4,500 by the end of December that year.[128] UAW leaders had hoped to delay the start of the GM strike until Michigan's New Deal Governor Frank Murphy took office on January 1, 1937, but they were unable to hold back the workers. The sit-down started at the Fisher Body plant in Cleveland on December 27, spreading the next day to the Fisher Body and Chevrolet plants in Flint. The targeting of these plants was strategic. They were key to production for roughly 75 percent of GM production nationally. Within a week, autoworkers were on strike in Anderson, Indiana, Norwood, Ohio, Janesville, Wisconsin, and Detroit.[129]

GM management—while itself refusing to abide by the Wagner Act—responded by declaring the sit-down strikes illegal: "Such strikers are clearly trespassers and violators of the law of the land. We cannot have bona fide collective bargaining with sit-down strikers in illegal possession of the plants. Collective bargaining cannot be justified if one party, having seized the plant, holds a gun at the other party's head."[130]

GM won a court injunction on January 2, 1937, restraining the strikers from remaining inside the plant and from picketing and confronting strikebreakers. But when the sheriff read the injunction aloud to the sit-down strikers, they laughed him "out of the plant." Judge Edward Black, who issued the injunction, as it turned out, owned $219,900 worth of GM stock.[131]

Alfred P. Sloan, president of the automaker, informed strikers that GM would "not recognize any union as the sole bargaining agency for its workers, to the exclusion of all others."[132] On January 11, management cut off all heat inside Flint's Fisher Body Plant No. 2, and company guards stopped all food from entering the plant. The strikers and their supporters confronted the guards at the plant gates—battling the police, who used clubs, tear gas, and riot guns against them. The strikers replied with door hinges and fire hoses. Thousands of supporters streamed in to defend the strikers, who finally succeeded in defeating the police, in what unionists later called "The Battle of the Running Bulls."[133]

But General Motors continued to refuse to negotiate with the UAW. Lewis issued this scathing rebuttal, using labor's electoral support as a direct challenge to Roosevelt:

> For six months during the presidential campaign the economic royalists, represented by General Motors and the DuPonts, contributed their money and used their energy to drive this administration from power. The administration asked labor to help repel this attack and labor gave it. The same economic royalists now have their fangs in labor. The workers of this country expect the administration to help the strikers in every reasonable way.[134]

Frances Perkins, Roosevelt's Labor Secretary, spoke defiantly: "There was a time when picketing was considered illegal. The legality of the sit-down strike has yet to be determined."[135] The UAW reacted to Sloan's refusal to negotiate by extending the sit-down strike to GM's motor assembly plant, Chevrolet No. 4, in Flint. Outsmarting police, the union pretended to target Chevrolet Plant No. 9—while quietly seizing No. 4.[136]

When the company secured a second injunction against the strike in early February, the workers met and voted to hold the plants at all costs, even as Governor Murphy threatened to call in troops to break the stalemate. The strikers from Fisher Body No. 1 responded to Murphy in writing:

We have decided to stay in the plant. We have no illusions about the sacrifices which this decision will entail. We fully expect that if a violent effort is made to oust us many of us will be killed, and we take this means of making it known to our wives, to our children, to the people of the state of Michigan and the country that if this result follows from an attempt to eject us, you [Governor Murphy] are the one who must be held responsible for our deaths.[137]

By the next morning, Preis wrote, "all the roads into Flint were jammed with unionists from Detroit, Lansing, Pontiac, and Toledo." The solidarity contingent, including more than a thousand veterans of the 1934 Toledo Auto-Lite strike, rubber workers from Akron, and coal miners from Pittsburgh, formed a ring around Fisher Body No. 1—ready to do battle. The sheriff refused to enforce the injunction.

GM again turned off all the heat to try and freeze out the strikers. In response, the sit-downers opened all the plant windows to let in the frigid January air—fully aware that if the plant's firefighting equipment froze, GM's insurance contract would not cover any damage that ensued.

Flint city officials, meanwhile, began arming antiunion vigilantes. The chief of police stated, "Unless John L. Lewis wants a repetition of the Herrin, Illinois, massacres he had better call off his union men. The good citizens of Flint are getting pretty nearly out of hand. We are organizing fast and will have between 500 and 1,000 men ready for any emergency." [138]

Lewis responded, "I do not doubt your ability to call out your soldiers and shoot the members of our union out of those plants, but let me say that when you issue that order I shall leave this conference and I shall enter one of those plants with my own people. And the militia will have the pleasure of shooting me out of the plants with them." [139] The police emergency order was pulled, and the Governor abruptly changed his mind about sending in the National Guard.

GM management, fearing for the safety of their plants and equipment, finally backed down, and on February 11, 1937, signed a six-month contract with the UAW. The strikers' willingness to disobey the "law"—in defense of workers' *legal* right to organize—proved the key to success. Indeed, roughly half of all sit-down strikes in this period demanded basic union recognition, granted by the 1935 Wagner Act yet denied by their employers.[140] As historian Walter Galenson commented,

The strikes were clearly illegal, and there was little disposition on the part of anyone to take an opposite point of view. Although they would be unthinkable today, they were tolerated in 1937, and even received substantial public support, mainly because large segments of American industry refused to accept collective bargaining. Trade unions were the underdogs, and they were widely represented as merely attempting to secure in practice the rights that Congress had bestowed upon them as a matter of law.... It is not at all unlikely that General Motors and other manufacturers could have resisted the UAW more successfully if the union had confined itself to more orthodox weapons." [141]

The strikers' ingenious tactical maneuver, occupying Chevrolet Plant No. 4, had been critical to winning the strike. In addition, during the strike the strikers organized a system of self-defense, food distribution, exercise, and even entertainment, with all decisions made at daily mass meetings. Strike leader and socialist Kermit Johnson described the immense satisfaction felt by the workers when, "herding the foremen out of the plant, we sent them on their way with the same advice that most of us had been given year after year during layoffs: 'We'll let you know when to come back!'" [142]

Women also played a decisive role in the Flint sit-down strike. Some 350 strikers' wives came together to form the Flint Women's Emergency Brigade after taking part in the Battle of the Running Bulls. Like the strike itself, the Emergency Brigade was organized along military lines, commanded by socialist and striker's wife Genora Johnson and staff captains overseeing individual squads. Far from a typical "women's auxiliary," the Brigade organized a women's speakers' bureau, day care centers for women on picket duty, and a line of defense, ready to battle the police at a moment's notice.

Their courage was every bit as great as the men's inside the plant. On January 20, Johnson instructed members, "We will form a line around the men, and if the police want to fire then they'll just have to fire into us." The Flint women's experience in the class struggle changed their lives forever, as this remark by one Brigade member shows clearly: "A new type of woman was born in the strike. Women who only yesterday were horrified at unionism, who felt inferior to the task of organizing, speaking, leading have, as if overnight, become the spearhead in the battle of unionism." [143]

The Flint victory impacted the class struggle nationally, raising working-class confidence still higher. The *New York Times* reported,

"By entirely stopping production of all General Motors cars in January and February and obtaining recognition in the first written and signed agreement on a national scale which that great citadel of the open shop had ever granted to a labor union, the CIO . . . opened the way for the remarkable upsurge in sentiment for union organization which is now going on in many sections of the country." [144]

Labor historian Sidney Fine commented, "the GM strike, as a spectacular and successful example of the sit-down, greatly increased the popularity of the tactic." He added, "The sit-downs involved every conceivable type of worker—kitchen and laundry workers in the Israel-Zion Hospital in Brooklyn, pencil makers, janitors, dog catchers, newspaper pressmen, sailors, tobacco workers, Woolworth girls, rug weavers, hotel and restaurant employees, pie bakers, watchmakers, garbage collectors, Western Union messengers, opticians, and lumbermen." [145]

The sit-down tactic also gained popularity as a form of protest in other arenas of struggle. As Nicholson commented, "People sat down in protest at relief offices, in employment agencies, against police in eviction demonstrations. Prisoners adopted the tactic in jails in Joliet, Illinois, and Philadelphia, Pennsylvania. Children did the same in movie theaters to protest program cuts." [146]

By the end of 1937, nearly a half-million workers all over the United States had taken part in a sit-down strike. The number of all strikes more than doubled between 1936 and 1937, from 2,172 to 4,740, involving nearly two million workers overall. [147]

In the auto industry, there were 170 sit-down strikes against General Motors alone between March and June 1937. As the *New York Times* observed, the sit-downs were due at least in part to "dissatisfaction on the part of the workers with the union itself," and the auto workers "are as willing in some cases to defy their own leaders as their bosses." [148] The Flint victory also helped the CIO organize other mass-production industries in its aftermath. On March 2, the giant United States Steel Corporation signed a CIO contract without a strike. [149]

The sit-down strike wave earned massive sympathy in the population at large. A *Fortune* magazine poll in July 1937 showed only 20.1 percent of respondents thought sit-downs should be stopped if the price was bloodshed. Even among corporate executives, just 32.9 percent thought this was a price worth paying to stop the illegal sit-downs. [150]

By September 1937, the CIO claimed a membership of 3,718,000. But the CIO's success also benefited the AFL, and both organizations grew significantly during the strike wave of the 1930s. The AFL garnered a million new members, bringing its total to 3.6 million. After its intransigence against industrial organizing that caused the CIO split, the AFL subsequently proved willing to organize unskilled workers into its ranks.

President Green reported to the AFL executive council in April 1937:

> At the present time it is almost impossible for me here, working 24 hours a day, to meet the requests that come in for our organization. Many of these requests are coming from employers suggesting they are ready to bow to the decision of the Supreme Court on the Wagner Act and they are ready to become organized. We are going forward in a wonderful way organizing, and I know most of our National and International Unions are meeting with the same situation, particularly those having jurisdiction in manufacturing and industry." [151]

The Communist Party Helps John L. Lewis Assert Control

When the Flint sit-down began, John L. Lewis was quick to issue a statement of support: "The CIO stands squarely behind these sit-downs." [152] He did so not because he approved of the tactic, but because the occupation was already under way, and he knew there was nothing he could do to talk the workers into leaving the plant. Above all, Lewis wanted to put the CIO at the head of the strike wave in auto in order to organize the industry under its banner.

But once the Flint sit-down strike ended, Lewis made clear that the CIO would not tolerate unauthorized strikes on any kind of permanent basis. "A CIO contract is adequate protection against sit-downs, lie-downs, or any other kind of strike," he announced afterward. Lewis' words fell on deaf ears, however. Autoworkers engaged in at least two hundred "quickie" strikes in the four months after the UAW and General Motors signed their first agreement. By mid-1937, the UAW leadership issued a formal statement that the "union will not support or tolerate" wildcat strikes, or strikes without union authorization. [153]

Although the union became more heavy-handed, autoworkers continued to try to take matters into their own hands. On March 8,

Chrysler workers sat down in nine plants when the company refused to recognize the UAW as the workers' sole bargaining agent, in a strike that lasted fifteen days. Lewis personally negotiated an agreement—one that did not grant the workers' key demand, sole representation by the UAW. Five votes had to be taken before workers occupying the Detroit Dodge plant finally agreed to end the sit-down.[154]

Lewis also shrewdly reversed his posture toward the Communist Party during the CIO strike wave. With the Popular Front well under way, the CP leadership made clear its willingness to uncritically serve top CIO officials. The communist membership represented an army of organizers, ready to work long hours for little or no pay. Lewis decided to use the communists to help reign in union militants and to help organize the CIO. In 1936, the CIO launched the Steel Workers Organizing Committee (SWOC), its campaign to unionize steel industry holdouts. In that year, sixty of SWOC's two hundred full-time organizers were members of the Communist Party. In Chicago, thirty-two of the thirty-three steel organizers were part of the communist caucus.[155]

Publicly, Lewis defended the communists from conservatives within the CIO. "I do not turn my organizers or CIO members upside down and shake them to see what kind of literature falls out of their pockets," he told red-baiters. But privately, Lewis made it quite clear that he was merely using the communists. He argued, "Who gets the bird, the hunter or the dog?" After SWOC finished unionizing the steel industry, and Lewis no longer needed them, he fired all the communists from the union's payroll.[156]

Communists strongly felt the need to prove their loyalty to Lewis in 1937. Some CIO leaders tried to blame the 1936–37 wildcat strike wave on communist agitation—but the party leadership vehemently denied this charge. "The Communist Party is not stirring up strikes," Browder protested. Meanwhile, B. K. Herbert, the party leader overseeing the work of communists in the auto industry, issued a directive that "unauthorized actions must not be tolerated." UAW vice-presidents Wyndham Mortimer, a party member, and Ed Hall, a communist sympathizer, also announced, "[W]e wish to emphatically deny that we are in any way responsible, or in any way encouraged, unauthorized sit-downs."[157]

Supporting Roosevelt's New Deal coalition had a devastating impact on the class struggle, as communists offered CIO officials, including John L. Lewis, their uncritical support. As a result, the

Communist Party used its enormous influence inside the unions to lead the most militant sections of workers *away* from militancy as it peaked in late 1937.

Communist Party leaders bent over backwards to make clear that their allegiance was to the New Deal coalition, not to rank-and-file workers outside its control. The *Daily Worker* ran a statement by William Weinstone, the party's Michigan state secretary, declaring, "unequivocally and emphatically that the Communists and the Communist Party had never in the past and do not now in any shape, manner, or form advocate or support unauthorized and wildcat action and regard such strikes as gravely injurious to the union's welfare." He continued, if party members were to initiate such strike action, it would be "gravely injurious . . . to the cause of cooperative action between labor and middle-class groups." [158]

But the CP leaders' newfound aversion to wildcat strikes did not immediately filter down to rank-and-file communists on the shop floor—many of whom continued to lead the wildcats and sit-downs that erupted during the course of 1937. Not only was confidence still rising among the rank and file, but that confidence also allowed workers to begin to try and assert some control over the pace of production and other working conditions.

In January 1937, soon after the Flint sit-down began, two hundred UAW delegates met and created a "board of strategy" that served General Motors a set of eight demands, including a demand for a thirty-hour workweek, a six-hour day, and union participation in regulating the pace of the assembly lines. After the Flint strike was won, union activists tried to incorporate a strong shop steward system into the first contract agreement with GM. Under their proposal, each work group of fifteen to a hundred workers would elect its own steward. Some GM plants already had a steward system in place.[159]

But it soon became clear that the UAW leadership was all too willing to bargain away this crucial control over working conditions. In the first contract, negotiated in March, GM management refused to recognize shop stewards, replacing them with a new structure of "committeemen"—who were far fewer in number and held less authority than stewards. The second GM settlement, negotiated in April, explicitly stated that shop stewards would not be authorized to handle grievances. The union implemented the April agreement without ratification by UAW members.

In April, after a month-long sit-down paralyzing nearly all Chrysler plants, the UAW secured an agreement that angered many Chrysler workers. As one union member said later, "It was not surprising that the Chrysler sit-down strikers balked at leaving the plants when this agreement was brought to them. They had been told that the union would insist on obtaining sole recognition in a contract, as well as in practice." [160]

As Chester argued, the March and April settlements were a setback for autoworkers: "Committeemen who had to service 400 workers could not possibly remain in direct contact with all of their constituents. Unlike shop stewards, who were themselves members of the work department whose grievances they sought to uphold, committeemen would often have to act as another outsider adjudicating the disputes of those directly involved." [161]

In May 1937, the *United Automobile Worker* warned, "nothing is to be gained and everything is to be lost by bleeding a union to death through a constant stream of wildcat strikes. . . . If the United Automobile Workers of America is to protect its right to strike it must strike when it is *right* to strike." [Emphasis in original.] The union's executive board voted to impose disciplinary action against workers engaging in unauthorized strikes. [162]

Meanwhile, General Motors demanded permission from the union to fire any worker who took part in unauthorized strikes—which the union granted in September 1937. Fear of discipline temporarily curtailed the number of wildcat strikes. But when GM negotiated an agreement with the UAW in November that was worse than the first contract—and included the new disciplinary provision—workers once more took matters into their own hands.

The Turbulent UAW

By 1937, the UAW was divided into two caucuses: the Unity Caucus and the Progressive Caucus. The leadership of the Unity Caucus included Flint organizer and communist Wyndham Mortimer and rank-and-file leader Walter Reuther, representing the socialist faction (although he had not been an SP member since 1933). The Progressive Caucus, in contrast, was an anticommunist formation led by UAW president Homer Martin. [163]

Martin demoted and dispersed leading members of the Unity Caucus, sending Mortimer to St. Louis and leaders Roy Reuther, Ralph Daly, and William Cody to other cities. Communist Henry Kraus was replaced as editor of the union's newspaper, the *United Automobile Worker*. The newspaper soon began carrying thinly veiled anticommunist editorials, such as this one in June, decrying the role played by radicals in wildcat strikes: "Its active opposition to the policy of the organization is of itself a menace to the continued effective functioning of the union." [164]

Nevertheless, the 1937 UAW convention "was one of the most disorderly conventions ever held by an American labor union," according to Galenson.[165] When the Unity Caucus claimed the union apparatus had failed to seat some its members, mayhem broke out, made clear by the record of the proceedings appearing in the *United Automobile Worker*:

President Martin: The next order of business before this convention . . . (President Martin was interrupted by loud and continued shouts of protest.)

President Martin: The next order of business before this convention . . .

(The shouting continued.)

I will recognize this brother.

Delegate Steinhardt, 156: . . . I would like to ask, at this time, with your permission, that you call the house to order and take another vote.

President Martin: Just a moment. Now, let me say this to you . . .

(Renewed shouting occurred, and there was a great deal of confusion.)

President Martin: I know you don't want me to speak. Where will the convention be next year?

(There were cries of "No, no," and the noise increased.)

President Martin: Where will the convention be next year?

(A number of delegates were standing on tables, and tables and floors were pounded with sticks, and there was a general condition of disorder.) . . .

President Martin: Where will the convention be next year?

(Disorder broke out again among the delegation.)

President Martin: Everybody take your seats, please. Just a moment . . .

(The noise and disorder was resumed.)

President Martin: I think all of you realize . . .

(President Martin was interrupted by cries of "Point of Order," and "We want Reuther. We want Reuther.")

The convention defeated the union president's right to remove union officers, as well as Martin's attempt to eliminate local newspapers, including Walter Reuther's *West Side Conveyor*.[166]

The Communist Party Leads the Movement—Backward

The conflict between the UAW's central leadership and rank-and-file militants finally reached a showdown during a five-day struggle in November 1937 at the Pontiac, Michigan, Fisher Body plant. After the company fired four union activists for leading a wildcat strike, five hundred workers occupied the plant of fourteen thousand workers on November 17 and vowed to stay until all four were reinstated. CP members and supporters played a key role in the strike. One of the fired workers was a communist sympathizer, George Method, and he was the unofficial leader of the sit-down strike. Mortimer himself backed the strike and, as a UAW vice president, tried (unsuccessfully) to convince the UAW executive board to grant strike authorization. The *Daily Worker* quickly ran a story supporting the strike, arguing that the four fired workers "had been unjustly treated." [167]

But UAW leaders were under enormous pressure to crack down on union militants. First, GM President William Knudsen (who succeeded Sloan) threatened to end all negotiations with the UAW unless it proved that it could control its members. New Deal governor Frank Murphy announced plans to send in the state militia to forcibly evacuate the plant. John L. Lewis instructed Martin to end the wildcat immediately. The UAW executive board condemned the strike, although both Mortimer and Reuther argued to sanction it. Soon thereafter, the UAW board voted to ban all local union newspapers.[168]

Martin's opposition to the Pontiac strike broke out into open accusations against the Communist Party when he declared, "there is every reason to believe that professional provocateurs were mixed up in the calling of the Pontiac strike and its continuation." [169]

But the Pontiac workers had no intention of ending the strike. UAW officials twice attended mass meetings and pleaded with workers to vacate the plant, and twice the workers voted to continue the strike. Instead of leaving the plant, they organized a large dance party, inviting autoworkers from all over the Detroit area to come and show their solidarity.

The Communist Party finally broke the stalemate—by condemning a strike led by its own members, which it had publicly supported only days earlier. After an article appeared in the *New York Times* blaming the strike on the Communist Party, the CP leadership immediately switched sides, fearing it might alienate its New Deal allies. Browder personally ordered the party's Pontiac autoworkers fraction to end the occupation.

Under orders, George Method used his role as strike leader to convince workers to leave the plant after just five days. He said, "We are all wrong. Let's go out of the plant and show we are behind the international union." Within an hour, the strikers had vacated the plant. The strike was lost. Afterward, a *Daily Worker* editorial argued that wildcats "only play into the hands of the bosses." Not long after the strike ended, communist leaders told UAW officials that the party supported their attempt to shut down all local rank-and-file newspapers.[170]

The Class Struggle Subsides

The Pontiac strike effectively marked the end of the CIO strike wave of the 1930s. The dynamic of class struggle is such that, if it does not continue to move forward, it very quickly begins to backslide. The monthly average of strikes fell by more than half between 1937 and 1939, while the CIO added only four hundred thousand new members—compared with nearly four million in its first two years.[171]

By late 1937, recession once again set in. Between August and November 1937, the industrial production index dropped by 27 percent, once again throwing millions of workers into unemployment. Between November 1937 and January 1938, U.S. auto production fell from 295,000 to 155,000. Employment in the auto industry dropped from 517,000 in 1937 to 305,000 in 1938.[172]

With the 1936 presidential election out of the way and world war on the horizon, Roosevelt quickly shifted gears. As Mike Davis argued, "FDR's overriding desire to win support for an increasingly interventionist foreign policy, preempted further reform initiatives or new concessions to labor."[173] As Roosevelt began his war buildup, he looked to reestablish his ties with big business.

Thus, Roosevelt slashed relief and works programs for the poor and unemployed in 1938 and again in 1939, although unemployment was rising sharply. Courts ruled in 1938 that sit-down strikes for union recognition were illegal, while the rival AFL and CIO leaders battled each other over jurisdiction.[174]

But Roosevelt made a decisive turn against the labor movement in 1937. Although U.S. Steel had granted union recognition just two months earlier, a group of virulently antiunion steel manufacturers, known as "Little Steel," decided to use every means at their disposal to prevent the CIO from organizing their companies. Before the strike even began, they had already stockpiled millions of dollars' worth of arms and ammunition and had begun organizing squads of armed strikebreakers.

But the CIO leadership did nothing to prepare the strikers for the onset of violence. Union leaders told strikers they should "welcome" the National Guard when it was called in by New Deal governors—telling workers the Guard was there to *protect* their right to unionize. The communists echoed this advice. Instead, the National Guard traveled from one steel town to another to force the mills open, smashing up picket lines and escorting scabs through, beating and arresting strikers, and raiding and ransacking workers' homes. The most violent attack took place at a strikers' Memorial Day meeting outside the Republic Steel plant in South Chicago on May 30, 1937:

> Union leaders, including Stalinists, told [the workers] that Roosevelt, the Wagner Act and Chicago's own "New Deal" Democratic Mayor Kelly had "guaranteed" the right to peaceful picketing. . . . The police then charged with swinging clubs and blazing guns, beating down or shooting every laggard. In a couple of minutes, ten lay dead or fatally wounded—every one shot in the back. Another 40 bore gunshot wounds—in the back. One hundred and one others were injured by clubs—including an eight-year-old child.[175]

All told, eighteen workers were killed during the Little Steel strike, which ended in defeat soon after the Chicago Memorial Day massacre. Yet Roosevelt refused to intervene in the face of this vicious—and obviously illegal—assault on workers' right to unionize. His only statement came after the strike was over, when he condemned both sides, quoting Shakespeare's *Romeo and Juliet:* "A plague on both your houses!"[176]

Although a Paramount News cameraman captured the Republic Steel massacre on film, the news agency refused to make it public.

When *Life* magazine published photos of the shootings, the captain claimed the police were acting in self-defense. That same year, the National Association of Manufacturers published more than two million copies of a pamphlet, "Join the CIO and Help Build a Soviet America." [177]

In 1938, Congress formed the Special Committee on Un-American Activities (later known as HUAC) to investigate so-called radical subversives. As Nicholson pointed out, "the first HUAC victim was Governor Murphy of Michigan, who was publicly pilloried for his failure to use force to break the Flint strike the previous year." [178]

It was to be expected that Roosevelt would turn his back on the labor movement—and that the CIO leadership would not lead a fight against Roosevelt. But by the time workers learned this bitter lesson, the greatest working-class upsurge in U.S. history was over. The Communist Party had played a crucial role. The CP had an impact inside the labor movement that reached far beyond its own membership: not only did the Communist Party maintain a substantial base among industrial workers, but by 1937, CP members held top leadership posts in 40 percent of CIO unions. [179]

The working-class movement of the 1930s lacked a decisive element: an organization of revolutionaries that was large enough to influence the course of the struggle. The Communist Party was large enough, but whatever its claims to the contrary, it had long ceased to function as a revolutionary organization. So instead of leading workers forward, the CP left thousands of workers defenseless against the employers. Most workers who had joined the CP during the course of the 1930s left by the end of the decade, undoubtedly confused and demoralized by the experience, with a grossly distorted vision of socialism. In the eyes of the many militant workers, the Communist Party discredited itself when it turned its back on the class struggle at its turning point in 1937.

The Communist Party experienced yet a third about-face in policy before the decade ended, when Stalin signed a short-lived truce with Adolph Hitler in 1939. Suddenly, five years of alliances with liberals and support for Roosevelt went out the window. The war buildup that the party had enthusiastically supported was condemned as a war between "rival imperialisms for world domination." The Stalin-Hitler pact resulted in an exodus of members from the CP, including a large number of African Americans, who could not stomach the idea of defending a Soviet alliance with the world's most renowned fascist.[180]

One of the most important lessons to be learned from the 1930s, however, is how it might have ended differently. If sections of the labor movement had *broken* with the Democrats, and if the sit-down strikes had escalated instead of subsiding in 1937—both of which were possible—the potential existed to build a revolutionary workers' party. Instead, the 1930s era ended in a series of defeats, followed by World War II.

Nevertheless, the working-class upheavals of the 1930s succeeded in shifting the balance of class forces in favor of the labor movement. The New Deal recognized this fact and could not easily be dismantled without provoking another rise in struggle. While employers would begin to consolidate their efforts to reverse labor's gains by the end of World War II, they could not succeed without uprooting the radicals and militants who had built the CIO. Indeed, the top income tax rate rose to 91 percent during World War II, and stayed there until 1964.

Would a Labor Party Have Made a Difference?

Revolutionary organization might have been possible if a mass working-class party had been built in the 1930s. But that did not happen. Yet, the question remains whether American workers would have been better off if a labor or social democratic party had developed during this tumultuous period. Trotsky, who was closely acquainted with the U.S. working-class movement, offered a number of useful insights in his discussions with American revolutionaries during this period.

Trotsky argued that it was "commonplace for a Marxist" to understand that the working class in the United States needed to develop its own political tradition independent of the two capitalist parties.[181] The question remained, however, whether a labor party would help or hinder this process, given the conditions that existed in the United States at the time. Trotsky changed his own position on this question during the course of the 1930s.

In 1932, Trotsky opposed socialist support for forming a labor party in the United States. He argued that the trade union leadership was so conservative and tied to the two-party system that "the creation of a labor party could be provoked only by a mighty revolutionary pressure from the working masses and by the growing threat of communism." But if there were a revolutionary alternative, "under these conditions the labor party would signify not a progressive step but a hindrance to the progressive evolution of the working class." [182]

By 1938, Trotsky had shifted from this position. He said that in 1930, "I personally didn't see that this sharp crisis or series of crises would begin in the next period, and become deeper and deeper." [183] Moreover, "No one in our own ranks foresaw during that period the appearance of the CIO with this rapidity and power." [184] Given the weakness of the revolutionary socialist movement, combined with the potential the CIO created for the working-class movement, Trotsky argued that a labor party would have been a step forward—if only because it would have meant a break with the Democrats.

Trotsky concluded, "economic action is not enough. We need political action." [185] Given the historic weakness plaguing the U.S. working-class movement—the absence of its own political tradition—such a development could only have been positive. While it is unlikely that a labor party alone would have changed the overall outcome of the 1930s, it could have prevented the repeated derailment of the working-class movement behind the Democrats in the decades that followed.

A labor party could have exposed the corporate base of the Democratic Party and given workers the opportunity to develop a greater sense of independent class politics. This would have made a difference not only during the Depression but also in its aftermath.

But this history has been largely forgotten, even by many labor historians. As Davin observed,

> The collapse of the "popular collective movement" for a labor party after "Roosevelt's Revolution" caused a similar washing out of historical consciousness. So complete is the amnesia that neither labor and political historians nor even the children of the militants recall that it ever commanded the imagination, loyalty, and dedicated energy of so many working people for so long. The oblivion has been so total that it is as if it had never been. Not only did labor's future belong to the Democrats, but the Democratic tide even claimed labor's past. [186]

PART III

The Employers Strike Back

CHAPTER FIVE

From World War to Cold War

On October 30, 1940, on the eve of his third-term election, Roosevelt promised voters that he would not lead the United States to war: "And while I am talking to you, fathers and mothers, I give you once more assurance. I have said this before, but I shall say it again, and again, and again: Your boys are not going to be sent into any foreign wars."[1]

By the time of that impassioned speech, however, Roosevelt had already set the U.S. war machine in motion. In June 1940, he created the National Defense Advisory Commission, appointing CIO leader Sidney Hillman to serve alongside an assortment of business and government leaders. The Commission quickly condemned any strike in defense industries that might interfere with war preparedness.

Indeed, U.S. rulers had long anticipated another Great War against their imperialist rivals. Secretary of War Henry L. Stimson noted in his diary on November 25, 1941, "The question [at a White House conference] was how we should maneuver them [the Japanese] into the position of firing the first shot without allowing danger to ourselves."[2] Less than two weeks later, on December 7, 1941, the Japanese bombing of Pearl Harbor provided the immediate justification for the United States to enter into the war. World War II, as Nicholson commented, proved "the most destructive and horrific conflagration of human violence ever carried out." He added,

> Most of the estimated 55 million people killed by military power were civilians, and most of those were workers with very limited or no political capability to influence the war's causation. That number does not

include the workers who were killed in industrial accidents, but when predictably caused by wartime speedups and safety lapses, should better be known as collateral losses. In the United States, there were over 88,000 workers killed in various industries, more than 11 million seriously maimed or injured from 1941 to 1945, according to the U.S. Bureau of Labor Statistics.[3]

The No-Strike Pledge

On December 8, 1941, the day after the Pearl Harbor bombing, CIO leader Philip Murray declared that CIO members were "ready and eager to do their utmost to defend our country against the outrageous aggression of Japanese imperialism, and to secure the final defeat of the forces of Hitler."[4] The next day, the AFL Executive Committee followed suit, issuing the following statement: "Labor knows its duty. It will do its duty, and more. No new laws are necessary to prevent strikes. Labor will see to that. American workers will now produce as the workers of no other country have ever produced."[5]

On December 15, the AFL banned its members from striking in defense industries, and extended the ban to cover the AFL's entire membership the following day. Not to be outdone by his AFL rivals, in 1942 Murray demanded a government ban on overtime pay scales for Saturdays and Sundays. To enforce the no-strike pledge, Roosevelt assembled the National Defense Mediation Board, closely modeled after Wilson's Council of National Defense during the First World War. The Board's twelve representatives—four each from labor, business, and "public" leaders—were entrusted to "prevent the interruption of production by labor disputes during the period of the war."[6]

UMWA leader John L. Lewis, who had left the CIO leadership in 1940, further estranged himself from the New Deal coalition when he refused to surrender his union's right to strike in the lead-up to war. Lewis voiced support for the war effort, but nonetheless led UMWA members out on strike numerous times throughout 1941—winning union recognition and significant wage hikes for miners. When the National Defense Mediation Board refused to grant the union shop to the miners, Lewis still wielded enough influence to force the CIO representatives to resign from the board in protest. Lewis' days in the CIO, however, were numbered. He led the UMWA out of the CIO in 1942, and back into the AFL in 1944.

Just two months after leaving the Defense Mediation Board, CIO leaders eagerly joined Roosevelt's new War Labor Board in January 1941—empowered with binding government authority. Most business interests were pleased to enter into a pact with the labor movement, ostensibly united by love for their country. When the CIO's Sidney Hillman proposed the unity slogan, "No strikes as usual, no business as usual," corporate representatives agreed enthusiastically, adding their own slogan: "Equality of Sacrifice."[7] Behind all the patriotic posturing, business leaders had a compelling motive to pursue the no-strike pledge. They aimed to use it as a weapon to curb the confidence that still characterized the working-class movement. The CIO doubled its membership in 1941, finally organizing the last auto holdout, the Ford Motor Company, and the antiunion Bethlehem Steel under conditions of full employment.[8] The number of strikes also rose sharply in 1941. "One out of every twelve workers took part in a strike at some time during the year," Cochran noted, adding, "this was the identical proportion as in 1916, the Preparedness year preceding United States entry into the First World War."[9]

Corporations were anxious to prevent a repeat of the class warfare of the mid-1930s—and the cause of war provided an easy justification. Some corporate leaders, emboldened by the favorable atmosphere, ventured to admit their "war aims" at home. Admiral Emory S. Land of the U.S. Maritime Commission in October 1942, declared, "[Union] organizers ought to be shot at sunrise."[10]

The Rise of the "Labor Statesmen"

The no-strike pledge was unconditional. Most union leaders agreed to it without polling their own members. But UAW leaders who proposed an "Equality of Sacrifice" program to the union's April 1942 convention met such strong opposition from delegates that Vice President Richard Frankensteen retorted, "Are you going to tell the President of the United States to go to hell?" One delegate from Flint argued,

> I was certainly going to represent the local union that sent me down here and that was for the purpose of defeating the Equality of Sacrifice Program because we figured there would be no such thing as equality

of sacrifice. . . . The only ones that were going to sacrifice would be the workers themselves. . . . That was our first no-strike pledge. . . . The only effective weapon the worker has and we gave it away.[11]

In 1942, the government froze wages—although workers were offered the opportunity of plenty of extra work hours to raise their incomes. Union leaders were granted two major government concessions in return for their assistance in implementing the no-strike pledge. A "maintenance of membership" provision made it illegal for union members in defense industries to quit their jobs for the duration of the war—but also required workers in these industries to join unions. In addition, unions were granted dues check-off, enabling the deduction of members' dues automatically from their paychecks. While the provisions gave management a stable workforce, union membership increased by 40 percent during World War II.[12]

The character of labor negotiations shifted markedly during the war. As Nicholson commented,

An extensive body of law and precedent setting standards built up. Court and NLRB (National Labor Relations Board) rulings set standards and precedents for thousands of other settlements, and unions became administrative agencies that were quasi-governmental themselves. The need for expertise in these matters created specialists, and more elaborate administration organization by business and unions. Negotiations took on fixed stylistic practices, becoming almost ritualistic. A bargaining table decorum set in as the law increasingly set the parameters for collective bargaining.[13]

Rapid union dues growth—without the expense of depleted strike funds—allowed the CIO to buy an enormous office building in Washington, D.C., in 1942, at the cost of $300,000, and to hire a staff to fill it. In 1943, the CIO set up a Political Action Committee (PAC) to campaign for Democrats.[14]

This coincidence of interests between business and labor leaders undoubtedly fueled the patriotic fervor of both, however reluctant many rank-and-file workers were to relinquish the strike weapon. With wartime production, not the threat of strikes, providing the key to union growth, the UAW executive board proposed to the CIO in November 1942, "Labor organizations should place greater emphasis on participation in the national war problem than on organizing efforts." UAW leaders Walter Reuther, Wyndham Mortimer, and Homer Martin—all on the same side when it came to the war—

negotiated an agreement allowing the union's legendary opponent, General Motors, to fire wildcat strikers.[15]

To amplify its commitment to uninterrupted wartime production, the CIO announced it would "redouble its energies to promote and plan for ever-increasing production." CIO leader Philip Murray told workers in a radio message they should "Work! Work! Work! Produce! Produce! Produce!"[16]

Communists as Super-Patriots

The Stalin-Hitler Pact was shattered when Germany invaded Russia in June 1941, abruptly ending the communist Party's opposition to the Second World War. The party immediately resumed the pro-Roosevelt stance it had abandoned two years earlier, as if there had been no interruption. Party leader Earl Browder argued that if the war was to be won, "the main sacrifice" must come from workers.[17]

This support was significant, as communists made up roughly one-third of the CIO's executive board by the Second World War—and they led unions representing over a million members.[18] Communist leaders not only embraced the no-strike pledge, but also took it much further than other CIO officials were willing—pushing for incentive pay (piece rates) and even proposing drafting workers into the military.[19]

The communists also enthusiastically supported speedups in production. As Harry Bridges, leader of the CIO's International Longshoremen's and Warehousemen's Union (ILWU), stated, "To put it bluntly, I mean your unions today must become instruments of speed-up of the working-class of America."[20] Bridges also ordered the members of his union to confront and physically break a 1944 strike by Chicago warehouse workers against the Montgomery Ward Company. The *Daily Worker* justified Bridges' action with this no-nonsense statement: "Those who violate the no-strike pledge are scabs and should be so treated. Scabs were never handled with kid gloves."[21]

The management magazine *Business Week* heaped these words of praise on communist-led unions in 1944:

> Since Russia's involvement in the war, the leadership in these unions has moved from the extreme left-wing to the extreme right-wing position in the American labor movement. Today they have perhaps the

best no-strike record of any section of organized labor; they are the most vigorous proponents of labor-management cooperation; they are the only serious labor advocates of incentive wages. . . . In general, the employers with whom they deal now have the most peaceful labor relations in industry.[22]

As the Communist Party carried the theme of labor-management cooperation to its furthest extreme, the patriotic themes of the Popular Front reemerged, in a yet more exaggerated form. The communists even supported Roosevelt's "evacuation" order in 1942, which forcibly "relocated" one hundred and twenty thousand Japanese-Americans to West Coast concentration camps. Two-thirds of those relocated were U.S. citizens—most lost their homes and jobs while they were detained for the duration of the war.[23]

Indeed, the war against Japan was justified through virulent racism. Mississippi Representative John Rankin declared on the floor of Congress, "This is a race war. . . . The white man's civilization has come into conflict with Japanese barbarism. . . . I say it is of vital importance that we get rid of every Japanese, whether in Hawaii or on the mainland. . . . Damn them; let's get rid of them now."[24] *Time* magazine echoed this sentiment, commenting, "the ordinary unreasoning Jap is ignorant. Perhaps he is human. Nothing . . . indicates it."[25]

In this context, Browder declared in 1943, "the prevailing 'American way of life,' which is dominated by its capitalist foundation in many and most decisive ways, determines that our national unity cannot find expression in the forms and modes followed by the Soviet peoples." He continued,

> In the United States, national unity can be achieved only through compromise between the conflicting interests, demands, and aspirations of various class groupings (primarily between those usually spoken of as "capital and labor"), a compromise which agrees to reach at least provisional settlement of all disputes through arbitration. The motive power behind such a compromise can only be something which all parties hold in common—that is, patriotism. . . . The Communist Party of the United States foresees that out of victory for the United Nations will come a peace which will be guaranteed by the cooperation of the United States, the Soviet Union, Britain, and China. . . . This will make possible the solution of reconstruction problems with a minimum of social disorder and civil disobedience. . . . We offer our cooperation to all like-minded persons and groups.[26]

Browder extended this offer to even the biggest capitalists: "If J. P. Morgan supports this coalition, I as a Communist am prepared to clasp his hand and join with him in realizing it. Class divisions or political groupings have no significance now." Since even the barest elements of class struggle appeared no longer necessary, Browder temporarily dissolved the Communist Party in January 1944, reorganizing it as the Communist Political Association.[27]

Not surprisingly, the Communist Party's credibility was further diminished in the eyes of workers who refused to sacrifice the right to strike during the war. The effect was to leave a vacuum of left leadership inside the unions—which was quickly filled by *anti*communists. This would have far-reaching consequences after the war, when the anticommunist witch-hunt reached fruition. As Davis argued,

> The Communists' abdication of leadership opened the way for anti-Communist forces within the CIO to manipulate rank-and-file unrest to their own factional advantage. . . . Within the important United Electrical Workers [UE], for example, anti-Communist dissident James Carey and his Jesuit-led allies from the American Catholic Trade Unionists (ACTU) (who modeled their organization on CP factory cells) profited from grassroots dissatisfaction with the Communist-dominated international leadership. In the UAW, the explosive issues of incentive pay and speedup—both of which were defended by Communists and their allies in the Addes-Frankensteen leadership—provoked a deep split in the leadership. The Reuther faction alone reoriented itself to the rebellion of the locals and outflanked the Communists and their central allies by appearing as the most militant wing of the national leadership.[28]

Anticommunism strengthened within the CIO as early as 1940 and continued to grow throughout the war. Yet, the CP refused to confront red-baiting as a matter of policy, believing it was better to avoid conflict with its New Deal allies. In so doing, the Party allowed anticommunism to grow inside the union movement unchallenged. In 1940, the CIO passed a resolution at its convention stating, "[W]e firmly reject consideration of any policies emanating from totalitarianism, dictatorships, and foreign ideologies such as Nazism, Communism, and Fascism." CIO attorney Lee Pressman, a close sympathizer of the Communist Party, *presented* the resolution. Party leaders considered it a "smart move" that "avoided an ugly showdown." But it only laid the groundwork for a much more ugly showdown in the years to come.[29]

The Smith Act

Anticommunism, however, was directed against all socialists, not merely those who uncritically followed the directives of Joseph Stalin. The government's first crackdown targeted not communists, but Trotskyists from the Socialist Workers Party (SWP). Congress passed the Alien Registration Act [30] (Smith Act) in 1940, making it a crime to "knowingly or willfully advocate, abet, advise, or teach the duty, necessity, desirability, or propriety of overthrowing the Government of the United States or of any State by force or violence, or for anyone to organize any association which teaches, advises, or encourages such an overthrow, or for anyone to become a member of or to affiliate with any such association."

In June 1940, International Brotherhood of Teamsters (IBT) president Daniel Tobin alerted Roosevelt to a "subversive" conspiracy afoot in Minneapolis—immediately after the Trotskyist-led Local 544 voted to sever relations with the IBT-AFL and affiliate instead with the CIO's Motor Transport and Allied Workers Industrial Union. Tobin held considerable sway with the Roosevelt administration, since he was then chair of the Democratic Party's National Labor Committee.[31]

Within a matter of weeks, the government took action. On June 30, the FBI raided the SWP's Minneapolis headquarters. Although the evidence gathered consisted of widely available Marxist publications, including the *Communist Manifesto*, twenty-nine leaders of the Socialist Workers Party were indicted in August 1941 for "seditious conspiracy" and violating the Smith Act. All but three of those indicted were "present or former members of Minneapolis unions," Preis noted. Farrell Dobbs, Karl Skoglund, and the Dunne brothers, who had led the 1934 Minneapolis strike to victory, were among them.[32]

On June 28, the CIO issued a statement in Local 544's defense, calling its leaders' pending indictment "nothing but a smear campaign against the CIO." The statement also acknowledged Tobin's role in instigating the attack: "Unable to bend the workers to his will by the other vicious tactics which he has employed, Dan Tobin has persuaded Roosevelt to carry out this action in payment of his political debt to Tobin. . . . It is deplorable that the functions of the U.S. Department of Justice have been perverted in this reprehensible manner." [33]

Yet the Communist Party did nothing to defend Local 544, both because communists preferred to avoid the issue of red-baiting and because the Party remained highly antagonistic toward Trotskyists. Indeed, the August 16 edition of the communist *Daily Worker* enthused, "The Communist Party has always exposed, fought against and today joins in the fight to exterminate the Trotskyite Fifth Column from the life of our Nation." [34]

In December 1941, eighteen Trotskyists were acquitted on sedition charges but found guilty of violating the provisions of the Smith Act. Over the next two years, the U.S. Supreme Court declined to review the case three times, and the eighteen were finally sent to federal prisons in December 1943, to serve sentences of twelve to eighteen months.[35] With its leaders in prison, Local 544 was easily destroyed. Meanwhile, the infamously corrupt Jimmy Hoffa used the opportunity to expand his own control over the Teamsters union, with Tobin's blessing.[36]

Within a decade, the Smith Act took aim with a vengeance against the Communist Party itself. Twelve communist leaders were indicted in 1948 as the anticommunist witch-hunt reached its full fury. In 1958, when McCarthyism was already receding, a United States Court of Appeals finally ruled that teaching or advocating the overthrow of government does not constitute "a call to action" and is therefore not a felony.[37] But by then the damage had already been done.

Wartime Strike Wave

Although the U.S. enjoyed enormous domestic support for the war after Pearl Harbor, rank-and-file workers were quick to show their widespread hostility to the no-strike pledge. As an interviewer described of Chrysler workers who struck five plants in May 1943, "Without exception, so far as I was able to discover, they maintain that they have never agreed to any such thing." [38] In fact, many more workers went out on strike during the four years of U.S. involvement in the Second World War than in the first four years of the CIO's formation. All told, 6,774,000 workers took part in a total of 14,471 strikes during the war—the vast majority wildcat strikes—that grew in frequency as the war years dragged on.[39]

John L. Lewis was the only leader of a major union to openly defy the no-strike pledge during the war. Lewis led 530,000 miners out on strike three times in 1943. The rebellious mood of the miners was such that, when the War Labor Board ordered the UMWA *not* to strike on April 22, as historian Martin Glaberman wrote, "[t]he miners responded by beginning walkouts in Alabama and Western Pennsylvania." On May 1, 1943, Roosevelt ordered "government seizure" of the mines and the War Labor Board ordered the miners to return to work, on the grounds that miners were working "for the government." The miners refused. Even after Lewis declared a "truce" beginning on May 3, UMWA locals voted to wait until May 4 to return to work.[40]

The War Labor Board's tough stance against the miners met with the approval of both its AFL and CIO representatives. UAW president R. J. Thomas was quick to condemn the miners' strike as a "political strike against the President." But rank-and-file autoworkers sided overwhelmingly with the miners:

> [A] thousand delegates representing 350,000 members of the United Auto Workers in Michigan overrode their national officers and adopted by overwhelming vote a resolution to support not only the UMW's demands but the strike as well. The UAW national leaders, which included President Thomas and Vice-President Reuther, introduced and backed a minority resolution opposing the strike.... But the delegates would not be swayed. Only a half dozen or so . . . openly voted against the majority resolution to back the coal strike.[41]

In June, mine operators quietly began negotiating wage increases directly with the UMWA. This did not sit well with the War Labor Board, which refused to sanction the agreement. Miners again responded by walking out. After yet another round of strikes in October, the government finally backed down. *The miners had defied the no-strike pledge and won.*

Their victory opened the floodgates for other workers to take strike action. As labor historian Nelson Lichtenstein described, "Wildcat strikes were centered in the highly integrated mass-production rubber and converted automobile factories, where half or more of all workers took part in wartime strikes in 1944 and

1945. Of the 16 strikes involving over 10,000 workers each in 1944, 11 took place in the auto-aircraft industry." [42]

Union officials took disciplinary action against strike leaders—including blacklisting known militants. But fear of reprisal apparently had little impact, as momentum only continued to grow. The vast majority of the wildcats were "quickie" work stoppages disputing immediate working conditions, often involving just one or two departments within a plant.

The following examples are typical of the disputes at the center of most wildcat strikes during this period. The incident leading to a December 1, 1944, strike by GM's sand-blast workers was explained as follows: "Sand-blast employees demanded ten minutes to clean up at end of shift; walked out when not granted." On December 5, a strike at Ford's Rouge plant was explained this way: "Protest against suspension of two committeemen for countermanding orders of supervision and reading newspapers on the job." On December 15, workers struck at the Chicago Chrysler Dodge plant, claiming "band-saw blades not sharp." Later in the day, the same workers struck again "in protest when notified that they would not be paid for time not worked during above stoppage." [43]

The examples above illustrate the degree to which rank-and-file workers in key industries were intent on exercising control over the shop floor, using methods learned during the 1930s, with a fair amount of success. Testimony presented at Senate hearings on the defense industry in March 1945 demonstrates the impact of this success. Below, M. F. McCauley, a manager at the Packard Motor Company, explained why Packard management was unable to conduct time-motion studies to improve the efficiency of its aircraft engine:

> Mr. McCauley: "We weren't allowed in there for two years to time-study the job."
> Senator Ferguson: "Wait a minute. You say you weren't allowed in?"
> Mr. McCauley: "No, sir."
> Senator Ferguson: "Who kept you out?"
> Mr. McCauley: "The stewards of the plant objected every time we went in to study them. . . . [A] number of times they told the time-study man to get out of the department. So, as to avoid trouble, he got out."
> Senator Ferguson: "Well, now, I am just unable to . . . understand it, if a steward tells an employee of the company to get out of the factory, that he gets out. I am not able to understand it. Will you explain it?"

Mr. McCauley: "You would either have that or trouble or a walk-out on you or bodily throw him out . . ."

Senator Ferguson: "So, one of two things happens: That if the steward tells an employee of the company to get out of the factory, and he doesn't go out voluntarily, they will do one of two things—walk out themselves or throw him out bodily."

Mr. McCauley: "That is correct."

Senator Ferguson: "Well, have you ever had anybody thrown out" . . .

Mr. McCauley: "No; I haven't on time study because they just got out before they got into trouble."

Senator Ferguson: "Have you ever had anybody thrown out by the stewards on any other study of any other work?"

Mr. McCauley: "Well, I think Mr. Patzkowsky can tell you some foremen who were walked out of the plant."

Senator Ferguson: "You mean the stewards took the foreman out of the plant?"

Mr. McCauley: "That is correct." [44]

The wartime strike wave was accompanied by a concerted attempt to rescind the no-strike pledge within the still turbulent UAW. During the summer of 1944, a small group of radicals, led by Trotskyists from the Socialist Workers Party, joined forces with local union officials to form the Rank and File Caucus in the UAW—organized for the express purpose of voting down the no-strike pledge at the union's September convention.[45] At the convention, the caucus was surprised by its own success: nearly 40 percent of delegates supported the caucus' resolution against the no-strike pledge. When the UAW held a referendum a few months later, 35 percent voted against continuing the no-strike pledge.[46]

Segregation in the "World's Greatest Democracy"

The widespread sentiment against the no-strike pledge clearly demonstrated the mood of defiance that carried over from the 1930s among many thousands of rank-and-file workers. In addition, Black workers took advantage of wartime full employment to escalate the battle against segregation in the military and at the workplace.

Roughly half a million African-American soldiers served in the Second World War. Yet the military fighting on behalf of the "world's greatest democracy" remained segregated throughout the war, while not a single Black soldier was awarded a Medal of Honor. Back at home, Black workers were systematically denied access to higher-paying defense industry jobs during the initial phase of wartime production.

These contradictions were too great to ignore. A. Philip Randolph organized the March on Washington movement in 1941, threatening to bring fifty thousand African Americans to the U.S. Capitol to march against segregation. In response to this call, tens of thousands of African Americans joined demonstrations in New York, Chicago, and St. Louis, demanding that Roosevelt establish a Fair Employment Practices Committee to open defense industry jobs to Black workers. As Randolph argued,

> The Negro's stake in national defense is big. It consists of jobs, thousands of jobs. It may represent millions, yes, hundreds of millions of dollars in wages. It consists of new industrial opportunities and hope. This is worth fighting for. Most important and vital of all, Negroes by the mobilization and coordination of their mass power, can cause PRESIDENT ROOSEVELT TO ISSUE AN EXECUTIVE ORDER ABOLISHING DISCRIMINATION IN ALL GOVERNMENT DEPARTMENTS, ARMY, NAVY AIR CORPS, AND NATIONAL DEFENSE JOBS.[47]

Under pressure, Roosevelt was indeed forced to sign an executive order abolishing discrimination in all government departments and defense jobs, and finally establishing a Fair Employment Practices Committee.[48] In 1943, the War Labor Board issued a specific appeal to African Americans: "Whether as vigorous fighting men or for production of food and munitions, America needs the Negro; the Negro needs the equal opportunity to work and fight. The Negro is necessary for winning the war, and at the same time, is a test of our sincerity in the cause for which we are fighting."[49]

Roosevelt's order did not, however, come close to ending discrimination against African Americans. Indeed, the U.S. Army remained segregated until 1948 (as did major league baseball until 1947). The Fair Employment Practices Committee, while forcing defense employers to hire Black workers, did nothing to defend those Black workers who then faced workplace segregation and were offered only the worst job assignments. Tens of thousands of Black workers joined in demonstrations and strikes against workplace discrimination in the following years. The biggest was a wildcat strike at Ford's Rouge plant in April 1943, when twelve thousand Black workers walked out to demand the hiring of more African Americans.[50]

The Black struggle significantly impacted the racial composition of the industrial workforce. Between 1940 and 1945, the number of Black men employed in agriculture fell from 41 percent to 28 percent, and the number of Black workers employed in industry nearly doubled (from 5.9 percent to 10.1 percent). African-American women did not fare as well. While Black women's overall employment increased during the war, most were denied access to higher-paying industrial jobs and remained concentrated as domestic servants and in other service occupations.

White women, on the contrary, made up a large proportion of workers in defense industries. Between three hundred thousand and four hundred thousand women joined the UAW during the Second World War, forming a third of the union's membership. Most women in World War II defense industries were not new to the labor force. As Glaberman noted, "It is clear that the picture of housewives rushing to become Rosie the Riveter and rushing back to the home after the end of the war is inaccurate. Most of the women working in war plants had had earlier [work] experience."

All told, two in five Black women and one in three white women were in the workforce by 1944.[51]

Radicalization Averted

Thus, the war years witnessed a sharp rise in class struggle, broad sentiment against the no-strike pledge, a militant movement against racial discrimination and a significant influx of women into industrial unions. These should have been the ingredients for the renewed growth of radicalism inside the working-class movement.

But the Communist Party, still by far the largest organization on the left, made that possibility much more unlikely. The communists' uncritical support of Roosevelt and the no-strike pledge only succeeded in alienating militant workers who went on strike during the war. The much smaller groups of genuine radicals held virtually no influence over the direction of the class struggle, with the notable exception of the UAW's Rank and File Caucus. As a result, while World War II ranks among the most militant periods of class struggle in history, this was not a period when radicalism developed on any significant scale. In fact, the political climate significantly shifted *rightward* from the previous decade.

This was evidenced by a rise in racism among white workers that peaked in 1943. Mobs of white workers often forcibly blocked African Americans migrating North from settling in previously all-white industrial areas. These confrontations frequently turned violent. The June 1943 Detroit race riot, one of the worst incidents of racist violence during this period, left thirty-four people dead.[52] As Bert Cochran pointed out, overcrowding provided the backdrop for this explosion of racist bigotry:

> As soon as Michigan became a major war production center, there was an ingathering of masses of new workers, many from the South. By mid-1941 in Detroit alone there were over 350,000 new workers, 50,000 of them Blacks. No provisions worth talking about had been made to accommodate the newcomers. All facilities were monstrously overcrowded; there was an acute housing shortage; the Blacks . . . were forced into decaying, infested ghetto slums and were hemmed in by walls of hatred.[53]

This rise in racism among white workers spilled over into a spate of racist "hate strikes" during the same period. The hate strikes were a temporary development, peaking in June 1943 and subsiding soon thereafter. Nevertheless, their significance should not be underestimated, for they mark a sharp backslide from the racial unity that had grown inside the labor movement throughout the 1930s.

In general, the hate strikes were protests against the hiring or promotion of Black workers, or the transfer of a Black worker into a previously all-white department. Like other wildcats during the war, most were "quickie" actions of workers. But for a short period of time they were quite frequent. At their height, between March and June 1943, over a hundred thousand work hours were lost to hate strikes. And larger hate strikes did take place. Twenty-five thousand white workers struck Detroit's Packard Works in April 1943 to protest an earlier sit-down of Blacks demanding job promotions.[54]

However, even at their height, the hate strikes represented only a minority of the wartime work stoppages taking place. In many more instances, Black and white workers struck together in genuine solidarity. But the hate strikes demonstrate how, without significant pressure from labor radicals to challenge the right-wing climate that grew throughout the Second World War, white unionists could quickly begin venting their frustrations not at those in power—but by turning on African-American workers. Wildcat strikes could thus display remarkable solidarity one day, only to foment racist hatred the next.

Postwar Upsurge

Even before the war finally ended in August 1945, union officials proudly declared a postwar era of continued labor-management co-operation. Together, the AFL and CIO signed a "Charter of Industrial Peace" with the Chamber of Commerce in March. The *CIO News* ran a banner headline that month announcing, "It's Industrial Peace for the Post-War Period!" And the Communist Party once again outflanked the CIO, declaring bluntly soon after the war was over, "The no-strike pledge was not declared only for the duration of the war." [55]

But these predictions were nothing more than wishful thinking. The end of the war brought with it an explosion of class struggle that continued through the end of 1946. Workers who had risked their lives fighting in the war returned home to a recession economy and, in many cases, to find they'd lost their jobs. Those who still had jobs faced sharply lower wages. During the war years, productivity had risen by 11 percent, but average hourly raises had totaled only 0.6 percent. In addition, four million women workers who had landed industrial jobs during the war years were thrown out of work immediately afterward. Within a week after "Victory over Japan Day" (known as V-J Day) in August 1945, the unemployed were organizing mass demonstrations, drawing fifty thousand in New York City and thirty thousand in San Francisco. [56]

The first six months of 1946 marked "the most concentrated period of labor-management strife in the country's history," according to the U.S. Bureau of Labor Statistics. In January of that year, auto, steel, electrical, and packinghouse workers were all on strike at the same time, paralyzing the industrial base of the economy. During the twelve months after V-J Day, more than five million workers were involved in strikes, which lasted on average four times longer than those during the war.[57] By 1946, 69 percent of all production workers in manufacturing were union members.[58] Total union membership continued rising during the immediate postwar period, peaking at roughly 35 percent of the U.S. labor force by 1954.

Meanwhile, those soldiers remaining overseas after the war organized a "Bring us home now!" movement in late 1945 and 1946, involving troops abroad and their family members at home. Trains carrying troops through Minneapolis were adorned with signs complaining, "We're being sold down the river while Congress vacations."[59] Thousands of U.S. soldiers demonstrated in Seoul, Manila, Guam, Frankfurt, and Paris—often using tactics learned in the 1930s labor movement. One commander told a rowdy demonstration of four thousand U.S. soldiers in Manila, "You men forget you're not working for General Motors. You're still in the Army." Thousands of troops marched through the streets of Paris, chanting "Get us home!" Troops in Seoul adopted the following resolution: "We cannot understand the War Department's insistence on keeping an oversized peacetime army overseas under present conditions."[60]

Sentiment was widespread among Black soldiers that "we know our fight for democracy will really begin when we reach San Francisco on our way home." By January 1946, Black veterans were already demonstrating for voting rights in the South. In 1947, A. Philip Randolph again began to organize a movement against segregation in the U.S. Army. He declared, "I personally will advise Negroes to refuse to fight as slaves for a democracy they cannot possess and cannot enjoy."[61] Randolph organized a picket outside the 1948 Democratic Party convention, demanding an end to segregation in the military. An opinion poll at the time showed 71 percent of Black youth in Harlem would refuse to be drafted into a segregated army. The government finally gave in, formally ending segregation in the U.S. Army that year.[62]

Truman's Assault on Labor

However determined workers were to regain lost ground after the war, the employers were just as determined to prevent them from doing so. As GM president Alfred Sloan declared at the end of World War II, "It is going to take a good while to rid the country of the New Deal, but sooner or later the ax falls and we get a change."[63]

They found a capable ally in President Harry Truman, who succeeded Roosevelt after his death in April 1945. Truman's first significant presidential act was to order two atomic bombs dropped on the Japanese cities of Hiroshima and Nagasaki in August 1945, killing an estimated two hundred thousand Japanese, the vast majority civilians. Truman did not have a liberal reputation to protect.

Truman quickly joined forces with antiunion employers. For more than a year after the war ended, the War Powers Act entitled the government to continue to seize entire industries in order to break strikes. Truman made good use of this power, successfully breaking strikes by oil workers, packinghouse workers, railroad workers, and miners by the end of 1946. Explaining his numerous interventions in the 1946 strikes, he said, "[I]t was clear to me that the time had come for action on the part of the government."[64] By 1947, 90 percent of union contracts contained clauses pledging no strikes during the course of the agreement. As Brecher remarked, "Indeed, by May 1947—a year after the big strikes—the average worker had less purchasing power than he had had in January 1941; in March 1947, auto and basic steelworkers were making almost twenty-five cents less than two years before."[65]

Workers expressed their disillusionment with the Democrat in the White House through mass abstention from the 1946 Congressional election, which drew only three-eighths of eligible voters and elected a Republican majority.[66] The new Congress wasted no time in launching a frontal assault on labor, passing the Taft-Hartley Act in 1947—which imposed a multitude of restrictions on organized labor and working-class solidarity.[67]

Taft-Hartley

The Taft-Hartley Act of 1947, officially titled the Labor-Management Relations Act, outlawed wildcat strikes, solidarity strikes, secondary boycotts, and mass picketing. It required all union officials to sign affidavits stating that they were not members of the Communist Party and had no relationship with any organization seeking the "overthrow of the United States government by force or by any illegal or unconstitutional means." Taft-Hartley allowed states to pass laws banning the closed union shop, in a goodwill gesture to Southern employers. The president of the United States was given authority to impose an eighty-day "cooling-off period" on strikes that threatened the "national interest." Moreover, Taft-Hartley held union organizations and their leaders legally responsible—that is, subject to lawsuits—for damages incurred by wildcat strikes or any other "breach of contract." [68]

Truman vetoed the Taft-Hartley Act in June 1947, knowing that Congress had more than enough votes to override his veto. As Nicholson wrote, "More Democrats joined Republicans in voting for the bill and the override than voted against it." [69] Truman's claimed opposition to Taft-Hartley was also belied by his own actions. By the middle of 1948, Truman had used it twelve times to break strikes. [70]

"Although both the AFL and the CIO initially favored a boycott of Taft-Hartley," Lichtenstein commented, "such a nullification would also deprive them of access to the NLRB [National Labor Relations Board], to bargaining unit election procedures, and to what protections the labor law still afforded them against anti-union employers." [71] CIO leaders continued to support the Democrats and vigorously campaigned for Truman in the 1948 election—based upon his (never fulfilled) campaign promise to repeal Taft-Hartley. But union officials were also enjoying their status as "labor statesmen" and wished to continue the collaborative relationships they had established with government representatives during the war. Unions' support for Truman proved decisive in the 1948 election. After Truman won a surprise victory against his Republican opponent, Thomas E. Dewey, he declared, "Labor did it!" [72] Labor's continued backing for the Democrats had further implications, as Mike Davis argued:

> [T]hey chose to reconsolidate their shaken alliance with Truman and the national Democratic Party, allowing the CIO in the process to become an integral component of the administration's escalating anti-communist crusade. . . . [T]he CIO's one-sided and obsequious tie to the Presidential level of the Democratic Party—like Gompers' earlier reliance upon Wilson—bound it naturally to the twists and turns of American foreign policy from the ephemeral 'one world' enthusiasms of the Teheran Conference period to the nuclear imperialism of the late forties. [73]

Just over a year after Taft-Hartley passed, eighty-one thousand union officers from roughly 120 unions had filed non-communist affidavits with the government.[74] By 1957, Taft-Hartley had completely altered the political complexion of the U.S. labor movement. In July of that year, as David Caute, author of *The Great Fear*, noted, "the NLRB announced that about 250 international unions were in compliance (involving about 2,750 affidavits) and 21,500 locals (involving some 193,500 affidavits)."[75]

After Taft-Hartley was passed, the number of strikes declined significantly—never again approaching the 1945–46 level.[76] In 1953, the CIO's research department reported, "no significant industry or service which was not organized before 1945–46 has been organized since then."[77] By the end of the 1950s, the labor movement had entered its long-term decline.

Liberals Unite to Stamp Out the "Red Menace"

The anticommunist witch-hunt of the 1940s and 1950s is generally regarded as a Republican creation—in the likeness of the ruthless Republican Senator Joseph McCarthy and the reactionary FBI director J. Edgar Hoover. To be sure, McCarthyism peaked during the Eisenhower administration. And right-wing Republican Richard Nixon launched his Congressional career by claiming in his 1946 campaign, "A vote for Nixon is a vote against the Communist-dominated [CIO] PAC with its gigantic slush fund."[78] Nixon built his political reputation as a vitriolic member of the House Un-American Activities Committee.

But the anticommunist crusade achieved such overwhelming success only because *liberal Democrats* pursued it with equal ferocity. Roosevelt, of course, signed the Smith Act into law in 1940, setting the legal precedent for prosecuting radicals. And a host of Democrats, including Senators John F. Kennedy and Hubert Humphrey, spearheaded the liberal embrace of anticommunism. Kennedy's role paralleled Nixon's, as Caute describes:

> After the war the lead in the red-baiting of unions was taken by the House Committee on Education and Labor under its chairman Fred Hartley, coauthor of the Taft-Hartley Act. This committee, hostile to the New Deal and graced by such freshman starts as Nixon of California and John F. Kennedy of Massachusetts, fastened its claws into the Communist militant who had led highly publicized strikes in 1941 and 1947 at the Allis-Chalmers Company in Wisconsin. What happened to Harold Christoffel could well serve—and was intended to serve—as an

example to any other union leader tempted to adhere to the Marxist principles he had absorbed in the thirties. . . . A grand jury indicted him for perjury, and in March 1948 he was convicted. After the Supreme Court had thrown out the verdict on a technicality, he was tried and convicted again. In May 1953, though he was relentlessly pursued by John F. Kennedy, Christoffel's sentence was reduced from four years to sixteen months.[79]

After sponsoring a bill to make Communist Party membership a crime, Hubert Humphrey successfully supported the Communist Control Act of 1954, stripping the CP of all legal "rights, privileges and immunities."[80] Humphrey was also a founder of the liberal Americans for Democratic Action (ADA) in 1954, which quickly made clear its dedication to stamping out the "red menace." An ADA supporter made the following observation about liberal infighting, "In the course of this battle liberals attacked liberals with more venom than they had ever directed at any economic royalist."[81]

The American Civil Liberties Union (ACLU)—created to defend the right to free speech and individual liberty—was one of the first liberal organizations to conduct its own internal campaign against communism. In 1940, veteran IWW leader Elizabeth Gurley Flynn was expelled from the ACLU's Board of Trustees (an elected position) for being a member of the Communist Party. Just one year earlier, the ACLU had published the pamphlet, *Why We Defend Free Speech for Nazis, Fascists, and Communists*. The ACLU also reversed its earlier opposition to labor policies that barred communists from running for union office. And throughout the 1950s, leading members of the ACLU played the role of informers, tipping off the FBI about anyone who approached them asking them to join a campaign against HUAC or otherwise expressing hostility to McCarthyism.[82]

The Truman Doctrine

In the mid-1940s, Truman himself launched the full-throttled anticommunist crusade that paved the way for McCarthyism in the 1950s. After the Democrats' resounding defeat in the 1946 Congressional elections, Truman consciously steered the Democrats to the right in an attempt to steal the Republicans' anti-New Deal thunder.

But anticommunism was also the centerpiece of Truman's foreign policy, ostensibly to defend the "free world" from the "Soviet threat." Fighting as allies during World War II, the United States and the USSR emerged from the Second World War as the world's largest superpowers, although the United States was by far the stronger of the two. Their wartime alliance was quickly severed once hostilities came to a close. Nevertheless, before the conclusion of World War II, the United States was forced to share the spoils of war not only with Britain, its long-standing ally, but also with its Russian nemesis. The three leaders of the victor nations—Churchill, Roosevelt, and Stalin—met at Yalta in February 1945 to carve up control of Europe. In his memoirs, Churchill described the Yalta meeting with Stalin to divide the European continent:

> The moment was apt for business, so I said, "Let us settle our affairs in the Balkans. Your armies are in Rumania and Bulgaria. We have interests, missions and agents there. Don't let us get at cross-purposes in small ways. So far as Britain is concerned, how would it do for you to have 90 percent predominance in Rumania, for us to have 90 percent of the say in Greece, and go 50–50 about Yugoslavia?" While this was being translated I wrote on half a sheet of paper:
>
> *Rumania: Russia 90%—The others 10%*
> *Greece: Great Britain 90%—Russia 10%*
> *Yugoslavia: 50–50%*
> *Hungary: 50–50%*
> *Bulgaria: Russia 75%—The others 25%*
>
> I pushed this across to Stalin, who had by then heard the translation. There was a slight pause. Then he took his pencil and made a large tick upon it, and passed it back to us. It was all settled in no more time than it takes to set down. . . . After this there was a long silence. The penciled paper lay on the center of the table. At length I said, "Might it not be thought rather cynical if it seemed we had disposed of these issues, so fateful to millions of people, in such an off-hand manner? Let us burn the paper." "No, you keep it," said Stalin.[83]

Although leaders of the conquering nations had so calmly divided control at Yalta, Republicans afterward bitterly accused New Deal Democrats—the now deceased Roosevelt in particular—of having ceded too much ground to Russia.

The Truman Doctrine, unveiled on March 12, 1947, institutionalized a power struggle between the United States and the Soviet Union, launching the Cold War that dominated world politics until the unraveling of the USSR fifty years later. The Marshall Plan, central to the Truman Doctrine, dangled the offer of economic aid to countries resisting "Communist domination" in order to buy their allegiance to the United States. "Communism" was broadly defined to include militant workers' movements from below in addition to Soviet intervention from above.

While gaining little notice at the time, the Truman administration was already aiding France's colonial efforts in the war in Vietnam, bearing up to 50 percent of the financial cost by 1952. As Caute noted, "It was the Truman government that very energetically planted the disastrous harvest of the late 1960s." [84]

The U.S. State Department, under the auspices of the Marshall Plan, quickly enlisted the assistance of American labor leaders in crushing left-wing workers' movements in Europe and Latin America. By 1948, as Preis noted, "CIO Secretary Treasurer [James] Carey threatened the Italian workers that if they did not vote against the Communist-Socialist ticket in the April 18 elections, 'they could hardly expect to share in the benefits of the ERP [European Recovery Plan].'" [85] CIO officials thus graduated from the role of "labor statesmen" to international operatives for the U.S. government.

The Truman Doctrine called for the containment of the "Soviet threat" primarily because the Soviet Union interfered with the right of U.S. imperialism to single-handedly dominate the world. To be sure, the United States spoke of promoting democracy and human rights, but its actual plan was far more pragmatic. As State Department planner George Kennan argued in an internal document in 1948:

> [W]e have about 50 percent of the world's wealth, but only 6.3 percent of its population. . . . In this situation, we cannot fail to be the object of envy and resentment. Our real task in the coming period is to devise a pattern of relationships which will permit us to maintain this position of disparity without positive detriment to our national security. To do so, we will have to dispense with all sentimentality and day-dreaming; and our attention will have to be concentrated everywhere on our immediate national objectives. [86]

America thus based its Cold War alliances not on any commitment to democracy but on other governments' willingness to advance the aims of U.S. imperialism. As Nicholson remarked, "Governments, no matter how tyrannical, that provided unrestricted access to labor, natural resources, markets, and opportunities for investment were to be protected by the United States and its allies." [87]

McCarthyism Under Truman

Truman's anti-Russian foreign policy translated into a domestic witch-hunt only because it provided an opportunity to launch an employers' backlash against the working-class radicalization of the 1930s. While European social democracy flourished after the war, the U.S. ruling class stood alone in lurching rightward. Caute argued pointedly, "We need only glance momentarily outside the borders of the United States to notice that Britain also committed itself to a political and military alliance against the Soviet Union, *but without the corollary of domestic red-baiting and witch-hunting.*"[88]

As historian Victor Navasky, author of *Naming Names,* commented,

> To underwrite the costs of containment abroad, Truman over-sold the Communist menace at home. Ten days after promulgating the Truman Doctrine for Greece and Turkey, in March 1947, he signed Executive Order 9835, which established a loyalty and security program for all federal employees and revived the attorney general's old list of subversive organizations. Many former isolationists quickly adapted Truman's anti-Communist foreign policy to their 'politics of revenge' against the New Deal.[89]

In March 1947—the same month he announced the Truman Doctrine and two months before the Taft-Hartley Act sailed through Congress—Truman instituted the Loyalty Act by Executive Order 9835, authorizing the Attorney General to compile a list of "subversive" organizations. Within a year, the list had grown to include six categories and 78 organizations.[90] The Loyalty Act authorized the FBI and the Civil Service Commission (CSC) to begin surveillance activities on federal employees, in addition to members of any organizations on the Attorney General's list. In its first six years, the program resulted in 4,666,122 sets of fingerprints, 4,756,705 loyalty oaths, and 26,236 investigations of federal employees or applicants. By 1955, the CSC announced that the FBI maintained intelligence files on two million people. That same year, roughly one in five U.S. workers was required to submit a loyalty oath or pass security clearance for their jobs.[91]

The security agents were empowered to scour the personal as well as political activities of their suspects—from their sex lives to their reading material. Journalist Elmer Davis later described an incident in which a young woman was being screened for a civilian job with the U.S. Navy. When Davis complimented her intelligence, the investigating officer remarked, "These intelligent people are very likely to be attracted to Communism." [92]

Between 1947 and 1956, twenty-seven hundred civilian workers were fired from their jobs, while twelve thousand more resigned after the experience of being investigated. In a single day during this period, three Chicago electric companies fired over five hundred stewards and officials of the communist-led United Electrical Workers (UE). The NLRB upheld the mass firings as valid under Taft-Hartley. [93]

The charges against most suspects ranked far below actual membership in the Communist Party. One civil servant lost his job in 1949 after he was accused of being "unduly critical of the United States Government and unduly praiseful of the Communist Government of Russia." The sum total of his "subversive" activity was having signed a Progressive Party petition in 1948. Another employee was confronted by an informant's testimony that, while visiting his apartment, he had "listened for three hours to a recorded opera entitled *The Cradle Will Rock.*" The informer explained that the plot of this opera "followed along the lines of a downtrodden laboring man and the evils of the capitalist system." [94]

"Questions of social philosophy, supposedly protected by the First Amendment, were grist to the mill," Caute observed. A geographer employed by the government was asked:

> Have you provided any sort of religious training for your children?
> Do you believe in government ownership of public utilities as a general proposition?
> Have you indicated that you favor redistribution of wealth?
> What do you consider "reactionary" to be?
> Do you think that workers in the capitalist system get a relatively fair deal?
> In your opinion should Guatemala be both legal and Communistic [*sic*]? [95]

Mississippi Democrat John E. Rankin and Texas Democrat Martin Dies set the political tone for HUAC. Dies was chairman of HUAC's predecessor, the Special Committee on Un-American Activities, from 1938 to 1944. When the Special Committee subpoenaed the membership list of the American League for Peace and Democracy, he estimated that "there are not less than 2,000 outright

Communists and Party-liners still holding jobs in the government in Washington." [96]

Rankin hailed from the voting district that imposed the highest poll tax in the country and, as a KKK sympathizer, insisted that slavery was "the greatest blessing the Negro people ever had." [97] Rankin considered the Fair Employment Practices Committee "the beginning of a Communist dictatorship the like of which America never dreamed." Rankin was also a vocal anti-Semite, whose "convictions led him to attribute all the horrors of the Russian Revolution to Trotsky [a Jew] and to see Stalin as a kind of reformer, a seminary student who opened the churches, got rid of the commissars, and drove the local Reds to America." [98] According to Rankin, Jesus Christ himself had been "hounded" by (presumably Jewish) communists, who persecuted him and then "gambled for his garments at the foot of the cross." [99]

The Communist " Conspiracy"

During the 1948 election campaign, Truman faced a third-party challenge from former New Dealer Henry Wallace. Wallace had served as Roosevelt's vice president between 1941 and 1945, but Democratic Party leaders replaced Wallace with the more conservative Truman as Roosevelt's running mate in the 1944 election. Truman fired Wallace as Secretary of Commerce in 1946, after Wallace voiced criticism of Truman's aggressive hostility toward Russia.

The Democrats successfully closed ranks against Wallace's 1948 presidential candidacy, and Truman was assured of the CIO's support. The Communist Party, however, endorsed Wallace, and Truman worried that Wallace could siphon off working-class votes in a close race. Truman took aim at Wallace's liberalism, referring to "Henry Wallace and his Communists" on the campaign trail. Rhode Island Senator Howard McGrath, chairman of the Democratic National Committee, was more explicit, arguing, "[A] vote for Wallace . . . is a vote for the things for which Stalin, Molotov, and Vishinsky stand." [100] Wallace was trampled on Election Day, receiving just over 2 percent of the vote.

Four months before the 1948 election, Truman brandished his anticommunist credentials by using the Smith Act to conduct a show trial against twelve leading members of the Communist Party, eventually leading to 145 indictments against communists.[101] In the process, Truman lowered the bar for indicting radicals yet further from the 1940 trial against Trotskyists—from *advocating* revolution to *conspiring to advocate* revolution. As Caute described,

> These Communist leaders, it should be noted, were not accused of attempting to overthrow the government or even of teaching the technology of such an overthrow. The gist of the indictment was that, in dissolving the Communist Political Association and resurrecting the CPUSA, they entered into a conspiracy dating from April 1, 1945 until July 20, 1948 (the day of their indictment). The crucial notion here is *conspiracy to advocate;* by introducing the charge of conspiracy, the Justice Department opened the door to drag-net trials based on sympathetic association and obviated the hard task of proving the case against each defendant at the same level of rigor. Now, at last, the Justice Department and the FBI were on the verge of achieving their ambition of imprisoning Communists simply for being Communists.[102]

The government's "evidence" in the 1948 Smith Act trials consisted of (out-of-context) quotes from Lenin and Stalin, along with the testimony of thirteen professional witnesses, all ex-communist and FBI informers, who traveled from one courtroom to the next giving identical testimony. Although many passages in Communist Party literature renounced the use of violence, one former communist witness assured the Court that such passages were written in code and were always understood to denote violent overthrow. Another witness claimed that, at one Communist Party meeting, a member had argued that for a revolution to succeed in the United States, the Red Army might have to march from Siberia through Alaska and Canada to Detroit.[103]

Truman enjoyed the backing of virtually the entire ruling elite in ratcheting up the level of hysteria. The National Industrial Conference Board, an influential business organization, was only too happy to encourage Truman's crusade against communism to crack down on militant workers. Its outreach to other employers made the connection vividly: "industrial security can . . . help you rid your plant of agitators who create labor unrest. . . . The spies, traitors, and the misguided fools who promote Communism constitute our number one industrial security problem today." [104] The Chamber of Commerce was an early advocate of crushing the communist threat, having published a thirty-eight-page booklet in 1938, *Communist Infiltration in the United States: Its Nature and How to Combat*

It. In 1947, the chamber published another pamphlet: *Communist Ideas, Loyalty, and Espionage*, explicitly linking the New Deal Democrats with the advance of Communism.[105]

The sensational trial and conviction of Alger Hiss on charges of perjury dominated headlines from 1948 until 1950. Hiss was a 1930s New Deal Democrat who had quit the State Department in 1947 to assume the presidency of the Carnegie Endowment for International Peace. He was convicted of having passed state secrets to the Soviet Union and sentenced to five years in prison in 1950, based on flimsy evidence and even flimsier testimony from ex-communist Whittaker Chambers.

In 1949, the Senate Judiciary Committee launched an attack on the United Nations, accusing it of harboring communists disguised as diplomats. In 1951, HUAC chairman John S. Wood called the United Nations Educational, Scientific, and Cultural Organization (UNESCO) "the greatest subversive plot in history."[106]

McCarthyism

The hysteria associated with McCarthyism was spinning out of control before Senator Joe McCarthy took center stage. HUAC itself had already been conducting its sensational show trials for several years, with newsreel and television camera lights blinding witnesses as they testified. As Caute remarked, "The Committee and its subcommittees customarily rode into town like a sheriff's posse. . . . The Committee's lust for publicity was unquenchable. . . . Witnesses faced storms of exploding flashbulbs, sudden sunrises and sunsets from the klieg lights, a stifling atmosphere as reporters pushed for places at the overcrowded long tables."[107]

McCarthy seized the opportunity—with gusto—to drive the campaign to its most extreme conclusions. McCarthy raised the level of paranoia during a speech to a Republican women's club on February 9, 1950, in which he waved a piece of paper at the audience while claiming, "I have here in my hand a list of 205 that were known to the secretary of state as being members of the Communist Party and are still making and shaping the policy of the State Department."[108]

McCarthy chaired the Senate's Permanent Subcommittee on Investigations, the Senate's counterpart to HUAC. His unrelenting theme was that "the Communists within our borders have been more responsible for the success of Communism abroad than Soviet Russia." [109] McCarthy claimed that communists had infiltrated everywhere, from the factory floor to the uppermost echelons of government. To drive home the notion that communists had "burrowed from within," McCarthy accelerated the pace of show trials against alleged communists, socialists, left sympathizers, and liberals, holding 169 Senate hearings between 1953 and 1954.

Meanwhile, over three thousand witnesses testified at 230 HUAC hearings between 1945 and 1957. [110] Hundreds of investigating committees and sub-committees conducted their own separate hearings at the federal, state, and local level. The hearings were designed to publicly humiliate radicals and liberals of every stripe into submission, whichever investigative committee was holding them. Their goal was to hound left-wingers out of Hollywood, liberal teachers and lawyers out of their professions, and perhaps most importantly, to drive radicals out of unions and workplaces across the country. As Caute observed, "HUAC's ultimate mission and highest delight was to hound radicals out of their jobs." [111] Between 1949 and 1959, HUAC furnished information on sixty thousand people to employers who wanted to know the political backgrounds of their workers.

In the process, thousands of people were investigated, fined thousands of dollars, sent to prison, fired from their jobs or deported—for such "crimes" as having once been a member of the Communist Party, having signed a petition for peace or against fascism, or having been friendly with people who had done so. Lawyers were subpoenaed for having once belonged to the National Lawyers Guild. [112] Revered civil rights leader W. E. B. Du Bois was indicted by a Washington grand jury at the age of eighty-three for sitting on the board of the Peace Information Center—because it failed to register as an "agent of a foreign power." He was "handcuffed, fingerprinted, bailed, and remanded for trial." [113]

The "American Way"

Ironically, as the U.S. government was touting its principled defense of the "free world," it was trampling on the Bill of Rights, including the rights of free speech and due process in a court of law. One of the pinnacles of the "American way" of democracy, declaring every person innocent until proven guilty of a crime, was openly flouted during the anticommunist crusade.

Those who tried to exercise their right to invoke the First Amendment frequently found themselves thrown in jail for contempt of court. Courts ruled that the right to free speech covered by the First Amendment did not apply when there was a "clear and present danger" such as communism. Meanwhile, invoking the right to not incriminate oneself, protected by the Fifth Amendment, was considered tantamount to admitting guilt. Many of those who took the Fifth Amendment automatically lost their jobs and were blacklisted.

Committee members, however, often refused to allow witnesses to invoke either the First or Fifth Amendments. In 1946, Rankin threatened an Austrian-born witness, "Do you realize that you are violating your oath of citizenship when you show contempt for this Committee, and are likely to have that citizenship cancelled?" Another uncooperative witness was told by Rankin, "You are rubbing your nose right up against the gates of the penitentiary here." [114]

Mass Paranoia

In 80 percent of cases filed during the Korean War, the NLRB, the government agency assigned to protect the rights of workers, sided against workers who were fired for alleged radical activity.[115] Those who lost their jobs after appearing before HUAC were denied unemployment benefits.[116] But the hearings were just one aspect of the massive cloud of paranoia that enveloped U.S. society in the early 1950s. The witch-hunt was a massive ideological crusade that reached into every corner of society.

Communist Party members were barred from receiving passports and were banned from using the U.S. Postal Service. Congress passed the Internal Security Act in 1950, granting government authorities the right, among other things, to round up members of the Communist Party and put them into concentration camps in a time of national emergency. After passage of the Immigration and Nationality Act of 1952, immigrants could be arrested without a warrant, held without bail, and deported for actions (such as joining the Communist Party) that were legal when they were committed.[117]

In 1950, the Pennsylvania state Democratic committee issued

a pamphlet entitled *Fellow-Traveling Pa. GOP [Republican] Congressmen Follow Red-Party Line*.[118] In 1954, the Senate Internal Security Subcommittee issued a report, *Interlocking Subversion in Government Departments*, claiming to trace communist infiltration at every level of U.S. government since the New Deal. The report stated, "They colonized key committees of Congress, they helped write laws ... advised Cabinet members ... staffed interdepartmental committees which prepared basic American and world policies." The Republican National Committee footed the bill for fifty thousand copies of the report, and Texas millionaire H. L. Hunt sprung for another fifty thousand. [119]

In 1953, an Indiana citizen campaigned to remove all copies of the subversive *Adventures of Robin Hood* from the shelves of school libraries.[120] In the late 1940s and early 1950s, a number of states outlawed the Communist Party, while the state of Texas considered a bill to make membership in the Communist Party punishable by death. In the end, Texas passed a "watered down" law making the penalty for CP membership twenty years in prison and a $20,000 fine. Indiana law was changed to carry a three-year prison term for engaging in any "un-American activities." In 1947, the State of Washington created a Joint Legislative Fact-Finding Committee on Un-American Activities, instructed to investigate anyone "whose activities are such to indicate a purpose to foment strife, discord, and dissension." [121]

Often, the level of paranoia crossed the line from ridiculous to absurd. The right-wing John Birch Society infamously claimed that the fluoridation of water was a communist plot. But this was just the tip of the iceberg. Frank S. Tavenner, HUAC's general counsel from 1949 to 1956, claimed that the Library of Congress was a "haven for aliens and foreign-minded Americans." His successor, Richard Arens (who obsessively repeated the phrase, "Stand up like a red-blooded American," when interrogating witnesses) counted among his own accomplishments having successfully prevented twenty-five thousand displaced German Jews from emigrating to the United States after the Second World War.[122]

One Michigan police chief warned residents in a radio telecast, "Soviet agents are coming into the United States disguised as Jewish rabbis." [123] Albert Cantwell, the chairman of yet another anticommunist committee, informed those helping to weed out the communist conspiracy to beware of anyone who advocated racial equality.

He said, "If someone insists there is discrimination against Negroes in this country . . . there is every reason to believe that person is a Communist."[124]

The virulently anticommunist American Legion picketed films starring left-wing actors (Charlie Chaplin was a favorite target), while in 1951 its *American Legion Magazine* published a report by Joe McCarthy's underling asking ominously, "Did the Movies Really Clean House?"[125] William E. Jenner, chairman of the Senate Internal Security Subcommittee, called for firing schoolteachers whose communist past might be "not easily provable." He justified this drastic measure as necessary to "safeguard academic freedom"—which, he argued, could not exist "until this Soviet conspiracy hidden in our schools and colleges is exposed."[126]

Anticommunist Hollywood

Hollywood movie studios enthusiastically joined in the anticommunist hysteria. The Hollywood Ten, a group of left-wing writers and directors, refused to cooperate when subpoenaed by HUAC in 1947, citing their First Amendment rights. Under the banner of the Committee for the First Amendment, Hollywood stars Humphrey Bogart, Lauren Bacall, Groucho Marx, and Frank Sinatra—accompanied by a planeload of other supporters—arrived to back the Ten during the hearings.

Before the Hollywood Ten hearings, Eric Johnston, president of the Motion Picture Association, pledged, "As long as I live I will never be party to anything as un-American as a blacklist." Afterward, however, Johnston suspended the Ten without pay and vowed Hollywood would never again "knowingly" employ other Communists.[127] The Hollywood Ten were convicted of contempt of Congress, and after exhausting all appeals in 1951, each went to prison for up to one year.

While blacklisting hundreds of Hollywood actors, writers, and directors, the studios produced more than thirty-five anticommunist films during this period, with titles such as *The Red Menace* (1949) and *I Was a Communist for the FBI* (1951), in which the set-piece communists were portrayed as beady-eyed conspirators. Writer Nora Sayre described the Hollywood stereotype of communists during this era as follows:

Bereft of any humor, they grimly demand explanations of "jokes," and are incapable of asking civil questions, except when they're offering "More Scotch?" to a possible recruit. . . . Often they can be detected by their style of inhaling [cigarette smoke]: they expel smoke very slowly from their nostrils before threatening someone's life, or suggesting that "harm" will come to his family.[128]

The Short But Significant Career of Joe McCarthy

The paper-waving Senator McCarthy fueled mass paranoia as he leveled ever more grandiose charges—based on "secret" evidence that could be shared neither with the public nor the accused. As Caute noted, McCarthy's accusations were typically backed up by "half-truths, warmed over 'revelations,' or just plain lies."[129] McCarthy injected a strong dose of populism, albeit of the right-wing variety, to stoke class resentment against New Deal liberals. When accusing communists of infiltrating the State Department, he said, "It is not the less fortunate, or members of minority groups who have been selling this nation out . . . but the bright young men who are born with silver spoons in their mouths."

By all accounts, McCarthy's arrogance seemed to know no bounds. He frequently heaped contempt on his critics, as in this 1951 remark: "Let me assure you that regardless of how high-pitched becomes the squeaking and screaming of left-wing, bleeding heart, phony liberals, this battle is going to go on."[130] In 1951, McCarthy denounced General George C. Marshall, the U.S. Chief of Staff during World War Two, as a pro-Soviet traitor whose transgressions were responsible for the 1949 Chinese Revolution. In a televised speech in 1953, McCarthy accused President Eisenhower of sending "perfumed notes" to countries that traded with communist China. In 1953, McCarthy claimed to have unearthed a communist spy ring inside the Voice of America, a wing of the U.S. State Department that transmitted *anti*communist radio messages to countries behind the Iron Curtain.[131]

But when McCarthy targeted the Pentagon in 1954, accusing those in the highest reaches of the U.S. Army of harboring Russian spies, he had gone too far. He alienated the very forces in U.S. society who were his strongest backers. Caute described McCarthy's downfall as follows:

> All this came about because McCarthy's hungers were unappeasable—this baron of bastard feudalism was capable of subpoenaing God Almighty. . . . In a crowded caucus room the subcommittee convened to adjudicate between its chairman and the Army. His face covered in cream-colored makeup, constantly interrupting with "points of order" in his strong, low voice and generally disregarding acting chairman Karl Mundt's attempts to exercise authority. . . . [A]lthough he remained a senator, McCarthy's wings were clipped.[132]

McCarthy's downfall marked the beginning of the end of the anticommunist crusade. But this did not happen soon enough to save the lives of Ethel and Julius Rosenberg. They were arrested in 1950 and were tried, convicted, sentenced, and killed within three years. The Justice Department charged the Rosenbergs with *conspiracy* to commit espionage, allowing the prosecution to introduce evidence based on second-hand conversations that would otherwise have been ruled out as hearsay. The judge who sentenced the Rosenbergs to death, Caute commented, "went so far as to insist that the Rosenbergs had put the atomic bomb into the hands of Russia and had thus caused the Communist aggression in Korea, with its cost to America of 50,000 casualties."[133] On June 19, 1953, Ethel and Julius Rosenberg, the parents of two young boys, became the first people executed under the provisions of the 1917 Espionage Act.

McCarthyism had succeeded in its aims, ruining thousands of lives in the process. The anticommunist crusade transformed the political climate—even in Flint, Michigan, where the solidarity of the sit-down strike gave way to an angry anticommunist mood. After HUAC swept through Flint in 1953, suspected radicals were beaten and run out of their factories by fellow autoworkers. Representative Kit Clardy, known as "Michigan's McCarthy," who had invited HUAC to town, made this revealing comment after the violence: "This is the best kind of reaction there could have been to our hearings."[134]

The CIO and the CIA

The most damaging to socialists in the working-class movement was, of course, the witch-hunt conducted by union leaders themselves. Before the Hollywood Ten were convicted, Screen Actors Guild leader Ronald Reagan declared, "We will not be party to a blacklist." Soon thereafter, however, the union banned all noncooperative witnesses from membership and, beginning in 1953, also required its members to sign the loyalty oath.[135]

Even during the 1946 strike wave, CIO leaders were already preparing an internal anticommunist purge that became their main preoccupation for the next five years. Once CIO leaders had been enlisted as fighters in the Cold War, internal CIO politics emulated the foreign policy pursued by the U.S. State Department.

The CIO's postwar statement on foreign policy read, "The American labor movement has channels of communication and relationships in foreign countries, the use of which is essential to the successful prosecution of a democratic foreign policy. Labor's participation in the ECA [European Cooperation Administration] has accounted for much of the popular success of the recovery program; labor's moral appeal and experience have helped avert policies that might have weakened the understanding of the ECA by the great mass of European workers." [136] By 1948, both the AFL and the CIO joined with British trade unions to form the anti-Soviet International Confederation of Free Trade Unions to advance the cause of pro-American (as opposed to radical) labor unions worldwide. As Cochran noted,

> It was not long before American labor officials suffered a bad reputation for being mere creatures of the State Department, and got into a false position in their relationships with labor officials of other countries. . . . They were adjuncts of the State Department, the CIA, and the ECA missions, institutions whose interest in foreign labor movements or worker uplift was limited to making use of such groups and endeavors for the struggle against Communism or insurgencies in which Communists figured, and for the stabilization of capitalist infrastructures and markets.[137]

The labor movement's enthusiastic support for the Truman Doctrine led union leaders not only to support the United States in Korea, but also every successive U.S. military intervention in the name of "fighting communism," including the war in Vietnam. In 1950, the CIO and the AFL secretly began a decades-long collaboration with the CIA, channeling hundreds of millions of dollars to form and sustain anticommunist labor movements around the world.

CIO Witch-Hunt

As U.S. hostility toward the Soviet Union grew, so did CIO leaders' hostility toward communists and other union radicals. By 1948, the

Communist Party (after another about-face in policy) began to express reservations about Truman's Cold War policies and refused to back Truman in the 1948 election. Instead, the CP supported the independent candidacy of Henry Wallace, providing ammunition for the CIO's now open warfare against communists.

In 1948, the CIO expelled Harry Bridges from his post as its Northern California director, on the grounds that he refused to endorse Truman's Marshall Plan and supported the candidacy of Henry Wallace against Truman. In 1949, the CIO passed its own anticommunist statutes, barring any member of the Communist Party from holding union office, and giving the CIO the power to expel any unions with communists in their leadership. Next the convention voted to expel two CP-led unions, the United Electrical Workers and the Farm Equipment Workers. Soon thereafter, Walter Reuther, now second-in-command of the CIO, authorized CIO raiding of communist-led unions.

At the 1949 convention, CIO leader Philip Murray called communists "skulking cowards . . . apostles of hate . . . lying out of the pits of their dirty bellies." [138] In 1950, the final purge took place, when the convention voted to expel nine more CP-led unions. All told, the CIO had expelled roughly 20 percent of its membership, nearly 250,000 workers. [139] But most workers were relatively indifferent to the expulsions, however unjust. The CP had long since alienated the very layer of workers who would have fought hardest to defend union democracy. [140]

The CIO purge did not stop with the expulsion of CP-led unions. Indeed, that was the launching pad for the remaining CIO unions to weed out their own radical "trouble-makers," often working hand in glove with HUAC and other investigative committees. By 1954, fifty-nine out of a hundred unions had changed their constitutions to bar communists from holding union office, and forty unions had barred communists from membership. [141]

During this period, labor unions "enacted rituals and vendettas of their own to pulverize the radical, dissenting spirit that had characterized the CIO in its formative years," Caute commented. Such rituals followed a clear pattern:

> During or after a hotly contested union election, the anti-Communist faction, particularly if disappointed, would talk to the FBI; the FBI would talk to the company's security men; word would reach the staff

of HUAC, the SISS, or the McCarthy subcommittee; the government Screening Panel, having consulted FBI files, would deny the radicals access to classified material; the rival anti-Communist union or a friendly company would demand an NLRB election; the Justice Department would attempt an indictment under the Taft-Hartley Act's non-Communist affidavit; Congressional committees, armed with subpoenas, would swoop down on the area; the press would publicize the latest exposures in lurid headlines; there would be much talk of potential sabotage; and finally the company would fire a bunch of tight-lipped, amendment-invoking radicals.[142]

Crushing the Left in the UAW

Nowhere was the purge more ferocious than in the UAW, forcing a final showdown between the leadership and its long-standing radical wing. In 1941, years before Taft-Hartley, UAW vice president Walter Reuther proposed and won, by a two-thirds margin, a resolution barring communists from holding union office. During the debate, George F. Addes, secretary-treasurer, argued that socialists and other radicals should be barred in addition to communists. The debate was thus about whether to include other radicals in the ban, not whether the ban should be instituted.[143]

Two years later, Reuther used anticommunist smear tactics against Addes himself in a struggle for leadership of the union. Reuther's faction circulated a campaign song charging Frankensteen and Addes with taking orders from Joseph Stalin: *"Who are the boys who take their orders straight from the office of Joe Sta-leen? No one else but the gruesome twosome, George F. Addes and Frankensteen."*[144]

Reuther, who assumed the UAW presidency in 1946, embraced the opportunity offered by the witch-hunt to finally rid himself of the union's communist (and radical) opposition. Reuther was no stranger to the left, having been a willing collaborator with the Communist Party and a member of the Socialist Party in the 1930s. In 1937, in fact, Reuther himself had been the victim of red-baiting attacks. At the time, he argued, "So let's all be careful that we don't play the bosses' game by falling for their red scare. . . . No union man worthy of the name will play the bosses' game. Some may do so through ignorance. But those who peddle the red scare and know what they are doing are dangerous enemies of the union."[145]

Soon thereafter, however, Reuther joined labor's anticommunist camp, promoting the American Catholic Trade Unionists (ACTU) as a counterweight to the radical wing of the UAW. Interestingly, even while communists were baited as taking orders from Moscow, ACTU was never charged with receiving its orders from Rome and emerged unscathed from the witch-hunt.

Reuther's rallying cry was "Get the Commies!" as his faction succeeded in driving Thomas, Addes, and their supporters from UAW office at the 1947 UAW convention. As Preis commented, "Reuther emerged from the convention not only as a one-man ruler of the UAW—his machine had captured all top officerships and 18 out of 22 members of the National Executive Board—but as chief spokesman for the Truman Doctrine inside the labor movement." [146]

When HUAC set its sights on the alleged "un-American" activities among Detroit unionists, it zeroed in on the militant UAW Local 600, questioning more than a hundred of its members in preliminary hearings. The fact that none of the local's four top officers were members of the Communist Party had no deterrent effect, since the witch-hunt had long ago been extended to include all union militants who opposed the witch-hunt (so-called *anti*-anticommunists).

Local 600 stood firm, and its president, Carl Stellato, wrote, "[T]he politicians are building up a scare hysteria second to none. . . . Why? So that the unemployed, standing in the soup lines in Hamtramck, talking about the unemployment, the graft, the corruption in America, can have their attention diverted by the Un-American Activities Committee." Because these union activists stood together, HUAC was forced to leave town without indicting any member of Local 600. Even their employer, the Ford Motor Company, did not fire a single worker. Yet Reuther immediately suspended all functions of Local 600 and its executive board, taking over its administration. *Business Week* observed, "[T]his week Reuther and [HUAC] were working together on the UAW like a well-rehearsed vaudeville team." [147]

Retreat and Surrender

Even at the height of the McCarthy purge, the Communist Party did not fight back in any principled way. The party newspaper never once mentioned the Rosenbergs' espionage trial while it was taking place.[148] In 1948, party leaders were unwilling to organize a political defense when faced with expulsion from the CIO and indictment under the Smith Act. But even if they had tried to do so, they would likely have had a difficult time finding significant numbers of non-communist workers who would be willing to come to their defense.

Having supported the Smith Act until it took aim at the CP leadership made it difficult for communists to take anything resembling a principled stand on the right to freedom of speech.

Communist Party members had for many years dealt with red-baiting by simply denying party membership, and sometimes joining in the red-baiting. Some communist union leaders signed the Taft-Hartley affidavit swearing they were not communists, only to be thrown in prison afterward on charges of perjury. Instead of fighting McCarthyism, the CP sent hundreds of party members to live underground lives, under assumed names, while weathering the reactionary storm. The communists' courtroom strategy rested on invoking the Fifth Amendment. In the lynch mob atmosphere surrounding the hearings, taking the Fifth Amendment added to the prevailing sentiment that it was a crime to be a radical.

Nor was the Communist Party strong enough to wage a serious defense against the purge. The horrors of Stalinism finally led to an ideological crisis for communism internationally during this period, culminating in 1956 with Nikita Khrushchev's "secret speech" to the Twentieth Congress of the Russian Communist Party. In it, he detailed decades of Stalin's crimes, including the massacres of virtually all Bolsheviks who had taken part in the 1917 Russian Revolution, and labeled Stalin's self-glorification and distortion of history the "cult of the personality." The final straw occurred after Khrushchev's speech, when the Russian army invaded Hungary and crushed a workers' uprising there, leading to a mass exodus of long-standing party members. By 1957, the Communist Party had shrunk to less than ten thousand demoralized members, a skeleton of what it had been in the 1930s.[149]

Since the left did not stand together to fight McCarthyism, those victimized by HUAC were forced to choose between remaining silent and informing—the government's litmus test for "cooperation." The former meant risking prison and certainly losing one's jobs; the latter required witnesses to betray people they had worked alongside for many years. Navasky estimated that up to one-third of all those brought before HUAC from the entertainment industry turned over the names of those they suspected as Communist Party members. Some liberal celebrities, including respected filmmaker Elia Kazan, grabbed headlines when they became informers.[150]

Most witnesses, however, refused to cooperate, and some openly vented hostility toward their interrogators. Elizabeth Gurley Flynn refused to inform and made a courtroom speech in which she denounced "the motley array of bought and paid for informers, stool pigeons and renegades." Gurley Flynn was locked up five times between 1951 and 1955 for her defiance.[151] Black singer Paul Robeson told interrogators who asked why he did not go back to Russia, "Because my father was a slave, and my people died to build this country, and I'm going to stay here, and have a part of it just like you." Actor Lionel Stander offered to name "a group of fanatics who are desperately trying to undermine the constitution," referring, of course, to HUAC itself.[152]

Right-Wing Society

By its end, the McCarthy witch-hunt transformed U.S. society, from the heyday of the 1930s—when the self-confidence of the working class grew in leaps and bounds, and radical politics influenced a significant section of workers—to the right-wing paranoia of the 1950s. The anticommunist purge succeeded at excising the socialist tradition from inside the U.S. working-class movement. By 1957, more than two hundred thousand shop-floor union leaders had signed affidavits swearing that they did not belong to the Communist Party or believe in its ideals.[153] It is no exaggeration to say that the U.S. left was all but destroyed in the 1950s.

The broader political climate can be measured in a variety of ways. A 1954 opinion poll showed 80 percent of the population wanted to bar all communists from any rights of U.S. citizenship. But the hostility was directed at all radicals and to dissension as a whole: 45 percent were against allowing socialists to publish their own newspapers and 42 percent were in favor of banning criticism of the "American form of government" from the mainstream press. Another survey that year showed 20 percent of white Americans refused to say what country their ancestors came from.[154]

McCarthyism engendered widespread fear of political protest, in particular those regarding U.S. military interventions. As early as 1951, a Gallup poll showed 66 percent of Americans wanted U.S. troops to pull out of the Korean War. In 1952, 51 percent agreed that it was a "mistake" to intervene in Korea at all. Nevertheless, no movement materialized against the war, which killed roughly five million people—four million of them Korean civilians.[155]

The effects of McCarthyism long outlasted the career of Joe McCarthy. With the civil rights movement on the ascendancy in 1960, Harry Truman still felt comfortable declaring that "Communists" were behind the student sit-ins at Southern lunch counters. When civil rights leaders Martin Luther King, Jr., and Roy Wilkins demanded proof of this claim, Truman replied, "I know that usually when trouble hits the country the Kremlin is behind it." [156] It wasn't until 1967 that the U.S. Supreme Court finally ruled that forcing communist-affiliated organizations to register with the government was a violation of the Fifth Amendment of the Constitution.

In 1976, the ACLU formally reinstated Elizabeth Gurley Flynn, admitting that her 1940 expulsion "was not consonant with the basic principles on which the ACLU was founded." But Gurley Flynn had died in 1964.[157] In September 1997, the AFL-CIO finally removed its rule, in place since the McCarthy era, banning members of the Communist Party from holding union office. Shortly afterward, the Screen Actors Guild and the Directors Guild formally apologized to the scores of Hollywood actors, writers, and directors who were blacklisted during the McCarthy witch-hunt of the 1950s. But those who were witch-hunted out of Hollywood had lost their careers decades earlier. Most of the socialists who were targeted by McCarthyism were driven from political activity by the end of the 1950s. The McCarthy witch-hunt is the main reason why the socialist movement—which played such a central role in building industrial unions—remains marginalized five decades later.

As radical author Harvey Swados remarked in the 1950s, "Not only is Marx held posthumously accountable for all the crimes committed in his name or in the name of socialism—from the Stalinist slave-labor camps to the Socialist management of imperialist pacification in Algeria—but he is also charged with having failed to foresee that capitalism would be able to provide not less and less, but more and more and more of the good things of life for its proletariat." [158]

From the other side of the political spectrum, a top State Department official bragged in 1947, "While the rest of the world has moved to the left, has admitted labor into government, has passed liberalized legislation, the United States has become anti-social change, anti-economic change, anti-labor." The political climate, he commented, "is not moving to the right, it *has been moved*—cleverly—to the right." [159]

CHAPTER SIX

Social Contract?

The purge of radicals set the labor movement on a conservative course for decades to come. Some of the consequences were felt immediately; others would not become apparent until the end of the postwar economic boom.

Perhaps the most immediate consequence was labor's failure to organize the South. In 1946, the CIO launched its "Operation Dixie" Southern organizing campaign—dovetailing with the postwar strike wave then under way. Full of confidence, Philip Murray declared at the start of Operation Dixie, "You remember we started this [union] crusade in the North just ten years ago, and we are now going into the South. . . . Thank God we have an institution that can go into the South—the CIO."[1] The AFL followed the CIO southward, in hot pursuit of new members.

But neither federation succeeded in organizing the South. A 1951 Senate report showed that membership in the Textile Workers Union *fell* from 20 percent to 15 percent during this period. Although the unions pumped more than a million dollars into the campaign, the CIO lacked the political tools necessary for success. As Cochran wrote in 1959, "Ordinary trade union techniques could not break through the tangled skein of race hatreds, small town provincialism, backwoods prejudices, and the militant opposition of the government-employer alliance."[2]

Labor's unflinching support for the Democratic Party left it unable to confront the party's Southern segregationist wing. Moreover, Taft-Hartley's 1947 assault on workers' rights allowed Southern states to outlaw the union shop and the use of mass picketing—

under the guise of defending nonunion workers' "right to work." Only a confrontation with Southern white supremacy could have paved the way for organizing success. Instead, the CIO concentrated its efforts on the nearly all-white textile industry, using a staff of two hundred organizers who were also overwhelmingly white. These organizers were screened ahead of time to weed out radicals and instructed to avoid any racial or social controversies that would antagonize mill owners. The campaign aimed to focus only on "bread and butter" issues and organizers maintained a disciplined silence even when bigots and anti-Semites embarked on a campaign of slander—from billboards to newspaper ads.

It would be mistaken, however, to assume that Southern white workers were incapable of embracing unionism. Southern whites had joined Blacks in migrating to Northern industrial centers in the 1930s—and there, as Cochran noted, "when thrust into the environment of modern industry in the North, became . . . one of the mainstays of the CIO uprising in Detroit, Flint, Akron." [3]

Operation Dixie marked the last major effort by the labor movement to organize the low-wage, nonunion South. Its failure effectively precluded a national breakthrough for organized labor to win a majority of workers into its ranks. As Lichtenstein commented,

> The failure of Operation Dixie ensured that the political weight of an essentially undemocratic Southern polity would continue to inject a distorting "Prussian element" into American statecraft. Even as union densities rose to European levels in the late 1940s, an alliance of Republicans and Dixiecrats in Congress vetoed union-Democratic Party efforts to bolster the American welfare state or defend the Wagner-era labor relations regime. And because of the vital role the South still played in national Democratic Party politics, even those liberals elected from solidly pro-labor constituencies were drawn into compromise and coalition with the right.[4]

From McCarthy to Landrum-Griffin

Following closely on the heels of the McCarthy witch-hunt in the 1950s, Congress took aim at noncommunist union leaders. Indeed, one of its first targets was Teamsters president Dave Beck, an honorary member of the American Legion. Beck's Labor Day statement in 1953 read, in part,

If labor and management could rid themselves of old-fashioned—
actually Marxian—notions that they are forever locked in bitter
opposition . . . then our country would soar to new heights of accom-
plishment. The key to this magnificent future is not industrial peace,
which implies a compact between two warring factions, but industrial
fellowship, based on common understanding for a common goal.[5]

In 1957, the Senate formed a Select Committee on Improper
Activities in the Labor and Management Field, justified as a government effort to "clean up" union corruption and racketeering.
Chaired by Arkansas Senator Robert McClellan, the committee's
majority was composed of senators from "right to work" states,
while liberal Massachussetts attorney Robert F. Kennedy served as
its counsel.

As the committee's televised hearings in 1957 scrutinized the underworld activities of Beck (who led the union from 1952 to 1957)
and Jimmy Hoffa (who succeeded Beck in 1957), public support
for unions plummeted. Opinion polls showed popular approval of
unions standing at 76 percent before the hearings, falling to below
64 percent immediately afterward and to 56 percent several years
later.[6] The now-united AFL-CIO expelled the Teamsters union in
1957, after conducting its own internal hearings that emulated those
of the Senate.

Riding the wave of declining union sentiment, Congress passed
the Labor-Management Reporting and Disclosure Act—also known
as the Landrum-Griffin Act—in 1959. Among its provisions, the act
allowed the U.S. Department of Labor to directly oversee the financial records of unions. In addition, Landrum-Griffin expanded Taft-
Hartley's definition of secondary boycotts to bar any union from
taking solidarity action with another union on strike—a provision
with no connection to combating union corruption.[7]

For its part, the IBT—and its corrupt leadership—continued
to prosper even after the union was expelled from the labor federation. By 1969, the IBT was the nation's largest union, with
more than two million members. The Teamsters, alongside a number of other former AFL unions, continued to enjoy friendly relations with prominent Republicans throughout this period. Even
after Hoffa was sent to prison in 1967, the Teamsters remained
mired in corruption for many years to come. It is also worth noting that only a fine line separated respectable union officials from

their underworld counterparts. As historian Daniel Guérin argued of the "exorbitant salaries" and "well-heeled lifestyles" of American trade union leaders, "[T]he lifestyle of 'honest' labor leaders bears a strange resemblance to that of the corrupt leaders. . . . [I]n the United States, expense accounts for trade-union officials are so commonplace that none of them could be accused of 'immoral earnings' merely by reference to these 'extras.'"[8]

Landrum-Griffin meanwhile destroyed whatever rank-and-file organization and consciousness—on a class-wide basis—that remained after the McCarthy witch-hunts. As Nicholson described,

> Popular democratic vitality nearly disappeared from union leadership. The rank and file stopped singing at union meetings. Class conflict and worker consciousness were replaced by civic responsibility and patriotic loyalty. Cold War patriotism and good citizenship gave union workers clear benefits as their former identity dissolved and was replaced by a suburban middle-class imagined unity with employers.[9]

Labor Racketeering

The Landrum-Griffin Act had little impact on the racketeering and corruption that had plagued sections of the labor movement since its inception. Labor unions' first foray into the mob underworld was in answer to employers' picket line violence. If the employers hired private armies, unions that were able to hired street thugs in defense and appointed them as union officials. Labor corruption thus began with "the early full-time officials who were labor's answer to the violent employer offensive following the Haymarket Affair of 1886," according to left historian Dennis Anderson.[10]

In addition, craft unionism could easily lend itself to financial "cooperation" with employers, as union leaders sought to establish union dominance in a particular trade. In return, employers could ask for an agreement not to strike. In this way, bribery entered into management-labor relations in the early twentieth century building trades.[11] Racketeering was virtually exclusive to AFL unions and all but absent in the CIO before the two organizations merged in 1955. The typical corrupt union leader, Anderson described,

> worked at his trade, became a full-time official, and followed the lure of the dollar rather than the call of working-class solidarity—often with the daring of the robber barons who were spawned by the same grow-

ing capitalist system. In the 1920s, outsiders began to discover the material advantages offered by the business of labor. Gangsters, brought in originally as mercenaries for the combatants of industrial warfare, gained control of some of the unions that employed them. By the early 1930s, organized crime had successfully infiltrated important segments of the big city labor movement. Alongside the individual corruption of the home-grown labor racketeer was erected an apparatus which could systematically channelize profits to the underworld.[12]

In a striking illustration, the era of Prohibition between 1919 and 1933 created an entire underworld industry of alcoholic beverages, involving the Teamsters and, not surprisingly, the AFL's Distillery Workers. The Eighteenth Amendment, passed in 1919, banned the manufacture, sale, and transportation of alcohol within U.S. borders (in an interesting addition to the antiradical labor legislation that swept the nation after World War I). Trucks carrying alcohol became part of an enormous network involving unions, organized crime, and the paid-off judges, politicians, and law-enforcement officers who agreed to look the other way.

Hoffa and Beck were able to build their own personal fiefdoms under similar sets of arrangements. Hoffa created a truck-leasing company, whose stockholders consisted only of Mrs. James Hoffa and Mrs. Bert Brennan (wife of another Teamster official), earning them $125,000 between 1949 and 1956. Among Hoffa's other dubious dealings was arranging for the insurance carrier for the IBT's welfare fund to fall into the hands of close acquaintance—and mob racketeer—Paul Dorfman.[13]

Beck was unapologetic about making money on the side, arguing that his business relationships benefited the union's membership. He had no interest in promoting labor solidarity and was proud to admit that, under his leadership, "Teamsters went through picket lines many times."[14] Hoffa shared Beck's values but was far more beloved by rank-and-file Teamsters. He owned no swimming pool and refused to wear flashy clothes. More importantly, he negotiated significant wage increases and spearheaded the establishment of a national freight contract, the National Master Freight Agreement, covering four hundred thousand workers, in the decentralized trucking industry in 1964.[15]

The Triumph of Business Unionism

The anticommunist purges gave way to a more lasting political conservatism on the part of CIO leaders, and laid the basis for the victory of business unionism in the postwar era. As Nelson Lichtenstein argued in *Labor's War at Home: The CIO in World War II,*

> [T]he expulsion of the Communist unions narrowed drastically the limits of internal political life within the union movement. As we have seen, the institutional pressures creating a bureaucratic style of union leadership had been powerfully advanced by support from the state's labor relations apparatus during the war. By accepting the discipline of the Cold War mobilization, the industrial unions themselves advanced this process by identifying industrial radicalism with political subversion. Even in the UAW ... the purge of Communists undermined the legitimacy of all opposition groups, Communist and anti-Stalinist alike, and inaugurated the reign of a one-party regime that co-opted or suppressed potential rivals.[16]

The consequences were felt immediately inside the UAW, perhaps the most dynamic and activist union in the 1930s. Reuther had risen from the UAW ranks as an active (socialist) leader of the1930s class struggle. But in securing the union's presidency, he crushed all left-wing opposition.

Until 1948 the standard UAW contract lasted only one year. In 1948, the UAW agreed to the employers' demand for a two-year contract. In 1950, Reuther negotiated unprecedented five-year contracts with General Motors, Ford, and Chrysler. The contracts contained agreements that wages would rise as long as productivity increased by a specified amount. But as Art Preis points out, "Since General Motors had already intensified the speed-up in its plants, this alone would have insured a rate of productivity increase annually greater than the rate of wage increases." In return, workers gave up the right to strike for the duration of the contract.[17] It is no wonder that *Business Week* applauded the five-year auto contract, arguing that after five years of enforced labor peace, the workers "will almost forget they are union men." [18] As Cochran commented,

> In the course of a few years the UAW was transformed from an insurgent, membership-participatory, bellicose union into a progressive, efficiently run, machine-controlled union that traded off long-term contracts, management prerogatives, and stable relations for economic benefits like an annual improvement factor, a cost-of-living escalator

clause (actually proposed initially by General Motors management), supplemented unemployment benefits, and pension benefits.[19]

The AFL and CIO Reunite

The 1955 AFL-CIO merger symbolized the triumph of business unionism in the U.S. With no clear principles left to divide them by the 1950s, it was almost inevitable that the AFL and CIO would reunite in a common union federation. The AFL dominated the new leadership, since the AFL entered the merger with a membership more than double the size of the CIO. AFL president George Meany (who had succeeded William Green) assumed the presidency, while Reuther became vice president.

Meany served as president of the AFL-CIO for its first twenty-four years. His qualifications as a labor leader were obvious only to employers. In a 1958 speech to the National Association of Manufacturers (NAM), Meany stated,

> I never went on strike in my life, never ran a strike in my life, never had anything to do with a picket line. . . . In the final analysis, there is not a great deal of difference between the things I stand for and the things that NAM leaders stand for. I stand for the profit system; I believe in the profit system. I believe it's a wonderful incentive. I believe in the free enterprise system completely.[20]

Elsewhere, Meany summed up the political philosophy that would guide the AFL-CIO: "To be frank, we American trade unionists like the capitalist system. Naturally we well intend to preserve it in our efforts aimed at bettering the standard of living of the workers by improving the system itself. But we do not intend to abandon it for some pipe-dreams or some ideological fantasies invented by those who do not understand the workers' real needs and aspirations."[21] Under Meany's leadership union membership in the U.S. began its steady decline. When confronted with this problem, however, he remarked dismissively, "it doesn't make any difference."[22]

The AFL-CIO functioned as a loyal servant of U.S. imperialism after the merger. Both the AFL and CIO had established a relationship with the CIA and the State Department after the war. These relationships flourished under the new federation. The AFL-CIO willingly provided union "cover" to CIA operations enabling many a military junta. By 1985, the AFL-CIO had helped to set up and sustain anticommunist unions in eighty-three different countries, mainly in Asia, Africa, and Latin America, with a budget of $43 million—90 percent of it financed by the U.S. government.[23] As Cochran argued, this

> initiated a three-way partnership with the State Department and major United States corporations for the purpose of setting up the American Institute for Free Labor Development (directed at Latin America), the Asian-American Free Labor Institute, and the African-American Labor Center. All these, financed by United States government agencies except for nominal and largely cosmetic contributions by the two other partners, were "an exercise in trade union colonialism," as Victor Reuther would call it later.[24]

Walter Reuther, Cold War Liberal

Reuther served as AFL-CIO vice president, leading the federation's liberal wing until he died in a plane crash in 1970. But liberalism was a relative phenomenon in the Cold War era—since liberals remained part of the anticommunist coalition, itself beholden to the segregationist, antiunion South. Reuther's politics were inconsistent at best.

While agreeing to a 1948 contract with GM, Reuther took a defiant posture, declaring, "General Motors workers cannot be bribed with the wooden nickels of inflation into withdrawing from the fight against the greedy industrialists and subservient politicians who caused and condoned the price rises which are now undermining the living standards of millions."[25] Yet Reuther sounded much like Meany when he told the *New York Times* on March 28, 1958, "[W]e don't believe in the class struggle. The labor movement in America has never believed in the class struggle."[26]

Reuther was among the few union leaders to voice support for civil rights and to march in civil rights demonstrations in the early 1960s. Meany refused to authorize AFL-CIO endorsement for the 1963 March on Washington, and Reuther was the only white labor leader to join Martin Luther King, Jr., at the front of the march. But Reuther was far less supportive of the delegation from the Mississippi Freedom Democratic Party (MFDP), which demanded to be seated at the party's 1964 convention in a direct challenge to Dixiecrats.

Reuther joined King in supporting President Lyndon Johnson's "compromise," offering the Black delegation just two seats—to be chosen by the national party, not the MFDP. Rejecting the compromise, MFDP leader Fannie Lou Hamer responded eloquently, "We didn't come all this way for no two seats."[27] As historian Peter B. Levy described in *The New Left and Labor in the 1960s,* "almost all the participants in the Mississippi project saw Reuther's actions as contemptible."[28] Later, Reuther was openly hostile to the rise of the Black Power movement when it appeared inside the UAW in 1968, in the form of the Dodge Revolutionary Movement (DRUM). He denounced DRUM leaders as "extremists" and "terrorists."[29]

Reuther and the UAW played a role in launching the New Left of the 1960s. In the early 1960s, the UAW provided thousands of dollars to the League for Industrial Democracy, which gave birth to Students for a Democratic Society (SDS). The AFL-CIO offered up printing services and meeting halls to the young organization. SDS leaders wrote their 1962 Port Huron Statement at the UAW's summer retreat. Reuther himself lauded SDS as "the vanguard student organization dedicated to the forces of progress in America."[30] Reuther also voiced support for women's rights, and in 1970 the UAW endorsed the Equal Rights Amendment (ERA) to establish legal equality for women. Soon after, the UAW created the Network of Economic Rights, to join feminists in lobbying for passage of the ERA.[31]

But friction between the New Left and organized labor grew as the war in Vietnam progressed. Student activists protested at the AFL-CIO's 1965 convention, chanting, "Get out of Vietnam!" while delegates shouted back, "Get a haircut." Pounding his gavel, Meany instructed underlings to "clear these Kookies out of the gallery." After the students were ejected, Reuther joined in the round of denunciations, declaring, "protesters should be demonstrating against Hanoi and Peking . . . [who] are responsible for the war." The convention then passed the following resolution: "The labor movement proclaim[s] to the world that the nation's working men and women do support the Johnson administration in Vietnam."[32]

While King denounced the war in Vietnam in 1967, Reuther continued to support the war until shortly before his death. After Nixon invaded Cambodia in 1970, Reuther joined other union leaders in finally speaking out. These leaders were undoubtedly emboldened after the 1968 election, when Republican President Richard Nixon took charge of the war that had been escalated by his Democratic predecessor, Lyndon B. Johnson. Reuther urged Nixon, "We must mobilize for peace rather than wider theaters of war."[33]

The "American Dream"

"What's good for General Motors is good for America" is the slogan that was emblematic of the promise of the American Dream of the 1950s and 1960s. The prosperous postwar era, coinciding with Cold War ideology, fit neatly with the global aspirations of the U.S. ruling class in promoting the economic opportunities for workers in the "free world." During this same period, the superpower status of the United States allowed American capital to experience an unprecedented economic boom and to offer workers steadily rising wages through the 1950s and early 1960s.

During this period, income inequality declined significantly. Tax rates rose to 91 percent for those in the highest income bracket. The minimum wage rose as fast as, and sometimes faster than, inflation rates. Tax breaks for suburban homeowners and veterans' programs made home ownership possible for millions of working-class families for the first time. During the postwar period, more than 70 percent of whites were able to afford their own homes.[34]

Thus, during the same period in which the United States rose as the world's dominant power, its workers achieved wages and living standards that were the highest in the world. Many of that era's intellectuals concluded that the American Dream would prevent the reemergence of class struggle in the United States. Sociologist Daniel Bell, who expounded on this theme repeatedly during this period, argued in 1956, "Few autoworkers today have a future beyond their job. Few have a chance of social advancement. But they are not radical. . . . A worker sees himself as 'getting ahead' . . . because he is working toward a 'nice little modern house.'"[35]

Bell was not entirely off the mark in his observations. Indeed, popular culture in the 1950s centered on consumption—as more American workers used credit to purchase cars, televisions, and a steady stream of modern new gadgets churned out by entirely new industries. Families gathered around the television nightly to watch corporate-sponsored shows such as "Westinghouse Playhouse" and "The U.S. Steel Hour." As Cochran commented at the time, "There is much validity to Bell's thesis: if we take the present social climate as unchangeable, unions are not going to make any noteworthy advances. . . . A political and social shift has to pave the way for organization."[36]

A 1946 photo spread in *Life* magazine laid out a "roseate and wondrous" American Dream, accompanied by pictures of what it called a "family utopia"—complete with a brand new suburban home, a white picket fence, a convertible car, a television set, lawn furniture, and a swing set for the kids. Dangling such comforts before a generation of Depression-era working-class people—at the very same time that the left was being crushed by McCarthyism—ensured the idea's success.

The notion of an American Dream was just one part of U.S. capital's postwar ideological offensive—the flip side of the anticommunist coin. Employers were motivated not by generosity toward working-class people but by a desire to maximize their own profits. This required them to seek a way to prevent workers from engaging in regular work stoppages, with the strike weapon still very much in evidence during the immediate postwar years. In 1951 the editors of *Fortune* magazine congratulated U.S. capital in finding a uniquely "American" solution to the "problems of class struggle and proletarian consciousness."[37]

The American Dream was clearly something to which vast numbers of workers aspired, demonstrated by the large number of Americans who considered themselves middle class. In 1964, 44 percent of respondents to a survey saw themselves as middle class or higher, compared with 37 percent in 1952.[38] As Nicholson commented, "Nonwhites or immigrants were thought to belong to the 'working class,' or, more commonly, the 'lower class.' Class consciousness was based on what people thought or bought, not on what they objectively were."[39]

Average weekly earnings for U.S. manufacturing workers rose by 84 percent between 1950 and 1965, while prices rose by only 31 percent during the same period.[40] But while the relative affluence of the U.S. working class is undeniable, it was by no means uniform. Even in 1959 more than one in five people lived below the official poverty line.[41] Wages for unorganized workers rose far more slowly than for those in unions, and the significant gap between Black and white incomes remained. Throughout the 1950s and 1960s, the median income of Black Americans still hovered at about 55 percent of whites. Even in Detroit, the center for world auto production, the median Black family income was only two-thirds that of white families in 1954.[42]

Even for those workers whose living standards did not rise, however, their aspirations did—particularly their hopes that their children might escape from the working class into a middle-class occupation. The rise of community colleges and subsidized tuition made college education an attainable goal for millions of working-class children.

Labor Relations in the New Era of Postwar Prosperity

Unionized industrial workers in particular experienced dramatic improvements in their living standards, but they paid the price of a drastic rise in the rate of exploitation. Output per worker more than doubled between 1947 and 1967.[43] Corporations were willing to grant workers higher wages in order to preempt or shorten strikes and other interruptions in production during the long boom.

But the employers did not rely entirely on rising wages to ensure labor peace. Corporations spent large amounts of money on union-busting firms, to stop the spread of union membership—which still rose by 25 percent between 1945 and 1955.[44] Companies such as Sears, Blue Cross, All-State Insurance, American Express, Macy's, and United Parcel Service all invested in the union-busting firm of Labor Relations Associates of Chicago, one of the biggest union-busting companies at the time.[45] And employers did not hesitate to use violence against workers during the 1950s. For example, a September 8, 1953, *New York Times* story on a coal strike reported, "Eight organizers have been shot, one of them died, another is completely paralyzed. Cars have been dynamited, and union meeting places, members' homes and friendly merchants' stores have been blasted or fired upon. The union and its local leaders have been sued, indicted or even jailed." [46]

Still, corporations were not entirely successful at winning labor peace, even among the best-paid union members. Even at the height of the boom years, steelworkers struck for forty-five days in 1949, fifty-nine days in 1952, thirty-six days in 1956, and one hundred and ten days during a bitter battle in the recession of 1959. In 1957, a rank-and-file slate challenged union leaders' "tuxedo unionism" and demanded more democracy within the United Steel Workers of America (USWA).[47]

Although negotiated and lengthy agreements were hailed as proof of labor-management collaboration, labor relations were far from amicable in the auto industry during the 1950s and 1960s. The five-year contract negotiated in 1950 deprived workers of the right to stop production over grievances. The right to strike had been a key weapon of union militants in settling shop floor grievances. Without it, the grievance procedure turned into a bureaucratic nightmare: grievances were left unresolved for long periods of time by an increasingly remote union leadership. Frustrations erupted in periodic wildcat strikes during this entire period—so much so that Reuther was forced to shorten the length of the contract to three years in 1955 and even to authorize occasional local strikes over working conditions. As historian and labor activist Stan Weir described the situation in 1967:

> The General Motors Corporation employs as many workers as all other auto manufacturers combined. In 1955, UAW president Walter Reuther signed a contract with GM which did not check the speedup or speed the settlement of local shop grievances. Over 70 percent of GM workers went on strike immediately after Reuther announced the terms of his agreement. A larger percentage "wildcatted" after signing the 1958 contract because Reuther had again refused to do anything to combat speedup. For the same reason the autoworkers walked off their jobs again in 1961. The strike closed every GM and a number of large Ford plants.[48]

The number of strikes across all U.S. industries in the 1950s was only slightly lower than during the strike wave that marked the second half of the 1940s. But strikes tended to be shorter and involve fewer workers in the 1950s—and still fewer in the first half of the 1960s.[49] The resolve that typified early CIO picket lines was gradually replaced by passivity, as workers became accustomed to waiting out strikes, rather than playing any meaningful role. This was bound to have an effect on the class consciousness of white workers, who formed a politically conservative bloc, with little sympathy for either the civil rights movement or the antiwar movement until the late 1960s.

The Bloated Union Bureaucracy

In January 1946, Henry Ford II declared, "We of the Ford Motor Company have no desire to 'break the unions,' or to turn back the

clock," adding, "we must look to an improved and increasingly responsible [union] leadership for help in solving the human equation
in mass production." [50]

There was no shortage of "responsible" union leaders to help
Ford achieve his goal. The labor movement during this era increasingly relied on the legal expertise of its enormous professional staff,
rather than on shop-floor activism, to enforce contracts. In the mid-
1950s, B. J. Widick, a shop steward at Chrysler, commented, "[O]ur
contracts are becoming such legalistic documents as to be unwork-
able in terms of real, genuine labor relations. . . . In the old days, he
[the steward] was the Union, he was the Contract. . . . Now he is a
Philadelphia lawyer. It's embarrassing." [51]

As Lichtenstein noted, American unions grew to employ

> the largest and best-paid stratum of full-time salaried officers in the
> labor-movement world. . . . Functionary worker ratios in the United
> States were something like one in three hundred at the end of the 1950s,
> while the European average was about one full-time officeholder per
> two thousand unionists. The U.S. had sixty thousand full-time union
> officers in 1960, compared to just four thousand in Great Britain. [52]

This expansive bureaucracy developed in part because of the
vastly different political course taken by the United States and Europe after the Second World War. In Social Democratic Europe,
the government administered medical care and other government-
subsidized social programs, whereas in the United States social welfare was largely confined to privatized "fringe benefits," available
only to workers whose employers provided them. Lichtenstein correctly states, American unions "were burdened with a set of servic-
ing functions unknown in countries where either a labor party or a
stronger welfare state assumed those responsibilities." [53]

He continued, "Many unions in the United States . . . were responsible for the negotiation and administration not just of wage
schedules and seniority systems, but of pension benefits, health insurance, and various kinds of supplemental unemployment aid. In
addition, unions at the local, regional, and national levels directly
lobbied state and national officeholders, endorsed candidates, and
raised money and troops for their campaigns." [54]

This statement is true, but it is also worth exploring how much
of this situation was of labor's own making. America's union bu-

reaucracy is not qualitatively different from those in Europe or else-where. The job of full-time union officials is to negotiate settlements with employers that will satisfy both bosses and workers. Union of-ficials' own jobs do not depend on the contracts they sign since they are paid through union funds, and they do not directly experience the consequences of poor contracts on the shop floor.

Nevertheless, since Gompers, the U.S. labor officialdom has had an exaggerated tendency to steer toward collaboration and away from confrontation. The period after the Second World War proved decisive for the American labor movement. By choosing a course of collaboration rather than class struggle, union leaders relied in-creasingly on a professional staff far removed from the pressures of, or accountability to, rank-and-file workers. The sheer size of labor's apparatus has had long-standing consequences for the U.S. labor movement. Elected shop floor militants dominated CIO union conventions during the heyday of the 1930s. But in the age of an increasingly entrenched bureaucracy, the presence of a small army of loyal staffers gave the existing leadership an in-built advantage in voting and elections.

In addition, labor's reliance on friendly relationships with gov-ernment decision-makers required unions to devote substantial financial and staff resources to election campaigns and lobbying ef-forts. To this end, the AFL-CIO developed an elaborate network of PACs, COPEs (Committees on Political Education), and lobbyists. But even when Democrats dominated Congress and held the White House between 1961 and 1969, the labor movement won no signif-icant pro-labor legislation that could reverse the overriding down-ward trend.[55]

The Price Paid by Workers

If aspirations for creating a labor party had been defeated by the end of the 1930s, then any hopes for the development of a genuine welfare state disappeared by the 1950s. During the immediate af-termath of the Second World War, Lichtenstein wrote, "[T]he trade unions hoped that as in Britain the social solidarity generated by the wartime experience would give rise to a universal system of health insurance and higher social-security benefits."[56] Such a develop-ment was not forthcoming, however. American employers instead went on the attack with Taft-Hartley by 1947. Universal health care could not be won without a massive social struggle.

Rather than insisting that health and welfare benefits should be the right of every individual, unions increasingly accepted that these should be relegated to the arena of collective bargaining. The biggest and most powerful unions—in auto, steel, rubber, trucking, and mining—led the way. In 1946, the first health and welfare benefits were included in union contracts. In 1949, the first retirement pensions were negotiated.

By 1970, 90 percent of all unionized workers were covered by a health plan of some kind.[57] But even at the high point of the mid-1970s, just two-thirds of U.S. workers had health insurance, provided mainly by their employers.[58] Because there was no welfare state, an enormous disparity thus existed between union and non-union workers, since the poorest workers often had few or no health or other "fringe benefits." This significant minority of the population without health care undoubtedly impacted the willingness to struggle among those workers fortunate enough to land a job with an employer that offered coverage.

The problems with this arrangement were not apparent at the time, since the postwar economic boom allowed wages and benefits to rise steadily. By all appearances, workers were making great strides forward during this period. But, as Lichtenstein argued,

> Indeed, if such [a labor-management] accord could be said to exist during these years, it was less a mutually satisfactory concordat than a dictate imposed upon an all-too-reluctant labor movement in an era of its political retreat and internal division. At best it was a limited and unstable truce, largely confined to a well-defined set of regions and industries. It was a product of defeat, not victory.[59]

While other industrial societies, including Canada, recognized health care as a basic right, medical insurance has been firmly established as a privilege of employment in the United States since the 1950s. And that which corporations give can easily be taken away, as U.S. workers learned quite dramatically once the postwar boom came to an end in the 1970s and employers began attacking health and pension benefits, along with wages. The fact that U.S. workers had never won the right to even the most minimal national health care made it that much easier for corporations to leave millions more working-class people with no benefits.

In the long run, business unionism marked a decisive step backward, as union leaders agreed to whittle away workers' basic rights in return for better pay. The AFL-CIO merger marked the end of the era in which the U.S. working class had shown its willingness to struggle and had shown its power—and even its revolutionary potential.

The Social Consequences of Reaction

The era of the American Dream was hardly the idyllic period that the mass media typically depicts. The political repression of McCarthyism was accompanied by extreme social repression on every front. Indeed, one of the many "un-American" activities included in the anticommunist witch-hunt was homosexuality. In 1950, the Senate began investigating alleged homosexuals "and other perverts" in federal jobs. The Senate justified this investigation on the basis of national security: its report stated that gays "lack the emotional stability of normal persons"; "sex perversion weakens the individual"; and "espionage agents could blackmail them." President Eisenhower issued an executive order calling for the dismissal of homosexuals from government service. Two thousand gay people lost federal jobs every year during the 1950s; the figure rose to three thousand or more per year into the 1960s.[60]

African-Americans were systematically shut out of partaking in the American Dream. Racist segregation exposed the pretense that the new prosperity was meant to include Black people. Jim Crow segregation in the South had its counterpart in de facto segregation in the North. Even if African Americans could afford a new home in the suburbs, racists (usually with the support of the local police) would organize to violently bar them from or force them out of most suburban neighborhoods. These racists had the law on their side. As Nicholson noted, "Racial segregation in the booming suburbs was underwritten by the Federal Housing Administration and Veteran's Administration, the two most important federal mortgage insurance firms. The federal courts allowed racially exclusive covenants in titles to new homes in securing all-white suburbs."[61]

Three million African Americans left farm work in the South and migrated to the ten largest industrial cities in the Midwestern "rust belt" between 1940 and 1960 in the hopes of finding well-

paying industrial jobs. By 1962, roughly 70 percent of Black workers were employed in blue collar and service work, but the vast
majority remained stuck in unskilled or semi-skilled jobs. Nearly
two-thirds of all Northern Blacks found themselves living in urban
slums.[62] Black children still could not attend schools alongside white
children. These are the most important reasons why the civil rights
movement grew with urgency in the 1950s, accelerating after the Supreme Court's 1954 *Brown v. Board of Education of Topeka* ruling,
finally striking down the "constitutionality" of school segregation.

The labor movement at best, however, paid only lip service in
support of Black activists battling against segregation in Birmingham, Alabama, and Little Rock, Arkansas. Cochran commented in
1959,

> The pious pronouncements have been placed on record, but the unions
> have kept clear of actual involvement. In his current battle to break
> the age-old shackles in the South, the Negro, for a variety of reasons,
> is getting powerful support from the federal judiciary, but he cannot
> count on support, beyond some verbal encouragement, from the labor
> movement. This is a tragic turn of events, since it means that labor is
> again missing the Southern bus. . . . The result is that labor is on the
> sidelines in this historic crisis.[63]

Images of happy white families living in all-white suburbs on
such television shows as *Ozzie and Harriet* and *Leave It to Bea-
ver* dominated popular culture throughout this era. These shows
demonstrated not only the degree of extreme racism that characterized the 1950s, but also the heightened women's oppression that
accompanied it. According to 1950s mores, women should follow
June Cleaver, cheerfully burying themselves in housework while
their husbands drove off to their well-paying jobs.

According to Betty Friedan, the "spic-n-span" cleaning standards of the 1950s meant that in the typical household, the sheets
on the beds were washed two times per week.[64] Alongside the image
of the family-oriented housewife dangled the image of the blonde
buxom bimbo as the object of male sexual desire. Friedan claims
that three out of every ten women bleached their hair blonde in the
1950s and that, between 1939 and 1960, women's average dress
sizes became three or four sizes smaller. "Women are out to fit the
clothes, not vice versa," one buyer explained.[65]

The ideal housewife during the 1950s was expected to devote her life to pleasing her husband and family. In 1956, the following passage from *The Bride's Reference Book* admonished working wives,

> From the day you say "I do," your home and your husband come first. . . . From the practical, human point of view, do not expect your husband to accept cheerfully a slap-dash sort of housekeeping system such as you may have done fairly well with as a bachelor business girl. He may have found it amusing during courtship, but he is not going to think it is funny any more for you to arrive home breathless at 7:30 with the last minute groceries on your arm.[66]

The 1960s Radicalization

The revival of radicalism in the 1960s, not surprisingly, included an explosion of anger against the extreme ideological and social repression of the 1950s. Indeed, the late 1960s and 1970s was a period of social upheaval, witnessing a mass antiwar movement, the rise of the Black Power movement, and the women's liberation and gay liberation movements. But this revival took place largely outside the arena of organized labor and without a clear sense of class politics. Again, the reasons can be traced to McCarthyism. As Lichtenstein observed, "the elimination of the Communists from so much of American political life diminished the role to which the issues of class and union power would play in the emergence of the Civil Rights Movement and the New Left little more than a decade later."[67]

The New Left peaked in the late 1960s among a new generation of students who had been radicalized by the civil rights and antiwar movements. In spite of the role that the UAW and other unions played in helping to launch SDS in the early 1960s, animosity between the student movement and organized labor grew over the war in Vietnam—evidenced by the shouting match at the 1965 AFL-CIO convention.

Many workers harbored deep resentment toward student radicals. Some of this resentment was based on the overwhelmingly working-class composition of the troops drafted to fight in Vietnam. Working-class high schools sent 20 to 30 percent of their graduates to Vietnam every year. In contrast, college graduates made up just 2 percent of all troops sent to Vietnam in 1965 and 1966. Out of the twelve hundred students who graduated from Harvard Uni-

versity in 1970, only *two* went to Vietnam.[68] Hence, the denunci-
ation of campus antiwar activists as "draft-dodgers" was as often
based on class anger as support for the war. Many workers shared
the views of the so-called "silent majority" and negatively associated
student radicals with drug use, promiscuity, and other aspects of an
alien "youth counterculture."[69]

"Hard-hats" versus "Longhairs"

Hostility between the unionists and the antiwar movement was sym-
bolically captured by the May 8, 1970, rampage of two hundred
New York City construction workers against peaceful antiwar protesters, in which the "hardhats" brutally beat hundreds of "long-
hairs" while chanting "Love it or leave it!" A few days later, two
thousand construction workers and longshoremen marched in New
York in support of the war, carrying signs such as, "Don't worry,
they don't draft faggots."

These labor protests were not "spontaneous" outpourings of
pro-war anger as the media depicted, but had been instigated by contractors, some of whom reportedly offered cash bonuses to workers
who participated.[70] There is also evidence, as Levy noted, "that a
right-wing organization with business funding helped organize the
assault in the first place." But on May 20, 1970, labor unions joined
in the pro-war frenzy when New York City's Building Trades Council president Peter Brennan sponsored a demonstration in support
of Nixon's invasion of Cambodia that drew a flag-waving crowd
of between sixty thousand and one hundred thousand. Nixon soon
rewarded Brennan by appointing him Secretary of Labor.[71]

After this demonstration, SDS activist Cliff Sloan commented
in disgust, "If this is what the class struggle is all about . . . there is
something wrong here."[72] Sloan's opinion was shared by the bulk of
1960s student radicals. Most of those in SDS, inspired by the insurgency of the National Liberation Front in Vietnam, looked primarily
to the Third World for revolutionary struggle and regarded the U.S.
working class as "bought off." This sentiment had been deepened by
revelations by Victor Reuther (brother of Walter) that exposed the
AFL-CIO's long-standing participation in CIA covert operations.[73]

With few exceptions, New Left radicals regarded the working class in the heart of the imperialist beast as a [big] part of the

problem, and they looked elsewhere for allies.[74] The bulk of student radicals joined Maoist and Stalinist organizations, which took inspiration from nationalist movements in the Third World. Although the Maoist left numbered in the thousands in the early 1970s, it quickly disintegrated along with the Maoist left internationally by the decade's end.[75] Nixon's visit to China in 1972, Mao's death in 1976, and a change in policies launched by his successors all contributed to the disillusionment of a generation of radicals. The decline of Maoism was also a symptom of a more generalized retreat and decline of the organized left internationally during this period.

The Soldiers' Revolt

By the late 1960s, the growing rebellion among antiwar troops helped to transform the class character of the antiwar movement. Although the mass media depicted peace activists spitting on returning Vietnam vets, in actuality, troops were welcomed into the folds of the antiwar movement.[76] Vets marched in antiwar demonstrations, soldiers published antiwar newspapers from their military bases, and together they played a central role in shaping the politics of the antiwar movement, stateside and in Vietnam itself.

By 1971, Vietnam Veterans Against the War (VVAW) was at the forefront of antiwar struggle at home. VVAW's membership was predominantly working class—half coming from manual labor backgrounds and just 30 percent from professional or managerial families. The emergence of this organized opposition among vets helped to challenge the media's caricature of antiwar activists as frivolous middle-class rebels.[77] From April 19 to 23, 1971, two thousand Vietnam veterans sat in at the Supreme Court to protest the war, demanding that Congress enact an immediate and unconditional withdrawal of all U.S. forces from Indochina. When hundreds of vets ceremoniously discarded their war medals, ex-Marine sergeant Jack Smith apologized to the Vietnamese people, "whose hearts were broken, not won" because of "genocide, racism, and atrocity."[78]

The year 1968 marked a turning point in the war in Vietnam, when North Vietnamese forces launched the Tet Offensive in January, demonstrating that a decisive victory for U.S. forces was impossible. In Vietnam, soldiers refused combat orders sixty-eight times that year. By 1970, the number rose to thirty-five in the 1st Air Cavalry Division alone. During this same period, rebellious U.S. troops began "fragging" their commanding officers with grenades—with an estimated eight hundred to a thousand attempts to kill commanding officers on record. Veteran antiwar activist Joel Geier described, "Mutiny and fraggings expressed the anger and bitterness that combat soldiers felt at being used as bait to kill Communists. It forced the troops to reassess who was the real enemy." [79] As Geier wrote,

> An observer at Pace, near the Cambodian front where a unilateral truce was widely enforced, reported, "The men agreed and passed the word to other platoons: nobody fires unless fired upon. As of about 1100 hours on October 10, 1971, the men of Bravo Company, 11/12 First Cavalry Division, declared their own private cease-fire with the North Vietnamese." [80]

In June 1971, Marine Colonel Robert D. Heinl, Jr., wrote an article in the *Armed Forces Journal* whose title said it all: "The Collapse of the Armed Forces" reported on the severe deterioration of U.S. armed forces in Vietnam, and described the military as being "clobbered and buffeted from without and within by social turbulence, pandemic drug addiction, race war, sedition, civilian scapegoatings, draft recalcitrance and malevolence, barracks theft and common crime." [81]

1970: Labor Turns Against the War in Vietnam

After the Tet Offensive, popular support for the war diminished rapidly. By July 1968, disapproval reached 52 percent, reaching a majority for the first time. As Levy argued, "Contrary to the stereotype of 'hardhats' as hawks, virtually every survey demonstrated that at any given time, manual workers were just as likely to oppose the war as were youths, the archetypal doves." [82]

Students and organized labor reached a major rapprochement in 1970, when many unionists joined the massive outpouring of protest after Nixon announced that the United States had invaded Cambodia on April 30. As Joe Allen described in an article published in the *International Socialist Review:*

> The country literally exploded in rage. Within four days of the announced invasion, strikes were in progress at more than a hundred

campuses. Symbols of the military were under attack everywhere, especially ROTC buildings on campuses. Then the anger spread beyond the campuses. "It was something I'd never seen before . . ." remembered one activist in New York: "I could feel the polarization. You could cut that with a knife in society, it was so incredible. . . . On that day or two after the Cambodian invasion, this whole city was filled with thousands of people all over the street debating. You could just go from group to group arguing." [83]

Government authorities responded with a spree of violence against student protesters. On May 4 National Guard troops opened fire on students at Kent State University in Ohio, killing four and wounding nine. Ten days later, Mississippi police killed two Black students and wounded four at Jackson State College. Student strikes spread to thirteen hundred college campuses, and unionists began to appear in much larger numbers at antiwar marches, including the March Against Racism and Repression in Georgia protesting the Jackson State murders. On May 8, Nixon was forced to announce that U.S. troops would leave Cambodia by the end of June. In 1971, New York City labor leaders joined with VVAW and student activists to sponsor a memorial rally for students murdered at Kent State. [84]

In the fall of 1971, Gallup opinion polls showed 61 percent of the public wanted U.S. troops out of Vietnam by the year's end. This sentiment was strongest among nonwhites and those from union households. [85] The unity displayed in 1970 and 1971 between student and labor antiwar activists showed the potential power of a social movement with the strength of organized labor behind it. Unfortunately, this unity did not surface until the war in Vietnam was already in the process of winding down. SDS itself had collapsed into a number of competing factions and organizations at its 1969 convention. The opportunity for significant working-class participation in 1960s social movements had passed.

Rank-and-File Rebellion

Mass protest profoundly impacted the U.S. political climate during the 1960s and early 1970s. Under sustained pressure from the massive civil rights movement, Congress finally passed the Civil Rights Act in 1964 and the Voting Rights Act in 1965. Medicare was introduced and programs for the poor were expanded in response to the urban rebellions of the 1960s. By the early 1970s, the women's movement won the right to legal abortion, and the civil rights movement won affirmative action programs.

But no such political pressure was mounted by the leaders of organized labor during this entire period. In the 1960s, the Supreme Court further restricted the rights of union workers to take part in job actions not authorized by their union contracts. In 1970, Lichtenstein wrote, "the high court made virtually all work stoppages illegal during the term of the contract, in the process again legitimizing labor injunctions of the sort that had once so crippled the union movement during the nineteenth century." [86]

But a seismic rebellion was brewing among rank-and-file workers as the 1960s decade drew to a close. Wages stagnated in the late 1960s as the postwar economic boom began to falter. Anger at stagnating wages, combined with growing frustration at production speedups and the disinterested union bureaucracy, exploded into a series of working-class revolts beginning in 1968. These revolts were frequently spearheaded by young workers who were influenced by the anti-war or Black Power movements and by the radicalization of the period.

Black workers often led the most overtly radical struggles. Black autoworkers in Detroit, for example, raised demands against what they called "niggermation"—the combination of speedup and racial discrimination. Black workers had been virtually excluded from higher-paying skilled jobs at all the Big Three auto plants: in 1968, 3 percent of all skilled trades jobs at Chrysler were held by Blacks, 3 percent at Ford, and 1.3 percent at GM. The UAW, despite lip service to the contrary, was equally racist in practice: while Blacks made up one-fourth of the UAW's membership, they found themselves shut out of its leadership. Only six Black delegates attended the 1968 UAW convention, and of the union's top twenty-six officers, only one was African American. [87] As Dan Georgakas and Marvin Surkin described in *Detroit, I Do Mind Dying,*

> On May 2, 1968, 4,000 workers shut down Dodge Main in the first wildcat strike to hit that factory in 14 years. The immediate cause of the strike was speed-up and both Black and white workers took part, but the driving force was . . . DRUM. The activities and ideas of DRUM were to inspire Black workers throughout the United States. No less an authority than the *Wall Street Journal* took them very seriously

from the day of the first wildcat, for the *Wall Street Journal* understood something most of the white student radicals did not yet understand: the Black revolution of the sixties had finally arrived at one of the most vulnerable links of the American economic system—the point of mass production, the assembly line.[88]

DRUM's successes at Dodge Main inspired a number of spin-off RUMs (Revolutionary Union Movements) at other auto plants, and a Black Panther caucus at the Fremont, California, GM plant. The RUMs came together to form the League of Revolutionary Black Workers in 1969. The League was a Black nationalist formation and maintained a formal policy of discouraging white support, which no doubt blunted the actual potential that existed for building Black and white unity. Nevertheless, a significant minority of white workers supported the strikes led by the RUMs.[89]

The United Black Brothers, who led a wildcat strike at the Ford plant in Mahwah, New Jersey, in 1969, is less known but distinctive because the Mahwah workers understood the need to build solidarity with white workers at the plant. The United Black Brothers was formed out of a wildcat strike in 1967, when five hundred Black workers walked out after a foreman called a Black worker a "Black bastard." In 1969, when the Brothers organized a strike against racism at the Ford plant, with a workforce that was one-third African-American, the organization directed an appeal to white workers to join the strike:

> Why do we ask your support? Because the same thing can happen to you. The company has been laying off men by the dozens, but the lines have not slowed up a bit. You have been given more work, and if you can't do it, you lose your job or get time off. The supervisors are harassing the men and calling them all kinds of names such as "Dirty Guinea Bastard," "Black SOB," and "Stinking Spick," to name a few. . . . We ask that all of you stay out and support us in this fight![90]

The number of wildcat strikes across all industries doubled, from one thousand to two thousand between 1960 and 1969. In 1970, the strike wave peaked. General Motors weathered a sixty-seven-day strike. Forty thousand coal miners struck in three states to demand benefits for disabled miners. Postal workers went on strike across the country, shutting down the U.S. Postal Service in two hundred cities. When the government brought in the National Guard, the troops expressed sympathy with the postal strikers. After two weeks, postal workers, who are legally prohibited from striking, won a 14 percent wage increase. On April 1, rank-and-file Teamsters went out on strike and many stayed out for up to a month after IBT president Frank Fitzsimmons ordered them back to work.[91]

While 1970 marked the high point, the rank-and-file upsurge continued for several years thereafter. In 1972, the Miners for Democracy elected reform candidate Arnold Miller for union president. Also in 1972, eight thousand workers at GM's Lordstown, Ohio, plant went on strike against speedups. To be sure, union leaders were not happy with the rise in wildcat strikes and moved to reimpose their authority over strikers, sometimes violently. In 1973, Douglas Fraser, then head of the UAW's Chrysler division, organized a mob of one thousand union loyalists to attack a picket line at Chrysler's Mack Avenue Stamping Plant in Detroit. They beat up the strikers while the police stood by, watching. A Detroit television reporter commented, "for the first time in the history of the UAW, the union mobilized to keep a plant open." Fraser explained bluntly, "The wildcat violated our constitution, the law, the contract, and it really upset our bargaining strategy." [92]

But the outlook seemed promising for the rank-and-file rebellion to lead to a broader class radicalization. Small sections of the left developed a working-class orientation in the early 1970s, and in 1975, Teamsters for a Decent Contract (later renamed Teamsters for a Democratic Union) was formed. In 1975, dissident steelworkers launched the Fight Back campaign to elect reformer Ed Sadlowski as United Steel Workers president. Sadlowski won a formidable 43.1 percent of the vote against incumbent Lloyd McBride's 51.9 percent when the election took place. In 1976, a national Teamsters strike paralyzed the freight trucking industry.[93]

Many on the left predicted that the recession of 1973–75 would produce another round of class struggle. But none of the rank-and-file movements was—or could have been—prepared for what was to follow over the next few years. American capital united in a grand coalition to decisively shift the balance of class forces, determined not only to stop granting wage increases, but also to start forcing workers' wages down sharply. The result has been a sustained employers' offensive that has continued for three decades, with no sign of abating.

With the benefit of hindsight, it is easier to see that the short-term economic gains unions made in the 1950s and 1960s were far outweighed by the rights workers lost in exchange. Indeed, the era of the American Dream set the stage for the employers' offensive that would inevitably follow when the boom gave way to recession. The lasting impact of McCarthyism left the rank and file with few existing structures to challenge corrupt or moribund union leaders, much less to launch an aggressive defense of workers' rights.

PART IV

One-Sided Class War

CHAPTER SEVEN

The Employers' Offensive

I n 1971, former Pentagon staffer Daniel Ellsberg leaked seven thousand pages of secret Pentagon documents to the *New York Times*. The Pentagon Papers, as they came to be known, proved that Secretary of Defense Robert McNamara and other Pentagon officials had systematically lied to the public about the war in Vietnam—stating that victory in Vietnam was "just around the corner" while knowing the war was unwinnable and the death toll would be enormous. Soon afterward, a group of White House "plumbers" broke into the offices of Ellsberg's psychiatrist in an effort to discredit him publicly. The same "plumbers" were caught breaking into Democratic National Committee offices at the Watergate complex in 1972 to install wiretapping devices.

For nearly two years, Nixon maintained his innocence, and that he knew nothing about the break-ins, stating famously, "I'm not a crook," on November 17, 1973.[1] Finally, under court order, the White House grudgingly released official White House tape recordings. On one of the tapes, recorded just days after the Watergate burglary, Nixon could be heard concocting a plan to have the CIA claim that issues of "national security" were involved in order to block any further investigation. With Richard Nixon's administration publicly exposed as thoroughly corrupt, he was forced to resign in August 1974 or face impeachment.

Even as the Watergate scandal was still unfolding, Congress began investigating leaked FBI documents that revealed an expansive domestic counterintelligence program—known by its acronym

COINTELPRO—stretching from the FBI and the White House to local and state law enforcement. Hoover had initiated the program in 1956 to use against the Communist Party, but its targets expanded to include thousands of individuals and organizations during the turbulent 1960s. COINTELPRO's stated purpose was to use any tactic, from infiltration to sabotage, to "expose, disrupt, misdirect, discredit, and otherwise neutralize" political dissidents.[2] The FBI was proven to have maintained surveillance files on and infiltrated a wide range of organizations, including the Socialist Workers Party, the Black Panther Party, Martin Luther King, Jr., the Southern Christian Leadership Conference (SCLC), and the Ku Klux Klan.[3]

By the mid-1970s, the U.S. ruling class had reached a crisis point, extending far beyond the excesses of Nixon and Hoover. The world's largest military power had been defeated in Vietnam, in a war that killed over two million Vietnamese and other Southeast Asians and over fifty-eight thousand U.S. soldiers. U.S. rulers were also humiliated by a massive antiwar movement at home. The war's enormous unpopularity saddled U.S. rulers with the risk of provoking mass domestic discontent if they attempted to start another major war—what became commonly known as the "Vietnam Syndrome." In addition, the postwar boom was over. While the United States had been pouring investment into producing weaponry, its economic competitors, Japan and Germany in particular, had been investing in manufacturing—outstripping U.S. manufacturing productivity by the 1970s. The recession of 1973 signaled the onset of decline and a long-term economic crisis for capitalism internationally:

> While it was highlighted by the 1973–75 recession, the economic deterioration that drove this process began before, and continued after, that catastrophic event. . . . At the bottom line, profits of U.S. firms declined after 1965 and failed throughout the next 15 years to regain their early 1960s levels. Annual net investment in plant and equipment followed suit, falling from an average 4 percent of GNP during 1966–70 to 3.1 percent over 1971–75 and 2.9 percent over 1976–80. Productivity suffered in turn, as the annual growth of output per worker employed in non-residential business fell from 2.45 percent over 1948–73 to 0.08 percent over 1973–79.[4]

The U.S. share of world trade and world GNP continued to fall throughout the 1970s. The U.S. trade balance moved into negative territory in 1971 for the first time since 1893, marking the beginning of a trade deficit that would grow to mammoth proportions during the Reagan administration. By 1979, American auto companies produced only 28 percent of world car output. By 1981 the U.S. share of world steel production dropped to 15 percent.[5]

The Selling Job

In 1974 and 1975, a group of CEOs assembled under the auspices of the Conference Board to commiserate about this crisis and brainstorm for the future. One corporate leader summed up the sense of the attendees when he said, "We have been hoisted with our own petard. We have raised expectations that we can't deliver on."[6] The consensus was that business interests must unite to shift the balance of class forces back toward capital. This required dramatically lowering working-class living standards—that is, increasing the level of class inequality. But the strike wave—official or wildcat—between 1968 and 1974 showed clearly that workers were not in the mood to accept a wage freeze, much less wage cuts.

In the mid-1970s, *Business Week* summarized the challenge that lay ahead: "It will be a hard pill for many Americans to swallow—the idea of doing with less so that business can have more. . . . Nothing that this nation, or any other nation, has done in modern economic history compares in difficulty with the selling job that must now be done to make people accept the new reality."[7] Corporate forces geared up for this "selling job." As journalists Alexander Cockburn and Ken Silverstein noted in *Washington Babylon:*

> In 1973, as the reputation of big business plummeted, corporate leaders formed the Business Roundtable. They reactivated the moribund Chamber of Commerce and made it a potent lobbying force. Intensive recruitment of "opinion makers" went into high gear. Led by the John M. Olin Foundation—chaired by former Treasury Secretary William Simon—corporations and wealthy individuals were soon funneling tens of millions of dollars annually to right-wing thinkers. . . . Since then, [Joseph Coors] has funded Paul Weyrich's Free Congress Foundation, the reclusive Council for National Policy (the far right's answer to the Council on Foreign Relations), the Hoover Institution, the American Defense Institute and Accuracy in Media.[8]

The "Great Society" of the 1960s, during which Presidents Kennedy and Johnson increased welfare spending to attract African-American votes, was to prove short-lived. In inflation-adjusted terms, Aid to Families with Dependent Children (AFDC) payments fell by 29 percent between 1969 and 1981, the year Ronald Reagan took office.[9] Taxes followed a regressive route over roughly the same period: between 1965 and 1975 corporate income taxes declined as a percentage of gross federal receipts from 21.8 percent to 14.6 percent, while personal income taxes for the bottom tenth of the population tripled and the next lowest tenth more than doubled.[10]

Wages had risen steadily throughout most of the 1960s. The gap between rich and poor had continued to close throughout the boom until 1973, when trends started to reverse.[11] In the early 1970s the wave of strikes and wildcats kept wages afloat, but by 1974 real wages began to fall. By 1980, the downward trend began to accelerate.

Reaganism Before Reagan

Ronald Reagan and the Republican Party have received most of the credit for implementing tax cuts for the rich and slashing social spending for the poor—steps that greatly increased inequality in the United States throughout the 1980s. But the employers' offensive has been a bipartisan project from the beginning.

Jimmy Carter, a Democrat, took office in time to oversee the first stage of the employers' offensive. Since the New Deal, the Democrats had succeeded in containing social upheaval by promoting certain reforms and implementing fewer. But in the late 1970s, the Democrats joined forces with their Republican counterparts in clamoring for a new social program: one that would openly attack workers' living standards and organization, while conjuring up images of overpaid union workers and freeloading poor people.

In 1975, the labor movement was on the verge of winning a significant piece of pro-labor legislation, the Common Situs picketing bill, which would have weakened Taft-Hartley restrictions on secondary boycotts. The bill passed Congress, but was vetoed by Nixon's successor, Gerald Ford, in 1975. When the bill returned to Congress in 1976, Jimmy Carter was in the White House. But the mood in Washington had changed: key Democrats voted against it, and it failed in the House.[12] In 1978, Carter himself attempted to use Taft-Hartley to break a bitter strike by one hundred sixty thousand coal miners.[13]

During his tenure, Carter instituted key policies that set the stage for Reagan's more draconian measures. Carter, not Reagan, took the first stab at deregulation, which in the 1980s would leave big business and banking unencumbered by environmental, worker safety, or other "social" restraints. In 1978, Carter signed legislation deregulating the airline industry, and in 1980, he began deregulating trucking.[14]

Carter authorized a whopping 5 percent annual increase in military spending coupled with massive cuts in poverty programs.[15] After the fall of the Shah of Iran in 1979, Carter warned the world, "An attempt by any outside force to gain control of the Persian Gulf region will be regarded as an assault on the vital interests of the United States of America, and such an assault will be repelled by any means necessary, including military force." [16]

In 1978, Congress passed a tax reform bill that cut the top capital gains rate for businesses by more than 40 percent—from 48 to 28 percent—while the social security tax (a regressive tax in which the same rate is paid by everyone, no matter what their income) increased dramatically.[17] Meanwhile, Carter did nothing to intervene on behalf of workers when employers began union-busting in earnest in the late 1970s. The number of charges of unfair labor practices filed against employers swelled by 750 percent between 1957 and 1980, at a time when union representation elections had increased by only 54 percent.[18]

During this same period union membership fell to 23 percent of the labor force—roughly 10 percentage points lower than in the mid-1950s. The AFL-CIO estimated that more than a thousand union-busting consultant firms were operating across the United States in 1979. According to the *Economist* magazine they were collectively making over $100 million a year, issuing promises like these to employers: "In Chapter Two we will show you how to screw your employees (before they screw you) and how to keep them smiling on low pay—how to maneuver them into low-paying jobs they are afraid to walk away from—how to hire and fire so you always make money." By the mid-1980s, U.S. corporations were spending an estimated half-billion dollars on union-busting.[19]

Collaboration and Concessions

In 1978, UAW president Doug Fraser declared angrily,

> I believe leaders of the business community, with few exceptions, have
> chosen to wage a one-sided class war in this country—a war against
> working people, the unemployed, the poor, the minorities, the very
> young and the very old, and even many in the middle class of our soci-
> ety. The leaders of industry, commerce, and finance in the United States
> have broken and discarded the fragile, unwritten compact previously
> existing during a period of growth and progress.[20]

But Fraser himself clung to the familiar collaborationist methods. In 1979, the Carter administration intervened to rescue the
smallest of the Big Three automakers, Chrysler, from bankruptcy.
Although the UAW agreed to concessions amounting to $200 mil-
lion, Congress refused to give Chrysler its $1.2 billion loan guarantee
unless workers gave concessions totaling $462 million. This included
a wage freeze and giving up seventeen paid vacation days. By the
next contract Chrysler chairman Lee Iacocca was again demanding
more concessions, which this time totaled $673 million—including
a pay *cut* of $1.15 per hour and the loss of three more vacation days.
By 1985, when Chrysler had been restored to profitability, Iacocca
had risen to the second-highest-paid U.S. executive, with a salary of
$11.4 million.[21] By this time, all told, Chrysler had cut fifty thousand
jobs.[22] The Chrysler bailout marked the beginning of a new era in
collective bargaining.

The Republocrats

The employers' offensive could not succeed in its aims without an
ideological assault on the social movements that had shifted the political climate so far to the left in the late 1960s and early 1970s. The
Carter administration oversaw the first attacks on the right to abortion and affirmative action, firing the opening shots in what would
become a relentless pursuit under Reagan.

In 1976, Jimmy Carter, a southern evangelical Christian, won
the presidential race over Gerald Ford. While he was more liberal
than Ford, historian Kenneth O'Reilly noted,

> Carter also sent mixed messages during the 1976 push for the White
> House. The most controversial were his remarks about busing and use

of the phrase "ethnic purity" to describe white-ethnic enclaves and
neighborhood schools. . . . Follow-up questions . . . led to additional
warnings from the candidate about "alien groups" and "black intru-
sion." "Interjecting into [a community] a member of another race" or
"a diametrically opposite kind of family" or a "different kind of person"
threatened what Carter called the admirable value of "ethnic purity."[23]

No sooner had Carter taken office than he endorsed the Hyde
Amendment, cutting off federal funding for poor women's abortions—which has never been restored. By 1990, only thirteen states
still provided Medicaid funding for abortions, and thirty-two states
denied funding even to victims of rape or incest. Carter defended
the Hyde Amendment as a necessary consequence of class society,
"There are many things in life that are not fair, that wealthy people can afford and poor people can't. But I don't believe the federal
government should take action to try to make these opportunities
exactly equal, particularly when there is a moral factor involved."[24]

Another key issue that was used to roll back the social reforms of
the 1960s was the attack on affirmative action. In 1978, the U.S. Supreme Court reached its landmark *Bakke v. Regents of the University of California* decision, setting in motion more than two decades
of attacks on affirmative action programs. The Court ruled that
Allan Bakke, a white male, had been denied a place at the University
of California at Davis medical school due to "reverse discrimination" policies that victimized white males. The medical school's policy of setting aside just sixteen of its one hundred annual openings
for nonwhite students was found to be discriminatory against "better qualified" whites. But several important facts about the *Bakke*
case never surfaced in the mass media. First, the medical school at
Davis also reserved a certain number of spots each year for the sons
and daughters of wealthy alumni, also known as "legacies." Secondly, thirty-six of the eighty-four *white* students admitted the year
Bakke applied had lower test scores than Bakke. In addition, ten
other medical schools had also turned down Bakke's application.[25]

Affirmative action programs were necessary to finally force racial integration upon recalcitrant employers and educational institutions. As late as 1948, twenty-six of the twenty-seven medical
schools in the United States openly practiced racial segregation.
In the year that Bakke applied to medical school, Blacks made up
about 12 percent of the U.S. population, but just over 2 percent

were doctors and less than 3 percent were medical students. Racial quotas were needed because segregation was alive and well.[26] By upholding the notion of "reverse discrimination," however, the Supreme Court succeeded at recasting the debate over affirmative action. Thereafter, "reverse racism" provided the justification for undermining affirmative action programs.

By the time Jimmy Carter left office, his administration had paved the way for Ronald Reagan's frontal assault on the working class.

Looting Decade

In 1981, just as the economy entered a new recession, the employers' offensive took a qualitative leap forward. Behind Reagan's "trickle down" economics was an economic program for a massive arms buildup, an attack on social spending and working-class living standards, and huge tax breaks for the rich.

One of Reagan's first moves upon taking office in 1981 was to announce plans for major corporate tax cuts. As Thomas Ferguson and Joel Rogers describe in *Right Turn: The Decline of the Democrats and the Future of American Politics,* "big business mobilized rapidly. Immediately after the Administration's announcement, the Business Roundtable called an emergency meeting. Executives of America's top firms descended on Washington in droves for an orgy of lobbying that became known as the 'Lear Jet Weekend.'"[27] Democrats and Republicans set out on a bidding war, each party trying to outdo the other in inventing tax breaks, including special breaks for oil, real estate, and high-tech firms, to ingratiate themselves to the business leaders. As David Stockman later described the scene, "The hogs were really feeding. The greed level, the level of opportunism, just got out of control."[28]

Unemployment broke the 10 percent barrier at the height of the 1981–82 recession. Between 1978 and 1982, employment in large manufacturing plants fell by an estimated 25 percent (3.5 to 4 million jobs). Many manufacturing employers took the opportunity to relocate to Southern right-to-work states, and increasingly to Mexico and Southeast Asia.[29] But high unemployment was part of the plan. As Reagan's Budget Director David Stockman explained to a Chamber of Commerce breakfast meeting in 1982, a period of sustained unemployment was "part of the cure, not the problem" for the U.S. economy.[30] By 1983 more than 15 percent of the population was living below the official poverty level.[31]

Business tax rates were effectively halved, from 33 percent to 16 percent between the Economic Recovery Tax Act passed in 1981 and the 1982 Tax Equity and Fiscal Responsibility Tax Act. These reforms were widely supported by Democrats in both houses of Congress. More than half of House Democrats voted in favor, as did more than 80 percent of Democrats in the Senate.[32] Meanwhile, the capital gains tax was capped at 20 percent, down still further from Carter's cuts. The 1986 Tax Reform Act cut tax rates for the richest individuals from 70 percent in 1981 to 28 percent for 1988. Yet between 1982 and 1984, the working poor—those earning below $10,000 a year—saw their taxes rise by 22 percent.[33] As Kevin Phillips argued in *Politics of Rich and Poor*:

> By the middle of Reagan's second term, official data had begun to show that America's broadly defined "rich"—the top half of 1 percent of the U.S. population—had never been richer. Federal policy favored the accumulation of wealth and rewarded financial assets, and the concentration of income that began in the mid-1970s was accelerating. . . . *No parallel upsurge of riches had been seen since the late 19th century, the era of the Vanderbilts, Morgans and Rockefellers.*[34]

According to official government figures, the number of U.S. taxpayers reporting more than one million dollars in gross income increased fourteen-fold between 1980 and 1989. As a group, their total income grew by 1,630 percent. And the number of taxpayers reporting more than half-million-dollar incomes rose more than tenfold.[35]

Reagan, again with barely a peep from the Democratic Congress, massively increased military spending. Under Reagan, like Carter before him, defense spending rose in symmetry with cuts in social spending. Social spending was reduced from 28 percent of the federal budget to 22 percent between 1980 and 1987; military spending, on the other hand, rose from 23 percent to 28 percent over the same period. This was not how Reagan explained it, of course. He conjured up images of "welfare queens" driving around in fancy cars as he dropped millions from welfare rolls and slashed prenatal care programs for poor women. He argued that the government should only fund programs for the "truly needy" while his administration cut poor children from school lunch programs. To reduce costs further, Reagan's Food and Nutrition Service even reclassified ketchup as a "vegetable" in children's school lunches.[36]

By the end of the 1980s, the United States had achieved the dubious status as the most unequal society among Western industrial countries, as measured by the gap between the richest and the poorest fifths of the population. An end-of-decade report on salaries in ten leading companies showed that, while the average CEO earned thirty-four times more than his employees in the mid-1970s, he earned 110 times more by the late 1980s. By February 1992, *BusinessWeek* reported that, on average, U.S. executives earned 160 times the pay of their employees and three to six times the salary of their European and Japanese counterparts.[37]

Corporate Swindles

But the rich didn't get richer only because of tax breaks. There was an orgy of speculation. Even after the economy had been pulled out of recession in 1983 and productivity began to rise, the temptation was to use profits for speculation—a much more lucrative endeavor than capital investment. Nowhere was this more evident than in the savings and loan (S&L) industry. Here again the stage was set during the Carter administration. In 1980, Congress voted to provide federal insurance to any and all S&L deposits up to $100,000 apiece, up from the $40,000 cap in place since 1974. In 1982, Congress did the S&Ls another favor: they deregulated, removing all limits on interest rates. This meant that corporations and wealthy individuals could divide up their fortunes into $100,000 deposits and place them in S&Ls all over the country, at exorbitantly high interest rates—all of it completely insured with taxpayers' money:

> To complete the felonious scene, the new law (1) permitted [real estate] developers to own S&Ls and (2) permitted the owners of S&Ls to lend to themselves. In short, the vault was not only opened to the crooks, it could be owned by them. No wonder, then, at the Rose Garden signing of the bill, President Reagan, with his customary talent for the unconscious confession, chortled, "All in all, I think we've hit the jackpot." [38]

If the S&Ls had been shut down as soon as they became insolvent, there would have been no need for a colossal bailout. But federal regulators waited years before they stepped in, allowing insolvent thrifts to lose billions of dollars—only to have taxpayers bail them out. The total cost of the S&L bailout to taxpayers was an estimated $300 billion.

Charles Keating's fairy tale existence at the helm of American Continental and Lincoln Savings gives an accurate picture of the wealth and power enjoyed by those running the savings and loan industry. Over a period of five years, Keating paid himself and his family almost $39 million, not including stocks and options. The whole family flew to Europe fifteen times in a corporate jet with gold-plated trim, leather seats, a wet bar, and the best audio and video equipment money could buy. One Christmas, the family flew in an entire orchestra from New York to entertain a party for top corporate employees. Meanwhile, when American Continental and Lincoln Savings became insolvent, seventeen thousand bondholders, most of them elderly depositors, lost $200 million. Many were thrown into poverty.[39]

The politically connected Neil Bush sat on the board of the Silverado, a Denver S&L, which cost taxpayers an estimated $1 billion to bail out. A phone call from the White House to federal examiners in mid-1988 convinced them to hold off from seizing Silverado's assets until after the 1988 presidential elections. They did, and Silverado was seized on December 9, just one month after George H. W. Bush was elected President.[40]

The fruits of the S&L swindle extended far beyond those running the S&Ls. The fate of the S&L industry was closely bound to that of junk bonds: by 1989, S&Ls owned $14 billion worth of junk bonds.[41] Generous campaign contributions kept both houses of Congress from blowing the whistle. The "Keating Five," the five senators accused of fronting for Charles Keating, represented only the tip of the iceberg. They included four Democrats (Senators Alan Cranston of California, Donald Riegle of Michigan, Dennis DeConcini of Arizona, and John Glenn of Ohio) and one Republican (Senator John McCain of Arizona). It has been estimated that members of Congress officially received $11 million, and unofficially twice that amount, from S&L interests in the 1980s.[42]

The Working Class under Attack

For many years, government reports cloaked statistics on rapidly falling real wages with cheerful statements that median family incomes had remained stable in the 1980s. But such reports were misleading, since families compensated for lower wages by adding wage earners, working longer hours, and going deeper into debt.

In 1989, nearly 60 percent of women were in the labor force, compared with less than 40 percent in the 1960s. The figures are similar even for married women with children under age six, whose labor force participation rose from 36.7 percent to 58.4 percent in 1989. But even two-earner families couldn't keep pace. A Joint Economic Committee report showed that adults in 80 percent of two-parent families with children worked longer hours in 1989 than in 1979, but their incomes did not rise commensurately. Real hourly pay for husbands fell in 60 percent of families, while women's wages still averaged only 65 percent of men's. In 1988, the Bureau of Labor Statistics reported that the number of women working two or more jobs rose from 2.2 percent of working women in 1970 to 5.9 percent in 1989. Only families in the top income quintile showed "clear gains in their standard of living." [43]

Meanwhile, deregulation of the banking industry increased the number of credit cards in circulation from 12 million in 1980 to 289 million by 1990. As more people went into debt to keep up, personal credit card debt rose from $853 in 1980 to $2,350 in 1990. [44] But even median family incomes dropped for those under the age of thirty. Families in this age group had a median income in 1991 that was 13 percent lower in inflation-adjusted terms than such families earned in 1973. And more than one-third of all single-parent families—one in every four families with children in 1987—lived below the poverty line. For the roughly one in two single-parent families headed by Black women, two-thirds lived in poverty. [45] Yet, between fiscal years 1982 and 1985, Congress cut $5 billion from school lunch, breakfast, and summer food programs for poor children.

The ranks of the working poor swelled during Reagan's two terms in office. The minimum wage of $3.35 an hour remained the same from 1981 until 1989, a drop in real income of 36 percent. In 1986, workers received the same disposable income as in 1961, and 20 percent less than in 1972. Real hourly wages were no higher in 1989 than they had been in 1966.[46] Thanks to Reagan-era cuts that halved the duration of unemployment benefits from fifty-two to twenty-six weeks, only one in three of the unemployed were entitled to collect benefits in 1990, compared with two in three in 1981.

Close to forty million Americans had no health insurance coverage by the early 1990s—more than 85 percent of them workers or their dependents.[47] Like the S&L debacle, the U.S. health care industry, which was raking in $700 billion a year by 1990, is the story of greed gone mad. For decades a conglomeration of insurance companies, drug companies, doctors, and hospitals has ensured that neither the laws of competition nor state intervention would interfere with the flow of profits. In 1992, the Families USA Foundation reported that the cost of the three most common prescriptions sold in the U.S. had risen 80 percent between 1985 and 1991.[48] Like the S&Ls, the health care giants have been willing to pay Congress generously not to meddle. More than two hundred PACs, representing the various wings of the medical industry, together contributed more than $60 million in campaign contributions to members of Congress between 1980 and 1991.[49]

Occupational safety and health also deteriorated in the 1980s. Workplace injury rates doubled thanks to speedups: more overtime, smaller work crews, and faster assembly lines. In the 1980s, the United States had the highest occupational fatality rate of any Western industrialized nation. A September 1991 fire at a North Carolina poultry processing plant highlighted the nineteenth-century working conditions experienced by a significant number of nonunion factory workers. When the fire broke out at the plant, the ninety workers inside rushed to the exits, but only one of the nine doors would open. The owner had blocked or padlocked the other doors to prevent workers from stealing his chickens.[50] The plant had only one fire extinguisher and no sprinkler system. Passers-by reported hearing workers screaming and beating on plant doors, but it was too late. Of the ninety workers, mostly Black women, twenty-five died in the fire, and fifty-three others were injured.

After the fire, an agricultural inspector told a Congressional committee that he had received phone calls from colleagues in the poultry industry from as far away as Texas "going around with bolt cutters the day after the fire unlocking doors" in their own plants.[51] It was also revealed in the aftermath of the fire that North Carolina had only enough occupational safety inspectors to visit each workplace once every seventy-five years. Nationally, there were only twelve hundred inspectors for five million workplaces.[52]

Rise of the New Right

Ronald Reagan's 1980 election fueled the confidence of the Republican Party's conservative wing, propelling the formation of a loose coalition known as the "New Right." The New Right took aim at virtually all the gains made by the social movements of the 1960s, uniting under its umbrella religious and political organizations ranging from Reverend Jerry Falwell's Moral Majority to the National Conservative Caucus. The New Right's most prominent members had one thing in common: all had already established their right-wing credentials. In the late 1970s, Phyllis Schlafly's "Stop ERA" organization campaigned as ardently against the Equal Rights Amendment as the "National Right to Life" campaigned against abortion. Anita Bryant, who achieved fame as a television vendor for Florida orange juice, spearheaded a legal assault on gay rights in Florida in the late 1970s. A campaign by Bryant's organization, "Save the Children," successfully repealed an ordinance prohibiting discrimination against gays in Dade County in 1977.[53]

The New Right's allies in Congress worked hard to achieve results, targeting abortion rights. California Republican Representative Robert K. Dornan (unsuccessfully) sponsored the "Human Life Amendment," that would ban abortion under all circumstances—for rape and incest victims, and even if the woman would die if she gave birth.[54] The New Right's success should be measured, however, by its impact on mainstream political discourse. Its alliance of Protestant fundamentalists, old-time segregationists, antiabortion crusaders, and antigay bigots succeeded in shifting the political climate far rightward in the course of a mere decade. The Christian Right, which ascended into the political mainstream in the 1990s, was launched out of the New Right—touting the familiar "family values" mantra that politicians of both major parties by then enthusiastically embraced and actively promoted.

Race and Class

The degree of racism coming from the Reagan White House was frequently staggering. Reagan courted the white racist vote in 1980 by repeatedly assuring white audiences that he had consistently opposed civil rights, while resurrecting the slogan of Southern segregationists, "The South will rise again!"[55] Not surprisingly, many members of the Democratic Party's Southern segregationist wing began to abandon the New Deal coalition, defecting to the Republicans during Reagan's presidency.

Reagan aimed to deepen the wedge between white workers and those of oppressed national minorities, African Americans in particular. Nearly every social spending cutback was justified with a racist stereotype. "Welfare," "drugs," and "crime" became permanently etched as racist code words in election campaigns henceforth. Although two-thirds of welfare recipients were white, the "welfare cheats" Reagan complained about were always understood to be Black. When Bush ran for president in 1988, he ran a television ad depicting his Democratic opponent, Michael Dukakis, as "soft on crime"—using the police photograph of a recidivist Black convict, Willie Horton, to prove his point. In a 1988 survey that asked African Americans whether the Reagan administration "tended more to help Blacks or . . . to keep Blacks down," an overwhelming 78 percent answered, "to keep Blacks down."[56]

Every aspect of life got worse for Blacks under Reagan. Whereas in 1975 the average annual income of Blacks was 63 percent that of whites, by 1991 the figure had fallen to 56 percent—the same as before the "Great Society" programs of the 1960s. One in every three Black families fell below the poverty line. The poverty rate for Latinos was only slightly lower, at 26.8 percent, but more than 40 percent of Puerto Ricans lived in poverty. Black infant mortality rates were double that for white children. Unemployment rates for young African Americans skyrocketed: the national rate stood at 34 percent by 1987 and ranged as high as 50 percent in some cities.[57]

In 1988, life expectancy for African Americans fell for the fourth year in a row. The homicide rate among young Black men nearly doubled between 1984 and 1988, in some areas exceeding the casualty rate among U.S. soldiers in the war in Vietnam. The *New England Journal of Medicine* reported by the early 1990s that a young

Black man in Harlem had less chance of living to the age of 65 than a man in Bangladesh. Homicide was the leading cause of death.[58]

By the early 1990s, 86 percent of suburban whites lived in communities that were less than 1 percent Black. More than 8 percent of the Black population was arrested each year in the 1980s. The sheriff of Jefferson Parish, Louisiana, an all-white suburb of New Orleans, called a press conference in 1986 specifically to announce that he was instructing his police force to arrest any young Black males seen in the area after dark.[59] Once these young men were arrested the U.S. "justice" system could be counted upon to take over. As a former director of the National Conference of Black Lawyers commented,

> someone poor and Black tried for stealing a few hundred dollars has a 90 percent likelihood of being convicted of robbery with a sentence averaging between 94 and 138 months. A white business executive who has embezzled hundreds of thousands of dollars has only a 20 percent likelihood of conviction with a sentence averaging about 20 to 48 months.[60]

But all African Americans did not suffer equally under Reagan. The Black middle class grew in size and income in the 1970s and 1980s. Affirmative action programs finally began to open occupations and professions that had been tightly closed to African Americans before then. Blacks remained shut out of the ruling class—as of 1985 only one Black businessman, John Johnson, publisher of *Ebony* and *Jet,* had made it onto the lower end of the Forbes 400 list.[61] Still, class polarization among Blacks had surpassed that of whites. The NAACP, the traditional middle class Black organization, saw its membership plunge from 550,000 in the mid-1970s to about 150,000 ten years later.[62] As Manning Marable wrote at the time:

> Now, in the post civil rights era of the 1980s and 1990s, even the definition of the term "Black community" is up for debate. The net result of affirmative action and civil rights initiatives was to expand the potential base of the African-American middle class, which was located primarily outside the neighborhood confines of the old ghetto. By 1989, one out of seven African-American families had incomes exceeding 50,000 dollars annually, compared to less than 22,000 dollars for the average Black household. Black college educated married couples currently earn 93 percent of the family income of comparable white couples.[63]

The Role of Black Democrats

In the mid-1970s, many African-American activists entered the folds of the Democratic Party, aiming to change it from within. By that point, however, the Democrats were moving rightward, and, after Reagan's election, were consciously orienting to win back so-called "Reagan Democrats"—white Democrats who shifted over to vote for Republicans during the 1980s. There was no room for civil rights activism on the party agenda. By 1985, leading conservative Democrats formed the Democratic Leadership Council (DLC), intent on institutionalizing the party's rightward orientation.

By January 1990, there were 7,370 Black elected officials, the vast majority of them Democrats, across the country.[64] Many major cities elected Black mayors, who then found themselves carrying out the same cuts in social programs as their white counterparts—with the same net result: greater poverty and unemployment for the Black population and a continuation of segregation and police brutality.

While solidly Democratic, the National Conference of Black Mayors went so far as to support a 1985 Reagan proposal to reduce Black youth unemployment through the establishment of a sub-minimum wage for teenagers. Explained then-Mayor Johnny L. Ford of Tuskegee, Alabama: "If 2.50 dollars an hour is all we can go with at this time, we'll take whatever we can."[65] In 1985, Philadelphia Mayor Wilson Goode ordered a bomb dropped on a residential neighborhood. The victims were members of a countercultural Black group, MOVE, who refused to allow city officials into their homes. Eleven people were killed, including five children, and dozens of homes were destroyed.[66] Tom Bradley, mayor of Los Angeles, posed for photographs for the *South African Digest* presenting the key to the city of Los Angeles to the pro-apartheid South African General Consul.[67]

The class stratification, and the related political shift rightward, in the Black population grew, so that by 1990, Virginia Governor Douglas Wilder felt no need to identify himself with the civil rights movement. He admitted, "I never viewed myself as an activist. . . . Of course everybody says they marched on Washington now. I was not there. I didn't even participate in pickets here in Richmond, but I felt I had to make my contribution in other ways."[68] As Black sociologist Manning Marable noted at the time, "These charlatans rely on the old nationalist rhetoric of racial solidarity, but lack any progressive content because they are detached from any social protest movement for empowerment or resistance." [69]

Rainbow Coalition

Civil rights leader Jesse Jackson founded the Rainbow Coalition, a grassroots antiracist movement, to campaign in the 1984 presidential election. Although the coalition was organized as part of Jackson's bid for the Democratic Party nomination, he made clear that he intended the Rainbow Coalition as an inclusive movement— that would welcome African Americans, Latinos, and other racially oppressed groups, as well as women, gays, workers, the poor, and left-wing activists—into a common progressive organization.

The Rainbow Coalition quickly gained the feel of a broad popular movement, although its demands were far to the left of the Democratic Party platform, including:

- dismantling Reagan's tax cuts for the richest ten percent of Americans to finance social welfare programs
- cutting the budget of the Department of Defense by up to 15 percent
- designating South Africa as a rogue nation as long as it practices apartheid
- an immediate freeze on nuclear weapons and beginning disarmament negotiations with the Soviet Union
- a single-payer system of universal health care
- ratifying the Equal Rights Amendment
- increasing federal funding for public education and providing free community college to all
- stricter enforcement of the Voting Rights Act
- the formation of a Palestinian state

As Ron Walters, who was Jackson's campaign manager for political issues, remarked later, "No one else at that level was talking about environmental racism, 'no first use' of nuclear weapons; antiapartheid (remember, the ANC was a 'terrorist organization'); the Arab-Israeli situation." [70] Perhaps for this reason, Jackson attracted thousands of active supporters and placed third in 1984, after winning five party primaries, with 3.5 million votes.

Jackson's 1984 speech to the Democratic Party convention could have been a call to arms, had it not taken place within the confines of a party that rejected its central theme:

> America is not like a blanket—one piece of unbroken cloth, the same color, the same texture, the same size. America is more like a quilt—many patches, many pieces, many colors, many sizes, all woven and held together by a common thread. The white, the Hispanic, the black, the Arab, the Jew, the woman, the Native American, the small farmer, the businessperson, the environmentalist, the peace activist, the young, the old, the lesbian, the gay and the disabled make up the American quilt.
>
> Even in our fractured state, all of us count and all of us fit somewhere. We have proven that we can survive without each other. But we have not proven that we can win and progress without each other. We must come together.
>
> From Fannie Lou Hamer in Atlantic City in 1964 to the Rainbow Coalition in San Francisco today; from the Atlantic to the Pacific, we have experienced pain but progress as we ended American apartheid laws, we got public accommodation, we secured voting rights, we obtained open housing, as young people got the right to vote. We lost Malcolm, Martin, Medgar, Bobby, John and Viola. The team that got us here must be expanded, not abandoned.[71]

In 1988, Jackson received over seven million votes and won eleven primaries, placing him a close second to Massachusetts Governor Michael Dukakis. Indeed, after Jackson won 55 percent of the vote in the Michigan primary, he briefly surpassed all other candidates and was the front-runner in total number of pledged delegates. Despite the close race, however, nominee Michael Dukakis did not consider Jackson as his running mate. As journalist JoAnn Wypijewski commented recently, "Again the pundits, here in the *New Republic*, warned of 'certain and apocalyptic defeat' if Jackson were given a spot on the Democratic ticket. He wasn't, and Michael Dukakis, as heedless as Mondale and hitched to Lloyd Bentsen, a DLC Democrat, suffered his own private apocalypse."[72]

Even with the handwriting on the wall, the Democratic Party forgot how to mouth the rhetoric for its voting base. The Democratic Party's leadership abandoned its appeals to African Americans and labor, known in party circles as "special interest groups," after the Democrats' resounding defeat to Reagan in the 1984 presidential election. Even the Black political establishment inside the Democratic Party had shunned Jackson. They "wanted very much not to anoint Jesse Jackson," Walters argued.[73]

Jackson's loyalties remained with the Democratic Party, unlike many on the left who saw the Rainbow Coalition as a springboard to a "new movement." In 1984 and 1988, he advised Rainbow delegates to support the Democrats' chosen presidential nominees, Walter Mondale and Michael Dukakis. Jackson dissolved the Rainbow Coalition as an organization after the 1988 election. The Rainbow's so-called "inside-outside" strategy—ostensibly a campaign with one foot inside and one foot outside the Democratic Party—was, in reality, never outside the folds of the Democratic Party.

The Democratic establishment could continue to take the Black vote for granted while appealing to conservative votes. Party leader Robert Strauss put it bluntly: "Women, Blacks, teachers, Hispanics. They have more power, more money than ever before. Do you think these groups are going to turn the party loose? Do you think labor is going to turn the party loose? Jesse Jackson? The others? Forget it." [74]

Labor Movement in Retreat

Within a few months of taking office Ronald Reagan forced a showdown with the labor movement for which unionists were ill-prepared. Reagan chose one of the very few unions that had supported his candidacy for president as his first target. The twelve thousand members of the Professional Air Traffic Controllers Organization (PATCO) walked off their jobs on August 3, 1981, over unsafe and stressful working conditions. Within four hours, President Ronald Reagan was on national television, warning the controllers that if they didn't return to work within forty-eight hours, they "will have forfeited their jobs and will be terminated." Reagan was perfectly ready to carry out this threat. Jimmy Carter had planned ahead: twelve months before the PATCO contract was due to expire, Carter set up the Management Strike Contingency Force, which prepared a plan to run air traffic without the controllers if they went on strike. [75]

AFL-CIO leaders talked tough, but did nothing to build solidarity with the PATCO strikers. AFL-CIO president Lane Kirkland (who succeeded Meany in 1979) called Reagan "harsh and vindictive," but then sent out a letter to all AFL-CIO locals urging them *not* to join in a nationwide job action to support the strike. Kirkland wrote, "I personally do not think that the trade union movement should undertake anything that would represent punishing or incon-

veniencing the public at large for the sins and transgressions of the
Reagan administration." [76] The president of the International Association of Machinists (IAM), the union representing airline machinists, refused to call his members out on strike to support PATCO,
arguing, "It should be recognized that the IAM has a no-strike clause
with the airlines." [77]

The AFL-CIO had already planned a Labor Day "Solidarity
Day" march in Washington, D.C., taking place a few weeks after
the strike began. Yet PATCO barely got a mention in the speeches
to the half-million workers who participated. Instead, speaker after
speaker urged workers to vote for the Democrats the next time
around. Left to fight alone, the twelve thousand striking air traffic
controllers lost their jobs. PATCO had been crushed.

Green Light for Union-Busting

The PATCO strike represented a turning point from which the labor
movement has yet to recover. Reagan's crushing of the air traffic
controllers' union, played out on national television, signaled a go-
ahead to business to engage in union-busting on a massive scale. The
AFL-CIO had also sent a signal: unions had no intention of fighting
back. Years of conservatism had made them believe they could negotiate more favorable deals with employers and continue to rely on
Democrats in Congress to reverse the tide. They feared the prospect
of rank-and-file militancy more than they feared the employers' attacks. Indeed, top union officials felt no organized pressure to their
left to goad them out of their executive suites to lead the movement
forward. Instead, they searched for ways to salvage the comfortable
relationships they had nurtured with the employers for decades.

The labor movement's only response to the employers' offensive
was more of the same. Labor unions' financial contributions to election campaigns increased more than threefold between 1974 and
1982.[78] The AFL-CIO supported the Democrats while the Teamsters
and a few others supported the Republicans, but the strategy was the
same: collaboration, rather than any form of confrontation. Nevertheless, Reagan won the 1980 election by eight million votes, as a
right-wing backlash swept the country. Although the AFL-CIO dil-
igently endorsed Democrats, 40 percent of Reagan's votes in 1980
came from union households; in 1984, the figure rose to 46 percent.

Overall voter turnout fell from 70 percent in the 1960s to just 60 percent of eligible voters in the 1980 election. Voter participation would continue to decline, with just 50 percent of eligible voters taking part in the 2000 election.[79]

The full implication of the unions' collaborationist approach was revealed when UAW president Doug Fraser (who as vice president of the union led the attacks on the Chrysler wildcat strikes in 1973) agreed to massive concessions in the 1979 Chrysler bailout: he was awarded a seat on Chrysler's board of directors. One local UAW official had warned workers who hesitated to grant concessions, "Those of you who don't want to take a wage cut, go out and find another job. No one's stopping you from leaving this organization."[80]

While initially firms claimed they needed concessions to stay afloat, once Reagan had crushed PATCO in 1981, concessions and union-busting became the order of the day. A 1982 *BusinessWeek* survey of four hundred executives reported that nearly one in five admitted, "Although we don't need concessions, we are taking advantage of the bargaining climate to ask for them." In 1983, one-third of all workers with new contracts had agreed to wage cuts. By 1987, in the midst of economic recovery, almost three-quarters of all contracts covering a thousand or more workers included concessions. For manufacturing workers, the figure was 90 percent.[81] After extracting their demands from workers desperate to save their jobs, many plants closed down anyway. In fact, employers often used the savings they squeezed out of workers to finance their plans for rationalization. As Kim Moody argued,

> In 1983, the same year that it received concessions from the USW, U.S. Steel announced plans to close one-third of its remaining steel capacity as well as various finishing and fabricating mills. Chrysler, of course, closed several plants as part of the bail out operation and continued closing plants after returning to profitability. In March 1987 Chrysler announced that it would buy AMC (American Motors Corporation) from Renault for 1 billion dollars; in that same week, it also announced that it would close a parts plant in Indiana.[82]

Gone were the days when industry standards were negotiated into a single industry-wide contract. Here too, union leaders allowed contract negotiations to set groups of workers in competition with those from other plants, companies, and other countries. Union leaders' only response when plants closed down in search of cheaper labor was to clamor for protectionism.

Employers, knowing they had a staunch ally in the White House, began to exercise their legal right to hire permanent replacements for striking workers to break unions. That right had been upheld by the Supreme Court in 1938, but had rarely been used before the 1980s. Although the United States is a member of the International Labor Organization (ILO), which sets global labor standards, the United States refused to ratify the ILO's convention establishing workers' right to return to their old jobs after a strike.[83] Many employers forced their workforces on strike with proposals for drastic wage cuts, and then hired scabs as permanent replacements as soon as the strikes began. After twelve months, the scabs could then legally hold an election to decertify the union. About two hundred thousand workers became nonunion thanks to decertification elections in the 1980s. Other employers chose to simply lock out their workers, effectively forcing them to strike.[84]

Union membership had been in decline since the mid-1950s, but in the 1980s it entered a downward spiral. By 1989, union membership had fallen to 16 percent of the workforce. By 1987, strike levels had fallen to record lows, although statistics are much harder to measure for the 1980s since the Bureau of Labor Statistics stopped including strikes involving fewer than one thousand workers in its strike statistics. Even so, the strike level fell dramatically, an important gauge of the level of demoralization felt by most workers. Groups of workers fought back against the employers' offensive in the 1980s, but they often found themselves engaged in long-term, bitter disputes that pitted them against their own union leaders as well as their employers.

Union Leaders versus Strike Leaders

While the number of strikes fell in the early 1980s, the workdays lost rose, indicating longer walkouts.[85] Rather than lasting days or weeks, many strikes lasted months or even years and, with few exceptions, ended in defeat. One important exception is the Watsonville Cannery strike that began in 1985. Of the thousand Watsonville workers who struck, most of them Latinas, not one union member crossed the picket line during the entire eighteen-month strike. The company did not succeed in busting the union. As labor activist Jim

Woodward commented afterward in *Labor Notes,* a newsletter for union reformers, such defiant tactics might not guarantee success, but "the old ones guarantee defeat." [86]

Union leaders deserve little or no credit for the few examples of working-class militancy and solidarity that took place in the 1980s. Machinists' union president William Winpisinger pledged his support to the Rhode Island machinists at Brown and Sharpe during their 1981 strike. When they battled with police on their picket line, he proclaimed, "Labor history is being written" in Rhode Island. Yet in two years he never even bothered to visit the picket line of one of the longest strikes in U.S. history, and the union eventually cut off strike benefits to the strikers, forcing an end to the strike. [87]

P-9 Strikes Hormel in Austin, Minnesota

Union leaders, in fact, consistently played the role of discouraging, forbidding, or even sabotaging militancy and solidarity. The Hormel meatpackers' strike that began in 1985 and stretched into 1986 saw the most bitter clash between striking workers and their union leaders during the Reagan era. Workers at Hormel's Austin, Minnesota, meatpacking plant had already agreed to an eight-year concessionary contract in 1978. But the profitable Fortune 500 company wanted more, and unilaterally imposed a wage cut. In Austin, the company offer sought to impose a two-tier wage system, offering $10 per hour to current workers, but just $8 for new hires.

When the fifteen hundred members of Local P-9 of the United Food and Commercial Workers (UFCW) finally voted to strike in August 1985, however, their national union wasn't behind them. On the contrary, UFCW leaders did everything they could to undermine the strike. UFCW president William Wynn had already agreed to concessions for the rest of the industry and sent a letter to every local in the country casting the P-9 local as breaking union solidarity:

> The P-9 story is not one of "solidarity" in action. It is the converse of that honored union principle. Local P-9's leaders refused to act in solidarity with other Hormel workers. Instead of acting together with other Hormel workers to accomplish the most good for the greatest number of Hormel workers, Local P-9 leaders sought a better deal for Austin alone. [88]

When P-9 organized roving pickets to call out nearby Hormel plants in solidarity, Wynn sent out a telegram to union locals, urging them to have no part of the "plague" from P-9. UFCW official Lynn Hansen sent a letter to the strikers, explicitly stating,

> I truly believe that extending the picket lines would only compound the suffering—not only for the UFCW members at other plants who would be jeopardizing their jobs, but also for P-9 members. Therefore, I will not recommend that the International Union sanction extension of picketing and the International Union will not sanction such picketing regardless of the outcome.[89]

Thousands of P-9 supporters traveled repeatedly to Austin for solidarity rallies—the Reverend Jesse Jackson among them—raising money and food donations to get the strikers through the long months.[90] But in March, after eight months on strike, the national union revoked even its formal sanction of the strike, put the P-9 local into trusteeship, and stopped all strike benefits. Although the Hormel strikers continued to fight on for another six months, the national union took over their union local and negotiated a contract for the scabs who stole their jobs, formally ending the strike in September 1986.

Forcing Down Labor Standards

The Reagan administration quickly began lowering labor standards in a series of administrative decisions. In 1985, Reagan's assistant secretary of labor for the Occupational Safety and Health Administration opposed farm workers' request to require employers to "provide toilets, fresh drinking water, and cleanup facilities wherever more than ten workers are employed in the field." By administrative order, the Department of Labor removed the ban on homework in the manufacture of jewelry, buttons and buckles, handkerchiefs, and gloves in 1988.[91]

The NLRB, set up as an objective third-party arbitrator to settle labor disputes, was stacked with conservative, antilabor appointees during the Reagan era. As Nicholson described,

> The Business Roundtable, the National Right-to-Work Committee, and the conservative think tank, the Heritage Foundation, set the board agenda when they controlled the majority of seats on the NLRB. The Board cut sharply into the rights of unions, and made it harder

to pass out leaflets and easier to fire workers. Delays by the board in reaching decisions favorable to labor could take five years. Illegal business actions to break union organizing drives resulted in small fines or reinstatement rulings long after the union defeat.[92]

Workers who attempted to defend their living standards in the 1980s had neither a political party nor a labor movement to bolster their struggles. Wages in 1990, which stood at 346 dollars per week before taxes, were almost 20 percent lower than in 1972 when adjusted for inflation. Average hourly wages of U.S. production workers in manufacturing were surpassed by workers in Germany, Norway, Switzerland, Sweden, Netherlands, Denmark, Belgium, and Finland, and were nearly matched by those in Japan, Canada, France, and Italy.[93] As Vicente Navarro described:

> The average worker in the U.S., for example, works longer hours and has less paid vacation than workers in the majority of advanced capitalist countries. The average workweek for full time U.S. workers in 1986 was 42.3 hours, compared with 37 in Denmark, 37.5 in Norway and Finland and 39 in France and Britain and 37 in West Germany. . . . The level of disposable income of U.S. workers is lower than that of workers in the majority of advanced capitalist countries. Disposable income as percentage of gross earnings is 78.9 percent in the U.S., lower than in France (98.72 percent), Japan (89.10 percent), Canada (88.03 percent), Italy (86.19 percent), West Germany (79.22 percent), and the United Kingdom (78.98 percent).[94]

Reaganism After Reagan

As the 1980s came to a close, the vast majority of unionists had painfully learned that, although Reagan had promised that wealth would "trickle down," instead it flooded in the other direction. When George H. W. Bush was running for president in 1988, he promised to be a "kinder, gentler" president, but Bush's presidency just ushered in the next phase of Reaganism. Indeed, virtually every attack on workers' rights implemented under Reagan has yet to be reversed nearly two decades later.

Bush was sworn in as president in 1989, when the economy first hit the doldrums, in what turned out to be the longest recession since the Second World War. Reagan's supply-side economy had been built upon quicksand: in order to fund the tax cuts for the rich and the massive military build-up, the Reagan administration needed to borrow huge sums of money at high interest rates. In 1985, the United States became a debtor nation for the first time since 1914. The annual deficit had already reached the $200 billion range when Reagan left office. Just funding the interest on the debt cost $129 billion in 1983, $178 billion in 1985 and $216 billion in 1988.[95] The manufacturing sector restored its productivity during the 1980s, in some fields surpassing even the rates of Japan. But even after more than a decade of concessions and layoffs, U.S. manufacturing had not been able to reverse its global decline. Moreover, productivity in the service sector remained stagnant.[96]

Voices of dissent began emanating from sections of the ruling class by the decade's end. They argued that Reagan's policies had actually contributed to declining U.S. hegemony. Rising right-wing criticisms of the United States' relative share of world military spending grew in the 1980s and rose to a feverish pitch during the 1991 Gulf War against Iraq. The complaints centered on comparisons between the U.S. share of military spending and that of its main economic competitors, Germany and, with particular acrimony, Japan. Among the top five most advanced economies in 1983 (the USA, Britain, France, West Germany, and Japan), the U.S. share of combined defense spending amounted to 56.7 percent, while Japan's stood at only 3.3 percent.[97] A 1987 *Wall Street Journal* article summarized the gloomy outlook for U.S. imperialism:

> The U.S. now sits in the bottom corner, where Britain was from 1926 to 1944. Such nations live on past credit, suck in foreign capital and can't save enough to finance domestic investment. Two rankings higher stands Japan: a strong country with a trade surplus, saving more than it spends and sending excess money abroad. That puts Japan among other nations at the height of their strength, including the U.S. from 1946 to 1970 and Britain from 1851 to 1890.[98]

The Reagan Revolution should have been over, but Bush had nothing with which to replace it. His administration pursued familiar supply-side policies, while the scale of poverty reached crisis proportions during the second recession in a decade. By 1989, total consumer credit had risen to $775 billion, equal to almost one-fifth of total personal income. A Florida study reported that among 16 percent of families there at least one family member went to bed hungry in the early 1990s. The number of personal bankruptcies in 1991 was triple the annual rate during the 1981–82 recession.

Yet Bush wondered aloud why "consumer confidence" was so low during the 1991 holiday shopping season, since the 1981–82 recession had been "deeper." [99]

Where the federal government slashed social spending ten years earlier, local city and state budgets began doing so in earnest. States began to cut welfare spending, removing the last cushion available to millions of the poor. Sixteen states made cuts by the early 1990s—Michigan completely eliminated its general welfare program in the autumn of 1991, leaving ninety thousand of the state's poorest citizens without an income. New York City, with massive job losses, had an estimated ninety thousand homeless by 1991, one-third of whom was HIV-positive. By early 1992, federal health officials had declared the spread of tuberculosis—a disease of poverty—"out of control" as they reported cases in sixteen states.[100]

With the typical California welfare family living 30 percent below the poverty line, California Governor Pete Wilson proposed a "Tax Protection Plan," which would immediately cut payments by 10 percent, soon to be followed by a 15 percent cut in six months. Women on welfare who gave birth to any more children would be denied any additional payments. Teenage mothers would be required to live with their parents.[101]

The Rise and Fall of George H. W. Bush

One of Reagan's aims had been to reestablish the dominance of U.S. imperialism on a world scale, primarily through a massive military budget. Indeed, the collapse of Eastern European regimes, leading to the downfall of the USSR, convinced many that Reagan had achieved his aims. But the U.S. military's actual interventions under Reagan had been limited to an ill-fated invasion of Lebanon between 1982 and 1984, the U.S. invasion of the tiny island of Grenada in 1986, and the one-off bombing of Libya in 1986. In addition, during the Reagan years, the CIA also covertly supported the mercenary war against the revolutionary Sandinista government in Nicaragua, while funding and training an Islamic fundamentalist army against the Soviet occupation of Afghanistan.

U.S. imperialism came roaring back under Bush. Within his first two years in office, the elder Bush invaded Panama and carpet-bombed Iraq, ostensibly to rid the world of two "madmen," Manuel

Noriega and Saddam Hussein. Through strict control over the news media, which offered their full cooperation, Bush managed to keep the public from finding out about the thousands of Panamanians and hundreds of thousands of Iraqis killed in these two wars.[102] Even the one hundred fifty thousand antiwar protesters who marched in Washington, D.C., during the first Gulf War never made an appearance on the national news.

For U.S. rulers, the war against Iraq wasn't just another war. It was an opportunity for the United States to flex its military muscles in the immediate aftermath of the implosion of the Soviet Bloc, effectively ending the Cold War—and eliminating the United States' only rival superpower. The 1991 Gulf War was the largest U.S. military intervention since its defeat in Vietnam. U.S. planes dropped more explosives onto Iraq each day than were dropped on Hiroshima and Nagasaki. Bush's triumph over Iraq showed that, even if the U.S. economy was stalling, the United States remained the world's main military power. Bush felt confident enough to proclaim at the end of the war, "The Vietnam Syndrome is over." As he said toward the end of the war, "When we win, and we will, we will have taught a dangerous dictator, and any tyrant tempted to follow in his footsteps that the U.S. has a new credibility, and that *what we say goes.*"[103]

As wars have been known to do in the short term, the United States' six-week victory over Iraq sent Bush's popularity soaring to 90 percent. But it soon became apparent that the long-term U.S. war aims were unsatisfied: Saddam Hussein remained in power, and stability was not forthcoming anywhere in the Middle East. Moreover, the massive military victory over Iraq did nothing to arrest the recession at home. After the unification of Germany and the collapse of Stalinism, Bush didn't predict that his own chest-beating about the wonders of the free market would focus Americans' attention on their own lack of health care. Bush's popularity plunged to 51 percent by November 1991. Moreover, only one in four approved of Bush's handling of the economy, a level of discontent not approached since the final days of Jimmy Carter.[104]

Health care was one of the main issues on voters' minds—an issue that Bush had all but ignored, claiming that the U.S. health care system didn't need reform because it was the best in the world. In a Time/CNN News survey, 91 percent of the respondents said, "our health care system needs fundamental change." In addition, 70 percent said they would be willing to pay higher taxes to guarantee that all Americans have health coverage.[105] Another survey showed a majority opposed further capital gains cuts for the rich, yet Bush proposed that Congress further cut capital gains taxes for the rich, while he refused to support raising income taxes on the rich to 33 percent.[106] In yet another poll, 71 percent agreed that "a few big interests" run the U.S. government.[107]

In the face of a deepening recession, Bush faced comparisons with the clueless Herbert Hoover during the Great Depression. Bush finally admitted that the recession wasn't over. In 1990, Bush raised the tax rate for the wealthiest Americans to 31 percent. With pressure coming from both the left and the right, Bush was forced to backtrack at the end of 1991, but he couldn't figure out in which direction he should go—giving the White House the appearance of panic and disarray. Bush signed a bill temporarily extending workers' unemployment payments by twenty weeks—the same bill he'd vetoed only a month earlier, claiming workers didn't need additional benefits because the recession would be "short and shallow." [108]

Bush's blunders did not sit well with business interests, to whom it was apparent that he had no actual plan for jump-starting the economy. Corporate giants, saddled with rising health care costs, raised the demand for a national health care plan. *Business Week* announced, "We're for a Universal Health Care System," and issued a six-page proposal for one.[109] When Bush loaded up a plane with corporate executives to barter with Japan, he was likened to a traveling salesman. The business weekly *Barron's* quipped, "Bush returned from his arduous undertaking with nothing to show but bad publicity and solemn promises (which, close inspection revealed, were dated 1987)." [110]

The bottom line for Bush was the state of the economy. As one White House aide said of his reelection prospects in late 1991, "If the economy comes back in six months, nothing else matters. If it doesn't, nothing else matters." [111] U.S. employers had been successful in forcing workers to pay the cost of a major restructuring of U.S. capital. But in the process they also greatly increased the bitterness and anger of millions of working-class people. No longer could it be said that American workers unequivocally thought of themselves as middle class.

The U.S. working class had changed dramatically since the 1950s. For most workers then, expectations of higher living standards were in part matched by reality. U.S. rulers claimed conditions would only continue to improve and that the "American way" stood in the face of "totalitarianism." By the early 1990s, workers had been stripped of such illusions. Whether Black, white, or Latino, male or female, employed or unemployed, conditions for all workers declined markedly. The expectation of upward mobility had been replaced by the reality of downward mobility. The economic expansion of the 1980s created hundreds of thousands of jobs, but 85 percent of the jobs created were in low-paying or part-time service work. By 1992, of the more than twenty million workers in part-time jobs, six million said they wanted to be working full time.[112] Nearly forty million people had no health insurance, and 40 percent had no pension coverage. And a stunning 22 percent of children were living in poverty.[113]

As economist Lester Thurow wrote,

> A few years after [the] increase in inequality began (1973 to be precise), inflation-corrected real wages started to fall for males. As with inequality, real wage reductions gradually spread across the workforce so that, by 1992, real wages for males were falling for all age groups, for all industrial and occupational classifications, and for all educational groups, including those with five or more years of university education. . . . And the wages of those in their prime working years (ages forty-five to fifty-four) took an even bigger fall—17 percent from 1987 to 1992. . . . And although real wage reductions started later for women than for men, by 1992 real wages were falling for all female workers except those with four or more years of university education.[114]

Mass Anger

In the absence of mass struggle, the dramatic shift in consciousness could only be measured through opinion polls. In February 1991, 39 percent of those polled believed the United States was headed in the right direction. Eight months later, in October, that proportion had dropped to 26 percent. However low Bush's popularity dipped, however, few seemed to consider the Democrats to be an alternative. According to a December 1991 *Newsweek* poll, while only 31 percent of U.S. adults approved of Bush's "economic management," just 28 percent believed the Democrats would do a better job.[115] When asked whether they agreed with the statement, "I don't think that public officials care much about what people like me think," 59 percent agreed.[116]

Time magazine declared in 1990, "The upshot is that most Americans are entering the 1990s worse off than they were in the early 1970s. Only those Americans whose incomes are in the top 20 percent have escaped stagnation; their incomes have grown significantly."[117] Some political analysts began to worry out loud that the shift in working-class consciousness was laying the basis for a revival of class conflict. As one sociologist remarked at the time, "When you talk to people, you get an awful lot of this kind of generalized anger. From a political point of view, I think the potential for a lot of very difficult and dangerous things is there, but it hasn't been happening yet."[118] As if to amplify this statement, Los Angeles erupted into a massive, four-day riot in April 1992, in outrage over the acquittal of the four white police officers who had beaten Black motorist Rodney King. Change was in the air, demonstrated by the success of the 1989–1990 Pittston miners' eleven-month strike. After a three-day occupation and solidarity strikes involving thirty thousand miners from seven states, the miners kept the company from busting their union or getting major concessions.

Teamster Reform

Workers scored an additional victory in 1991. For the first time in the history of the Teamsters union, the rank and file democratically elected its leadership, and an entire reform slate was voted in. The Teamsters, with 1.5 million members, had finally broken the long history of embezzlement, corruption, and mafia involvement among its top officials. Three of its last five presidents had wound up in prison. A fourth indicted president, Jackie Presser, died before his case reached court. Finally, in 1989, the U.S. government used racketeering statutes to intervene in the union, setting up, among other things, elections.

In the past, delegates at Teamster conventions, held once every five years, were overwhelmingly tilted toward full-time union officials. And they were known mainly for their lavish social gatherings, which typically began around 4 p.m. At the last convention before government intervention, Joseph Trerotola, a New York Teamster leader, threw a party costing $648,000.[119]

But at the 1991 IBT convention, union delegates booed outgoing union president William McCarthy. They also booed President George Bush's videotaped message. Discontent had been brewing inside the Teamsters for many years. The reform slate, headed by New York Teamster official Ron Carey, was backed by the union reform organization Teamsters for a Democratic Union (TDU). While Carey himself (a former Republican) was no left-winger, he broke the trail of IBT corruption stretching back for generations.

CHAPTER EIGHT

The Neoliberal President Dismantles the New Deal

The 1992 election took place amid a wave of corporate down-sizing that cut 300,000 jobs in 1990, 550,000 in 1991, and 400,000 in 1992.[1] Voter turnout ticked up to 55 percent on Election Day in 1992. Voter frustration was so great that billionaire Ross Perot, a right-wing populist whose campaign centered on complaints about American jobs moving overseas, garnered 19 percent of the vote—drawing an equal number of votes away from Democrats and Republicans.

But Arkansas Governor Bill Clinton defeated Bush with ease, pledging to "put people first" and end the misery caused by "twelve years of trickle-down economics." He told voters, "I feel your pain," while promising a tax cut for the "middle class." Clinton bemoaned the fact that "American CEOs were paying themselves 100 times more than their workers" under the Bush administration.[2] And he promised to overhaul the health care system to provide every American with affordable medical coverage.[3]

Clinton made a number of specific promises aimed at the Democratic Party's traditional voting base. He told union leaders he would work for legislation to ban employers' use of permanent replacements against strikers and fight to raise the minimum wage. He assured feminists that he would pass a "Freedom of Choice Act" guaranteeing the right to legal abortion. He proposed to end the ban on gays in the military. His speeches frequently referenced Dr. Martin Luther King, Jr., to indicate his appreciation of the gains of the civil rights movement.

260

But there was another side to Clinton. He was a new breed of Democrat, at the helm of a conservative faction that formed the DLC in 1985 to break the Democratic Party's identification with so-called "special interests"—organized labor, civil rights, and other traditionally liberal causes. Bill Clinton chaired the DLC in 1990 and 1991, and used his position as a launching pad for his presidential campaign. In late 1992, the DLC hosted a $15,000-a-plate dinner for Clinton, sponsored by such corporate leaders as the American Bankers Association, Occidental Petroleum, Merrill Lynch, and Coca-Cola.[4]

Thus, Clinton's other 1992 campaign promises were explicitly directed toward conservatives. He promised to "end welfare as we know it," while promoting "personal responsibility" to end "the cycle of dependence" among the poor. He chastised welfare recipients, arguing that welfare should provide "a second chance, not a way of life."[5] To send a signal that he would be "tough on crime," Clinton interrupted his campaign schedule to rush back to Arkansas and oversee the execution of a brain-damaged man, Ricky Ray Rector, on January 24, 1992.[6] Two weeks later, Clinton sent a coded message to segregationists by golfing at a segregated Little Rock country club in full view of a television camera crew.[7] To calm any jittery nerves among business leaders about his intentions, Clinton assured *Business Week* he hoped his administration would "generate a lot of millionaires."[8]

Promises Kept, Promises Broken

Democrats held a majority in Congress during Clinton's first two years in office, making significant reform a real possibility. Yet Clinton never mentioned the minimum wage during this period. The "middle-class tax cut" also fell by the wayside. Legislation against permanent replacements quickly died without a fight from Clinton. The Freedom of Choice Act never saw the light of day. And instead of granting gays the right to serve openly in the military, Clinton adopted the "Don't ask, don't tell" policy proposed by Christian conservatives, forcing gays to remain in the closet or face discharge.

Clinton's corporate loyalty doomed his pledge for health care reform. Having received $85,000 in his 1992 campaign coffers from health insurance interests, he rejected a single-payer plan like the Canadian system. Thus his health care reform proposal revolved

around greater *privatization* rather than greater government responsibility. His health care team, headed by wife Hillary, dubbed
the plan "managed competition"—a complex network of for-profit
medical, insurance, and drug companies that was incomprehensible
to the average consumer. Although a few health care giants stood
to make hefty profits through the plan, the notion of "reigning in
costs" lit a fire under the health care lobby and employers reluctant
to pay for their employees' insurance. As Alexander Cockburn and
Ken Silverstein described,

> During 1993 and 1994, some 660 groups shelled out more than $100
> million to thwart health reform. Organizations with health care inter-
> ests funneled some $25 million to members of Congress, according to
> a report from the Center for Public Integrity. About one-third of that
> amount went to members sitting on one of the five committees over-
> seeing health care. . . . More than 130 members [of Congress], their
> spouses or dependent children, had investments in health care compa-
> nies, most prominently drug makers.[9]

Health care reform never even made it to the floor of Congress.
Roughly 39 million Americans had no health coverage when Clinton was elected; eight years later the figure had risen to roughly 45
million. By 2003, a study in the *New England Journal of Medicine*
estimated that 31 cents out of every dollar the United States spent on
health care went to administrative costs—care deniers, advertising,
executive salaries, and shareholders—compared with only 17 cents
under Canada's single-payer plan.[10]

Clinton did succeed in passing the Family and Medical Leave
Act, finally giving workers the right to take up to three months of
unpaid leave from their jobs to care for a newborn or a sick family
member. He also instituted tax credits to help pay for college tuition.
But, as socialist Lance Selfa observed,

> All of these share similar characteristics. They sounded like good reforms
> of a deeply flawed system, and sometimes they even addressed critical so-
> cial needs. But they were usually so minimal as to come nowhere near fill-
> ing the social need they were supposed to meet. What's more, they tended
> to stress private-sector initiatives, as when the administration marketed
> tax breaks for business as its antipoverty program during its 1999 "pov-
> erty tour" of depressed areas.[11]

Clinton's economic plan instituted "deficit reduction" as its
central theme. Clinton raised taxes on the wealthiest Americans to

38.6 percent in 1993 (still much lower than the 70 percent rate in place until Reagan) and expanded the earned income tax credit for the working poor, but also increased a variety of regressive taxes, including one on gasoline. Moreover, the Clinton administration expanded the number of tax loopholes companies could use to lower—or eliminate—their federal income taxes. Such loopholes included research, oil drilling, and employee stock options.

Indeed, many profitable companies not only paid no taxes in the Clinton years, but also received enormous rebates. A study by the Institute on Taxation and Economic Policy reported, "In 1998, twenty-four corporations got tax rebates. These twenty-four companies—almost one out of ten of the companies in the study—reported U.S. profits before taxes in 1998 of $12.0 billion, yet received tax rebates totaling $1.3 billion." The companies that received government rebates that year included Texaco, Chevron, CSX, Pepsico, Pfizer, J. P. Morgan, Goodyear, Enron, General Motors, Phillips Petroleum, and Northrop Grumman.[12]

Clinton's tax policy thus continued the trend since Reagan that sharply shifted the tax burden away from corporations and onto the shoulders of workers. The share of federal revenue received from corporate taxes dropped from 23 percent to only 7.6 percent between 1966 and 2001, while social insurance payroll taxes rose from 19.5 percent to 34.9 percent in the same period. "Americans have the lowest corporate taxes in the world—and far fewer social services" than in Europe, argued Robert McIntyre of Citizens for Tax Justice.[13]

Clinton won praise on Wall Street for generating record budget surpluses and maintaining "fiscal discipline" in driving down social spending—achieving the lowest level of government spending since the Eisenhower administration. Wall Street also applauded the Clinton administration's support for Federal Reserve Chairman Alan Greenspan, who controlled inflation by raising short-term interest rates repeatedly during the Clinton boom of the late 1990s.[14]

The Art of "Triangulation"

In the 1994 election, voters expressed their dissatisfaction with Clinton in the only way possible in a two-party system: throwing the "bums" out from the party in power, and replacing them with the "bums" from the other party. Republicans swept the 1994 congressional elections. Newt Gingrich, the new Speaker of the House, wasted no time in announcing the congressional Republicans' "Contract with America"—a strident agenda with a host of reactionary policies, including eliminating welfare for the poor.

As social policy expert Mimi Abramovitz noted, by 1994, Clinton's "talk of personal responsibility had been upstaged by the Republicans' Personal Responsibility Act, which was part of the Contract with America and called for ending welfare altogether." [15] Moreover, as Alexander Cockburn and Jeffrey St. Clair commented, the Republican-dominated Congress let Clinton off the hook with liberals:

> Yet for Bill Clinton the Democratic defeat held its paradoxical allure. . . . The White House no longer had to dicker with hostility to its agenda from New Deal–oriented Democrats. Without the threat of a presidential veto to lend clout to their resistance, the liberal Democrats on the Hill were as impotent against the Republicans flourishing their Contract with America. Thus unencumbered, the Clinton administration could cut deals with the Republican leadership. . . . All this strategy needed was a name, and soon after the election Clinton summoned in the man who would introduce "triangulation" into the lexicon of the late 1990s. [16]

Political consultant Dick Morris was the man for the job, hired by Clinton in 1995 to help reshape his image. The poll-driven strategy of triangulation was simple: steal the essence of the Republicans' program, effectively pulling the rug out from under them—while glossing it over with liberal-sounding rhetoric. Clinton's presidency tacked firmly rightward thereafter, adopting a variety of hitherto Republican positions as his own. Amid right-wing attacks on affirmative action programs, for example, Clinton responded, "Mend it, don't end it"—while opposing the quotas that provided the only means for enforcement. Clinton told voters he aimed to "save" the government's Social Security pension fund for the elderly—by privatizing it. [17]

The Clinton administration signed the 1997 Kyoto Agreement targeting global warming—yet did not try to win ratification in the U.S. Senate. The pro-environment rhetoric from the Clinton administration belied its firm commitment to corporate deregulation. Industry lobbies were virtually assured of the administration's cooperation. "We just don't have unlimited resources to enforce all these measures and that can create a backlash [from corporations]," said Environmental Protection Agency administrator Carol Browner. With the EPA's blessing, the mining industry continued to pillage federal lands, and the timber industry to clear-cut old-growth forests. In 1995, the EPA opened some federal land holdings to oil drilling, further enriching Occidental Petroleum—and Vice President Al Gore, an Occidental stockholder.[18]

In 1993, Clinton declared that U.S. borders "leak like a sieve," adding to anti-immigrant hysteria.[19] Under Morris' encouragement, he pledged to double the number of immigrants turned back at border crossings and to expand workplace raids for undocumented workers. In 1996, Clinton signed the Immigration Act requiring the deportation of all immigrants ever convicted of "aggravated felonies"—even those whose convictions occurred decades earlier. Thousands of immigrants who had lived most of their lives in the United States faced deportation under this draconian law, for crimes many had committed when they were teenagers.[20]

Clinton also embraced the Christian conservatives' "family values" slogan (however infrequently he practiced them), bringing Vice President Al Gore on board early on for this project. Gore and wife Tipper would crusade against TV and movie violence, finally zeroing in on the hip-hop music industry. Clinton signed the Defense of Marriage Act in 1996, barring same-sex couples from marrying. During his second term, Clinton also took aim at teen pregnancy, promoting abstinence programs and pushing for teen curfews.

Incarceration Nation

Clinton made good on his "tough on crime" persona. In 1994, Congress passed Clinton's Omnibus Crime Control Act, which expanded the use of the federal death penalty to sixty crimes, and included financing for a hundred thousand more local police. Under Clinton's watch, the prison population nearly doubled. In 1996, Congress passed Clinton's Anti-Terrorism and Effective Death Penalty Act, severely limiting death row inmates' right to habeas corpus appeals and shortening time limits on filing for appeals. During Clinton's presidency, the number of executions surged to the highest level in four decades.[21]

Two-thirds of those who entered the prison system between 1980 and 1995 were Black, Latino, or poor, the vast majority nonviolent drug offenders. With the prison population swollen to more than two million, African Americans, who made up just 12 percent of the U.S. population and only 13 percent of drug users, accounted for 35 percent of drug arrests, 53 percent of drug convictions—and 43 percent of those on death row.[22] In 2002, the U.S. Bureau of Justice estimated that 30 percent of twelve-year-old Black boys would spend time in jail at some point in their life—more than will attend college.[23]

Because many states have laws denying present and former inmates the right to vote, an estimated 13 percent of all Black men—one in every three in Alabama and Florida—has been disfranchised. As Marable pointed out, "[M]ore than 4.2 million Americans were prohibited from voting in the 2000 presidential election because they were in prison or had in the past been convicted of a felony. . . . In effect, it was the repressive policies of the Clinton-Gore administration that helped to give the White House to the Republicans."[24]

Cockburn and St. Clair commented, "The spectre and reality of incarceration would have the traditional effect of suppressing the dangerous classes, as a time when the gap between the rich and the poor grew wider than at any point in recent history."[25]

In 1994, Clinton stripped public housing residents of their most basic constitutional rights. He endorsed routine "police sweeps" throughout high-rise public housing—without requiring that police first either go to court to get search warrants or ask for residents' permission. A federal court judge in Chicago had earlier ruled that such police sweeps were unconstitutional, on the grounds that they amount to "a chaotic invasion of privacy." The judge went on to argue that many of the same people who support the idea of police sweeps "would not dream of allowing police to search their own homes without their consent or without warrants."[26]

The case that prompted the ruling came after some Chicago public housing tenants filed legal complaints when their apartments were searched by the Chicago Police Department. Bands of up to two hundred police—most of whom were ostensibly in search of drugs and guns—began regularly sweeping through the city's enormous public housing complexes, which together house 150,000 of the city's poor. Clinton was unmoved by the judge's talk of poor people's right to privacy. He denounced the ruling, and vowed to increase the number of police sweeps in public housing. "We must not allow criminals to find shelter in the public housing community they terrorize," he said.[27]

The Democratic President Dismantles the New Deal

But welfare reform was Clinton's trump card, as he made good on his pledge to "end welfare as we know it." In 1994, he instituted new requirements for welfare, transforming AFDC into a temporary program that required all able-bodied recipients to go to work after two years. In addition, Clinton's Department of Health and Welfare Services allowed individual states to waive federal regulations and experiment with stricter programs, granting nineteen states waivers for a more stringent time limit. As Wisconsin Governor Tommy Thompson was in the process of eliminating that state's welfare program—reducing the welfare caseload by 62 percent, from 100,000 to 38,000 families—he ranted, "There will be no more welfare offices, no more welfare checks, no more welfare families." He added, "Families are working. They're living the American Dream."[28]

In 1996, Clinton signed the Republican-sponsored Personal Responsibility and Work Opportunity Act, dismantling the hallmark of the New Deal in place for sixty years, relieving the government of any responsibility to care for the poorest members of its population. The bill not only limited poor women and children to a five-year lifetime limit, but also denied federal services to legal immigrants and included a $2.5 billion cut in food stamps. Cockburn and St. Clair observed, "It's likely that these two Republican add-ons were what allured the White House, because . . . Clinton could then turn to the liberals saying they needed him to be elected president so he could repair part of the damage wrought by the very bill he had just signed."[29]

While welfare rolls shrank and work rates soared over the following years, most former welfare families joined the ranks of the working poor. Five years later, 40 percent of former welfare recipients were still not able to find and keep jobs. Most of those who did succeed in finding work were earning some $6 to $8 an hour. In one study, 33 percent had to cut the size of meals because there wasn't enough food. Peter Edelman, who resigned from the Clinton administration in protest over welfare reform, estimated that roughly three million families who left the welfare system had become part of America's "disappeared." [30]

Clinton was reelected in 1996 when he ran against the droopy Senator Bob Dole —but with a voter turnout that dipped to less than 50 percent. Voter participation varied greatly according to income. In 1996, 74 percent of those with household incomes above $75,000 cast a vote, while 61 percent of those whose family incomes fell between $10,000 and $15,000 did not bother.

Clinton Attacks Labor; Labor Supports Clinton

Clinton came to the presidency having already built an antilabor reputation in Arkansas, a right-to-work state. In Clinton's successful campaign for state attorney general in 1976, he opposed efforts by the state AFL-CIO to allow union shops if members of the union local and management agreed to it. "I don't think it will pass, and I so far have very serious reservations about it," Clinton said at the time.[31] In 1986, state AFL-CIO leader Bill Becker told the *Wall Street Journal,* "almost any [Clinton] activity, insofar as our folks are concerned, is reminiscent of what Reagan is doing to us." Four years later, Becker stated more bluntly, "This guy will pat you on the back and piss down your leg." [32]

One of Clinton's first accomplishments as president was the successful ratification of the North American Free Trade Agreement (NAFTA) in 1993. Deregulation and open markets were the watchwords of the Clinton administration, and protests from labor and environmentalists were not about to get in the way. "If the 1993 budget plan enshrined 'deficit reduction' as a domestic economic strategy, NAFTA established 'free trade' as the holy writ of the Clinton-Gore foreign economic strategy," Selfa noted.[33] Clinton went on to pursue other free trade initiatives—including the 1994 ratification of the World Trade Organization (WTO) and the 2000 approval of "permanent normal trade relations" with China, further advancing the cause of unbridled corporate greed around the globe.

By Clinton's second term, economist Leo Troy observed, "Organized labor is one Clinton constituency that cannot say it is better off after four years, and that will likely feel the pain even more acutely as it crosses his bridge into the next century."[34] In 1997, Clinton used the provisions of the 1926 Railway Labor Act to ban a strike by American Airlines pilots. Although the U.S. economy gained 12.2 million jobs between 1992 and 1995, mass layoffs continued at recession levels. Between 1993 and 1995, 8.5 million workers lost their jobs involuntarily. Low unemployment rates were meaningless to the millions of workers downsized during this period.[35]

Clinton's labor secretary, Robert Reich, summing up Clinton's first year in office, stated, "We essentially have collaborated and responded to the business community."[36] At Clinton's behest, Reich set up a commission to study how to rewrite 1930s-era labor laws to allow for greater "cooperation" between labor and management. *Business Week* magazine acknowledged in 1994, "Few American managers have ever accepted the right of unions to exist . . . [but] over the past dozen years, U.S. industry has conducted one of the most successful antiunion wars ever, illegally firing thousands of workers for exercising their right to organize. To ease up now, many executives feel, would be to snatch defeat from the jaws of victory."[37] In 1994, twenty-five thousand workers filed lawsuits claiming they were illegally fired, compared with just two hundred workers per year in the late 1970s.[38]

AFL-CIO's "New Voices" Leadership

In 1995, there were promising signs of labor revitalization. The AFL-CIO witnessed the first contested election for leadership in its history. Prior to 1995, the federation had had only two presidents, George Meany from 1955 to 1979, and Lane Kirkland since 1979. But the 1995 convention was marked by heated debate, in sharp contrast to the typical week of banquets and backslapping followed by a ritual coronation.

That year, roughly 56 percent of delegates from the federation's seventy-eight affiliated unions rejected Lane Kirkland's designated successor, Tom Donahue. Instead they elected Service Employees International Union (SEIU) president John Sweeney and his "New Voices" reform slate for top leadership in AFL-CIO posts.

Sweeney's SEIU had been one of the few major unions to grow in the 1980s (although two-thirds of the growth came through mergers with other unions). Nevertheless, the SEIU had adopted aggressive organizing methods with considerable success in its Justice for Janitors campaigns in Los Angeles and Washington, D.C. As SEIU president, Sweeney devoted 30 percent of the union's operating budget to organizing, targeting low-paid service workers such as janitors and health care workers, with a great deal of success.

The "New Voices" leader pledged that no longer would the AFL-CIO top brass hold its annual meeting at its traditional luxurious Bal Harbour, Florida, meeting spot. He argued that the mass media seized upon images from the meeting as "'symbols of the labor federation's complacency—often with photos of older men lounging at poolside.' Sweeny pledged that organized labor would henceforth be meeting at the sites of major organizing drives." [39]

Sweeney demonstrated a sense of urgency in his 1996 book, *America Needs a Raise:* Under Clinton, "labor continued to lose almost as many legislative battles in Washington as we won. . . . Our sense of alarm increased with the November 1994 elections, when Republicans, intent on repealing 60 years of social progress, captured control of both houses of Congress." [40] In a 1996 speech to the Rainbow Coalition, Sweeney argued, "There's a free-floating anger among hardworking people for whom the American dream is turning into a nightmare of unpaid bills and unfulfilled aspirations. Increasingly, American workers are down on their government, down on their employers, and down on their future. American workers are running out of hope." [41]

But Sweeney was an AFL-CIO insider, having served on its Executive Council and tolerated Kirkland during his sixteen-year reign. As SEIU president, Sweeney drew two union salaries: on top of his $200,000 salary, he continued to draw a paycheck from his old New York City local for "consultant's fees," which earned him an additional $450,000 over a period of thirteen years. [42] While "consulting," however, he ignored corruption in his own local, and as SEIU president he put Los Angeles Local 399 into receivership after Black and Latino reformers won union office. He quickly offered an olive branch to the AFL-CIO Executive Council, when the federation needed a major overhaul.

Like Donahue, Sweeney pledged the AFL-CIO's support for

Clinton's 1996 reelection campaign—before it even began. "We truly believe President Clinton has done a great job as president." Clinton, who received a standing ovation at the AFL-CIO convention, wasn't even questioned as to why he had not fulfilled the two promises he made to workers in the last campaign: to raise the minimum wage and to pass a bill banning the union-busting tactic of permanently replacing workers who go on strike.[43]

Unlike John L. Lewis in 1935, Sweeney had no clear alternative direction in mind for the union movement.[44] As socialist Lee Sustar argued, "Rather than fight, the trade union bureaucracy accepted concessions to reestablish 'partnership' with employers. Union officials embraced management's 'teamwork' and 'jointness'— 'cooperative' work programs that supposedly replaced adversarial labor-management relations."[45] In April 1996, Sweeney argued in the *AFL-CIO News,* "We can no longer afford the luxury of pretending that productivity, quality, and competitiveness are not our business. They are our business, our jobs, and our paychecks."[46]

Later that year, Sweeney assured members of Business for Social Responsibility: "We want to help American business compete in the world and create new wealth for your shareholders and your employees. We want to work with you to bake a larger pie which all Americans can share, and not just argue with you about the existing pie."[47] But business leaders had no intention of resuming a cooperative relationship with the labor movement. The relatively peaceful 1950s and 1960s were the exception, not the rule, of American capital's relations with labor.

A large part of the problem was that the labor movement's flabby and conservative leadership remained reluctant to lead the sort of fight required to turn the tide. "We're not a strike-happy union," UAW president Ronald A. Gettelfinger declared in 2002.[48] In 1997, having pledged to organize a million new workers per year, Sweeney seemed oblivious to the fact that AFL-CIO unions had lost a half-million members since he took over. "I really think things are going great," he stated.[49]

In 1996, pay increases for union workers ranked *below* those for nonunion workers. Nor did the new leadership initiate a fightback. Work stoppages (strikes and lockouts) involving a thousand or more workers increased to a meager thirty-seven in 1996, from a fifty-year low of thirty-one in 1995.[50]

Nine years later, the failures of its reform leadership were obvious in the chosen location for its executive council's meeting: a luxury resort in Bal Harbour, Florida. In 2004, the Bureau of Labor Statistics had announced that private sector union membership had hit a record low of 8.2 percent—roughly one million lower than when Sweeney took over running the AFL-CIO.[51] Nothing much had changed, from the AFL-CIO's unflinching support for Democrats to its leaders' disdain for initiating class struggle. This strategy had proven disastrous for organized labor.

The Return of Class Struggle

Whether or not Sweeney intended to make good on his promise to rebuild a fighting labor movement, his rhetoric fit the mood among rank-and-file unionists. The goal of the employers' offensive remained the same: fewer workers laboring much harder for falling wages, preferably without union representation. But in the 1990s, industrial workers began to struggle with a degree of determination and solidarity not shown since Reagan's election in 1980, as both employers and workers dug in their heels in a number of bitter, protracted disputes.

But these strikes rarely made national headlines. As journalist William Serrin commented,

> Much of the labor movement and much of the United States—including the nation's newsrooms—believed in the 1980s and 1990s that nothing was going on in labor. . . . In truth, industrial America, the labor movement and the lives of America's working people were being turned upside down. It was just that almost no one could see this, including the last few labor correspondents and a handful of reporters often reduced to covering work, not labor, and quickly ready to say so.[52]

The strikes of this period demonstrated the enormous capacity for solidarity that existed among rank-and-file workers, but the New Voices leadership rarely tapped that capacity and discouraged anything beyond symbolic gestures. This weakness was evident in the defeat of the twenty-six hundred workers on strike between 1995 and 1997 against Detroit's two main newspapers, the *Detroit Free Press* and the *Detroit News*. Under a joint agreement, the Detroit Newspaper Agency managed both papers, owned by newspaper chains Gannett and Knight-Ridder.

The strike began after management gutted work rules and issued new work schedules. At the beginning of the strike in July 1995, *Detroit News* publisher Robert Giles made the employers' strategy clear: "We're going to hire a whole new workforce and go on without unions, or they can surrender unconditionally and salvage what they can." [53]

Thousands of strikers and supporters turned out to mass pickets, with some success. Round-the-clock mass pickets over Labor Day weekend in 1995 prevented, with some confrontation, the newspaper from getting through the plant gates for hours at a time. But the police force, which had received a $400,000 "donation" from the newspaper owners, stood by and watched when scab trucks drove into the pickets, injuring five. Then a judge granted the paper owners what they'd sought: an injunction limiting pickets to no more than five strikers at a time at the main printing plant. The strikers responded by moving their pickets to distribution centers and called on union leaders to organize a national solidarity march through Detroit, to "shut down Motown." [54]

The leaders of the six local unions endorsed the march, but the AFL-CIO was not enthusiastic. The strike became a war of attrition. The unions promoted a labor boycott of the struck newspapers, which drove down circulation by 37 percent, and published their own newspaper, the *Sunday Journal,* that reached a circulation of 165,000 in 1997. [55] But Gannett and Knight-Ridder were prepared to weather a long-term dispute to cripple the union.

In the end, the unions made an unconditional offer to return to work without a contract, while calling on the NLRB to rule that the strike was over unfair labor practices. Only then did the AFL-CIO organize the long-awaited march on Detroit. As Sustar argued, "The unions and the AFL-CIO have tried to cover up this surrender by claiming that this was a 'new stage' in the struggle to win back workers' jobs. But Sweeney's announcement of a national march could not disguise the fact that the unions had surrendered in a key battle in the archetypical union town of Detroit." [56]

Illinois "War Zone"

By 1995, Decatur, Illinois—dubbed the "war zone" by those in the labor movement—had become emblematic of the bitterness of the class struggle. More than 750 workers at A.E. Staley, a corn processing plant owned by the British multinational Tate & Lyle, had been locked out of their jobs for two and a half years. Another nineteen hundred workers had been on strike against Caterpillar, the earth-moving equipment manufacturer, for more than a year and a half.[57] When rubber workers ended their ten-month strike against Bridgestone/Firestone in May, only 371 of 1,209 union members had crossed the picket line to return to work.[58] Altogether, these three corporations employed a third of Decatur's working class, and in 1995 one in four Decatur households had a family member who was either on strike, locked out, or permanently replaced while on strike.[59]

Workers from the three striking unions faced common problems: ten- to twelve-hour workdays, sixty-hour workweeks, and speedups— in the name of corporate "competitiveness" in an increasingly global economy. Their union leaders—the United Paperworkers International Union (UPIU) at Staley, the UAW at Caterpillar, and the United Steel Workers at Bridgestone/Firestone (which absorbed the United Rubber Workers during the strike)—were reluctant participants in a showdown forced by the employers. As journalist Stephen Franklin, documenting the Decatur struggles, argued in *Three Strikes*:

> But in Decatur the three global giants that were taking on the unions— Caterpillar, Bridgestone/Firestone, and A.E. Staley—were the reigning powers in their industries. They were not fighting to stay alive. They were not racing to keep ahead of ruthless competitors about to overtake them. They were monoliths, and they had prevailed because they had the power to do so.[60]

The Staley struggle began in 1992 when Staley demanded twelve-hour rotating shifts for all employees. The union initiated a corporate campaign to pressure Staley clients Miller Beer and the Pepsi Corporation to withdraw their contracts. Inside the plant, workers slowed down production by half using a tightly coordinated "running the plant backward" strategy. But as Moody commented, "The Staley workers ran the plant backward so well that, in August 1994, the company locked them out."[61]

The strike won the formal backing of the AFL-CIO, but little more. Leaders of UPIU Local 7837 had no plan for stopping production, and building trades union members and Teamsters crossed picket lines throughout the strike. Local leaders, themselves facing court injunctions, actively discouraged mass pickets. Police attacked hundreds of peaceful protesters with pepper gas during a demonstration on June 25, 1994. Finally, two and a half years after they were locked out, the workers voted to accept Staley's original offer. Only a handful of the locked-out workers were given back their jobs.[62] "What was clear," Moody wrote, "was that the strike had not only lost because of the weak position of the workers at this single plant, but because the UPIU leadership had been willing to accept defeat." [63]

" Kick the Cat"

Caterpillar CEO Donald Fites made no secret of the fact that he intended to drive wages down in any future contract with the UAW. Caterpillar's U.S. workforce was 75 percent nonunion by the 1990s.[64] Fites told the *New York Times* in 1991, "There is a narrowing of the gap between the average American's income and that of the Mexicans. As a human being, I think what is going on is positive. I don't think it is realistic for 250 million Americans to control so much of the world's GNP." [65] Fites himself had taken home $545,000 in wages and benefits the previous year.[66]

When Caterpillar workers went on strike in 1995, they had been working without a union contract for more than two years, after losing a six-month strike in 1992. Between 1992 and 1994, class war raged inside the plant. Management systematically harassed union members, while workers maintained their sense of solidarity by wearing T-shirts with slogans such as "Cat treats workers like dogs" and chanting anti-company slogans inside the plant. At eight different Caterpillar plants, workers took unauthorized strike action to protest management policies, which pressured the UAW to call an unfair labor practices strike in 1994.[67]

Yet, eighteen months into the second strike, the UAW surrendered for the second time—and again *without a contract*. Fully 80 percent of Caterpillar workers voted against returning to work, but the UAW cut off their strike benefits. Within a month, they were back at work. Once back, union members were banned from wearing union buttons, hats, or T-shirts and even fired for refusing to shake hands with scabs or opening their lunch boxes too slowly for inspection by company security guards.[68] The demoralization of the defeat was so great that twelve workers committed suicide shortly after the strike ended in December 1995.[69]

Caterpillar, however, saw its profits soar by 155 percent between 1993 and 1997.[70] Profits surged to $836 million. *Fortune* magazine added Caterpillar to its list of the "World's Most Admired Companies"—which Fites stated "clearly reflects on our highly motivated employees who are committed to meeting the needs of customers around the world."[71] Between 1992 and 1997, Caterpillar opened fifteen new nonunion plants, eleven in the largely nonunion South.[72] In 1998, Fites' salary rose to $3.5 million, plus $7 million worth of stock options.[73]

At the insistence of UAW leaders, Caterpillar workers finally accepted a contract by a narrow margin in March 1998, but only after the company agreed to rehire all one hundred sixty union militants, and arbitrate the fate of two hundred more who had been fired.[74]

Solidarity and Politics

The solidarity among the Decatur strikers was such that the three unions were able to unite locally to organize teams of strikers, dubbed "road warriors," to visit hundreds of union locals across the country to appeal for solidarity. The strategy worked. Donations came in from locals and supporters across the country, and thousands of supporters traveled to Decatur to take part in solidarity rallies. Road warrior Dan Lane, for example, roused the audience at the Chicago Teamsters hall to "wild, foot-stomping applause," when he told them: "we're sick of workers dying, of twelve-hour shifts, of watching communities die because there aren't enough jobs when there are too many jobs that need doing. We're tired of being second-class citizens. We need to start making laws. This fight in Illinois has to be won."[75]

And Lane himself underwent a seismic change in consciousness. A Vietnam vet, he had gone to work at Staley, where his own father had worked for twenty-five years. As he traveled across the country, he said, "[W]hat became even more real to me was that this was not an isolated situation. It became not just Decatur—not just Decatur that was being exploited. All of a sudden I'm in the middle of people in a struggle, and it was a very real part of my life."[76]

Meanwhile, as Franklin noted, "within the union's leadership, some became uncomfortable with Lane's growing alignment with some of the leftist groups that identified with the Staley workers' struggle. They feared that his rhetoric was turning off other union members and dividing the local." [77] These leaders were missing the depth of class anger and bitterness, accumulated over nearly two decades, which had finally begun to translate into action. A layer of workers was beginning to conclude that the only way to turn the tide for labor was for workers to take matters into their own hands. For example, Bridgestone/Firestone worker Robert Borders argued—in the newspaper of one such "leftist group":

> I'm working for a company that treats me like a dog. That makes me want to fight back. It makes me dislike the people that are doing this to me. And eventually if they keep doing this all over the country there's going to be a revolution. . . . I'm not trying to sound radical or off the wall, but there's getting to be an underlying feeling in this country by people who are suppressed and kept down, and someday in the future that's going to explode, because they're not going to be able to keep it under control forever. [78]

Caterpillar had set out to destroy the union but did not succeed. As George Boze, vice president of Local 974 in Peoria, Illinois, commented in February 1998, "The company has made radicals of so many people." [79] The 1998 contract did not end the dispute but opened up a new chapter in the struggle. A group of Caterpillar workers began publishing a newsletter, *Kick the Cat,* aimed at building a network of rank-and-file union activists from different plants. As the newsletter explained:

> We have endured a long and bitter struggle as UAW members at Cat and our families have endured as well. We have made many sacrifices and we have lost many members along the way. We must never forget we have been the victims of a brutal and vicious employer who will not rest until the UAW is destroyed at Cat. . . . UAW leadership has for a very long time followed patterns of bargaining that have failed, and failed miserably, to protect our jobs and provide fundamental union values mandated by our constitution. . . . The battle with Cat is win or lose. There is no middle ground. [80]

"Part-Time America Doesn't Work!"

The Teamsters union won labor's first major victory in decades in a strike against United Parcel Service (UPS) in August 1997. IBT President Ron Carey had been reluctant to call the one hundred eighty-five thousand UPS workers out on strike but had little choice after UPS management refused to budge as the national contract expired. Within days, Carey was leading a crusade against corporate greed on behalf of millions of working-class people.

Not only was the UPS strike the first national strike of any kind in fourteen years, it was also the first strike in generations to win widespread popular support. Two weeks into the strike, opinion polls showed support for the strikers beating support for management by a two-to-one margin. Pollster Daniel Yankelovich argued, "This strike is a consciousness-raising event. What so often happens is that an event like this suddenly and unexpectedly focuses attention on something that is on people's minds and makes their concerns more of a political issue." [81] Even the *Wall Street Journal* was forced to begrudgingly admit, "The strike, oddly popular with the inconvenienced, has wide public support." [82]

Before the strike the news media paid little attention to the plight of low-paid workers. But for two short weeks, the UPS strikers' demands were featured on the front page of every newspaper, and as the most important news items in virtually every broadcast. Millions of television viewers saw a triumphant Ron Carey emerge from negotiations to declare victory on August 18: "This fight with UPS shows what working people can accomplish when they all stick together." Viewers also saw UPS' chief negotiator, who had arrogantly declared at the start of the strike that the company would not shift from its "last, best, final offer," shamefacedly admit that UPS had given in to most of the union's demands. [83]

UPS made more than $1.1 billion in profits in 1996, ranking thirty-seventh in the Fortune 500—ahead of Coca-Cola—and was an obvious symbol of the shameless greed of U.S. corporations. UPS had more than doubled its profits since 1992, yet the real wages of its full-time workforce had not risen since 1987. The company had also come to rely increasingly upon part-time workers, who made up 60 percent of its workforce by 1997, up from 42 percent ten years earlier. UPS's part-time starting wage of $8 to $9 an hour had not risen since 1982. Even after two years of employment, part-timers still earned as little as $9 an hour compared with a $20 hourly wage for full-time workers. [84]

The situation of the UPS workforce roughly mirrored that of

workers across the United States, and the strike's slogan, "Part-time America doesn't work!" resonated with broad swaths of working-class people. As Deepa Kumar commented, "What is truly remarkable in this context is how the UPS strike affected media coverage of economic issues and opened up a space for deliberation on questions of economic and political inequality."[85] *New York Times* columnist Bob Herbert went so far as to call the UPS strike a "workers' rebellion," "the angry, fist-waving response of the frustrated American worker, a revolt against the ruthless treatment of workers by so many powerful corporations."[86]

UPS management was financially far better prepared for a strike than the Teamsters' union, which was forced to borrow money from other unions to pay workers just $55 per week in strike pay. Management hired off-duty police to harass and, given the opportunity, beat up strikers. But UPS' vast fortune couldn't buy public sympathy. Its slick public relations team issued full-page newspaper ads calling upon the Teamsters' union to allow workers to vote "democratically" on management's offer and persuaded the National Association of Manufacturers to demand that Clinton intervene to stop the strike to avert economic disaster. Both these plans backfired.[87]

Ron Carey quickly pointed out that union members were "voting" against UPS by honoring the picket line by a margin of more than 95 percent. Clinton, meanwhile, despite daily requests from UPS and other business interests to intervene in the strike, was openly unenthusiastic about the prospect of doing so. He would have had to invoke Taft-Hartley legislation last used by Carter against the national miners' strike in 1978. Indeed, in a mid-August Gallup poll, 75 percent of the respondents said that Clinton should not intervene to stop the strike.[88]

Two weeks into the strike, UPS was running at less than 10 percent of its normal capacity, and claimed to be losing $50 million per day with its mainly managerial scab workforce.[89] While Carey ran the UPS strike in a standard nonconfrontational fashion, flying pickets in Chicago shut down operations at skyscrapers such as the Sears Tower and the Amoco Building, drawing out all the buildings' janitors and other union workers until management agreed to refuse to accept any packages from UPS scabs. Picket lines in Somerville, Massachusetts, and Warwick, Rhode Island, erupted into confrontations with police, as hundreds of workers tried to stop trucks from crossing the picket line.[90] If UPS had attempted to resume its ground operations with a scab workforce, more confrontations were likely.

As in Detroit and Decatur, union members from a variety of occupations visited the picket lines regularly. In New York, more than a thousand members of the Communications Workers of America (CWA) joined the picket line on August 7, chanting, "Big Brown, shut it down!" When strikers thanked the CWA workers, one replied, "No, thank *you*. You're fighting for all of us."[91] The Independent Pilots Association (IPA), representing UPS pilots—whose own union contract had been in limbo for months—honored the Teamsters' picket lines throughout the strike. "This airline is closed until you give us the okay to return," vowed UPS pilot Rich Henry at a support rally.[92]

After the strike ended, newspapers were filled with pictures of cheering strikers celebrating their victory. The Teamsters' strike marked the first major strike victory since the defeat of PATCO in 1981, and pointed the way forward for the labor movement as a whole. "It ends the PATCO syndrome. A 16-year period in which a strike was synonymous with defeat and demoralization is over," argued labor historian Nelson Lichtenstein.[93] UPS driver Robert Ridley said in Austin, Texas, "This was labor against Corporate America."[94] And labor won.

Carey's Downfall

Just one year after Carey led the UPS strike to victory, however, he was removed from office and expelled from the IBT. A government commission took this action on the basis of corruption charges against Carey—which were found to be baseless in federal court years later.[95] Officially, Carey was accused of having "failed to exercise his required duty of inquiry" when one of the organizers of his 1996 presidential campaign took part in a financial swap scheme to funnel money into the Carey campaign.

Carey was not accused of participating in the underhanded deal, but merely of not knowing about it. Yet such transactions are "business as usual" in the world of America's top-heavy union bureaucracy. The commission acknowledged, in fact, that Carey's opponent, James Hoffa, Jr. (son of the famed mobster), was suspected of impropriety when he claimed to have received $2 million in small notes from bingo games and bake sales. The commission decided, however, not to discipline Hoffa, who went on to win the Teamsters presidency in the rerun of the election.

At the age of sixty-two, Carey was banned from membership in the union to which he had belonged since his first job at UPS in 1956. In reality, Carey's expulsion from the IBT was an act of revenge by the employers, and an attempt to squash a rising labor movement by removing one of its key leaders. It also helped to discredit a union reformer, since Carey won the Teamsters union presidency in 1991 at the helm of a democratic reform movement. Republicans in Congress, not to mention UPS management, openly embraced the return of the Teamsters union to the Hoffa empire. Senator Orrin Hatch predicted, "Hoffa is going to be the labor leader of the 21st century." [96]

Shutting Down General Motors

By 1995, union membership in auto-parts plants had fallen to just 18 percent, down from 70 percent in 1976.[97] Yet in 1998, UAW auto-parts workers were still able to paralyze General Motors in a fifty-four-day strike.[98] GM generated record net profits of $1.6 billion in the first quarter of 1998, but its productivity still lagged behind that of its competitors.[99] In 1997, GM made $850 in profits for every car it produced; the figure for Ford was $1,520 per car. For this reason, General Motors' management pleaded poverty to justify slashing jobs—nearly eighty thousand in the previous six years—from a North American total of three hundred seventy thousand. All told, twenty-seven plants had been closed down, while GM announced it planned to close yet more.[100]

On June 5, 1998, ninety-two hundred UAW members went on strike at two auto-parts plants in Flint to protest GM's decision to send union work to outside suppliers elsewhere in the United States and in Mexico. GM provoked one strike when management moved machinery for a new car model out of the plant, implying the new model would be built elsewhere. Within weeks, the strike shut down twenty-seven of GM's twenty-nine North American assembly plants, forcing GM to lay off 192,000, costing the company more than $2 billion during the fifty-four-day strike. While the union did not win a clear victory, the agreement kept the status quo until the 1999 national contract. GM certainly did not win, which was itself a victory after two decades of concessions. Symbolically, GM management was forced to move the contested machinery back into the plant, as workers stood arm-in-arm on the picket line singing "Solidarity Forever." [101]

Like the UPS workers a year earlier, the Flint autoworkers demonstrated the enormous power of the strike weapon against even the most profitable corporations. Yet the mainstream media repeatedly declared the strike the antiquated technique of an obsolete labor movement. The *New York Times* even concluded that the Caterpillar strike provided "a stark demonstration of the increasing futility of a weapon with which unions could once paralyze whole industries in promoting their members' interests." [102]

The Battle of Seattle

When thirty thousand unionists and environmentalists marched against the World Trade Organization (WTO) in downtown Seattle on November 30, 1999, carrying signs and chanting against "corporate bloodsuckers," they gave voice to the seething anger felt by millions of people across the United States and around the world. Thousands of protesters linked arms for hours, preventing officials from entering the conference center and delaying the start of the meeting. [103] Hundreds of Seattle port workers called a one-day strike on November 30 and blockaded the doors of the WTO's conference center. More than ninety-six hundred dockworkers up and down the West Coast went on strike in solidarity with their Seattle union brothers and sisters. [104]

Trapped in his hotel room, United Nations Secretary General Kofi Annan missed his scheduled address. Secretary of State Madeleine Albright was also pushed off the speaking schedule. Washington's governor declared a state of emergency, while Seattle Mayor Paul Schell called in the National Guard to crack down on protesters. Schell declared the downtown area of Seattle surrounding the WTO talks a "no protest zone" and vowed that anyone in the area after a 7 p.m. curfew would be arrested. [105]

City officials blamed "hooligans"—a small number of anarchists who broke store windows—for starting the violence. But it was the overwhelming show of police force unleashed by government officials, not the protesters, that turned the city of Seattle into a battle scene for three days, until the WTO talks ended on December 3. Police shot rubber bullets, tossed percussion grenades, and sprayed pepper gas at thousands of protesters, while armored personnel carriers roamed the streets, tear-gassing and terrorizing entire residential neighborhoods until late into the night. The protesters chanted, "The whole world is watching" as they were pepper-gassed by Seattle police. By the end of the second day, more than six hundred protesters had been rounded up and thrown into jail. As eyewitness Bill Capowski of the Center for Campus Organizing reported, "Several neighborhoods are, at 1 a.m. Pacific Time, still . . . deluged by police running through their streets and throwing tear gas canisters . . . regular non-political neighborhood, middle-aged folks, residents, are out in the streets, with their kids watching them out the windows, yelling at the police to go home, while their eyes and throats are burning [from the tear gas]." [106]

Hundreds of protesters—including unionists, students, and other activists—who had been arrested during the police sweep on December 1 remained in jail two days later. Police threw tear gas canisters into buses holding protesters. Once protesters reached the jail, the police targeted individual activists and threw them into solitary confinement. On the inside, the prisoners organized themselves as one group, refusing to be arraigned in court until those in solitary were released. Meanwhile, several thousand demonstrators rallied for their release outside the jail in a spontaneous outpouring of anger. On the last day of the WTO talks, with the protesters still jailed, the King County Labor Council called a demonstration at the courthouse, inside the "no-protest zone." [107]

For days, city newspapers all across the United States featured front-page photos of the violence. Newspapers felt compelled to document the evidence against the WTO, so ordinary people could read in a single news article how the WTO forbade South Africa from producing lower-cost AIDS drugs because they were the "intellectual property" of pharmaceutical corporations; how the WTO's notion of free trade included child and sweatshop labor; and how corporations produced dangerous genetically engineered food to maximize their profits. People were able to see for themselves pictures of the mass demonstrations of workers, students, and environmentalists. Television news featured footage of police in riot gear, tear-gassing and kicking peaceful demonstrators, as well as shots of looting and window-breaking at McDonald's and Gap.

Mainstream news reports left no doubt that police were targeting not the anarchists, but the thousands of peaceful protesters who had linked arms to stall WTO officials. The *Chicago Tribune*, for example, wrote, "when more than 35,000 people had gathered in the streets of the Emerald City and started to accomplish their goal, police in riot gear fired tear gas to control the crowd to keep the conference running on time. . . . Initially, police allowed vandals and looters to roam the streets with impunity, because they were blocks from the convention center." [108]

Chicago Tribune columnist Mary Schmich was direct. She wrote, "People who last week had never heard about the World Trade Organization are now wondering, rightly, who are these trade guys? And are they really running the world behind our backs? People who don't usually pay attention to business news are suddenly talking about child labor, environmental abuses, and low wages in countries they couldn't find on a map." [109] A *BusinessWeek* poll conducted during the Seattle protests found that 52% of Americans supported the protesters. [110]

The outcry against the WTO shifted the ideological terrain in mainstream society. The widely televised and reported-on demonstrations and confrontations served as a reminder that protest was both urgent and effective. In one antiracist struggle that subsequently emerged in January, forty-six thousand mostly Black protesters demonstrated in front of South Carolina's state capitol, demanding the state stop flying the Confederate flag—many with signs bearing the slogan, "Your Heritage Is My Slavery." [111]

Inequality Grows in the "Miracle Economy"

The economic recovery of the early 1990s evolved into a long boom, lasting until the end of Clinton's presidency. As the boom entered its seventh straight year, economists sounded much like their 1920s predecessors in describing the boom as a new type of "miracle economy." "From boardrooms to living rooms and from government offices to trading floors, a new consensus is emerging," the *Wall Street Journal* enthused: "The big, bad business cycle has been tamed." [112] Clinton bragged, "America's economy is the strongest it's been in a generation," noting that the economy had "added 12.3 million new jobs since I took office, and unemployment has now been below 6 percent for almost three years." [113] When the unemployment rate dipped to 4.9 percent in May 1997, lower than at any time since 1973, writers for *BusinessWeek* could barely contain themselves, bleating, "Is this economy on a roll, or what?" [114]

As Joel Geier and Ahmed Shawki remarked of Clinton's appearance at the G-7 (plus Russia) meeting in 1997,

> Bill Clinton used the opportunity to swagger in front of the media and share his wisdom on economic matters. The *Chicago Tribune* reported: "Sounding like Ronald Reagan a decade earlier, President Clinton delivered a free-market economic lecture . . . to other world leaders skittish about voter protests to budget cuts and freer trade." The other G-7 members were encouraged to emulate the strategy employed by the U.S. ruling class in cutting wages and social benefits, raising rates of exploitation, maximizing profit, and developing an edge in global markets.[115]

The consistently low level of unemployment did not bring economic security to workers in the 1990s. In 1997, almost 30 percent of all U.S. workers had jobs that were not regular full-time jobs. Downsized or laid-off workers earned an average of 13 percent less in their next job, and more than one-fourth lost employer-provided health insurance. By 1990, U.S. manufacturing employees worked 320 more hours—the equivalent of two months—than manufacturing workers in West Germany or France.[116] Yet the typical married-couple family worked 247 hours—more than six weeks—longer per year in 1996 than in 1989. African Americans in married-couple working families worked almost five hundred more hours per year than white families in 1996, showing the consequences of wage disparities between Blacks and whites due to racism.[117]

But even working longer hours did not provide financial security to working-class families, who were more frequently forced to borrow money just to pay their bills. Personal debt levels had reached their highest point in history, pushing more and more "typical American families" toward bankruptcy. It is no exaggeration to say that the miracle economy was built on the backs of the working class.

The wave of corporate downsizing during the early 1990s recession continued into the economic boom that followed it. In 1993, jobs lost to downsizing reached a record six hundred thousand.

During the month of January 1994 alone, corporations announced job cuts of 104,000 due to downsizing. Of those workers who lost their jobs between 1990 and 1992, 12 percent left the labor force, and an additional 17 percent were still unemployed two years later. Of the 71 percent who found new jobs, 31 percent had to take a wage cut of 25 percent or more, while 31 percent took a wage cut of up to 25 percent. Only 37 percent found new jobs at comparable wages. For example, of those downsized by RJR Nabisco in 1993, 72 percent found new jobs—earning an average of just 47 percent of their previous wages.[118] The share of jobs paying less than a "poverty-level wage" stayed the same between 1989 and 1997, making it virtually impossible for poor families to lift themselves out of poverty, no matter how many hours they worked.

A May 1997 survey by the *Wall Street Journal* reported that 46 percent of workers were "frequently concerned" about losing their jobs, compared with 31 percent in 1992.[119] As John A. Challenger, an executive vice president at Challenger Gray, admitted, "Companies are using downsizing to control wage pressures."[120] Meanwhile, manufacturing productivity grew by an average of 1.7 percent annually in the mid-1990s, compared with 2.9 percent during the postwar boom.[121]

By 1996—six years into the "miracle economy"—average weekly earnings in constant dollars were 19 percent lower than they had been in 1973, falling from $315 to $256.[122] Thurow observed, "[T]his is the first time since the collection of income data began that the median real wages of American males have consistently fallen over a twenty-year period. And never before have the majority of American workers suffered real wage reductions while the per capita gross domestic product (GDP) was increasing."[123] Economist David Gordon documented that the per capita real gross output of the U.S. economy was 53 percent larger in 1994 than it had been in 1973, yet real hourly take-home pay was four cents lower.[124]

According to the Economic Policy Institute's extensive report, *The State of Working America 2000–2001*, median family income in 1996 was $1,000 *lower* than in 1989. The report noted of the 1990s economic boom, "[O]nly corporate profits, the stock market and top executive pay are doing better than in the past." Author John Schmitt concluded, "The stock market boom has not rescued working families. Most Americans own no stock in any form, and those who do typically own very little." Ninety percent of the value of all stock remained in the hands of the top 10 percent of households.

The average corporate executive's (CEO) pay doubled between 1989 and 1997, while workers' real wages fell by 3.1 percent—down 6.7 percent for men and up just 0.8 percent for women—in the same period. Wage declines were worst among entry-level workers, whose real hourly wages fell by 7.4 percent among men and 6.1 percent among women. When benefits such as health insurance are included in the calculation, the drop was steeper. The number of employers offering health coverage dropped 4.2 percent—and 7.8 percent for male workers—between 1989 and 1997.[125]

Despite the economic boom, inequality grew virtually without interruption throughout the 1990s. Though Clinton had complained on the 1992 campaign trail that American CEOs were "paying themselves 100 times more than their workers," that figure rose to 209 times by 1997.[126] The share of wealth owned by the richest 1 percent of households rose from 37.4 percent of the national total in 1989 to 39.1 percent in 1997. Yet annual taxes paid by the wealthiest 1 percent of families fell by $36,710 between 1977 and 1997. Indeed, in 2004, the Associated Press reported, "Most American and foreign corporations operating in the United States paid no income tax between 1996 and 2000."[127] The audit, conducted by the General Accounting Office, found that 61 percent of American corporations and 71 percent of foreign corporations paid no income tax.[128] In 2000, 94 percent of American corporations and 89 percent of foreign corporations paid less than 5 percent of their total incomes in taxes.[129]

Yet the Clinton administration appeared oblivious to rising class inequality throughout the boom. Gordon recalled an April 1994 report on the economic recovery by a Clinton economic advisor, in which he "applauded the Federal Reserve's and the markets' continuing restraint in interest rates and pointed proudly to the tepid pace of inflation." Then, without comment, the advisor "projected 1994 real wage growth at zero percent." Gordon remarked on this apparent lack of concern about wages "from a key economic advisor to the president who had promised, in his initial economic message to Congress, that 'our economic plan will redress the inequities of the 1980s.'"[130]

For the Love of Enron

Enron's CEO, Kenneth Lay, was a close friend of George W. Bush and firmly established within Republican Party political circles. Cockburn and Silverstein remarked, "Perhaps it is a mere coincidence, simply the normal workings of the bourgeoisie's executive committee, but Enron has done remarkably well during the Clinton years." As Cockburn and Silverstein noted of Clinton's Treasury Secretary Robert Rubin,

> Shortly after Clinton selected him to head the NEC, Rubin sent a letter, written on Goldman Sachs stationery, to hundreds of former business clients, saying he "looked forward to continuing to work with you in my new capacity." One recipient of the letter was natural gas giant Enron, listed on Rubin's 1993 financial disclosure statement as one of 44 firms with which he had "significant contact" while at Goldman Sachs.[131]

In March 1994, Enron executives were part of Commerce Secretary Ron Brown's twenty-eight-company entourage when he traveled to Russia. On the trip, Enron successfully reached a deal to "develop new European markets for Russian gas." By November 1993, Enron reached a $1 billion deal with Turkey to construct two power stations.

In May 1994, U.S. State Department officials lobbied Indonesian dictator Mohamed Suharto on behalf of Enron's effort to build power plants there. In August 1994, Enron reached a $2.5 billion deal for a power plant in India. That same month, Enron arranged to build two power plants in the Philippines. The following month, an Enron representative was part of a fifty-executive troupe that traveled to Pakistan with Energy Secretary Hazel O'Leary. In November, Enron won a contract to build a power plant in China's Hainan province.[132]

The Democratic Party's 2004 presidential candidate John Kerry also had connections to Enron in the 1990s, via wife Teresa Heinz. Ken Lay sat on the board of the Heinz Foundation, and was put in charge of the Foundation's global warming work. Even after Enron's financial meltdown in December 2001 exposed the company's systematic and brazen looting of energy markets, the Heinz Foundation issued this statement of support: "Whatever troubles he had at Enron, Ken Lay had a good reputation in the environmental community for being a business man who was environmentally sensitive. When someone does something wrong in one part of their life, it doesn't mean they can't do good in another part of their life."[133]

Corporate Bailouts and Personal Bankruptcy

Long-Term Capital Management was known as the "Rolls Royce" of investment hedge funds that rose to prominence amidst the Wall Street feeding frenzy of the mid-1990s. Founded in 1994 by a particularly arrogant band of Wall Street bond traders, physicists, Nobel laureate economists, and computer programmers, Long-Term Capital's "rocket scientists"—as they became known on Wall Street—claimed to have found a foolproof method of betting on bond prices. They based their betting strategy on computer models and mathematical equations that compared the current prices of bonds, stocks, and currencies with their historical values. In return for their guidance, they demanded a 2 percent management fee, and a 25 percent annual "incentive" fee. A writer for the business newspaper, *Barron's,* later described them as "affluent, BMW-driving, Dom Perignon-drinking, Vail-vacationing, Hampton-weekending, Greenwich-living erstwhile masters of the universe."[134]

Long-Term Capital's chief officer, John W. Meriwether, achieved stardom in the 1980s as a Wall Street bond trader for Salomon Brothers. True, he was forced out after his department was caught making trades on behalf of clients who knew nothing about them. And he had been known to wage multi-million dollar bets for a lark: once on a golf outing, he bought a dozen lobsters, taped numbers to their backs, and raced them against his golf partners. A 1989 book, *Liar's Poker,* describes Meriwether and his Salomon Brothers boss making a $10 million bet on the serial number of a dollar bill. But to the cutthroats on Wall Street these displays of arrogance only added to Meriwether's legendary status.[135]

Wealthy investors—including the government of China and the Bank of Italy—lined up to invest the $10 million minimum demanded by Long-Term Capital.[136] They accepted that the bets were shrouded in secrecy, as required by Meriwether, who was based far from Wall Street, in Greenwich, Connecticut. Financial giants like Merrill Lynch, J. P. Morgan, Goldman Sachs, and Europe's largest bank, Switzerland's UBS, loaned freely to Long-Term Capital, lured by its high returns—20 percent in 1994, 43 percent in 1995, and 41 percent in 1996. In the first three years, investors more than doubled their money.[137]

But the rocket scientists' formula was flawed, as it turned out. Two factors threw them off. First, their formula was based upon "historical values" and did not predict the possibility of the massive financial meltdown that began on August 17, 1998, when Russia devalued its currency and defaulted on part of its debt. Long-Term Capital had bet massively that U.S. long-term bond prices would go down and other bond prices would go up. But instead the trends went in the opposite direction—investors pulled out of Russia and fled to the so-called "safe havens" of U.S. bond treasuries, driving prices up. Secondly, a growing number of hedge and other investment funds were waging the same bets using similar formulas in the same markets, and they all tried to bail out at the same time.

Long-Term Capital's equity stood at $4.1 billion on August 1, $2.3 billion on September 1, and plunged to $600 million by September 21. In just fifty-five days 90 percent of its equity was wiped out. But the bankers who had lent so freely to Long-Term Capital over the previous few years were not about to let it go under. Federal Reserve Chairman Alan Greenspan explained that, if Long-Term Capital went bankrupt, it would lead to a "fire sale" of its gigantic portfolio of bonds onto the market, causing prices to fall and interest rates to rise—with devastating reverberations throughout the world economy. The New York Federal Reserve organized an emergency bailout on September 23, involving an array of international lenders, including six banks, along with Merrill Lynch and Goldman Sachs, who together coughed up $3.5 billion to keep the firm afloat. But all they did was buy some time—by most estimates, no more than six months. By October 9, Long-Term Capital had already used up about $1.9 billion of the bailout money. Merrill Lynch, which estimated its losses from the Long-Term Capital debacle at $1.4 billion, announced on October 13 that it would cut its global workforce by more than 5 percent—eliminating thirty-four hundred jobs.[138]

The week after Long-Term Capital came within hours of going belly-up, Congress was busy considering a bill tightening up bankruptcy law. "Congress is sending a strong message that no one should be allowed to act irresponsibly and simply wash their hands of the consequences, leaving others to pay the price," Republican demagogue Dick Armey told the House of Representatives.[139] Armey was not, however, directing his fury at the seventy-one financial institutions that carelessly lent Long-Term Capital $90 billion, enabling the hedge fund to use its mere $4 billion capital base to wage bets involving $1.25 trillion.[140]

The House was acting on the behest of major credit card companies, and cracking down on the growing number of ordinary consumers filing for personal bankruptcies after becoming buried in debt. The credit giants claimed current bankruptcy laws were too lenient on consumers—"welfare on demand" for borrowers, according to Tom Layman, chief economist for Visa.[141] The number of Americans filing personal bankruptcies swelled to 1.4 million in 1997—up 400 percent from the figure for 1980.[142] Millions of people who were downsized or became ill resorted to borrowing simply to pay for necessities and medical bills.

Congress finally succeeded in passing a punitive personal bankruptcy bill in 2005. Although the vast majority of personal bankruptcies are due to medical bills, job loss, and divorce, Congress refused to make exceptions even for active duty soldiers and vets—or Hurricane Katrina survivors. Republican Senator Charles Grassley ranted during the Congressional debate, "People who have the ability to repay some or all of their debt should not be able to use bankruptcy as a financial planning tool so they get out of paying their debt scot-free, while honest Americans who play by the rules have to foot the bill."[143]

Yet a Harvard University study showed that during the two years before filing for bankruptcy, "19 percent of families went without food, 40 percent had their phone service shut off, 43 percent could not fill a doctor's prescription and 53 percent went without important medical care."[144]

As economist Paul Krugman commented,

> The bankruptcy bill was written by and for credit card companies, and the industry's political muscle is the reason it seems unstoppable. But the bill also fits into the broader context of what Jacob Hacker, a political scientist at Yale, calls "risk privatization": a steady erosion of the protection the government provides against personal misfortune, even as ordinary families face ever-growing economic insecurity. . . . Some of these changes are the result of a changing economy. But the underlying economic trends have been reinforced by an ideologically driven effort to strip away the protections the government used to provide.[145]

Senator Hillary Rodham Clinton recently boasted in Senate testimony, "I'm very proud of the fact that during the 1990s, with the
greatest expansion of economic prosperity that our country or any
country has ever known, we did create a lot of millionaires and mul-
timillionaires." [146] Former Clinton Labor Secretary Robert Reich, in
an article titled "Why Gore Is Good for Business," explained why
the capitalist class was not worried by a Gore victory in the 2000
election:

> No administration in modern history has been as good for American
> business as the Clinton-Gore team. None has been as solicitous of the
> concerns of business leaders, none has generated as much profit for
> business, and none has presided over as buoyant a stock market or as
> huge an increase in executive pay. And no vice-president in modern
> history has had as much influence in setting an administration's agenda
> as Mr. Gore. [147]

Resurgent Imperialism; Collapse of Liberalism

Bill Clinton was the first post–Cold War president, but his administration ensured that there would be no "peace dividend." By December 1991, Clinton the candidate had made clear he would not
hesitate to use military power when necessary. He argued, "To
protect our interests· and our values, sometimes we have to stand
and fight." Historian Andrew J. Bacevich remarked, "On this point,
Clinton proved true to his word; as president, he intervened with
greater frequency in more places for more varied purposes than any
of his predecessors." [148]

Before launching the U.S./NATO war against Yugoslavia in
1999, Clinton had already sent U.S. forces into combat situations
forty-six times. This figure compares to twenty-six times for Presidents Ford (four), Carter (one), Reagan (fourteen), and Bush (seven)
combined. Clinton's foreign policy picked up where Bush's left off.
His administration continued Bush's 1992 invasion of Somalia, invaded Haiti in 1994, bombed Serbia in 1995 and 1999, and bombed
Sudan and Afghanistan in 1997. [149]

In his approach to Iraq, likewise, Clinton differed little from his
Republican predecessor (or successor). Clinton and British prime
minister Tony Blair bombed Iraq's "no fly zone" regularly for
eight years, killing many hundreds of Iraqi civilians. And the U.S.-

sponsored sanctions against Iraq killed well over a million people in the decade after the end of the 1991 Gulf War.[150] On May 12, 1996, one of the few occasions when the media reported the sanctions' death toll, Clinton's Secretary of State Madeline Albright was asked by Leslie Stahl on *60 Minutes,* "We have heard that half a million children have died. I mean that's more children than died in Hiroshima. And—you know—is the price worth it?" Albright replied, "I think this is a very hard choice, but the price—we think the price is worth it." [151]

In 1998, Clinton signed the Iraq Liberation Act, which stated, "It should be the policy of the United States to seek to remove the regime headed by Saddam Hussein from power in Iraq and to promote the emergence of a democratic government to replace the regime." That regime change would be carried out by his successor, George W. Bush, in 2003. By 2000, France's foreign minister complained of the Clinton administration: "We cannot accept either a politically unipolar world, nor a culturally uniform world, nor the unilateralism of a single hyperpower." [152]

Clinton, true to form, justified the invasions of Somalia and Haiti as "humanitarian" missions, gaining broad support at home. Many antiwar activists who had opposed the Gulf War in 1991 remained silent during Clinton's "humanitarian" invasions. In 1999, Clinton again gained widespread domestic approval when he launched a war against Serbia, ostensibly to "protect" Kosovo from Serbian domination. Because a Democrat and not a Republican launched the attack on Kosovo—while claiming to support an oppressed people—the U.S. left abandoned its once consistent opposition to U.S. imperialism by the end of the 1990s.[153]

Indeed, Clinton succeeded in shifting the political parameters of mainstream discourse, as the Democratic Party lurched rightward in the 1990s. American liberals continued to support Clinton as he embraced a range of conservative domestic policies. The feminist movement never protested against Clinton, even as he allowed the erosion of legal abortion and dismantled welfare for poor women and children. Most gay rights organizations maintained their loyalty even after Clinton signed the Defense of Marriage Act. In essence, the collapse of liberalism as a force during the Clinton era allowed mainstream politics to shift rightward in the years *before* George W. Bush took office in 2001. The 1996 Defense of Marriage Act paved the way for Bush's more draconian proposal for a federal ban on gay marriage, while the Anti-Terrorism and Effective Death Penalty Act made palatable the even more repressive USA PATRIOT Act that passed after September 11, 2001. By the time Bill Clinton left office, income inequality in the United States had reached a level not seen since Herbert Hoover was president. In 1999, according to the U.S. Census Bureau, wealth was apportioned as follows: the poorest fifth of the U.S. population received less than 4 percent, the second poorest fifth received 9 percent, the middle fifth received 15 percent, the second richest fifth received 23 percent, and the richest fifth received 49 percent.[154]

As economist Edward N. Wolff described, "In 1976, the richest 10 percent of U.S. families held 50 percent of the nation's wealth; by 1995 they held 70 percent of all wealth, and the top 20 percent of families owned 83 percent of wealth—with the remaining 80 percent of families holding only 17 percent." [155] This concentration of wealth, furthermore, was a global phenomenon. In 1995 the world's 358 top billionaires were worth $760 billion, the same as the poorest 20 percent of the world's people.[156]

Wages had barely begun to tick upward in the late 1990s before the speculative bubble burst in 2000, plunging the economy into recession.

CHAPTER NINE

Rule of the Neocons

President George W. Bush and his band of neoconservatives quickly seized upon the September 11, 2001, attacks on the World Trade Center and the Pentagon as an excuse to wage an all-out war against the Arab and Muslim world. No sooner had the United States attacked Afghanistan as its first target in the "war on terror" than neoconservatives began preparing the ground to invade Iraq. Indeed, well before September 11, then-Assistant Secretary of Defense Paul Wolfowitz had already called for the United States to strike Baghdad as soon as "we find the right way to do it."[1]

In early October, a group of neoconservatives, including Richard Perle, then-chairman of the Defense Policy Board Advisory Committee, issued an open letter to Bush stating, "It may be that the Iraqi government provided assistance in some form to the recent attack on the United States. But even if the evidence does not link Iraq directly to the attack, any strategy aiming at the eradication of terrorism and its sponsors must include a determined effort to remove Saddam Hussein from power."[2] On October 21, Air Force General Richard Myers, chairman of the Joint Chiefs of Staff, was asked on ABC's *This Week* whether he had "started to prepare targets in Iraq." He replied without responding directly to the question: "This is a global war on terrorism—and weapons of mass destruction . . . Afghanistan is only one small piece. So, of course, we're thinking very broadly. I would say, since World War Two, we haven't thought this broadly about a campaign."[3]

Once again, war abroad was accompanied by a wave of political repression at home. From the outset, the war on terror was accompanied by virulent racism against Arabs and Muslims—inside and outside U.S. borders. In November 2001, Georgia Republican Saxby Chambliss, chairman of the House Subcommittee on Terrorism and Homeland Security, suggested that Georgia police should "arrest every Muslim that comes across the state line" to combat terrorism.[4] Meanwhile, Assistant Attorney General Michael Chertoff told the Senate Judiciary Committee, "[L]et's be clear. . . . [T]hey've overstayed their welcome. . . . They don't belong here."[5]

War at Home

As hundreds of Arabs and Muslims were being rounded up and detained by authorities, the USA PATRIOT Act swept through Congress without debate—passing the Senate by a margin of ninety-eight to one and Congress by 356 to sixty-six. Bush signed the PATRIOT Act into law on October 26, severely curtailing civil liberties, granting federal authorities broad surveillance powers, and allowing the U.S. government to place non-citizens in mandatory detention without any right to due process. Much like the Espionage and Sedition Acts of 1917–18 and the Smith Act of 1940, the USA PATRIOT Act allowed FBI and immigration officials to deport immigrants based on mere "association" with a broad list of organizations designated by the secretary of state as "foreign terrorist organizations (FTOs)."

As Nancy Chang, an attorney for the Center for Constitutional Rights, argued,

> If the FTO statute had been on the books during the 1970s and 1980s, the African National Congress—another group that has resorted to violence—could have been designated as an FTO at the discretion of the secretary of state. Had the African National Congress been designated, the many thousands of Americans who volunteered their time to, and made charitable contributions toward, the group's struggle to end apartheid in South Africa might have found themselves staring at long prison sentences.[6]

On November 13, Bush issued an executive order giving him the sole authority to order a secret military tribunal for any "individual who is not a United States citizen with respect to whom I determine from time to time."[7] That same month, Attorney General John Ashcroft warned critics with McCarthyite resolve, "[T]o those who scare peace-loving people with phantoms of lost liberty, my message is this: Your tactics aid terrorists, for they erode our national unity and diminish our resolve. They give ammunition to America's enemies, and pause to America's friends." [8]

By April 2002, the Justice Department had detained an estimated two thousand Arabs and Muslims, many held "indefinitely." Nine months after September 11, not one of these detainees had been charged in connection with the attacks or was even certified as a "terrorist." Nevertheless, the Justice Department called on another five thousand Arab and Muslim men between the ages of eighteen and thirty-three who had *legally* migrated to the U.S. during the previous two years to "voluntarily" submit to an "interview" and a process of "special registration." Despite a number of false arrests, these dragnets did not succeed in tracking down terrorists. They did, however, allow federal authorities to scrutinize the paperwork of thousands of immigrants, leading to a spate of deportations based solely on legal technicalities. [9]

On May 30, 2002, Attorney General John Ashcroft implemented new intelligence-gathering guidelines that set the stage "for a replay of the worst abuses of the FBI's infamous COINTELPRO program," according to Chang. Under the banner of "national security," the FBI was given the authority to resume its long-standing vendetta against the U.S. left. In collaboration with the FBI and Justice Department, local police departments in major cities across the United States resurrected "red squads" that had been dormant since COINTELPRO. [10]

Well before September 11, the FBI had taken aim at the global justice movement that grew after the Seattle demonstrations in 1999. In congressional testimony in May 2001, FBI director Louis J. Freeh described "domestic terrorists" as including "left-wing groups" who "generally profess a revolutionary socialist doctrine and view themselves as protectors of the people against the 'dehumanizing effects' of capitalism and imperialism. They aim to bring about change in the United States through revolution rather than through the established political process." [11] After September 11, socialist Candace Cohn noted,

> [T]he FBI [did] not stop at harassing global justice protesters. The agency *expressly* extend[ed] its "antiterrorist" net to Puerto Rican independence activists, environmentalists, anarchists, socialists, Women in Black (a vigil-oriented women's peace group). . . . Protests, pickets, marches, rallies, and demonstrations qualify as "terrorist" under the

act's definition if the government determines that activity "dangerous to human life" is involved—which could conceivably cover acts of minor vandalism, resisting arrest, or violent provocations by police agents; and if they *"appear* to be intended . . . to influence the policy of a government by intimidation." [12]

The speed and aggression with which the Bush administration pursued its agenda was possible only because it was a bipartisan project, in which the Democrats enabled *all* Bush's policies to pass, often enthusiastically. "The Bush administration deserves to be savagely criticized for the timing and the conduct of the Iraq war," political commentator Anatol Lieven remarked. But, he added, "Future historians may, however, conclude that President Bill Clinton's strategy of the 1990s would also have made the conquest of Iraq unavoidable sooner or later; and that given the realities of Iraqi society and history, the results would not have been significantly less awful." [13]

The USA PATRIOT Act was not a departure from, but an acceleration of, repressive legislation passed during the Clinton era. Chang observed, "Under the 'material support statute,' which was introduced in the Anti-Terrorism and Effective Death Penalty Act of 1996 but was strengthened considerably in the USA PATRIOT Act, it is a crime punishable by a fifteen-year prison sentence, or by a life sentence if the death of any person results, to provide material support to any organization that the secretary of state designated as an FTO." [14]

The Employers' Offensive Unhinged

With the war on terror raging in the background, the Reagan revolution entered its second incarnation at the dawn of the twenty-first century, far outstripping the excesses of the first. Like Reagan, Bush made tax cuts for the rich the ideological centerpiece of his economic agenda. This was just the tip of the iceberg in a frontal assault on workers, as already-battered working-class living standards entered another downward spiral. A 2005 study on wealth inequality by the *New York Times* revealed stunning class disparities:

> Under the Bush tax cuts, the 400 taxpayers with the highest incomes—a minimum of $87 million in 2000, the last year for which the government will release such data—now pay income, Medicare

and Social Security taxes amounting to virtually the same percentage of their incomes as people making $50,000 to $75,000. . . . The hyper-rich have emerged in the last three decades as the biggest winners in a remarkable transformation of the American economy characterized by, among other things, the creation of a more global marketplace, new technology and investment spurred partly by tax cuts. The stock market soared; so did pay in the highest ranks of business. . . . From 1950 to 1970, for example, for every additional dollar earned by the bottom 90 percent, those in the top 0.01 percent earned an additional $162, according to the *Times* analysis. From 1990 to 2002, for every extra dollar earned by those in the bottom 90 percent, each taxpayer at the top brought in an extra $18,000.[15]

Because the study above examined only tax returns, *Times* reporter David Cay Johnston commented, "[T]he gap between the very richest and everyone else is almost certainly much larger." More than three million Americans lost their jobs between 2000 and 2003, most unable to find work in the jobless recovery that began in November 2001. "We close factories in America today," wrote liberal commentator Harold Meyerson in 2003. "In the past four years, the United States has lost nearly one in nine manufacturing jobs, including 20 percent in durable-goods industries such as autos."[16] The Midwestern industrial "Rust Belt," once the thriving center of auto and steel production, was hardest hit by job loss, as once well-paid industrial workers were thrown into poverty by unemployment. To compensate for lost income, workers increasingly relied on borrowing, often using credit cards to buy necessities such as food, as consumer debt topped $2 trillion and personal bankruptcies reached a record 1.6 million in 2003.[17]

Two million out of Ohio's eleven million people were forced to turn to charity to put food on the table in 2002, after the state lost one in six of its manufacturing jobs.[18] In 2004, the U.S. Department of Agriculture reported that sometime during the year, twelve million families "were uncertain of having, or unable to acquire, enough food for all their members because they had insufficient money or other resources. . . . One-third of these families went hungry, while the other two-thirds obtained enough food to avoid hunger using a variety of coping strategies, such as eating less varied diets, participating in federal food assistance programs, or getting emergency food from community food pantries or emergency kitchens."[19]

Downward Mobility

With a four-year university education out of reach for a growing number of working-class families, "this may be the first generation in American history that won't be better educated" than the one before, argued National Center for Public Policy and Higher Education president Patrick Callan.[20] This is also the first generation of young workers in U.S. history that faces a substantially lower standard of living than that of their parents. The employment rate for teenagers during the first eleven months of 2004 stood at just 36.3 percent, the lowest since 1948, when the federal government began tracking teenage employment. The figures were far worse for African Americans and Latinos. In Chicago, for example, just one of every ten Black teenagers was employed in 2004. That year, the employment rate for those age twenty to twenty-four years old stood at only 67.9 percent in a typical month. Andrew Sum, director of Northeastern University's Center for Labor Market Studies at Northeastern University commented, "Two-thirds of this generation are not living up to their parents' standard of living."[21]

Life expectancy in the United States has also been falling behind that of other countries in the twenty-first century. People live longer on average in Costa Rica, a country with a per capita gross national product one-tenth that of the United States. Infant mortality in the United States is higher than in Cuba. And more than one in four workers have no access to employer-based health insurance. As James Lardner of Inequality.org argued in 2004, "In the developed world, at least, population health appears to depend less on national or per capita income than on the way income is apportioned. Thus, Greece, where the average citizen earns about one-half as much as the average American, outdoes the United States in most indices of good health, including longevity."[22]

The United States also remains the only wealthy society in the world without a system of universal health care, leaving more than forty-five million Americans without medical insurance. An estimated one in six Americans of working age are without any health care coverage. Some 13 percent of whites are uninsured, while 21 percent of African Americans and 34 percent of Latinos have no health care insurance. Babies born into an uninsured household face a 50 percent higher probability of death before reaching age one.[23]

Sweatshop production, so central to global labor injustice in the early twenty-first century, has also seen a resurgence in the United States since the 1980s. Activist author Miriam Ching Yoon Louie reported in 2001, "According to the U.S. Department of Labor, *more than half* of the estimated 22,000 garment shops in the United States—where many immigrant women find their first U.S. jobs—violate multiple wage, hour, and safety laws." [24]

Even industrial homework—the bottom rung of sweatshop labor—in which entire families labor long hours at piece rates, is again on the rise in seasonal industries. In the early 1990s—thirty years after the New York State Labor Department shut down its homework unit because of its "apparent success"—homeworkers made up an estimated 20 percent of New York City's garment labor force, numbering roughly thirty thousand workers. [25]

Indeed, sweatshops were never wiped out in the United States after the 1930s, as is widely believed. As labor historian Nancy L. Green argued in 2003, the "sweatshop has never really gone away . . . [E]xplaining the *return* of the sweatshop on industrial decline in the 'First World' fails to see how similar conditions have prevailed ever since the late nineteenth century period of *growth*." [26]

Silent Depression

Significantly, wages fell faster in the years *after* the economy pulled out of recession and moved into recovery in 2001. In 2003, liberal economists began to take note of the extraordinarily low proportion of corporate incomes going to wages compared with profits. In December 2003, the Economic Policy Institute (EPI) reported that just 29 percent of corporate incomes went to labor compensation, two years into the recovery. That amounts to roughly half of labor's typical share of income—61 percent, and never less than 55 percent—at a similar stage of previous recoveries dating back to 1949. The money instead flowed upward, with 46 percent going to profits, nearly double the typical 26 percent share. [27]

After three years of decline, new jobs were added to the economy beginning in 2004, but the new jobs on offer—overwhelmingly in the service sector—paid far less than the industrial jobs that were lost. [28] In September 2004, the EPI reported,

Contracting industries paid $61,983 in annual *compensation,* including all wages and benefits, while expanding industries paid $35,546 in compensation ($26,437, or 42.7 percent, less). Contracting industries paid annual *wages* of $51,270, while expanding industries paid $30,368 ($20,902, or 40.8 percent, less). On the benefits side, the reduction in quality was even greater: contracting industries paid $10,713 per year for *benefits* but expanding industries paid $5,178— less than half as much. Income inequality in the U.S. is far greater than that of all other advanced countries, as is poverty, particularly of children.[29]

In 2005, the federal minimum wage, unchanged for eight years, fell to its lowest level in fifty-six years—equaling just 32 percent of the average wage for private sector, nonsupervisory workers.[30] In October 2005, EPI economist Jared Bernstein reported that real wages were falling at a faster rate than during the Reagan years. Although employers' wage costs grew by 2.3 percent in the previous twelve months, Bernstein noted, "Factoring in the recent energy-driven increase in inflation, the real wage is down 2.3 percent, also the largest real loss on record for this series that began in 1981. . . . This 2.3 percent rate is a slight tick down from the 2.4 percent—the previous historical low—that prevailed for the last four quarters." He added, "With hourly wages falling in real terms, the only way working families can raise their incomes is by working more hours—certainly not the path to improving living standards that we would expect in an economy posting strong productivity gains." [31]

In the twenty-first century, U.S. workers labor two hundred hours more per year than Canadians and roughly four hundred hours more than Germans, while also surpassing the annual work hours of Japanese workers.[32] Yet the median family income *fell* by 3.8 percent between 1999 and 2004. In the worst-hit industrial Midwest, household income fell dramatically during this period: falling by 12.2 percent in Illinois and 18 percent in Michigan.[33] In Illinois, which lost two hundred twenty thousand manufacturing jobs by 2004, median family income fell by $6,383 between 1999 and 2004.[34]

Race to the Bottom

With well-paying jobs increasingly scarce, strike levels fell at the turn of the century after rising slightly in the late 1990s. Employers took advantage of widespread fears of unemployment to further weaken unions. In 2004, according to National Labor Relations Board statistics, companies illegally disciplined or fired twenty thousand workers a year for union activity. Fully half of the companies facing union drives threatened to close their plants, while one-fourth fired at least one union supporter.[35] As *New York Times* columnist Bob Herbert remarked, "Workers have been so cowed by an environment in which they are so obviously dispensable that they have been afraid to ask for the raises they deserve, or for their share of the money derived from the remarkable increases in worker productivity over the past few years. And from one coast to the other, workers have swallowed draconian cuts in benefits with scarcely a whimper." [36]

Like Reagan before him, Bush gave employers the green light to up the ante against unions. In 2002, the Bush administration claimed a possible work stoppage by West Coast members of the International Longshore and Warehouse Union (ILWU) would endanger "national security"—and threatened to use the military to break any strike on West Coast docks. Even after the employers' Pacific Maritime Association locked out workers after a safety dispute in September, Bush invoked Taft-Hartley to impose an eighty-day "cooling off" period on dockworkers working without a contract for months. In an October 12 radio address, Bush claimed he had acted because "the crisis in our Western ports is hurting the economy," and "the work stoppage also threatens our national defense." [37] In reality, he did so at the behest of top officials from the National Association of Manufacturers, who had lobbied heavily for the imposition of Taft-Hartley.[38]

The employers' demands for massive concessions resumed full throttle in 2002, as major airlines such as United, facing bankruptcy, set the concessionary pattern for the entire airline industry—and ultimately for industry as a whole. United Airlines demanded, and received, cuts totaling $2.56 billion in each year of a six-year contract. U.S. Airways entered bankruptcy court next, winning $7.9 billion in concessions over seven years and terminating its pilots' pension plan. American Airlines followed suit, this time merely *threatening* bankruptcy to win $1.8 billion annually from its workers over four years, while granting a bankruptcy-proof pension plan to the company's top executives. These enormous concessions were extracted from the heavily unionized airline industry, where roughly

39 percent of workers belonged to a union in 2002, setting a new precedent in labor negotiations.[39]

Delta and Northwest Airlines headed to bankruptcy court in September 2005, demanding job, wage, and pension cuts from their workers. Northwest declared bankruptcy just one day after it began hiring permanent replacements for mechanics and cleaners who went on strike after management demanded a 26 percent wage cut in August. Afterward, aerospace investment banker Tom Gallagher stated bluntly, "You have to convince people that the value of their labor is no longer what it was. People have to understand that I'm willing to fly [discount carrier] JetBlue, and I don't care about the difference in service."[40]

Bankruptcy courts first allowed steel and then airline industry giants, including U.S. Steel, LTV, US Airways, Northwest, and United Airlines, to bail out on pension payments negotiated in previous labor contracts, saddling union retirees with hundreds of dollars in monthly payments—leaving those who could not afford to pay without crucial health and welfare benefits. "Employers in heavily unionized U.S. industries are turning to bankruptcy courts as a strategy for gutting union contracts and imposing layoffs and givebacks even deeper than those workers made in the concessions of the early 1980s," activist and *Labor Notes* editor Chris Kutalik observed in 2005. He added,

> After the long boom of the 1990s, many U.S. companies found themselves with problems created by rapid economic expansion. Competition with newer or foreign companies; high debt loads from mergers and expanding business efforts; general overcapacity (overproduction of goods or too many planes or plants); and the 2001–2002 recession put affected employers more in the mood to use bankruptcy as their battering ram. . . . Many companies started underpaying into their pension funds in the late 90s. As the 2001 recession hit, these companies were under funding to the tune of hundreds of billions of dollars: $305 billion in 2002, $278 billion in 2003, and $354 billion in 2004, according to the PBGC [Pension Benefit Guarantee Corporation]. To restore investor confidence, managers sought a way out of paying up on their obligations. Chapter 11 fit the bill.[41]

In 2005, auto industry giants jumped on the bankruptcy bandwagon, demanding massive concessions from their workers. In October, Delphi, the world's largest auto parts manufacturer—spun off by General Motors in 1999—filed for Chapter 11, while announcing plans to cut two-thirds of its thirty-four thousand hourly U.S. workforce and to slice wages from an average of $26 an hour to $12.50.[42] In addition, Delphi chief executive Steve Miller told the *Wall Street Journal* he planned to eliminate all supplementary health insurance coverage once retirees become eligible for Medicare at age sixty-five.[43] "This is a tradeoff," Miller remarked disdainfully. "I can't satisfy what everyone would like to have." [44] Ironically, Delphi's website continued to boast, "As a world-class employer, Delphi offers its full-time employees world-class benefits," even as Miller told reporters that Delphi's hourly workers were overpaid, but its executives were underpaid.[45]

Bankruptcy or Not: Concessions Demanded

Delphi's move set the pattern for concessions at GM, Ford, and DaimlerChrysler. General Motors, amid bankruptcy rumors after it posted a record $1.1 billion third-quarter loss in October 2005, announced plans to cut its domestic manufacturing workforce to eighty-six thousand by the end of 2008—down from roughly six hundred thousand at its peak.[46] The contagion quickly spread to Ford: "Now Ford has just reported a $284 million third-quarter loss, and wants the same kind of deal the UAW gave GM," noted Robert Kuttner.[47]

In a climate so favorable to employers, profitable companies have been emboldened to demand drastic wage and benefit cuts from their workers—claiming these are necessary to remain "competitive" in an increasingly global economy. With the brazen arrogance of the robber barons a hundred years earlier, Jerry Jasinowski, president of the Manufacturing Institute at the National Association of Manufacturers, made employers' intentions clear: "From airline pilots to auto assembly workers, employees need to help reduce their costs," he said in 2005. "We can't afford to live with the very generous benefits we provided 10, 15 years ago." Economist Peter Morici, a Clinton-era trade negotiator, remarked, "Companies cannot provide gold-plated healthcare benefits and open-ended pension commitments." He added, "The UAW should have educated" its members long ago "and been realistic" in its demands.[48]

Yet corporate executives apparently considered granting themselves "gold-plated" increases in compensation to be perfectly "realistic." While demanding wage cuts of up to two-thirds, Delphi management offered its executives a plan for cash and bonuses estimated at $500 million in its 2005 bankruptcy plan.[49] Between 2003 and 2004, as wages entered their unprecedented downward spiral, CEO pay grew into the stratosphere. According to an August 2005 report by United for a Fair Economy and the Institute for Policy Studies, "The ratio of average CEO pay (now $11.8 million) to worker pay (now $27,460) spiked up from 301 to 1 in 2003 to 431 to 1 in 2004. If the minimum wage had risen as fast as CEO pay since 1990, the lowest paid workers in the U.S. would be earning $23.03 an hour today, not $5.15 an hour."[50]

The problem has not been low manufacturing productivity. The U.S. steel industry produced more in 2005 than it did twenty years earlier, after eliminating two-thirds of its jobs.[51] Multinationals have been eager to put their U.S. workforces into direct competition with low-wage labor across the globe. Wilbur Ross, the Wall Street financier who built the International Steel Group (ISG) on the ruins of LTV Steel and Bethlehem Steel, sold an entire former LTV steel mill and shipped it to China, putting additional low-priced steel on the market.[52] By 2005, more than two-thirds of Delphi's 185,000 employees were already outside the United States—with workers at its China operations earning only $3 an hour.[53] As Kuttner argued,

> [I]t would be a mistake to conclude that high wages or excess health benefits are bankrupting U.S. industry. Look at our competitors. Japanese labor costs in the auto industry are comparable to American ones and German wages are far higher. There are, however, two offsetting differences. First, the Japanese and Germans are ahead technologically and have a knack for making reliable cars that consumers want to buy. Second, their healthcare is financed socially.[54]

By 2005, only 60 percent of U.S. companies provided a health insurance plan to their workers, down from 69 percent in 2000.[55] But union retirees were hardest hit, when a spate of manufacturers that once defined the "American Dream" cut or eliminated defined-benefit pension and health care plans. Between 1988 and 2004, companies with two hundred or more workers offering retiree health benefits fell from 66 percent to 36 percent. Between 2001 and 2004, nearly two hundred corporations on the Fortune 1000 list eliminated or froze their plans for retirees. By 2005, United Airlines and

US Airways had eliminated guaranteed pension plans, while Delta and Northwest had slashed their pension funds for employees.[56]

American Nightmare

General Motors no longer sets the standard for wages. The virulently antiunion Wal-Mart—where full-time employees earn an average of $17,500 a year—now sets that standard, in a race to the bottom.[57] In 2004, less than 45 percent of Wal-Mart's 1.33 million U.S. workers received company health benefits, while 38 percent of Wal-Mart employees spent more than one-sixth of their income on medical expenses. That same year, Wal-Mart raked in $10.5 billion profits on sales of $285 billion.

Yet Wal-Mart's top management launched a new plan to push down health care costs for its workers in 2005. An internal memo sent to Wal-Mart's board of directors by M. Susan Chambers, Wal-Mart's executive vice president for benefits, proposed, among other things, hiring more part-time workers while finding ways to drive out older, less healthy, full-time employees. The memo made this less-than-subtle point: "It will be far easier to attract and retain a healthier work force than it will be to change behavior in an existing one." Chambers noted that workers with seven years' seniority earned more than new workers yet were no more productive. Thus, she proposed that Wal-Mart change policy for "all jobs to include some physical activity (e.g., all cashiers do some cart-gathering)." The memo continued, "These moves would also dissuade unhealthy people from coming to work at Wal-Mart."[58]

Chambers admitted, "Wal-Mart's critics can easily exploit some aspects of our benefits offering to make their case; in other words, our critics are correct in some of their observations. Specifically, our coverage is expensive for low-income families, and Wal-Mart has a significant percentage of associates and their children on public assistance."[59] In a move aimed to improve Wal-Mart's anti-worker image, the company announced a new health plan that would allow some employees to pay just $11 a month in premiums. Health experts quickly denounced this smoke-and-mirrors stunt, noting that under the plan, Wal-Mart workers could still end up paying out-of-pocket expenses exceeding $2,500 a year.[60]

The aggressiveness with which employers have attacked union-negotiated benefits in recent years is without historical parallel. As *Time* reporters Donald L. Bartlett and James B. Steele asked, "How can this be legal?" as they described the situation facing growing numbers of workers:

> [T]he ranks of workers and their spouses—previously invisible but now fast growing ... believed the corporate promises about retirement and health care, often affirmed by the Federal Government: they would receive a guaranteed pension; they would have company-paid health insurance until they qualified for Medicare; they would receive company-paid supplemental medical insurance after turning 65; they would receive a fixed death benefit in the event of a fatal accident; and they would have a modest life-insurance policy.
>
> They didn't get those things. And they won't.
>
> Corporate promises are often not worth the paper they're printed on. Businesses in one industry after another are revoking long-standing commitments to their workers. It's the equivalent of your bank telling you that it needs the money you put into your savings account more than you do—and then keeping it. Result: a wholesale downsizing of the American Dream. It began in the 1980s with the elimination of middle-class, entry-level jobs in lower-paying industries—apparel, textiles and shoes, among others. More recently it spread to jobs that pay solid middle-class wages, starting with the steel industry, then airlines and now autos—with no end in sight.[61]

The Way Forward

Work stoppages, including both strikes and lockouts, inched upward by 14 percent in 2005, according to the Bureau of National Affairs—which counted 231 stoppages at the end of August, compared with 202 in the same period a year earlier.[62] The UAW, the IBT, Service Employees International Union, International Association of Machinists, and the United Steel Workers of America all took part in more stoppages than in the previous year. The Teamsters led the pack with forty-seven work stoppages, up from thirty-eight in the previous year.[63] This rise in struggle, while small, marked a significant departure from previous years, representing "a sign of frustration, almost to the point of desperation," argued Professor Gary Chaison of Clark University. "For many workers there's no alternative."[64]

Wall Street Journal reporter Kris Maher commented, "More major unrest could be on the horizon. Some analysts predict the showdown between the UAW and Delphi Corp., which is seeking sharp cuts in union pay, health-care benefits and pensions, could culminate in a strike—potentially crippling auto plants that depend on steady supplies of Delphi parts." Ron Blackwell, chief economist for the AFL-CIO, argued, "Employers are taking a much harder bargaining position, and that's naturally going to be met by an elevated level of worker militancy. Given what we see going on this year, you have to expect the level of strike activity would increase." [65] Bruce Raynor, president of UNITE HERE, representing 450,000 hotel and apparel workers, echoed this sentiment: "There have been efforts in a number of industries by employers to take a hard line unnecessarily. Unions are fed up with it," he stated. "Unions are in a fighting mode." [66]

Beyond the level of rhetoric, however, there was little indication that union leaders had risen to confront employers' frontal assault on labor as 2005 drew to a close. By the time Delphi entered bankruptcy court in October 2005, the UAW had already agreed to allow management to cut $15 billion, almost 20 percent, from its retiree health care plan—raising retirees' payments to as much as $752 a year.[67] The UAW, which led the working class in fighting for higher wages and union recognition during the 1930s, had long since reversed course. To ensure seamless success for the Delphi deal, the union leadership took the unprecedented action of filing a lawsuit to *prevent* its retired members from challenging the cuts.[68]

At the formal level, some progress has been made in recent years. In 2004, the AFL-CIO reversed its decades-long opposition to undocumented immigrants, finally endorsing broad amnesty and an end to federal sanctions against employers who hire undocumented workers. On July 26, 2005, the federation passed a resolution opposing a major U.S. war for the first time in its fifty-year history. The resolution called for a "rapid" withdrawal of U.S. troops from Iraq, expanded benefits for veterans, unconditional cancellation of Iraq's foreign debt, and the right of Iraqi workers to freely organize and bargain in unions of their choice.[69]

The same week as it adopted this historic antiwar resolution, however, the AFL-CIO experienced a major split. At the federation's fiftieth anniversary convention in June 2006, the SEIU, Teamsters, UNITE HERE, and the UFCW exited to form a rival union federation—the Change to Win coalition—accounting for approximately one-third of the federation's membership. The split marked the biggest fissure in organized labor since the CIO split from the AFL in the 1930s. But the CIO break with the AFL in 1938 represented the triumph of industrial unionism, a breakthrough for organized labor that led to its biggest gains historically. In contrast, the 2005 split merely highlighted the failure of the AFL-CIO to reverse the decline of unions in its fifty years of existence. When the AFL and CIO merged in 1955, one out of every three private-sector workers belonged to a union. When the AFL-CIO split in 2005, less than 8 percent of private-sector workers were unionized.

The breakaway unions that came together to form the Change to Win coalition claimed they were forced to leave the AFL-CIO because they wanted to devote more resources to aggressively organizing new members, but their strategy represented little more than a nuanced difference from business as usual. As JoAnn Wypijewski noted shortly before the split, "It would be pleasant to set forth the impending showdown in Chicago as one in which the mutineers have a convincing plan for regenerating a labor movement, a plan made credible and compelling by their own past achievements. . . . The cliché is true: unions are in crisis. But an honesty equal to the crisis is not forthcoming." [70] Although IBT president James Hoffa, Jr., accused AFL-CIO leaders of "throwing money at Democrats," his SEIU collaborators had spent $65 million, *more than the total spent by the AFL-CIO,* on John Kerry's ill-fated, labor-unfriendly 2004 presidential campaign. [71] The questions that remained unanswered of the upstart coalition were many. Wypijewski asked these crucial questions: "Would they purge themselves of corruption, sexism, racism and arrogance? . . . Could they develop a disciplined, independent political strategy, not simply to elect politicians but to challenge the corporate state and leverage power? Would they confront their own failings in order to act globally, to cooperate locally, to revive the strike as a weapon . . . ?" [72]

The prospects for change within the aging dinosaur of the AFL-CIO, to be sure, were less encouraging. The federation remained especially reluctant to confront its own past collaboration with the CIA at its historic 2005 convention. As labor activist Jerry Tucker described,

> Among the Convention's last morning's unfinished business was what some had hoped would be a full debate on the controversial role of the AFL-CIO American Center for International Solidarity (ACILS). Now called the Solidarity Center for short, the ACILS has over the years re-

ceived significant monies from the U.S. Government's National Endowment for Democracy (NED). The National Endowment for Democracy is cited by critics for its "dubious history, having been deployed frequently to promote U.S. government foreign policy objectives, including assisting in overthrowing democratically elected governments and interfering in the internal affairs of the labor movements of other countries." Such an unprecedented open debate was not to be. In its place, by use of arbitrary Resolution Process rules, was an administration-backed resolution which under those rules represented the final and only resolution to be voted on in the matter of the AFL-CIO's Solidarity Center.[73]

Reversing the Balance of Class Forces

The present crisis for the American working class has been many decades in the making. It can no more be resolved by a change in the cast of characters who lead organized labor than by replacing the Bush administration with the next election slate offered by Democrats, who long ago abandoned any pretense of fighting for working-class interests. The Democratic Party has successively represented the interests of slaveholders intent on instituting a system of white supremacy in the post–Civil War South; the New Deal coalition that enlisted labor as a key government collaborator to ensure a working-class voting base between the 1930s and the 1970s; and the corporate-backed "New Democrats" since the 1980s, determined to dismantle the New Deal coalition and turning its back on workers.

Many observers who consider themselves pro-labor have remained pessimistic about—or outrightly hostile to—the idea of breaking with the Democratic Party. Labor historian Nelson Lichtenstein, for example, argued in 2002, "[L]abor must function as an independent, and sometimes as a disloyal, component of the Democratic Party Coalition, at least until a reassessment of its political options can take place."[74] Viewed historically, however, the ebbs and flows of class conflict have had little to do with election cycles. Labor's most significant gains have taken place in periods of social and political upheaval—at the dawn of the twentieth century, during and after the First World War, and during the 1930s Depression decade. During these periods, the most successful labor organizers embraced a broad social vision of transforming society, rather than "bread-and-butter" trade unionism or relying on either political party to promote reform.

In contrast, labor's most sustained backward slide has occurred over the last thirty years, a period marked by a prolonged employers' offensive, the politics of business unionism by labor leaders, and a corresponding decline in class struggle. The result has been a seismic shift in the balance of class forces. As Krugman argued, "You can't understand what's happening in America today without understanding the extent, causes, and consequences of the vast increase in inequality that has taken place over the last three decades, and in particular the concentration of income and wealth in just a few hands."[75]

The rise and fall of wages has little to do with labor productivity, but rather with the shifting balance of class forces, as recent labor history proves. For the past thirty years, productivity increases have drastically outpaced wages, reflecting the decisive shift in favor of capital over labor. Since 1973, productivity has grown by more than 70 percent, yet the median wage is worth *less* today than in 1973.[76] As economist Max B. Sawicky argued, "the longer-term trend indicates the problem is bigger than Republicans running all three branches of the federal government." He added, "Realizing the fruits of one's labor has always been a political struggle, not some inescapable economic market outcome. People don't need to settle for normal and not-good-enough, but without a fight, that's what we will get."[77]

Indeed, a return to class struggle is the only strategy that will shift the balance of class forces in the twenty-first century. Corporate greed apparently knows no bounds. At the end of 2005, House Republicans' budget proposals eliminated free school lunches for forty thousand children and food stamps for 225,000 working families, and cut $12 billion from Medicaid, on which 25 percent of children rely for access to medical care.[78] Economist Robert H. Frank warned of the gaping disparity between the rich and poor in the United States in 2005,

> History has repeatedly demonstrated that societies can tolerate income inequality only up to a point, beyond which they rapidly disintegrate. . . . Major social upheavals are sometimes preceded by years or even decades of rising levels of social unrest. If such unrest is currently building in the United States, it remains well hidden. But as recent experience has made clear, social upheavals often occur with virtually no warning. Almost no one predicted the fall of the Eastern European gov-

ernments in 1989. Because revolutions almost always entail important elements of social contagion, even small changes can launch political prairie fires once a tipping point is reached. . . . As Plutarch wrote almost 2000 years ago, "An imbalance between rich and poor is the oldest and most fatal ailment of all republics." [79]

Hurricane Katrina: Race and Class Exposed

Hurricane Katrina hit the U.S. Gulf Coast on August 29, 2005. Katrina was a natural disaster, but the scale of its devastation was thoroughly man-made, exposing the hideous level of inequality in the world's most prosperous society, still steeped in racism nearly 150 years after the formal end of legal slavery.

Three years earlier, in 2002, the New Orleans *Times-Picayune* reported that, according to a vice president for disaster services for the American Red Cross, between twenty-five thousand and one hundred thousand of New Orleans' poorest residents would die in the event of a major hurricane.[80] Yet when Katrina arrived, city officials still had no evacuation plan and made no attempt to help the city's poor escape the city ahead of time, despite warnings of impending disaster. Those who could afford it left the city in the days before Katrina arrived, yet scores of city buses sat idle while the poor were left to fend for themselves. Thousands of New Orleans' poorest residents died for no reason other than government neglect.

A year before Katrina struck, the Louisiana Army Corps of Engineers identified $18 billion in urgently needed improvements to prevent massive flooding in New Orleans in the event of a major hurricane.[81] But work to shore up Lake Pontchartrain's levees was never completed.[82] The Bush administration, while slashing taxes for the rich and building up its massive war machinery, had nearly halved the Army Corps' funding to the region between 2001 and 2005. "It appears that the money has been moved in the president's budget to handle homeland security and the war in Iraq, and I suppose that's the price we pay," Walter Maestri, emergency management chief for Jefferson Parish, told the New Orleans *Times-Picayune* in June 2004.[83]

Television viewers around the world were horrified to see tens of thousands of desperate African Americans pleading for help days after Katrina swept through New Orleans. TV reporters were often overwhelmed with emotion as they described the wretched conditions at the government's two "evacuation" sites at the city's Super-dome and Convention Center. "What a shocked world saw exposed in New Orleans last week wasn't just a broken levee. It was a cleavage of race and class, at once familiar and startlingly new, laid bare in a setting where they suddenly amounted to matters of life and death," observed one *New York Times* reporter.[84]

"This looks like the hull of a slave ship," commented Reverend Jesse Jackson as he viewed the thousands of Black hurricane victims still stranded without food or water outside the New Orleans Convention Center five days after Katrina struck. The Convention Center was on dry ground and easily accessible by land, but hurricane survivors waited in sweltering heat, surrounded by filth and decomposing corpses, for buses that authorities promised would take them to safety but didn't arrive, day after day.[85]

"We had to wrap dead people in white sheets and throw them outside while the police stood by and did nothing," a 19-year-old meat cutter told reporters, after he had waded two miles through waist-high toxic water littered with floating bodies to reach the Convention Center. "The police were in boats watching us. They were just laughing at us. . . . We were pulling people on bits of wood, and the National Guard would come driving by in their empty military trucks."[86]

New Orleans' poor—and predominantly Black—population was literally trapped inside the ravaged city throughout the crisis. Police from the predominantly white suburb of Gretna, on the other side of the Mississippi River, sealed off the bridge crossing to New Orleans. When hundreds of hurricane survivors tried to walk across the bridge to safety, they were greeted with gunfire from Gretna's police force, shooting over the evacuees' heads to force them to turn back. But Arthur Lawson, Gretna's police chief, justified sealing the bridge, arguing, "If we had opened the bridge, our city would have looked like New Orleans does now—looted, burned, and pillaged."[87]

Gretna's police force showed equally little compassion for its own poor, also struggling without food and water and surviving amidst open sewerage. One Gretna resident, still waiting for help two weeks after the hurricane, reported that when he asked police what he should do, "they just yelled at me for not leaving."[88]

During a nationally televised "Concert for Hurricane Relief" on

September 2, 2005, rap star Kanye West ad-libbed, "George Bush doesn't care about Black people," adding that the U.S. government intends "to help the poor, the black people, the less well-off as slow as possible." While West's statement was carried live on the East Coast, it had been censored from the taped program three hours later when it played on the West Coast.[89]

Indeed, federal authorities appeared thoroughly indifferent to the plight of the Katrina victims.[90] Vice President Dick Cheney continued vacationing at his Wyoming ranch for the entire week of the crisis. Secretary of State Condoleezza Rice was spotted shopping for shoes and attending a Broadway play in New York City during the disaster.[91]

Bush himself did not step foot in New Orleans until five days after the hurricane. When he did, as columnist Bob Herbert wrote, he "proved (as if more proof were needed) that he didn't get it. Instead of urgently focusing on the people who were stranded, hungry, sick, and dying, he engaged in small talk, reminiscing at one point about the days when he used to party in New Orleans, and mentioning that Trent Lott had lost one of his houses but that it would be replaced with 'a fantastic house—and I'm looking forward to sitting on the porch.'"[92]

Former First Lady Barbara Bush added to the air of cheerful indifference when she accompanied her husband on a tour of hurricane relief centers in Texas, where tens of thousands of evacuees were eventually transported. After viewing the throng of stunned hurricane survivors crammed into the Houston Astrodome, she chuckled as she told reporters, "So many of the people here, you know, were underprivileged anyway, so this is working very well for them."[93]

Michael Brown, then director of the Federal Emergency Management Agency (FEMA), initially blamed the victims who were killed by the hurricane. He told CNN that the large death toll was "going to be attributable a lot to people who did not heed the evacuation warnings."[94] Despite the virtual absence of emergency relief in the devastated region, Bush praised FEMA's director several days after the hurricane. "Brownie, you're doing a heck of a job," he enthused.[95] Within a week of this statement, "Brownie" was forced to resign amid a torrent of outrage over FEMA's incompetence.

During the days before food and water were delivered to the stricken region, Bush condemned the many desperate people who were taking food, water, diapers, and other necessities from stores—calling for "zero tolerance" against looting and lawlessness. (Local police, also without food, were given permission to break into stores and help themselves.)[96]

When a detachment of three hundred National Guard troops arrived in New Orleans, Louisiana Governor Kathleen Blanco ordered them to shoot and kill "hoodlums": "These troops are fresh back from Iraq, well trained, experienced, battle-tested, and under my orders to restore order in the streets. They have M-16s and they are locked and loaded. These troops know how to shoot and kill and they are more than willing to do so if necessary and I expect they will."[97]

Brigadier General Gary Jones, commander of the Louisiana National Guard's Joint Task Force, announced he would treat the area as a war zone. "This place is going to look like Little Somalia," he told the *Army Times*. "We're going to go out and take this city back. This will be a combat operation to get this city under control."[98]

City officials added to the hysteria. New Orleans Police Chief Eddie Compass reported from the Convention Center on September 1: "We have individuals who are getting raped; we have individuals who are getting beaten." New Orleans Mayor C. Ray Nagin told television host Oprah Winfrey five days later, "They have people standing out there, have been in that frickin' Superdome for five days watching dead bodies, watching hooligans killing people, raping people."[99]

Within a month, however, police admitted most of these allegations had no basis in fact. "It was a chaotic time for the city. Now that we've had a chance to reflect back on that situation, we're able to say right now that things were not the way they appeared," Police Captain Marlon Defillo explained to reporters.[100]

Moreover, officials who furiously denounced the alleged "lawlessness" of African Americans had nothing to say about the squads of white racists roaming the area throughout the crisis, shooting and assaulting Black residents. "There are gangs of white vigilantes near here riding around in pickup trucks, all of them armed, and any young Black they see who they figure doesn't belong in their community, they shoot him," New Orleans resident, Black Panther Party veteran, and Green Party activist Malik Rahim reported from his Algiers neighborhood.[101]

As the hurricane debacle unfolded, numerous reports high-lighted the racial and class divide in New Orleans. As the *Financial Times* described,

> [W]hile nearly 1 million people evacuated the region before the hurricane, New Orleans' poor—most of them black—were left behind. Two-thirds of the city is black, and nearly one-third of those is poor, while the city's overall poverty rate is 28 per cent, more than double the national average. Those who remained were probably not any braver than their wealthier white counterparts. Instead, many did not own cars or otherwise lacked the resources to leave the city. They waited behind and hoped. Many are still waiting.[102]

"The Great American Dream Is an Ongoing Nightmare"

Katrina gave the world a glimpse of the gaping chasm between rich and poor in the world's wealthiest society. The same week the hurricane hit, the Census Bureau reported that another 1.1 million Americans dropped below the poverty line in 2004. Between 2000 and 2005, the number of Americans living in poverty grew from 11.3 percent to 12.7 percent of the population, a higher percentage than during the 1970s.[103]

Meanwhile, the UN released its 2005 Human Development Report, accusing the United States of pursuing "an overdeveloped military response to collective security threats and an underdeveloped human strategy response."[104] According to the report, poverty levels of the poorest Americans parallel those in parts of the Third World.[105] A reporter for the *Independent* (UK) concluded, "[The] UN report provides statistical proof that for many—well beyond those affected by the aftermath of Hurricane Katrina—the great American Dream is an ongoing nightmare."[106]

The gap between the rich and poor has reached record levels in present-day America, comparable to only two previous points in U.S. history: the 1890s, during the era of the steel and railroad barons, and the "Roaring" 1920s.[107] Each of those two eras subsequently produced powerful explosions in class struggle.

Recently, some of U.S. capitalism's most ardent supporters have begun warning that the present scale of inequality could also threaten the stability of the system. Federal Reserve Chairman Alan Greenspan, testifying before the U.S. Senate on February 16, 2005, said of the widening income gap, "In a democratic society, such a stark bifurcation of wealth and income trends among large segments of the population can fuel resentment and political polarization. These social developments can lead to political clashes and misguided economic policies that work to the detriment of the economy and society as a whole." [108]

Such warnings, however, are likely to fall on deaf ears. The U.S. ruling class is rapacious, arrogant, and overconfident. The last three decades have only further deepened their belief that they are destined to dominate the world. But this is wishful thinking on their part. The history of the U.S. working-class movement has shown time and again that such a system will of necessity produce revolt. The coming period will inevitably witness social explosions on a massive scale.

Rebuilding the Class Struggle

If viewed in each of its components separately, the crisis facing workers and the labor movement today is daunting: breaking labor's reliance on the Democratic Party; organizing the vast unorganized labor force; raising the living standards of low-wage workers, be they in the U.S. South or the global South. But the sum total of all these components is easier to confront when viewed in its essence, as shifting the balance of class forces. The crucial element of class struggle Marx described in the *Communist Manifesto* remains key: "This organization of proletarians into a class, and consequently into a political party, is continually being upset again by the competition between the workers themselves. But it ever rises up again, stronger, firmer, mightier." [109] Solidarity *among* workers is the only antidote to competition *between* workers.

More than a few parallels exist between the balance of class forces today and that of the late 1920s. Then also, union membership had fallen to skeletal levels, working-class struggles were overwhelmingly defensive, and the forces of the organized left were comparatively small. But despite the dramatic setbacks suffered by the labor movement in the 1920s, these proved only temporary. As historian David Montgomery has argued, "No historical resolution of the conflict between labor and capital, however, has enjoyed a permanent lease on life." [110] Moreover, those activists and organizations who remained committed to the ideas of class struggle often played a central organizing role in this period and helped lay the basis for the mass struggles of the 1930s. With the onset of mass struggle in the mid-1930s, the left was able to grow massively.

This simple truth remains valid. Today, as then, nothing short of mass struggle will reverse the balance of class forces. The opportunities for such a level of struggle, however, are self-evident. Left historian Stanley Aronowitz argued after the 2005 AFL-CIO split,

> [W]hat would constitute an effective politics and strategy adequate to stop the rapid deterioration in workers' living standards? What can arrest the decline of real wages, the proliferation of temporary and contingent work and the profound regression in the already weakened system of industrial and labor relations? That's the first question. *I want to suggest that organizing more workers is only one and perhaps not the most important condition for mounting a counter-offensive.* The sufficient condition is the emergence of a Left within the labor movement that forces the issues, that opens wide a discussion in both major sections of Organized Labor. For this is the first period in recent history when there is no organized left to pose the uncomfortable questions. But this is also the first time in decades when those questions are getting a hearing, even if they are uttered in incoherent and fragmented ways.[111]

Tucker made a similar point, remarking on the opportunities offered by the 2005 AFL-CIO split: "The breakup of monopoly unionism, even one precipitated by the barons of the bureaucracy with similarly anemic agendas could force a sinking labor movement to rediscover its greatest strength—its membership and its larger social constituency."[112] Progressive commentator Seth Sandronsky argued pointedly, "[T]he Sword of socialism will remain the humane alternative to business as usual."[113] Labor history shows that the socialist tradition has never been imposed from the outside, but rather is a product of class struggle. McCarthyism erased that tradition from memory, yet as Moody argued,

> Modern socialism as anything more than an idea or theory is a creature of the labor movement. Its ideas would have moldened in old books or died with Karl Marx and a handful of other radical intellectuals around a hundred years ago, if millions of workers, hundreds of trade unions and labor federations, and scores of working-class political parties had not embraced the ideas and perspectives they called socialism. Its appeal to these workers and their organizations as the movement gained momentum over a hundred years ago was simple: socialism was the rule of the working class.[114]

The Populists' preamble to its 1892 program remains as relevant today, more than one hundred years later: "We meet in the midst of a nation brought to the verge of moral, political, and material ruin. Corruption dominates the ballot-box, the Legislatures, the Congress, and touches even the ermine of the bench. . . . The fruits of the toil of millions are boldly stolen to build up colossal fortunes for a few, unprecedented in the history of mankind; and the possessors of these, in turn, despise the Republic and endanger liberty." [115]

The possibility for international class solidarity would seem discouraging, were it not for the international character of production in the era of globalization. As Moody argued, "If capitalism is now more global than ever, so too is the working class it begets. . . . To put it one way, it is not simply that the makers of a single automobile are found in many countries, but that the making of the car requires the increased input of workers in telecommunications, transportation, and countless 'services' in many countries." [116]

The living standards of the U.S. working class will either continue to fall drastically to approximate those of the poorest workers of the world, or American workers will unite in solidarity to fight to raise the living standards of the world's poorest workers, thereby salvaging their own. The material possibility for this outcome is promising, as Moody argues: "Even within most nations, the world-wide class that is still forming also crosses borders with greater regularity, is more ethnically diverse, and international in nature. . . . The material substance of working-class internationalism is at hand." [117] Such an outcome requires the rebuilding of a radical labor tradition inside the U.S. labor movement—thereby resurrecting the *Communist Manifesto*'s most famous slogan, more relevant than ever before: "The proletarians have nothing to lose but their chains. They have a world to win. WORKERS OF ALL COUNTRIES, UNITE!" [118]

PART V

From George W. Bush to Donald J. Trump

CHAPTER 10

Manufactured on Wall Street: The Great Recession

The year 2006 witnessed a rise in struggle, as a new immigrants' rights movement drew hundreds of thousands of migrants and their supporters onto the streets in more than a hundred cities on April 10. Those numbers grew to the millions on May Day—marking the first time in six decades that International Workers Day was celebrated on May 1st on U.S. soil with mass working-class demonstrations.

Movement organizers had called on migrant workers to "boycott" their jobs on May Day, naming the protest "A Day without Immigrants," thereby tying workers' ability to withhold their labor to this struggle for civil rights. Millions of migrant workers responded to this call, often shutting down entire workplaces to take part in mass May Day demonstrations in cities, large and small, across the country. In so doing, these workers demonstrated the potential to finally begin to reverse decades of working-class retreat and setback.[1]

But the immigrants' rights movement was stopped in its tracks—first by congressional Democrats who played both sides of the immigration debate and ultimately did very little to advance immigrants' rights. Second, by the onset of the worst financial crisis since the Great Depression of the 1930s.

The U.S. economy had been booming in the mid-2000s, thanks to a financial feeding frenzy engineered by Wall Street bankers gambling with other people's money. One of the consequences was the creation of an enormous housing bubble—which burst in 2007, plunging the entire economy into recession.

Financial Meltdown

This financial perfect storm was set in motion by Bill Clinton some years before the crisis hit. In one of his last acts as president, in December 2000, Clinton signed into law the Commodity Futures Modernization Act, which formally deregulated companies sponsoring derivatives schemes. The legislation was sponsored by Texas Republican Phil Gramm, later to become vice chairman of the Swiss bank UBS. This legislation repealed the Glass-Steagall Act of 1933—the New Deal legislation requiring the separation of investment and commercial banks during the Great Depression—and single-handedly enabled banks to run the unaccountable shadow banking system at the center of the 2008 financial crisis.

In the 1990s, Wall Street investment firms began orchestrating investment schemes that operated free of government regulation or oversight, creating that shadow banking system, which operated in virtual secrecy, accountable to no one, based on mathematical models that investors could not possibly understand. The system was leveraged by borrowed money many times the actual equity invested—at terms always skewed in favor of the short-term gains for fund managers.

The schemes Wall Street orchestrated first included get-rich-quick schemes based on a model of betting using the odds of Russian Roulette: Managers offered investors opportunities to make fast money in new high-risk transactions, conducted through hedge funds, Structured Investment Vehicles (SIVs) and other "innovative" derivative instruments, such as Collateralized Debt Obligations (CDOs). In the 2000s, managers added yet another high-risk formula to this bag of tricks: predatory lending via sub-prime mortgages. Sub-prime mortgages targeted low-income families who did not otherwise qualify, dangling the promise of low "teaser" interest rates that later rose sharply and added more fees. Many working-class families took out second or third mortgages on their homes during this time simply to pay their bills in the face of falling incomes, subjecting them to this form of predatory lending.

Bankers immediately carved up these mortgages and rushed them into investments that changed hands before the ink was dry, bundling the debts and passing them on in a global game of "hot potato." In so doing, they passed on risks to the entire international banking system, while feeding an unsustainable real estate bubble. The sub-prime formula worked only as long as housing prices kept rising. But once the real estate bubble burst in 2007 and housing prices collapsed, an estimated two and a half million homes, the vast majority of them owner-occupied with mortgages acquired between 2005 and 2008, were lost to foreclosure.[2]

"Too Big to Fail"

On March 13, 2008, the Carlyle Capital Corporation hedge fund collapsed with debts amounting to thirty-two times its capital. The significance of Carlyle's demise was overshadowed by the collapse of Bear Stearns, one of Wall Street's five largest investment banks, on March 19—when its high-flying management team informed its stunned investors that the bank had lost $17 billion of wealth five days earlier. The Federal Reserve stepped in to rescue Bear Stearns from collapse by obtaining emergency funding to allow commercial titan JPMorgan to take over Bear Stearns, the first time the Fed had engineered such a rescue since the 1930s.

Two of Bear Stearns' hedge funds went under due to disintegrating sub-prime mortgage holdings. But as the subsequent string of Wall Street crises exposed, the shadow banking system increasingly intersected with commercial banks. It was difficult to know where one ended and the other began, since banks were allowed—legally—to keep such investment vehicles off their balance sheets.

The Bear Sterns debacle was just the first market convulsion in a succession of bank and corporate failures that brought Wall Street to the brink of collapse in 2008, infecting the entire global financial system. The list of insolvencies included Wall Street giants Lehman Brothers and Merrill Lynch; Wachovia, the largest savings and loan in the U.S.; Washington Mutual, the fourth-largest bank; and AIG, the world's largest insurer.

The federal government responded with lightning speed, arguing that the banks were "too big to fail." The Federal Reserve invoked emergency authority and, along with the Treasury Department, launched a $700-billion corporate bailout swiftly passed by Congress in October 2008, paid for with taxpayer dollars. That figure ballooned into the trillions over the next years, as the list of corporations lining up for handouts, including the automakers General Motors, Ford and Chrysler, grew exponentially.

As it turned out, much of the bailout money went toward financially solvent investment firms. The $182 billion bailout of AIG, for example, went not only to AIG but also to its debtors—Goldman Sachs, Morgan Stanley, Bank of America, and Merrill Lynch (not to mention AIG's European trading partners)—to cover AIG's bad debts.

Goldman Sachs, which reported earnings of $2.32 billion in 2008, received 100 cents on the dollar for its CDOs. Although AIG had intended to offer only 60 cents on the dollar, reflecting market value, New York Fed president Timothy Geithner (soon to become Treasury Secretary under Obama) overruled AIG's decision for unstated reasons.[3] As *Bloomberg* reported,

> The deal contributed to the more than $14 billion that over 18 months was handed to Goldman Sachs, whose former chairman, Stephen Friedman, was chairman of the board of directors of the New York Fed when the decision was made. Friedman, 71, resigned in May, days after it was disclosed by the Wall Street Journal that he had bought more than 50,000 shares of Goldman Sachs stock following the takeover of AIG.[4]

Friends in High Places

The financial crisis provided a rare glimpse at the private club of government and corporate cronies who together run the financial system from behind closed doors. All its members are culpable in the financial meltdown of 2008. To be sure, the banks conned their clients in a manner befitting a Mafia family. But the government institutions empowered to police them were all too happy to look the other way until the deals went sour—en masse. Even three decades of deregulation legislation had not entirely removed Wall Street oversight. Between them, the Security and Exchange Commission (SEC), the Treasury Department and the Federal Reserve surely could have taken action against the bankers while the good times were still rolling.

The SEC was not simply asleep at the wheel while the financial system careened toward disaster. In 2004, it designed a special program, known as the "consolidated supervised entities" program, which enabled the reckless borrowing that later caused the banking crisis. The special program was created, according to the *New York Times*, "after heavy lobbying for the plan from all five big investment banks. At the time, Mr. Paulson was the head of Goldman Sachs. He left two years later to become the Treasury Secretary."[5]

The same five investment banks—Goldman Sachs, Morgan Stanley, Bear Stearns, Lehman, and Merrill Lynch—immediately "volunteered" to enroll in the new SEC program that was created at their behest. Through this special program, the SEC allowed these Wall Street giants to vastly increase their amount of debt. SEC rules had long required banks to hold roughly $1 of equity for every $15 of debt, or a 15-to-1 debt-to-net-capital ratio. The new program lifted these limits. As journalist Ben Protess reported, "Merrill Lynch's leverage ratio was possibly as high as 40-to-1 [in 2008], and Lehman Brothers faced a ratio of about 30-to-1, according to *Bloomberg*."[6]

In return for this cash cow, the banking behemoths agreed to allow the SEC to regulate their holding companies. But this also was at the banks' request. Voluntarily submitting to SEC oversight would allow their overseas operations to avoid European Union regulators. They preferred the SEC for reasons that later became obvious: their backslapping pals at the SEC provided virtually no regulatory supervision.

By the time the SEC dissolved the program on September 26, 2008, none of the five investment banks remained as such, although their trail of poison was still working its way through the global financial system.

Indeed, the Goldman Sachs brass had long enjoyed an especially cordial relationship with government regulatory agencies. Goldman Sachs executives had transitioned habitually to employment at the U.S. Treasury Department—as did Bill Clinton's Treasury Secretary Robert Rubin, along with Paulson. And Paulson's Treasury Department collaborated with Goldman Sachs apparently more than any other Wall Street firm during the 2008 financial collapse. The line between banks and their overseers has become so blurred because watchdog agencies actively recruit from big banks and vice versa, in a revolving door of golfing partners.

Upon taking office in June 2006, to avoid a conflict of interest with his former employer, Paulson ruled out any official contact with Goldman Sachs. But just over two years later, he requested and received an "ethics waiver" voiding that pledge. That was on September

17, 2008, just one day after the government agreed to come up with its initial $85 billion for insurance giant AIG to pay off its substantial debts to Goldman Sachs and other big banks.

Goldman Sachs was the largest recipient of the payoff. According to the *New York Times*, during the week of the AIG bailout, Paulson spoke to Goldman Sachs CEO Lloyd Blankfein "two dozen times, the calendars show, far more frequently than Mr. Paulson did with other Wall Street executives."[7] At the end of that tumultuous week, the Federal Reserve rushed through emergency requests by Goldman Sachs and Morgan Stanley to change their status from investment banks to traditional bank holding companies, bypassing, with the flick of a pen, the legal five-day antitrust waiting period.

That deal was struck over a single weekend, and Goldman Sachs and Morgan Stanley emerged on Monday morning as entirely new entities—a signal from the Fed that it would not allow these two firms to fail. Interestingly, their new status switched their holding companies from SEC to Federal Reserve supervision.

In a note of bitter irony, during the 2010 congressional hearings investigating the financial crisis, Ben Bernanke (by then Obama's Treasury Secretary) rejected proposals to cap the proposed payout to failed executives taking advantage of the federal bailout as unnecessarily "punitive."[8] Perhaps more importantly, no politician suggested that Corporate America be barred from policing itself.

Merrill Lynch passed into Bank of America's hands on January 1, 2009; just weeks before, it paid out $3.6 billion in bonuses—its four top executives alone shared $121 million in cash and stocks—while the company posted a loss of $27 billion for 2008. The bonuses were given about a month ahead of Merrill's normal schedule, without explanation.[9]

The federal government's ability to bail out the nation's most corrupt capitalists appeared inexhaustible, yet little was on offer for those who work for a living. Wall Street insiders fed at a bottomless trough that was funded by the millions of workers facing mass unemployment, wage and health insurance cuts, and home foreclosures. Yet no relief was forthcoming from the same government powerbrokers so eager to aid their banking brethren who had caused the financial crisis. Even the *Wall Street Journal* observed this glaring discrepancy, commenting, "Why a 'bailout' for Wall Street, and none for homeowners?"[10]

The credibility of the entire financial system was in shambles, yet corporate executives remained remarkably insulated from the working-class anger they had provoked. When the clueless CEOs from the "Big Three" auto companies, General Motors, Chrysler, and Ford, flew from Detroit to Washington, D.C., in November 2008, to plea for $2.5 billion in bailout money, each traveled in his own luxurious private jet.[11]

Just days after its initial $85 billion bailout, AIG executives treated themselves to a luxury resort costing $440,000. Two weeks later, the company's top brass jetted off to England for a weekend of fox hunting, with a price tag of $85,000. At year's end, after receiving a total of $182 billion in bailout money (and posting a $40.5 billion loss for 2008), AIG awarded its top seventy-three executives bonuses totaling $165 million.[12]

President Barack Obama Raises Expectations

Senator Barack Obama ran for president as the U.S. economy was spiraling downward, and he reaped the political gains, since most working-class people blamed both Wall Street and Republican George W. Bush's administration for the financial meltdown. Obama was all but assured victory in the 2008 presidential election, as he told throngs of cheering supporters across the country that he represented "change you can believe in" and encouraged crowds to chant "Yes, we can!" borrowing directly from the immigrants' rights 2006 movement slogan "¡Si, se *puede!*" In so doing, Obama raised expectations and energized the U.S. population on a scale not experienced in decades.

Thus, Obama's election brought widespread optimism to millions of people: Not only was the despised Bush finally leaving the White House, but he was also being replaced by the first Black president in history. At long last, in a country built upon slavery, a majority of American voters elected an African-American to the U.S. presidency.

Obama's election was partly due to changed demographics in the U.S., in which the combined votes of African-Americans, along with Latino, Arab, Muslim, and other racially oppressed populations, helped to shift the electoral terrain. But Obama's victory was only possible, even decisive, because 43 percent of white voters cast a vote for him. A higher percentage of white men voted for Obama than for Bill Clinton in the 1990s.[13] A 2008 Newsweek poll showed roughly 70 percent of voters agreeing that the country is ready for a Black man to serve as president, up from just 37 percent in the 2000 election.[14]

The weeks following Obama's election in November 2008 witnessed two important struggles—one, a rising LGBTQ movement and the other, a factory occupation—each providing a glimpse of how widespread anger at the political and class status quo can transform into struggle.

Thousands of LGBTQ activists took to the streets in California the day after the 2008 election, when voters narrowly passed a ban on same-sex marriage. The ban overruled a California Supreme Court decision that had legalized same-sex marriage just months earlier. Some eighteen thousand California couples had already been married when the ban was passed, spurring a spontaneous outpouring of fury that this hard-fought victory could be taken away.

In Los Angeles, outraged activists marched through city streets, blocking traffic and sparring with police, inspiring activists across the country to demonstrate their support. That support jelled into a nationwide movement that culminated in a march on Washington, D.C., the following year that drew hundreds of thousands of equal-marriage supporters.

Like the immigrants' rights movement, the struggle for same-sex marriage merged a fight for civil rights with a working-class demand. Without the right to legally sanctioned marriage, LGBTQ couples are denied basic human rights—including the right as the legal "next of kin" to be with their partners at their deathbeds. At the workplace, LGBTQ people who are denied the right to marry are usually denied the right share their job benefits—including medical coverage and Social Security—with their partners or to be eligible for the Family Medical Leave Act in order to care for sick family members or newborn children.

The weeks after Obama's election also witnessed an eruption of class struggle at the point of production, when workers at the Republic Windows and Doors factory in Chicago occupied their workplace for six days. The two hundred fifty workers were notified with just three days' notice that they would lose their jobs so that their financially insolvent employer could shut down their union plant to open up a non-union plant in Iowa. The company had violated any number of the few remaining workers' rights in U.S. labor law yet claimed that it had no choice because Bank of America, its main creditor, refused to make any more loans to the company.

The Republic Windows and Doors workers, members of United Electrical, Radio and Machine Workers of America (UE) refused to leave the plant on December 5, its last day of operation, and vowed to stay inside until they were given the $1.5 million in severance and vacation pay owed to them by management. News of the occupation spread quickly, electrifying both labor and immigrants' rights activists who rushed to Republic Windows and Doors to provide support for the largely Black and Latino workforce.

Facing bitter winter weather, the union and thousands of its supporters from Chicago and around the Midwest immediately began organizing deliveries of food and blankets to the workers, who faced frigid conditions *inside* the plant—while organizing fundraising and labor rallies outside the plant. Carrying signs with messages such as "Bank of America got bailed out, we got sold out!" workers and supporters also rallied outside the bank, demanding that it cough up the money to pay the company's debts to its workers.

On December 10, the bank and other lenders agreed to fund about $2 million in severance and vacation pay as well as health insurance. The workers then voted unanimously to end their six-day occupation. With 600,000 manufacturing jobs lost in the recession the previous year, support for the Republic Windows and Doors workers was widespread among the broader population. Even President-elect Obama felt compelled to voice support for the occupation. When asked about it at a news conference, he replied, "The workers are asking for the benefits and payments that they have earned," adding, "I think they're absolutely right and understand that what's happening to them is reflective of what's happening across this economy."[15]

But the Republic Window and Doors struggle did not lead to a broader rise in class struggle, as many had hoped. Once Obama took office, his supporters waited for him to make good on the many promises he had made while on the campaign trail. He had pledged to close down the infamous Guantanamo Bay detention camp. He had promised to pass a Freedom of Choice Act, guaranteeing women the right to legal abortion. He had told workers he would pass the Employee Free Choice Act, allowing workers to unionize

simply by signing union cards—thereby avoiding employer intimidation during union elections.

Once in the White House, however, Obama kept none of these
promises. He had benefited handsomely from Wall Street donations in his election campaign, and he returned the favor. Obama's
approach to the banking crisis was as generous to the bankers as
Bush's, effectively handing Wall Street a blank check from the Treasury Department. Even when its bailouts gave the government con-
trolling shares in company stocks—at insurer AIG and Citibank, for
example—the Obama administration did not take control but left
managers in charge.

"Recovery" for the Few

Years after the recovery officially started in 2009, the lives of workers remained grimmer than when the recession began. The gap between the rich and poor likewise reached levels not seen in a century,
with the percentage of income going to the top 10 percent of the U.S.
population exceeding that of the bottom 90 percent. As Berkeley
economist Emmanuel Saez observed, "The top decile share in 2012
is equal to 50.4 percent, a level higher than any other year since 1917
and even surpasses 1928, the peak of stock market bubble in the
'roaring' 1920s."[16]

Journalist Caroline Fairchild summarized, "Income of the top 5
percent of Americans rose last year, while median household income
fell, keeping inequality at a record high, according to Census Bureau
data."[17] The top one percent fared even better. During the economic
recovery from 2009 and 2012, the incomes of the top 1 percent of
the U.S. population soared by more than 31 percent, compared with
0.4 percent for the bottom 99 percent of the population.[18]

The ranks of the poor expanded beneath the corporate class's surge
in wealth, with rates of long-term unemployment, poverty and hunger
accelerating after 2008. In 2011, the Census bureau of the U.S. government measured the official poverty rate at 15 percent of the overall
population. The same survey showed that four in ten U.S. adults find
themselves living in poverty for at least one year of their lives.

But this official statistic underestimates the scale of deprivation
in the U.S. during the recovery from the Great Recession. A more
comprehensive study, published in 2013, showed that eight in ten

U.S. adults face "economic insecurity," for at least parts of their lives by the time they reach age sixty. Economic insecurity is defined as "a year or more of periodic joblessness, reliance on government aid such as food stamps, or income below 150 percent of the poverty line."[19]

According to the report, racial disparities in the rate of economic insecurity have closed significantly over the last three decades. The study showed that while the rate of economic insecurity described above afflicts racially oppressed groups at the astronomical rate of 90 percent, the white population is affected at a rate of 76 percent by the time they reach age sixty. Roughly half of all children in the U.S. live for some period of time in a household that relies on food stamps to eat.[20] Census data for the last several decades have shown that about two-thirds of those living in poverty describe themselves as white.[21]

As social welfare scholar Mark R. Rank described, "The typical pattern is for an individual to experience poverty for a year or two, get above the poverty line for an extended period of time, and then perhaps encounter another spell at some later point. Events like losing a job, having work hours cut back, experiencing a family split or developing a serious medical problem all have the potential to throw households into poverty."[22]

Persistently high rates of unemployment combined with the prevalence of part-time, low-wage jobs and a shredded social safety net greatly contributed to the economic distress of working-class families during the early years of the economic recovery. The rate of joblessness in 2012 stood at more than 21 percent among those earning less than $20,000, roughly the rate experienced during the Great Depression. But this statistic downplays the effect of the jobs crisis following 2008, which, four years later, left 40 percent of workers in households making less than $20,000 a year either unemployed, underemployed (working part-time while seeking full-time jobs), or among the millions of long-term unemployed who are too discouraged to actively seek work.[23]

The foreclosure crisis left entire working-class neighborhoods peppered with repossessed homes, standing empty. Yet as the *Financial Times* observed, "Remarkably, bankruptcy laws currently provide that almost every form of property (including business property, vacation homes, and those owned for rental) except an individual's principal residence cannot be repossessed if an individual has a suitable court-approved bankruptcy plan."[24]

The Economic Consequences of Racism

Racism is a defining feature of U.S. capitalism, and even in the best of economic times Black unemployment is twice that of whites. This simple fact guarantees that in any economic crisis, Black communities will suffer by far the most, and the most recent crisis followed this familiar pattern, leaving fully 48.4 percent of Black workers in households earning less than $20,000 per year, under- or unemployed well after the recession ended. Latinos in this same household income category faced an under- and unemployment rate of 38 percent, while white households earning less that $20,000 also faced a similarly high rate of 36.8 percent.[25]

Between the beginning of 2007 and the end of 2009, lenders foreclosed on about two and a half million homes. Roughly 8 percent of African American and 8 percent of Latino homeowners—compared with 4.5 percent of whites—lost their homes to foreclosure during this period.[26]

The expansion of financial distress among the broader working-class population thus does not diminish the much deeper and persistent poverty experienced by Blacks, Latinos and other racially oppressed populations. It does, however, show that white workers have reaped no gains from it. On the contrary, white workers have found their own living standards deteriorating along with rising class inequality.[27]

CHAPTER 11

The Flashpoints
of a New Resistance

The Great Recession and its aftermath exposed not only the
excesses of corporate greed in the U.S. today but also the
grotesque level of inequality that is the bedrock of capitalism itself—and this has led to resistance after four long decades of
setback and retreat. It was inevitable that this new resistance would
emerge in fits and starts, as a new generation of workers and students moved into struggle without the lessons that can only come
from experience, which were once passed down from generation to
generation. The struggles that began to emerge to in the years following the Great Recession centered on both class inequality and
racism, while, for the most part, workplace-centered class struggle
remained muted.

The year 2011 began on a very promising note the world over.
A mass uprising in Tunisia had toppled its brutal dictator the previous month, and the struggle quickly spread to Egypt and beyond,
launching what soon became known as the Arab Spring. The victorious revolution in Egypt, removing despised dictator Hosni Mubarak
in a matter of weeks, elated activists around the world, stirring hopes
among workers as far away as Madison, Wisconsin.

Uprising in Madison

On February 11, 2011, Wisconsin Governor Scott Walker introduced a so-called "budget repair bill," which was a frontal assault on
public-sector workers. Walker enjoyed the support of the right-wing
"Tea Party" movement, with significant backing from billionaires
Charles and David Koch.

Besides gutting wages and healthcare benefits, Walker's bill laid waste to public-sector unions' collective bargaining rights. Perhaps the most devastating part of the bill was its requirement that public-sector unions hold annual elections in order to be recertified as the bargaining agents for their members the following year.

As tens of thousands of union members and supporters poured into the streets surrounding the Wisconsin state capitol in Madison, the inspiration coming from the Egyptian Revolution was clear in the signs they carried—including "This Is Our Tahrir Square" (referring to the central location where activists gathered during the Egyptian revolution) and "Treat Us Like Egyptians"—while waving placards with photos of Walker and Mubarak side-by-side. Days later, thousands of protesters, including entire working-class families, occupied the three floors on the interior of the capitol building, hanging banners and chanting slogans such as "Tell me what does democracy look like? THIS is what democracy looks like!" and "What's disgusting? Union busting!"

Egyptian revolutionaries soon began expressing solidarity with Wisconsin workers. When a local pizza store announced it would begin only taking orders for delivery to the protesters, pizzas began arriving from Tahrir Square. One Egyptian protester, Muhammad Saladin Nusair, posted a photo of himself on Facebook standing in Tahrir Square holding a sign that read "Egypt Supports Wisconsin Workers—One World, One Pain."[1]

The struggle to "kill the bill" in Wisconsin marked a turning point in recent U.S. labor history, when the one-sided class war showed signs of producing significant working-class resistance from below. Madison teachers, while legally prevented from going on strike, staged a mass "sickout" and joined the protests at the capitol. So great was the firestorm of struggle that enveloped Madison in those weeks that fourteen Wisconsin senate Democrats fled the state on February 17 to prevent the quorum necessary for a vote on the bill, while protesters began occupying the senate chambers.

Days later, the Madison-based South Central Federation of Labor (SCFL), representing one hundred unions, passed resolutions raising the possibility of a general strike if Walker's bill passed, reading in part: "The SCFL endorses a general strike, possibly for the day Walker signs his 'budget repair bill,' and requests the education committee (of the SCFL) immediately begin educating affiliates and members on the organization and function of a general strike."[2]

The raised stakes in the Wisconsin battle quickly led to a showdown that would impact the balance of class forces for the foreseeable future. Governor Scott Walker and his Republican cronies were determined to win. In the end, they passed the bill by using a procedural ploy on March 10, in a resounding defeat for Wisconsin's working class.

Yet no general strike call came from the SCFL. Two days later, the fourteen Democrats who had fled the state received a hero's welcome from a crowd of seventy thousand gathered at the capitol. But the politicians used their hero status to urge the protesters to accept defeat, telling reporters "They won the battle; we're going to win the war," while promising to soon move to "phase two" of the fight.[3]

Phase two turned out to be an electoral campaign to recall the Republican Walker from office and replace him with a governor from the Democratic Party. Union activists enthusiastically gathered nine hundred thousand signatures to initiate the recall election. But a mood of intense demoralization set in soon thereafter, as public-sector workers were forced to absorb the effects of the legislation stripping them of bargaining rights.

More than a year later, on June 5, 2012, Scott Walker was easily reelected governor of Wisconsin, as Republicans cheered. Significantly, the Democratic Party machine allowed the war on Wisconsin workers to unfold without comment. Even the possibility of replacing Walker with a Democrat did not gain significant support from federal Democrats, including President Obama.

Apparently, they did not support a Democratic electoral gain if it also scored a victory for the grassroots of the Wisconsin labor movement. Indeed, Obama said and did nothing to support public-sector workers—even as the state legislatures of Ohio, Indiana, and Michigan followed Walker's example and pushed through legislation crippling unions in these once densely unionized manufacturing states.[4]

By 2015, Wisconsin's unionization rate had plummeted to just 8.3 percent, compared with 13.3 percent in 2011. Meanwhile, two of every three members of the public-sector union the American Federation of State, County and Municipal Employees (AFSCME) had dropped from its membership rolls in Wisconsin by 2015.[5]

Occupy Wall Street:
The 99 Percent vs. the 1 Percent

The rise of Occupy Wall Street that same year was also inspired in part by the Tunisian and Egyptian revolutions. On July 13, 2011, the Canadian anti-consumerist Adbusters Foundation posted the following call on its site, using the hash tag #OCCUPYWALLSTREET: "Are you ready for a Tahrir moment? / On Sept 17th flood into lower Manhattan, set up tents, kitchens, peaceful barricades and occupy Wall Street."[6] On September 17, a group of dedicated activists staked their tents at Zuccotti Park, located in the heart of New York's financial district, and fewer than one thousand turned out for its first protest on Wall Street.

But the protesters' message, "The 99% vs. the 1%," soon struck a chord with the many millions of people still reeling from the Great Recession and the colossal hypocrisy of the bank bailouts. As the mainstream media began covering the story, the protesters spoke about the foreclosure crisis, skyrocketing student debt, graduating from college with no jobs on offer, and low-paying jobs that left young people with no future. Soon, thousands of working-class and student New Yorkers were visiting Zuccotti Park on a daily basis, while many became involved in its daily "general assemblies," open air meetings to decide next steps, which grew in size to one thousand or more on any given evening.

Occupy Wall Street reached out to local unions and gained the support of the transit workers and other major New York City unions. This support proved crucial in the weeks that followed. After police arrested seven hundred peaceful protesters on the Brooklyn Bridge in October, a coalition of union and community groups organized a demonstration of more than twenty thousand in downtown Manhattan.

On October 13, New York City Mayor Michael Bloomberg announced plans to evict the Occupiers from Zuccotti Park at seven o'clock the next morning for "sanitation" reasons. As soon as they were alerted, thousands of activists began mobilizing—gaining three hundred thousand signatures on a petition against eviction. In the middle of the night, New York City unions called out their members, and students and workers who supported the movement's goals flooded the park to physically defend the encampment from police.

The following morning, Bloomberg announced that the city's eviction had been called off, injecting the movement with a strong dose of confidence. The next day, an estimated one hundred thousand jubilant Occupy supporters demonstrated in Times Square.[7]

Occupy protests quickly spread across the country. The protests drew many thousands of activists into the struggle, including substantial numbers who had become radicalized through disillusionment with Obama. That radicalization deepened as police repeatedly assaulted peaceful protesters and engaged in mass arrests to quell protests.

The first major attack in New York City came on September 24, less than a week after the occupation began. A video posted online showed police squirting pepper spray at a group of women protesters—after they were *already* trapped in orange police netting. Incident after incident of police brutality made its appearance online, so activists across the country could offer support and organize solidarity protests with each other.

On October 25, cops from a dozen police forces in the Oakland area moved in before dawn to evict the Occupy Oakland encampment, using tear gas, beanbag rounds and rubber bullets to awaken protesters as they slept. Later that day, as a thousand Occupiers marched to protest the eviction, police again attacked them, using teargas and rubber bullets, leading to numerous injuries. A thirty-four-year-old Iraq War veteran was so badly injured that he suffered a life-threatening lacerated spleen. The protesters used the media outrage at police brutality to successfully reoccupy the plaza the following day, without police interference.

Thus, both Occupy Wall Street and Occupy Oakland had managed to thwart police attempts to evict them, humiliating city administrators while fueling confidence among Occupiers across the country. In November, the Obama administration moved in via its Department of Homeland Security (DHS) to coordinate a national campaign to defeat Occupy forcibly.

As progressive journalist Dave Lindorff described, the DHS used its various agencies to organize "a series of multi-city law enforcement calls to coordinate the police response to Occupy, which led immediately to the wave of violent crackdowns. It was at those meetings that police were advised, among other things, to act at night, to use aggressive tactics and weapons like tasers and pepper spray, and to take steps to remove journalists and cameras from the scene of crackdowns."[8] The result, in the four days between November 12 and 15, was the successful eviction of protesters in New York City, Denver, Portland, Oregon, Salt Lake City, and Oakland, using the methods of police repression described above—with the aim of shutting down the movement nationwide.

After the evictions, Occupy Wall Street protesters issued the following statement: "Some politicians may physically remove us from public spaces—our spaces," adding, "You cannot evict an idea whose time has come."[9] The Occupy movement did not recover. But its theme, "the 99% vs. the 1%," has been embedded in mass consciousness ever since.

Chicago Teachers Point the Way Forward

In September 2012, the twenty-six thousand members of the Chicago Teachers Union (CTU) went on strike for nine days. This was the first strike in twenty-five years for the CTU, the nation's third-largest teachers union, and it was called in the midst of the massive assault that stripped collective bargaining rights from public sector workers in Wisconsin and throughout the Midwest.

The CTU leadership had been elected as a reform slate from the Caucus of Rank and File Educators (CORE), a coalition of progressive teachers, including a small but significant number of socialists and other radical activists, committed to fighting the privatization of public schools and to democratizing the union from below. Two years after winning the union leadership, they led a strike against Chicago mayor Rahm Emanuel—a cold-blooded champion of school privatization who made no secret of his plan to fight the union tooth and nail. Emanuel had left his job as chief of staff in Obama's White House to run for mayor of Chicago in 2011, with the aim of showcasing his ability to run a major urban city to further his long-term political ambitions.

Emanuel's program for education "reform" included a plan to first close public schools en masse, on the grounds that they were "failing children." The second part of the plan involved replacing them with for-profit and nonunion "charter" schools, along with competitive "magnet" schools that choose their students through lotteries or scholastic requirements.

The schools targeted for closure were almost exclusively located in working-class Black and Latino neighborhoods, while new magnet schools catered primarily to "high-achieving" (disproportionately white and middle-class) students. New charter schools often took over the public school buildings they replaced. (Wealthy Chicagoans, including Mayor Emanuel, sent their children to expensive private schools.)

Upon taking office, Emanuel immediately set his sights on preventing a teachers' strike, successfully convincing state lawmakers to pass a law requiring 75 percent of all union members (not just voting members) to authorize a strike. Emanuel thought the CTU would never be able to meet this preposterous threshold, thereby preempting even the possibility of a teachers' strike in the foreseeable future. Meanwhile, Emanuel floated his intention to impose merit pay on teachers, which would base teachers' wage increases on how well their students perform on standardized tests.

The future looked grim for the CTU in the spring of 2012, when it became clear that Emanuel was preparing to close an unprecedented number of schools. [10]

Nevertheless, although CORE members were inexperienced as union leaders, these activists already had plenty of experience at grassroots organizing in Chicago—forging links between teachers, parents, and community organizations while fighting together against the (unelected) Chicago Board of Education's relentless assault on so-called underperforming schools. These included not only school closures but also "turnarounds"—firing the entire school staff while blaming teachers for the school's problems. These attacks made teachers threatened with job losses the natural allies of the parents and students whose schools were facing the possibility of closure and turnaround.

As Robert Bartlett described in *Monthly Review*:

> People who wanted to fight back against the encroaching privatization began to be attracted to CORE, which started a series of audacious actions against school closings. When a school was targeted for closing or turnaround, CORE members went to the school and met the teachers and parents who wanted to fight the closings and did whatever they could to help build a resistance in that community. This ranged from leafleting at the school to camping out overnight in front of the Board of Education in January or in front of schools with parents....

> Most teachers threatened with losing their jobs do not automati-
> cally respond by trying to fight back, but a critical layer started going to
> school board meetings, bringing with them parents and teachers from
> the affected schools, as well as community organizations that were also
> opposed to board policies, to testify at board meetings and become a
> public opposition to privatization.[11]

The CTU continued this method of community activism
against school closures while beginning to prepare for a possible
strike as soon as they took office. The union's Black president,
Karen Lewis, sparred publicly with Emanuel on a regular basis—to
the delight of CTU members and the disdain of corporate media
outlets (which labeled her "confrontational").[12] When Emanuel
blamed teachers for the low quality of education in the city schools,
the CTU retorted that the problem was the city's *underfunding* of
public schools due to its *undertaxing* of corporations. In February
2012, the CTU released a well-researched report, *Schools Chicago's Students Deserve*,[13] highlighting the racism that led to a system
of "educational apartheid" in Chicago.

The CORE union leadership, unlike its predecessors, cut its own
pay and put financial resources into its organizing department, whose
members spent more time at the schools than in the union's offices.
Perhaps most importantly, the CTU leadership recognized that a
union is no stronger than the commitment of its rank and file. As Lee
Sustar noted in the *International Socialist Review*, "Training for delegates and other CTU members went well beyond the usual network
of activists to create an organizational backbone of one thousand to
three thousand teachers and paraprofessionals who led discussion
about contract demands and made the argument that a strike would
be necessary."[14]

When the strike authorization vote took place in June, it not only
met but vastly exceeded Emanuel's required 75 percent authorization threshold—when nearly *90 percent of eligible union members
voted to authorize a strike*. The CTU spent the summer preparing
members through strike training to lead the picketing and organizing at every school.

As Sustar described, when the CTU finally declared a strike on
September 10, "tens of thousands of red-shirted members of the Chicago Teachers Union (CTU) and supporters swarmed downtown,
shutting down traffic around the Board of Education headquarters
and City Hall in what a local radio news reporter aptly called 'an

older and more polite version of Occupy Chicago.'"[15]

Every day during the nine-day strike, parent, student, and community supporters joined striking teachers at school pickets across the city. Teachers organized marches through their schools' local neighborhoods and repeatedly marched by the thousands through downtown Chicago, circling the school board and City Hall. The strikers enjoyed widespread popularity among bus drivers, truckers and other passers-by, who honked their horns in solidarity whenever they saw a red CTU shirt on the street. Opinion polls showed 66 percent of parents sided with the union in the strike, a remarkably high number, given that working parents were largely left to scramble for childcare as long as the walkout continued.

The CTU leadership's commitment to rank-and-file democracy meant that, even after union negotiators reached a tentative contract agreement with the city, they brought the details of the contract for a vote by the union's eight hundred delegates. At that meeting, the delegates voted to extend the strike by two extra days in order to take the agreement to the picket lines for discussion by the entire membership. For the next two days, while they debated the terms of the contract, members took part in meetings that lasted for hours on sidewalks in front of schools across the city. On September 18, the CTU House of Delegates voted to end their strike and resume work the next morning.

The new contract defeated merit pay in favor of continuing seniority pay increases, in a major setback for a centerpiece of the mayor's plan. But the contract also contained a number of important teacher concessions—most importantly, it left open the possibility of more school closures.

The strike's success, however, must be measured by its context. Taking place in the midst of the staggering assault on public sector unions, Chicago teachers scored a significant advance not only for public sector unions but also for all unions. With all the chips stacked against them, they stood up as a united force and forced Democratic Party powerbroker Rahm Emanuel to face a major strike in Obama's home city. This was a far cry from the mayor's expectations when he took office.

In this context, the CTU scored a rare victory for organized labor, using a strategy of social justice unionism. In so doing, they pointed the way forward for a revival of the entire labor movement. (To be sure, Emanuel struck back in the spring of 2013—threatening to close fifty-four public schools and laying off thousands of teachers and staff, the largest numbers in Chicago history, while agreeing to finance the construction of a local basketball stadium for the private DePaul University. Thousands of teachers, parents, and students again took to the streets in protest, but they were only able to save four schools from closing.)

The Battle Against Racist Police Violence: The Road to #BlackLivesMatter

The Chicago teachers strike took place as the level of class struggle remained low compared to the scale of radicalization in working-class consciousness. But the emergence of a new struggle against racism—which reached massive proportions in the #BlackLivesMatter movement—has been one of the most important struggles to sweep the U.S. in decades.

The rampant police murders of unarmed Black people and the blatant racism of the entire criminal justice system, combined with the lasting economic devastation inflicted upon the Black population by the Great Recession, made it inevitable that such a movement would eventually materialize. It is not irrelevant that America's first Black president was mostly silent about the ever-worsening conditions facing the vast majority of the Black population, including the sharp rise in racism and police brutality. The movement developed over a period of years during which racist police violence became an epidemic and people in power failed to act.

In 2009, Oscar Grant III, a twenty-two-year-old, unarmed Black man, was murdered in the early morning hours of New Year's Day on the platform of Fruitvale Station by BART police officer Johannes Mehserle. Mehserle shot Grant execution-style, in the back, as he lay face down on the floor. After shooting Grant, the officer handcuffed him.[16] Numerous videos of Grant's murder went viral on both social and broadcast media, enraging millions of viewers, while angry protests took place in Oakland. On July 8, 2010, Mehserle was found guilty of involuntary manslaughter but not guilty of second-degree murder or voluntary manslaughter. He was released after serving just 11 months of his two-year sentence, all of it in a private cell in the Los Angeles County Jail in protective custody.[17]

Soon thereafter, an ongoing struggle to stop the execution of Troy Anthony Davis intensified in 2010 and 2011. He was accused of murdering, on August 19, 1989, Mark Allen MacPhail, a twenty-seven-year-old police officer from Savannah, Georgia, while MacPhail was working off duty as a security guard. MacPhail was shot twice and later died. Davis maintained his innocence until the time of his execution.

According to police, eyewitnesses to this shooting identified Davis as the culprit, and he was later convicted and sentenced to death based solely on this testimony; no murder weapon or physical evidence ever linked him to the crime. Indeed, no murder weapon was ever found. But as the Campaign to End the Death Penalty (CEDP), which played a major role in the years-long struggle to prevent Davis' execution argued, the evidence that convicted Davis eventually fell apart:

> Years after Troy was convicted, new evidence surfaced showing that one of the nine witnesses who labeled Troy as the shooter may have, in fact, committed the crime himself, and deflected blame onto Troy in order to avoid prosecution. Seven of the eight witnesses have since recanted their original testimony, with many saying they were threatened and coerced by police to implicate Troy....
>
> Racism cannot be separated out from what is happening in the case of Troy Davis. In fact, racism has everything to do with how the death penalty is carried out in this country. Southern states where slavery was still legal 150 years ago carry out over 80 percent of all executions.[18]

Davis had already been given execution dates in July 2007, September 2008, and October 2008—but in each case the execution was stayed shortly before it was carried out. The human rights organization Amnesty International, along with the NAACP and other organizations took on Davis' case and stepped up their campaign for his exoneration as the years passed. But a Georgia trial judge ruled against Davis in June 2010 in an evidentiary hearing, despite the fresh evidence of his innocence. Crushing all hopes for a new trial, the U.S. Supreme Court failed to challenge that decision.

Pope Benedict XVI, Archbishop Desmond Tutu, and former U.S. President Jimmy Carter all called for clemency for Troy Davis. Activists from around the country (and internationally) turned out to support Davis, desperately trying to prevent his state-sponsored killing.

Nevertheless, the Georgia Board of Pardons and Paroles denied Davis' plea for clemency the morning before he was due to die. On the night of Davis' scheduled execution, the U.S. Supreme Court also declined to intervene, without explanation. The state of Georgia put Troy Anthony Davis to death by lethal injection on September 21, 2011, at 11:08 p.m., after he had served nearly twenty years on death row for a crime he insisted until the end he did not commit.

On the day of Troy Davis' execution, president of the Georgia State Conference of the NAACP Edward Dubose stated, while visiting with Davis, "It is bigger than Troy. It really reflects the attitude of a country and a state that still sees black life as meaningless."[19] Troy Davis issued this final statement on the day of his death:

> The struggle for justice doesn't end with me. This struggle is for all the Troy Davises who came before me and all the ones who will come after me. I'm in good spirits and I'm prayerful and at peace. But I will not stop fighting until I've taken my last breath. Georgia is prepared to snuff out the life of an innocent man.[20]

Meanwhile, right-wing pundit Ann Coulter mocked Davis' execution with her trademark contempt, tweeting "One Troy Davis flame-broiled, please."[21]

While the struggles for justice for Oscar Grant and Troy Davis did not become mass movements, they did break through into national consciousness. The video footage of Grant's execution created outrage around the country, while in New York City the protests for Troy Davis joined together with the Occupy movement, helping to educate young activists about the racism ingrained throughout the criminal justice system, and setting the stage for an increasing number of struggles in 2012. Often waged by family members, these struggles were a fight for justice on behalf of young Black victims killed by police violence. They would eventually form the basis for the Black Lives Matter movement. Eighteen-year-old Ramarley Graham was unarmed when he was shot and killed by NYPD officer Richard Haste after police illegally followed him as he entered his grandmother's Bronx apartment on February 2, 2012. Although police lacked a search warrant before barging in and shooting Graham in the bathroom, Haste never faced a trial.[22]

Graham was a casualty of New York City's "stop-and-frisk" program, allowing police to detain anyone deemed to appear vaguely suspicious in an individual cop's subjective opinion—which amounted to a massive racial profiling policy. Police overwhelmingly targeted young Black and Latino males between the ages of fourteen and twenty-four, who accounted for just 4.7 percent of the city's population yet 40 percent of police stops in 2012. After studying the 2012 data, the New York Civil Liberties Union (NYCLU) concluded:

> The NYPD stopped and interrogated people 532,911 times, a 448-percent increase in street stops since 2002–when police recorded 97,296 stops during Mayor Bloomberg's first year in office. Nine out of ten of people stopped were innocent, meaning they were neither arrested nor ticketed. About 87 percent were black or Latino. White people accounted for only about 10 percent of stops.[23]

The NYPD's racist approach has not been the exception, but the rule, in policing. In 2014 alone, Chicago police stops targeted Blacks 72 percent of the time, even though Black people made up just 32 percent of the city's population. In Ferguson, Missouri, Blacks were 67 percent of the population but accounted for 89 percent of those stopped by police for traffic violations.[24] In September 2016, the Massachusetts Supreme Judicial Court argued that, due to the frequency of racial profiling by police, Black males may have a legitimate reason to flee from police officers. "Such an individual, when approached by the police, might just as easily be motivated by the desire to avoid the recurring indignity of being racially profiled as by the desire to hide criminal activity," the court wrote in an opinion. It added, "Rather, the finding that black males in Boston are disproportionately and repeatedly targeted . . . suggests a reason for flight totally unrelated to consciousness of guilt."[25]

Arrest and incarceration rates have risen in recent years, even as crime rates have fallen—which is also tied to the neoliberal agenda—government welfare for corporations, combined with austerity for the working class and the poor. As Black scholar and activist Keeanga-Yamahtta Taylor argued in her critically-acclaimed book, *From #BlackLivesMatter to Black Liberation*, "The social consequences of austerity budgets have effectively made the police stormtroopers for gentrification, as cities compete to attract businesses and young white professionals with disposable incomes."[26] She added:

> Aggressive policing not only leads to an increasing arrest rate of African Americans, but every encounter with law enforcement draws working-class and poor Blacks into a matrix of fines and fees. . . . Because politicians have been reluctant to raise taxes on wealthy individuals and corporations, police are increasingly responsible for municipal revenue. . . . The rebellion in Ferguson uncovered how the local government was literally extorting the Black population, to such a degree that monies derived from these fines and fees were the second largest source of revenue.[27]

On March 21, 2012, twenty-two-year-old Rekia Boyd, who was relaxing outdoors with friends in her neighborhood on Chicago's West Side, was shot and killed by Dante Servin, an off-duty Chicago police detective. Boyd was unarmed when Servin shot her in the back of the head with five bullets from an unregistered handgun. She had been scheduled to start nursing school the following week and was excited about her future before her life was snuffed out.

Servin was charged with involuntary manslaughter, reckless discharge of a firearm, and reckless conduct in the shooting death of this unarmed woman in March 2012.[28] But the irony ran deep in this case: the judge stopped the trial and dismissed the charges—not because there was any doubt that Servin killed Boyd, but because "The act of intentionally firing a gun at some person or persons on the street is an act that is so dangerous it is beyond reckless; it is intentional and the crime, if there be any, is first-degree murder." On this basis—*that the charges against Servin were not serious enough*—Servin walked free. The case was not subject to appeal because Servin was found "not guilty."[29]

On May 6 that same year, Oakland police officer Miguel Masso shot and killed high school senior Alan Blueford. That fact is not in dispute. But his parents' account of the events leading to Alan's death differs considerably from that of the police every step of the way. Police claimed that they stopped Blueford and his two friends because they suspected them of conducting a drug deal; his parents, Adam and Jeralynn Blueford, allege that the police racially profiled them. The police insisted that Masso had shot in self-defense, while the Bluefords maintained that Alan was unarmed at the time of the shooting. Police at first claimed that the teen had shot Masso, but later admitted that Blueford had not fired a gun and Masso shot himself in the foot.[30] A coroner's report on the teen found no gunpowder residue on his hands and no drugs or alcohol in his system, which supported the Bluefords' assertions about their son.[31]

Jeralynn Blueford reconstructed the scene of her son's murder, based on reports from bystanders:

> Officer Masso had on a lapel camera, but he turned it off and chased my Alan for about five city blocks, then took out his gun. Accounts diverge here: either Alan was shot once, stumbled into a driveway, and was shot twice more while lying on his back, or he stumbled into a gate, fell into the driveway and was then shot three times. Either way, the

officer stood over him and shot him, center mass. According to multiple witnesses, Alan screamed "I didn't do anything!" One of the bullets went through his armpit, proving his hands were up at the time. His last words were "Why did you shoot me?"[32]

These are just a few cases among many more in which family members waged years-long struggles for justice for their murdered loved ones, expressing a new determination to fight on a local level against racist police violence. It was in the midst of this epidemic of racist police violence that Trayvon Martin was killed, and the movement took on a national character.

On February 25, 2012, seventeen-year-old high school student Trayvon Martin was shot and killed in Sanford, Florida, while he and his father, Tracy Martin, were visiting his father's fiancée at her townhome community there. George Zimmerman, the neighborhood watch captain for the subdivision, who was a frequent caller to the local police, fired the fatal shot to Martin's heart. As it turned out, Zimmerman had made at least forty-six calls to the Sanford Police Department over the previous eight years about suspicious behavior of Black males in the area.

Martin's dad later explained that his son had walked to a local 7-Eleven to buy Skittles for himself and an Arizona Iced Tea for his younger stepbrother in the middle of watching the NBA All-Star Game. But Trayvon never returned.

Zimmerman, who was a twenty-eight-year-old part-time criminal justice student at Seminole State College, called 911 that evening to report, "There's a real suspicious guy. This guy looks like he's up to no good or he's on drugs or something." Although the dispatcher told Zimmerman, who was carrying a permitted black Kel Tek 9mm semi-automatic weapon, that he didn't need to follow the teen and the police would "handle it," Zimmerman apparently did not heed the advice and left his vehicle. Moments later, several residents made calls to 911, telling police that two men were fighting outside and shots had been fired. There were no witnesses to the actual shooting.[33]

The packet of Skittles and the can of iced tea were still in Martin's hoodie jacket pockets when police found his young body face down on the grass, bleeding to death from a gunshot wound to the chest. Police did not arrest Zimmerman for forty-five days, however, prompting nationwide protests. Eventually charged with second-degree murder, Zimmerman claimed he shot the unarmed teenager in self-defense. On

July 13, 2013, a six-person, all-woman jury found Zimmerman not guilty because he believed that deadly force to was "necessary to prevent imminent death or great bodily harm" to himself, which is Florida's definition of self-defense.[34]

The jury included five white women and one Puerto Rican woman. Afterward, the Puerto Rican juror, known only as "Maddy," said on television that George Zimmerman "got away with murder" but Florida law prevented a guilty verdict by allowing Zimmerman to claim he shot in self-defense.[35]

The response to Zimmerman's acquittal was immediate, as protests broke out in cities across the country, while activists in Florida launched civil disobedience actions and formed the new Florida-based Dream Defenders.[36] Activists Patrisse Cullors, Opal Tometi, and Alicia Garza founded the #BlackLivesMatter movement in response, a refrain that not only captured mass sentiment but also galvanized a new generation of antiracist activists.[37]

Thus, well before the rebellion in response to Michael Brown's murder in Ferguson, Missouri, on August 9, 2014, a general awakening around issues of racist violence had already begun to express itself in a higher level of struggle and greater radicalization, bringing new people into political activity. While most of these individual struggles have been short-lived, together they have translated into a broad-based movement extending far beyond organized forces and also deep into the Black working class.

"Hands up, don't shoot!"

The murder of Michael Brown, an unarmed Black teenager, by white police officer Darren Wilson provided the spark that brought outraged crowds into streets across the country. Many witnesses reported that Brown had his hands in the air when Wilson fired the shots that killed him, inspiring the chant "Hands up, don't shoot!" that became common on Black Lives Matter protests. The Ferguson police left Michael Brown's dead body lying in the street for four hours after the shooting, incensing local witnesses.

After seven days of daily protests that were violently suppressed by police using military-grade vehicles, hardware, and guns, Missouri Governor Jay Nixon declared a state of emergency and declared nightly curfews from midnight to five o'clock a.m. Two days later, he called in the National Guard against the protesters. The Guard described the protesters as "enemy forces" when they moved into Ferguson, revealing exactly whose side they were on.[38]

Protests in Ferguson continued on and off through September with remarkable resilience. On September 29, after a peaceful night of protests, Ferguson police declared they would begin to impose a "five-second rule," arresting anyone who stood in one place for that fleeting length of time. They would also arrest anyone protesting outside the police station after eleven o'clock p.m. Police then moved forward, reaching six feet from the protesters. But twenty of the young protesters linked arms and stood their ground, daring the police to arrest them "for standing up for our constitutional rights." As Brittany Farrell shouted to the police, "We're not going nowhere. We're getting smarter and we're going to keep fighting." By midnight, Captain Ron Johnson of the Missouri Highway Patrol, was forced to concede that the five-second rule would not be enforced.[39]

Governor Nixon again declared a state of emergency on November 17, this time in anticipation of the protests that would follow the grand jury's decision whether to indict Darren Wilson for murdering Michael Brown. Seven days later, the grand jury announced it would not indict Wilson. In the protests that followed, Ferguson police arrested sixty-one protesters as the National Guard was called in, while multiracial throngs of demonstrators took to the streets in at least one hundred seventy cities across the country to voice their anger.

On the following Sunday, November 30, St. Louis Rams players Stedman Bailey, Tavon Austin, Chris Givens, Kenny Britt, and Jared Cook all entered the football stadium during pregame introductions with their hands in the air in a "Hands up, don't shoot!" gesture of solidarity with Ferguson protesters. Cook explained to reporters, "We wanted to do something. . . . So, we wanted to come out and show our respect to uh, to the protesters and people that have actually been doing a heck of a job around the world." Although the St. Louis Police Officers Association demanded that the National Football League (NFL) discipline the players for their protest, the NFL declined to do so.[40]

On March 4, 2015, the Department of Justice announced it would also not pursue charges against Wilson—dashing the hopes of those who had believed the "feds" would step in to crack down on racism in the Ferguson Police Department. The Department of Justice stated that there was there was "no evidence upon which prosecutors can rely to disprove Wilson's stated subjective belief that he feared for his safety"—the same rationale used by the grand jury.[41]

This scenario is all too familiar. Just weeks before the shooting of Michael Brown, Staten Island policeman Daniel Pantaleo used a chokehold to kill unarmed Eric Garner—a father of six who was selling loose cigarettes on the street. Although Pantaleo was caught on video continuing to choke Garner as he repeatedly gasped "I can't breathe!" a Staten Island grand jury cleared the cop of all wrongdoing.[42] Pantaleo even received a pay raise, earning $119,996 while on desk duty during fiscal year 2016—a 40 percent increase from fiscal year 2015.[43]

Just two days after the Missouri grand jury declined to indict Brown's killer Darren Wilson in 2014, twelve-year-old Tamir Rice, who was playing in a Cleveland, Ohio park with an Airsoft toy gun, was killed by police. On November 22, 2014, police fired and killed Rice within two seconds of arriving on the scene—and without warning him that he should drop his "weapon." Rice died the following day. A grand jury declined to indict the police officer who killed him, on the grounds that the child did not drop the toy gun—which they perceived as an actual threat to the police who shot him. The mainstream media assisted in helping to justify the killing of this child by claiming Rice looked "large" for a child his age, while the neighborhood had a history of violence that endangered police in the area.[44]

Police departments are not required to report how many people they kill to the Department of Justice, and the vast majority do not. Eric Garner and Tamir Rice, for example, were both missing from the FBI's list of police homicides in 2014.[45] Those researchers hoping to count the number of police killings must therefore rely on various other sources, which can only estimate the total. The Washington Post calculated that 995 people were killed by police in 2015, and 963 in 2016.[46] The British newspaper The Guardian estimated a larger number: 1,146 people in 2015 and 1,093 in 2016.[47] It is safe to conclude, however, that roughly a thousand people are murdered by police every year.

A study of data from 2010 and 2014, conducted by Dr. James Buehler of the Dornsife School of Public Health at Drexel University, found that among males, who accounted for 96 percent of police killings, Black men are 2.8 times more likely to be killed by police than white men, while Latinos are 1.7 times as likely.[48] But the rate of fatal police shootings is far higher for Black teens compared to white teens—and got dramatically higher between 2006 and 2012. From 2006 to 2008, Black males age fifteen to nineteen were killed at a ratio of nine to one compared with white males in the same age group. By 2010, the ratio was seventeen to one, and by 2012 it rose to twenty-one to one.[49]

The Murder of Freddie Gray and the Black Political Establishment

The death of twenty-five-year-old Freddie Gray, at the hands of the Baltimore police on April 12, 2015, exposed yet another dimension of racist police violence: the dubious role played by the Black political establishment in the face of massive protests against police violence.

Police chased Gray after they noticed him "running while Black," even though they had not been pursuing him beforehand. Although police claimed they arrested Gray for possessing an illegal switch-blade, witnesses' cell phone videos of Gray's arrest showed that he had no switchblade in either of his hands as police roughed him up and then shoved him head first into a police van. Later on, officials discovered that the knife that had remained in his pocket during the entire altercation was perfectly legal for him to possess.[50]

Cell phone video taken before Gray entered the van also recorded him pleading for his inhaler, since he was asthmatic and having trouble breathing, while police did not respond to his request or provide medical assistance. Police put Freddie Gray in leg irons during the ride, but did not restrain his body with a seatbelt, violating department policy. They did not respond to the young man's repeated calls for medical help from the back of the van, making a total of five stops during the thirty minutes before they finally called for medical assistance.[51] By the time he was delivered to paramedics, Freddie Gray had entered a coma from which he never recovered. He died exactly one week after his arrest.

The Gray family's lawyer, Bill Murphy, reported that an autopsy showed that his "spine was 80 percent severed at his neck." Such an injury could have only occurred as a result of "significant force," similar to that of a "car accident." Gray was conscious and speaking when he was put into the van, but unconscious and unable to breathe when he finally received medical attention.[52] The state medical examiner ruled his death a "homicide" rather than an "accident," and suggested that police had committed a crime. As the *Baltimore Sun* reported, "In concluding his death was a homicide, Assistant Medical Examiner Carol H. Allan wrote that it was 'not an unforeseen event that a vulnerable individual was injured during operation of the vehicle, and that without prompt medical attention, the injury would prove fatal.'" [53]

The injustice of Freddie Gray's arrest and subsequent murder spurred Baltimore's Black working-class into action, beginning before he died on April 19 and growing day by day afterward. After Gray's densely packed funeral on April 27, thousands of Black citizens of Baltimore, many of them teenagers, took to the streets in protest, some of them burning and looting in outrage, which is a perfectly understandable response when there is no other option in finding justice.

These protesters were right: Although all evidence pointed to the role of Baltimore police in murdering Freddie Gray, the six officers involved in Gray's death paid no price, as described below. Without addressing these valid concerns on the part of Baltimore's Black residents, Baltimore's Black mayor, Stephanie Rawlings-Blake, announced a weeklong citywide curfew beginning at ten o'clock each night until five o'clock the following morning, while the governor called in the National Guard and declared a state of emergency. As Taylor described:

> What distinguishes Baltimore's uprising from Ferguson's is that the Black political establishment runs the city: African Americans control virtually the entire political apparatus. Mayor Stephanie Rawlings-Blake and police commissioner Anthony Batts were the most prominent faces of political power in Baltimore during the rebellion, but Black power runs deep in the city: Baltimore's city council has fifteen members, eight of whom are African American, including its president. . . .
> Despite the lawlessness of the Baltimore Police Department, Mayor Rawlings-Blake reserved her harshest comments for those involved in the uprising, describing them as "criminals" and "thugs." A few days later, President Obama took the mayor's lead when he referred to "criminals and thugs who tore up the place.". . .
> There have always been class differences among African Americans, but this is the first time those class differences have been expressed in the form of a minority of Blacks wielding significant political power and authority over the majority of Black lives.[54]

In the end, the six police officers who were charged by Baltimore State's Attorney Marilyn Mosby with manslaughter and murder for killing Freddie Gray went free. The first three were acquitted at trial, while the fourth's case ended in a mistrial. Ultimately, Mosby dropped the remaining charges.

The Justice Department also decided not to pursue federal charges against them, stating in a press release on September 12, 2017, "the evidence was insufficient to prove beyond a reasonable doubt that" the six police officers "willfully violated Gray's civil rights." All six continued to be employed by the Baltimore Police Department in mid-2017.[55]

Thus, the legal outcomes were identical in Ferguson and Baltimore, at both the local and federal level: both Michael Brown's and Freddie Gray's killers escaped punishment, as do the overwhelming majority of police who murder Black people and other people of color each year. More and more often, witnesses have provided video recordings that offer irrefutable documentation of lawless police conduct as incidents occur in real time. The Black Lives Matter movement shined a spotlight not only on the role of racism in individual acts of police violence, but also on the connection between racism and the capitalist system—at a time when a new generation of young people were already becoming radicalized by the class and social inequality inherent to capitalism revealed so starkly during and after the Great Recession. And perhaps most importantly, #BlackLivesMatter demonstrated the importance of mass protest against racial injustice as an ongoing feature of the youth radicalization.

It is telling that in an August 2016 USA Today opinion poll of people aged thirty-five and under, while the economy and jobs were named as the most important issues, more than seven in ten respondents said "police violence against Black people" was a problem—up by 10 percentage points from January of that same year.[56]

The End of the Obama Era

This is the political context in which Barack Obama's presidency came to a close. While Obama was easily reelected in 2012 and maintained a high popularity rating through the end of his second term, the raised expectations generated by his 2008 campaign for "change you can believe in" remained unfulfilled.

The struggles that emerged after the start of the Great Recession were significant due to their mass character, but each individual struggle was short-lived, involving outpourings of anger followed by retreat. This makes sense for a working class attempting to rebuild its own organizations after four decades of one-sided class war. Moreover, the overwhelming dominance of the Democrats and Republicans, the two corporate parties that together rule U.S. society, have thus far acted as a restraint on the political expression of struggles that have developed.

The Great Recession was caused by neoliberal policies, yet these remained firmly in place when it ended—and will remain so until they are pushed back through struggle from below. The disappointment in Obama hangs heavily on those who placed their hopes and expectations in his presidency. While right-wing Tea Partiers reveled in labeling Obama a "socialist," the president left no doubt about his class loyalties in a speech to a meeting of top CEOs in late 2013:

> People call me a socialist sometimes, but you've got to meet real socialists, you'll have a real sense of what a socialist is. I'm talking about lowering the corporate tax rate, my health care reform is based on the private marketplace, the stock market is doing pretty good the last time I checked and it is true that I am concerned about growing inequality in the system, but nobody questions the efficacy of a market economy in terms of producing wealth and innovation and keeping us competitive.[57]

However, the working class scored an important victory through the 2008 LGBTQ movement described above, which offered a glimpse of the transformative possibilities ahead. This movement was not centered at the workplace but teaches the crucial lessons of the importance of integrating of social and class struggle. On October 11, 2009, more than one hundred thousand LGBTQ activists rallied in the National Equality March in Washington, D.C. As union leader Stuart Appelbaum, the first openly gay president of a major labor union argued to the crowd, "Nobody should be patient when it comes to the denial of their human rights."[58]

In this way, LGBTQ activists spawned a new movement that changed the hearts and minds of the U.S. population. Obama himself reversed his earlier opposition to this basic civil right in 2012, due to pressure from below. By 2013, a majority of the U.S. population approved of same-sex marriage, compared with just 27 percent in 1996—representing a sea change in consciousness.[59] In June 2013, the U.S. Supreme Court finally ruled against the Defense of Marriage

Act (DOMA) and California's Prop 8, both of which banned same-sex marriage as unconstitutional, and California was one of sixteen states that had legalized same-sex marriage by the end of the year.

While LGBTQ activists scored the most important victory during the Obama years, most of the other struggles taking place were relatively small but contained the seeds of future mass struggle. Low-wage retail and fast food workers began organizing, staging small-scale strikes and protests at corporate giants such as Wal-Mart, McDonalds, and Whole Foods. With the backing of the SEIU—a union with a recent history of impeding democracy in its own affiliates[60]—these workers nevertheless organized a social justice movement addressing the plight of minimum-wage workers forced to survive on poverty wages.

The "Fight for 15" campaign—referring to the $15 per hour that could provide a substanital improvement in living standards for workers instead of the federal minimum wage of $7.25 per hour that remained in place in 2017—has gained substantial support in the larger population. One opinion poll in the summer of 2013 showed 80 percent of respondents supported raising the minimum wage to $10.10 per hour, with cost-of-living raises.[61] These attitudes point to the issues that can ignite a resurgence of working-class struggle in the future.

As labor scholar Kim Moody argued in early 2012:

> While there is no automatic mechanism that creates such an upturn in worker self-activity, the worker-led resistance that has commenced on a fairly large scale in Europe, Latin America, and more recently in China, suggests the possibility of a new upsurge. Even such seemingly disconnected events as the plant-occupation at Republic Doors and Windows in December 2008 and the spectacular mass-movement in Wisconsin in early 2011 may be signs of things to come.[62]
>
> Whether America's weakened labour-movement can rise to the occasion, as it did in the early 1930s when it had hit low levels of organisation comparable to those of today, is as much a matter of practice and politics as of economics.[63]

CHAPTER 12

The Rogue President

Very few political pundits expected the words "President" and "Trump" to ever appear together, but the handwriting had been on the wall throughout the 2016 primary season, when candidates Bernie Sanders and Donald Trump each attracted massive support on the left and the right, respectively. While Sanders was a self-described socialist and Trump was a bigoted demagogue, they both regularly chided the Washington political elite for failing to address the economic plight of ordinary people—even if Sanders and Trump offered wildly different solutions. The Democratic Party leadership successfully sidelined Sanders by the end of the primaries in favor of its anointed candidate, Hillary Rodham Clinton. Sanders remained disciplined to the party apparatus and withdrew from the race to support Clinton in the general election. But Trump thumbed his nose at the Republican Party establishment from the beginning, seeming to relish GOP leaders' overwhelming disapproval of his campaign—earning him the status of an "anti-establishment" candidate and boosting his popularity among a segment of angry white voters.

The election of Trump—who even as a candidate was clearly unable to muster the restraint expected of the leader of the world's main superpower—sent shock waves throughout U.S. society. It is no exaggeration to say that Trump's election stunned the Democratic Party establishment and its supporters into a state of near paralysis. After the election, Robert Reich, who served as Bill Clinton's secretary of labor in the 1990s, wrote an analysis of Trump that painted him as a unique figure in U.S. politics—one who resembles a nascent fascist dictator. Reich's essay, quoted below, expresses a view that was widespread in the Democratic Party and throughout the left after Trump's election:

Trump has finally reached a point where parallels between his presidential campaign and the fascists of the first half of the 20th century—lurid
figures such as Benito Mussolini, Joseph Stalin, Adolf Hitler, Oswald
Mosley, and Francisco Franco—are too evident to overlook. . . .

That older generation of fascists didn't bother with policy prescriptions or logical argument, either. They presented themselves as
strongmen whose personal power would remedy all ills.

They created around themselves cults of personality in which they
took on the trappings of strength, confidence, and invulnerability—all
of which served as substitutes for rational argument or thought.

The Tea Party: Precursor to Trumpism

To be sure, Trump's electoral victory emboldened the entire right
wing, including the far right, in the U.S. And on February 28, 2016,
Trump approvingly retweeted a quote widely attributed to Italian
fascist Benito Mussolini: "It is better to live one day as a lion than
100 years as a sheep." When a television news host asked Trump
about it, Trump replied, "Mussolini was Mussolini. It's a very good
quote, it's a very interesting quote. I know who said it, but what
difference does it make whether it's Mussolini or somebody else?"[1]

But Trump is less unique than Reich's words suggest. First, reactionary demagogues are no strangers to the Republican Party,
and the current crop is following a path blazed long ago. As political commentator Sam Tanenhaus observed, for more than the
last half century, "Each new insurrection [in the Republican Party]
feels spontaneous even as it revives antique crusades to abolish the
Internal Revenue Service, 'get rid' of the Supreme Court or—most
persistent of all—rejuvenate the Old South."[2] Tanenhaus offers numerous examples, including a mob action led by Dallas Republican
Bruce Alger, which culminated in spitting at Lady Bird Johnson:

> In November 1960, four days before the presidential election, he led a
> group of 300 protesters who converged on a downtown Dallas hotel and
> accosted Lyndon and Lady Bird Johnson when they entered the lobby.
> Television cameras captured the moment—along with Alger holding
> aloft a placard that read "L.B.J. Sold Out to Yankee Socialists"—helping
> to plant the image of Dallas as a "city of hate."[3]

Second, it is more historically useful to specifically understand the
Trump phenomenon—"Trumpism"—in the context of the evolution
of Republican Party politics since the late 1970s. As Chapter Seven
describes, the post-war economic boom that brought a degree of so-

cial stability in the 1950s and 1960s came to an abrupt halt with the crisis of corporate profitability beginning in the late 1960s. This crisis emerged as U.S. imperialism was suffering a humiliating defeat in Vietnam, alongside rising social and class struggle at home. The resignation of disgraced President Richard Nixon in 1974, and the credibility of the world's largest superpower was in tatters, at home and abroad.

In the face of this crisis, the U.S. ruling class united to shift the balance of class and social forces decisively back in its favor. One key element of this reassertion of ruling-class power was a sharp lurch rightward politically—personified by the election of Reagan in 1980. The centerpiece of this campaign was an all-out war on the working class to restore corporate profitability. This involved not only lowering wages at the workplace, but also stripping workers of their hard-won legal rights to organize unions and use the strike weapon, which was enabled by both the Democrats and Republicans. That war on the U.S. working class morphed into the global war on workers that later became known as neoliberalism, which had already been raging for four long decades by the time Trump took office.

Trump did not emerge out of the blue but rather represents the ongoing degeneration of Republican Party politics that began with Ronald Reagan's two terms, followed by the presidency of George H. W. Bush in 1988, and George W. Bush from 2000 to 2008. At each stage, Republicans in Congress could count on the support of a populist movement demanding the party's increasingly conservative program. The New Right in the 1980s was followed by the Christian Right in the 1990s and early 2000s, each able to turn out large numbers of conservative voters for conservative Republican candidates on Election Day.

But the emergence of the Tea Party as a reaction to Obama's election in 2009 perhaps illustrates most vividly how such right-wing populist movements were far less spontaneous or grassroots than they appeared. On the contrary, they were directly tied to the ruling class's neoliberal agenda.

Charles and David Koch, two brothers who at that time were each worth more than $20 billion and who own Koch Industries, the second-largest company in the U.S., provided the funding and directed the activities of Tea Party organizations across the country during Obama's presidency.[4] They did so from behind the scenes, primarily using their Americans for Prosperity Foundation as an intermediary. Investigative journalist Jane Mayer described a summit sponsored by Americans for Prosperity in which summit organizer Peggy Venable declared, "We love what the Tea Parties are doing, because that's how we're going to take back America!" while accusing Obama of promoting "a socialist vision for this country." Mayer continued:

> Five hundred people attended the summit, which served, in part, as a training session for Tea Party activists in Texas. An advertisement cast the event as a populist uprising against vested corporate power. "Today, the voices of average Americans are being drowned out by lobbyists and special interests," it said. "But you can do something about it." The pitch made no mention of its corporate funders. The White House has expressed frustration that such sponsors have largely eluded public notice. David Axelrod, Obama's senior adviser, said, "What they don't say is that, in part, this is a grassroots citizens' movement brought to you by a bunch of oil billionaires.[5]

Moreover, a New York Times/CBS News poll of the 18 percent of Americans who identified as Tea Party supporters in 2010 showed that they tended to be white, older than forty-five, male, married, and they almost always vote Republican.[6] They described themselves as "very conservative" and were more likely than most Republicans to depict themselves as "angry" at Washington. However, their anger appeared not to be based on their own financial situation; most were wealthier and better-educated than the general public, and were more likely to say that their personal financial situation was fairly good or very good.[7] This was certainly not the case for the majority of working-class people in the immediate aftermath of the Great Recession.

But more than 90 percent of the Tea Party supporters interviewed in the poll believed that the country (including the economy) was headed in the wrong direction, and nearly the same number disapproved of Obama's performance as president. Their views on race and class distinguished them from the general public. More than half stated that the policies of the Obama administration favored the poor, while roughly 25 percent said Obama favored Blacks over whites. Furthermore, they were more likely than either the general public or other Republicans to say that too much was being made of the problems facing Black people.[8]

A sixty-seven-year-old female respondent described the suspicion she felt about Obama, revealing her own racist prejudice: "I just feel he's getting away from what America is. He's a socialist. And to tell you the truth, I think he's a Muslim and trying to head us in that direction, I don't care what he says. He's been in office over a year and can't find a church to go to. That doesn't say much for him."[9]

It was just a short leap from these Tea Party themes to those espoused by Trump on the 2016 campaign trail—as the logical extension of the GOP's increasing captivity to right-wing populism, which was decades in the making.

But Trump's electoral aspirations also apparently motivated his embrace of right-wing populism, which required a political transformation for him. Trump had once traveled in Democratic Party circles. In 2005, Bill and Hillary Clinton even attended his wedding to third wife, Melania, at his Mar-a-Lago Florida estate.[10] At that time, he was most famous as the bombastic host of the reality show "The Apprentice," best known for shouting "You're fired!" at losing contestants. Trump's first major foray into national politics was in 2011, when he began exploring the possibility of a presidential run—by building his reputation as a leading spokesperson for the so-called "birther movement."

As soon as Barack Obama was elected as the nation's first Black president in 2008, right-wing conspiracy theorists and vocal racists began loudly questioning the legitimacy of his claim to be a U.S. citizen. Obama was born in Hawaii, with a U.S.-born mother, but because his father was Kenyan, the "birthers" demanded that Obama produce his birth certificate. Trump embraced this campaign in 2011 as he made the rounds on the talk show circuit, asking "Why doesn't he show his birth certificate?" on *ABC*'s "The View" and repeating his doubts about Obama's citizenship on *Fox News* and *NBC*'s "Today Show."[11]

Trump's campaign against Obama put him firmly on the right of the political spectrum while establishing his reputation as a racist. As the *New York Times* reported, "The more Mr. Trump questioned the legitimacy of Mr. Obama's presidency, the better he performed in the early polls of the 2012 Republican field, springing from fifth place to a virtual tie for first."[12] This is how Trump began to build his voting base years before he announced his 2016 candidacy.

Who Elected Trump?

As soon as Trump was declared the winner of the 2016 presidential election, mainstream news outlets all sounded the same alarm: white workers had gotten their "*revenge.*" Indeed, the headlines were stunningly similar: "How Trump won: The revenge of working-class whites" (*Washington Post*),[13] "The Revenge of the White Man" (*Time*),[14] "Revenge of the Forgotten Class" (*ProPublica*),[15] "Revenge of the Rural Voter" (*Politico*),[16] "Why Trump Won: Working-class Whites" (*New York Times*).[17]

In this way, the mainstream media created the liberal post-election narrative, parroting Democratic Party leaders frantically seeking to blame someone (other than themselves) for Hillary Clinton's loss. They settled on the slice of white voters from key Midwestern states who gave him the small margin of victory in states won by Trump in the general election.

But the mainstream media's "white working-class revenge" account was factually incorrect. Perhaps most importantly, the typical Trump voter was middle class, not working class. Trump's supporters in the 2016 primaries earned an average of $72,000 per year, well above the national median household income of $55,775—indicating a solid middle-class component among Trump's core backers. Trump voters in the general election mirrored this income distribution, with two-thirds earning above the national median income.[18]

It turned out that white working-class voters had not turned out in droves for Trump on Election Day. The *Washington Post* reversed its own earlier claim on June 5, 2017, with the headline, "It's time to bust the myth: Most Trump voters were not working class."[19] Based on the American National Election Study of the actual voting figures (rather than morning-after Election Day speculation), the article concluded, "White non-Hispanic voters without college degrees making below the median household income made up only 25 percent of Trump voters. That's a far cry from the working-class-fueled victory many journalists have imagined."[20]

Yet even in McDowell County, West Virginia, where voters gave Trump a 74 percent margin of victory over Clinton, most working-class voters did not participate in the election. As author Elizabeth Catte, a native of Appalachia, argued, "It is not immaterial to me that Trump won McDowell County during an election that had a historically low voter turnout for the county. With 17,508 registered voters, only 27 percent of McDowell County voters supported Trump."[21]

Catte added that depicting such communities as "Trump Country" erases much of their actual populations: "According to the bulk of coverage . . . nonwhite people, anyone with progressive politics, those who care about the environment, LGBTQ individuals, young folks, and a host of others do not exist in Appalachia."[22]

On the other hand, some commentators criticized the Clinton campaign for purportedly paying too much attention to those who are specially oppressed in society—front-loading what the media called "identity politics" (but in actuality is championing the rights of the oppressed)—speculating that this alienated white voters with "economic anxiety" who then had no choice but to reject Clinton and turn to Trump. Columbia University professor Mark Lilla put it perhaps the most crudely in the *New York Times*, claiming to "paraphrase" Bernie Sanders: "America is sick and tired of hearing about liberals' damn bathrooms, Lilla wrote."[23] [Fact check: Sanders declared his *support* for transgender bathroom rights in May 2016.[24]]

The mainstream debate thus counterposed "class" politics to so-called identity politics, as if combating class inequality and fighting racism, sexism, Islamophobia, transphobia, and other forms of oppression are necessarily mutually exclusive. It also left hanging the issue of whether Clinton was a *genuine* fighter against oppression, or just cynically chasing the votes that her campaign mistakenly calculated could win her a majority in the Electoral College.

The working class is no longer (if it ever was) predominantly white and male, even though this remains the caricature among most people. People of color will very soon become the majority in the U.S. population, and among younger generations make up already close to 50 percent.[25] Moreover, people of color have always been disproportionately represented within the working class and the poor, due to the economic consequences of racism. This demonstrates why combatting oppression is (and always has been) a working-class issue and will be vital to rebuilding a fighting class-based movement. Today's working class is multiracial, made up of multiple genders and nationalities, and of people with a variety of disabilities.

While white male workers have suffered enormously in recent decades, Black people and other oppressed sectors of the working class have suffered yet more. There is no reason to counterpose their interests, when solidarity between all workers will advance the entire working class, and all its oppressed members—while combatting Trumpism—if the movement champions the rights of all those who suffer oppression.

The Consequences of Political Polarization in a Two-Party Duopoly

Most in the media failed to ask the most important questions about the 2016 election before concluding that the white working class, especially in the "fly-over" country of the Midwest, has become a bastion of reaction. How many of these same people voted for Obama four years earlier? Millions of them did, a fact the Clinton campaign discovered months before the November election. As Nate Cohn described, "The [Clinton] campaign looked back to respondents who were contacted in 2012, and found large numbers of white working-class voters who had backed Mr. Obama were now supporting Mr. Trump."[26]

It is also the case that self-described socialist Bernie Sanders experienced a groundswell of support in the Midwest during the 2016 primaries, winning the Michigan, West Virginia, Indiana, and Wisconsin primaries, which all went to Trump in the general election.[27]

The real story of the 2016 election is the sharp political polarization that allowed both Sanders and Trump to attract mass popular support during the primary season. The bulk of the mainstream media, with their fleeting attention span, failed to appreciate this fact in their election post-mortem. Although Sanders spoke from the left and Trump from the right, both candidates acknowledged the *failures of the political status quo.*

Trump succeeded in winning the nomination, but Sanders did not. Unfortunately, Sanders ran as a Democrat—and the party's powerbrokers had decided on Clinton as their neoliberal candidate from the beginning. The 2016 election merely highlighted how the Democrats had frittered away their traditional voting base over a period of decades—taking their votes for granted yet offering less than nothing in return, even as working-class living standards plummeted in the wake of the 2008 financial crisis.

"Democrats for the Leisure Class"

As discussed in Chapter Eight, Bill and Hillary Clinton had been among the key architects of the Democratic Party's open embrace of neoliberalism, beginning in 1985 with the founding of the Democratic Leadership Council (DLC). The Rev. Jesse Jackson once called the DLC "Democrats for the Leisure Class," and with good reason: its board of trustees, made up of major donors, included Koch Industries, Aetna, and Coca-Cola, while its executive board included Enron, AIG, Texaco, Chevron, and AT&T, among other corporate giants. The DLC spawned a generation of "New Democrats," to carry out its mission—reshaping the Democratic Party as (more openly) probusiness and much less liberal.[28]

As Robert Dreyfuss described in *The American Prospect,* "The DLC thundered against the 'liberal fundamentalism' of the party's base—unionists, Blacks, feminists, Greens, and cause groups generally."[29] The DLC finally closed its doors in 2011 on the verge of bankruptcy, but it had already succeeded in its mission. The Clinton Foundation acquired its papers, in a fitting conclusion.

The New Democrats had assumed that they could maintain the party's voting base by offering a "Republican-lite" alternative as the "lesser evil" at the voting booth. But as the decades passed, the Democrats' voting base gradually faded as its members' suffering steadily worsened, especially among young people facing bleak futures. And many so-called low-information voters were nevertheless very much aware that mainstream Democrats had long ago turned their backs on them in search of a higher income constituency.

In his 1996 State of the Union Address, Bill Clinton stole the Republican Party's thunder, declaring "The era of big government is over." Reagan had invented the racist myth of the "welfare queen," but it was Bill Clinton who ended "welfare as we know it." He also oversaw the mass incarceration of Black and Latino nonviolent drug offenders in the name of the racist "War on Drugs," while Hillary Clinton demonized young Black men with the racially charged term "super-predator" to bolster her husband's efforts. Trump called for building a thousand-mile wall at the Mexican border, but Bill Clinton had already built a three-hundred-mile security "smart fence" in the 1990s, and both Hillary Clinton and Barack Obama voted for a seven-hundred-mile fence in 2006 when they were in the Senate.

Hillary Clinton voted in favor of the USA PATRIOT Act, enabling the massive roundup and deportation of Arabs and Muslims after September 11, 2001, which failed to generate a *single* charge of terrorism. Throughout her political career, she has without exception strongly supported U.S. military intervention abroad, including the invasions of Iraq and Afghanistan, still wreaking death and destruction in those countries with no end in sight. Indeed, just hours before the Trump Administration announced it had launched fifty-nine cruise missiles on a Syrian airfield on April 6, 2017, Clinton had argued that the U.S. "should take out [Assad's] air fields."[30]

Hillary Clinton's Dilemma with the Democrats' Voting Base

Surely, many would-be Democratic voters viewed Hillary Clinton with skepticism in 2016, since the Clintons' record was well known. Perhaps her scripted commitment to Black Lives Matter activists seemed both insincere and hypocritical, as did her support for immigrants' rights. The $675,000 she accrued giving just three speeches to Goldman Sachs and the hundreds of thousands more dollars she received for speaking to other Wall Street vultures could not have sat well with those who lost their homes and jobs during the financial crisis, while those same bankers got not only bailed out but rewarded with huge bonuses in the years that followed.[31]

Clinton demonstrated just how out of touch she was with the working class and once solidly Democratic voting base when she announced at a West Virginia campaign stop that she planned to "put a lot of coal miners and coal companies out of business"—without offering the promise of new training or help finding new jobs for those coal miners whose lives have been upended by job loss.[32] As Cohn observed, "In retrospect, the scale of the Democratic collapse in coal country was a harbinger of just how far the Democrats would fall in their old strongholds once they forfeited the mantle of working-class interests."[33]

Nature abhors a vacuum, the old saying goes. The same dictum holds true in politics, and a left—or even a genuinely liberal—flank has been missing in mainstream U.S. politics for decades, *in large part because of the rightward shift of the Democratic Party helmed by the Clintons.*

There is no doubt that Trump fed the racism, sexism, homophobia, and xenophobia that already exists among large swathes of the

U.S. population. Trump's speech announcing his run for president in the atrium of New York City's Trump Tower on June 16, 2015, included this openly racist assertion: "When Mexico sends its people, they're not sending their best. . . . They're sending people that have lots of problems and they're bringing those problems with us [sic]. They're bringing drugs, they're bringing crime, they're rapists, and some, I assume, are good people."[34]

Trump continued in this reactionary vein throughout his campaign—and just one month before the November 2016 election, a 2005 video was released discussing with Billy Bush, of "Access Hollywood," his strategy for sexually assaulting women, asserting, "I just start kissing them. It's like a magnet. Just kiss. I don't even wait. And when you're a star, they let you do it. You can do anything. . . . Grab 'em by the pussy. You can do anything."[35]

But as left-wing author Christian Parenti observed after watching many hours of Trump's speeches, "Contrary to how he was portrayed in the mainstream media, Trump did not talk only of walls, immigration bans, and deportations. In fact, he usually didn't spend much time on those themes." Mainly, Trump talked about bringing lost jobs back.[36] Trump, like Sanders, was addressing the burning issue that Clinton ignored: the economic hardship of the working class, which has only accelerated since the economic recovery began in earnest in 2010. Both these factors undoubtedly played a role in Trump's popularity.

But it is also the case that roughly 28 percent of Latino and 27 percent of Asian votes went to Trump, according to exit polls.[37] Within the confines of the two-party system, voters are not given the opportunity to vote for their ideal candidate, but rather must settle for who they perceive as the less harmful.

Clinton did, of course, win the popular vote by nearly three million yet lost the election; only 16 years earlier, Al Gore won the popular vote by roughly five hundred thousand, yet George W. Bush was elected president. The Electoral College in the so-called "world's greatest democracy" is inherently undemocratic. It is a holdover from slavery, originally designed to give disproportionate weight to Southern slave states in elections. It is no coincidence that the Constitutional Convention of 1787 that formed the Electoral College also determined that slaves (denied the right to vote) would be counted as three-fifths of a person for the sole purpose of inflating the representation of slaveholders.[38]

Even after her surprise loss, however, Clinton accepted the results without questioning the legitimacy of the Electoral College, speaking volumes about the party's commitment to preserving the political and social status quo that ultimately benefits both major parties, even when they lose elections. That status quo includes the power-sharing arrangement between the Democrats and Republicans, devised to prevent third parties from gaining a toehold. The two-party system and its limited choices go a long way toward explaining why voters are used to backing candidates with whom they disagree on many issues, often as a vote *against* the other candidate. Perhaps for this reason, voter turnout in the U.S. is historically low overall.

"The Unequal States of America" and the Race to the Bottom

The U.S. is strewn with the wreckage of neoliberalism, its landscape dotted with once-thriving communities built around manufacturing plants where Wal-Mart is now the biggest employer, setting the low standard for local wages. Well before Trump ever ran for president, the scale of class inequality in the U.S. was already the worst in the industrialized world. The Allianz's *Global Wealth Report 2015*, using figures from 2014, reported that the U.S. possessed a larger amount of personal wealth than any other country, at 41.6 percent of the global wealth total. At the same time, the report found that the U.S. also had the largest concentration of overall wealth in the hands of the proportionately fewest people, leading it to call the U.S. "the Unequal States of America."[39]

In January 2017, the British business magazine *The Economist* reported that its Intelligence Unit had downgraded the U.S. from a "full democracy" to a "flawed democracy," based on low voter turnout, the degree of distrust that the population holds toward government institutions, and the high level of class inequality. "Popular trust in government, elected representatives, and political parties has fallen to extremely low levels in the U.S. This has been a long-term trend and one that preceded the election of Mr. Trump as the U.S. president in November 2016," stated the report. It added, "[Trump] appealed to the angry, anti-political mood of large swathes of the electorate who feel that the two mainstream parties no longer speak for them."[40]

To be sure, Democrats and Republicans have often debated heatedly over the details of the neoliberal project over the last forty years but without either side challenging its overriding goals: allowing capital to cross national borders unrestrained in the search for low-wage labor and maximum profits around the world. Meanwhile, the global working class was yet more tightly controlled when attempting to migrate through borders, whether these migrants were fleeing from war, poverty and hunger, or violent dictators. The neoliberal agenda forced workers on a global scale yet more directly in competition with each other, in a race to the bottom.

Employers have always threatened to relocate their companies elsewhere as a tactic to keep workers from organizing unions and demanding higher wages. Throughout much of the twentieth century, such actions usually pitted workers in the U.S. North against those in the nonunion southern part of the country. Neoliberal globalization extended this competition among workers far beyond U.S. borders, as capitalists scoured the world in search of the cheapest wages and operating costs to maximize profits. Thus, the textile industry moved most of its operations to the southern U.S. by the mid-twentieth century, only to relocate to the Global South in the 1990s and 2000s.

Free trade agreements like NAFTA came to symbolize neoliberalism's assault on U.S. workers, but they were just one part of its multipronged attack—and far from its most destructive attack against the U.S. working class. There are plenty of reasons why socialists oppose NAFTA and other so-called free trade agreements. The most important should be opposition to U.S. imperialism. NAFTA was "sold" by then-President Bill Clinton partly on the basis that it would bring prosperity to ordinary Mexicans as well as U.S. workers.

Yet, over the course of more than two decades, because of U.S.-subsidized corn and other products, NAFTA resulted in the further impoverishment of Mexican workers and "wiped out" small farmers in Mexico, according the Center for Economic and Policy Research in 2014. "From 1994 to 2000, the annual number of Mexicans emigrating to the United States soared by 79 percent," the report stated. "The number of Mexican-born residents living in the United States more than doubled from 4.5 million in 1990 to 9.4 million in 2000 and peaked at 12.6 million in 2009."[41] This migration, in turn, seemed to bolster the right's (false) claim that Mexican workers were "stealing" American workers' jobs.

And while outsourcing U.S. jobs in recent decades, especially to low-wage workers in India and China, certainly played a role in the downward spiral of U.S. wages, increasing technology and automation played a larger role, allowing manufacturers to *increase* output with far fewer workers. As labor activist and scholar Kim Moody recently argued, "While manufacturing jobs disappeared by the millions [since 1980], manufacturing output increased, so that by 2010 manufacturing production workers were producing four times what they had in the 1950s and twice their production of 1983."[42]

Elsewhere he argued:

> A more likely explanation for manufacturing job losses on the scale of the last thirty years or so, one that is internal to the workings of U.S. capitalism and, indeed, capitalism generally, is to be found in the rise of productivity extracted after 1980 by the introduction of lean production methods, new technology, and capital's accelerated counteroffensive against labor—*an explanation based in class conflict itself*.[43] [Emphasis added.]

Losing the One-Sided Class War

But one of the most central goals of neoliberalism was simply crushing working-class organizations that could fight against falling wages. After Ronald Reagan took office in 1981, strike levels dropped significantly, falling steadily ever since. By February 2017, the Bureau of Labor Statistics reported that work stoppages over the last decade have been the lowest on record, noting that the "average number of major work stoppages by decade has declined over 95 percent since 1947."[44]

Over the last decades, union membership nearly halved, from 20.1 percent in 1983 to 10.7 overall in 2016—and just 6.4 percent in the private sector—a level comparable to that before the labor upheaval of 1930s won the legal right to organize unions.[45] As of 2014, only 7.4 percent of young workers aged eighteen to twenty-nine were members of unions, even though 55 percent of them viewed unions favorably.[46]

Indeed, the war on unions escalated over the last decade, as Republican-dominated state legislatures went on an antiunion rampage in the Midwest, passing a wave of "right to work" laws that, among other things, allowed nonunion workers to withhold union dues even when they benefit from union contracts. Once a hallmark of the antiunion, low-wage South, "right to work" was adopted by twenty-eight states by February 2017—including the once union-dense Midwestern states of Indiana, Michigan, Wisconsin, West Virginia, Kentucky, and Missouri—with no end in sight.

By May 2017, unemployment had dropped to 4.3 percent—a low not seen since 2001. Historically, low unemployment has led to rising wages and rising confidence among workers as employers facing labor shortages were forced to offer higher compensation.[47] But as *Wall Street Journal* reporter Justin Lahart argued:

> It took a long seven years for the unemployment rate to get to 4.3% from the peak of 10% in October 2009. Because of the sluggish growth, businesses never had to scramble, and pay more, to add workers. And at no point did workers feel they were awash in opportunity.
>
> This slow growth doesn't give people confidence to ask for higher wages. And plenty of workers have never experienced that kind of environment. . . . Only workers in their 40s and older remember the 1990s boom. Maybe the U.S. labor market is turning a bit like Japan's, where the unemployment has fallen to its lowest level in nearly a quarter-century, but after so many years of disappointment, workers are hesitant to demand higher wages, and employers are hesitant to give them.

The Disappearing Middle-Income Earner

The U.S. working class was the highest-paid in the world during the post-Second World War economic boom, but its wages began a downward slide in the mid-1970s. Today it is the lowest-paid among OECD countries, with the greatest proportion of low-wage jobs, (which are defined as paying less than two-thirds of the nation's median income). Twenty-six percent of jobs in the U.S. fell into this category, paying less than $23,390 in the OECD's 2014 report.[48]

While most media reports have described U.S. wages as "stagnating" over recent decades, the reality is far worse. Most middle-income earners have fallen off the face of the map, either advancing into the upper-income tier or, far more likely for the working and lower-middle class, joining lower income earners.[49] In addition, examining wages and incomes does not tell half the story about those in in the lower-income tier, now encompassing much larger numbers of workers as the category of middle-income earners has hollowed out.

Neoliberal policy has taken many forms that have severely eroded working-class living standards, including regressive taxes (such as skyrocketing sales taxes), cuts in emergency heating and food stamp subsidies, higher fees for everything from traffic tickets to public transportation, rising premiums and deductibles for health insurance coverage, higher rents, unaffordable childcare costs—among other expenses built into everyday life. Almost none of these are adequately incorporated into mainstream analyses of class inequality.

The political establishment perhaps believed that shielding this reality from mainstream discourse would fool those suffering because of these policies. "Poverty goes down, coverage goes up, and America gets a raise," announced *MSNBC* on September 13, 2016 about the Census Bureau finding that not only did all U.S. incomes rise in the previous year, but incomes also grew the fastest for the poorest people.[50]

We must ask whether this cheerful announcement fooled those workers whose lives have been turned upside down in recent decades. Even by the Census Bureau's own measurement, in 2015, median household income (which is the level at which 50 percent of the population makes more and the other 50 percent makes less) was lower than in 2007, and lower still than the all-time high in 1999. Further examination also reveals that people in rural areas didn't share in the increase, but rather experienced a 2 percent *decrease* in median income in 2015, which fell to just $44,657 for these households, far below the national median.

Defining Poverty in the Twenty-First Century

The Census Bureau generalizations about median income dramatically downplayed the deep concentrations of poverty that exist across the country. For example, North Dakota had the nation's biggest drop in child poverty between 2011 and 2016, but the poverty rate for Native American children, the majority living on reservations, is five times higher than for the rest of the state's children.[51] Likewise, buried within a *Detroit Free Press* article headlined "Michigan posts its largest income gain since the recession" is the admission that the majority-Black cities of Flint and Detroit continue to have some of the highest poverty rates in the U.S., at 40.8 percent and 39.8 percent, respectively. The child poverty rate is even higher; more than half of the children who lived in Detroit and Flint in 2015 lived in poverty, at a rate of 57.6 percent and 58.3 percent, respectively.[52]

The Census Bureau figures also ignore the enormous income disparities, often along racial lines, *within* individual cities. According to the Census Bureau, Washington, D.C.'s median household income rose to $75,600 in 2015, but that breaks down to $120,000 for white households compared to just $41,000 for Black households. The poverty rate for the city's Black population is 27 percent, and 75 percent of all D.C. residents living in poverty are Black.[53]

There is yet another way that the Census Bureau's poverty statistics skew lower while its median income figures skew higher. In the introduction to its Current Population Survey, the Bureau makes the following caveat about its "sample" population: "People in institutions, such as prisons, long-term care hospitals and nursing homes, are not eligible to be interviewed in the CPS [Current Population Survey] . . . people who are homeless and not living in shelters are not included in the sample." The list of those excluded from the survey thus includes millions of the most impoverished people in the U.S. Despite the flaws in the Census Bureau's findings, they still show roughly one in four African Americans and Native Americans and more than one in five Latinos living under the official poverty line. One in five children overall are living in poverty by official standards, and 10 percent of U.S. households are trying to survive on less than $13,300 a year.

But the most glaring problem with the Census Bureau's methodology is its appallingly low poverty threshold. If the poverty line were scaled upward to a more accurate level, the official poverty rate of the U.S. population would certainly skyrocket. The Social Security Administration developed the current poverty measure back in 1963, adopting a formula based on the minimum amount of money necessary to buy a subsistence level of food, using data from the 1955 Household Food Consumption Survey. On the assumption that food expenditures made up one-third of what a family of four needed to survive at the time, that amount was then multiplied by three to define the poverty line.

This definition, using obsolete, fifty-year-old consumption patterns and even more antiquated sixty-year-old prices (adjusted annually based on the also-inadequate consumer price index), is still in use today. If that formula (food expenses times three) was ever adequate for survival—and it most likely wasn't—it is preposterous today. In 2015, the poverty threshold was set at just at $24,250 for a family of four and $11,770 for an individual. While those cloistered in the bubble of the federal bureaucracy seem to find its poverty threshold adequate for survival, anyone with at least one foot in the real world is aware that no family of four can make ends meet on $24,250 a year.

The Rise in the Actual Cost of Living

Our World in Data compiled statistics documenting the change in consumer prices between 1997 and 2017 for the average urban consumer, based on Bureau of Labor Statistics data. They found that prices for household necessities rose as follows during that time period:

- Housing costs rose by nearly 58 percent.
- Household energy costs rose by more than 68 percent.
- Medical care costs rose by almost 100 percent.
- Childcare costs rose by more than 110 percent.
- Public transportation costs rose by more than 45 percent.
- Education costs rose by more than 151 percent.
- Food and beverage costs rose by more than 56 percent.
- College tuition rose by more than 170 percent.[54]

Determining a living wage therefore requires a realistic accounting for the cost of living, which also varies considerably by geographic region. Dr. Amy K. Glasmeier from the Massachusetts Institute of Technology (MIT) has developed a "living wage calculator" that estimates living wages for specific localities across the U.S. Glasmeier's calculation is based on fulfilling *only* basic necessities—housing, childcare, food, transportation and healthcare—not vacations, dining at restaurants, generous health insurance policies, savings, or college funds. The living wage can also be described as the "minimum subsistence wage."[55]

On this basis, the 2016 MIT living wage calculator estimated that the lowest livable wage was in Knoxville, Tennessee, at $54,745. The highest livable wage is in the Washington, D.C., metropolitan area, at $90,621.[56] In April 2017, the MIT researchers demonstrated the gross inadequacy of the official federal poverty level of $24,491 in 2016, estimating that the living wage was actually "$65,860 on average for two working adults, two children per year before taxes."[57]

Put differently, millions of working-class people in the U.S. today are deprived of basic necessities simply because they do not earn a minimum subsistence wage, while corporate profits soar.

A Georgetown University study on job creation showed that workers with a high school diploma or less lost the most income during the recovery, as more jobs go to those with at least some post-secondary education—likely reflecting a glut of "over-educated" applicants for low wage jobs. Recent college graduates are filling barista jobs at a higher level, as roughly 40 percent are "underemployed," often for a long time."[58]

The business magazine *Forbes* recently described that a new Amazon warehouse in Fall River, Massachusetts, offers starting pay for workers without college degrees at $12.75 per hour. Those with bachelor's degrees qualify for "junior inventory clerks," if they have prior "warehousing experience," at $14.70 an hour. *Forbes* headlined this story as "China-Like Wages Now Part of U.S. Employment Boom."[59] This downward trajectory for college grads has further impacted workers without higher education, as both are forced into competition even for low-paying jobs.

"Of the 7.2 million jobs lost in the recession," the Georgetown study states, "5.6 million were jobs for workers with a high school diploma or less. . . . On net, there are now more than 5.5 million fewer jobs for individuals with a high school education or less than there were in December 2007."[60] The downward trend in wages for this group of workers began well before the Great Recession. A report by the Hamilton Project of the Brookings Institution found that between 1990 and 2003, *real median wages had already fallen by 20 percent for male workers without a high school diploma age thirty to forty-five*, and by 12 percent for women in the same category. As the *New York Times* concluded, citing the report, "Less-educated Americans, especially men, are shifting away from manufacturing and other jobs that once offered higher pay, and a higher share are now working in lower-paying food service, cleaning, and groundskeeping jobs." [61]

But this decline in wages is tied to much more than the decline in manufacturing jobs. As the *Times* added, "Pay levels are declining in almost all of the fields that employ less-educated workers, so even those who have held onto jobs as manufacturers, operators, and laborers are making less than they would have a generation ago." Inflation-adjusted annual pay for manufacturing jobs fell from $33,600 in 1990 to $28,000 in 2013. The greatest damage from neoliberalism was done early on, from the late 1970s through the early 1990s.[62] The average real hourly wages of production and nonsupervisory workers fell by 15 percent between 1973 and the mid-1990s, lowering the ceiling for working-class wages ever since. Wages briefly rose during the economic boom of the late 1990s, only to be derailed by the early 2000s when wages began to stagnate again. The Great Recession once again accelerated the decline.

The Social Crisis Facing the U.S. Working Class

One of the most glaring inequalities in the U.S. today is the gross disparity in access to adequate and affordable healthcare coverage. While making medical insurance a "benefit" of employment was never sufficient—leaving millions of people in low-wage, nonunion jobs without such benefits even in the 1960s and 1970s—enough workers received medical benefits to give the appearance of corporate generosity during the post-war economic boom.

The neoliberal agenda has targeted healthcare benefits systematically during the last several decades, resulting in a social crisis for the working class. This crisis preceded Trump's election because the Affordable Care Act (ACA), often known as "Obamacare," relied on profit-making insurance companies to maintain it. As Fairness and Accuracy in Reporting (FAIR) described in March 2017:

> The truth is our healthcare system is sick, and the Affordable Care Act has been little more than a bandage on a compound fracture. The ACA cut the rate of the uninsured to an all-time low, and limited the health insurance industry's most outrageous consumer abuses, both important steps forward. At the same time, 29 million people remain uninsured, most of the non-elderly population who have employer-paid coverage are increasingly underinsured, and costs continue to soar at 200–400 percent of inflation.[63]

But the damage extended far beyond those enrolled directly in ACA plans, to the 177 million people who get their insurance through their employers. As the *FAIR* authors explained, for these workers:

> Their premiums went up more than 3 times faster than inflation.
> Their deductibles increased 89 percent, while their compensation went up just 14 percent.

Even though the U.S. has the lowest rate of un-insurance in our lifetimes, 31 percent of Americans told Gallup they either skipped or delayed necessary medical care last year because of costs, the majority for serious conditions.[64]

The *New York Times* reported on July 23, 2017, that a long line of cars formed overnight for a free medical clinic in Wise, Virginia, as would-be patients slept in their cars to receive treatment they desperately needed after the clinic opened at five o'clock a.m. All had urgent medical needs: "Patients passed the command tent of the charity that runs the clinic, Remote Area Medical, emblazoned with a plea and a promise: 'Stop the Suffering.' The group, staffed by medical volunteers, has treated more than 700,000 people at free clinics around the country and overseas since 1985." Some two thousand patients in total stood in line for medical care—for everything from rotting teeth to diabetes prescriptions that they could not afford.[65]

Youngstown, Ohio: A Microcosm of the Industrial Heartland

The Youngstown, Ohio, area provides a microcosm of once-thriving communities that have fallen into economic devastation after manufacturing employers abandoned them over recent decades. Until 1977, steel corporations offered decent paying jobs for those willing to work in grueling conditions in Mahoning Valley, Ohio. But on September 19 of that year, Youngstown Sheet and Tube announced it was laying off five thousand workers. Then U.S. Steel announced that it would be shutting down sixteen plants in the U.S., including their plant in Youngstown, leading to a loss of more than 4,000 jobs. Jones & Laughlin Steel Corp. soon announced that they would also be laying off thousands more workers. In the space of a decade, 40,000 jobs were eliminated, ravaging working-class living standards in the area.

Gary Steinbeck of nearby Warren, Ohio—who was twenty-five years old in 1977—told the *New York Post,* "Those numbers only reflect the jobs that were lost in the plant; the ripple effect was equally devastating. Grocery stores, pizza shops, gas stations, restaurants, department stores, car dealerships, barber shops all saw their business plummet and they started closing," He added, "No one never

[sic] calculated the cultural tragedy as part of the equation either. They didn't just dismantle the old mills, they dismantled the societal fabric of what made Youngstown Youngstown."[66]

In 2011, the Brookings Institute rated Youngstown as having the highest concentrated poverty rate among core cities in the United States' one hundred largest metropolitan areas, with an overall poverty rate of 49.9 percent.[67] Radical journalist Chris Hedges described the city this way in 2010:

> Youngstown, like many postindustrial pockets in America, is a deserted wreck plagued by crime and the attendant psychological and criminal problems that come when communities physically break down. The city's great steel mills have been leveled and replaced by America's new growth industry—prisons, including a so-called supermax facility.[68]

Vanity Fair reporter Ken Stern visited the greater Youngstown area in May 2017, and discovered that, far from being a solid Trump stronghold, it was divided between Trump and Clinton supporters—with a large layer of people who supported neither Trump nor Clinton and were fed up with both parties. That is, this community is as politically polarized as the rest of the country. Stern described one resident this way:

> Scott Seitz stares at me through red-rimmed eyes, recounting the economic devastation in his village of McDonald, Ohio. The town's fortunes have always been tied to the steel mills, for better, or, more recently, for much worse. With the flight of the steel industry, the tax base of tiny McDonald has gone too, along with its only pharmacy, all of its bars, and hope for replacing its failing sewer and gas lines. But it is not the state of McDonald that renders Seitz emotional, but the fate of his family, which is plagued with all the modern symptoms of the American working class: unemployment, heroin addiction, single fatherhood, and lost opportunity. It is enough to make a middle-aged steel worker teary-eyed and a little desperate, which is why Scott Seitz—a lifelong Democrat, a committed union man, a two-time Obama voter—voted for Donald Trump in 2016. Trump spoke in plain language on the only issue Seitz really cares about: jobs, jobs, jobs.[69]

The Unstable Narcissist Takes Office

As a candidate, Trump had routinely railed against Muslims, Black people, women, Mexicans, and immigrants in general, while promising to bring back good manufacturing jobs for American workers. His campaign slogan was "Make America Great Again!"; he spouted nationalist and protectionist rhetoric aimed at shoring up his base. But once Trump became president, his directives appeared to be guided primarily by his own enormously bloated ego. While his unstable and incompetent administration failed in its first nine months to advance its legislative agenda—most notably repealing Obamacare through Congress—his executive orders, cabinet, and Supreme Court appointments nevertheless managed to wreak havoc on the future of legal abortion and accessible birth control, immigrants' rights, transgender rights in the military and the workplace, the fight against global warming, indigenous rights, Muslim rights, and much more. His encouragement of the racist far right has emboldened that group to an extent not seen since the 1920s.

Trump has not shown mercy to officials in his own administration who got on his wrong side. For example, Trump tweeted shortly after six o'clock a.m. on July 25, 2017, "Attorney General Jeff Sessions has taken a VERY weak position on Hillary Clinton crimes (where are E-mails & DNC leaks) & Intel leakers!"[70] Indeed, Trump became dissatisfied with one after another of the top officials in his administration, resulting in a revolving door of prominent officials who Trump fired or drove out. In roughly the first nine months of Trump's presidency, these included, but were by no means limited to the following:

- Trump fired acting attorney general Sally Yates on January 30, after she ordered the Justice Department not to defend Trump's executive order on immigration and refugees, titled "Protecting the Nation from Foreign Terrorist Entry into the United States"—also known as the "Muslim Ban," for its obvious racism.
- Michael Flynn, Trump's national security adviser, resigned on February 13—after serving less than a month—when it became known that that he had discussed U.S. sanctions on Russia with the Russian ambassador to the United States before Trump became president.
- On May 9, Trump suddenly fired FBI director James Comey, who was leading an investigation into possible collusion between Trump's presidential campaign and Russia to influence the 2016 election.

- Press secretary and acting communications director Sean Spicer resigned on July 21 after Trump hired as communications director Anthony Scaramucci, who was obviously intended to replace him.
- Trump's chief of staff Reince Priebus was fired by Trump on July 28 after Congress failed to pass Trump's legislative agenda, including repealing the Affordable Care ACT (ACA).
- Anthony Scaramucci lasted just ten days on the job as communications director, leaving after he gave a profanity-laden interview with a reporter in which he called Reince Priebus a "paranoid schizophrenic."
- Trump fired the controversial white nationalist Stephen Bannon as his chief strategist on August 18. Bannon immediately returned to the far-right *Breitbart News*, which he edited before joining the Trump administration.[71]

Trump's administration was wracked by scandal soon after his inauguration. The many scandals, some of them related to the job turnover described above, led *Slate* journalist Phillip Carter to label the White House "one enormous undifferentiated scandal soufflé."[72] There were already enough improprieties to fill a book just twelve months into his presidency, and undoubtedly there will be many books written about this scandal-laden administration.

Trump's son-in-law Jared Kushner found himself at the center of several such improprieties. Trump appointed Kushner to powerful positions in his White House—among them, negotiating a peace deal in the Middle East, directing diplomacy with Mexico and China, battling opioid abuse, and improving veterans' care in the U.S. But Kushner had no previous experience in politics. Kushner, like Trump, is the son of a real estate tycoon and was CEO of the family business empire before joining the White House staff. In addition to Kushner's apparent lack of qualifications for these formidable responsibilities, a cloud of unseemliness seems to follow him everywhere. As journalist T.A. Frank described in *Vanity Fair*:

> It was Kushner who fumbled, it seems, in talks with Russians about setting up a communication backchannel. It was Kushner whose family went to China to promote a sleazy EB-5 visa scheme that allows you to effectively purchase U.S. citizenship by purchasing a $500,000

apartment. It was Kushner who was recently found to be conducting White House business on personal e-mail, right after a campaign during which Trump had hammered his opponent incessantly for the same sin. It was Kushner who kept looking for ways to keep his empire solvent, including looking for infusions of cash from titans in China and the Gulf states.[73]

Trump's frequent refrain during campaign rallies in 2016 was "Lock her up!" referring to Hillary Clinton's use of private emails to conduct official business while she was secretary of state. In October 2017, however, it was revealed that both Kushner and his wife Ivanka Trump—Donald Trump's daughter and also a White House aide—had sent hundreds of emails from a private Kushner family email domain, some of them involving official White House communications.[74]

Despite the unsavory inner workings of the Trump administration, the Republican Party establishment appeared willing to look the other way while waiting to reap the financial benefits of Trump's tax reforms. The corporate class hung its hopes on Trump's ability to deliver a tax overhaul skewed heavily in its favor—the same mythical "trickle-down economics" that has been the program of neoliberalism since Ronald Reagan. Trump did not disappoint when he unveiled the bare bones of the GOP tax reform proposal in September 2017, in full Reagan-speak:

> Under our framework, we will dramatically cut the business tax rate so that American companies and American workers can beat our foreign competitors and start winning again. We will reduce the corporate tax rate to . . . below the average of industrialized nations. This is a revolutionary change and the biggest winners will be the Middle Class (sic) workers as jobs start pouring into our country, as companies start competing for American labor and as wages continue to grow.[75]

It is astonishing that Trump managed to get through this speech without winking at his corporate brethren, because there is nothing in the GOP proposal that will help workers to "start winning again." *CNN's* Edward J. McCaffery bluntly labeled the proposal "Trump's massive tax cut—for the rich."[76] On December 21, 2017, Trump signed the sweeping tax reform bill into law, slashing the corporate tax rate to 21 percent from 35 percent—the largest cut since Reagan. An analysis by the Urban-Brookings Tax Policy Center estimated that "by 2027, the GOP tax plan would provide massive benefits to upper-income taxpayers even as it smacked large sections of the middle class with a net tax hike."[77]

Trump's tax reform pleased the corporate class enormously, but if he becomes a liability, it will not hesitate to throw him overboard. The Trump administration's many indiscretions will offer ample opportunity to do so.

Trump's Path of Destruction

To be sure, Republicans were unable to muster enough votes *from their own party* to repeal Obamacare—despite grandstanding on this slogan for the previous seven years. Repealing the ACA had been one of Trump's signature campaign promises.

Trump had also promised to defund Planned Parenthood while he was campaigning as an opponent of abortion rights, and the failed Republican proposal to repeal the ACA had included eliminating federal funds for Planned Parenthood for a year. In April 2017, congressional Republicans did, however, manage to narrowly pass a law—made possible by Vice President Mike Pence's tie-breaking vote—allowing states to withhold federal family planning funds to Planned Parenthood and other clinics that also perform abortions. This law potentially denies access to basic healthcare services to the millions of low-income women who rely on Planned Parenthood for this care.

In his early presidency, Trump forged his path of destruction primarily through executive channels. His administration frequently announced far-reaching policy changes with tweets or other terse notifications, without detailed guidance for their implementation, creating chaos and confusion as government agencies scrambled to carry them out. Using these means, Trump managed to inflict the following damage in his early months in office:

Sabotaging Healthcare for the Working Class

As it became clear that the GOP would fail to repeal the ACA in July, Trump tweeted, "As I said from the beginning, let ObamaCare implode, then deal. Watch!"—indicating that he would dismantle the ACA through executive orders.[78] He began this process in October. First, his administration exempted all employers and insurers from providing birth control coverage if they object to contraception due to "sincerely held religious beliefs," or other "moral convictions." As the *Atlantic* reported, "Half of all women receive their coverage through their employers, and the ACA's mandate has reduced the percentage of women from ages fifteen to forty-four who have to pay for contraceptive coverage through their employer from 20 to 3.6 percent."[79]

Next, Trump issued two new far-reaching directives. The first was an executive order allowing insurance companies to offer low-cost insurance policies that require higher out-of-pocket costs for subscribers than allowed under the ACA. The second was an announcement that his administration would no longer pay subsidies to compensate insurance companies that offer affordable health plans for low-income people; the intention was to drive these profit-seeking companies out of the ACA insurance markets altogether.[80]

Attacking Environmental Protections and Indigenous Rights

A well-known climate-change denier, Trump appointed former Oklahoma attorney general Scott Pruitt, a long-standing antienvironmentalist, to head the Environmental Protection Agency (EPA). He also cut the EPA budget by 31 percent, to its lowest level in four decades, with major reductions to research, clean air, and clean water programs.[81]

On February 7, just two months after the Obama administration ordered the Army Corp of Engineers to halt construction on the $3.8 billion Dakota Access Pipeline and seek an alternate route, Trump ordered construction to resume. In so doing, he overturned a crucial victory for the Standing Rock Sioux Tribe and its thousands of supporters, who had long struggled to stop the construction.

In 2015, Trump owned between $500,000 and $1 million in stock in the company responsible for the Dakota Access pipeline, Energy Transfer Partners, but this amount shrank to under $50,000 by the spring of 2016. Trump's order expediting approval of the pipeline canceled an environmental impact study already underway. On February 22, police in riot gear forcibly evicted the remaining Standing Rock water protectors from their encampments. By June, Energy Transfer Partners had already begun shipping crude oil from the Dakota Access pipeline between western North Dakota and southern Illinois.[82]

Trump also granted a permit to TransCanada Corp. for the cross-border construction of the $8 billion Keystone XL pipeline to deliver oil from the tar sands of Canada to the refineries of the Texas Gulf Coast. Obama had denied a permit for its construction only after environmental and indigenous activists' long-standing struggle against it.

On June 1, 2017, Trump announced that the U.S.—the world's second-largest polluter—would withdraw from the 2015 Paris Climate Accord on the grounds that it was "unfair to U.S. businesses and workers."[83]

Instituting the "Muslim Ban(s)"

While campaigning, Trump had promised a "total and complete shutdown of Muslims entering the United States," and one of his first acts as president, on January 27, was to impose an order that immediately became known as the "Muslim Ban". The order banned entry into the U.S., for ninety days, from seven majority-Muslim countries—Iran, Iraq, Libya, Somalia, Sudan, Syria and Yemen—and deferred the admission of all refugees for one hundred and twenty days, while indefinitely suspending the Syrian refugee program.

The United States had accepted only 12,486 Syrian refugees in 2016, compared with roughly 300,000 accepted by Germany that year. For the sake of comparison, Turkey received about 2.7 million refugees, Lebanon 1 million refugees and Jordan 650,000 since the Syrian civil war began—showing that the U.S. had been far from generous to the millions of Syrians escaping death and destruction in their homeland.[84]

Trump's vaguely worded order caused massive confusion and repression at airports around the world, as stranded travelers possessing visas or with permanent U.S. residency status were prevented from boarding flights to the U.S., while those in mid-flight when the ban was announced were detained at airports upon arrival. Before a judge placed a temporary restraining order on the Muslim Ban, more than seven hundred passengers were detained and up to sixty thousand visas were "provisionally revoked."[85]

Amid massive public outcry and a series of legal challenges about the order's constitutionality, Trump issued a slightly revised ban on March 6 that removed Iraq from the list, exempted permanent residents and travelers with current visas, and removed the indefinite ban on Syrian refugees (while placing them under the general ban). This ban, known as "Muslim Ban 2.0," was blocked by two federal judges a day before it was to take effect.[86] In late June, the U.S. Supreme Court upheld parts of the order, allowing the Department of Homeland Security to bar many nationals from Iran, Sudan, Libya, Somalia, Syria and Yemen from entering the U.S. for ninety days.

On September 24, the date that the second ban expired, Trump issued yet a third version, dropping Sudan but adding North Korea, Chad, and Venezuela to the list of targeted nations with restrictions on travel. Unlike the first two bans, Muslim Ban 3.0 had no expiration date and allowed Trump apparently to believe he had cleverly bypassed judicial scrutiny by adding two non-Muslim majority countries.[87]

Stoking Racism and Promoting Police Brutality

In a speech to Long Island law enforcement officers in July 2017, Trump referred to gang members as "animals," suggesting, amid laughter and applause from the police audience, that police should use "rough" treatment during arrests:

> When you see these thugs being thrown into the back of a paddy wagon—you just see them thrown in, rough—I said, please don't be too nice. Like when you guys put somebody in the car and you're protecting their head, you know, the way you put their hand over? Like, don't hit their head and they've just killed somebody—don't hit their head. I said, you can take the hand away, okay?[88]

In August 2017, Trump pardoned virulently racist Arizona police sheriff (and fellow "birther") Joe Arpaio, undoing his "contempt of court" conviction. In 2011, a federal district judge had ordered Arpaio to stop his department from racially profiling Latinos at traffic stops when there was no evidence that they had broken a state law.[89] Arpaio flouted the ruling, but years passed before he was convicted of contempt of court in July 2017. Trump pardoned him before his sentencing hearing.[90]

Terrorizing Mexican and Other Latin American Communities

Under Trump's watch, arrests by Immigration and Customs Enforcement (ICE) agents rose by almost 40 percent during the first half of 2017, compared with the same period in 2016, while arrests of undocumented immigrants without a criminal record more than doubled. Obama had been labeled by activists the "Deporter in Chief" for the large number of deportations during his tenure, which surpassed those of any previous president.[91] But the Trump administration is set to far surpass Obama's record once immigrants awaiting trial work their way through deportation hearings. The horror stories circulated rapidly through migrant communities:

- In February, ICE agents arrested an El Paso, Texas woman when she went to court to secure a protective order from her abusive partner, whose actions included "punching, kicking, choking, and [throwing] a knife . . . at her." The ICE agents sat through the hearing, and arrested her after the judge granted her a protective order. County officials suspected that her abuser had tipped off ICE to find her at the courthouse.[92]

- In March, a father of four who had lived in the U.S. for 25 years had just dropped off his 12-year-old daughter at school when ICE agents surrounded his vehicle. His wife and 13-year-old daughter were in the car at the time, and his daughter managed to record parts of his arrest. She is heard sobbing in the video as her father is taken away.[93]

- In September, the undocumented parents of a two-month-old baby with pyloric stenosis, a rare condition in infants that blocks food from entering the small intestine, were told by medical staff that they needed to transport their son from the Rio Grande Valley in Texas to a Corpus Christi hospital for surgery. This move required them to pass through a border patrol checkpoint. Apparently, someone from the hospital's staff alerted Customs and Border Patrol agents of their undocumented status, and agents appeared at the hospital before the traumatized parents could decide how to handle the situation. The agents followed the ambulance and then trailed the parents wherever they went inside the hospital, including the restroom. The next morning, Border Patrol arrested both parents, and took them to be fingerprinted and booked.[94]

Soon after taking office, Trump announced that self-declared "sanctuary cities"—cities that do not instruct law enforcement officers to report undocumented immigrants to ICE—would be stripped of various forms of federal funding. Once again, this order faced court challenges.[95] On September 29, ICE officials admitted the agency had specifically targeted sanctuary cities in a recent sweep that arrested roughly five hundred undocumented immigrants, because "ICE deportation officers are denied access to jails and prisons to interview suspected immigration violators."[96]

Perhaps Trump's most malicious act in his first year was ending the Deferred Action for Childhood Arrivals (DACA) program, which Obama had granted by executive order in 2012. DACA is hardly a blanket amnesty. Among other things, it specifically requires applicants to have been under the age of sixteen when they arrived in the U.S. and to have a high school diploma, GED certification, honorable discharge from the military, or to be still in school. Recipients cannot have a criminal record. DACA status is subject to renewal every two years. Nevertheless, almost eight hundred thousand undocumented youth had been granted legal status through DACA in 2017. And yet, unconscionably, Trump aimed to rescind the opportunity these young people had been granted to stay in the only country they had ever known.[97]

Attacking LGBTQ Rights

Trump did not specifically target LGBTQ people while he was campaigning for president, so many were surprised on February 2017 when the Trump administration rescinded all Obama-era neutral gender bathroom rights for transgender students, reversing Obama's order that they be allowed in public spaces, including high schools.[98]

In July, via Twitter, Trump announced that transgender people would no longer be allowed to serve in the U.S. military—reversing an Obama administration ruling that just one year earlier had permitted openly transgender people to serve.[99] In October, Trump's Attorney General Jeff Sessions "ordered the Justice Department to take the position in court cases that transgender people are not protected by a civil rights law that bans workplace discrimination based on sex."[100]

Trump's rapid-fire attacks have had a disorienting effect, which socialist author Alan Maass aptly described as "political whiplash."

As Maass explained, "The right-wing agenda is unpopular on almost every issue, so its champions need a blitzkrieg approach of pushing ahead, as fast and as far as they can go on every front, before resistance comes together."[101]

The Rising Far Right

Trump's openly racist agenda meanwhile greatly strengthened the confidence of the far right, including open fascists. When Trump picked as his chief strategist Steve Bannon, a white nationalist and the former executive chairman of *Breitbart News*, he gave a nod of approval to the movement Bannon represented. Bannon once described *Breitbart* as "the platform for the alt-right," the youth-driven white nationalist movement that rejects the Republican establishment as too tame.[102]

Just weeks after Trump's election, the National Policy Institute, which describes itself as "an independent organization dedicated to the heritage, identity, and future of people of European descent in the United States, and around the world," hosted a conference in Washington, D.C., to celebrate Trump's election. Richard Spencer, one of the alt-right's leading spokesmen, began his speech with a salute: "Hail Trump, hail our people, hail victory!" The conference drew more than two hundred overwhelmingly young, white, male attendees. The day of speeches was interspersed with many audience members standing to give the Nazi salute. Spencer has proposed "peaceful ethnic cleansing" and believes that a fifty-year ban on all immigration into the U.S. would help maintain the U.S.'s white majority.[103]

This sense of confidence—that its time had come—pervaded the racist right in the months after Trump's election. Alt-right spokesmen, including the preppy Spencer and the flashy Milo Yiannopoulos, embarked on national speaking tours aimed at broadening the base for the alt-right, claiming that liberal college campuses had robbed them of free speech rights. But Spencer also joined together with other far-right organizers in the project of organizing an activist, street-fighting movement with distinctly fascist components. "Free speech" quickly became the rallying cry for this movement, as far-right activists attempted to recast themselves as the victims of liberalism—even as they used hate speech to incite acts of violence against people of color and antiracist activists. Again, examples are plentiful:

- In May 2017, white University of Maryland student Sean Urbanski stabbed and killed Black student Richard Collins III after a bizarre tirade directed at Collins as he waited at a bus stop. Collins was set to graduate from nearby Bowie State University just days later. Urbanski was a member of the Facebook group "Alt-Reich," which spewed hatred directed against African-Americans and other people of color.[104]

- On a Portland, Oregon, train just days later, passenger Jeremy Joseph Christian began "ranting and raving" and shouting anti-Muslim threats at two young women (one of whom was wearing a *hijab*). When three other passengers stepped forward to defend the women, Christian, who "was a known white supremacist," stabbed all three antiracists. Two of the men, fifty-three-year-old Ricky John Best and twenty-three-year-old Taliesin Myrddin Namkai Meche, died from their wounds; the other, twenty-one-year-old Micah David-Cole Fletcher, was seriously injured but survived.[105]

- With Trump's winds in their sails, far right organizers aimed to expand their geographic reach outward from their traditional rural strongholds to liberal cities such as Berkeley, California, Portland, Oregon, and Boston, Massachusetts. They ambitiously organized rallies all over the country in Trump's first months as president, which included organizations such as Identity Evropa, Fraternal Order of Alt-Knights, the Oath Keepers, the Traditionalist Workers Party and the white male violent fraternity calling itself the Proud Boys.[106]

- After Yiannopoulos was prevented from speaking by a two-thousand-strong throng of protesters at the UC campus in February 2017, the far right struck back in March and then again in April. While the right's forces were outnumbered in March, they regrouped and overpowered their antifascist opponents in April—bringing more than one hundred fifty far-right goons to take their revenge in Berkeley. The violence they unleashed on their antifascist opponents resulted not only in punches, but pummeling with blunt instruments, including flag poles. In the end, eleven people were injured and six hospitalized.

The Resistance to Trump

Yet Trump's reactionary agenda, while bolstering the confidence of the far right, has also strengthened its opposition, making clear the urgent need for a united response against the onslaught of attacks. Indeed, a new generation of young activists, many of whom had been drawn to Senator Bernie Sanders' presidential campaign in 2016, took part in mass protests across the country in the days after Trump was elected on November 8, 2016. Chanting "Not my president," in cities and on campuses across the U.S., they demonstrated in the thousands.[107]

The day after Trump's poorly attended inauguration on January 20, 2017,[108] an overflow crowd of between five hundred thousand and a million protesters packed into the Women's March in Washington, D.C., while hundreds of thousands more demonstrated across the U.S. and around the globe. *USA Today* estimated that more than two and a half million people in total participated in Women's Marches on that day—and that could easily have been an underestimation. Besides in Washington, D.C., in many major cities, including New York City and Chicago, the crowds were so dense that it was difficult (or impossible) to actually march.[109] The Women's March developed as a call on Facebook and, in a groundswell of support, volunteers emerged from states all over the U.S. to help organize people from their localities to get to Washington, D.C., and/or organize their own local solidarity protests.[110]

After Trump announced the first Muslim Ban on January 27, thousands of people descended on airports across the country to defend Arab and Muslim immigrants held back from entering the U.S. These protests continued for a full week. In New York City, Yemeni bodega (convenience store) owners closed their doors for a day on February 2 to protest Trump's ban and rallied alongside thousands of others in Brooklyn.[111]

Soon afterward, a new arena for protest erupted. Republican politicians returning home for their week-long February congressional recess—the first since Trump took office—faced angry crowds crammed into their local town hall meetings. These were ordinarily lackluster events attended mainly by party loyalists and bored journalists. In February, however, these Republicans encountered hostile audiences, many of whom had never before taken part in a protest, chanting and waving signs against repealing the ACA, opposing the Muslim Ban, and defending Planned Parenthood, among a host of other issues.

On February 4, for example, California Republican Rep. Tom McClintock, apparently fearing for his safety, was escorted by police to an awaiting police vehicle, after he faced a raucous audience that followed him, chanting "This is what democracy looks like!"[112] On February 9, an overflow crowd of eleven hundred booed and chanted "Do your job!" at Utah Republican Rep. Jason Chaffetz, who later denounced the audience as intending "to bully and intimidate me."[113] In response to this unrest, some Republicans simply canceled their in-person meetings with constituents, while others opted for conference calls that would allow them to maintain control of the conversation with the touch of the "mute" button.[114]

Many of these new town hall protesters were mobilized by "Indivisible," an online liberal organization formed by some Democratic congressional staffers during Obama's administration. Indivisible produced "A Practical Guide for Resisting the Trump Agenda," which took the reactionary Republican "Tea Party" movement's playbook used against the Obama administration and provided guidelines for turning it against the GOP in the era of Trump.[115] As with Indivisible, most of the anti-Trump resistance has been organized by new and online formations.

Turning Point in Charlottesville, Virginia

After the upsurge immediately following the election, there was a lull in grassroots protest. Certainly, the sense of political whiplash among activists was a contributing factor, as each week brought multiple attacks from the Trump administration, producing widespread disorientation. However, the lull did not last long, as antiracist activists faced the need to confront the violence of the growing forces of the far right. The turning point came during the "Unite the Right" rally in Charlottesville, Virginia, on August 12, 2017—a gathering of white supremacists and fascists aiming to create a show of force in protest against the planned removal of Confederate General Robert E. Lee's statue from Lee Park (which has since been renamed Emancipation Park).

The evening before the planned rally, the group assembled an unannounced nighttime rally at the local University of Virginia campus. Hundreds of white supremacists and fascists wielded torches—the long-standing symbol of the KKK—while chanting "Jews will not replace us." They also chanted "blood and soil," based on the Nazi racial purity slogan *"blut und boden,"* while some gave Nazi salutes.[116] When they passed a smaller group of antifascist protesters chanting "Black Lives Matter," the white supremacists responded with the chant "White Lives Matter."[117]

The next day, the "Unite the Right" rally was aggressive from its start. Throngs of white supremacists marched in military style toward antifascists, wielding shields with neo-Nazi emblems and physically attacking the group with fists and any other objects they could use as weapons. After the Virginia State Police declared the far-right demonstration "unlawful" and ordered it to disperse, James Alex Fields Jr., a twenty-year-old fascist sympathizer who had marched with the neo-Nazi group Vanguard America drove his car at high speed to deliberately slam a car into a throng of antifascist protesters.

Fields killed thirty-two-year-old Heather Heyer and injured nineteen other antiracist protesters in that act. Heyer, a Charlottesville area native, was known to all her friends and coworkers as a passionate fighter for justice, whose Facebook page declared "If you're not outraged, you're not paying attention." Her grieving mother, Susan Bro, posted on a GoFundMe page in Heather's honor, "I want her death to be a rallying cry for justice and equality and fairness and compassion. No mother wants to lose a child, but I'm proud of her."[118]

President Trump, after issuing conflicting statements about the cause of Heyer's murder, settled on blaming both sides—while also praising both sides. On August 15, Trump said, "I think there is blame on both sides. You look at both sides. I think there is blame on both sides." But he also added, "You had some very bad people in that group. You also had some very fine people on both sides."[119]

Trump had attempted to call Susan Bro to offer condolences on the loss of her daughter. But after Trump stated that there were "fine people" on both sides, Heyer's mom refused to speak with the president, stating, "I'm not talking to the President now. . . . I saw an actual clip of him at a press conference equating the protesters like Ms. [Heather] Heyer with the KKK and the white supremacists."[120]

As news spread of Heyer's murder, local activists across the country organized solidarity demonstrations in response. The following weekend, a right-wing "Free Speech" rally in Boston drew just a few dozen—and was utterly overwhelmed by antiracist protesters numbering roughly twenty thousand—many of them new to protest.[121]

The balance of forces was shifting rapidly. Right-wing protests scheduled for August 26 and 27 in San Francisco and Berkeley were canceled by their organizers when it became clear that antiracists across the Bay Area were planning large counter-protests. Patriot Prayer leader Joey Gibson announced that its San Francisco demonstration scheduled for August 26 would not take place due to "safety concerns." Meanwhile, Amber Cummings, who had called a "No to Marxism" rally the following day in Berkeley effectively canceled it, stating "'I am asking that no one come to my event."[122] The antiracist counter protests turned into mass celebrations instead as right-wing forces fizzled in the face of mass opposition—exposing exactly how the left can defeat them.

Donald Trump, Colonial Master

Hurricane Maria, a devastating level 4 hurricane, swept through Puerto Rico on September 20, 2017, producing a catastrophe for its residents. The hurricane left most of the island without electricity, food, and potable water, while virtually destroying its entire infrastructure. The death toll is likely to rise as time passes, as people struggle to survive without food, water, medicine, flushing toilets, and other basic necessities.

Puerto Rico was a Spanish colony until 1898, but the U.S. took control as part of its victory in the Spanish-American war. The island remains a U.S. territory, or colony, to this day. Its nearly three-and-a-half-million residents are U.S. citizens but have fewer rights than residents of the U.S. mainland. Puerto Ricans have the "right" to serve in the U.S. military and die in its wars, but do not have the right to have a voting representative in Congress or to vote for the President of the United States in general elections. In June 2017, Puerto Ricans voted overwhelmingly for statehood, but the referendum was non-binding, leaving Congress to decide Puerto Rico's fate.[123]

The Jones Act of 1920—requiring that all shipping from one U.S. port to another take place on U.S.-built and U.S.-owned ships staffed by U.S. legal residents and citizens—was designed as a cash cow for the U.S. shipping industry. But this purely protectionist measure, which also includes tariffs and fees for all goods brought onto the island, drastically drives up prices for food and other goods sold there. The Jones Act, in other words, has guaranteed financial hardship for Puerto Rico even in the best of times for nearly a century.

In the aftermath of Hurricane Maria, the Jones Act was predictably debilitating to recovery efforts. Yet, for a full week, Trump refused to grant an emergency order waiving the Jones Act, admitting, "A lot of people who are in the shipping industry don't want" a waiver. And when he finally did grant one, it was for only ten days.[124]

More than two weeks after Hurricane Maria hit, Trump finally made his way to Puerto Rico for a brief "press conference," during which he took no questions, and a photo op in which he arrogantly tossed paper towels and bags of rice at the audience. In his speech, Trump praised the U.S. response at length—although at the time of his visit, only 5 percent of electric power grids had been fixed and half the island's residents were without running water. Even worse, Trump appeared to blame Puerto Ricans for the ongoing devastation, as Susanne Ramirez de Arellano described in the *Guardian*: "President Donald Trump arrived in Puerto Rico like an emperor, coming to scold his uncooperative subjects. 'I hate to tell you, Puerto Rico, but you've thrown our budget a little out of whack,' he said during a visit to the island on Tuesday. He might as well have blamed us for throwing ourselves in the path of a hurricane."[125]

One month after Hurricane Maria, amid ongoing devastation in Puerto Rico, Trump inexplicably gave the federal government "a ten out of ten" for its recovery efforts.[126]

"Taking a Knee" Against Racist Police Violence: NFL Players' Revolt

But Trump concerned himself with other matters entirely as Puerto Ricans endured this humanitarian crisis. Two days after Hurricane Maria hit, in a speech in Alabama, Trump unleashed the following vitriol at National Football League (NFL) players who had been kneeling during the playing of the national anthem to protest racist police violence: "Wouldn't you love to see one of these NFL owners, when somebody disrespects our flag, to say, "Get that son of a bitch off the field right now, out, he's fired. He's FIRED!"" Later in his speech, Trump urged fans to boycott games if players took a knee, arguing "if you see [players kneeling during the national anthem], even if it's one player, leave the stadium. I guarantee things will stop. Things will stop. Just pick up and leave. Pick up and leave."[127]

Trump's wrath was directed at Black NFL players, who had been kneeling in solidarity with former San Francisco 49ers quarterback Colin Kaepernick, who first refused to stand for the national anthem during the 2016 pre-game season. At that time, Kaepernick explained his silent protest, stating "I am not going to stand up to show pride in a flag for a country that oppresses Black people and people of color. To me, this is bigger than football and it would be selfish on my part to look the other way. There are bodies in the street and people getting paid leave and getting away with murder."[128]

While Kaepernick began his protest alone, he was soon joined in taking a knee during the anthem by a handful of fellow 49ers teammates and other Black players throughout the league. Kaepernick ended up paying a steep price: his career. At the end of the season, when he became a free agent, no NFL team offered to sign him. He remained unemployed as the 2017 season began.

Kaepernick chose to join the long-standing Black radical tradition, dating back to the time of slavery. As Black abolitionist Frederick Douglass famously argued in his 1852 speech, "The Meaning of July Fourth for the Negro," "What, to the American slave, is your 4th of July? I answer; a day that reveals to him, more than all other days in the year, the gross injustice and cruelty to which he is the constant victim."[129]

Kaepernick also stands in a long line of Black athletes who have used their celebrity to expose the hypocrisy of a flag and an anthem trumpeting a nation that claims to be "the land of the free," when racist violence has been embedded in its very foundation from its beginning. Kaepernick's words echoed those of Jackie Robinson, the first African-American to play in major league baseball in 1947. In his autobiography, Robinson shared his feelings as the national anthem played at his first World Series game:

> There I was, the black grandson of a slave, the son of a black sharecropper . . . a symbolic hero to my people. . . . The band struck up the

National Anthem. The flag billowed in the wind. It should have been a glorious moment for me as the stirring words of the National Anthem poured from the stands. Perhaps, it was, but then again. . . .

As I write this twenty years later, I cannot stand and sing the anthem. I cannot salute the flag; I know that I am a black man in a white world. In 1972, in 1947, at my birth in 1919, I know that I never had it made."[130]

But Kaepernick's supporters, both on the field and off, carried on his protest after none of the all-white NFL owners chose to hire him. Black players continued to take a knee during the anthem, while fans protested his collective punishment by the NFL owners, who had effectively prevented him from continuing his promising career. Civil rights organizations, including the NAACP, organized a "United We Stand" rally of several thousand for Kaepernick outside NFL headquarters in Manhattan during the pre-season in August 2017.[131] White players also began speaking out, including Green Bay Packers quarterback Aaron Rodgers, who argued, "I think he should be on a roster right now." He added, "I think because of his protests, he's not."

As radical sports writer Dave Zirin remarked in the *LA Times*:

> The NFL seems to believe that shutting out Kaepernick will be like a crack of the whip across the backs of its players, stamping out dissent, keeping everyone in line. But the opposite has been the case. During the preseason, and in the wake of events in Charlottesville, Va., more and more players stepped forward to sit, take a knee or raise a fist during the anthem, and they are not shy about telling the world why. Unlike last season, white players also have involved themselves in these protests.
>
> For most of the protesting players I've talked with, Kaepernick is not a "distraction" but a friend, a colleague or a teammate, and one whose fellow 49ers voted to give him the team's "courage award" at the conclusion of last season. NFL owners want Kaepernick to be a ghost story to scare players from speaking out. Instead, his absence haunts the NFL far more effectively than if he were where he deserves to be: on an NFL roster.[132]

Trump's contempt for players' protests merely added fuel to a fire that was already burning. After Trump used the term "son of a bitch" to describe any player taking a knee during the anthem, Kaepernick's mother tweeted, "Guess that makes me a proud bitch!"[133]

NFL players responded to Trump's attacks through a collective show of defiance and solidarity during the national anthem over the weekend that followed. Entire teams, including the Seattle Seahawks and Pittsburgh Steelers, joined by their coaches, chose not to take the field until after the anthem. Other teams chose to kneel, sit, or lock arms while the anthem played—some with fists in the air—while two national anthem singers also took a knee at the end of their song.[134]

The players' solidarity was so great that owners joined them on the field in a (very temporary) show of support, which was actually a transparent effort to curtail them. No owner was more obvious than Dallas Cowboys' owner and Trump supporter Jerry Jones, who took a knee with players *before* the national anthem played on September 25, 2017, while asking that all players stand when the anthem played. Two weeks later, Jones announced that any player who did not stand in respect for that national anthem would be benched for the entire game.[135]

Just two days later, NFL Commissioner Roger Goodell indicated that he was siding with Jones (and Trump) when he wrote in a letter to owners, "Like many of our fans, we believe that everyone should stand for the national anthem." Goodell also announced that an up-coming owners' meeting would decide policy on the issue. No fines against players not present and standing for the national anthem had yet been issued—and NFL rules did not currently require play-ers to stand.

Green Bay Packers tight-end Martellus Bennett quickly tweeted in reply to Goodell, "@nflcommish really bruh? It's hard trying to play both sides of the fence when it comes down to injustice and your money huh?" The collective bargaining agreement between NFL players and owners stated clearly that rules could not be changed after the start of training camp.[136]

After the owners met with player representatives on October 17, they emerged without a requirement that players must stand for the national anthem prior to games, in an obvious victory for the players. The player protests continued in week seven without repercussions.

Working-Class Radicalism Emerges in Unexpected Places

Few might have predicted that NFL players would be the new face of working-class solidarity in 2017. In hindsight, however, it made perfect sense. NFL players are 70 percent Black, and many hail from working-class, segregated communities with rampant racist police harassment and brutality.

Seattle Seahawks star player Michael Bennett—who had joined NFL players' national anthem protests—was assaulted and threatened by Las Vegas police in August 2017. As his lawyer described, "Mr. Bennett was face down on the ground when a Las Vegas Police officer placed his gun at the back of Mr. Bennett's head and shouted don't move or I'll blow your fucking head off." He added, "Bennett was in total compliance and scared for his life when a second officer for no apparent reason forcefully dug his knee into Mr. Bennett's back, making it difficult for him to breathe."[137]

Trump had followed up his first post-Hurricane Maria tirade against NFL players who chose to take a knee against racism with the following tweet: "If a player wants the privilege of making millions of dollars in the NFL, or other leagues, he or she should not be allowed to disrespect."[138]

But NFL players are very much a part of the U.S. working class, while working in one of its most dangerous occupations. According to the *Wall Street Journal*, based on data between 2008 and 2014, the average NFL career lasts just 2.66 years. The median annual income (meaning half earn above and half below) for NFL players was $860,000 in 2015—which is a small compensation given the brevity and danger of their careers.[139]

Many NFL players have been walking away from the sport because of emerging evidence of fatal health risks.[140] In July 2017, a Boston University study of a hundred eleven donated brains of former NFL players found that a hundred ten had chronic traumatic encephalopathy (CTE), caused by repeated blows to the head. The disease, which can only be diagnosed postmortem, can cause impaired judgment, aggression, memory loss, and depression.[141]

In the wake of this groundbreaking study revealing the severe health hazards of football, Trump nevertheless lamented even minimum safety protections for players in his Alabama speech:

> Today if you hit too hard—fifteen yards! Throw him out of the game! They had that last week. I watched for a couple of minutes. Two guys, just really, beautiful tackle. Boom, fifteen yards! The referee gets on television--his wife is sitting at home, she's so proud of him. They're ruining the game! They're ruining the game. That's what they want to do. They want to hit. They want to hit! It is hurting the game.[142]

NFL Players Association (NFLPA) executive director DeMaurice Smith responded to Trump on Twitter, "Whether or not Roger [Goodell] and the owners will speak for themselves about their view on player rights and their commitment to player safety remains to be seen." He added, *"This union, however, will never back down when it comes to protecting the constitutional rights of our players as citizens as well as their safety as men who compete in a game that exposes them to great risks."*[143] [Emphasis added.]

Those are precisely the kind of fighting words that have been lacking in the U.S. labor movement for the last four decades. We should not wait for the same old labor leaders who have surrendered to neoliberalism to lead the way forward for the working class today. While some labor leaders have been known to adapt to new situations historically, we also need to expect the unexpected today, as new initiatives, formations, and struggles are likely to emerge where and when we might least anticipate them.

Perhaps the most important lesson from the present political situation is that a youth radicalization is well underway, and history has shown that such a radicalization can shift the ground underneath us all in the foreseeable future. The current radicalization—compared with those decades ago—will most assuredly enable the class struggle to combat all forms of oppression. Whereas the struggles of the Great Depression in the 1930s were by and large limited to the class struggle, and the movements of the 1960s were primarily struggles against oppression, it is possible today to combine all struggles into one unified movement. This is the only way to enable the working class to advance at this historical juncture: if it champions the struggle against all forms of oppression. Only then will the revolutionary agency be enabled in ways that have not been possible in previous historical circumstances. We should not expect working-class history to repeat itself but rather to advance itself, while forging a new history of class struggle in the years ahead.

Notes

Epigraphs

Paul Avrich, *The Haymarket Tragedy* (Princeton, NJ: Princeton University Press, 1984), 287; Karl Marx, "The Eighteenth Brumaire of Louis Bonaparte," in Karl Marx and Frederick Engels, *Collected Works*, vol. 11 (New York: International Publishers, 1979), 103.

Preface to the Second Edition

1. *TIME* Staff, "700,000 Female Farmworkers Say They Stand With Hollywood Actors Against Sexual Assault," *TIME*, November 10, 2017. http://time.com/5018813/farmworkers-solidarity-hollywood-sexual-assault/

Introduction

1. See Brigitte Buhmann and others, "Equivalence Scales, Well-Being, Inequality, and Poverty: Sensitivity Estimates Across Ten Countries Using the Luxembourg Income Study (LIS) Database," *Review of Income and Wealth* 34 (June 1988): 126–33.

2. United Nations Development Program, *Human Development Report 2005: International Cooperation at a Crossroads: Aid, Trade and Security in an Unequal World* (New York: United Nations, 2005), 152.

3. Ibid., 58.

4. Ibid.

5. Ibid.

6. Kevin Phillips, *The Politics of Rich and Poor: Wealth and the American Electorate in the Reagan Aftermath* (New York: Random House, 1990).

7. Statistics cited in Paul Krugman, "For Richer: How the Permissive Capitalism of the Boom Destroyed American Equality," *New York Times Magazine*, October 20, 2002.

8. Richard Fletcher, "Buffett Lashes Out at Corporate Greed," *Sunday Telegraph* (UK), March 7, 2004.

9. Kim Moody, *An Injury to All: The Decline of American Unionism* (New York: Verso, 1988), 17.

10. U.S. Bureau of Labor Statistics, "Union Members Summary," press release, January 27, 2005, http://www.bls.gov.

11. Michael Zweig, *The Working Class Majority: America's Best Kept Secret* (Ithaca, NY: Cornell University Press, 2000), 32.

12. Ibid., 24–31.

13. Ibid., 30–31.

14. David Montgomery, *The Fall of the House of Labor: The Workplace, the State and American Labor Activism, 1865–1925* (New York: Cambridge University Press, 1987), 345.

15. *Seattle Union Record*, June 23, 1919, cited in Montgomery, *Fall of House of Labor,* 429.

16. Bert Cochran, ed., *American Labor in Midpassage* (New York: Monthly Review Press, 1959), 15–16 (emphasis in original).

17. Cochran notes, "The figures for the Knights of Labor are from the official membership tabulations of the Order in Norman J. Ware, *The Labor Movement in the United States* (New York, 1929). The figure for the early trade unions is estimated by Selig Perlman in John R. Commons and Associates, *History of Labor in the United States*, vol. 2, (New York, 1918). The figures for 1897 to 1934 are Leo Wolman's estimates in *Ebb and Flow in Trade Unionism* (New York, 1936). The figures from 1934 to 1943 are Florence Peterson's estimates in *American Labor Unions*, (New York, 1952). In all subsequent references, figures from 1934 up to 1951 are those from Florence Peterson. For more recent years, the figures are from the Bureau of Labor Statistics." Ibid., 16.

18. Quoted in Cochran, *American Labor in Midpassage*, 17.

19. Eric Thomas Chester, *True Mission: Socialists and the Labor Party Question in the U.S.* (London: Pluto Press, 2004), 22.

20. *To the Workingmen of America* (New York: I.W.P.A., Committee of Agitation, 1883), quoted in Avrich, *Haymarket Tragedy*, 75.

21. Ibid., quoted in Avrich, *Haymarket Tragedy*, 75.

22. Montgomery, *Fall of House of Labor*, 343.

23. Ibid., 425.

Chapter 1

1. Quoted in Avrich, *Haymarket Tragedy,* 184.

2. Quoted in Mike Davis, *Prisoners of the American Dream* (London: Verso, 1986), 32.

3. Letter from Frederick Engels to Florence Kelley Wischnewetsky, June 3, 1886, in Marx and Engels, *Selected Correspondence* (Moscow: Progress Publishing, 1982), 371.

4. Letter from Frederick Engels to Adolph Sorge, December 2, 1893, in *Marx and Engels on the United States,* (Moscow: Progress Publishers, 1979), 333.

5. Sidney Lens, *The Labor Wars: From the Molly Maguires to the Sitdowns* (New York: Doubleday & Company, 1973), 111.

6. Eric Hobsbawm, *Labouring Men: Studies in the History of Labor* (New York: Basic Books, 1964), 7.

7. Jeremy Brecher, *Strike!* (Boston: South End Press, 1972), 34.

8.   *Writings of Leon Trotsky [1934–1935]* (New York: Pathfinder Press, 1971), 74.

9.   Philip S. Foner, *Women and the American Labor Movement: From the First Trade Unions to the Present* (New York: The Free Press, 1982), 154. March 8 was adopted as International Women's Day at the International Socialist Congress in 1910.

10.   Quoted in B. C. Forbes, *Men Who Are Making America* (New York: B. C. Forbes Publishing Co., 1926), 316.

11.   Quoted in Michael Zuckerman, "The Dodo and the Phoenix," in Rick Halpern and Jonathan Morris, eds., *American Exceptionalism? U.S. Working-Class Formation in an International Context* (New York: St. Martin's Press, 1997), 18.

12.   Quoted in Brecher, *Strike!*, xxi.

13.   See, for example, Seymour Martin Lipset, *American Exceptionalism: A Double-Edged Sword* (New York: W. W. Norton & Company, 1996).

14.   Halpern and Morris, *American Exceptionalism?*, 2–3.

15.   Neville Kirk, "The Limits of Liberalism," in Halpern and Morris, *American Exceptionalism?*, 118.

16.   Ibid.

17.   For a fuller elaboration on these themes, see Mike Davis, "Why the American Working Class Is Different," in *Prisoners of the American Dream*, 3–51; Duncan Hallas, "The American Working Class," in *Socialist Review* 88 (1986): 17–18; Halpern and Morris, *American Exceptionalism?*

18.   Cited in Hallas, "American Working Class," 17–18.

19.   Frederick Engels, "Appendix to *The Condition of the Working-Class in England*," first American edition (New York: 1887), in Karl Marx and Frederick Engels, *Collected Works* (New York: International Publishers, 1990), 402–03.

20.   Hallas, "American Working Class," 17–18.

21.   Quoted in Irving Howe, *Socialism and America* (New York: Harcourt Brace Jovanovich, 1977), 117.

22.   Quoted in Montgomery, *Fall of House of Labor*, 272.

23.   Ibid., 70, 172.

24.   Daniel Bell, *The End of Ideology* (Glencoe, IL: The Free Press, 1960), 84; Daniel Bell, *The Cultural Contradictions of Capitalism* (New York: Basic Books, 1976), 251.

25.   Benjamin S. Kleinberg, *American Society in the Postindustrial Age: Technocracy, Power, and the End of Ideology* (Columbus, OH: Merrill, 1973), 37.

26.   Nelson Lichtenstein, *State of the Union: A Century of American Labor* (Princeton, NJ: Princeton University Press, 2002), 14–15; Krugman, "For Richer."

27.   Ibid., 213.

28.   Halpern and Morris, *American Exceptionalism?*, 1.

29.   Lipset, *American Exceptionalism*, 75–76.

30.   Ibid., 281–92.

31.   Herbert Marcuse, *One Dimensional Man* (Boston: Beacon Press, 1991), 1–2.

32.   Moody, *Injury to All*, 86–87; Glenn Perusek and Kent Worcester, eds., *Trade Union Politics: American Unions and Economic Change, 1960s–1990s* (Atlantic Highlands, NJ: Humanities Press, 1995), 8–10.

33.   Paul F. Clark, *The Miners' Fight for Democracy: Arnold Miller and the Reform of the United Mine Workers* (Ithaca, NY: Cornell University, 1981), 24; Dan

Georgakas and Marvin Surkin, *Detroit I Do Mind Dying: A Study in Urban Revolution* (New York: St. Martin's Press, 1975).

34. Karl Marx, *Capital*, vol. 1 (New York: International Publishers, 1996), 639.

35. Ibid.

36. Kim Moody, *Workers in a Lean World: Unions in the International Economy* (New York: Verso, 1997), 88.

37. Thomas Ferguson and Joel Rogers, *Right Turn: The Decline of the Democrats and the Future of American Politics* (New York: Hill & Wang, 1986), 49; Moody, *Injury to All*, 13; Nigel Harris, *The End of the Third World: Newly Industrializing Countries and the End of an Ideology* (London: Penguin Books, 1986), 106, 111.

38. James R. Green, *The World of the Worker: Labor in Twentieth Century America* (New York: Hill & Wang, 1980), 219–20; Stanley Aronowitz, *False Promises* (New York: McGraw-Hill, 1973), 21–50.

39. Studs Terkel, *Working: People Talk About What They Do All Day and How They Feel About What They Do* (New York: Pantheon Books, 1972), 261–62.

40. Hal Draper, *Karl Marx's Theory of Revolution, Vol. II: The Politics of Social Classes* (New York: Monthly Review Press, 1978), 42.

41. Davis, *Prisoners of the American Dream*, 4.

42. *Writings of Leon Trotsky*, 335.

43. Halpern and Morris, *American Exceptionalism?*, 125 (emphasis in original).

Chapter 2

1. Letter from Engels to Hermann Schlüter, March 30, 1892, in *Marx and Engels on the United States* (Moscow: Progress Publishers, 1979), 328.

2. Saul K. Padover, *The Letters of Karl Marx: Selected and Translated with Explanatory Notes and an Introduction* (Englewood Cliffs, NJ: Prentice-Hall, Inc., 1979), 341.

3. Quoted in Avrich, *Haymarket Tragedy*, 97.

4. Leo Huberman, "No More Class War?" in Cochran, *American Labor in Midpassage*, 87.

5. Stephen H. Norwood, *Strikebreaking and Intimidation: Mercenaries and Masculinity in Twentieth Century America* (Chapel Hill: University of North Carolina Press, 2002), 3–4.

6. Kirk, "The Limits of Liberalism," 118.

7. Ibid., 126.

8. Quoted in Lens, *Labor Wars*, 5.

9. Letter quoted in Matthew Josephson, *The Robber Barons: The Great American Capitalists, 1861–1901* (New York: Harcourt, Brace & World, 1962), 15.

10. Lens, *Labor Wars*, 5 (emphasis in original); Josephson, *Robber Barons*, 441.

11. U.S. National Advisory Commission on Racial Disorders, *The Kerner Report* (New York: Pantheon Books, 1988), 1–2.

12. Milton S. Eisenhower Foundation and the Corporation for What Works, executive summary, *The Millennium Breach: The American Dilemma, Richer and Poorer*, http://www.eisenhowerfoundation.org.

13. See Jonathan Kozol, *Shame of the Nation: The Restoration of Apartheid*

Schooling in America (New York: Crown Publishers, 2005).

14. Erica Frankerberg, Chungmei Lee, and Gary Orfield, *A Multiracial Society with Segregated Schools: Are We Losing the Dream?*, The Civil Rights Project of Harvard University, January 16, 2003, http://www.civilrightsproject.harvard.edu.

15. Diana Jean Schemo, "Neediest Schools Receive Less Money, Report Finds," *New York Times,* August 9, 2002.

16. Douglas S. Massey and Nancy A. Denton, *American Apartheid: Segregation and the Making of the Underclass* (Cambridge, MA: Harvard University Press, 1993), 2.

17. Paul Street, "A Whole Lott Missing: Rituals of Purification and Racism Denial" (ZNET, December 22, 2002), http://www.zmag.org.

18. Letter from Karl Marx to Pavel Vasilyevich Annenkov, December 28, 1846, in *Marx and Engels Collected Works,* vol. 38, (New York: International Publishers, 1975), 95.

19. Karl Marx, *Capital,* vol. 1, 925–26.

20. Theodore W. Allen, "On Roediger's *Wages of Whiteness," Cultural Logic: An Electronic Journal of Marxist Theory and Practice* 4, no. 2 (Spring 2001), http://eserver.org/clogic/4–2/allen.html.

21. Jack M. Bloom, *Class, Race, and the Civil Rights Movement* (Bloomington and Indianapolis: Indiana University Press, 1987), 29.

22. Ibid., 29–30.

23. W. E. B. Du Bois, *Black Reconstruction in America: An Essay Toward a History of the Part Which Black Folk Played in the Attempt to Reconstruct Democracy in America, 1860–1880* (New York: The Free Press, 1965), 670.

24. Bloom, *Class, Race, and Civil Rights,* 19.

25. Peter Camejo, *Racism, Revolution and Reaction, 1861–1877,* (New York: Monad Press, 1976), 88.

26. Ahmed Shawki, *Black Liberation and Socialism* (Chicago: Haymarket Books, 2005), 70.

27. Max Shachtman, *Race and Revolution* (London: Verso, 2003), 16–25.

28. Quoted in Paul Ortiz, *Emancipation Betrayed: The Hidden History of Black Organizing and White Violence in Florida from Reconstruction to the Bloody Election of 1920* (Berkeley: University of California Press, 2005), 10.

29. Ortiz, *Emancipation Betrayed,* 10.

30. Quoted in Ortiz, *Emancipation Betrayed* 18.

31. C. Vann Woodward, *Origins of the New South: 1871–1913* (Baton Rouge: Louisiana State University Press, 1951), 59.

32. Bloom, *Class, Race, and Civil Rights,* 33.

33. Ibid.

34. Ibid., 32–33.

35. Ibid., 28, 34.

36. Quoted in Angela Y. Davis, "From the Convict Lease System to the Super-max Prison," in *States of Confinement: Policing, Detention, and Prisons,* ed. Joy James, (New York: St. Martin's Press, 2000), 67–68.

37. Lee Sustar, "The Roots of Multi-Racial Labour Unity in the United States," *International Socialism Journal* 63 (Summer 1994): 91.

38. Bloom, *Class, Race, and Civil Rights,* 42; Norwood, *Strikebreaking and Intim-*

idation, 197.

39. Bloom, *Class, Race, and Civil Rights,* 43; Robin D. G. Kelley, *Hammer and Hoe: Alabama Communists During the Great Depression* (Chapel Hill: University of North Carolina Press, 1990), 16.

40. Norwood, *Strikebreaking and Intimidation,* 78–86; Charles C. Moskos Jr., "Racial Integration in the Armed Forces," in *The Making of Black America,* vol. 2: *The Black Community in the Modern America,* eds., August Meier and Elliott Rudwick (New York: Atheneum, 1969), 427–31.

41. Norwood, *Strikebreaking and Intimidation,* 82.

42. Bloom, *Class, Race, and Civil Rights,* 40.

43. Du Bois, *Black Reconstruction in America,* 706.

44. Ibid.

45. Michael Reich, "The Economics of Racism," in *The Capitalist System,* eds., Edwards, Reich, and Weisskopf (Englewood Cliffs, NJ: Prentice-Hall, 1972), 316, 318 (emphasis added).

46. Victor Perlo, *Economics of Racism U.S.A.: The Roots of Black Inequality* (New York: International Publishers, 1975), 168.

47. Du Bois, *Black Reconstruction in America,* 713.

48. Quoted in Bloom, *Class, Race, and Civil Rights,* 45.

49. Montgomery, *Fall of House of Labor,* 81.

50. Ibid., 67–68, 85–86.

51. Ibid., 460–61.

52. David Gersh, "The Corporate Elite and the Introduction of IQ Testing in American Public Schools," in Michael Schwartz, ed., *The Structure of Power in America: The Corporate Elite as a Ruling Class* (New York: Holmes & Meier, 1987), 164.

53. Quoted in Lens, *Labor Wars,* 143.

54. Gersh, "The Corporate Elite," 164–65.

55. Quoted in Gersh, "The Corporate Elite,", 165.

56. Bloom, *Class, Race, and the Civil Rights Movement,* 44.

57. Montgomery, *Fall of House of Labor,* 242–43.

58. Margaret Sanger, *An Autobiography* (W. W. Norton & Company, New York, 1938), 110–11.

59. Hartmann, *Reproductive Rights and Wrongs,* 99.

60. Ibid., 98.

61. Rickie Solinger, ed., *Abortion Wars: A Half Century of Struggle, 1950–2000* (Berkeley: University of California Press, 1998), 132.

62. Ibid.; Susan E. Davis, ed., *Women Under Attack* (Boston: South End Press, 1988), 28.

63. Hartmann, *Reproductive Rights and Wrongs,* 111–15, 232.

64. Davis, *Prisoners of American Dream,* 20.

65. David Brody, *In Labor's Cause: Main Themes on the History of the American Worker* (New York: Oxford University Press, 1993), 49–50.

66. Davis, *Prisoners of American Dream,* 28.

67. Lens, *Labor Wars,* 57.

68. Ibid.; Montgomery, *Fall of House of Labor,* 147.

69. Montgomery, *Fall of House of Labor*, 209.

70. Julius Jacobson, ed., *The Negro and the American Labor Movement*, (New York: Doubleday & Company, 1968) 28, 33; Montgomery, *Fall of House of Labor*, 85.

71. Quoted in Montgomery, *Fall of House of Labor*, 194; Lens, *Labor Wars*, 57–58.

72. Frederick Engels, *The Condition of the Working Class in England*, (Stanford, CA: Stanford University Press, 1968), 357.

73. Bernard Mandel, "Samuel Gompers and the Negro Workers, 1886–1914," in *The Making of Black America*, vol. 2, eds., Meier and Rudwick, 87.

74. Brody, *In Labor's Cause*, 114–15.

75. Montgomery, *Fall of House of Labor*, 31–32.

76. Quoted in Jacobson, *Negro and American Labor*, 159; Brody, *In Labor's Cause*, 117.

77. Quoted in Jacobson, *Negro and American Labor*, 159.

78. Ibid., 158.

79. Quoted in Philip S. Foner, *Organized Labor and the Black Worker, 1619–1973* (New York: International Publishers, 1974), 137; Jacobson, *Negro and American Labor*, 46.

80. Foner, *Organized Labor and the Black Worker*, 137.

81. Quoted in Jacobson, *Negro and American Labor*, 159.

82. Lens, *Labor Wars*, 143.

83. Montgomery, *Fall of House of Labor*, 338.

84. Quoted in Foner, *Organized Labor and the Black Worker*, 84.

85. Ibid., 100.

86. Montgomery, *Fall of House of Labor*, 339.

87. Lens, *Labor Wars*, 142.

88. Norwood, *Strikebreaking and Intimidation*, 107.

89. Ibid., 108.

90. Montgomery, *Fall of House of Labor*, 84–85 (emphasis added).

91. Ibid, 55.

92. Quoted in Michael Kazin, *The Populist Persuasion: An American History* (New York: Basic Books, 1995), 38.

93. Lens, *Labor Wars*, 147.

94. Quoted in Bloom, *Class, Race, and the Civil Rights Movement*, 40.

95. Ibid., 40–41.

96. Ibid., 41.

97. Ibid., 44.

98. Sustar, "Roots of Multi-racial Labour Unity," 90–98.

99. Quoted in Sustar, "Roots of Multi-racial Labour Unity," 93.

100. Ibid., 92.

101. Ibid., 94.

102. Ibid., 94.

103. Quoted in Montgomery, *Fall of House of Labor*, 111.

104. Shawki, *Black Liberation and Socialism*, 249.

105. David Roediger, *The Wages of Whiteness: Race and the Making of the American Working Class,* (London: Verso, 1991), 9.

106. Ibid.

107. Du Bois, *Black Reconstruction in America,* 700.

108. Ibid.

109. Ibid., 701.

110. Roediger, *Wages of Whiteness,* 176.

111. Brian Kelly, *Race, Class and Power in the Alabama Coalfields, 1908–1921* (Chicago: University of Illinois Press, 2001), 8 (emphasis in original).

112. Roediger, *Wages of Whiteness,* 175–76.

113. Ibid., 170.

114. Ibid., 14–15.

115. For a detailed analysis of identity politics, see Sharon Smith, "Mistaken Identity," *International Socialism* 62 (Spring 1994): 3–50.

116. Ernesto Laclau and Chantal Mouffe, *Hegemony and Socialist Strategy: Towards a Radical Democratic Politics* (London: Verso, 1985).

117. Ibid., 191 (emphasis in original).

118. Ibid., 180, 184.

119. Gregory Meyerson, "Rethinking Black Marxism: Reflections on Cedric Robinson and Others," *Cultural Logic: An Electronic Journal of Marxist Theory and Practice* 3, no. 2, (Spring 2000).

120. Roediger, *Wages of Whiteness,* 7 (emphasis in original).

121. Meyerson, "Rethinking Black Marxism."

122. Karl Marx, *Capital,* vol. 1, chapter 10 "The Working Day," section 7 (New York: International Publishers, 1967), 301.

123. Frederick Douglass, "Life and Times of Frederick Douglass," in *The Oxford Frederick Douglass Reader* (New York: Oxford University Press, 1996), 267.

124. Frederick Douglass, *My Bondage and My Freedom,* William L. Andrews, ed. (Chicago: University of Illinois Press, 1987), 188.

125. Roediger, *Wages of Whiteness,* 9.

126. Karl Marx and Frederick Engels, *The Communist Manifesto: A Road Map to History's Most Important Political Document,* Phil Gasper, ed. (Chicago: Haymarket Books, 2005), 68.

127. Marx and Engels, *Communist Manifesto,* 53.

128. Karl Marx, *The German Ideology* (New York: International Publishers, 1947), 95 (emphasis in original).

129. Josephson, *Robber Barons,* 347.

130. See Davis, *Prisoners of American Dream,* 19. The first workers' organizations to formally enter the Democratic Party were the New York Workingmen's Parties, calling themselves "Locofocos," which tried to form a workers' rights wing of the Democrats in the 1830s. In response, the Democratic President Martin Van Buren proposed (but did not win) a ten-hour day for federal workers.

131. Brody, *In Labor's Cause,* 50.

132. Quoted in Noam Chomsky, *Year 501: The Conquest Continues* (Boston: South End Press, 1993), 201.

133. David Sprague Herreshoff, *The Origins of American Marxism, from the Tran-*

scendentalists to De Leon (New York: Monad Press, 1967), 123–4.

134. Brody, *In Labor's Cause*, 56, 60.

135. Quoted in Lichtenstein, *State of the Union*, 25.

136. Quoted in Lenni Brenner, *The Lesser Evil: The Democratic Party* (Secaucus, NJ: Lyle Stuart Inc., 1988), 63–64.

137. Lens, *Labor Wars*, 246–47.

138. Letter from Franklin Delano Roosevelt to Felix Frankfurter, February 9, 1937, http://newdeal.feri.org/court/fdr01.htm.

139. Quoted in Davis, *Prisoners of American Dream*, 5.

140. Ferguson and Rogers, *Right Turn*, 46–47; Brenner, *Lesser Evil*, 62.

141. Ferguson and Rogers, *Right Turn*, 46.

142. Marx, Engels, *Selected Correspondence* (Moscow: Progress Publishers, 1982), 374.

143. Kelley, *Hammer and Hoe*, xii–xiii.

144. Davis, *Prisoners of American Dream*, 15–16.

145. Brecher, *Strike!*, 57–58.

146. Ibid., 58–63; Guérin, *100 Years of American Labor*, 62.

147. Lens, *Labor Wars*, 112–13.

148. Ibid., 148; Montgomery, *Fall of House of Labor*, 345–50.

149. Quoted in Lens, *Labor Wars*, 96.

150. Quoted in Lens, *Labor Wars*, 95–96.

151. Guérin, *100 Years of Labor*, 64.

152. Lens, *Labor Wars*, 95–109.

153. Quoted in Lens, *Labor Wars*, 107.

154. Ibid.

155. Ibid.

156. Ibid., 100–101.

157. Ibid., 97.

158. Avrich, *Haymarket Tragedy*, 35.

159. Brecher, *Strike!*, 38–39.

160. Quoted in Lens, *Labor Wars*, 59.

161. Brecher, *Strike!*, 43–46; Avrich, *Haymarket Tragedy*, xi.

162. Ibid.; Lens, *Labor Wars*, 64.

163. Quoted in Lens, *Labor Wars*, 63.

164. Quoted in Avrich, *Haymarket Tragedy*, 216–17.

165. Ibid., 218–9.

166. Ibid., 222; Lens, *Labor Wars*, 63–64.

167. Philip Yale Nicholson, *Labor's Story in the United States* (Philadelphia: Temple University Press, 2004), 191–92.

168. Howe, *Socialism and America*, 42.

169. Montgomery, *Fall of House of Labor*, 376.

170. David Caute, *The Great Fear: The Anti-Communist Purge Under Truman and Eisenhower* (New York: Simon and Schuster, 1978), 62.

171. Ibid., 64.

172. Ibid., 67.

173. Quoted in Caute, *Great Fear*, 68.

174. Joy James, ed., *States of Confinement: Policing, Detention and Prisons* (New York: St. Martin's Press, 2000), xii.

175. Ibid., xi.

Chapter 3

1. Quoted in Lance Selfa, "U.S. Imperialism: A Century of Slaughter," *International Socialist Review* 7, (Spring 1999): 16–21.

2. Quoted in Harvard Sitkoff, *A New Deal for Blacks: The Emergence of Civil Rights as a National Issue*, vol. 1: *The Depression Decade* (New York: Oxford University Press, 1978), 19.

3. Sitkoff, *New Deal for Blacks*, 18.

4. Nicholson, *Labor's Story in the United States*, 199.

5. Sitkoff, *New Deal for Blacks*, 18.

6. Nicholson, *Labor's Story in the United States*, 145.

7. Lens, *Labor Wars*, 137.

8. Nicholson, *Labor's Story in the United States*, 142–43.

9. Lens, *Labor Wars*, 138.

10. Nicholson, *Labor's Story in the United States*, 144.

11. Ibid., 144–45.

12. Lens, *Labor Wars*, 135.

13. Ibid., 136.

14. The information in this section is from Meredith Tax, *The Rising of the Women: Feminist Solidarity and Class Conflict, 1880–1917* (New York: Monthly Review Press, 1980), 205–40.

15. Lens, *Labor Wars*, 138.

16. Howe, *Socialism and America*, 3–5.

17. Nicholson, *Labor's Story in the United States*, 149.

18. Report by the Executive Committee, National Lettish [Latvian] Organization, to the SP National Convention, May 1912, in *Proceedings: National Convention of the Socialist Party, 1912*, John Spargo, ed. (Chicago: The Socialist Party), 244–48.

19. Biographical Directory of the United States Congress, 1774 to the present. Available online at http://bioguide.congress.gov.

20. Chester, *True Mission*, 39–65.

21. Nicholson, *Labor's Story in the United States*, 180.

22. Ibid., 181.

23. Ibid.

24. Howe, *Socialism and America*, 42–43.

25. Ibid., 43.

26. Rhonda F. Levine, *Class Struggle and the New Deal: Industrial Labor, Industrial Capital, and the State* (Lawrence, Kansas: University Press of Kansas, 1988), 38.

27. U.S. Supreme Court: Debs v. U.S., 249 U.S. 211 (1919), http://www.justia.us/us/249/211/case.html.

28. Eugene V. Debs, "The Canton, Ohio, Speech,"(June 16, 1918), *International Socialist Review* 20, (November–December 2001): 80–91; Jean Y. Tussey, ed., *Eugene V. Debs Speaks* (New York: Pathfinder Press, 1970), 251–52, 253, 256–57, 260–61, quoted in Howard Zinn and Anthony Arnove, eds., *Voices of the People's History of the United States* (New York: Seven Stories Press, 2004), 295–297.

29. Biographical Directory of the United States Congress, 1774 to the present. Available online at http://bioguide.congress.gov.

30. See Duncan Hallas, *The Comintern* (London: Bookmarks, 1985).

31. Quoted in Ira Kipnis, *The American Socialist Movement, 1897–1912* (Chicago: Haymarket Books, 2004), 202.

32. Duncan Hallas, "American Working Class," 17–18.

33. Quoted in Kipnis, *American Socialist Movement,* 169–70.

34. Leon Trotsky, *My Life: An Attempt at an Autobiography* (London: Penguin, 1975), 282–84.

35. Tussey, *Eugene Debs Speaks,* 293.

36. Ibid., 65.

37. Quoted in Philip S. Foner, *American Socialism and Black Americans: From the Age of Jackson to World War II* (Westport, CT: Greenwood Press, 1977), 105–06.

38. Kipnis, *American Socialist Movement,* 130–32.

39. Quoted in Manning Marable and Leith Mullings, eds., *Let Nobody Turn Us Around; Voices of Resistance, Reform and Renewal: An Afro-American Anthology* (Lanham, MD: Rowan & Littlefield, 1999), 232–33.

40. Tussey, *Eugene Debs Speaks,* 92.

41. Quoted in Philip S. Foner, *American Socialism and Black Americans: From the Age of Jackson to World War II* (Westport, CT: Greenwood Press, 1977), 114.

42. Quoted in Tax, *Rising of the Women,* 194.

43. Quoted in Kipnis, *American Socialist Movement,* 278–80.

44. Ibid., 287.

45. Kipnis, *American Socialist Movement,* 288.

46. Quoted in Kipnis, *American Socialist Movement,* 284.

47. Quoted in Lens, *Labor Wars,* 151.

48. Ibid., 152.

49. Ibid., 140, 152, 155.

50. Ibid., 152.

51. Quoted in Lens, *Labor Wars,* 152–53.

52. Ibid., 153.

53. Lens, *Labor Wars,* 154.

54. Ibid.

55. Ibid., 153.

56. Ibid.

57. Ibid., 155.

58. Ibid.

59. Ibid.

60. Ibid., 156.

61. Tax, *Rising of the Women*, 242.

62. Ibid., 243.

63. Quoted in Tax, *Rising of the Women*, 243–44.

64. Lens, *Labor Wars*, 172–74.

65. Tax, *Rising of the Women*, 248; Lens, *Labor Wars*, 174.

66. Lens, *Labor Wars*, 173.

67. Ibid., 179–80.

68. Ibid., 175.

69. Tax, *Rising of the Women*, 248.

70. Quoted in Tax, *Rising of the Women*, 248.

71. Ibid., 249.

72. Ibid., 256.

73. Lens, *Labor Wars*, 181.

74. Ibid., 183.

75. Ibid.

76. Guérin, *100 Years of Labor*, 32, 79; Howe, *Socialism and America*, 14; Lens, *Labor Wars*, 159.

77. Lens, *Labor Wars*, 223.

78. Kipnis, *American Socialist Movement*, 381.

79. Ibid., 386.

80. Quoted in Kipnis, *American Socialist Movement*, 386.

81. Ibid., 382.

82. Ibid., 408.

83. Ibid., 407.

84. Ibid., 417–18.

85. Brody, *In Labor's Cause*, 60–61.

86. Montgomery, *Fall of House of Labor*, 402.

87. Quoted in Brecher, *Strike!*, 104.

88. Montgomery, *Fall of House of Labor*, 401.

89. Brecher, *Strike!*, 104–14.

90. Ibid., 104.

91. Ibid., 106–7.

92. Montgomery, *Fall of House of Labor*, 389.

93. Nicholson, *Labor's Story in the United States*, 188.

94. Quoted in Nicholson, *Labor's Story in the United States*, 111.

95. Quoted in Brecher, *Strike!*, 113.

96. Ibid., 104–5.

97. Howe, *Socialism and America*, 41.

98. Ibid., 41, 46.

99. Ibid., 49–50.

100. This foolish squabbling continued through most of 1920. See, for example, R. A. Archer, trans., *Second Congress of the Communist International: Minutes of the Proceedings*, vol. 2 (London: New Park Publications, 1977), 151–53.

101. Hallas, "American Working Class," 17–18.

102. Alix Holt and Barbara Holland, trans., *Theses Resolutions and Manifestos of the First Four Congress of the Third International* (London: Ink Links, 1980), 267.

103. Montgomery, *Fall of the House of Labor,* 432.

104. Ibid., 436–47.

105. Nicholson, *Labor's Story in the United States,* 182.

106. Ibid.

107. Ibid., 189.

108. Ibid., 190.

109. Montgomery, *Fall of the House of Labor,* 394–95.

110. Lens, *Labor Wars,* 222.

111. Levine, *Class Struggle and the New Deal,* 38–39.

112. Montgomery, *Fall of the House of Labor,* 461.

113. Quoted in Montgomery, *Fall of the House of Labor,* 461.

114. Montgomery, *Fall of the House of Labor,* 400–401.

115. Ibid., 135.

116. Ibid., 463.

117. Ibid., 395.

118. Eric Leif Davin, "Defeat of the Labor Party Idea," in *We Are All Leaders: The Alternative Unionism of the Early 1930s* (Chicago: University of Illinois Press, 1996), 120.

119. Levine, *Class Struggle and the New Deal,* 23.

120. Ibid., 24.

121. Ibid., 26.

122. Quoted in Brecher, *Strike!,* 144; Louis Corey, *The Decline of American Capitalism* (New York: Covici Friede Publishers, 1934), 16.

123. Nicholson, *Labor's Story in the United States,* 196.

124. Levine, *Class Struggle and the New Deal,* 36.

125. Lens, *Labor Wars,* 223.

126. Ibid.

127. Guérin, *100 Years of Labor,* 95.

128. Nicholson, *Labor's Story in the United States,* 198.

129. Irving Bernstein, *The Lean Years: A History of the American Worker, 1920–1933* (Baltimore: Penguin Books, 1966), 2.

130. Ibid., 10.

131. Quoted in Bernstein, *Lean Years,* 10.

132. Bernstein, *Lean Years,* 3.

133. Quoted in Bernstein, *Lean Years,* 8.

134. Bernstein, *Lean Years,* 2–3.

135. Quoted in Bernstein, *Lean Years,* 8.

136. Bernstein, *Lean Years,* 6.

137. Quoted in Bernstein, *Lean Years,* 10.

138. Ibid., 11.

139. Ibid., 17.

140. Ibid.

141. Ibid., 17–18.

142. Ibid., 19–20.

143. For a fuller elaboration of this argument, see *Russia: From Workers' State to State Capitalism,* (Chicago: Haymarket Books, 2004).

144. Quoted in Harvey Klehr, *Heyday of American Communism* (New York: Basic Books, 1984), 171. For an analysis of Stalinism in Russia, see Tony Cliff, *Trotsky: The Darker the Night the Brighter the Star, 1927–1940,* vol. 4 (London: Bookmarks, 1993).

145. See Leon Trotsky, *The Revolution Betrayed: What Is the Soviet Union and Where Is It Going?* (New York: Pathfinder, 1970). First published in 1937.

146. Quoted in Klehr, *Heyday of American Communism,* 13–14.

147. See Cliff, *Trotsky: Darker the Night,* 381.

148. See James P. Cannon, *The History of American Trotskyism* (New York: Pathfinder Press, 1972), 65–74, 123–24.

149. Bernstein, *Lean Years,* 20–22.

Chapter 4

1. Levine, *Class Struggle and the New Deal,* 52.

2. Nicholson, *Labor's Story in the United States,* 200.

3. Levine, *Class Struggle and the New Deal,* 1.

4. Art Preis, *Labor's Giant Step* (New York: Pathfinder Press, 1972), 9.

5. Nicholson, *Labor's Story in the United States,* 200.

6. Ibid., 202.

7. Ibid.

8. Quoted in Klehr, *Heyday of American Communism,* 63, 67.

9. Norwood, *Strikebreaking and Intimidation,* 196.

10. Ibid., 207, 217.

11. Nicholson, *Labor's Story in the United States,* 208.

12. Bert Cochran, *Labor and Communism: The Conflict that Shaped American Unions* (Princeton, NJ: Princeton University Press, 1977), 84.

13. Brecher, *Strike!,* 172.

14. Quoted in Brecher, *Strike!,* 177.

15. Quoted in Cochran, *Labor and Communism,* 35.

16. Brecher, *Strike!,* 172–73.

17. Lens, *Labor Wars,* 262.

18. Brecher, *Strike!,* 174–75.

19. Ibid., 169, 175.

20. Lens, *Labor Wars,* 262.

21. Davin, "Defeat of the Labor Party," 126.

22. Ibid., 129.

23. Ibid., 131.

24. Lens, *Labor Wars*, 246.

25. Ibid., 264.

26. Muste shunned the Communist Party and briefly united with Trotskyists. He soon reunited with religious pacifists, however. See A. J. Muste, "My Experience in the Labor and Radical Struggles of the Thirties," in Rita James Simon, ed., *As We Saw the Thirties: Essays on Social and Political Movements of a Decade* (Chicago: University of Illinois Press, 1969), 123–150.

27. Quoted in Lens, *Labor Wars*, 264–65.

28. Lens, *Labor Wars*, 265–66.

29. Although Bridges always denied that he was a Communist Party member, he was certainly a very close sympathizer who adhered to party discipline.

30. Lens, *Labor Wars*, 250.

31. Quoted in Lens, *Labor Wars*, 250.

32. Lens, *Labor Wars*, 250–53.

33. Ibid., 255.

34. Ibid., 256.

35. Preis, *Labor's Giant Step*, 32.

36. Brecher, *Strike!*, 157. See also Klehr, *Heyday of American Communism*, 126–27.

37. Nicholson, *Labor's Story in the United States*, 211.

38. Preis, *Labor's Giant Step*, 25.

39. Ibid., 28.

40. Brecher, *Strike!*, 162.

41. Ibid.; Lens, *Labor Wars*, 268.

42. Lens, *Labor Wars*, 269; Brecher, *Strike!*, 162–63.

43. Farrell Dobbs, *Teamster Rebellion* (New York: Pathfinder Press, 1972), 80–81.

44. Ibid., 88.

45. Quoted in Brecher, *Strike!*, 166.

46. Preis, *Labor's Giant Step*, 29.

47. Brecher, *Strike!*, 165.

48. Preis, *Labor's Giant Step*, 29.

49. Ibid., 30.

50. Guérin, *100 Years of Labor*, 101.

51. Brody, *In Labor's Cause*, 104; Foner, *Organized Labor and the Black Worker*, 218; Guérin, *100 Years of Labor*, 151.

52. Nicholson, *Labor's Story in the United States*, 201.

53. Cited in Guérin, *100 Years of Labor*, 152.

54. Ibid.

55. Walter Galenson, *The CIO Challenge to the AFL: A History of the American Labor Movement, 1935–1941* (Cambridge, MA: Harvard University Press, 1960), 3.

56. Klehr, *Heyday of American Communism*, 224–25.

57. Cochran, *Labor and Communism*, 48.

58. Brecher, *Strike!*, 177.

59. Guérin, *100 Years of Labor*, 102–03; Cochran, *Labor and Communism*, 95.

60. Jacobson, *Negro and American Labor*, 188–89.

61. Foner, *Organized Labor and the Black Worker*, 231.

62. Preis, *Labor's Giant Step*, 16.

63. Brecher, *Strike!*, 177.

64. Davis, *Prisoners of American Dream*, 62–63.

65. Foner, *Organized Labor and the Black Worker*, 200–01.

66. Davis, *Prisoners of American Dream*, 63 (emphasis in original).

67. Cochran, *Labor and Communism*, 156.

68. Ibid.

69. Davin, "Defeat of the Labor Party," 122.

70. Ibid., 123.

71. Davis, *Prisoners of American Dream*, 63; Brody, *In Labor's Cause*, 68.

72. Nicholson, *Labor's Story in the United States*, 213.

73. Cited in Davin, "Defeat of the Labor Party," 123.

74. Davin, "Defeat of the Labor Party," 141–42.

75. Ibid., 136.

75. Davis, *Prisoners of American Dream*, 67; Brody, *In Labor's Cause*, 69.

76. Davin, "Defeat of the Labor Party," 140.

77. Quoted in Chester, *Ballot Box*, 69; Davin, "Defeat of the Labor Party," 140.

78. Preis, *Labor's Giant Step*, 47–48.

79. Quoted in Davin, "Defeat of the Labor Party," 144.

80. Ibid., 145.

81. Preis, *Labor's Giant Step*, 48.

82. Ibid., 49.

83. Levine, *Class Struggle and the New Deal*, 16.

84. Cochran, *Labor and Communism*, 46; Klehr, *Heyday of American Communism*, 171–72, 366.

85. Roger Keeran, *The Communist Party and the Auto Workers' Unions* (Bloomington: Indiana University Press, 1980), 185.

86. Cochran, *Labor and Communism*, 107n.

87. Nicholson, *Labor's Story in the United States*, 213.

88. Cited in Mark Naison, *Communists in Harlem During the Depression* (New York: Grove Press, 1983), 18–19.

89. Quoted in Kelley, *Hammer and Hoe*, 73–75.

90. Ibid., 74.

91. Ibid., 72–73.

92. Ibid., 29.

93. Ibid., 45.

94. Kelley, *Hammer and Hoe*, 102.

95. Ibid, 161.

96. Ibid., 74.

97. Ibid., 102, 161–67.

98. Ibid., 51, 132.

99. Ibid., 51, 132, 163.

100. Naison, *Communists in Harlem,* 37, 87.

101. Cited in Naison, *Communists in Harlem,* 149.

102. Dave Zirin, *What's My Name Fool? Sports and Resistance in the United States* (Chicago: Haymarket Books, 2005), 28; Naison, *Communists in Harlem,* 213–14.

103. Naison, *Communists in Harlem,* 58.

104. Quoted in Naison, *Communists in Harlem,* 62.

105. Ibid., 58.

106. Ibid., 82.

107. Theodore Draper, *American Communism and Soviet Russia* (New York: Vintage Books, 1986), 55; Klehr, *Heyday of American Communism,* 348.

108. Kelley, *Hammer and Hoe,* 143–44; Foner, *Organized Labor and the Black Worker,* 231.

109. Quoted in Klehr, *Heyday of American Communism,* 178; Chester, *Ballot Box,* 45.

110. Quoted in Klehr, *Heyday of American Communism,* 205.

111. Chester, *Ballot Box,* 43; Klehr, *Heyday of American Communism,* 206.

112. Naison, *Communists in Harlem,* 37–38.

113. Ibid., 65–66.

114. Ibid., 174.

115. Ibid., 182.

116. Ibid., 170; Chester, *Ballot Box,* 45.

117. Klehr, *Heyday of American Communism,* 207.

118. Quoted in Chester, *Ballot Box,* 45–46; Klehr, *Heyday of American Communism,* 222.

119. Membership statistics are cited in Chester, *Ballot Box,* 58.

120. See Naison, *Communists in Harlem,* 290–91.

121. Brecher, *Strike!,* 185.

122. Ibid., 184–85.

123. Irving Bernstein, *Turbulent Years: A History of the American Worker, 1933–1941* (Boston: Houghton Mifflin Co., 1971), 595.

124. Cochran, *Labor and Communism,* 114.

125. Preis, *Labor's Giant Step,* 53.

126. Norwood, *Strikebreaking & Intimidation,* 203.

127. Ibid., 194.

128. Cochran, *Labor and Communism,* 118.

129. Galenson, *CIO Challenge to the AFL,* 135–36.

130. Quoted in Galenson, *CIO Challenge to the AFL,* 136.

131. Ibid., 137.

132. Ibid.

133. Galenson, *CIO Challenge to the AFL,* 138.

134. Quoted in Galenson, *CIO Challenge to the AFL,* 138–39.

135. Ibid., 139.

136. Galenson, *CIO Challenge to the AFL,* 139.
137. Quoted in Preis, *Labor's Giant Step,* 60.
138. Galenson, *CIO Challenge to the AFL,* 140.
139. Quoted in Galenson, *CIO Challenge to the AFL,* 140.
140. Preis, *Labor's Giant Step,* 63.
141. Galenson, *CIO Challenge to the AFL,* 146–48.
142. Quoted in Preis, *Labor's Giant Step,* 54, 59–60.
143. Quoted in Sidney Fine, *Sit-Down: The General Motors Strike of 1936–1937* (Ann Arbor, MI: University of Michigan Press, 1969), 201.
144. Galenson, *CIO Challenge to the AFL,* 141.
145. Fine, *General Motors Strike,* 331.
146. Nicholson, *Labor's Story in the United States,* 220.
147. Preis, *Labor's Giant Step,* 61.
148. Cited in Brecher, *Strike!,* 203.
149. Fine, *General Motors Strike,* 229.
150. Ibid., 332.
151. Quoted in Galenson, *CIO Challenge to the AFL,* 31.
152. Quoted in Preis, *Labor's Giant Step,* 54.
153. Brecher, *Strike!,* 205; Chester, *Ballot Box,* 73.
154. Guérin, *100 Years of Labor,* 115.
155. Cochran, *Labor and Communism,* 96–97.
156. Quoted in Cochran, *Labor and Communism,* 97, 100.
157. Quoted in Chester, *Ballot Box,* 73–74.
158. Cochran, *Labor and Communism,* 138; Chester, *Ballot Box,* 83.
159. Preis, *Labor's Giant Step,* 53–54; Chester, *Ballot Box,* 71, 73–74.
160. Quoted in Galenson, *CIO Challenge to the AFL,* 149.
161. Chester, *Ballot Box,* 71–72.
162. Cited in Galenson, *CIO Challenge to the AFL,* 154.
163. Galenson, *CIO Challenge to the AFL,* 150–51.
164. Cited in Galenson, *CIO Challenge to the AFL,* 154.
165. Galenson, *CIO Challenge to the AFL,* 154.
166. Cited in Galenson, *CIO Challenge to the AFL,* 156.
167. Cited in Chester, *Ballot Box,* 80.
168. Galenson, *CIO Challenge to the AFL,* 158, 159.
169. Quoted in Galenson, *CIO Challenge to the AFL,* 158.
170. For a more detailed account of the Pontiac strike, see Chester, *Ballot Box,* 78–83.
171. Preis, *Labor's Giant Step,* 72.
172. Ibid., 73; Chester, *Ballot Box,* 90.
173. Davis, *Prisoners of American Dream,* 68.
174. Nicholson, *Labor's Story in the United States,* 220.
175. Preis, *Labor's Giant Step,* 69.
176. Ibid., 70.

177. Nicholson, *Labor's Story in the United States,* 225.

178. Ibid., 225–26.

179. Guérin, *100 Years of Labor,* 105.

180. Cochran, *Labor and Communism,* 143, 145–47.

181. Leon Trotsky, "The Labor Party Question in the United States," (May 19, 1932), in *Writings of Leon Trotsky [1932]* (New York: Pathfinder, 1981), 94.

182. Ibid., 95.

183. Leon Trotsky, "US and European Labor Movements: A Comparison" (May 31, 1938), in *The Transitional Program for Socialist Revolution* (New York: Pathfinder, 1977), 164.

184. Leon Trotsky, "How to Fight for a Labor Party in the United States" (March 21, 1938) in *The Transitional Program,* 82.

185. Trotsky, "U.S. and European Labor Movements: A Comparison," 166.

186. Davin, "Defeat of the Labor Party," 158.

Chapter 5

1. Quoted in Preis, *Labor's Giant Step,* 134.

2. Ibid.

3. Nicholson, *Labor's Story in the United States,* 230.

4. Quoted in Martin Glaberman, *Wartime Strikes: The Struggle Against the No-Strike Pledge in the UAW During World War II* (Detroit: Bewick Editions, 1980), 2.

5. Ibid.

6. Glaberman, *Wartime Strikes,* 3–7.

7. Preis, *Labor's Giant Step,* 148.

8. Davis, *Prisoners of American Dream,* 74–75.

9. Cochran, *Labor and Communism,* 160.

10. Quoted in Preis, *Labor's Giant Step,* 150.

11. Quoted in Glaberman, *Wartime Strikes,* 7.

12. Nicholson, *Labor's Story in the United States,* 230; Brecher, *Strike!,* 223.

13. Nicholson, *Labor's Story in the United States,* 232.

14. Cochran, *Labor and Communism,* 231.

15. Glaberman, *Wartime Strikes,* 10, 14.

16. Quoted in Brecher, *Strike!,* 221.

17. Guérin, *100 Years of Labor,* 121.

18. Glaberman, *Wartime Strikes,* 70.

19. Ibid., 67–68; Guérin, *100 Years of Labor,* 122.

20. Quoted in Guérin, *100 Years of Labor,* 121; Glaberman, *Wartime Strikes,* 68.

21. Cited in Glaberman, *Wartime Strikes,* 67–68.

22. Cited in Brecher, *Strike!,* 221.

23. Davis, *Prisoners of American Dream,* 90.

24. Quoted in Page Smith, *Democracy on Trial* (New York: Simon & Schuster, 1995), 120.

25. Cited in Howard Zinn, *A People's History of the United States* (New York: Harper Perennial, 1995), 412.

26. Cochran, *Labor and Communism,* 229.

27. Quoted in Cochran, *Labor and Communism,* 230–31.

28. Davis, *Prisoners of American Dream,* 80.

29. Cochran, *Labor and Communism,* 145.

30. Nicholson, *Labor's Story,* 227.

31. For a detailed account, see Preis, *Labor's Giant Step,* 139–43.

32. Preis, *Labor's Giant Step,* 139.

33. Cited in Preis, *Labor's Giant Step,* 140.

34. Ibid., 143.

35. Ibid.

36. Nicholson, *Labor's Story in the United States,* 228.

37. Preis, *Labor's Giant Step,* 143.

38. Glaberman, *Wartime Strikes,* 98.

39. Preis, *Labor's Giant Step,* 236.

40. Glaberman, *Wartime Strikes,* 94–95.

41. Quoted in Glaberman, *Wartime Strikes.*

42. Lichtenstein, *Labor's War at Home: The CIO in World War II* (New York: 1982), 134–35.

43. Glaberman, *Wartime Strikes,* 51–53.

44. Quoted in Glaberman, *Wartime Strikes,* 45–46.

45. Although a range of socialists and independent leftists were involved in the Rank and File Caucus, the driving force came from the Workers' Party.

46. Guérin, *100 Years of Labor,* 129. For a full account of the Rank and File Caucus' attempt to rescind the UAW's no-strike pledge, see Glaberman, *Wartime Strikes,* 101–20.

47. Quoted in Bloom, *Class, Race, and Civil Rights,* 78 (emphasis in original).

48. Bloom, *Class, Race, and Civil Rights,* 78–79.

49. CIted in Bloom, *Class, Race, and Civil Rights,* 234.

50. Lichtenstein, *Labor's War at Home,* 125.

51. Davis, *Prisoners of American Dream,* 75; Glaberman, *Wartime Strikes,* 17–20.

52. Nicholson, *Labor's Story in the United States,* 234.

53. Cochran, *Labor and Communism,* 221.

54. Davis, *Prisoners of American Dream,* 81; Cochran, *Labor and Communism,* 221–22.

55. Cited in Guérin, *100 Years of Labor,* 122; Brecher, *Strike!,* 226.

56. Preis, *Labor's Giant Step,* 258, 260.

57. Ibid., 228; Davis, *Prisoners of American Dream,* 86.

58. Brecher, *Strike!,* 223.

59. Preis, *Labor's Giant Step,* 273.

60. Ibid., 272–75.

61. Quoted in Bloom, *Class, Race, and Civil Rights,* 79.

62. Bloom, *Class, Race, and Civil Rights,* 78.

63. Nelson Lichtenstein, *State of the Union: A Century of American Labor* (Princeton, NJ: Princeton University Press, 2002), 107.

64. Quoted in Brecher, *Strike!,* 228.

65. Brecher, *Strike!,* 228–30; Preis, *Labor's Giant Step,* 258.

66. Caute, *The Great Fear,* 27.

67. Davis, *Prisoners of American Dream,* 87.

68. For a summary of the many provisions of Taft-Hartley, see Guérin, *100 Years of Labor,* 161–63; Nicholson, *Labor's Story in the United States,* 251.

69. Nicholson, *Labor's Story in the United States,* 252.

70. Preis, *Labor's Giant Step,* 353.

71. Lichtenstein, *State of the Union,* 117.

72. Quoted in Lichtenstein, *State of the Union,* 368.

73. Davis, *Prisoners of American Dream,* 88.

74. Nicholson, *Labor's Story in the United States,* 252.

75. Caute, *Great Fear,* 356.

76. Nicholson, *Labor's Story in the United States,* 253.

77. Robert Zieger, *The CIO: 1935–1955* (Chapel Hill: University of North Carolina Press, 1995), 344.

78. Quoted in Caute, *Great Fear,* 27.

79. Caute, *Great Fear,* 358–59.

80. Ibid., 50.

81. Quoted in Victor Navasky, *Naming Names,* (New York: Viking Press, 1980), 48.

82. Cited in Navasky, *Naming Names,* 48–51.

83. Quoted in Gabriel Kolko, *The Politics of War* (New York: Pantheon Books, 1968), 251.

84. Caute, *Great Fear,* 44.

85. Preis, *Labor's Giant Step,* 355.

86. State Department Policy Planning Study, February 23, 1948, cited in Noam Chomsky, *On Power and Ideology: The Managua Lectures* (Boston: South End Press, 1987), 15–16.

87. Nicholson, *Labor's Story in the United States,* 250.

88. Caute, *Great Fear,* 30 (emphasis in original).

89. Navasky, *Naming Names,* 21.

90. Ibid., 22.

91. Caute, *Great Fear,* 112, 270–71, 275.

92. Quoted in Caute, *Great Fear,* 273.

93. Davis, *Prisoners of American Dream,* 92.

94. Cited in Caute, *Great Fear,* 280–81.

95. Ibid., 281.

96. Ibid., 89.

97. Ibid., 166.

98. Quoted in Navasky, *Naming Names,* 109.

99. Caute, *Great Fear,* 90; Navasky, *Naming Names,* 109.

100. Quoted in Caute, *Great Fear,* 252.

101. Ibid., 208.

102. Ibid., 187–88 (emphasis in original).

103. Navasky, *Naming Names,* 31–36.

104. Cited in Caute, *Great Fear,* 369.

105. Navasky, *Naming Names,* 24.

106. Quoted in Caute, *Great Fear,* 43, 60–61, 325.

107. Caute, *Great Fear,* 94.

108. Navasky, *Naming Names,* 23.

109. Caute, *Great Fear,* 46.

110. Ibid., 96.

111. Ibid., 102.

112. Navasky, *Naming Names,* 37.

113. Caute, *Great Fear,* 176.

114. Quoted in Caute, *Great Fear,* 95.

115. Caute, *Great Fear,* 360–75.

116. Ibid., 182–83.

117. Ibid., 230; Navasky, *Naming Names,* 23.

118. Cited in Caute, *Great Fear,* 38.

119. Ibid., 57.

120. Dell H. Hymes, "Robin Hood Goes to College," *Nation* 178, no. 0023, (June 5, 1954).

121. Caute, *Great Fear,* 71–72, 78–79.

122. Ibid., 93.

123. Ibid., 122.

124. Ibid., 168.

125. Cited in Navasky, *Naming Names,* 86.

126. Quoted in Caute, *Great Fear,* 105.

127. Quoted in Navasky, *Naming Names,* 82–83.

128. Ibid., 15.

129. Caute, *Great Fear,* 47.

130. Ibid., 48.

131. Ibid., 321–24.

132. Ibid., 107–8.

133. Ibid., 67.

134. Ibid., 364.

135. Navasky, *Naming Names,* 87; Nicholson, *Labor's Story in the United States,* 255.

136. Cochran, *Labor and Communism,* 317–18.

137. Ibid., 319.

138. Quoted in Caute, *Great Fear,* 353.

139. Nicholson, *Labor's Story in the United States,* 254.

140. Preis, *Labor's Giant Step,* 358, 401, 404–05, 410–11; Guérin, *100 Years of Labor,* 176.

141. Caute, *Great Fear,* 353.

142. Ibid., 354.

143. Cochran, *Labor and Communism,* 192–95.

144. Cited in Cochran, *Labor and Communism,* 221.

145. Preis, *Labor's Giant Step,* 460.

146. Cochran, *Labor and Communism,* 193; Preis, *Labor's Giant Step,* 341.

147. Preis, *Labor's Giant Step,* 459–60.

148. Caute, *Great Fear,* 67.

149. Navasky, *Naming Names,* 333.

150. Ibid., xii–xiii.

151. Caute, *Great Fear,* 198, 211.

152. Navasky, *Naming Names,* 188; 84.

153. Caute, *Great Fear,* 356.

154. Ibid., 215–25.

155. Preis, *Labor's Giant Step,* 417–18.

156. Quoted in Caute, *Great Fear,* 35.

157. Quoted in Navasky, *Naming Names,* 49.

158. Quoted in Cochran, *Labor at Midpassage,* 75.

159. Quoted in Noam Chomsky, *Necessary Illusions: Thought Control in Democratic Societies* (Boston: South End Press, 1989), 30.

Chapter 6

1. Cochran, *Labor at Midpassage,* 46.

2. Ibid., 48.

3. Ibid., 50.

4. Lichtenstein, *State of the Union,* 113.

5. Leo Huberman, "No More Class War?" in Cochran, *Labor at Midpassage,* 84.

6. Nicholson, *Labor's Story in the United States,* 267.

7. Ibid., 267–68.

8. Guérin, *100 Years of Labor,* 191.

9. Nicholson, *Labor's Story in the United States,* 268.

10. Dennis Anderson, "Corruption and Racketeering," in Cochran, *Labor at Midpassage,* 151.

11. Ibid., 151–52.

12. Ibid., 153.

13. Ibid., 160.

14. Nicholson, *Labor's Story in the United States,* 265.

15. Anderson, "Corruption and Racketeering," 161; Nicholson, *Labor's Story in the United States,* 264–66.

16. Lichtenstein, *Labor's War at Home,* 237.

17. Preis, *Labor's Giant Step,* 412.

18. Ibid.

19. Cochran, *Labor and Communism,* 330.

20. Ibid, 85.

21. Guérin, *100 Years of Labor,* 185.

22. Lichtenstein, *State of the Union,* 129.

23. Nicholson, *Labor's Story in the United States,* 256; Sharon Smith, "Twilight of the American Dream," *International Socialism Journal,* 54 (Spring 1992).

24. Cochran, *Labor and Communism,* 320.

25. Lichtenstein, *State of the Union,* 123.

26. Cochran, *Labor at Midpassage,* 85.

27. Peter B. Levy, *The New Left and Labor in the 1960s* (Urbana, IL: University of Illinois Press, 1994), 39.

28. Levy, *New Left and Labor,* 39; Bloom, *Class, Race, and Civil Rights,* 182–83.

29. Nicholson, *Labor's Story in the United States,* 263.

30. Levy, *New Left and Labor,* 14.

31. Ibid., 175.

32. Ibid., 47–48.

33. Ibid., 60.

34. Nicholson, *Labor's Story in the United States,* 257.

35. Cochran, *Labor at Midpassage,* 32.

36. Ibid., 45.

37. Quoted in Davis, *Prisoners of American Dream,* 102.

38. Sharon Smith, "Twilight of the American Dream."

39. Nicholson, *Labor's Story in the United States,* 258.

40. Kim Moody, "The American Working Class in Transition," *International Socialism* 36 (old series), (October–November 1969): 13.

41. Sharon Smith, "Twilight of the American Dream."

42. Sidney M. Peck, "The Economic Situation of Negro Labor," in Julius Jacobson, ed., *The Negro and the American Labor Movement* (New York: Anchor Books, 1968), 212–13.

43. Lichtenstein, *State of the Union,* 99.

44. Cochran, *Labor in Midpassage,* 87.

45. Huberman, "No More Class War?" 90–91.

46. Ibid., 88.

47. Stan Weir, "U.S.A.: The Labor Revolt," *International Socialism Journal* (April–June, 1967); James Green, *The World of the Worker: Labor in Twentieth Century America* (New York: Hill & Wang, 1980), 213.

48. Weir, "U.S.A.: The Labor Revolt," 280.

49. Moody, *Injury to All,* 68.

50. Perusek and Worcester, *Trade Union Politics,* 8.

51. Lichtenstein, *State of the Union,* 125.

52. Ibid., 144.

53. Ibid., 143.

54. Ibid., 143–44.

55. Nicholson, *Labor's Story in the United States,* 243.

56. Lichtenstein, *State of the Union*, 126.

57. Lichtenstein, *Labor's War at Home*, 240.

58. Lichtenstein, *State of the Union,* 127.

59. Ibid., 99.

60. John D'Emilio, *Sexual Politics, Sexual Communities: The Making of a Homosexual Minority in the U.S. 1940–1970* (Chicago: University of Chicago Press, 1983), 46, cited in Sherry Wolf, "The Roots of Gay Oppression," *International Socialist Review* 37: 55 (September–October 2004).

61. Nicholson, *Labor's Story in the United States*, 257.

62. Sidney M. Peck, "The Economic Situation of Negro Labor," in *The Negro and the American Labor Movement, Julius Jacobson,* ed., (New York: Anchor Books, 1968), 212–13.

63. Cochran, *Labor at Midpassage*, 58–59.

64. Betty Friedan, *The Feminine Mystique* (New York: W. W. Norton & Company, 1997), 18.

65. Ibid., 17.

66. Bride's Magazine, *The Bride's Reference Book* (New York: M. Barrows & Company, 1956), 299–301.

67. Lichtenstein, *State of the Union*, 117.

68. James Fallows, "What Did You Do in the Class War, Daddy?" *Vietnam: Anthology and Guide to a Television History,* Steven Cohen, ed. (New York: Alfred A. Knopf, 1983), 384, cited in Joel Geier, "Vietnam: The Soldier's Revolt," *International Socialist Review* 9 (August–September 2000): 39.

69. Levy, *New Left and Labor*, 53.

70. Ibid., 61.

71. Ibid., 1–2, 61.

72. Ibid., 2.

73. Ibid., 50.

74. See Levy's *New Left and Labor* for an overview of the politics of the New Left in the 1960s.

75. See Chris Harman, *The Fire Last Time: 1968 and After* (London: Bookmarks, 1988).

76. See Jerry Lembcke, *The Spitting Image: Myth, Memory, and the Legacy of Vietnam* (New York: New York University Press, 1998).

77. Levy, *New Left and Labor*, 56.

78. Gerald Nicosia, *Home to War* (New York: Three Rivers Press, 2001), 141, quoted in Joe Allen, "Vietnam: The War the U.S. Lost: From Quagmire to Defeat," *International Socialist Review* 40 (March–April 2005): 45.

79. Geier, "Soldier's Revolt," 46. Fragging statistics cited in this article are from: Matthew Rinaldi, "The Olive-Drab Rebels: Military Organizing during the Vietnam Era," *Radical America* 8, no. 3 (May–June 1974): 29; Richard Moser, *The New Winter Soldiers: GI and Veteran Dissent During the Vietnam Era (Perspectives in the Sixties)* (New Brunswick: Rutgers, 1996), 48; and Christian Appy, 246.

80. Richard Boyle, *GI Revolts: The Breakdown of the U.S. Army in Vietnam* (San Francisco: United Front Press, 1972), 28.

81. Quoted in Andrew Bacevich, *The New American Militarism: How Americans Are Seduced by War* (New York: Oxford University Press, 2005), 36.

82. Levy, *New Left and Labor,* 57–58.

83. Quoted in Tom Wells, *The War Within: America's Battle Over Vietnam* (New York: Henry Holt, 1994), 421 and Allen, "War the U.S. Lost," 42.

84. Levy, *New Left and Labor,* 60–62.

85. Ibid., 62.

86. Lichtenstein, *State of the Union,* 175–76.

87. Foner, *Organized Labor and the Black Worker,* 411–12.

88. Georgakas and Surkin, *Detroit: I Do Mind,* 24.

89. See Georgakas and Surkin, *Detroit: I Do Mind.*

90. Foner, *Organized Labor and the Black Worker,* 423.

91. Moody, *Injury to All,* 86–87.

92. Aaron Brenner, "Rank-and-File Teamster Movements," in Perusek and Worcester, *Trade Union Politics,* 114.

93. Moody, *Injury to All,* 223–26.

Chapter 7

1. John Herbers, "The 37th President; in Three Decades, Nixon Tasted Crisis and Defeat, Victory, Ruin and Revival," *New York Times,* April 24, 1994.

2. David Cunningham, "What the G-Men Knew," *New York Times Magazine,* June 20, 2004.

3. See *Brian Glick, War at Home: Covert Action Against U.S. Activists and What We Can Do About It* (Boston: South End Press, 1989).

4. Ferguson and Rogers, *Right Turn,* 79–80.

5. Joshua Cohen and Joel Rogers, "Reaganism After Reagan," in *Socialist Register 1988: Problems of Socialist Renewal: East and West,* eds. Ralph Miliband, Leo Panitch, et al. (London: The Merlin Press, 1988), 390; Nigel Harris, *The End of the Third World,* 106, 111.

6. Alexander Cockburn and Ken Silverstein, *Washington Babylon* (New York: Verso, 1996), 8.

7. Ibid.

8. Ibid., 11.

9. Holly Sklar, Barbara Ehrenreich, Karin Stallard, et al., *Poverty in the American Dream: Women and Children First* (Boston: South End Press, 1983), 31.

10. Ferguson and Rogers, *Right Turn,* 67.

11. Philip Mattera, *Prosperity Lost* (Reading, MA: Addison-Wesley Publishing Company, Inc., 1990), 15.

12. Perusek and Worcester, *Trade Union Politics,* 10.

13. Moody, *Injury to All,* 138.

14. Nicholson, *Labor's Story in the United States,* 318–19.

15. Ferguson and Rogers, *Right Turn,* 111.

16. Quoted in Bacevich, *New American Militarism,* 181.

17. Ferguson and Rogers, *Right Turn,* 109.

18. Mattera, *Prosperity Lost,* 107.

19. Quoted in Michael Goldfield, *The Decline of Organized Labor in the United*

States (Chicago: University of Chicago Press, 1987), 109, 193.

20. Quoted in Moody, *Injury to All,* 148–49.

21. Moody, *Injury to All,* 155, 165–66.

22. Nicholson, *Labor's Story in the United States,* 297.

23. Kenneth O'Reilly, *Nixon's Piano: Presidents and Racial Politics from Washington to Clinton,* (New York: The Free Press, 1995), 339.

24. Quoted in Laurence H. Tribe, *Abortion: The Clash of Absolutes* (New York: W. W. Norton & Company, 1990), 154.

25. Alphonso Pinkney, *The Myth of Black Progress* (Cambridge: Cambridge University Press, 1984), 153–54.

26. J. Harvie Wilkinson, III, *From Brown to Bakke—The Supreme Court and School Integration: 1954–1978* (New York: Oxford University Press, 1979), 267, 275.

27. Ferguson and Rogers, *Right Turn,* 121. See also Kim Moody, "Reagan, the Business Agenda and the Collapse of Labor," in *Socialist Register 1987* (London: The Merlin Press, 1987), 165–66.

28. Quoted in Ferguson and Rogers, *Right Turn,* 122.

29. Perusek and Worcester, *Trade Union Politics,* 36.

30. Quoted in Ferguson and Rogers, *Right Turn,* 119.

31. Phillips, *Politics of Rich and Poor,* 53.

32. Cohen and Rogers, "Reaganism After Reagan," 395–96.

33. Phillips, *Politics of Rich and Poor,* 80; Ferguson and Rogers, *Right Turn,* 123.

34. Phillips, *Politics of Rich and Poor,* 10 (emphasis in original).

35. Paul Farhi, "Number of U.S. Millionaires Soars; Boom in Highest Incomes Raises Debate on Equity, Class," *Washington Post,* July 11, 1992.

36. Quoted in Phillips, *Politics of Rich and Poor,* 87; Sklar, Ehrenreich, Stallard, et al., *Poverty in the American Dream,* 42.

37. Phillips, *Politics of Rich and Poor,* 8, 180. See also Labor Research Association, *Economic Clips,* (November–December 1990); Judith H. Dobrzynski, "CEO Pay: Something Should Be Done—But Not by Congress," *BusinessWeek* 3250 (February 3, 1992): 29.

38. Robert Sherrill, "The Looting Decade: S&Ls, Big Banks and Other Triumphs of Capitalism," *Nation* 251, no. 17 (November 19, 1990): 589–622.

39. Elliot Blair Smith, "Keating Clan Tears Down Walls: Exec's Family Still Open, Unified Despite Uncertainty," *Chicago Tribune,* January 5, 1992.

40. Sherrill, "Looting Decade," 609–10.

41. Ibid., 599.

42. Ibid., 590.

43. U.S. Dept of Commerce, Bureau of the Census, *Statistical Abstract of the United States, 1991,* (Washington, DC, 1991), 391; Albert R. Karr, "A Special News Report on People and Their Jobs in Offices, Fields and Factories," *Wall Street Journal,* January 21, 1992; Kevin Phillips, *Boiling Point: Democrats, Republicans and the Decline of Prosperity* (New York: HarperCollins, 1994), 158.

44. Chris Toulouse, "Political Economy After Reagan," in *Trade Union Politics,* Perusek and Worcester, 36.

45. Aaron Bernstein, "What Happened to the American Dream—The Under-30 Generation May Be Losing the Race for Prosperity," *BusinessWeek,* August 19,

1991, 80; Mattera, *Prosperity Lost,* 139; Manning Marable, "Black Politics in Crisis," *Progressive* 51, no. 1 (January 1987): 20.

46. Vicente Navarro, "Social Movements and Class Politics in the United States," in *Socialist Register 1988: Problems of Socialist Renewal: East and West,* eds. Ralph Miliband, Leo Panitch, and John Saville (London: Merlin Press, 1988), 390, 437; Mattera, *Prosperity Lost,* 18.

47. Susan B. Garland, "The Health Care Crisis—a Prescription for Reform," *Business Week,* October 7, 1991, 59.

48. Phillips, *Boiling Point,* 152.

49. Vicki Kemper, "The Great American Health-Care Sellout," *Washington Post,* October 13, 1991, 28.

50. Mark Feinberg, "Warning: Work Is Hazardous to Your Health," *Progressive* 56, no. 1 (January 1992): 26.

51. M. L. Kerr, "Chickens Come Home to Roost," *Progressive* 56, no. 1 (January 1992): 29.

52. Rae Tyson and Mark Mayfield, "How Safe Is Your Workplace?" *Chicago Sun-Times,* September 5, 1991.

53. Sharon Smith, *Women and Socialism: Essays on Women's Liberation* (Chicago: Haymarket Books, 2005), 73; Michael Bronski, "Shove, the second time around: Those who remember the past are doomed to repeat it," Boston Phoenix, September 12–19, 2002.

54. Sharon Smith, *Women and Socialism,* 51. During the 1980s, Republicans sought repeatedly, but unsuccessfully, to win the passage of a Constitutional ban on abortion, known as the Human Life Amendment.

55. Manning Marable, "Race and Realignment in American Politics," in *The Year Left:* An American Socialist Yearbook Vol. 1, eds. Mike Davis, Fred Pfeil, and ·Michael Sprinker (London: Verso, 1985), 19.

56. Lee Sigelman and Susan Welch, *Black Americans' Views of Racial Inequality: The Dream Deferred* (Cambridge: Cambridge University Press, 1991), 36.

57. Manning Marable, "Black America in Search of Itself," *Progressive* 55, no. 11 (November 1991): 22; Kevin Davis, "Latino Poverty Grew Over Decade, Study Finds," *Los Angeles Times,* December 16, 1989; J. T. Gibbs, *Young, Black and Male in America: An Endangered Species* (Dover, MA: Auburn House Publishing Co., 1988), 7.

58. Cited in Don Colburn, "The Risky Lives of Young Black Men; Key Factors in Soaring Homicide Rate: Poverty, Drug Culture, Guns," *Washington Post,* December 18, 1990. See also C. McCord and H. P. Freeman, "Excess Mortality in Harlem," *New England Journal of Medicine* 322, no. 3 (January 18, 1990): 173–77.

59. Dennis R. Judd, "Segregation Forever," *Nation* 253, no. 20 (December 9, 1991): 742; Manning Marable, *How Capitalism Underdeveloped Black America* (Boston, 1983), 127; Gibbs, *Young, Black and Male,* 3.

60. Quoted in Marable, *How Capitalism Underdeveloped,* 127.

61. Bart Landry, *The New Black Middle Class* (Berkeley: University of California Press, 1987), 229.

62. Manning Marable, "The Contradictory Contours of Black Political Culture," in *The Year Left 2: Toward a Rainbow Socialism,* eds., Mike Davis, Manning Marable, Fred Pfeil, Michael Sprinker, (London: Verso, 1987), 6.

63. Marable, "Black America in Search of Itself," 22.

64. David A. Bositis, *Black Elected Officials: a Statistical Summary* (Washington, D.C.: Joint Center for Political and Economic Studies, 2001), 13.

65. "Black Mayors Back Subminimum Wage for Youth," *New York Times,* May 6, 1984.

66. Lindsey Gruson, "Expert Disputes Decision on Bomb," *New York Times,* November 6, 1985.

67. Lenni Brenner, *The Lesser Evil: the Democratic Party,* (Seacaucus, NJ: Citadel Press, 1988), 188, 278–79.

68. Sharon Smith, "Twilight of the American Dream," 22.

69. Manning Marable, "A New Black Politics," *Progressive* 54, no. 8 (August 1990): 21.

70. Quoted in JoAnn Wypijewski, "The Instructive History of Jackson's Rainbow," in *A Dimes' Worth of Difference: Beyond the Lesser of Two Evils,* eds. Alexander Cockburn and Jeffrey St, Clair (Petrolia and Oakland, CA: CounterPunch and AK Press, 2004), 80.

71. Jesse Jackson, "Excerpts from Jackson to Convention Delegates for Unity in Party," *New York Times,* July 18, 1984.

72. JoAnn Wypijewski, "The Rainbow's Gravity," *Nation* 279, no. 4 (August 2–9, 2004): 83.

73. Ibid.

74. Quoted in Ferguson and Rogers, *Right Turn,* 9.

75. Moody, *Injury to All,* 139–41.

76. Quoted in Editorial, *Socialist Worker* (U.S.), September 1981.

77. Quoted in "Solidarity Forever," *Socialist Worker* (U.S.), October 1981.

78. Moody, *Injury to All,* 148.

79. Nicholson, Labor's *Story in the United States,* 300.

80. Quoted in Moody, *Injury to All,* 148, 154, 166.

81. Cited in Mattera, *Prosperity Lost,* 112–13.

82. Moody, *Injury to All,* 185.

83. Nicholson, *Labor's Story in the United States,* 302.

84. Moody, *Injury to All,* 116–17.

85. Goldfield, *Decline of Organized Labor,* 46.

86. Quoted in *Trade Union Politics,* Perusek and Worcester, 181.

87. Sharon Smith "Brown and Sharpe: How Not to Win," *Socialist Worker* (U.S.), February 1983.

88. Quoted in Ahmed Shawki and Alan Maass, "Victory to the P-9 Strike!" *Socialist Worker* (U.S.), April 1986.

89. Cited in Dave Hage and Paul Klauda, *No Retreat, No Surrender: Labor's War at Hormel* (New York: William Morrow and Company, Inc., 1989), 242.

90. Hage and Klauda, *No Retreat, No Surrender,* 346–51.

91. Nicholson, *Labor's Story in the United States,* 302.

92. Ibid., 303.

93. Labor Research Association, *Economic Notes,* January–February 1990 and May–June 1991.

94. Navarro, "Social Movements and Class Politics," 429.

95. Phillips, *Politics of Rich and Poor,* 89–90.

96. Sylvia Nasar, "Employment in Service Industry, Impetus to Boom in 80's, Falters," *New York Times,* January 2, 1992.

97. Phillips, *Politics of Rich and Poor,* 133.

98. Michael R. Sesit, "Global Finance (A Special Report): Japan's Challenge—When Tokyo Picks Up the Tab: America's Appetite for Japanese Capital Grows Producing Worries on Both Sides of the Pacific," *Wall Street Journal,* September 18, 1987.

99. Mattera, *Prosperity Lost,* 22; Mike Dorning, "Bankruptcy filings gaining with the public," *Chicago Tribune,* January 5, 1992.

100. Lawrence K. Altman, "Deadly Strain of Tuberculosis Is Spreading Fast, U.S. Finds," *New York Times,* January 24, 1992; Mireya Navarro, "New York Asks U.S. Help in Tracking New TB Cases," *New York Times,* January 24, 1992.

101. Susan C. Faludi and Marilyn Chase, "Surging Welfare Costs, Struggle to Control Them Join Health-Care Expense as Hot Political Issue," *Wall Street Journal,* December 11, 1991; Jason DeParle, "California Plan to Cut Welfare May Prompt Others to Follow," *New York Times,* December 18, 1991.

102. See the Independent Commission of Inquiry on the U.S. Invasion of Panama, *The U.S. Invasion of Panama: The Truth Behind Operation "Just Cause"* (Boston: South End Press, 1991) and Anthony Arnove, ed., *Iraq Under Siege: The Deadly Impact of Sanctions and War* (Boston: South End Press, 2002).

103. Quoted in Julius Jacobson, "Pax Americana: The New World Order," *New Politics* 111, no. 3 (new series), (Summer 1991): 18 (emphasis added).

104. Joe Klein and Anne McDaniel, "What Went Wrong?" *Newsweek,* August 24, 1992, 22; Robin Toner, "Casting Doubts: Economy Stinging Bush," *New York Times,* November 26, 1991.

105. Janice Castro, "Condition: Critical," *Time* 138, no. 21 (November 25, 1991): 36.

106. Mark N. Vamos and Judith H. Dobrzynski, "Prescriptions for a Sick Economy," *Business Week* 3242 (December 2, 1991): 32.

107. Dan Balz and Richard Morin, "A Tide of Pessimism and Political Powerlessness Rises," *Washington Post,* November 3, 1991. See also Phillips, *Boiling Point,* 75.

108. See William J. Eaton and Michael Ross, "President Signs Measure to Extend Jobless Benefits," *Los Angeles Times,* November 16, 1991; Mitchell Locin, "Bush, Congress OK Extending Jobless Benefits," *Chicago Tribune,* November 14, 1991; and "Bush Gets Jobless Bill—Demos Assail Veto Vow," *San Francisco Chronicle,* October 10, 1991.

109. Editorial, "We're for a Universal Health Care System," *Business Week,* October 7, 1991, 158.

110. Alan Abelson, "Up and Down Wall Street," *Barron's,* January 13, 1992.

111. Quoted in Maureen Dowd, "White House Isolation," *New York Times,* November 22, 1991.

112. Phillips, *Boiling Point,* 156.

113. Sharon Smith, "Twilight of the American Dream," 37–38.

114. Lester Thurow, "Almost Everywhere: Surging Inequality and Falling Wages," in *The American Corporation Today,* ed. Carl Kaysen (New York: Oxford University Press, 1996), 384.

115. Marc Levinson with Eleanor Clift, Daniel Glick, and Rich Thomas, "Capitol Gridlock," *Newsweek* 118, no. 24 (December 9, 1991): 45.

116. Balz and Morin, "Tide of Pessimism."

117. Cited in Phillips, *Boiling Point*, 3.

118. Christopher Jenks quoted in Irene Sege, "Growing Gap Shown Between Rich, Poor," *Boston Globe*, May 15, 1989; Phillips, *Politics of Rich and Poor*, 209.

119. William Serrin, "Negotiating Democracy: The Teamsters' Toughest Contract," *Nation* 253, no. 4 (July 29, 1991): 151.

Chapter 8

1. Thurow, "Almost Everywhere," 386.

2. Quoted in David M. Gordon, *Fat and Mean: The Corporate Squeeze of Working Americans and the Myth of Managerial "Downsizing"* (New York: The Free Press, 1996), 35.

3. For a summary of the Clinton presidency, see Alexander Cockburn and Jeffrey St. Clair, *A Dimes' Worth of Difference*. Also see Lance Selfa, "Eight Years of Clinton-Gore: The Price of Lesser-Evilism," *International Socialist Review* 13 (August–September 2000): 7–15.

4. Cockburn and Silverstein, *Washington Babylon*, 17.

5. Quoted in Mimi Abramovitz, *Under Attack, Fighting Back: Women and Welfare in the United States* (New York: Monthly Review Press, 1996), 14.

6. Harley Sorensen, "Dems Have Only Themselves to Blame," *San Francisco Chronicle*, November 11, 2002.

7. O'Reilly, *Nixon's Piano*, 410.

8. Cited in Alan Maass, "Anybody But Bush?" *International Socialist Review* 30 (July–August 2003): 19; "A Talk with Bill Clinton," *BusinessWeek* 3257 (March 23, 1992): 28.

9. Cockburn and Silverstein, *Washington Babylon*, 68–69.

10. Cited in Paul Krugman, "The Medical Money Pit," *New York Times*, April 15, 2004.

11. Selfa, "Eight Years of Clinton-Gore," 8.

12. Bob McIntyre, Institute on Taxation and Economic Policy, "Study Finds Resurgence in Corporate Tax Avoidance," press release, October 19, 2000.

13. Quoted in Lee Sustar, "U.S. Tax System: Rigged in Favor of the Rich," *Socialist Worker* (U.S.), June 13, 2003.

14. Selfa, "Eight Years of Clinton-Gore," 8.

15. Abramovitz, *Under Attack, Fighting Back*, 14.

16. Alexander Cockburn and Jeffrey St. Clair, "War on the Poor," in *Dimes' Worth of Difference*, Cockburn and St. Clair, 45.

17. See Robin Blackburn, "How Monica Lewinsky Saved Social Security," in *Dimes' Worth of Difference*, Cockburn and St. Clair, 31–42.

18. Quoted in Jeffrey St. Clair, "Oil for One and One for Oil," in *Dimes' Worth of Difference*, Cockburn and St. Clair, 195–214; Selfa, "Eight Years of Clinton-Gore," 8.

19. David Lauter, "Clinton Asks New Rules on Asylum Immigration," *Los Angeles Times*, July 28, 1993.

20. Jonathan S. Landay, "Legal Immigrants Deported If They Have a Criminal Past," *Christian Science Monitor*, September 5, 1996.

21. Robert Scheer, "New National Monument: The Jailhouse," *Los Angeles Times,* August 27, 1995.

22. Marc Mauer and The Sentencing Project, *Race to Incarcerate,* revised ed. (New York: The New Press, 2006). Also cited in "Insights Into the Inmate Population," *Washington Post,* May 21, 2003.

23. Salim Muwakkil, "Have We Put Racism Behind Us? Don't Kid Yourselves," *Milwaukee Journal Sentinel,* September 29, 2003.

24. Manning Marable, *The Great Wells of Democracy: The Meaning of Race in American Life* (New York: Basic Books, 2003), 88–89.

25. Cockburn and St. Clair, "War on the Poor," 60.

26. Harvey Grossman, "Gun Sweeps in Public Housing," Congressional Testimony by Federal Clearing House, April 22, 1994; Lynn Sweet and Daniel J. Lehmann, "Clinton Pushes Housing Sweeps; Judge Rules Searches Are Unconstitutional," *Chicago Sun-Times,* April 8, 1994.

27. Sharon Smith, "War on the Poor," *Socialist Review* (UK) 175 (May 1994.

28. Quoted in "As of Now, Everybody Works in Wisconsin," *Seattle Times,* September 1, 1997.

29. Cockburn and St. Clair, "War on the Poor," 52.

30. Quoted in Ellen Goodman, "In 'Ending Welfare as We Know It,' We've Left Many Families in Poverty," *Boston Globe,* January 4, 2001.

31. Cockburn and Silverstein, *Washington Babylon,* 258.

32. Quoted in Cockburn and Silverstein, *Washington Babylon,* 258.

33. Selfa, "Eight Years of Clinton-Gore," 8.

34. Leo Troy, "Unions 'Charge' Into the 21st Century," *Wall Street Journal,* March 18, 1997.

35. *Socialist Worker,* January 31, 1997, cited in Lee Sustar, "A New Labor Movement?" *International Socialist Review* 1 (Summer 1997): 21.

36. Mara Liasson, "Business Support of Clinton's Policies Not Solid," *All Things Considered,* National Public Radio, April 26, 1994.

37. Aaron Bernstein, "Why America Needs Unions, But Not the Kind It Has Now," *BusinessWeek* 3373 (May 23, 1994): 70.

38. Sharon Smith, "Dogs Bite Back," *Socialist Review* (UK) 178 (September 1994).

39. Robert Fitch, *Solidarity for Sale: How Corruption Destroyed the Labor Movement and Undermined America's Promise* (New York: Public Affairs, 2006), 3.

40. John Sweeney, *America Needs a Raise* (Boston and New York: Houghton Mifflin, 1996), 90.

41. AFL-CIO news release, March 1996, quoted in Sustar, "A New Movement?," 22.

42. Robert Fitch, "Labor Pain," *Nation* 263, no. 17 (November 25, 1996).

43. Quoted in Frank Swoboda, "AFL-CIO Chief in Close Contest for Top Union Post," *Washington Post,* September 4, 1995; Peter G. Gosselin, "Clinton Pushes Pact at AFL-CIO Convention," *Boston Globe,* October 5, 1993; Jim McKay, "Labor Embraces Clinton for Stand on Workers," *Pittsburg Post-Gazette,* October 24, 1995.

44. Fitch, "Labor Pain;" Sustar, "A New Movement?," 22.

45. Sustar, "A New Movement?" 22.

46. AFL-CIO news release, April 1996, quoted in Sustar, "A New Movement?," 22.

47. Quoted in Jane Slaughter, "AFL-CIO's Report Card: Sweeney; Pass, Fail or In-

complete?" *Against the Current* 12, no. 1, special issue (March–April 1997): 7.

48. Joann Muller, "Has the UAW Found a Better Road?" *Business Week* 3791, (July 15, 2002): 108.

49. Quoted in Steven Greenhouse, "Labor's Lost Love," *New York Times,* June 8, 1997.

50. "Work Week," *Wall Street Journal,* May 20, 1997.

51. Fitch, *Solidarity for Sale,* 3.

52. William Serrin, foreword to *Three Strikes: Labor's Heartland Losses and What They Mean for Working Americans,* Stephen Franklin (New York: Guilford Press, 2001), x.

53. Kim Moody, *Workers in Lean World,* 29.

54. Ibid.

55. Ibid., 28.

56. Sustar, "A New Movement?," 24.

57. Associated Press, Christopher Wills, "Three Big Strikes Make Decatur Labor-Management Battleground," *Buffalo News,* July 18, 1994.

58. "Strikes, Scabs and Tread Separations: Labor Strife and the Production of Defective Bridgestone/Firestone Tires." National Bureau of Economic Research Website. Available online at http://papers.nber.org/papers/w9524.

59. Moody, *Workers in a Lean World,* 27; Sharon Smith, "Fighting Talk," *Socialist Review* (UK) 192 (December 1995).

60. Franklin, *Three Strikes,* 2.

61. Moody, *Workers in Lean World,* 26.

62. "Locked-out Staley Workers Speak Out: Lessons from the War Zone," Interviews with Staley workers Art Dhermy, Dan Lane, and Lorell Patterson by Lance Selfa, Carole Ramsden, and Paul D'Amato, *Socialist Worker,* January 19, 1996.

63. Moody, *Workers in Lean World,* 27.

64. Ibid., 26.

65. Quoted in Franklin, *Three Strikes,* 44.

66. Franklin, *Three Strikes,* 43.

67. Associated Press, "UAW Strikes at Caterpillar Plant Over Banned Slogans," June 8, 1994.

68. Kim Moody "Caterpillar: UAW Ends Strike, But Workers Refuse to Ratify Contract," *Labor Notes* 202 (January 1996): 14–16.

69. Sustar, "A New Movement?" 22.

70. Franklin, *Three Strikes,* 255.

71. Quoted in Bill Roberts, "Caterpillar Report," *Socialist Worker,* January 19, 1996.

72. Sustar, "A New Movement?," 24.

73. Franklin, *Three Strikes,* 283.

74. Christopher Wills, "UAW OKs 6-Year Caterpillar Contract," Associated Press, March 23, 1998; "Union to Drop 441 Unfair Labor Practice Charges for Contract at Caterpillar," *Labor Notes* (March 1998).

75. Franklin, *Three Strikes,* 176–77.

76. Ibid., 175.

77. Franklin, *Three Strikes,* 176.

78. "Interview with Robert Borders," *Socialist Worker* (U.S.), September 1994.

79. Carl Quintanilla and Robert L. Rose, "Caterpillar-UAW Feud Drags On," *Wall Street Journal,* February 24, 1998.

80. Quoted in Sharon Smith, "Kick the Cat," *Socialist Review* (UK) 218 (April 1998).

81. Louis Uchitelle, "Strike Points to Inequality in 2-Tier Job Market," *New York Times,* August 8, 1997.

82. Christina Duff, "We Are So Attached to Our UPS Man, We Feel for Him," *Wall Street Journal,* August 14, 1997.

83. Brian Jenkins and Lou Waters, "Long-time Union Vet Carey Wins Results, Applause Once More," CNN, August 20, 1997; Dave Murray, UPS chief negotiator at Washington, DC, press conference, "Teamsters Union and UPS Have Made a Tentative Agreement," CNN, August 19, 1997.

84. Deepa Kumar, *Outside the Box: Corporate Media, Globalization, and the UPS Strike* (Urbana Champaign: University of Illinois Press, forthcoming).

85. Ibid.

86. Bob Herbert, "A Workers' Rebellion," *New York Times,* August 7, 1997.

87. Sharon Smith, "A crusade against corporate greed," *Socialist Review* (UK) 211 (Sept. 1997).

88. USA Today/CNN/Gallup poll cited in David Field, "Poll: 55% Support Strikers at UPS," *USA Today,* August 15, 1997.

89. Robert A. Rosenblatt, "Teamsters, UPS Hint at Progress," *Chicago Sun-Times,* August 18, 1997.

90. Bernard J. Wolfson et al., "15 Arrested as Cops Clash with Striking UPS Workers," *Boston Herald,* August 6, 1997; C. Eugene Emery Jr., "UPS Strike Hits Home," *Providence Journal-Bulletin,* August 5, 1997.

91. Smith, 'Crusade Against Corproate Greed."

92. Ibid.

93. Steven Greenhouse, "A Victory for Labor, But How Far Will It Go?" *New York Times,* August 20, 1997.

94. Dirk Johnson, "Rank and File's Verdict: A Walkout Well Waged," *New York Times,* August 20, 1997.

95. Lee Sustar, "The Labor Movement: State of Emergency, Signs of Renewal," *International Socialist Review* 34 (March–April 2004): 39.

96. Quoted in Sharon Smith, "A Striking Contrast," *Socialist Review* (UK) 222 (Aug./Sept. 1998).

97. Simon Head, "The New, Ruthless Economy," *New York Review of Books* 43, no. 4 (February 29, 1996): 47.

98. James R. Healey, "GM Strike: It's Over," *USA Today,* July 29, 1998.

99. Robert L. Simison, "GM Profit Falls 11% Due to Asia, Sale of Hughes Defense Assets," *Wall Street Journal,* April 20, 1998.

100. Warren Brown and Frank Swoboda, "At GM, a Stalled Revolution," *Washington Post,* July 12, 1998.

101. Associated Press, Brian S. Akre, "GM-UAW Strike Talks Press into Morning," July 27, 1998; Reuters News Service, "GM Returns Machinery to Plant," *St. Louis Post-Dispatch,* July 27, 1998.

102. Peter T. Kilborn, "Caterpillar Workers Forced to Crawl," *New York Times,* De-

cember 5, 1995.

103. Robert Evans, "WTO Chief Says Protesters Working Against Poor," Reuters News, November 30, 1999; see also "Organizing to Fight Corporate Greed: The Battle in Seattle," *Socialist Worker,* December 10, 1999.

104. Rick DelVecchio and Stacy Finz, "Dockworkers Shut Down Oakland Port," San Francisco Chronicle, December 1, 1999.

105. Robert Collier, "Turmoil in Seattle Streets," *San Francisco Chronicle,* December 1, 1999; Patrick McMahon, "Seattle Police Chief Resigns in Wake of WTO Riots," *USA Today,* December 8, 1999; Rebecca Cook, "More Arrests at WTO Meeting," *Chicago Sun-Times,* December 1, 1999.

106. Letter from Bill Capowski, "WTO and the Real Story," December 2, 1999. Konformist Newswire, www.konformist.com/1999/wto/wtoreports.htm.

107. See Alexander Cockburn and Jeffrey St. Clair, *Five Days That Shook the World: Seattle and Beyond* (New York: Verso, 2000); Lee Sustar, "Organizing to fight corporate greed: The battle in Seattle," *Socialist Worker* (US), December 10, 1999.

108. David Mendell and David Greising, "Seattle Cops Retake Streets: Anatomy of a Riot," *Chicago Tribune,* December 2, 1999.

109. Mary Schmich, "WTO Protests Catch Attention of Dozing Nation," *Chicago Tribune,* December 3, 1999.

110. Cited in Kumar, *Outside the Box.*

111. David Firestone, "46,000 March on South Carolina Capitol to Bring Down Confederate Flag," *New York Times,* January 18, 2000.

112. Jacob Schlesinger, "Scary Optimism: The Business Cycle Is Tamed, Many Say, Alarming Some Others," *Wall Street Journal,* November 15, 1996.

113. David Wessel and David Schlesinger, "U.S. Economy's Report Card: Not All A's," *Wall Street Journal,* May 5, 1997; Hubert Herring, "Diary," *New York Times,* June 8, 1997.

114. James C. Cooper and Kathleen Madigan, "Enjoy the Ride, But Keep Your Seat Belt Fastened; Labor Costs Will Stay Subdued Only If the Economy Slows," *Business Week* 3526 (May 12, 1997).

115. Joel Geier and Ahmed Shawki, "Contradictions of the 'Miracle' Economy," *International Socialist Review* 2, (Fall 1997): 6.

116. Juliet Schorr, *The Overworked American* (New York: Basic Books, 1991), 2.

117. Lawrence Mishel, Jared Bernstein, and John Schmitt, *The State of Working America, 2000–2001,* Economic Policy Institute. (Ithaca: Cornell University Press, 2001)

118. Thurow, "Almost Everywhere," 386–88.

119. Carl Quintanilla, "Work Week: Getting Fired," *Wall Street Journal,* May 27, 1997.

120. Aaron Bernstein, "Commentary: Who Says Job Anxiety Is Easing?" *Business-Week* 3521 (April 7, 1997), cited in Geier and Shawki, "Contradictions of the 'Miracle' Economy," 22.

121. Geier and Shawki, "Contradictions of the 'Miracle' Economy," 7.

122. Marc Miringoff and Marque-Luisa Miringoff, *The Social Health of the Nation: How America Is Really Doing* (Oxford: Oxford University Press, 1999), 92.

123. Thurow, "Almost Everywhere," 383.

124. Gordon, *Fat and Mean,* 20.

125. See Economic Policy Institute, *State of Working America, 2000–2001,*

126. Marc Cooper, "The Heartland's Raw Deal: How Meatpacking Is Creating a New Immigrant Underclass," *Nation* 264, no. 4 (February 3, 1997).

127. Government Accounting Office report cited in Associated Press, "Most Corporations Paid No U.S. Taxes in Late 1990s," April 2, 2004.

128. Asociated Press and Reuters, "Washington in Brief," *Washington Post,* April 3, 2004.

129. Ibid.

130. Gordon, *Fat and Mean,* 17.

131. Cockburn and Silverstein, *Washington Babylon,* 293.

132. Ibid.

133. Quoted in Cockburn and St. Clair, *Dimes' Worth of Difference,* 213.

134. Kathryn M. Welling, "Up and Down Wall Street: Crony Capitalism?" *Barron's,* September 28, 1998.

135. Michael Lewis, *"Liar's Poker: Rising Through the Wreckage on Wall Street,* (New York: Norton, 1989).

136. Ben Laurance and Anthony Browne, "Panic Grips the Markets," *Observer* (UK), October 4, 1998; Peter Truell, "Fallen Star: The Managers," *New York Times,* September 25, 1998; Steven Mufson, "What Went Wrong?," *Washington Post,* September 27, 1998.

137. Sharon Smith, "Up Like a Rocket," *Socialist Review* (UK) 224 (November 1998).

138. Ibid.

139. Associated Press, Marcy Gordon, "House Passes Bill to Make Bankruptcy Less Easy," *Los Angeles Daily News,* October 10, 1998.

140. Associated Press, "Critics Raise Questions About the Propriety of the Hedge Fund Rescue," *St. Louis Post-Dispatch,* October 11, 1998.

141. Quoted in David Cay Johnson, "Narrowing the Bankruptcy Escape Hatch," *New York Times,* October 4, 1998.

142. Katherine Pfleger, "Proposed Bancruptcy Law Has Tougher Look," *St. Petersburg Times,* April 17, 1998.

143. Interview with Senator Charles Grassley by Kitty Pilgrim, *Moneyline,* CNN, July 7, 2003.

144. Molly Ivins, "Bad to Worse: Republicans Vote Down Military Exemption to Bankruptcy Bill, Add Loopholes for Rich," Working for Change, March 3, 2005. Online journal, available at www.workingforchange.com/about/index.cfm.

145. Paul Krugman, "The Debt-Peonage Society," *New York Times,* March 8, 2005.

146. Senator Hillary Rodham Clinton testimony to the Senate, "Keep America Working: Restoring Jobs to Ensure American Prosperity," March 3, 2004, http://clinton.senate.gov/news/statements/details.cfm?id=233755.

147. Robert Reich, "Why Gore Is Good for Business," *Financial Times,* July 14, 2000.

148. Bacevich, *New American Militarism,* 120.

149. Robert L. Borosage, "Money Talks: The Implications of U.S. Budget Priorities," in *Global Focus,* eds. Martha Honey and Tom Barry (New York: St. Martin's Press, 2000), 12.

150. See Arnove, *Iraq Under Siege.*

151. Madeleine Albright, interview by Leslie Stahl, "Punishing Saddam," *60 Minutes,* CBS, May 12, 1996; Cited in Edward S. Herman, "The 'Price Is Worth It,' "

ZNET, September 25, 2001, www.zmag.org.

152. Quoted in Steve Chapman, "Clinton Is Gone, But His Policies Carry On," *Chicago Tribune,* June 27, 2004.

153. See Lance Selfa, "From Cold War to Kosovo," *International Socialist Review* 8 (Summer 1999).

154. U.S. Census Bureau, 1999 Income, Table F. http://www.census.gov/.

155. Quoted in Americans for Democratic Action, *Income and Inequality: Millions Left Behind,* 3rd ed., (Washington, D.C.: Americans for Democratic Action, 2004), 9.

156. David Korten, *When Corporations Rule the World,* (Bloomfield, Connecticut: Kumarian Press, 1995), 83.

Chapter 9

1. Quoted in Karen DeYoung and Rick Weiss, "U.S. Seems to Ease Rhetoric on Iraq," *Washington Post,* October 24, 2001.

2. Quoted in Matthew Rothschild, "Iraq, Anthrax, and the Hawks," *Progressive* 65, no. 12 (October 22, 2001): 9–10.

3. Response to George Stephanopoulos, Air Force General Richard Myers, *This Week,* ABC, October 21, 2001.

4. Quoted in Derrick Z. Jackson, "The Masking of a Conservative," *Boston Globe,* November 23, 2005.

5. Quoted in Candace Cohn, "The Assault on Civil Liberties," *International Socialist Review* 22 (March/April 2002): 21.

6. Nancy Chang and the Center for Constitutional Rights, *Silencing Political Dissent* (New York: Seven Stories Press, 2002), 107.

7. "President Bush's Order on the Trial of Terrorists by Military Commission," *New York Times,* November 14, 2001.

8. Quoted in Susan Milligan, "Critics Aid Terrorists, AG argues," *Boston Globe,* December 7, 2001.

9. Cohn, "Assault on Civil Liberties," 21.

10. Chang and CCR, *Silencing Political Dissent,* 119.

11. Louis J. Freeh testimony to United States Senate Committees on Appropriations, Armed Services, and Select Committee on Intelligence, "Threat of Terrorism to the United States," May 10, 2001, http://www.fbi.gov/congress/congress01/freeh051001.htm.

12. Cohn, "Assault on Civil Liberties," 26 (emphasis added).

13. Anatol Lieven, "Decadent America Must Give Up Imperial Ambitions," *Financial Times,* November 29, 2005.

14. Chang and CCR, *Silencing Political Dissent,* 105.

15. David Cay Johnston, "Richest Are Leaving Even the Rich Far Behind," *New York Times,* June 5, 2005.

16. Harold Meyerson, "In Wal-Mart's America," *Washington Post,* August 27, 2003.

17. William Branigin, "U.S. Consumer Debt Grows at Alarming Rate: Debt Burden Will Intensify When Interest Rates Rise," *Washington Post,* January 12, 2004.

18. Julian Borger, "Long Queue at Drive-In Soup Kitchen," *Guardian* (UK), November 3, 2003.

19. Quoted in Bob Herbert, "Shhh, Don't Say 'Poverty,' " *New York Times*, November 22, 2004.

20. Quoted in William C. Symonds, "Colleges in Crisis," *Business Week* 3830 (April 28, 2003): 72.

21. Quoted in Bob Herbert, "The Young and the Jobless," *New York Times*, May 12, 2005.

22. James Lardner, "Many Causes, One Obstacle," updated paper presented at national conference on "Income Inequality, Socioeconomic Status, and Health: Exploring the Relationships," June 4, 2004, http://www.inequality.org.

23. United Nations Development Program, *Human Development Report 2005: International cooperation at a crossroads: Aid, trade and security in an unequal world*, 58.

24. Miriam Ching Yoon Louie, *Sweatshop Warriors: Immigrant Women Workers Take on the Global Factory* (Boston: South End Press, 2001), 4 (emphasis in original).

25. Daniel E. Bender and Richard A. Greenwald, eds., *Sweatshop USA: The American Sweatshop in Historical and Global Perspective* (New York: Routledge, 2003), 47.

26. Nancy L. Green, "Fashion, Flexible Specialization, and the Sweatshop," in Bender and Greenwald, *Sweatshop USA* (emphasis in original).

27. Robert Kuttner, "Growth Without Jobs," *Boston Globe*, December 9, 2003.

28. Jared Bernstein, "The Fog Machine," *American Prospect*, web exclusive, August 9, 2004, http://www.prospect.org/web/page.ww?section=root&name=ViewWeb&articleId=8316.

29. Economic Policy Institute, "Recovery Yet to Arrive for Working Families," press release, September 5, 2004 (emphasis in original).

30. Jared Bernstein and Isaac Shapiro, "Unhappy Anniversary: Federal Minimum Wage Remains Unchanged for Eighth Straight Year, Falls to 56-Year Low Relative to the Average Wage," Center on Budget and Policy Priorities and Economic Policy Institute, September 1, 2005, http://www.epi.org/content.cfm/epi_cbpp_20050901. Available as a PDF.

31. Jared Bernstein, "Wages Picture: Economy Continues to Expand, While Real Average Wages Experience Fastest Decline on Record," Economic Policy Institute, October 28, 2005, http://www.epi.org/content.cfm/webfeat_econindicators_wages_20051028.

32. Lichtenstein, *State of the Union*, 14.

33. Bernstein, "Economy Continues to Expand."

34. The Center for Tax and Budget Accountability and Northern Illinois University, *2005 State of Working Illinois*, http://www.stateofworkingillinois.niu.edu/swil/index.html. Available as PDF.

35. Steven Greenhouse, "How Do You Drive Out a Union? South Carolina Factory Provides a Textbook Case," *New York Times*, December 14, 2004.

36. Herbert, "Young and the Jobless."

37. George W. Bush, "President's Remarks on West Coast Ports," press release, October 8, 2002.

38. Lee Sustar, "An Attack on All Workers," *Socialist Worker*, October 18, 2002.

39. Sustar, "Labor Movement: State of Emergency," 22.

40. Mark Skertic and Michael Oneal, "Chapter 11 Closing in for Delta, Northwest

Bankruptcy Filings Possible This Week," *Chicago Tribune*, September 14, 2005.

41. Chris Kutalik, "The Bankruptcy Bomb: Companies Use Bankruptcy Threats and Courts to Force Bigger Givebacks, Break Unions," *MRZine*, October 25, 2005, http://mrzine.monthlyreview.org/kutalik251005.html.

42. Danny Hakim, "For a G.M. Family, the American Dream Vanishes," *New York Times*, November 19, 2005.

43. Robert J. Samuelson, "The Fate of 'Made in the USA,' " *Washington Post*, October 19, 2005.

44. Hakim, "For G.M. Family."

45. David Streitfeld, "U.S. Labor Is in Retreat as Global Forces Squeeze Pay and Benefits," *Los Angeles Times*, October 18, 2005.

46. Hakim, "For G.M. Family."

47. Robert Kuttner, "Desperation Deal at GM," *Boston Globe*, October 22, 2005.

48. Streitfeld, "U.S. Labor Is in Retreat."

49. Jeffrey McCracken, "UAW Files Protest to Delphi Bonuses for Top Executives," *Wall Street Journal*, November 25, 2005.

50. United for a Fair Economy and the Institute for Policy Studies, "CEO/Worker Pay Ratio Shoots Up to 431:1," press release, August 30, 2005.

51. Samuelson, "The Fate of 'Made in the USA.' "

52. "Shuttered Steel Plants Sail from U.S. to China," *Wall Street Journal*, December 8, 2003.

53. McCracken, "UAW Files Protest"; Streitfeld, "U.S. Labor Is in Retreat."

54. Kuttner, "Desperation Deal at GM."

55. Streitfeld, "U.S. Labor Is in Retreat."

56. Donald L. Bartlett and James B. Steele, "The Broken Promise," *Time* 166, no. 18 (Oct. 31, 2005).

57. Meyerson, "In Wal-Mart's America;" Bartlett and Steele, "Broken Promise."

58. Steven Greenhouse and Michael Barbaro, "Wal-Mart Memo Suggests Ways to Cut Employee Benefit Costs," *New York Times*, October 26, 2005.

59. Ibid.

60. Ibid.

61. Bartlett and Steele, "Broken Promise."

62. Kris Maher, "Strikes Multiply Amid Increase in Labor Fights," *Wall Street Journal*, November 15, 2005. The Washington, D.C., based Bureau of National Affairs, Inc. tracks work stoppages at companies of all sizes, unlike the U.S. Bureau of Labor Statistics, which only counts work stoppages involving one thousand or more employees.

63. Ibid.

64. Ibid.

65. Ibid.

66. Ibid.

67. Hakim, "For G.M. Family."

68. The UAW New Directions Movement, "Protect UAW Retirees: Their Future Is Our Future," *MRZine*, October 26, 2005, http://mrzine.monthlyreview.org/ndm261005.html.

69. U.S. Labor Against War, "AFL-CIO Calls for Rapid Return of U.S. Troops,"

press release, July 27, 2005.

70.   JoAnn Wypijewski, "Showdown in Chicago: Is This *Really* an 'Insurgency' to Shake Up the Labor Movement?" CounterPunch.org, July 22, 2005, http://www.counterpunch.org/jw07222005.html.

71.   Robert Fitch, "A More Perfect Union? Why Andy Stern Isn't Helping the American Labor Movement," *Slate,* July 27, 2005, http://www.slate.com/id/2123481/?nav=navoa.

72.   Wypijewski, "Showdown in Chicago."

73.   Jerry Tucker, "Whither Labor? A House Divided: For Better or for Worse" *MR-Zine,* August 6, 2005, http://mrzine.monthlyreview.org/aflcio2005.html.

74.   Lichtenstein, *State of the Union,* 276.

75.   Krugman, "For Richer,"63–64.

76.   Max B. Sawicky, "The Fruits of One's Labor," TomPaine.com, May 13, 2005, http://www.tompaine.com/articles/20050513/the_fruits_of_ones_labor.php.

77.   Ibid.

78.   Robert H. Frank, "The Income Gap Grows," *Philadelphia Inquirer,* November 27, 2005.

79.   Ibid.

80.   John Clizbe, quoted in John McQuaid and Mark Schleifstein, "The Big One: A Major Hurricane Could Decimate the Region, But Flooding from Even a Moderate Storm Could Kill Thousands," *Times-Picayune* (New Orleans), June 24, 2002.

81.   Edward Alden, "Bush's Policies Have Crippled Disaster Response Capabilities," *Financial Times,* September 3, 2005.

82.   Christopher Drew and Andrew C. Revkin, "Design Shortcomings Seen in New Orleans Flood Walls," *New York Times,* September 21, 2005.

83.   Sheila Grissett, "Shifting Federal Budget Erodes Protection from Levees," *Times-Picayune* (New Orleans), June 8, 2004.

84.   Jason DeParle, "What Happens to a Race Deferred," *New York Times,* September 4, 2005.

85.   John M. Broder, "Amid Criticism of Federal Efforts, Charges of Racism Are Lodged," *New York Times,* September 5, 2005.

86.   Jamie Doward, "They're Not Giving Us What We Need to Survive," *Observer* (UK), September 4, 2005.

87.   Gardiner Harris, "Police in Suburbs Blocked Evacuees, Witnesses Report," *New York Times,* September 10, 2005; Andrew Buncombe, " 'Racist' Police Blocked Bridge and Forced Evacuees Back at Gunpoint," *Independent* (UK), September 11, 2005.

88.   Scott Gold, " 'Forgotten' Forced to Survive on Katrina's Edge," *Los Angeles Times,* September 16, 2005.

89.   Associated Press, Frazier Moore, "Kanye West Rips Bush During NBC Concert," September 3, 2005; Lisa de Moraes, "Kanye West's Torrent of Criticism, Live on NBC," *Washington Post,* September 3, 2005.

90.   See Scott Henkel, "Bush Ignoring Poverty in the U.S.," *South Bend Tribune,* September 9, 2005.

91.   "Four Bloggers Make Their Marks and Money, Too," *Crain's Business New York* 21, no. 45 (November 7, 2005): 22; Maureen Dowd, "United States of Shame," *New York Times,* September 3, 2005.

92. Bob Herbert, "A Failure of Leadership," *New York Times,* September 5, 2005.

93. Associated Press, "White House Says Barbara Bush Was Making a 'Personal Observation,' " September 7, 2005; Bob Moon, "Houston, We May Have a Problem," *Marketplace,* American Public Media, September 5, 2005, http://marketplace.publicradio.org/shows/2005/09/05/PM200509051.html.

94. Michael Brown speaking on *The Situation Room,* CNN, September 1, 2005; Cynthia Tucker, "Hurricane Katrina: Poor Didn't Deserve This; Neglected by Nation, They Had No Options," *Atlanta Constitution-Journal,* September 7, 2005; Henkel, "Bush Ignoring Poverty."

95. Gannett News Service, Chuck Raasch, "Katrina Aftermath Spins Off Political Problems for Bush, Other Politicians," September 3, 2005; Dowd, "United States of Shame."

96. Dow Jones Commodities Service, "Special Summary of Hurricane Katrina's Impact," September 1, 2005; Associated Press, Kevin McGill, "Mayor of New Orleans Stepping Up Enforcement of Looting," September 1, 2005; Knight Ridder Newspapers, "Police, residents loot New Orleans stores after storm, Wednesday, August 31, 2005.

97. AFP/Reuters, "Troops Told 'Shoot to Kill' in New Orleans," September 2, 2005.

98. Joseph R. Chenelly, "Troops Begin Combat Operations in New Orleans," *ArmyTimes.com,* September 2, 2005, http://www.armytimes.com/story.php?f=1-292925-1077495.php.

99. Associated Press, Michelle Roberts, "Reports of New Orleans Mayhem Probably Exaggerated," September 28, 2005.

100. Ibid.

101. " 'This Is Criminal': Malik Rahim Reports from New Orleans," SF Bayview.com, September 1, 2005, http://www.sfbayview.com/083105/thisiscriminal083105.shtml.

102. Alden, "Bush's Policies Have Crippled Disaster Response."

103. David Leonhardt, "U.S. Poverty Rate Was Up Last Year," *New York Times,* August 31, 2005.

104. UN Development Program, *Human Development Report 2005,* 152.

105. Ibid.

106. Paul Vallely, "UN Hits Back at US in Report Saying Parts of America Are as Poor as Third World," *Independent* (UK), September 8, 2005.

107. See Phillips, *Politics of Rich and Poor.*

108. Testimony by Alan Greenspan, Chairman of the Board of Governors of the U.S. Federal Reserve System, before the Committee on Banking, Housing, and Urban Affairs, U.S. Senate, Washington, DC, February 16, 2005, FDCH transcripts, Congressional Hearings, http://cq.com/.

109. Marx and Engels, *Communist Manifesto,* 53.

110. Montgomery, *Fall of the House of Labor,* 464.

111. Stanley Aronowitz, "On the AFL-CIO Split," *Logos* 4, no. 3, Summer 2005, http://www.logosjournal.com/issue_4.3/aronowitz.htm. (emphasis added).

112. Tucker, "Whither Labor?"

113. Seth Sandronsky, "GM, the UAW, and U.S. Health Care," *MRZine,* August 18, 2005, http://mrzine.monthlyreview.org/sandronsky180805.html.

114. Moody, *Lean World,* 294.

115. Richard Hofstadter, *The Age of Reform from Bryan to F.D.R.* (New York: Vin-

tage, 1955), 66–67.

116.   Moody, *Lean World,* 309.

117.   Ibid.

118.   Marx and Engels, *Communist Manifesto,* 89.

Chapter 10

1.   See, for example, Mark Engler and Paul Engler, "The massive immigrant-rights protests of 2006 are still changing politics," *Los Angeles Times,* March 4, 2016. http://beta.latimes.com/opinion/op-ed/la-oe-0306-engler-immigration-protests-2006-20160306-story.html.

2.   Debbie Gruenstein Bocian, Wei Li, and Keith S. Ernst, "Foreclosures by Race and Ethnicity: The Demographics of a Crisis, Center for Responsible Lending Research Report," *Center for Responsible Lending,* June 18, 2010. http://www.responsiblelending.org/mortgage-lending/research-analysis/foreclosures-by-race-and-ethnicity.pdf.

3.   The Goldman Sachs Group, "Goldman Sachs Reports Earnings per Common Share of $4.47 for 2008," press release, December 16, 2008. http://www.goldmansachs.com/media-relations/press-releases/archived/2008/pdfs/2008-q4-earnings.pdf.

4.   Richard Teitelbaum and Hugh Son, "New York Fed's Secret Choice to Pay for Swaps Hits Taxpayers," *Bloomberg,* October 27, 2009. http://www.bloomberg.com/apps/news?pid=newsarchive&sid=a7T5HaOgYHpE.

5.   Stephen Labaton, "S.E.C. Concedes Oversight Flaws Fueled Collapse, *The New York Times,* September 27, 2008. http://www.nytimes.com/2008/09/27/business/27sec.html?pagewanted=print&_r=0.

6.   Ben Protess, "'Flawed' SEC Program Failed to Rein in Investment Banks,"*ProPublica,* October 1, 2008. http://www.propublica.org/article/flawed-sec-program-failed-to-rein-in-investment-banks-101.

7.   Gretchen Morgenson and Don Van Natta, Jr., "Paulson's Calls to Goldman Tested Ethics," *The New York Times,* August 9, 2009. http://www.nytimes.com/2009/08/09/business/09paulson.html?pagewanted=all.

8.   Greg Hitt, Sudeep Reddy, and Deborah Solomon, "Bernanke, Paulson Face Skeptics On the Hill Despite Dire Warnings," *The Wall Street Journal,* September 24, 2008. http://online.wsj.com/news/articles/SB122217048963566935.

9.   Michael J. de la Merced and Louise Story, "Nearly 700 at Merrill in Million-Dollar Club," *The New York Times,* February 11, 2009. http://www.nytimes.com/2009/02/12/business/12merrill.html?_r=0.

10.   David Wessel, "After Bear, a New Game: Line Between Banks, Securities Firms Blurs; Homeowner Bailout?" *The Wall Street Journal,* March 20, 2008. http://online.wsj.com/news/articles/SB120596496618950023.

11.   Dana Milbank, "Flying from Detroit on Corporate Jets, Auto Executives Ask Washington for Handouts," *The Washington Post,* November 20, 2008. http://www.washingtonpost.com/wp-dyn/content/article/2008/11/19/AR2008111903669.html.

12.   Elizabeth McDonald, "American Inconscionable Group," *Fox Business News,* March 17, 2009. http://www.foxbusiness.com/markets/2009/03/17/american-inconscionable-group/.

13.   David Paul Kuhn, "Exit polls: How Obama won," *Politico,* November 5, 2008.

https://www.politico.com/story/2008/11/exit-polls-how-obama-won-015297.

14. Lance Selfa, *The Democrats: A Critical History* (Chicago: Haymarket Books, 2008), 6.

15. Monica Davey, "In Factory Sit-In, an Anger Spread Wide," *The New York Times*, December 7, 2008. http://www.nytimes.com/2008/12/08/us/08chicago.html?_r=0.

16. Emmanuel Saez, UC Berkeley, "Striking it Richer: The Evolution of Top Incomes in the United States" (updated with 2012 preliminary estimates), September 3, 2013. http://elsa.berkeley.edu/~saez/saez-UStopincomes-2012.pdf.

17. Caroline Fairchild, "Top-Tier CEO Pay Grew Nearly 15 Times Faster Than Worker Pay Last Year," *Huffington Post*, October 22, 2013. http://www.huffingtonpost.com/2013/10/22/ceo-pay-worker-pay_n_4143859.html.

18. Connie Stewart, "Income gap between rich and poor is biggest in a century," *The Los Angeles Times*, September 11, 2013. http://articles.latimes.com/2013/sep/11/nation/la-na-nn-income-inequality-20130910.

19. Associated Press, "80 percent of U.S. adults face near-poverty, unemployment, survey finds," *CBS News*, July 28, 2013. http://www.cbsnews.com/news/80-percent-of-us-adults-face-near-poverty-unemployment-survey-finds/.

20. Ibid.

21. Mark R. Rank, "The Great Divide: Poverty in America is Mainstream," *The Opinion Pages, The New York Times*, November 2, 2013. http://opinionator.blogs.nytimes.com/2013/11/02/poverty-in-america-is-mainstream/?_r=0.

22. Ibid.

23. Hope Yen, "Rich-Poor Employment Gap Now Widest On Record," *Huffington Post*, September 16, 2013. Online at http://www.huffingtonpost.com/2013/09/16/rich-poor-employment-gap_n_3933757.html.

24. Lawrence Summers, "America needs a way to stem foreclosures," *The Financial Times*, February 24, 2008. http://www.ft.com/cms/s/0/471e6794-e2e7-11dc-803f-0000779fd2ac.html.

25. Yen, op cit.

26. Bocian et al, op cit.

27. Yen, op cit.

Chapter 11

1. Medea Benjamin, "From Cairo to Madison: Hope and Solidarity Are Alive," *Huffington Post*, February 21, 2011. http://www.huffingtonpost.com/medea-benjamin/from-cairo-to-madison-hop_b_826143.html.

2. Roger Bybee, "Presidential Ambitions Behind Wis. Gov. Walker's Unionbusting Stance?" *In These Times*, February 22, 2011. http://inthesetimes.com/working/entry/6991/wisconsins_walker_like_wallace_tries_hard-line_stance_presidential_amb/.

3. Bill Glauber and Tom Held, "Democratic senators return to Madison to tell crowd fight isn't over," *Milwaukee Journal Sentinel*, March 12, 2011. http://www.jsonline.com/news/statepolitics/117862214.html.

4. Andrew Cole and Phil Gasper, "Wisconsin: From the uprising to Recall Walker," *International Socialist Review* 83, May 2012. https://isreview.org/issue/83/wisconsin-uprising-recall-walker.

5. Molly Beck, "5 years after Act 10: Union membership, clout has suffered," *Wisconsin State Journal*, February 11, 2016. http://host.madison.com/wsj/news

/local/govt-and-politics/years-after-act-union-membership-clout-has-suffered/article_2abae2a5-17a1-53f0-9d6d-8b837be0506d.html.

6. Thomas Stackpole, "Meet the Ad Men Behind Occupy Wall Street, *The New Republic*, November 12, 2011. http://www.newrepublic.com/article/politics/97353/adbusters-kalle-lasn-occupy-wall-street.

7. Doug Singsen, "A balance sheet of Occupy Wall Street," *International Socialist Review* 81, January 2012. https://isreview.org/issue/81/balance-sheet-occupy-wall-street.

8. Dave Lindorff, "White House and Dems back banks over protests: Newly discovered Homeland Security files show Fed central to Occupy crackdown," *Nation of Change*, May 15, 2012. http://www.nationofchange.org/white-house-dems-back-banks-over-protests-newly-discovered-homeland-security-files-show-feds-central.

9. Occupy Wall Street, "You can't evict an idea whose time has come," Occupy-WallStreet: We are the 99 Percent, November 15, 2011. http://occupywallst.org/article/you-cant-evict-idea-whose-time-has-come/.

10. Eric (Rico) Gutstein and Pauline Lipman, "The Rebirth of the Chicago Teachers Union and Possibilities for a Counter-Hegemonic Education Movement," *Monthly Review* 65, no. 02, June 2013. http://monthlyreview.org/2013/06/01/the-rebirth-of-the-chicago-teachers-union-and-possibilities-for-a-counter-hegemonic-education-movement.

11. Robert Barlett, "Creating a New Model of a Social Union: CORE and the Chicago Teachers Union," *Monthly Review* 65, no. 02, June 2013. http://monthlyreview.org/2013/06/01/creating-a-new-model-of-a-social-union.

12. Cynthia Dizikes and John Byrne, "She will not cower: Union President Karen Lewis forged her confrontational style in the classroom," *Chicago Tribune*, September 11, 2012. http://articles.chicagotribune.com/2012-09-11/news/ct-met-teachers-strike-karen-lewis-20120911_1_chicago-teachers-union-union-president-chemistry-teacher.

13. Available online at http://www.ctunet.com/blog/text/SCSD_Report-02-16-2012-1.pdf.

14. Lee Sustar, "Toward a renewal of the labor movement: U.S. labor after the Chicago teachers' strike," *International Socialist Review* 89, May 2013. http://isreview.org/issue/89/toward-renewal-labor-movement.

15. Lee Sustar, "What the Chicago teachers accomplished," *International Socialist Review* 86, November 2012.

16. Jesse McKinley, "In California, Protests After Man Dies at Hands of Transit Police," *New York Times*, January 8, 2009. http://www.nytimes.com/2009/01/09/us/09oakland.html?mcubz=0.

17. "Ex-BART Officer Johannes Mehserle Released From Jail," *CBS SF Bay Area*, June 13, 2011. http://sanfrancisco.cbslocal.com/2011/06/13/ex-bart-officer-johannes-mehserle-released-from-prison/.

18. "CEDP Special Alert on Troy Davis," *Campaign to End the Death Penalty*, April 11, 2011. http://www.nodeathpenalty.org/organizing-updates/april-22-2011-organizing-update/cedp-special-alert-troy-davis.

19. Trymaine Lee, "Troy Davis' Execution Eve Sees Last-Minute Efforts To Save His Life," *Huffington Post*, September 20, 2011. http://www.huffingtonpost.com/2011/09/20/on-eve-of-troy-daviss-exe_n_972291.html.

20. Richard Kim, "Supreme Court Rejects Stay of Execution for Troy Davis," *The Nation*, September 21, 2011. https://www.thenation.com/article/supreme

-court-rejects-stay-execution-troy-davis/.

21. Ibid.

22. Daniel Beekman, "Grand jury will not re-indict cop Richard Haste who shot Bronx teen Ramarley Graham," *New York Daily News,* August 7, 2013. http://www.nydailynews.com/new-york/bronx/grand-jury-not-re-indict-shot-bronx-teen-article-1.1420828.

23. "Analysis finds racial disparities, ineffectiveness in NYPD stop-and-frisk program; links tactic to soaring marijuana arrest rate," New York Civil Liberties Union, May 22, 2013. https://www.nyclu.org/en/press-releases/analysis-finds-racial-disparities-ineffectiveness-nypd-stop-and-frisk-program-links.

24. Keeanga-Yamahtta Taylor, *From #Black Lives Matter to Black Liberation* (Chicago: Haymarket Books, 2016), 126, 122.

25. Alan Neuhauser and Steven Nelson, "Black Men May Have Reason to Run from Police, Mass. High Court Finds," *U.S. News & World Report,* September 21, 2016. https://www.usnews.com/news/articles/2016-09-21/black-men-may-have-reason-to-run-from-police-massachusetts-high-court-finds.

26. Taylor, 125.

27. Taylor, 126–27.

28. Associated Press, "Chicago Police Detective Cleared of Manslaughter in Shooting Death, *New York Times,* April 20, 2015. https://www.nytimes.com/2015/04/21/us/chicago-police-detective-cleared-of-manslaughter-in-shooting-death.html?_r=1.

29. *Chicago Tribune* Editorial Board, "Rekia Boyd shooting was 'beyond reckless,' so cop got a pass," *Chicago Tribune,* April 22, 2015. http://www.chicagotribune.com/news/opinion/editorials/ct-cop-verdict-servin-edit-0423-20150422-story.html.

30. Bay City News, "Family of teen killed by Oakland police receives $110K settlement," *ABC 7 News,* June 4, 2014. http://abc7news.com/news/family-of-teen-killed-by-oakland-police-receives-$110k-settlement/94178/.

31. Aaron Sankin, "Alan Blueford Killing: Officer At Center Of Controversial Police Shooting Escapes Charges," *Huffington Post,* October 11, 2012. http://www.huffingtonpost.com/2012/10/10/alan-blueford-killing-off_n_1955211.html.

32. Jeralynn Blueford, "Stop Police Officers from Killing Our Children," *Common Dreams,* December 03, 2014. https://www.commondreams.org/views/2014/12/03/stop-police-officers-killing-our-children.

33. CNN Library, "Trayvon Martin Shooting Fast Facts, *CNN,* June 22, 2017. http://www.cnn.com/2013/06/05/us/trayvon-martin-shooting-fast-facts/index.html. Peter Andrew Bosch, "A teen was shot by a watchman 5 years ago. And the Trayvon Martin case became a cause," *Miami Herald,* February 28, 2017. http://www.miamiherald.com/news/state/florida/article135413214.html.

34. Yamiche Alcindor, "George Zimmerman found not guilty," *USA Today,* July 13, 2013. https://www.usatoday.com/story/news/nation/2013/07/13/george-zimmerman-found-not-guilty/2514163/.

35. Alyssa Newcomb, "George Zimmerman Juror Says 'In Our Hearts, We Felt He Was Guilty,'" *ABC News,* July 25, 2013. http://abcnews.go.com/US/george-zimmerman-juror-murder/story?id=19770659.

36. See *Dream Defenders* at http://www.dreamdefenders.org/.

37. "About the Black Lives Matter Network," *Black Lives Matter,* undated. http://blacklivesmatter.com/.

38. Barbara Starr and Wesley Bruer, "Missouri National Guard's term for Fergu-

son protesters: 'Enemy forces,'" *CNN,* April 17, 2015. http://www.cnn.com /2015/04/17/politics/missouri-national-guard-ferguson-protesters/index.html.

39. Robert Samuels, "Protesters in Ferguson, Mo., stand their ground, police ease up," *Washington Post,* September 30, 2014. https://www.washingtonpost.com /news/post-nation/wp/2014/09/30/police-in-ferguson-mo-ease-up-on-peaceful -protesters/?utm_term=.15d48fbd83f1.

40. Cory Howard, "NFL won't discipline Rams players for 'Hands up, don't shoot' gesture," *KULR News,* December 1, 2014. http://www.kulr8.com/story /27517799/nfl-wont-discipline-rams-players-for-hands-up-dont-shoot-gesture.

41. Sari Horwitz, "Justice Department clears Ferguson police officer in civil rights probe," *Washington Post,* March 4, 2015. https://www.washingtonpost.com /world/national-security/justice-dept-review-finds-pattern-of-racial-bias-among -ferguson-police/2015/03/03/27535390-c1c7-11e4-9271-610273846239_story .html?utm_term=.506105855299.

42. Larry Celona, Kirstan Conley, and Bruce Golding, "Cop cleared in chokehold death of Eric Garner," *New York Post,* December 3, 2014. http://nypost.com /2014/12/03/cop-cleared-in-eric-garner-chokehold-death/.

43. Carimah Townes, "The officer who killed Eric Garner got a big raise. The man who filmed him is in jail," *Think Progress,* September 13, 2016. https:// thinkprogress.org/the-police-officer-who-killed-eric-garner-just-got-a-huge-pay -bump-9d854e6e9d65/.

44. Timothy Williams and Mitch Smith, "Cleveland Officer Will Not Face Charges in Tamir Rice Shooting Death," *New York Times,* December 28, 2015. https://www .nytimes.com/2015/12/29/us/tamir-rice-police-shootiing-cleveland.html?_r=0.

45. John Swaine and Oliver Laughland, "Eric Garner and Tamir Rice among those missing from FBI record of police killings," *The Guardian*, October 15, 2015. https://www.theguardian.com/us-news/2015/oct/15/fbi-record-police-killings -tamir-rice-eric-garner.

46. Database, "Fatal Force," *The Washington Post,* September 22, 2017. https:// www.washingtonpost.com/graphics/national/police-shootings-2016/.

47. Database, "The Counted: People killed by police in the US," *The Guardian*, September 22, 2017. https://www.theguardian.com/us-news/ng-interactive /2015/jun/01/the-counted-police-killings-us-database.

48. Alan Neuhauser, "Black Males 3 Times More Likely to Be Killed by Police," *U.S. News & World Report*, December 21, 2016. https://www.usnews.com/news /national-news/articles/2016-12-21/black-males-nearly-3-times-more-likely-to -be-killed-by-police-than-whites.

49. Taylor, 131.

50. "Freddie Gray's death in police custody - what we know," *BBC News,* May 23, 2016. http://www.bbc.com/news/world-us-canada-32400497.

51. Scott Dance, "Freddie Gray's spinal injury suggests 'forceful trauma,' doctors say," *Baltimore Sun*, April 21, 2015. http://www.baltimoresun.com/health/bs-hs -gray-injuries-20150420-story.html.

52. Op cit. *BBC News,* May 23, 2016.

53. Justin Fenton, "Autopsy of Freddie Gray shows 'high-energy' impact," *Baltimore Sun,* June 24, 2015. http://www.baltimoresun.com/news/maryland/freddie -gray/bs-md-ci-freddie-gray-autopsy-20150623-story.html.

54. Taylor, 76–80.

55. Jon Schuppe, "Justice Department Won't Charge Six Officers in Freddie Gray

Death," *NBC News*, September 12, 2017. https://www.nbcnews.com/storyline /baltimore-unrest/justice-department-won-t-charge-six-officers-freddie-gray-death -n800786.

56. Susan Page and Fernanda Crescente, "Police violence a rising concern for Millennials, new poll shows," *USA Today*, August 14, 2016. https://www .usatoday.com/story/news/politics/elections/2016/08/14/police-violence-rising -concern-millennials-new-poll-shows/88712432/.

57. Rebekah Metzler, "Obama: I Am Not a Socialist: At CEO Council, Obama says Washington must shed rhetoric to work," *U.S. News & World Report*, November 19, 2013. http://www.usnews.com/news/articles/2013/11/19/obama-i-am -not-a-socialist.

58. Applebaum was the then-president of the Retail, Wholesale and Department Store Union (RWDSU). Rob Roehr, "National Equality March draws 100,000 to DC, *The Bay Area Reporter*, October 15, 2009. http://www.ebar.com/news /article.php?sec=news&article=4270.

59. Huffpost Gay Voices, "Gallup Gay Marriage Poll Finds Majority Of U.S. Citizens Would Support Nationwide Marriage Equality Law," *Huffington Post*, July 31, 2013. Frank Newport, "For First Time, Majority of Americans Favor Legal Gay Marriage, *Gallup Politics*, May 20, 2011. http://www.gallup.com /poll/147662/first-time-majority-americans-favor-legal-gay-marriage.aspx.

60. Dan Clawson, "SEIU: How Democratic?" *MR Online*, May 20, 2008. https:// mronline.org/2008/05/20/seiu-how-democratic/.

61. David Winograd, "80 Percent Want Minimum Wage Raised To $10.10 Per Hour: Poll," *Huffington Post*, August 1, 2013. http://www.huffingtonpost.com /david-winograd/.

62. Kim Moody, "Contextualising Organised Labour in Expansion and Crisis: The Case of the US," *Historical Materialism* Brill, 20.1 (2012), 25.

63. Ibid.

Chapter 12

1. Neetzan Zimmerman, "Trump retweets Mussolini quote," *The Hill*, February 28, 2016. http://thehill.com/blogs/blog-briefing-room/news/271078-trump-responds -to-retweet-Mussolini.

2. Sam Tanenhaus, "Book Review: 'Nut Country' and 'Right Out of California,'" *The New York Times*, December 14, 2015. https://www.nytimes.com/2015/12/20 /books/review/nut-country-and-right-out-of-california.html?rref=collection %2Fbyline%2Fsam-tanenhaus&action=click&contentCollection=undefined &region=stream&module=stream_unit&version=search&contentPlacemen t=5&pgtype=collection.

3. Ibid.

4. Tim Dickinson, "Inside the Koch Brothers' Toxic Empire," *Rolling Stone*, September 24, 2014. http://www.rollingstone.com/politics/news/inside-the-koch -brothers-toxic-empire-20140924.

5. Jane Mayer, "Covert Operations: The billionaire brothers who are waging a war against Obama," *The New Yorker*, August 30, 2010. https://www.newyorker .com/magazine/2010/08/30/covert-operations.

6. Kate Zernike and Megan Thee-Brenan, "Poll Finds Tea Party Backers Wealthier and More Educated," *The New York Times*, April 14, 2010. http://www.nytimes .com/2010/04/15/us/politics/15poll.html.

7.   Ibid.

8.   Ibid.

9.   Ibid.

10. Maureen Dowd, "When Hillary and Donald were friends," *The New York Times*, November 2, 2016. https://www.nytimes.com/2016/11/06/magazine/when -hillary-and-donald-were-friends.html?_r=0.

11. Ashley Parker and Steve Eder, "Inside the Six Weeks Donald Trump Was a Non-stop 'Birther,'" *The New York Times*, July 2, 2016. https://www.nytimes.com /2016/07/03/us/politics/donald-trump-birther-obama.html.

12. Ibid.

13. "How Trump won: The revenge of working-class whites," *Washington Post*, November 9, 2016. https://www.google.com/search?q=Revenge+of+white+working +class+voters&oq=Revenge+of+white+working+class+voters&aqs=chrome ..69i57.11521j0j1&sourceid=chrome&ie=UTF-8#q=Revenge+of+white+voters.

14. "The Revenge of the White Man," *Time*, http://time.com/4566304/donald -trump-revenge-of-the-white-man/.

15. "Revenge of the Forgotten Class," *ProPublica*, https://www.propublica.org /article/revenge-of-the-forgotten-class.

16. "Revenge of the Rural Voter," *Politico*, http://www.politico.com/story/2016/11 /hillary-clinton-rural-voters-trump-231266.

17. "Why Trump Won: Working-class Whites," *New York Times*, November 9, 2016, https://www.nytimes.com/2016/11/10/upshot/why-trump-won-working-class -whites.html.

18. Nate Silver, "The Mythology of Trump's 'Working Class' Support," *FiveThirty Eight*, May 3, 2016. https://fivethirtyeight.com/features/the-mythology-of-trumps -working-class-support/. For the general election income data on Trump voters, see Nicholas Carnes and Noam Lupu, "It's time to bust the myth: Most Trump voters were not working class," *Washington Post*, June 5, 2017. https://www .washingtonpost.com/news/monkey-cage/wp/2017/06/05/its-time-to-bust-the -myth-most-trump-voters-were-not-working-class/?utm_term=.94cf625e601c.

19. Carnes and Lupu, op cit.

20. Ibid.

21. Elizabeth Catte, "The Mythical Whiteness of Trump Country," *Boston Review*, November 7, 2017. http://bostonreview.net/race-politics/elizabeth-catte-mythical -whiteness-trump-country.

22. Ibid.

23. Mark Lilla, "The End of Identity Liberalism," *The New York Times*, November.18, 2016. https://www.nytimes.com/2016/11/20/opinion/sunday/the-end-of-identity -liberalism.html.

24. Bryanna Cappadona, "Here's what Bernie Sanders had to say about transgender bathroom rights: He shared his thoughts on last night's 'Jimmy Kimmel Live!'" *Boston.com*, May 27, 2016. https://www.boston.com/culture/tv/2016/05/27 /heres-bernie-sanders-say-transgender-bathroom-rights.

25. William H. Frey, "Five Charts That Show Why a Post-White America Is Already Here," *New Republic*, November 21, 2014. https://newrepublic.com /article/120370/five-graphics-show-why-post-white-america-already-here.

26. Nate Cohn, "How the Obama Coalition Crumbled, Leaving an Opening for Trump," *The New York Times*, December 23, 2016. https://www.nytimes.com /2016/12/23/upshot/how-the-obama-coalition-crumbled-leaving-an-opening-for

-trump.html.

27. The 2016 Cooperative Congressional Election Survey concluded that 12 percent of Sanders' primary supporters ended up voting for Trump in November 2016. While this is a small portion overall, *Newsweek* writer Jason Le Miere reported, "In each of the three states that ultimately swung the election for Trump—Michigan, Wisconsin and Pennsylvania—Trump's margin of victory over Clinton was smaller than the number of Sanders voters who gave him their vote." Jason Le Miere, "Bernie Sanders Voters Helped Trump Win and Here's Proof," *Newsweek,* August 23, 2017. http://www.newsweek.com/bernie-sanders-trump -2016-election-654320?amp=1.

28. Robert Dreyfuss, "How the DLC Does It," *The American Prospect,* December 19, 2001. http://prospect.org/article/how-dlc-does-it.

29. Ibid.

30. Feliz Solomon, "Hillary Clinton Called for Strikes on Syrian Airfields Shortly Before Trump's Announcement," *Time,* April 6, 2017. http://time.com/4730416 /syria-missile-attack-hillary-clinton-assad/.

31. Marisa Schultz, "Inside Hillary's $675K worth of Goldman speaking fees," *New York Post,* February 5, 2016. http://nypost.com/2016/02/05/inside-hillarys -675k-worth-of-goldman-speaking-fees/.

32. Daniel Strauss, "Clinton haunted by coal country comment," *Politico,* May 10, 2016. http://www.politico.com/story/2016/05/sanders-looking-to-rack-up-west -virginia-win-over-clinton-222952.

33. Cohn, op cit.

34. Adam B. Lerner, "The 10 best lines from Donald Trump's announcement speech," *Politico,* June 16, 2015. http://www.politico.com/story/2015/06 /donald-trump-2016-announcement-10-best-lines-119066.

35. "Transcript: Donald Trump's Taped Comments About Women, *The New York Times,* October 8, 2016. https://www.nytimes.com/2016/10/08/us/donald -trump-tape-transcript.html.

36. Christian Parenti, "Listening to Trump," *CommonDreams,* November 21, 2016. https://www.commondreams.org/views/2016/11/21/listening-trump.

37. "Election 2016: Exit Polls," *CNN Politics,* November 23, 2017. http://www .cnn.com/election/results/exit-polls.

38. See, for example, Akhil Reed Amar, "The Troubling Reason the Electoral College Exists," *Time,* November 8, 2016 [updated November 10, 2016]. http:// time.com/4558510/electoral-college-history-slavery/.

39. Erik Sherman, "America is the richest, and most unequal, country, *Forbes,* September 30, 2015. http://fortune.com/2015/09/30/america-wealth-inequality/.

40. "Declining trust in government is denting democracy: According to a new index, America's democracy score deteriorated in 2016," *The Economist,* January 25, 2017. http://www.economist.com/blogs/graphicdetail/2017/01/daily-chart-20 Elena Holodny, "The U.S. has been downgraded to a 'flawed democracy,'" *Business Insider,* January 25, 2017. http://www.businessinsider.com/economist -intelligence-unit-downgrades-united-states-to-flawed-democracy-2017-1.

41. Mark Weisbrot, Stephan Lefebvre, and Joseph Sammut, "Did NAFTA Help Mexico? An Assessment After 20 Years," *Center for Economic and Policy Research,* February 2014. http://cepr.net/documents/nafta-20-years-2014-02.pdf.

42. Kim Moody, "U.S. Workers in the Late Neoliberal Era," *International Viewpoint,* August 13, 2017. http://www.internationalviewpoint.org/spip.php?article5093.

43. Kim Moody, *On New Terrain: How Capital Is Reshaping the Battleground of Class War*, (Chicago: Haymarket Books, 2017).

44. Economic News Release: Work Stoppages summary, *Bureau of Labor Statistics*, February 9, 2017. https://www.bls.gov/news.release/wkstp.nr0.htm.

45. Bureau of Labor Statistics, U.S. Department of Labor, "Union membership rate 10.7 percent in 2016," *The Economics Daily*, February 9, 2017. https://www.bls.gov/opub/ted/2017/union-membership-rate-10-point-7-percent-in-2016.htm.

46. Charity Jackson, "18 to 29 things you didn't know about young workers," *Main Street, a project of Working America*, March 12, 2015. http://blog.workingamerica.org/2015/03/12/18-to-29-things-you-didnt-know-about-young-workers/. Elizabeth Bruenig, "Even Conservative Millennials Support Unions, *New Republic*, May 1, 2015. https://newrepublic.com/article/121688/pew-releases-new-labor-survey-millennials-supports-unions.

47. Justin Lahart, "If Jobs are Plentiful, How Come No One is Getting a Raise?" *Wall Street Journal*, June 2, 2017. https://www.wsj.com/articles/if-jobs-are-plentiful-how-come-no-one-is-getting-a-raise-1496420365.

48. Andy Kiersz, "America Is No. 1 In Low-Paying Jobs," *Business Insider*, September 23, 2014. http://www.businessinsider.com/oecd-low-wage-paying-jobs-by-country-2014-9.

49. Paul Mason, "The strange case of America's disappearing middle class," *The Guardian*, December 14, 2015. https://www.theguardian.com/commentisfree/2015/dec/14/the-strange-case-of-americas-disappearing-middle-class.

50. Steve Benen, "Poverty goes down, coverage goes up, and America gets a raise," *MSNBC*, September 13, 2016. http://www.msnbc.com/rachel-maddow-show/poverty-goes-down-coverage-goes-and-america-gets-raise.

51. Census Bureau, "ND child poverty data highlights local racial disparities," *KFGO*, September 20, 2016. http://kfgo.com/news/articles/2016/sep/20/nd-child-poverty-data-highlights-local-racial-disparities/.

52. Kristi Tanner, "Michigan posts its largest income gain since the recession," *Detroit Free Press*, September 15, 2016. http://www.freep.com/story/news/local/michigan/2016/09/15/michigan-posts-its-largest-income-gain-since-recession/90308316/.

53. Claire Zippel, "As DC has grown, so has its racial prosperity gap," *Greater Greater Washington*, September 22, 2016. https://ggwash.org/view/42944/as-dc-has-grown-so-has-its-racial-prosperity-gap.

54. Max Roser, "Price changes in consumer goods and services in the USA, 1997-2017," *Our World in Data*, accessed September 29, 2017. https://ourworldindata.org/grapher/price-changes-in-consumer-goods-and-services-in-the-usa-1997-2017.

55. Dr. Amy K. Glasmeier, "Introduction to the living wage model," MIT Department of Urban Studies and Planning, 2017. http://livingwage.mit.edu/pages/about.

56. Dr. Carey Anne Nadeau, "A Calculation of the Living Wage," MIT Department of Urban Studies and Planning, February 7, 2017. http://livingwage.mit.edu/resources/Living-Wage-Findings-2016.pdf.

57. Dr. Amy K. Glasmeier and Carey Anne Nadeau, "Results from the 2016 data update," *OpenDataNation.com*, April 13, 2017. http://livingwage.mit.edu/articles/23-results-from-the-2016-data-update.

58. Richard Vedder and Justin Strehle, "The Diminishing Returns of a College Degree," *Wall Street Journal*, June 4, 2017. https://www.wsj.com/articles/the-diminishing-returns-of-a-college-degree-1496605241.

59. Kenneth Rapoza, "China-Like Wages Now Part Of U.S. Employment Boom," *Forbes*, August 4, 2017. https://www.forbes.com/sites/kenrapoza/2017/08/04/china-like-wages-now-part-of-u-s-employment-boom/#4bf5b926128a.

60. "America's Divided Recovery: College Haves and Have-Nots 2016," Georgetown University, Center on Education and the Workforce, McCourt School of Public Policy, June 30, 2016. https://cew.georgetown.edu/cew-reports/americas-divided-recovery/.

61. Neil Irwin, "Why American Workers Without Much Education Are Being Hammered," *The New York Times*, April 21, 2015. https://www.nytimes.com/2015/04/22/upshot/why-workers-without-much-education-are-being-hammered.html.

62. David R. Howell, "The Collapse of Low-Skill Wages: Technological Change or Institutional Failure?" National Jobs for All Coalition, February 1998. http://njfac.org/index.php/us13/.

63. Jessica Contrera and Bonnie Jo Mount, "The Sickness of American Healthcare," *Fairness and Accuracy in Reporting (FAIR)*, March 11, 2017. http://us10.campaign-archive1.com/?e=a96e35dd0a&u=8c573daa3ad72f4a095505b58&id=a7ba35e111.

64. Ibid.

65. Trip Gabriel, "When Health Law Isn't Enough, the Desperate Line Up at Tents," *The New York Times,* July 23, 2017. https://www.nytimes.com/2017/07/23/us/healthcare-uninsured-rural-poor-affordable-care-act-republicans.html?_r=0.

66. Salena Zito, "The day that destroyed the working class and sowed the seeds of Trump," *New York Post*, September 16, 2017. http://nypost.com/2017/09/16/the-day-that-destroyed-the-working-class-and-sowed-the-seeds-for-trump/.

67. William K. Alcorn, "Youngstown leads nation with poverty rate of 49.7%," *The Valley's Homepage: Vindy.com*, November 3, 2011. http://www.vindy.com/news/2011/nov/03/youngstown-leads-nation-poverty-rate-497/.

68. Chris Hedges, "Heroes for the Beaten, Foreclosed on, Imprisoned Masses," *Truthdig*, October 18, 2010. http://truth-out.org/archive/component/k2/item/92361:heroes-for-the-beaten-foreclosed-on-imprisoned-masses.

69. Ken Stern, "In Trump country, true believers are still holding their breath for the embattled president," *Vanity Fair,* May 30, 2017. https://www.vanityfair.com/news/2017/05/in-trump-country-true-believers-are-still-holding-their-breath.

70. Jennifer Calfas, "President Trump Tweets Attorney General Jeff Sessions Is 'Very Weak' on Hillary Clinton," *Time*, July 25, 2017. http://time.com/4872242/trump-tweet-sessions-hillary-clinton/.

71. Reuters, "Factbox: Price Resignation Is Latest Trump Administration Departure," *U.S. News & World Report,* September 29, 2017. https://www.usnews.com/news/top-news/articles/2017-09-29/factbox-price-resignation-is-latest-trump-administration-departure.

72. Phillip Carter, "The Four Big Scandals of the Trump Administration," *Slate*, July 11, 2017. http://www.slate.com/articles/news_and_politics/politics/2017/07/the_four_big_scandals_of_the_trump_administration.html.

73. T. A. Frank, "Can Jared Kushner be put out of his misery?" *Vanity Fair,* October 4, 2017. https://www.vanityfair.com/news/2017/10/can-jared-kushner-be-put-out-of-his-misery.

74. John Dawsey and Andrea Peterson, "Hundreds of White House emails sent to third Kushner family account," *Politico, October 2, 2017.* http://www.politico.com/story/2017/10/02/jared-kushner-email-account-white-house-243389.

75. Kathryn Watson, "Trump tax plan remarks—live updates," *CBS News*, Septem-

ber 27, 2017. https://www.cbsnews.com/live-news/trump-tax-plan-remarks-live
-updates/.

76. Edward J. McCaffery, "Trump's massive tax cut -- for the rich," *CNN*, September
     27, 2017. http://www.cnn.com/2017/09/27/opinions/trump-tax-plan-opinion
     -mccaffery/index.html.

77. Editorial Board, "Will Trump's tax cuts profit Trump?" *The Washington Post*,
     October 1, 2017. https://www.washingtonpost.com/opinions/will-trumps-tax
     -cuts-profit-trump/2017/10/01/6858c8dc-a54c-11e7-ade1-76d061d56efa_story
     .html?utm_term=.81535b124f6e.

78. Cristiano Lima, "After health care loss, Trump tweets 'let ObamaCare implode,'"
     Politico, July 28, 2017. http://www.politico.com/story/2017/07/28/trump-tweets
     -let-obamacare-implode-241068. Ali Vitali, "After Health Care Defeat, Trump
     Pushes Obamacare Implosion," *NBC News*, July 28, 2017. https://www.nbcnews
     .com/politics/white-house/after-healthcare-defeat-trump-pushes-obamacare
     -implosion-n787591.

79. Vann R. Newkirk II, "Trump Reverses Obama Rule on Birth Control," *The At-
     lantic*, October 6, 2017. https://www.theatlantic.com/politics/archive/2017/10
     /the-trump-administration-dismantles-the-contraceptive-mandate/542298/.

80. Robert Pear, Maggie Haberman, and Reed Abelson, "Trump to Scrap Criti-
     cal Health Care Subsidies, Hitting Obamacare Again," *The New York Times*,
     October 12, 2017. https://www.nytimes.com/2017/10/12/us/politics/trump
     -obamacare-executive-order-health-insurance.html.

81. Stephanie Ebbs and Gloria Riviera, "Trump's budget cuts funding for Superfund
     sites, clean air and water programs," *ABC News*, May 23, 2017. http://abc-
     news.go.com/Politics/trumps-budget-cuts-epa-31-percent-campaign-promise
     /story?id=47583180.

82. Robinson Meyer, "Oil Is Flowing Through the Dakota Access Pipeline," *The
     Atlantic*, June 9, 2017. https://www.theatlantic.com/science/archive/2017/06/
     oil-is-flowing-through-the-dakota-access-pipeline/529707/.

83. Michael D. Shear, "Trump Will Withdraw U.S. From Paris Climate Agreement,"
     The New York Times, June 1, 2017. https://www.nytimes.com/2017/06/01/cli-
     mate/trump-paris-climate-agreement.html.

84. Alan Yuhas and Mazin Sidahmed, "Is this a Muslim ban? Trump's executive order
     explained," *The Guardian*, January 31, 2017. https://www.theguardian.com
     /us-news/2017/jan/28/trump-immigration-ban-syria-muslims-reaction-lawsuits.

85. Matt Zapotosky, "The government now says 746 people were held due to
     the travel ban. Here's why that number keeps changing," *The Washington
     Post*, February 24, 2017. https://www.washingtonpost.com/news/post-nation
     /wp/2017/02/24/the-government-now-says-746-people-were-held-due-to-the
     -travel-ban-heres-why-that-number-keeps-changing/?utm_term=.2c929278fec7.

86. Anjali Singhvi and Alicia Parlapiano, "Who Would Be Barred by Trump's Latest
     Immigration Ban," *The New York Times*, March 6, 2017. https://www.nytimes
     .com/interactive/2017/03/06/us/politics/trump-travel-ban-groups.html.

87. Marjorie Cohn, "Trump's Muslim ban 3.0 is still unconstitutional," *Truthout*,
     September 27, 2017. http://www.truth-out.org/news/item/42079-trump-s-muslim
     -ban-3-0-is-still-unconstitutional.

88. Philip Bump, "Trump's speech encouraging police to be 'rough,' annotated," *The
     Washington Post*, July 28, 2017. https://www.washingtonpost.com/news/politics
     /wp/2017/07/28/trumps-speech-encouraging-police-to-be-rough-annotated/?utm
     _term=.d85110b994a3.

89. Julie Hirschfeld Davis and Maggie Haberman, "Trump Pardons Joe Arpaio, Who Became Face of Crackdown on Illegal Immigration," *The New York Times,* August 25, 2017. https://www.nytimes.com/2017/08/25/us/politics/joe -arpaio-trump-pardon-sheriff-arizona.html.

90. Jacey Fortin, "A Guide to Joe Arpaio, the Longtime Sheriff Who Escaped Strife," *The New York Times*, August 27, 2017. https://www.nytimes.com/2017/08/27 /us/joe-arpaio-sheriff-pardon.html?action=click&contentCollection=Politics &module=RelatedCoverage&region=EndOfArticle&pgtype=article.

91. Tal Kopan, "ICE: Arrests still up, deportations still down," *CNN,* August 11, 2017. http://www.cnn.com/2017/08/11/politics/trump-administration -deportations/index.html. Serena Marshall, "Obama Has Deported More People Than Any Other President," *ABC News,* August 29, 2017. http://abcnews .go.com/Politics/obamas-deportation-policy-numbers/story?id=41715661.

92. Tom Dart, "Undocumented Texas woman arrested while seeking domestic violence help," *The Guardian,* February 16, 2017. https://www.theguardian.com /us-news/2017/feb/16/texas-undocumented-woman-arrested-el-paso-domestic -violence.

93. Andrea Castillo, "Immigrant arrested by ICE after dropping daughter off at school, sending shockwaves through neighborhood, *Los Angeles Times,* March 3, 2017. http://www.latimes.com/local/lanow/la-me-immigration-school-20170303 -story.html.

94. John Burnett, "Border Patrol Arrests Parents While Infant Awaits Serious Operation," *NPR,* September 20, 2017. http://www.npr.org/2017/09/20/552339976 /border-patrol-arrests-parents-while-infant-awaits-serious-operation.

95. Erik Ortiz, "'Sanctuary' Cities Targeted by ICE in Immigration Raids as Nearly 500 Arrested," *NBC News,* September 29, 2017. https://www.nbcnews.com /storyline/immigration-border-crisis/sanctuary-cities-targeted-ice-immigration -raids-nearly-500-arrested-n805796.

96. Eric Westervelt, "ICE Raids Target Sanctuary Cities," *NPR,* September 29, 2017. http://www.npr.org/2017/09/29/554424186/ice-raids-target-sanctuary-cities.

97. John Roberts, Kaitlyn Schallhorn, Brooke Singman and Alex Pappas, "Trump administration ends DACA, with 6-month delay," *Fox News,* September 5, 2017. http://www.foxnews.com/politics/2017/09/05/trump-administration-ends -daca-with-6-month-delay.html.

98. Daniel Trotta, "Trump revokes Obama guidelines on transgender bathrooms," *Reuters,* February 22, 2017. https://www.reuters.com/article/us-usa-trump-lgbt /trump-revokes-obama-guidelines-on-transgender-bathrooms-idUSKBN161243.

99. Julie Hirschfeld Davis and Helene Cooper, "Trump Says Transgender People Will Not Be Allowed in the Military," *The New York Times,* July 26, 2017. https:// www.nytimes.com/2017/07/26/us/politics/trump-transgender-military.html.

100. Charles Savage, "In Shift, Justice Dept. Says Law Doesn't Bar Transgender Discrimination," *The New York Times,* October 5, 2017. https://www.nytimes .com/2017/10/05/us/politics/transgender-civil-rights-act-justice-department -sessions.html.

101. Alan Maass, "Our resistance in the era of political whiplash," *Socialist Worker.org,* September 13, 2017. https://socialistworker.org/2017/09/13/our-resistance-in -the-era-of-political-whiplash.

102. Ben Mathis-Lilley, "How Trump Has Cultivated the White Supremacist Alt-Right for Years," *Slate,* August 14, 2017. http://www.slate.com/blogs/the_slatest /2017/08/14/donald_trump_s_ties_to_alt_right_white_supremacists_are _extensive.html.

103. Adam Gabbatt, "Hitler salutes and white supremacism: a weekend with the 'alt-right,'" *The Guardian*, November 21, 2016. https://www.theguardian.com/world /2016/nov/21/alt-right-conference-richard-spencer-white-nationalists.   Daniel Lombroso and Yoni Appelbaum, "'Hail Trump!': White Nationalists Salute the President-Elect," *The Atlantic*, November 21, 2016. https://www.theatlantic.com /politics/archive/2016/11/richard-spencer-speech-npi/508379/.

104. Holly Yan, Darran Simon, and Aileen Graef, "Campus killing: Suspect is a member of 'Alt-Reich' Facebook group, police say," *CNN*, May 22, 2017. http:// www.cnn.com/2017/05/22/us/university-of-maryland-stabbing/index.html.

105. Amy B. Wang, "'Brave and selfless' Oregon stabbing victims hailed as heroes for standing up to racist rants," *The Washington Post*, May 28, 2017. https:// www.washingtonpost.com/news/post-nation/wp/2017/05/28/brave-and-selfless -oregon-stabbing-victims-hailed-as-heroes/?utm_term=.4b5fbe04e7cd.

106. Ibid.

107. See, for example, Alan Taylor, "'Not My President': Thousands March in Protest," *The Atlantic*, November 10, 2016. https://www.theatlantic.com/photo /2016/11/not-my-president-thousands-march-in-protest/507248/.

108. Matt Ford, "Trump's Press Secretary Falsely Claims: 'Largest Audience Ever to Witness an Inauguration, Period,'" *The Atlantic*, January 21, 2017. https://www .theatlantic.com/politics/archive/2017/01/inauguration-crowd-size/514058/.

109. Heidi M. Przybyla and Fredreka Schouten, "At 2.6 million strong, Women's Marches crush expectations," *USA Today*, January 21, 2017. https://www .usatoday.com/story/news/politics/2017/01/21/womens-march-aims-start -movement-trump-inauguration/96864158/.

110. Nina Agrawal, "How the women's march came into being," *LA Times*, January 21, 2017. http://www.latimes.com/nation/la-na-pol-womens-march-live-how -the-women-s-march-came-into-1484865755-htmlstory.html.

111. Liam Stack, "Yemenis Close Bodegas and Rally to Protest Trump's Ban," *The New York Times*, February 2, 2017. https://www.nytimes.com/2017/02 /02/nyregion/new-yorks-yemeni-owned-bodegas-close-to-protest-trumps -immigration-ban.html?_r=0.

112. Angela Hart, "McClintock exits with police escort after raucous town hall meeting in Roseville," *Sacramento Bee*, February 4, 2017. http://www.sacbee .com/news/politics-government/capitol-alert/article130781279.html.

113. Andrew Kaczynski, "Rep. Jason Chaffetz: People at my town hall 'intended to bully and intimidate' me," *CNN*, February 23, 2017. http://www.cnn .com/2017/02/22/politics/kfile-chaffetz-bullied/index.html.

114. Bartholomew Sullivan, "Some members of Congress keep angry public at phone line's distance," *USA Today*, February 14, 2017. https://www.usatoday.com /story/news/politics/2017/02/14/some-congress-keep-angry-public-phone-lines -distance/97889920/.

115. "Indivisible: A Practical Guide for Resisting the Trump Agenda," December 17, 2016. Accessed on October 15, 2017. https://docs.google.com/document /d/1dzoz3y6d8g_mnxhnmjyaz1b41_cn535au5usn7lj8x8/preview#.

116. Jon Queally, "Proud Mother Says Charlottesville Victim Heather Heyer 'Was About Stopping Hatred,'" *Common Dreams*, August 13, 2017. https://www .commondreams.org/news/2017/08/13/proud-mother-says-charlottesville-victim -heather-heyer-was-about-stopping-hatred.

117. Adam Gabbatt, "'Jews will not replace us': Vice film lays bare horror of neo-Nazis in America," *The Guardian*, August 16, 2017. https://www.theguardian

.com/us-news/2017/aug/16/charlottesville-neo-nazis-vice-news-hbo.

118. Ibid.

119. Meghan Keneally, "Trump lashes out at 'alt-left' in Charlottesville, says 'fine people on both sides,'" *ABC News*, August 15, 2017. http://abcnews.go.com/Politics /trump-lashes-alt-left-charlottesville-fine-people-sides/story?id=49235032.

120. Eugene Scott, "Mother of Charlottesville victim says she won't speak with Trump," *CNN*, August 18, 2017. http://www.cnn.com/2017/08/18/politics /heather-heyer-susan-bro-donald-trump/index.html.

121. Doug Stanglin, "'Free Speech' rally fizzles as thousands of counterprotesters swarm Boston," *USA Today*, August 19, 2017. https://www.usatoday.com /story/news/nation/2017/08/19/boston-cradle-liberty-expects-thousands-protests -week-after-deadly-demonstration/582868001/.

122. Chris Benderev, "2 Far-Right Rallies In Bay Area Fizzle While Counterprotesters Rejoice," *NPR*, August 26, 2017. http://www.npr.org/sections /thetwo-way/2017/08/26/546397619/2-far-right-rallies-in-bay-area-fizzle -counterprotesters-rejoice.

123. Tim Webber, "What Does Being A U.S. Territory Mean For Puerto Rico?" *NPR*, October 13, 2017. http://www.npr.org/2017/10/13/557500279/what -does-being-a-u-s-territory-mean-for-puerto-rico.

124. Matthew Yglesias, "The Jones Act, the obscure 1920 shipping regulation strangling Puerto Rico, explained," *Vox*, October 9, 2017. https://www.vox.com /policy-and-politics/2017/9/27/16373484/jones-act-puerto-rico.

125. Susanne Ramirez de Arellano , "Trump came to Puerto Rico like an emperor: with pomp and little sympathy," *The Guardian*, October 4, 2017. https://www .theguardian.com/commentisfree/2017/oct/04/trump-puerto-rico-emperor -pomp-hurricane-maria.

126. Lauren Gambino, "Donald Trump awards himself 10 out of 10 for Puerto Rico hurricane response," *The Guardian*, October 19, 2017. https://www.theguardian .com/world/2017/oct/19/donald-trump-puerto-rico-hurricane-response-10-out -of-10.

127. Aric Jenkins, "Read President Trump's NFL Speech on National Anthem Protests," *Time*, September 23, 2017. http://time.com/4954684/donald-trump-nfl -speech-anthem-protests/.

128. Mark Sandritter , "A timeline of Colin Kaepernick's national anthem protest and the athletes who joined him," *SBNation*, September 25, 2017. https://www .sbnation.com/2016/9/11/12869726/colin-kaepernick-national-anthem-protest -seahawks-brandon-marshall-nfl.

129. Frederick Douglass, "The Meaning of July Fourth for the Negro" (1852), *History is a Weapon*, accessed October 1, 2017. http://www.historyisaweapon.com /defcon1/douglassjuly4.html.

130. Jesse Jackson, "Kaepernick's protest is part of a patriotic tradition," *Chicago Sun Times*, August 28, 2017. https://chicago.suntimes.com/columnists/jackson -kaepernicks-protest-is-part-of-a-patriotic-tradition/.

131. Dave Zirin, "The NFL wants you to think Colin Kaepernick isn't being sidelined by politics. The NFL is wrong — again," *LA Times*, September 8, 2017. http:// www.latimes.com/opinion/op-ed/la-oe-zirin-kaepernick-20170908-story.html.

132. Ibid.

133. Tom Porter, "Trump wants 'son of a bitch' NFL players fired but Colin Kaepernick—and his mom—are fighting back," *Newsweek*, September 23, 2017. http://www.newsweek.com/trump-wants-nfl-police-brutality-protesters-colin

-kaepernick-sacked-heres-670001.

134. Eliott C. McLaughlin and Darran Simon, "These are the NFL players protesting today amid Trump criticism," *CNN*, September 25, 2017. http://www.cnn.com/2017/09/24/us/nfl-trump-take-knee-protests/index.html.

135. Sean Wagner-McGough, "Cowboys owner Jerry Jones: Players who disrespect the flag won't be allowed to play," *CBS Sports*, October 9, 2017. https://www.cbssports.com/nfl/news/cowboys-owner-jerry-jones-players-who-disrespect-the-flag-wont-be-allowed-to-play/.

136. Ken Belson, "Goodell and N.F.L. Owners Break From Players on Anthem Kneeling Fight," *The New York Times*, October 10, 2017. https://www.nytimes.com/2017/10/10/sports/football/nfl-goodell-anthem-kneeling.html?_r=0.

137. Jeremy Stahl, "Vegas Police Allegedly Threatened to Kill NFL's Michael Bennett During Random Arrest," *Slate*, September 6, 2017. http://www.slate.com/blogs/the_slatest/2017/09/06/vegas_police_allegedly_threatened_to_kill_nfl_s_michael_bennett.html.

138. Aric Jenkins, "Donald Trump Called for NFL Players to Be Fired for National Anthem Kneeling — And They Responded," *Fortune*, September 23, 2017. http://fortune.com/2017/09/23/donald-trump-nfl-players-anthem-response/.

139. Tom Gerencer, "How Much Money Do NFL Players Make?" *MoneyNation*, January 5, 2016. http://moneynation.com/how-much-money-do-nfl-players-make/.

140. SI Wire, "WSJ data analysis shows average length of NFL careers decreasing," *Sports Illustrated*, March 1, 2016. https://www.si.com/nfl/2016/03/01/nfl-careers-shortened-two-years-data-analysis#.

141. Chris Chavez, "Boston University Study Finds CTE in 110 Of 111 Brains of Former NFL Players," *Sports Illustrated*, July 25, 2017. https://www.si.com/nfl/2017/07/25/boston-university-study-cte-nfl-player-brains.

142. Jenkins, op cit.

143. Brandon Carter, "NFL union hits back at Trump over players' right to protest," *The Hill*, September 23, 2017. http://thehill.com/blogs/blog-briefing-room/news/352023-nfl-players-union-head-we-will-never-back-down-from-protecting.

Index

trucking industry:
  deregulation of, 231
  see also Teamsters
Truman, Harry S, 172–73, 175–81,
  190, 195
Truman Doctrine, 176–77, 178, 189,
  192
Trump, Donald, ix–xi, 359–60, 363–70,
  378, 380, 384–90, 392
Trump, Melania, 363
Tucker, Jerry, 310, 319
Tunisia, 335, 338
Tutu, Desmond, 345

unemployment:
  and 2016 election, 369
  of Blacks, 19, 241, 243, 300, 334
  and downsizing, 269, 285–86
  federal compensation for, 114–15
  in Great Depression, xxi, 102–3, 333
  in Great Recession, 333, 373, 377,
    380
  and hunger marches, 103–4
  illegal firings, 269
  and jobless recovery, 299, 300
  planned, 234–35
  and plant closings, 248, 281
  and public works programs, 119,
    132
  slashing benefits, 148–49, 184, 239,
    256
  solidarity with workers, 108
Union Pacific Railroad, 28
unions:
  and anarchists, xx
  and anticommunism, 63, 174,
    190–92
  bureaucracies of, 158, 202, 203–4,
    209–11, 220
  closed shops, 94, 109, 172
  collective bargaining of, 16, 137, 140,
    212, 232, 248–49
  concessions from, 232, 248, 250, 253,
    271, 304, 305
  cooperation with management,
    66–67, 89, 203–4
  corporations vs., 17, 65–66, 97,
    208–9, 222, 231–32, 269, 273,
    303, 312, 371
  corruption in, 163, 199–201, 258,
    259, 270, 310
  craft, 31, 33, 36, 52, 67, 79, 88,
    114–15, 200
  decertification elections of, 249

and Democratic Party, 49, 119–22,
  135, 138, 151, 152, 158, 173, 197,
  211, 272, 310, 311, 343, 361, 367,
  380
and election campaigns, 122, 173,
  180, 190, 211, 247, 271, 272
failure to fight, 247–49, 271, 310
government oversight of, 199–200
grievance procedures of, 209
hiring halls of, 109, 110, 111
and HUAC, 63, 174, 190
industrial, 31–32, 33, 36, 56, 79, 82,
  120, 202
jurisdiction battles of, 149
and LGBT rights, 356
membership in, xiv, xviii, 35, 67, 91,
  97, 168, 171, 197, 203, 208, 231,
  249, 271–72, 318, 372
and New Deal, 50, 103, 106, 107
and 1960s radicals, 215, 216–17
and occupy, 338
and open shops, 65, 141
racism in, xv, 11, 25, 33–34, 47,
  114–17, 169–70
reform as goal of, 87, 88
revolutionary, 80, 82, 86–87, 88,
  178
right to organize in, 16, 104, 106,
  117, 139–40, 149, 269
right to strike, 156, 202, 209
solidarity of, 40, 82, 84, 85–86, 108,
  139, 164, 250–51, 275, 276, 280
suppression of, xiv, 16, 37, 72, 94,
  208, 372
targeted by Congress, 96, 198–200
of teachers, x, 340–44
violence against, 52, 99–100, 127,
  137, 139, 200
violence promoted by, 9, 52
in Wisconsin, 336–37
women as members of, xvii, xviii, 32,
  47, 168
and yellow dog contracts, 56, 97,
  103, 106
see also specific unions; workers
United Airlines, 303, 304, 306–7
United Auto Workers (UAW), 120–21,
  136–41, 142–48, 205, 209
  concessions from, 232, 248, 305,
    309
  radicals purged in, 191–92, 202–3
  Rank and File Caucus of, 166, 169
  and strikes, 13, 274, 275–76, 281–82,
    308

Also from Haymarket Books

*Fuego Subterraneo: Historia del radicalismo
de la clase obrera en los Estados Unidos*
Sharon Smith

Women and Socialism: Class, Race, and Capital
Sharon Smith

*On New Terrain: How Capital is Reshaping
the Battleground of Class War*
Kim Moody

*Class War, USA: Dispatches from Workers' Struggles
in American History*
Brandon Weber

*Song of the Stubborn One Thousand:
The Watsonville Canning Strike, 1985–87*
Peter Shapiro

*Poor Workers' Unions: Rebuilding Labor from Below
(Completely Revised and Updated Edition)*
Vanessa Tait, Foreword by Bill Fletcher,
Afterword by Cristina Tzintzún

Organized Labor and the Black Worker , 1619–1981
Philip S. Foner, Foreword by Robin D. G. Kelley

*A Short History of the US Working Class:
From Colonial Times to the Twenty-First Century*
Paul Le Blanc

From #BlackLivesMatter to Black Liberation
Keeanga-Yamahtta Taylor

About Haymarket Books

Haymarket Books is a nonprofit, progressive book distributor and publisher, a project of the Center for Economic Research and Social Change. We believe that activists need to take ideas, history, and politics into the many struggles for social justice today. Learning the lessons of past victories, as well as defeats, can arm a new generation of fighters for a better world. As Karl Marx said, "The philosophers have merely interpreted the world; the point however is to change it."

We take inspiration and courage from our namesakes, the Haymarket Martyrs, who gave their lives fighting for a better world. Their 1886 struggle for the eight-hour day, which gave us May Day, the international workers' holiday, reminds workers around the world that ordinary people can organize and struggle for their own liberation. These struggles continue today across the globe—struggles against oppression, exploitation, hunger, and poverty.

It was August Spies, one of the Martyrs who was targeted for being an immigrant and an anarchist, who predicted the battles being fought to this day. "If you think that by hanging us you can stamp out the labor movement," Spies told the judge, "then hang us. Here you will tread upon a spark, but here, and there, and behind you, and in front of you, and everywhere, the flames will blaze up. It is a subterranean fire. You cannot put it out. The ground is on fire upon which you stand."

We could not succeed in our publishing efforts without the generous financial support of our readers. Many people contribute to our project through the Haymarket Sustainers program, where donors receive free books in return for their monetary support. If you would like to be a part of this program, please contact us at info@haymarketbooks.org.